Ellery Publications - EP.D115

Diesel Maintence, Tune-up and Management

Volume No2

A comprehensive diesel vehicle engine repair, maintenance and service manual.

This manual covers engine and fuel checks, timing belt replacement, engine tightening torque specifications, fuel system adjustments, fuel pre-heating, fuel system component checks, fuel system electrical circuits, terminal and ECU information, service details, engine diagnosis and trouble-shooting. Step by step instructions with plenty of illustrations and diagrams. Ideal for the DIY or mechanic.

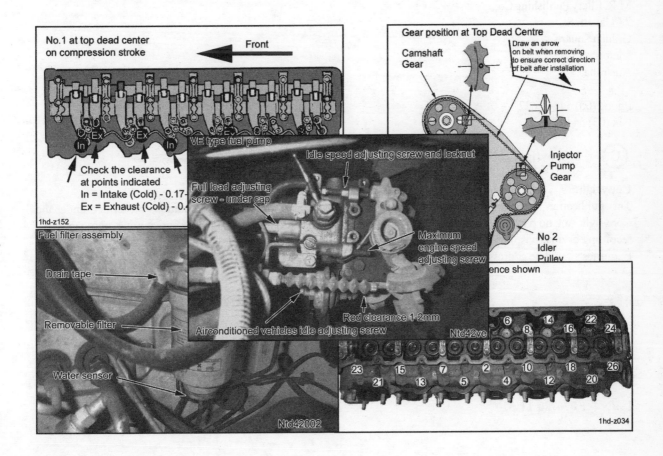

No.1 at top dead center on compression stroke — Front

Check the clearance at points indicated
In = Intake (Cold) - 0.17-
Ex = Exhaust (Cold) - 0.

1hd-z152

Fuel filter assembly
Drain tape
Removable filter
Water sensor
Ntd42002

VE type fuel pump
Idle speed adjusting screw and locknut
Full load adjusting screw - under cap
Maximum engine speed adjusting screw
Rod clearance 1-2mm
Airconditioned vehicles idle adjusting screw
Ntd42ve

Gear position at Top Dead Centre
Camshaft Gear
Draw an arrow on belt when removing to ensure correct direction of belt after installation
Injector Pump Gear
No 2 Idler Pulley
...ence shown

1hd-z034

This repair and maintenance manual has been published to help provide owners of diesel powered vehicles featured in this manuals with an invaluable, comprehensive and thorough guide to service, maintain and repair their diesel engines.

The manual is published from the latest information obtained at our factory. Where extensive research is undertaken to obtain the information for the benefit of people who purchase this manual.

DISCLAIMER

Every endeavour has been made to ensure all information in this manual is accurate. Mistakes and omissions can always occur, and the publisher does not assume any duty or care, or legal responsibility in relation to the contents of this book.

Maintenance, repair and tune-up are essential for safe and reliable use of all motor vehicles. These operations should be undertaken in such a manner as to eliminate the possibility of personal injury or in such a way that could damage the vehicle or compromise the safety of the vehicle, driver, passenger or a third party.

Published By:
M.R. Ellery Publishing Co.,
78 Hattam St,
Golden Square
Victoria, 3555
Australia.

Phone (03) 5444 5622
Fax (03) 5444 2660

National Library of Australia Card number and ISBN

ISBN   1 876720 11 5

VEHICLE INDEX

* When a model is stated as year XXXX On (eg 1986 On), this implies that the chapter will cover that engine for the time it is current or up to 2004

Diesel Maintence, Tune-up and Service Manual Volume No1
VEHICLE INDEX

Vehicle	Capicity	Engine and Year
Daihatsu		
Rocky	2765cc (2.8L)	DL42 and DL52 1984-1997
Ford		
Courier	2184cc (2.2L)	R2 Engine 1988-1996
Econovan	2184cc (2.2L)	R2 Engine 1984-1997
Isuzu / Holden		
Jackaroo	2238cc (2.3L)	C223T 1985-1988
Jackaroo	2771cc (2.8L)	4JB1-T - 2.8 Turbo 1984-1997
Rodeo	2499cc (2.5L)	4JA1 - 2.5 1988-1992
Land Rover		
Discovery	2495cc (2.5L)	2.5L Turbo TD200i Upto 1994
Mazda		
B2200	2184cc (2.2L)	R2 Engine (1988-1996)
E2200	2184cc (2.2L)	R2 Engine (1984-1997)
Mitsubishi		
Express	2447cc (2.5L)	SF- 4D56 Engine From 1986-1990
Triton	2447cc (2.5L)	ME - 4D56/4D56T Engine (1986-1988)
Pajero	2346cc (2.4L)	NA-NC 2.4 4D55T, Engine (1983 to 1985)
Pajero	2447cc (2.5L)	ND-NH 2.5 4D56T, Engine (1986 to 1993)
Pajero	2835cc (2.8L)	NJ 2.8L 4M4O Engine (1993-1996)
Nissan		
Cabstar	2488cc (2.5L)	F22/H40 SD25 Engine 1982 On
720	2164cc (2.2L)	SD22 (1979-1983)
720	2289cc (2.3L)	SD23 and SD25 (1983-1985)
Navara	2488cc (2.5L)	D21 - 2.5L SD 25 Engine (1986 On)
Patrol	3246cc (3.3L)	160 - SD33 and SD33 Turbo Diesel (1980-1987)
Urvan	2164cc (2.2L)	E23 - SD22 (1980-1983)
Urvan	2289cc (2.3L)	E23 - SD23 (1984-1986)
Toyota		
4 Runner	2446cc (2.5L)	LN60-61 - 2L(1984-1988)
4 Runner	2779cc (2.8L)	LN61 and LN130 - 3L 2.8 litre Enignie (1989-1996)
Dyna	2446cc (2.5L)	LY50/60 - 2L Engine (1984-1988)
Hiace	2446cc (2.5L)	LH50/51/61& 71 Series 2L Engine (1984 On)
Hilux	2446cc (2.5L)	LN 50/55/56/60/65 Series - 2L Engine (1983-1988)
Landcruiser	2446cc (2.5L)	LJ70 Series - 2L-T Engine (1986 On)
Landcruiser	3980cc (4.0L)	HJ60/HJ6/HJ75 - 2H Engine, HJ60-HJ75 - 12H-T Engine HJ61 (1986On)
Landcruiser	4164cc (4.2L)	HZJ 70-73-75, HZJ 80 Series - 1HZ Engine (1990-1998)

When a model is stated as 1998 on, this implies that the chapter will cover that engine for the time it is current or up to 2004

Diesel Maintence, Tune-up and Service Manual Volume No3

Vehicle	Capicity	Engine and Year
Ford		
Couier	2499cc (2.5L)	1996On
Isuzu / Holden		
Jackaroo	3059cc (3.1L)	1996-1998
Jackaroo	2999cc (3.0L)	1998 On
Rodeo	2999cc (3.0L)	1998 On
Landrover		
Defender	2405cc (2.5L)	1992 On
Discovery	2495cc (2.5L)	1994 On
Mazda		
Bravo	2499cc (2.5L)	1996 On
Econovan	2499cc (2.5L)	1999 On
Mitsubishi		
Pajero	2835cc (2.8L)	1996 On
Triton	2835cc (2.8L)	1996 On
Nissan		
Navara	3153cc (3.2L)	1997 On
Navara	2999cc (3.2L)	2001 On
Patrol	2826cc (2.8T)	1995 On
Patrol	4169cc (4.2L)	1997 On
Patrol	4169cc (4.2T)	1997 On
Patrol	2953cc (3.0T)	2000 On
Toyota		
Hilux	2986cc (3.0T)	1998On
Prado	2986cc (3.0T)	2000 On

* Provisional index, depending on availability of information at time of publishing

TOOLS, EQUIPMENT, ELECTRICAL SERVICE & SAFETY PRECAUTIONS

Diesel Engine Service and Repair Tools Listing & Description

Torque Wrench:

Torque wrenches are an important necessity for the work shop to allow bolts and screws to be tightened to the correct torque specifications. Torque wrenches are available in either lb. ft. or Nm, they are also available with both.

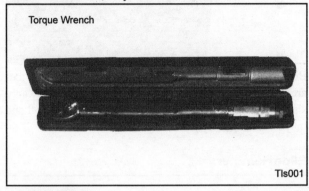

Torque Wrench

Tls001

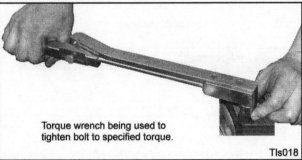

Torque wrench being used to tighten bolt to specified torque.

Tls018

Circlip/Snap-ring Pliers:

Cir-clip and Snap-ring pliers are essential for mechanical repairs. These are available as either individual pliers designed purely for certain types of clips or is available as a single set with interchangeable heads.

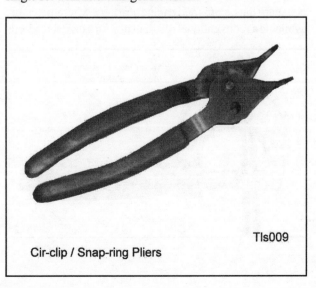

Cir-clip / Snap-ring Pliers

Tls009

Hammer/Mallet:

A good steel hammer preferably a ball-peen hammer and a rubber mallet are vital tools for all workshops. If possible it's best not to use a hammer, although at times they are required for removing or installing parts.

Steel hammers are also essential for when using punches and chisels.

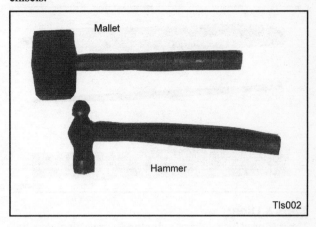

Mallet

Hammer

Tls002

Cold Chisels:

Cold chisels are generally used for removing seized or rusted bolt heads, or removing bolts which have had the heads rounded.

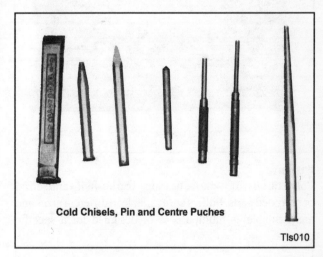

Cold Chisels, Pin and Centre Puches

Tls010

Centre/Pin Punches:

Punches are used for removing and installing roll pins and also for placing a small indent in a location to be drilled and is used to help centre and align the drill piece while starting.

Files:

Files are used for removing burrs and rough edges from parts of the transmission to assist in removal or before installation of parts. They are also used for marking parts, removing rust and filing of rivet and bolt heads where needed. Files are available in a number of shapes and sizes and are usually single-cut or double-cut files.

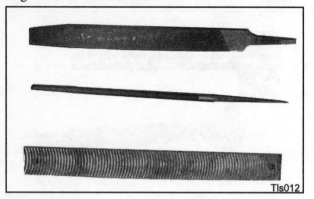

Tls012

Taps & Dies:

Taps are used for restoring and cutting internal threads to bolt holes, while dies are used for restoring and cutting external threads such as bolts.

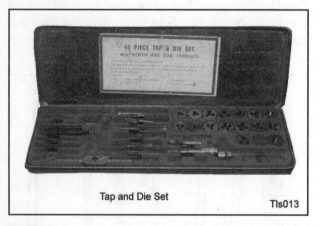

Tap and Die Set   Tls013

Pullers:

Pullers are used to remove bearings, bad bushings and seized or corroded parts. Pullers are available in different sizes and are available as multipurpose or designed for a specific purpose.

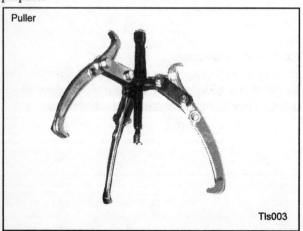

Puller

Tls003

Bench Vice:

Bench Vice

Tls004

Bench vices are a vital accessory for any workshop, vices are used for holding parts secure while working, soft jaws are also a necessity for the holding of parts which are soft and may be damaged by the hard jaws.

Slide Hammer:

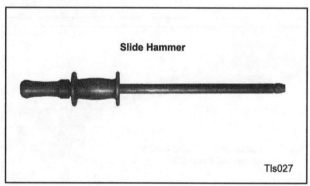

Slide Hammer

Tls027

Slide hammers are used to for bushing removal and other components as required.

Micrometer:

Micrometers are used for measuring the thickness of washers, snap rings, shims and engine bearings. Micrometers are available as conventional read-out or with a digital read-out.

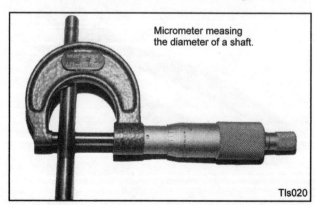

Micrometer measing
the diameter of a shaft.

Tls020

Dial Indicator:

Dial indicators are used to measure piston protrision measurements and can also be used on various other procedures. Ensure a good quality dial indicator is used with at least a one inch travel on the pin.

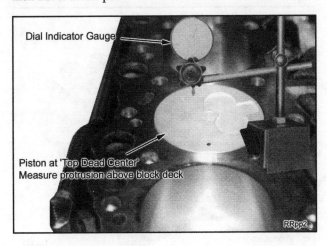

Dial Indicator Gauge

Piston at 'Top Dead Center'
Measure protrusion above block deck

RRpp2

Vernier Calipers:

Vernier calipers are used for measuring the diameter of parts or the inner diameter of holes. Vernier calipers are less accurate than micrometers but are also available in conventional and digital read-outs. The calipers can be used for measuring the inside and outside diameters as well as depth of various parts.

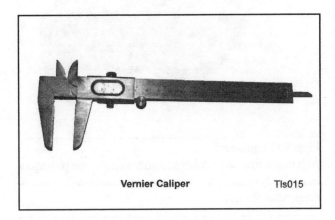

Vernier Caliper   Tls015

E-Z-Out Extractors:

E-Z-Out extractors are used for removing broken of studs and bolts, they are sold in sets and can be used for removing a number of different sized studs and bolts.

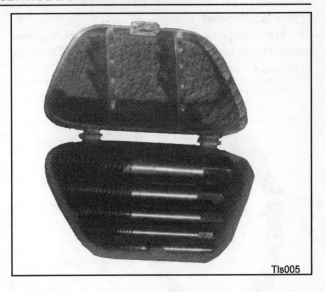

Tls005

Stethoscope:

Stethoscopes are very good in diagnosis of problems as they can be used to amplify noise to diagnose possible sources of trouble.

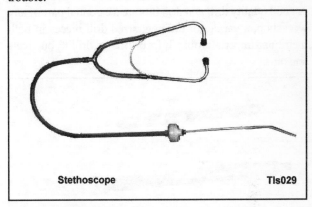

Stethoscope   Tls029

Vacuum Gauge:

Vacuum gauges are used to check the amount of vacuum at the intake manifold, and is required to check in certain modulator valves and solenoids on the engine.

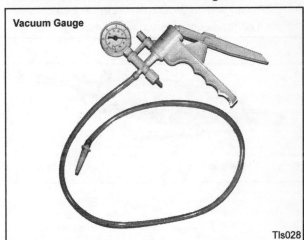

Vacuum Gauge

Tls028

9

Hydraulic Pressure Gauge:

The hydraulic pressure gauge is used to measure the oil pressure being generated by the engine oil pump. The gauge must read a minimum of 300 psi.

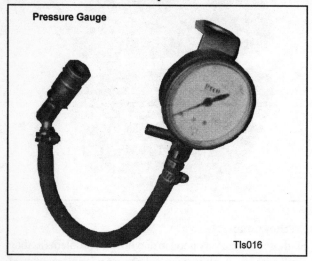

Pressure Gauge

Tls016

Drill/Drill Bits:

A good quality drill and drill bits are a essential part of any workshop, a variety of different sized drill pieces in both metric and imperial are handy for drill holes, drilling out rivets and pins.

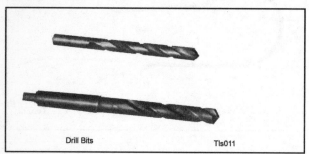

Drill Bits

Tls011

Die Grinder:

Die grinders are useful to chamfer oil holes, debar parts, cut and grind. They allow a job to be finished much quicker than doing it by hand although extreme care must be taken as they remove a large amount of material very quickly.

Die Grinder

Tls017

Work Gloves:

A good quality pair of heavy gloves are good for handling and components which are hot or have been heated for any reason. Also good for holding components with sharp edges to prevent cut hands.

Work Gloves

Tls023

Face Mask / Safety Glasses:

Face masks and especially safety glasses are very important protective wear which should be used whenever grinding, cutting or doing anything which could cause shrapnel or fluids to fly or splash into your face.

Saftey Glasses

Tls022

Fire Extinguisher:

A chemical fire extinguisher should be kept in close proximity incase of fire. As in workshop environments fire is a very dangerous hazard.

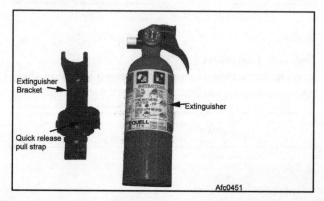

Extinguisher Bracket

Quick release pull strap

Extinguisher

Afc0451

Bench Grinder:

Bench grinders are a useful tool for removing rust and cleaning components, sharpening tools and grinding parts if required. Care must be taken to ensure the grinder is secured to a bench or stand and that it will not vibrate around.

Bench Grinder

Tls006

Sockets/Ratchet:

A good quality ratchet and socket set is the best way of removing bolts and nuts, as it is easier, quicker and most the time more secure on the bolt heads than conventional spanners.

Ratchet and socket sets are available in a number of drive sizes as well as being available in both metric and imperial.

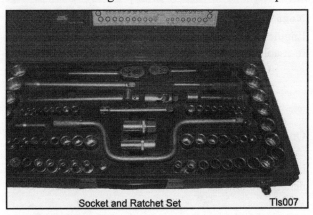

Socket and Ratchet Set

Tls007

Screw Drivers:

A large number of different sized screw drivers of both phillip head and flat blade screw drivers will be used frequently in disassembly of transmissions.

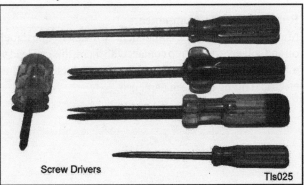

Screw Drivers

Tls025

Spanners:

A full set of metric and imperial spanners of both ring and open end are a essential set of tools to have in a work shop. Spanners are used allot in areas where access is not accessible with a ratchet and socket.

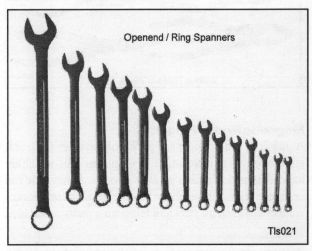

Openend / Ring Spanners

Tls021

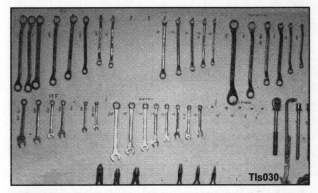

Tls030

Pliers:

Both small and large conventional and pointed nose pliers are used frequently in rebuild operations to disconnect springs remove clips and other small jobs.

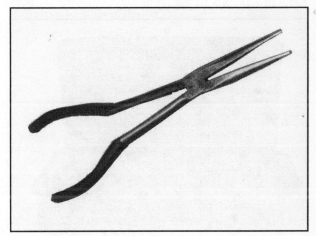

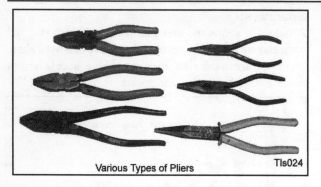

Various Types of Pliers   Tls024

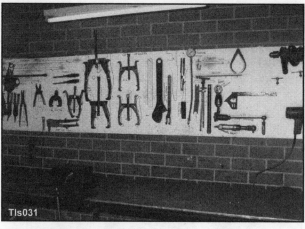

Tls031

Magnetic Rod or Finger:

A magnetic rod or finger and preferably an extendable unit is a necessity to remove small locking pins or balls, which are located in hard to access bores or cavities. A magnetic rod or finger is also particularly handy retrieve a small steel component or small steel tool falls into a partly assembled engine .

Sturdy Work Bench:

A good sturdy clean work bench is essential when working Ensure the bench has a large work area to enable the components to be laid out in order to assist in repairs and assembly of the relaevant component/assembly.

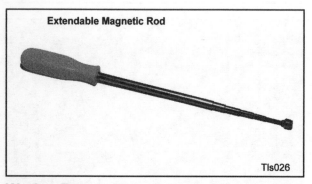

Extendable Magnetic Rod

Tls026

None Re-usable Parts

Engines, cooling systems and fuel systems utilise many non-re-usable parts such as:

O rings	D rings
Oil seals	Lock washers
Split pins	Self-locking nuts
Gaskets except rocker cover gaskets	

Once these none re-usable parts have been used, they shouldbe discarded and replacemeed, otherwise you may have an expesive repair due to a small inexpensive component not renewed.

Washup Bay:

A good washup bay is essential for cleaning components before inspecting for damage and before reassembly. A professional wash bay with flowing fluid can be purchased from a accessories/tools supplier or a bay can be made from using an old sink or similar.

Rubber / Plastic Components

Many rubber and plastic components will deteriorate if fuel, oil and solvents come into contact with them, this can lead to a break down and a badly performing vehicle if seal or electrical fitting has been damaged.

Washup Bay   Tls008

Gasket Sealants & Thread Sealants

Loctite 587

Anaerobic Sealant (Use as a gasket)

Anaerobic Form In Place Gasket (FIPG) products, such as Loctite 515 and Loctite 518 provide optimum sealing performance on ridged machined metal flanges with a minimum flange width of 5 mm. These products cure when confined between mated metal parts, covering the entire sealing surface and all surface irregularities, thus ensuring a complete seal. They are temperature resistant up to 150 degrees C and are suitable for use in contact with petrol.

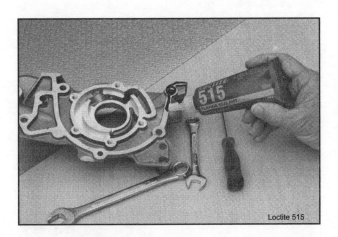

Loctite 515

Loctite 569

Silicone Sealant (Use at gasket joins and engine high temperature joins etc)

Silicones are used to seal joins with poor flange design and also critical areas like T-Joins where anaerobic or hard gaskets will have problems. It is important to select a low-volatile, neutral cure automotive silicone such as Loctite Blue Maxx, Black Maxx or Grey Maxx. Loctite Maxx silicones excel on so called "chamfer" design flanges and on pressed metal flanges, typical for pressed metal sumps. Silicones have a much higher temperature range than anaerobic FIPG products, and are oil resistant, however they are not suitable for use in contact with petrol.

Thread Sealant

Anaerobic thread sealants such as Loctite 567 and Loctite 577 are used for sealing threaded pipe fittings such as oil and coolant lines. These products seal to moderate pressure instantly and up to 68.9MPa (10 000 PSI) when fully cured.

Use of Loctite products on Cylinder Head Bolts

The success of the assembly of cylinder heads to the engine block solely relies on the clamp force created between the cylinder head and engine block during assembly.

To achieve the correct clamp force the car manufacturer specifies the correct torque settings and torque sequence for the cylinder head bolts.

The theory is that the torque setting translates into clamp force and that is correct. However in spite of applying the correct torque to the head bolts this is not a guarantee that the correct clamp force is achieved.

The cause usually is caused by extensive friction between the threads of the cylinder head bolts and that thread in the cylinder head.

One golden rule is to always use new cylinder head bolts when refitting the cylinder head. Secondly clean out the thread in the engine block.

Electrical Service Information

Once this is done Loctite offers special products suitable and recommended by major car manufactures.

Different car manufacturers may recommend a different Loctite product for this application.

Commonly used Loctite products are Loctite 243, Loctite 262 and Loctite 567.

These Loctite products have special lubricating properties ensuring the correct torque setting results in the correct clamp force. We call this torque / tension relationship.

Addition advantages of the Loctite products is:

No re-torque is required as the Loctite product cures and locks the bolt in place thus preventing loss of clamp force.

The Loctite product will create a permanent seal between head bolt and the thread in the engine block, preventing oil or coolant leaks.

Prevents over torque of the bolts, which can result in bolt failure.

Before performing an electrical repair work it is advisable to disconnect the battery negative terminal. Before disconnecting the terminal make sure all electrical units are turned off, including ignition.

Wiring Harness

Harness should be rerouted in the original position if removed for repairs. They should be fitted with no slack in the harness and if possible clamped at the same position from were the harness was removed. Make sure the harness will not rub on a sharp surface or a moving component such as a throttle cable or linkage.

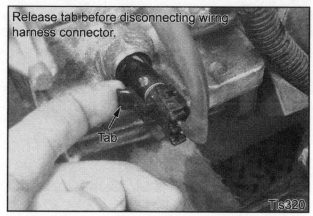

Release tab before disconnecting wiring harness connector.

Tab

Tls320

Wiring Harness Connectors

When seperating a connector, pull on the connector not the wiring leading into the connector.

Inspect the connector or a catch, many connectors have a small plastic tab that needs to be released before the connector can be seperated. quite oftewn the tab is released by pushing down on the tab with your finger, with age and engien heat deteriation the tab can become very brittle, sometimes it is prefferable to release the tab with a small screw driver.

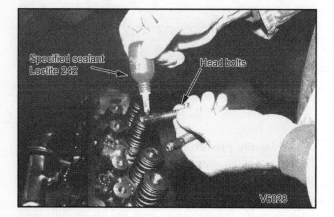

Specified sealant Loctite 242

Head bolts

V6028

Back Probing

When checking for continuity or voltage it is recommended that harness connectors remain connected and the test is carried out by back probing the connector or electrical unit. If the coupling is a weathproof type insert a fine probe in along the electrical wire to the terminal for testing.

If the harness coupling has been seperated do not force the probe into the female side of the terminl otherwise the probe will widen the terminal and possibly cause a bad connection.

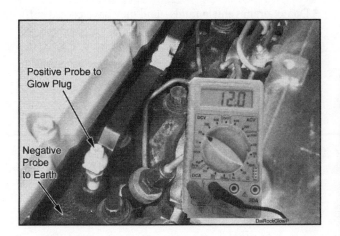

Ohm Meter / Volt Meter

A reliable digital ohm / volt meter is escential. Use a reputable brand instrument for acurate measurement of electrical current and resistance. A digital meter is more accuracte than an olague/dial type meter.

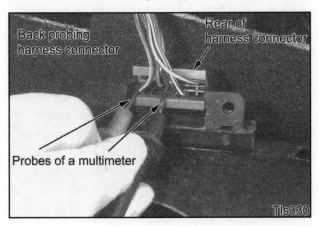

Electrical Componets

Sensors, relays, fuses and control units can be very sensitive to shock from droping, impact, electrical surge, to high voltage and excessive heat.

Never weld on the vehicle without disconnecting both battery terminals.

late model injector pumps incorporate electrical sensors and control valves. Do not drop an electrical component or strick with ahammer.

Never allow a component to over heat, take care if repairing the body and the body repairer uses a heat blower to dry heat or take moisture away from a panel.

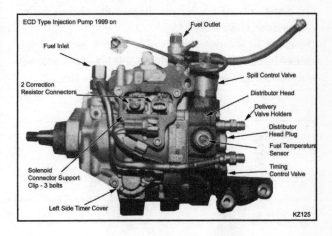

Fuses, Fusible Links and Relays

When replacing a fuse, fisible link or relay only use one that has the same rating as the one being replaced. If the fuse etc has a lower rating it will blow before necessary or if the rating is higher you may damage the electrical component or harness.

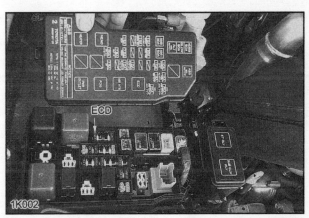

15

SAFETY PRECAUTIONS

Fire:
Remember that in a work shop you are working with and around flammable liquids. When working ensure nothing that can ignite is in the vicinity if possible especially when sparks are being created by the job. Ensure the chemical fire-extinguisher is available.

Note: Never use water on a fire in a work shop which is caused by electrical fault or a flammable liquid as water will only spread the flammable liquid enlarging the fire.

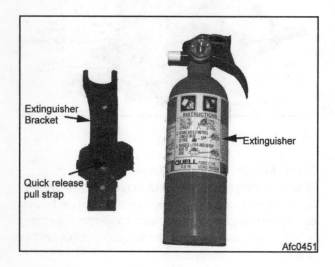

Afc0451

Electrical Equipment/Tools:
You must be extremely careful when using electrical equipment not to use in damp areas or have cords laying in water. Also becareful not to damage the power leads by cutting or having near heat as the result may be electrocution.

Fuels:
Do not store or use petrols or other fuels in plastic containers unless they are approved for transporting or storing fuels as many plastics will be eaten through (melted) by fuel. Metal or glass containers are best for storing and using fuels in.

Tls034

General Practice:

* When siphoning toxic chemicals never use your mouth to start the liquid drawing, always use a suction pump, or proper siphon hose.

* Do not remove radiator cap before firstly allowing coolant to cool down.

* Do not drain vehicle fluids until they have cooled sufficiently to prevent burning.

* Do not inhale brake or clutch dust as it is hazardous to health.

* Always ensure correct sized spanners are use to prevent slipping as it may cause injury.

* Wear protective clothing where necessary.

Ford Maverick TD42 4.2L Engine 1988 ON

CONTENTS   PAGE

CONTENTS   PAGE

Ford Maverick TD42 4.2L Engine 1988 ON

Engine Checks

Valve Clearance Check

Please Note: Valve clearance should only be made while the engine is warm but not running.

1. With the No1 cylinder set to TDC on the compression stroke adjust the valve clearances 1, 2, 4, 5, 8 and 9

2. With the No6 cylinder set to TDC on the compression stroke adjust the valve clearances 3, 6, 7, 10, 11 and 12

Intake valve clearances:

Valves 1, 3, 5, 7, 9 and 11 (0.35mm)

Exhaust valve clearances:

Valves 2, 4, 6, 8, 10 and 12 (0.35mm)

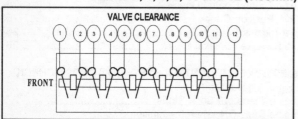

Compression Check

1. Run the engine to normal operating temperature, remove the glow plate or injector and the install a compression gauge adapter to the cylinder head.

2. Set the vehicle to 'No Fuel Injection Condition" by disconnecting the fuel cut solenoid wire **(VE Type Pump)** or by disconnecting the injection pump controller harness connector **(In Line Pump)**.

3. Crank the engine and record the compression pressure *(Please Note: On vehicle with an In Line Pump, press the throttle down fully and then crank the engine)*

Compression Pressure: **2,942 kpa (Standard)**

Differential Limit Between Cylinders: 294kpa

Compression Pressure: **2,452kpa (Minimum)**

4. If the compression reading in step 3 on one or more cylinders is low, pour a small amount of oil into the faulty cylinders through the glow plug holes and retest the faulty cylinders.

5. If by adding oil in step 4 the pressure increases, there is a possibility that the piston rings are worn or damaged, if the pressure stays low, there may be sticking valves or the valves may not be seating correctly.

6. If the compression in any two adjacent cylinders are low and adding oil does not increase the pressure, there may be a leak past the gasket surface and could cause oil and water to be present in the combustion chambers.

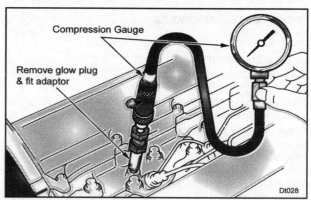

Piston Protrusion Check

1. Set each piston to TDC and with the piston set in that position record the measurement in each of the two positions shown. Calculate the average value of the two measurements and then check the protrusions on the other cylinders.

2. After calculating the measurements select the correct head gasket from the measurements shown below.

Average Piston Projection (mm)	Gasket Thickness (mm)	Gasket Grade Value
Less than 0.118	1.15	1
0.118-0.168	1.2	2
More than 0.168	1.25	3

Diagram is on the next page

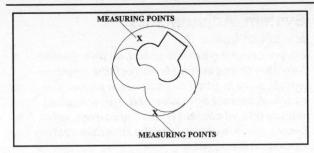

MEASURING POINTS

MEASURING POINTS

Cylinder Head Tightening Procedures

1. After selecting the correct grade of head gasket, apply oil to the thread of the head bolts and to the seat surface of the bolt.

2. Fit the gasket and cylinder head to the engine block and tighten the head bolts in two steps, 1ˢᵗ step tighten to between 49-59Nm, then 2ⁿᵈ stage tighten to between 98-108Nm in the sequence shown in the diagram.

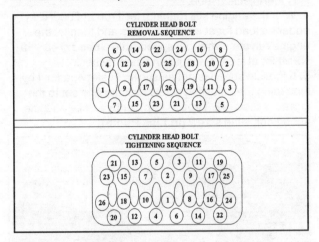

CYLINDER HEAD BOLT REMOVAL SEQUENCE

CYLINDER HEAD BOLT TIGHTENING SEQUENCE

Oil Pressure Check

Please Note: All oil pressure checks should be carried out with the transmission in the Neutral position.

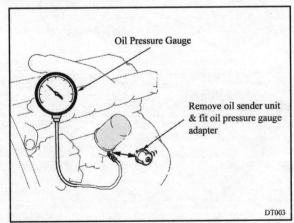

Oil Pressure Gauge

Remove oil sender unit & fit oil pressure gauge adapter

DT003

1. Check the oil level on the dipstick and if required fill as required, remove the oil pressure switch and install a pressure gauge to the engine.

2. Start the engine, let it run until normal operating temperature has been reached and then record the oil pressure shown on the gauge while the engine is

running under no load.

Oil Pressure: 78kpa (engine at idle)
Oil Pressure: 294-392kpa (engine at 3000RPM)

3. If the oil pressure in step 2 has an extreme variance, check the oil passage and oil pump for leaks and/or damage, if faults are found repair/replace as required.

Cooling System Thermostat Check

1. Remove the thermostat from the engine, place the thermostat into a suitable container of water and heat to normal operating temperature.

2. Check the valve opening temperature and maximum valve lift as shown below.

Valve Opening Temperature: 82°c
Maximum Valve Lift: 8mm @ 95°c

3. If the specifications shown in step2 are Ok, ensure that the valve now closes at 5°c below the valve operating temperature.

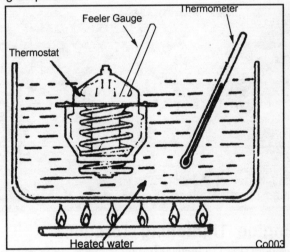

Feeler Gauge — Thermometer

Thermostat

Heated water   Co003

Fuel Filter Check and Replacement

1. Remove the fuel filter sensor, drain the fuel and then remove the fuel filter.

2. Clean the fuel filter mounting bracket and then coat the fuel filter sealing ring with some diesel fuel.

3. Screw the fuel filter on until a slght resistance is felt and then turn another 2/3 of a turn or until suitably tight.

4. Install the fuel filter sensor to the new filter and then bleed any air present from the system.

Draining Water From The Filter (VE Type Pump Only)

1. Loosen the drain cock 4 or 5 turns to allow the water to drain from the filter.

2. Retighten the drain cock and bleed any air present from the system

Diagram is on the next page

Bleeding the Fuel System (In Line Pump)

1. Remove the cap that covers the priming pump, turn the priming pump in an anti-clockwise direction and loosen the air vent screws.

2. Move the priming pump up and down until no more air-bleed comes out of the air vent screws.

3. Push and turn the priming pump in a clockwise direction, then refit the priming pump cap.

Bleeding the Fuel System (VE Type Injection Pump)

1. Loosen the air vent screw and move the priming pump up and down until no more air-bleed comes out of the air vent screws.

2. Re-tighten the air vent screws and then move the priming pump up and down until there is a sudden increase in the resistance when moving the priming pump up and down.

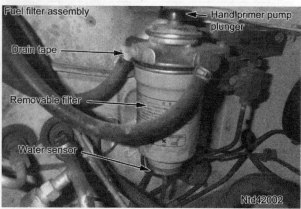

Engine Tightening Torques

Cylinder Head Tightening Torque 1st Stage: .. 49-59Nm
Cylinder Head Tightening Torque 2st Stage: 98-108Nm
Rocker Shaft Bracket Bolts: 20-25Nm
Rocker Shaft Lock Bolt: 10-13Nm
Rocker Arm Lock Bolt: 14-18Nm
Rocker Arm Lock Nut: 15-20Nm
Rocker Cover Bolts: 1-2Nm
Exhaust Manifold Bolts and Nuts: 15-20Nm
Inlet Manifold Bolts and Nuts: 25-29Nm
Exhaust Tube Nuts: 43-50Nm
Glow Plugs: 15-20Nm
Injection Nozzle: 54-64Nm
Flywheel: 147-167Nm
Main Bearing Caps: ....
167-167Nm (Tighten in two or three stages from the centre outwards)
Connecting Rod Caps: 78-83Nm
Crankshaft Pulley Bolt: 294-324Nm
Crankshaft Damper to Crankshaft Pulley Bolt:26-30Nm
Front Timing Cover: 16-21Nm
Camshaft Gear Centre Bolt: 78-88Nm
Idler Gear Bolt: 25-35Nm
Oil Pump Bolt: 13-19Nm
Oil Pump Relief Valve: 16-21Nm
Wheel Bearing Lock Nuts: 167-196Nm

System Adjsutments

Idle Speed Check

Before checking the idle speed, ensure that the injection timing setting is correct, the injection nozzle's are in good condition, the air cleaner is not blocked, correct operation of the glow system, the engine oil and coolant levels are correct, valve clearances are correct and the air intake system operation is correct.

1. Put the gear shift lever into Neutral, the parking brake is applied and then place wheel chocks on both the front and rear wheels.

2. Switch off the air conditioning and ensure all of the lights and accessories are switched off.

3. Run the engine to normal operating temperature, again ensure all the lights, heater fan and accessories are switched off and then fix a tachometer pick up to the No1 fuel injection tube.

4. With the engine still running, let it run at 2000RPM under no load for at least 2 minutes and then let the engine run at normal idle speed (**Idle Speed: 700 +50 RPM**) for at least 1 minute and then recheck.

5. If the idle speed is not as shown in step4, adjust by loosening the adjusting screw lock nut and set to the correct speed (**VE Type Pump**), or by turning the idle speed adjusting screw (**In Line Pump**).

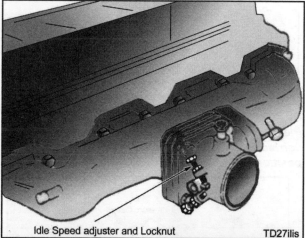

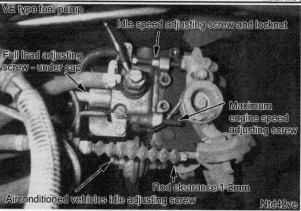

6. Once the idle speed is correctly set, race the engine a few times and ensure that the idle speed is still correct after the engine returns to normal idle speed.

7. If the engine does not return to the correct idle speed in step6, check the condition and/or operation of the throttle linkages, if faults are found repair/replace as required.

For Vehicles with Air Conditioning

8. Ensure that the clearance between the actuator idle control lever pin and the injector pump control lever are correct **(1-2mm)**. Adjust the idle speed setting to read **(850 -50Rpm)** without the air conditioning on, switch on the air conditioning and ensure that the idle speed setting is still correct

9. If the idle speed in step 8 is not correct, adjust the idle speed by turning the FICD actuator stroke adjusting screw.

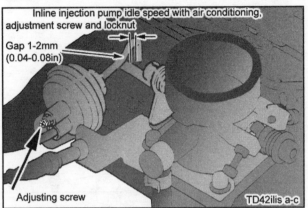

Inline injection pump idle speed with air conditioning, adjustment screw and locknut

Gap 1-2mm (0.04-0.08in)

Adjusting screw

TD42ilis a-c

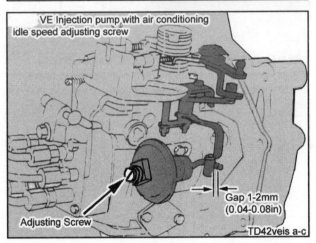

VE Injection pump with air conditioning idle speed adjusting screw

Gap 1-2mm (0.04-0.08in)

Adjusting Screw

TD42veis a-c

Injection Timing Check (In Line Pump)

1. Turn the crankshaft pulley in a clockwise direction and set the No1 piston to **16° BTDC**, remove all of the injection pipes and governor hoses.

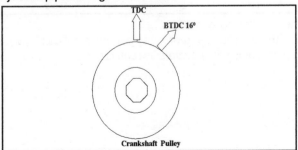

TDC

BTDC 16°

Crankshaft Pulley

2. Remove the No1 lockplate and delivery valve holder, pull out the delivery valve stopper (if fitted), delivery valve spring and delivery valve.

3. Install the delivery valve holder without the spring, valve and valve stopper, install a test tube to the No1 delivery valve holder and then push the injection pump assembly fully down towards the engine.

4. Feed the system fuel by using the priming pump, slowly move the injection pump until the fuel has stopped flowing from the No1 pipe and then tighten the fixing bolts in the injection pump.

5. Check to see if the injection marks on the front plate and the injection pump are lined up, if they are not, stamp a new mark on the front plate.

6. Remove the No1 test tube and delivery valve holder and install the delivery valve spring, stopper, valve holder and valve.

7. Install injection tubes and governor hoses and then if required bleed any air that may be present from the system.

Maximum Speed Adjustment (In Line Pump)
Please Note: The maximum speed adjusting screw is retained by sealing wire and under normal circumstances would not need adjustment.

1. If adjustment is needed, start the engine and let it run until normal operating temperature is reached, then connect a tachometer pick up to the No1 injection pipe.

2. With the engine still running, turn the adjusting screw in either direction while the throttle is being pressed down fully.

Maximum Engine Speed:
4,600 ± 100 RPM (Under No Load)

3. After the adjustment has been done, tighten the adjustment screw lock nut and wind up again with sealing wire.

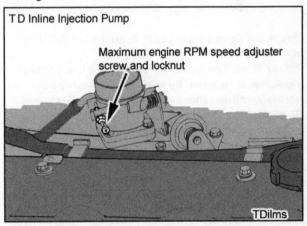

T D Inline Injection Pump

Maximum engine RPM speed adjuster screw and locknut

TDilms

Injection Timing Check (VE Type Injection Pump)

1. Remove the plug bolt from the injection pump distributor head and install a dial gauge to the distributor head.

2. Loosen off the injection pump mounting nuts and mounting bracket bolts.

3. Turn the crankshaft in an anti clockwise direction to a position of between 20-25° BTDC on the No1 piston.

4. With the dial gauge in a suitable rest position set the dial gauge to zero, turn the crankshaft in a clockwise direction until the No1 piston is set at TDC, and record the plunger lift measurement on the dial gauge.

Plunger Lift Measurement:

0.74±0.02mm (Equivalent to 6°BTDC)

5. If the plunger lift measurement in step 4 is not as shown, turn the injection pump body until the reading is correct, then tighten the injection pump mounting bracket and bolts.

Please Note: If the measurement is smaller than shown, turn the injection pump body in an anti clockwise direction, if the measurement is more than shown, turn the injection pump body in a clockwise direction.

6. After all the adjustments have been carried out, remove the dial gauge and refit the plug with a new washer, reconnect the injection pipes and bleed any air from the system that may be present.

Maximum Speed (Full Load) Adjustment (VE Type Injection Pump)

Please Note: The maximum speed (full load) adjusting screw is retained by sealing wire and under normal circumstances would not need adjustment. By disturbing the screw, this will cause the fuel flow to be changed and will cause incorrect adjustments on the engine. With this in mind, the injection pump timing will need to be adjusted again. If the maximum speed (full load) adjusting screw is turned in a direction that will increase the control lever angle, engine damage may occur

1. If adjustment is needed, start the engine and let it run until normal operating temperature is reached, then connect a tachometer pick up to the No1 injection pipe.

2. With the engine still running, turn the adjusting screw in either direction while the throttle is being pressed down fully.

Maximum Engine Speed:

4,600 ± 100 RPM (Under No Load)

3. If the engine speed is lower than shown in step 2, turn

the maximum speed (full load) adjusting screw anti-clockwise one or two full rotations, press down the throttle fully and record the engine speed.

4. If the engine speed is still lower than shown in step2, turn the maximum speed (full load) adjusting screw anti-clockwise one or two full rotations, press down the throttle fully until the correct engine speed is reached.

5. After the adjustment has been done, tighten the adjustment screw lock nut and wind up again with sealing wire.

Refer VE Idle Speed Diagrams

Injector Nozzle Check

1. Remove the injector from the vehicle, connect up to the pressure tester and check the initial pressure by pumping the tester handle a few times.

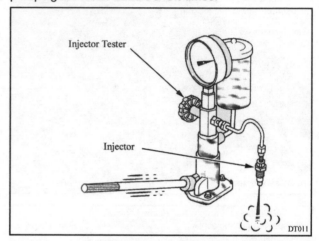

Initial Pressure: 9,807 to 10,297 (Used Nozzle).
Initial Pressure: 10,297 to 11,278kpa (New Nozzle).

2. Check the spray pattern by pumping the pressure tester handle 4-6 times or more per second , checking

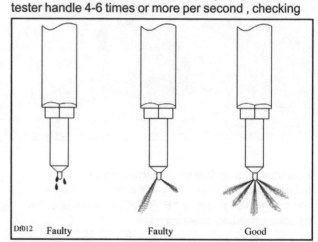

Df012   Faulty   Faulty   Good

the injection spray pattern.

3. If the operation and/or spray pattern is not as shown, repair/replace the nozzle/s as required.

Quick Glow System Check

1-If the engine fails to start or is hard to start, check the fuel level, condition and/or operation of the fuel supplying system and operation of the starter motor, if faults are found repair/replace as required.

2-If no faults are found in step1, check for correct installation of the glow plug connecting plate nuts, if faults are found repair/replace as required.

3-If no faults are found in step2, switch off the ignition for at least 10 seconds and then after switching on the ignition check if the glow plug indicator lamp comes on a few seconds after the ignition is switched on.

4-If the lamp comes on in step3, check the condition and/or operation of the glow plugs, if faults are found repair/replace as required.

5-If the glow plugs in step4 are OK, check the condition and/or operation of the glow plug relay, if faults are found repair/replace as required.

6-If the glow plug relay in step5 is OK, check the condition and/or operation of the "Start" signal input circuit, if faults are found repair/replace harness between the glow control unit and the ignition switch.

7-If the "Start" signal input circuit in step6 is OK, check the condition and/or operation of the glow control unit, if faults are found repair/replace as required.

8-If the glow control unit in step7 is Ok, check the condition and/or operation of the harness between the glow control unit and glow relay, and between the glow relay and the glow plug/s, if faults are found repair/replace as required.

9-If the glow plug indicator lamp in step3 does not come on, check the condition and/or operation of the indicator lamp globe, if faults are found repair/replace as required.

10-If the indicator lamp globe in step 9 is OK, check the condition and/or operation of the power supply circuit between the fuse and glow control unit, if faults are found repair/replace as required.

11-If no faults are found in the power supply circuit in step10, check the condition and/or operation of the glow control unit, if faults are found repair/replace as required.

12-If no faults are found in the control unit in step11, check for a short in the harness between the ignition switch and the glow indicator lamp, if faults are found repair/replace as required.

Quick Glow System Component Tests

With this system, when the ignition is switched ON, the relay is turned on and a high level electric current flows through the glow plugs and heats them up quickly. After between 2-6 seconds (depends on coolant temperature), the control unit turns off the glow indicator but the relay stays on. The relay will chop the electric current when the ignition switch has turned from ON to Start. The relay will have been chopping for 15 seconds after the ignition switch has gone back the ON position from Start. When the engine is not being cranked the relay chops the electric current, while 15 seconds or between 3-14 seconds (varies with glow plug terminal voltage) after the ignition switch has been turned to ON from

OFF.
Please Note: When the ignition is repeatedly turned ON amd OFF the 3-14 second time span will become shorter.

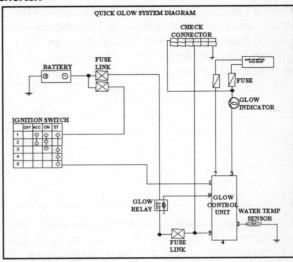

Glow Plug Check

1-Remove the glow plug connecting plate and check the continuity between each glow plug and the cylinder head.

2-If continuity exists the plug/s are OK, if no continuity exists repair/replace the plug/s as required.

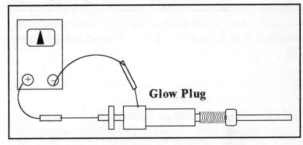

Water Temperature Sensor Check

1-Disconnect the sensor harness connector, install an ohmmeter to the sensor terminals and check the resistance at varying temperatures.

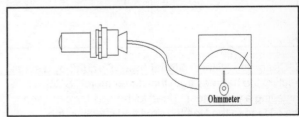

Coolant Temperature (°c)	Resistance (K/ohms)
-25	19.0
0	5.6
20	2.5
40	1.2

2-If the resistance is not as shown in step1, repair/replace sensor as required.

Quick Glow System Control Unit Check

1. Check the **"Power Supply Circuit"** by disconnecting the control unit harness connector, installing a voltmeter (+) lead to the harness connector terminal 7 and the (-) lead to terminal 4 and check the voltage with the ignition switch in the following position.

Ignition Switch Position OFF: **Voltage 0v**
Ignition Switch Position ON: **Voltage 0v**
Ignition Switch Position ACC: **Approx. 12v**

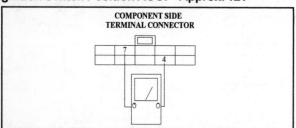

2. Disconnect the control unit harness connector, install an ohmmeter (+) lead to the harness connector terminal 4, (-) lead to body ground and check that continuity exists when the ignition switch is OFF.

3. If the voltage or resistance checks are not as shown, repair/replace as required.

4. Check the **"Water Temperature Sensor Circuit"** operation by disconnecting the control unit harness connector, installing an ohmmeter (+) lead to the harness connector terminal 2 and the (-) lead to terminal 4 and checking the resistance at varying temperatures.

Coolant Temperature (°c)	Resistance (K/ohms)
-25	19.0
1	5.6
20	2.5
40	1.2

5. If the resistance is not as shown in step4, repair/replace sensor, control unit and/or harness as required.

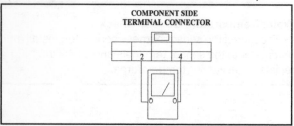

6. Check the **"Start" Signal Input Circuit** by disconnecting the harness from the starter motor "S" terminal, installing a voltmeter (+) lead to the No1 terminal and the (-) lead to the No4 terminal and checking the terminal voltage when the ignition switch is in the "START" position.

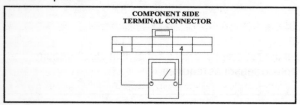

Voltage: **Approx. 12v**

7. If the voltage in step6 is not as shown repair/replace as required.

8. Check the **"Glow Indicator Control Circuit"** by switching off the ignition and leaving the harness connector connected to the control unit, installing a 3.4w test lamp between the No7 and No3 control unit harness connector terminals, switching on the ignition and recording the amount of time that the test lamp stays on.

Lamp Illumination Time Limit: Between 2 and 6 seconds (varying with coolant temperature)

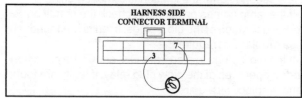

9. If the time limit is not as shown in step8, repair/replace as required.

10. Check the **"Glow Control"** by switching off the ignition, leaving the harness connected to the control unit and installing a 3.4w test lamp to the No9 and No4 terminals, switching on the ignition and recording the amount of time that the indicator lamp stays on.

Indicator Lamp Time Limit: **Between 3 and 14 seconds (varies with glow plug terminal voltage)**
Please Note: The above time will be shortened if the ignition switch is only OFF for a short time. So when checking this reading, leave the ignition off for at least 60 seconds and then turn the ignition on.
When the ignition is turned to "START" and returned to the "ON" position, the test lamp will come on and off between 3 and 6 times.

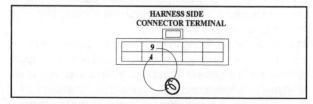

11. If the operation is not as shown in step10, repair/replace as required.

Injection Pump Control Lever Operation Check
Start Operation

1. Switch OFF the ignition, disconnect the harness connector from the starter motor "S" terminal.

2. Turn the ignition key to "Start" and ensure that the injection pump control lever moves to the start position.
Please Note: Diagram is on the next page

Drive Operation

1. Switch OFF the ignition, disconnect the harness connector from the oil pressure switch.

2. Turn the ignition key to the "ON" position and ensure that the injection pump control lever moves to the drive position.
Please Note: Diagram is on the next page

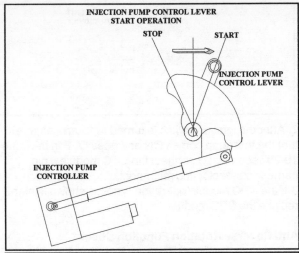

INJECTION PUMP CONTROL LEVER
START OPERATION

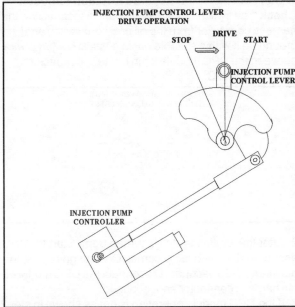

INJECTION PUMP CONTROL LEVER
DRIVE OPERATION

Stop Operation

1. Switch OFF the ignition and ensure that the injection pump control lever moves to the stop position.
2. Start the engine, disconnect and ground the oil pressure switch connector and ensure that the injection pump control lever moves to the stop position.

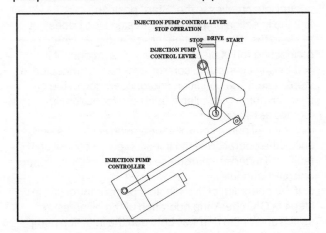

INJECTION PUMP CONTROL LEVER
STOP OPERATION

Injection Pump Controller Check
Motor Check

1. Switch OFF the ignition, disconnect the harness connector from the injection pump controller.
2. Apply battery voltage between the M (+) and M (-) terminals and ensure that the injector pump controller runs and that the control lever rotates.

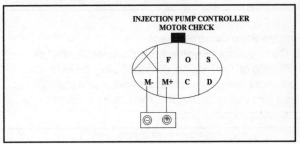

INJECTION PUMP CONTROLLER
MOTOR CHECK

3. If the operation is not as shown in step2, repair/replace as required.

Please Note: When replacing the controller, ensure that the 6-pin harness connector is disconnected and reconnected from controller after it has been fitted.

Lever Position Check

1. Connect a lead from the (+) battery terminal to the harness connector terminal F, a lead from the (-) battery terminal to the harness connector terminal M (-)
2. Connect another lead (1) from the (+) battery terminal to the harness connector terminals O, S and D and check the control lever stops in the relevant position.

Terminal Lead (1) Connected To Harness Connector Terminal	Injection Pump Lever Position
Terminal O	Start
Terminal S	Stop
Terminal D	Drive

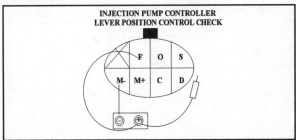

INJECTION PUMP CONTROLLER
LEVER POSITION CONTROL CHECK

3. If the operation is not as shown in step2, repair/replace as required.

Please Note: When replacing the controller, ensure that the 6-pin harness connector is disconnected and reconnected from controller after it has been fitted.

Injection Pump Control Unit Check
Preparation Check

1. Switch OFF the ignition, disconnect the "S" terminal from the starter motor, disconnect the 8 pin harness connector from the DPC module and install a test lamp between the M (+) and M (-) terminals.

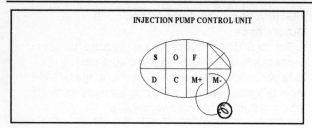

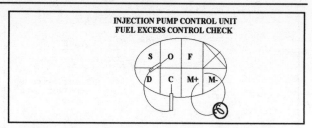

Engine Stop Control Check

1. Carry out the **"Engine Stop Control Check"** by switching off the ignition, disconnecting the harness connector from the oil pressure switch and installing a jump wire between the DPC module 8 pin harness connector terminal S and C.

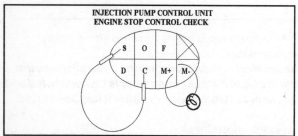

2. After the ignition switch is turned from OFF to ON, ensure that the test lamp comes ON and goes OFF in between 10-20 seconds. Disconnect the DPC module 6 pin harness connector and reconnect.
3-If the DPC module operation is not as shown in step2, replace the DPC module.

Drive Position Control Check

1. Carry out the **"Drive Position Control Check"** by switching off the ignition, disconnecting the harness connector from the oil pressure switch and installing a jump wire between the DPC module 8 pin harness connector terminal D and C.

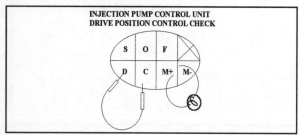

2. After the ignition switch is turned from Start to ON, ensure that the test lamp comes ON and goes OFF in between 10-20 seconds. Disconnect the DPC module 6 pin harness connector and reconnect.
3-If the DPC module operation is not as shown in step2, replace the DPC module.

Fuel Excess Control Check

1. Carry out the **" Fuel Excess Control Check "** by switching off the ignition, disconnecting the harness connector from the oil pressure switch and grounding it with a suitable cable, installing a jump wire between the DPC module 8 pin harness connector terminal O and C.

2. After the ignition switch is turned to "Start", ensure that the test lamp comes ON and goes OFF in between 10-20 seconds. Disconnect the DPC module 6 pin harness connector and reconnect.
3-If the DPC module operation is not as shown in step2, replace the DPC module.

Anti Reverse Rotation Function Check

1. Carry out the **" Anti Reverse Rotation Function Check "** by switching off the ignition, disconnecting the harness connector from the oil pressure switch and grounding it with a suitable cable, installing a jump wire between the DPC module 8 pin harness connector terminal S and C.

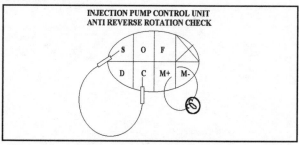

2. After the ignition switch is turned from "Start to "On", ensure that the test lamp comes ON and goes OFF in between 10-20 seconds. Disconnect the DPC module 6 pin harness connector and reconnect.
3. If the DPC module operation is not as shown in step2, replace the DPC module.

Injector Pump Control System Check
Engine Will Not Start

1. If the engine will not start, put the ignition switch into the "Start" position and ensure that the injection pump control lever moves to the "Start" position.
2. If the injection pump control lever in step1 does not move to the "Start" position, check and see if the connecting rod is disconnected, if it is reconnect it.
3. If the injection pump control lever rod is connected in step2, check the condition and/or operation of the injection pump controller, if faults are found repair/replace as required.
4. If the fuel pump controller operation is OK in step3, check the operation of the injection pump control unit, if faults are found repair/replace the injection pump control unit (DPC module).
5. If the operation of the injection pump control unit in step4 is OK, check the operation of the oil pressure switch and/or the harness between the injection pump control unit and the oil pressure switch, if faults are

found repair/replace as required.

6. If the injection pump control lever in step1 does move to the start position check the operation of the fuel system and/or the glow plugs, if faults are found repair/replace as required.

Engine Starts But Soon Stops

1. After the engine has been started (ignition switch ON), ensure that the injection pump control lever moves to the "Drive" position.

2. If the injection pump control lever in step1 does not move to the "Drive" position, with the ignition switch in the ON position disconnect the oil pressure switch harness connector and check if the injection pump control lever moves to the "Drive" position, if it does not check the condition and/or operation of the oil pressure lines and/or oil pressure switch, if faults are found repair/replace as required.

3. If the injection pump control lever in step2 does move to the "Drive" position, check the condition and/or operation of the injection pump controller, if faults are found repair/replace as required.

4. If the injection pump controller in step3 is OK, switch OFF the ignition, disconnect the oil pressure switch harness connector, install a jump wire between the D and C terminals and a test lamp between terminals M+ and M- on the 8 pin DPC harness connector, and ensure that when the ignition is switched to ON from START that then test lamp lights up and goes off in about 10-20 seconds. After checking the lamp operation disconnect and reconnect the DPC module 6-pin harness connector.

5. If the injection pump control unit check in step4 is not as shown, replace the injection pump control unit (DPC Module) as required.

6. If the injection pump control unit check in step4 is OK, check for a short in the harness between the injection pump control unit and the oil pressure switch, if faults are found repair/replace as required.

7. If the injection pump control lever in step1 does move to the drive position, check the condition of the fuel system components and/or venturi, if faults are found repair/replace as required.

Engine Runs On When the Ignition Switch is Turned Off

1. If the engine continues running when the ignition has been switched off, check whether the control lever rod is connected, if it is not, reconnect it.

2. If the connecting rod in step1 is connected, check the operation of the injection pump controller, if faults are found repair/replace as required.

3. If the injection pump controller in step 2 is OK, switch OFF the ignition, disconnect the harness from the oil pressure switch, install a jump wire between the S and C terminals on the 8 pin DPC module connector and when the ignition is switched to ON from the START position ensure that the test lamp goes ON and OFF in between 10-20seconds. Disconnect and reconnect the DPC module 6 pin harness connector.

If the operation is not as shown, replace the DPC module.

4. If the injection pump controller operation is not as shown in step3, check the condition and/or harness between the injection pump controller and the injection pump control unit, if faults are found repair/replace harness as required.

Engine Continues to Run in a Reverse Direction

1. If the engine continues to run in the reverse direction after the engine is turned off, carry out the test procedures shown above for the *Engine Runs On When the Ignition Switch is Turned Off*

2. If the engine does stop in step1, disconnect and ground the oil pressure switch connector with an earth lead and see if the engine stops, If the engine does stop, check the condition and/or operation of the oil pressure switch and/or oil pressure lines, if faults are found repair/replace as required.

3. If the engine does not stop in step2, switch OFF the ignition, disconnect the harness connector from the oil pressure switch and ground with a suitable wire, install a jump wire to the 8 pin DPC module connector terminals S and C, install a 3.4w test lamp to the 8 pin DPC module connector terminals M (+) and M (-), turn the ignition switch from "Start" to "On" and ensure that the test lamp comes on and then goes off in between 10-20 seconds, disconnect and reconnect the 6 pin DPC connector. If the operation is not as shown, replace the DPC module.

4. If the operation in step3 is OK, check the condition of the harness between the injection pump control unit (DPC Module) and the oil pressure switch, if faults are found repair/replace as required.

Vehicle Filling Capacities

Engine Oil with Filter: .... 9.2 Litres
Engine Oil without Filter: .... 8.0 Litres
Cooling System with Heater: .... 13.6 Litres
Cooling System without Heater: .... 12.8 Litres
Cooling System: .... 13.0 Litres
Manual Transmission: .... 3.9 Litres
Transfer Case: .... 2.2 Litres
Steering Box: .... 0.5 Litres
Front Differential (H233B): .... 5.4 Litres (Except Ute)
Front Differential (H233B): .... 4.3 Litres (Ute)
Rear Differential (H233B): .... 2.1 Litres
Rear Differential (H260): .... 4.7 Litres
Automatic Transmission: .... 8.5 Litres
Power Steering Fluid: .... 0.9-1.0 Litres

Vehicle Service Information

Adjust Valve Clearance:
> Every 20,000kms

Engine Coolant/Anti Freeze:
> Change Every 24 Months/40,000kms

Air Cleaner Element:
> Change Every 24 Months/40,000kms

Pre-Air Cleaner Element:
> Change Every 24 Months/40,000kms

Fuel Filter:
> Change Every 24 Months/40,000kms

Engine Oil:
> Change Every 3 Months/5,000kms

Engine Oil Filter:
> Change Every 6 Months/10,000kms

Brake Fluid:
> Change Every 24 Months/40,000kms

Manual Transmission Oil:
> Change Every 24 Months/40,000kms

Transfer Case Oil:
> Change Every 24 Months/40,000kms

Front Differential Oil:
> Change Every 24 Months/40,000kms

Rear Differential Oil:
> Change Every 24 Months/40,000kms

Repack Front Wheel Bearings:
> Every 24 Months/40,000kms

Repack Front Axle Joint Grease:
> Every 24 Months/40,000kms

Holden Jackaroo 4JG2 Engine 1992-1996

Holden Jackaroo 4JG2 Engine
1992-1996

Engine Checks

Valve Clearance Check

1. Check the rocker arm shaft bracket bolts and ensure that the bolts are tight, if not retighten to 54Nm.

2. Ensure that the No1 piston is at TDC by lining up the marks on the crankshaft pulley with the pointer on the front cover.

3. Ensure that the No1 cylinder push rods (both exhaust and inlet) are loose, this will indicate the No1 piston at TDC, check the valve clearances on the No1 and No3 exhaust valves and the No1 and No2 inlet valves with a feeler gauge.

Specified Clearance: 0.40mm

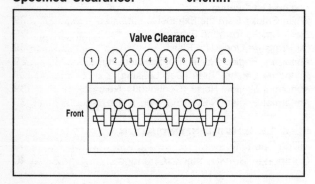

Valve Clearance

Front

4. If the clearance is not as shown, adjust to suit by loosening the lock nut on the adjusting screw and turning the adjusting screw until a resistance is felt when removing the feeler gauge.

5. Turn the crankshaft one full turn (360°) and ensure that the No4 cylinder push rods (both exhaust and inlet) are loose, this will indicate the No4 piston at TDC on its compression stroke. Record the valve clearances on the No2 and 4 exhaust valves and the 3 and 4 inlet valves with a feeler gauge.

Specified Clearance: 0.40mm

6. If the clearance is not as shown, adjust to suit by loosening the lock nut on the adjusting screw and turning the adjusting screw until a resistance is felt when removing the feeler gauge.

Compression Check

1. Start the engine and run until it is at normal operating temperature.

2. Remove the glow plugs, fuel cut solenoid connector and Quick ON Start System fuse link.

3. Install an adapter and compression gauge to the No1 cylinder, crank the engine and record the compression pressure.

Specified Compression Pressure:

2,942kpa @ 200RPM

Minimum Pressure: **2,157kpa**

Repeat procedure on remaining cylinders

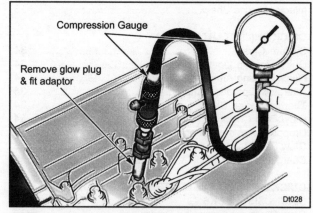

Compression Gauge

Remove glow plug
& fit adaptor

Dt028

4. If the pressure on one or more cylinders is low, pour a small amount of oil into the cylinder through the glow plug hole and check the compression pressure again. If it helps the pressure there are possibly faults with the piston rings or cylinder bores, if the oil does not help there may be a valve sticking or not seated correctly and/or leaks past the gasket.

Cylinder Head Tightening Procedures

1. The cylinder head bolts on this vehicle need to be tightened in three separate steps starting from the centre bolt outwards.

Cylinder Head Tightening Torque Bolts:
49Nm (First Stage)
Cylinder Head Tightening Torque Bolts:
Another 60-75° (Second Stage)
Cylinder Head Tightening Torque Bolts:
Another 60-75° (Third Stage)

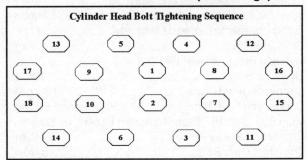

Cylinder Head Bolt Tightening Sequence

Piston Protrusion

1. Record the piston protrusion measurements at two separate points when the piston is in the TDC position.
2. All measuring points should be as close to the cylinder liner as possible.
3. Measure the projection at No1 and No3 on the cylinder head and at 2 and 4 on the cylinder body, then record the highest value from all cylinders. (This will determine the head gasket thickness).

Specified Protrusion Measurement: 0.658-0.814mm

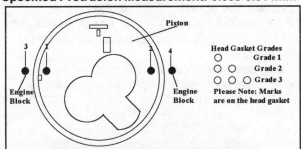

4. There are 3 different sizes of head gaskets, the difference between the highest and lowest measurments must not excedd the projection readings shown below.

Average Projection	Gasket Thickness (mm)	Gasket Grade
0.658-0.712	1.50	A(1Notch)
0.713-0.758	1.55	B(2Notch)
0.759-0.813	1.60	C(3Notch)

Oil Pressure Check (To Be Done)

1. Ensure that the engine oil level is correct, if not top up to suit.
2. Remove the oil pressure switch from the engine and install a pressure gauge to the engine block.
3. Start the engine and run to normal operating temperature and then record the oil pressure shown on the gauge.

Specified Oil Pressure: 19.6-49.00kpa (switch operating pressure)

4. If the oil pressure is not as shown, repair/replace as required.

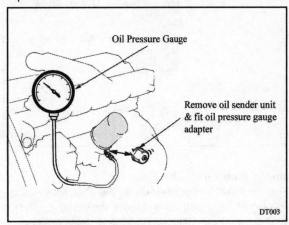

Cooling System Thermostat Check

1. Remove the thermostat from the engine and put into a suitable container of water.
2. Heat the water gradually and check the valve opening temperature and valve lift.

Valve Opening Temperature: 82-90°c

If the operation is not as shown above replace the thermostat.
3. Check that the valve spring is tight when the thermostat is fully closed, if not replace the thermostat.

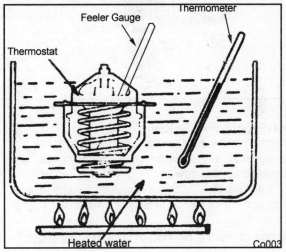

Fuel Filter Check and Replacement

1. Remove the fuel filter sensor, drain the fuel, then remove the fuel filter.
2. Clean the fuel filter mounting bracket and then coat the fuel filter-sealing ring with some diesel fuel.
3. Screw the fuel filter on until a slight resistance is felt and then turn another 2/3 of a turn or until suitably tight.
4. Install the fuel filter sensor (if fitted) to the new filter and then bleed any air present from the system.
Diagram is on the next page

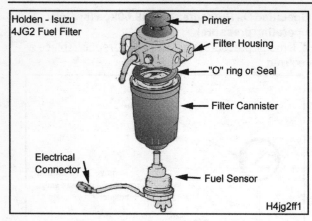

Holden - Isuzu 4JG2 Fuel Filter

- Primer
- Filter Housing
- "O" ring or Seal
- Filter Cannister
- Electrical Connector
- Fuel Sensor

H4jg2ff1

Draining Water from the Filter

1. Place a suitable container under the filter, loosen the drain plug of the separator and move the priming pump up and down about 10 times until the water is drained and then retighten the drain plug.

2. Move the priming pump up and down a few times, start the engine and ensure that there are no leaks from the drain plug.

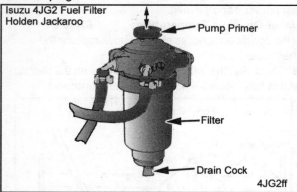

Isuzu 4JG2 Fuel Filter
Holden Jackaroo

- Pump Primer
- Filter
- Drain Cock

4JG2ff

Bleeding the Fuel System

1-Loosen the bleeder screw on the injection pump overflow valve and pump the primer pump until fuel flows from the bleeder screw.

2-Tighten the bleeder screw, operate the pump several times and check for fuel leaks in the system.

Timing Belt Removal and Replacement

Please Note: This engine has no timing belt and is driven by a gear system

Engine Tightening Torque's

Cylinder Head Tightening Torque Bolts: .... 49Nm (First Stage)
Cylinder Head Tightening Torque Bolts: .... Another 60-75° (Second Stage)
Cylinder Head Tightening Torque Bolts: .... Another 60-75° (Third Stage)
Rocker Shaft Bracket Bolts: 54Nm
Rocker Adjusting Screws: 15Nm
Exhaust Manifold Bolts and Nuts: 19.0Nm
Inlet Manifold Bolts and Nuts: 19.0Nm
Turbo Charger to Exhaust Manifold: 26Nm
Glow Plugs: 23Nm
Injection Pump Drive Pulley Nut: 76Nm
Flywheel Bolts: 118Nm
Connecting Rod Caps: .... 29Nm (First Stage)
Connecting Rod Caps: .... +40-60° (Second Stage)
Main Bearings:167.0Nm (Tighten in Two/Three Stages)
Crankshaft Pulley Bolt: 274Nm
Camshaft Gear Bolt: 64Nm
Oil Pump Bolt: 19.0Nm
Oil Sump Bolt: 19Nm

System Adjustments

Idle Speed Check

1-Run the engine to normal operating temperatures and then disconnect the engine control cable from the control lever.

2-Install a tachometer to the engine, and then with the engine still running record the engine idle speed.

Specified Idle Speed: 750-790RPM.

3-If the idle speed is not as shown, loosen the lock nut on the injection pump idling set bolt, and turn until the bolt setting is correct.

4-Re-tighten the lock nut and ensure that when the control cable is connected that there is no slack in it.

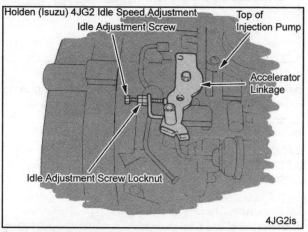

Holden (Isuzu) 4JG2 Idle Speed Adjustment

- Idle Adjustment Screw
- Top of Injection Pump
- Accelerator Linkage
- Idle Adjustment Screw Locknut

4JG2is

fast Idle Speed Check

1-Install a tachometer to the engine, disconnect the vacuum hose from the fast idle actuator on the injection pump, disconnect the other vacuum hose from the switching valve, connecting it to the fast idle actuator so as the vacuum line connects directly from the vacuum pump to the fast idle actuator.

2. With the engine still running record the fast idle speed.

Specified Idle Speed: 850-950 RPM

3. If the fast idle speed is not as shown, loosen the lock nut, turn the idle speed adjusting screw until the correct fast idle speed is set.

4. Retighten the lock nut, reconnect the vacuum hoses and any other removed parts in the reverse order of removal.

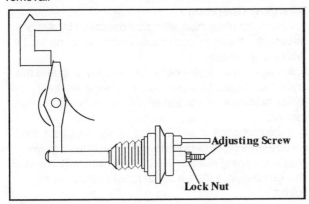

Injection Timing Check

1. Ensure that the No1 piston is at TDC on its compression stroke by checking that the push rods on the No1 valves are loose.

2. Remove the distributor head screw , cancel the WAX CSD with the handle of a screwdriver, install a static timing gauge and set lift to 1mm

3. Move the No1 piston to about 45° BTDC and then set the dial gauge to zero.

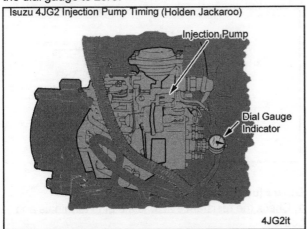

Isuzu 4JG2 Injection Pump Timing (Holden Jackaroo)

4. Turn the crankshaft slightly in both directions and ensure that the gauge indication is stable.

5. Turn the crankshaft in a clockwise direction and record a reading from the gauge when the timing marks in the crankshaft pulley lines up with its pointer (TDC).

Specified Timing Setting: 0.5mm

6. If the timing setting is not as shown, loosen the pump fixing nuts and bracket bolts and adjust the timing to its correct setting.

7. If the timing setting above is retarded, adjust the timing by moving the pump away from the engine.

8. If the timing setting above is advanced, adjust the

timing by moving the pump towards the engine.

9. After the adjustment has been done, retighten the pump and bracket nuts and bolts, remove the dial gauge and replace any removed parts in the reverse order of removal.

Injection Nozzle Check

Please Note: When checking the nozzle pressure use diesel fuel at 20°c

1. Set the nozzle on the injection nozzle tester and bleed the air by pumping the nozzle tester handle a few times.

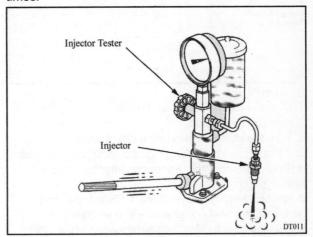

2. Slowly press down the nozzle tester handle and check the value shown on the pressure gauge.

Specified Injection Nozzle Pressure: 14,710kpa

3. If the pressure is not as shown in step2, adjust the nozzle pressure by changing the pressure adjusting shims.

Please Note: There are 27 different types of shims starting from 1.0-1.75mm in 0.01m increments. As an 0.01mm shim is added the pressure will increase by approximatley 147kpa.

4. If the spray condition of the injectors is bad, replace the injector/s as required.

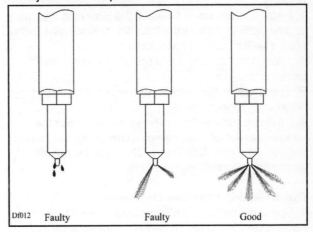

Quick ON Start (III) System.

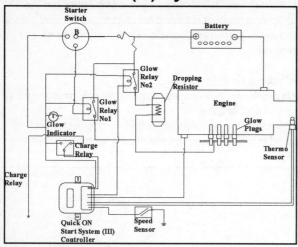

System Check

1. Disconenct the thermo switch connector on the thermostat outlet pipe.

2. Turn the starter switch to the ON position.

3. If the system is working OK, the glow relay will make a clicking sound within 7 seconds after the starter switch is turned ON.

4. Record the glow plug terminal voltage between the glow plug terminal and ground with a voltmeter imediatley after turning the starter switch to the ON position.

Glow Plug Voltage: 8-9volts

Please Note: The power to the quick on start system will be cut after the starter has been in the ON position for 20 seconds. Turn the starter switch to the OFF position and back to the ON position. (this will reset the Q.O.S (III) system)

System Operation Check
Quick Heating Operation

1. Check the quick heat operation by disconnecting the thermo switch harness connector on the thermostat housing.

2. Install a circuit tester between the glow plug and the engine earth and check the following operations with the starter switch in the ON position (engine OFF)

A. Glow indicator lamp lights up for between 1-6 seconds.

B. The circuit tester indicates power supply voltage for between 9-13 seconds

3. If the operation is not as shown above, check the condition of the relevant harness, glow relay and thermo sensor. If the operations were Ok, check the condition and/or operation of the glow plugs.

Quick Heating Afterglow Operation

1. Check the quick heat afterglow operation by disconnecting the thermo switch harness connector on the thermostat housing.

2. Install a circuit tester between the glow plug and the engine earth, start the engine and ensure that the circuit tester indicates power supply voltage for about 5 seconds.

3. If the operation in step2 is not OK, check the battery voltage, engine earth, wire harness and starter switch "ST" signal to the control unit.

4. If the operation in step2 is OK, check the condition and/or operation of the system harness, engine earth and/or starter switch, if faults are found repair/replace as required.

Afterglow Operation

1. Check the quick heat afterglow operation by disconnecting the thermo switch harness connector on the thermostat housing.

2. Install a circuit tester between the glow plug and the engine earth, start the engine and ensure that the circuit tester indicates 7.0 volts after 360 seconds of the engine running.

3. If the operation in step2 is not as shown, check the battery voltage, engine earth, system harness, glow plug/s, dropping resistor, No2 Relay, read switch and/or charge relay, if faults are found repair/replace as required.

Thermo Switch Check

1. Remove the sensor from the engine and place in a suitable container of water.

2. Heat the water gradually and make a continuity test across the terminal and body with a circuit tester.

Temperature (°c)	Current (mA)	Resistance (k/ohms)
19-21	1.0	2.0-3.0
49-51	1.0	0.6-1.0

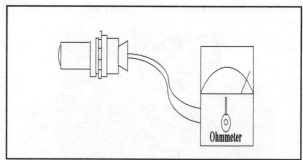

Glow Plug Check

1. Check the resistance across the plug terminals and body.

Specified Resistance: **0.8-1.0ohms**

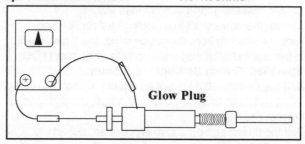

Dropping Resistor Check

1. Check for resistance across the resistor terminals A and B.

Specified Resistance: **224-236 m/ohms**

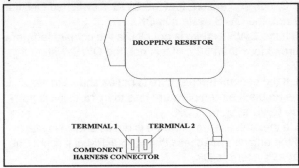

Glow Plug Relay No1 Check

1. Disconnect the relay harness connector and ensure that there is continuity between terminals 1-3 and none between terminals 2-4
2. Apply battery voltage between terminals 1-3 and ensure that there is continuity between terminals 2-4.
3. If the operation is not as shown above, replace the relay.

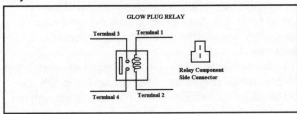

Charging Relay

1. Disconnect the relay harness connector and ensure that there is continuity between terminals 1-2, none between 1-3 and continuity between 4-5.
2. Apply battery voltage between terminals 4-5 and ensure that there is continuity between terminals 1-3 and none between 1-2.
3. If the operation is not as shown above, replace the relay.

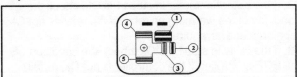

Quick ON Start Systen Trouble-Shooting and Diagnosis

Quick ON Start System.

Please Note: Disconnect the thermo switch connector, determine whether or not the glow plugs are receiving power by ensuring that the starter switch is off, installing a voltmeter between one of the glow plugs and the cylinder wall, move the starter switch to the ON position. If the voltmeter is showing the source voltage (12v) the glow plugs are receiving power, if the voltmeter does not move the glow plugs are not receiving power.

Glow Plugs are Receiving Power

1. If the glow plug light is not lighting up, check the condition and/or operation of the glow plug indicator globe, if faults are found repair/replace as required.
2. If no faults are found in step1, check the condition and/or operation of the Quick ON start timer, if faults are found repair/replace as required.
3. If no faults are found in step2, check that the glow indicator lamp turns ON for 0.3 seconds, if it does not there is a fault in the Quick ON start timer, repair/replace as required.
4. If the glow indicator lamp turns ON for 3.5 seconds in step3, put the starter switch back to the ON position from the Start position after the engine has started. If the glow plug relay stays ON for less than 14 seconds, the Quick ON start timer is faulty, repair/replace as required.
4A. If the glow indicator lamp turns ON for 3.5 seconds in step3, move the starter switch from the OFF to the ON position. If the glow plug relay stays ON for less than 14 seconds, the Quick ON start timer is faulty, repair/replace as required.
5. If the glow indicator lamp in step 4 and 4A is OK, check the condition and/or operation of the thermo switch, if faults are found repair/replace as required.
6. If no faults are found in step5, check the condition and/or operation of the glow plugs, if faults are found repair/replace as required

Glow Plugs are not Receiving Power

1. If the glow indicator lamp does not turn on check the condition and/or operation of the indicator light fuse, if faults are found repair/replace as required.
2. If no faults are found in step1, check the condition and/or operation of the Quick ON start timer, if faults are found repair/replace as required.
3. If no faults are found in step2, check that the glow indicator lamp turns ON for 3.5 seconds, if it does not check the condition and/or operation of the glow plug relay, Quick ON start timer, faults in the glow plug relay harness and/or faults in the fuse link and/or related harness, if faults are found repair/replace as required.
(Please Note: The glow plug relay turns on when the starter switch is moved from the OFF to the ON position)

QWS System Check

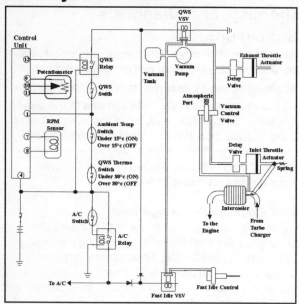

System Check

1. Disconnect the thermo switch harness connector from the thermostat housing. Disconnect the harness connecter from the ambient temperature sensor behind the radiator grille and short circuit the chassis side harness connecter by using a pin..
2. Start the engine and switch on the QWS switch on the console box.
3. Ensure that the fast idle control device operates and the engine RPM increases.
4. Ensure that the intake throttle operates, disconnect the exhaust shutter from the chassis and ensure that the exhaust throttle operates.
5. Push down the throttle pedal a little and ensure that the intake and exhaust throttle return a little.
6. Ensure that when the QWS is cancelled the throttle pedal is pushed down more than 60% (opening).

Thermo Switch Check

1. Remove the sensor from the engine and place in a suitable container of water.
2. Heat the water gradually and make a continuity test across the terminal and body with a circuit tester.

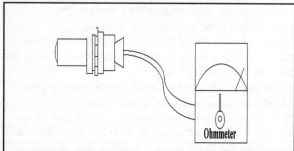

Switch ON>OFF: More than 73°c (Ambient Temperature More than 8°c)
Switch OFF>ON 76-84°c (Ambient Temperature 12-18°c)

QWS System Trouble-Shooting and Diagnosis

QWS Does Not Work

1. Check and ensure that the QWS is switched ON, if it is not, the QWS system is OK.
2. If the QWS system is not ON, is the coolant temperature at less than 80°c, if it is not, the QWS system is Ok.
3. If the coolant temperature is not as shown in step2, is the ambient air temperature less than 15°c, if it is not, the QWS system is OK.
4. If the ambient temperature is not as shown in step3, is the engine speed less than 1750RPM, if it is not, the QWS system is OK.
5. If the engine speed is not as shown in step4, is the throttle opening 50% or more, if it is not, the QWS system is OK.
6. If the throttle opening is not as shown in step5, check the condition of the thermo switch connector, if the connector is OK just disconnected and reconnect. If there are faults with the connector, repair/replace as required.
7. If the connector in step6 is Ok, check the condition of the ambient temperature switch connector, if the connector is OK but just disconnected reconnect. If there are faults with the connector repair/replace as required.
8. If the connector in step7 is Ok, check the condition of the potiometer connector, if the connectior is OK but just disconnected reconnect. If there are faults with the connector repair/replace as required.
9. If the connector in step8 is Ok, check the continuity of the thermo switch, if the continuity is not Ok, repair/replace as required.
10. If the continuity in step9 is Ok, check the continuity of the ambient temperature switch, if the continuity is not Ok, repair/replace as required.
11. If the continuity in step10 is Ok, check the condition of the potentionmeter, if the potentionmeter is not Ok, adjust/repair/replace as required.
12. If the potentionmeter in step11 is Ok, check the condition of the warming up relay, if the relay is not Ok, repair/replace as required
13. If the relay in step12 is Ok, check the condition of the EGR controller, if the controller is not Ok, repair/replace as required.
14. If the controller in step13 is Ok, check the condition of the vacuum hoses, if the hoses are not Ok, repair/replace as required
15. If the vacuum hoses are Ok in step14, check the condition and/or operation of the No1 VSV, if faults are found repair/replace as required.
16. If no faults are found in step15, check the condition and/or operation of the system wiring, if faults are found repair/replace as required.

Exhaust Throttle Fails to Close Fully
1. Check the condition and/or operation of the No1 VSV, if faults are found repair/replace as required.
2. If no faults are found in step1, check the condition and/or operation of the exhaust throttle, if faults are found repr/replace as required.
3. If no faults are found in step2, check the exhaust throttle fixings and/or play in the throttle, if faults are found repair/replace as required.

Only the Intake Throttle is Working
1. Check the condition and/or operation of the VCV pipes, if faults are found repair/replace as required.
2. If no faults are found in step1, check the condition and/or operation of the intake throttle, if faults are found repair/replace as required.

Intake Throttle Does Not Change its Opening at the Throttle Opening.
1. Check the condition and/or operation of the VCV pipes, if faults are found repair/replace as required.
2. If no faults are found in step1, check the condition and/or operation of the VCV, if faults are found repair/replace as required.

Neither the Intake or Exhaust Throttle is Actuated.
1. Check the condition and/or operation of the VSV-1 pipes, if faults are found repair/replace as required.
2. If no faults are found in step1, check the condition and/or operation of the VSV-1, if faults are found repair/replace as required.

Only the Fast Idle Does Not Work
1. Check the condition and/or operation of the VSV and FICD pipes, if faults are found repair/replace as required.
2. If no faults are found in step1, check the condition and/or operation of the VSV and FICD , if faults are found repair/replace as required.
3. If no faults are found in step2, check the condition and/or operation of the fast idle actuator, if faults are found adjust, re-adjust and/or replace as required.

Injection System and Engine Diagnosis and Troubleshooting
Engine Turns But Does Not Start
1. Check the operation and condition of the engine stop mechanism by checking condition and/or operation of the fuel cut solenoid, if faults are found repair/replace as required.

No Fuel to the Injetion Pump
1. Check the fuel level and ensure that there is enough fuel in the tank to carry out this test, if not fill as required.
2. If the fuel level in step1 is OK, check the fuel lines for blockage and/or damage, if faults are found repair/replace as required.
3. If no faults are found in step2, check the condition and/or operation of the fuel filter and/or overflow valve, if faults are found repair/replace as required.
4. If no faults are found in step3, check for air in the fuel system, if air is found bleed the system to suit.
5. If no air is found in the system in step4, check the condition and/or operation of the feed, if faults are found repair/replace as required.

Fuel is Being Delivered to the Injection Pump
1. Check the fuel in the tank and ensure that the correct fuel is being used and/or there is no water present in the fuel, if faults are found replace fuel as required.
2. If no faults are found in step1, check for air in the fuel injection pump, if air is found bleed the system to suit.
3. If no faults are found in step2, check the injection nozzles for sticking, wrong operating pressure and/or improper spray condition, if faults are found repair/replace as required.
4. If no faults are found in step3, check the injection pump and check for fuel drippage in the injector nozzles, if faults are found replace the fuel delivery valve.
5. If no faults are found in step4, check the injection pump control rack operation, if faults are found repair/replace the rack control as required.
6. If no faults are found in step5, check the injection pump plunger condition and/or operation, seized injection pump shaft and/or seized injection pump governor spring, if faults are found repair/replace as required.

Unstable Idling
1. With the engine running, check the engine idle speed setting, if the setting is not correct adjust as required.
2. If no faults are found in step1, check the condition and/or operation of the fast idle speed control device, if faults are found adjust and/or repair/replace as required.
3. If no faults are found in step2, check the condition and/or operation of the throttle control system, if faults are found, adjust and/or replace as required.
4. If no faults are found in step3, check the fuel system for leaks and/or blockages, air or water in the fuel, and/or damaged or blocked fuel filter, if faults are found repair/replace as required.
5. If no faults are found in step4, check the condition and/or operation of the fuel feed pump, if faults are found repair/replace as required.
6. If no faults are found in step5, check the injection nozzles for sticking, poor starting pressure and/or poor spray condition, if faults are found repair/replace as required.
7. If no faults are found in step6, check the operation of the injection pump by checking the condition and/or operation of the fuel delivery valve, injection timing setting, poor injection volume and/or faults in the idle spring, if faults are found adjust and/or repair/replace as required.
8. If no faults are found in step7, check the injection pump for faults in the governor lever operation, incorrect adjustment of the regulator valve, broken plunger spring, worn plunger, worn cam disc, if faults are found adjust/

repair/replace as required.

9. If no faults are found in step8, check the engine valve clearance adjustment, if faults are found adjust as required.

10. If the valve clearances are OK in step9, carry out a compression test on the engine, if faults are found repair/replace as required.

Insufficient Power

1. Check the condition and/or operation of the air cleaner, if faults are found repair/replace as required.

2. If no faults are found in step1, check for water in the fuel, if faults are found, replace the fuel as required.

3. If the fuel is OK in step2, check the condition and/or operation of the fuel filter, if faults are found repair/replace as required.

4. If no faults are found in step3, check the condition and/or operation of the fuel feed pump, if faults are found repair/replace as required.

5. If no faults are found in step4, check the injection nozzle/s for sticking, poor starting pressure and/or poor spray condition, if faults are found repair/replace as required.

6. If no faults are found in step5, check the condition and/or operation of the fuel injection pipes, if faults are found repair/replace as required.

7. If no faults are found in step6, check the condition of the injection pump by checking the condition and/or operation of the regulating valve, fuel delivery valve, faulty timer, worn cam disc, faulty control lever operation, injection timing setting and/or faults in the governor spring, if faults are found adjust and/or repair/replace as required.

8. If no faults are found in step7, check the injection pump for a worn plunger and worn cam disc, if faults are found repair/replace as required.

9. If no faults are found in step8, check the condition and/or operation of the Turbocharger by checking the condition and/or operation of the booster compensation pipe, leaks from the inlet and exhaust system and/or faults in the waste gate, if faults are found repair/replace as required.

10. If no faults are found in step9, carry out a compression test on the engine, if faults are found repair/replace as required.

11. If no faults are found in step10, check the engine valve clearance adjustment, if faults are found adjust to suit.

12. If no faults are found in step11, check the condition and/or operation of the engine valve springs, if faults are found repair/replace as required.

13. If no faults are found in step12, check the condition and/or operation of the exhaust system, if faults are found repair/replace as required.

14. If no faults are found in step13, check the condition and/or operation of the full load adjusting screw, if faults are found repair/replace as required.

Poor Fuel Consumption

1. Check the fuel system and related components for fuel leaks and/or damage, if faults are found repair/replace as required.

2. If no faults are found in step1, check the condition and/or operation of the air cleaner, if faults are found repair/replace as required.

3. If no faults are found in step 2 and with the engine running, check and record the engine idle speed, if the idle speed is not correct adjust to suit.

4. If no faults are found in step3, check the injection nozzle/s for poor starting pressure and/or improper spray condition, if faults are found repair/replace as required.

5. If no faults are found in step4, check the fuel injection timing setting, if the setting is not correct adjust to suit.

6. If no faults are found in step5, check the operation of the injection pump delivery valve, if faults are found repair/replace as required.

7. If no faults are found in step6, check the condition and/or operation of the turbocharger, if faults are found repair/replace as required.

8. If no faults are found in step7, check the engine valve clearances, if faults are found adjust to suit.

9. If no faults are found in step8, carry out a compression test on the engine, if the pressure is incorrect repair/replace faulty component/s as required.

10. If no faults are found in step9, check the condition and/or operation of the engine valve springs, if faults are found repair/replace as required.

Excessive Oil Consumption

1. Check the level of the engine oil and if the correct grade of oil is being used, if not correct fill or drain to the correct level.

2. If no faults are found in step1, check the engine for leaks from engine gaskets and/or seals, if faults are found repair/replace as required.

3. If no faults are found in step2, check the condition and/or operation of the air breather, if faults are found repair/replace as required.

4. If no faults are found in step3, check the inlet and exhaust valve stems and guides for wear and/or damage, if faults are found repair/replace as required.

Engine Overheating

1. Check the condition and/or level of the engine coolant in the radiator, if faults are found repair/replace as required.

2. If no faults are found check the condition of the fan coupling (if fitted), if faults are found repair/replace as required.

3. If no faults are found in step3, check the condition and/or operation of the fan belt, if faults are found repair/replace as required.

4. If no faults are found in step3, check the condition and/or operation of the radiator, if faults are found repair/replace as required.

5. If no faults are found in step4, check the condition

and/or operation of the water pump, if faults are found repair/replace as required.

6. If no faults are found in step5, check the condition and/or operation of the cylinder head and cylinder body-sealing cap, if faults are found repair/replace as required.

7. If no faults are found in step6, check the condition and/or operation of the thermostat, if faults are found repair/replace as required.

8. If no faults are found in step7, check the cooling system operation and/or for blockages, if faults are found repair/replace as required.

9. If no faults are found in step8, check the injection timing setting, if faults are found adjust to suit.

White Smoke From The Exhaust

1. Check the fuel in the system for water contamination, if faults are found repair/replace as required.

2. If no faults are found in step1, check the fuel injection timing setting, if the setting is incorrect adjust to suit.

3. If no faults are found in step2, carry out a compression test on the engine, if the pressure is not correct repair/replace as required.

4. If no faults are found in step3, check the condition and/or operation of the turbocharger, if faults are found repair/replace as required.

5. If no faults are found in step4, check the inlet and exhaust valve stems, oils seal and guides for wear and/or damage, if faults are found repair/replace as required.

Black Smoke From The Exhaust

1. Check the condition and/or operation of the air cleaner, if faults are found repair/replace as required.

2. If no faults are found in step1, check the condition of the injection nozzle/s for poor starting pressure and/or faulty spray pattern, if faults are found repair/replace as required.

3. If no faults are found in step2, check the fuel injection timing setting, if faults are found adjust to suit.

4. If no faults are found in step3, check the condition and/or operation of the injection pump for faults in the delivery valve and/or excessive injection volume, if faults are found adjust the injection volume and/or replace the delivery valve as required.

Oil Pressure Does Not Rise

1. Check the level and/or the quality of the engine oil, if faults are found replace or fill as required.

2. If no faults are found in step1, check the operation of the oil pressure gauge/switch and/or light, if faults are found repair/replace as required.

3. If no faults are found in step2, check the condition and/or operation of the oil filter, if faults are found repair/replace as required.

4. If no faults are found in step3, check the condition and/or operation of the relief valve and/or bypass valve, if faults are found repair/replace as required.

5. If no faults are found in step4, check the condition and/or operation of the oil pump and/or pump strainer, if faults are found repair/replace as required.

6. If no faults are found in step5, check the condition and/or operation of the rocker shaft, camshaft and bearings and crankshaft and bearings, if faults are found repair/replace as required.

Abnormal Engine Noise
Engine Knocking

1. Check the condition of the fuel in the system, if faults are found repair/replace as required.

2. If no faults are found in step1, check the fuel injection timing setting, if faults are found adjust to suit.

3. If no faults are found in step2, check the condition of the injection nozzle/s for poor starting pressure and spray pattern, if faults are found repair/replace as required.

4. If no faults are found in step3, carry out a compression test on the engine, if the pressure is not correct repair/replace as required.

Abnormal Engine Noise
Gas Leaking

1. Check the exhaust system for leaks from the pipes and/or gaskets, If faults are found repair/replace as required.

2. If no faults are found in step2, check the condition and installation of the injectors, if faults are found re-tighten and/or replace as required.

3. If no faults are found in step2, check the condition and/or operation of the exhaust manifold, if faults are found repair/replace as required.

4. If no faults are found in step3, check the condition of the head gasket, if faults are found repair/replace as required.

Abnormal Engine Noise
Continuous Noise

1. Check the condition and/or operation of the fan belt, if faults are found repair/replace as required.

2. If no faults are found in step1, check the condition and/or operation of the cooling fan, if faults are found repair/replace as required.

3. If no faults are found in step2, check the condition and/or operation of the water pump, if faults are found repair/replace as required.

4. If no faults are found in step3, check the condition and/or operation of the alternator and/or vacuum pump, if faults are found repair/replace as required.

5. If no faults are found in step4, check the engine valve clearances, if faults are found adjust to suit.

Abnormal Engine Noise
Slapping Noise

1. Check the engine valve clearances, if faults are found adjust to suit.

2. If no faults are found in step1, check the condition and/or operation of the rocker arm/s, if faults are found repair/replace as required.

3. If no faults are found in step2, check the flywheel for loose bolts, if faults are found tighten to suit.

4. If no faults are found in step3, check for worn and/or damaged crankshaft and/or thrust bearings, if faults are found repair/replace as required.

5. If no faults are found in step4, check for worn and/or damaged crankshaft and/or con rod bearings, if faults are found repair/replace as required.

6. If no faults are found in step5, check for worn and/or damaged con rod bushes and/or piston pins, if faults are found repair/replace as required.

7. If no faults are found in step6, check for worn and/or damaged pistons and/or cylinder liners, if faults are found repair/replace as required.

VEHICLE SERVICE INFORMATION

Vehicle Filling Capacities

Engine Oil with Filter: .... 5.0 Litres
Engine Oil without Filter: .... 6.0 Litres
Cooling System: .... 8.6 Litres
Manual Transmission: .... 2.95 Litres
Transfer Case: .... 1.45 Litres
Front Differential: .... 1.5 Litres
Rear Differential: .... 1.8 Litres

Vehicle Component Service Interval Changes

Valve Clearance
Check 24 months/40,000kms

Exhaust Manifold Nuts
Tighten Every 12 months/20,000kms

Engine Oil
Change Every 3 months/5,000kms

Engine Oil Filter
Change Every 6 months/10,000kms

Air Cleaner
Change Every 48 months/40,000kms

Fuel Filter
Change Every 18months/15,000kms

Engine Coolant
Check Every 12 months/20,000kms (Change as Required)

Brake Fluid
Change Every 48 Months/40,000kms

Manual Transmission Oil
Change at 10,000kms then every 48 Months 40,000kms

Transfer Case Oil
Change at 10,000kms then every 48 Months 40,000kms

Front/Rear Wheel Bearings
Repack Every 36 months/30,000kms

Front Axle Oil
Change at 10,000kms then every 48 Months 40,000kms

Rear Axle Oil
Change at 10,000kms then every 48 Months 40,000kms

Holden Rodeo 4JB1T Engine 1993-1997

1995 Rodeo

Holden Rodeo 4JB-1T Engine 1993-1997

Engine Checks

Valve Clearance Check

1. Check the rocker arm shaft bracket bolts and ensure that the bolts are tight, if not retighten to 53±4.9Nm.

2. Ensure that either the No1 and No4 pistons are at TDC by lining up the marks on the crankshaft pulley with the pointer on the front cover.

3. Ensure that the No1 cylinder push rods (both exhaust and inlet) are loose, this will indicate the No1 piston at TDC on its compression stroke. If the No1 push rods are depreseed this will indicate that the No4 piston is at TDC on its compression stroke. Check the valve clearances on the No1, No2, No3, No6 valves with a feeler gauge.

Specified Clearance: 0.40mm

4. If the clearance is not as shown, adjust to suit by loosening the lock nut on the adjusting screw and turning the adjusting screw until a resistance is felt when removing the feeler gauge.

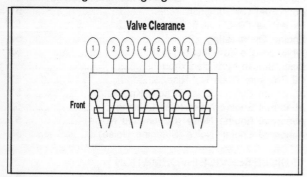
Valve Clearance

5. Turn the crankshaft one full turn (360°) and set the No4 piston to TDC on its compression stroke. Record the valve clearances on the No4, 5, 7 and 8 valves with a feeler gauge.

Specified Clearance: 0.40mm

6. If the clearance is not as shown, adjust to suit by loosening the lock nut on the adjusting screw and turning the adjusting screw until a resistance is felt when removing the feeler gauge.

Compression Check

1. Start the engine and run until it is at normal operating temperature.

2. Remove the glow plugs and fuel cut solenoid connector.

3. Install an adapter and compression gauge to the engine, crank the engine and record the compression pressure.

Specified Compression Pressure: 3,038kpa @ 200RPM

Minimum Pressure: 2,156kpa

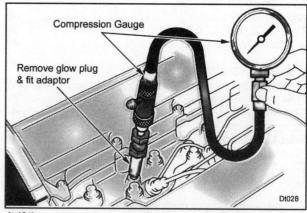

4. If the pressure on one or more cylinders is low, pour a small amount of oil into the cylinder through the glow plug hole and check the compression pressure again. If it helps the pressure there are possibly faults with the piston rings or cylinder bores, if the oil does not help there may be a valve sticking or not seated correctly and/or leaks past the gasket.

42

Cylinder Head Tightening Procedures

1. The cylinder head bolts on this vehicle need to be tightened in three separate steps starting from the centre bolt outwards.

Step1: Tighten to 49±4.9Nm
Second Step: Tighten again another 60°-75°
Third Step: Tighten again another 60°-75°

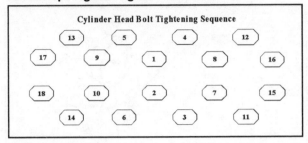

Cylinder Head Bolt Tightening Sequence

Piston Protrusion

1. Record the piston protrusion measurements at two separate points when the piston is in the TDC position.
2. All measuring points should be as close to the cylinder liner as possible.
3. Measure the projection at No1 and No2 and then at 3 and 4, then record the difference between No1 and No2 and then at 3 and 4 on each cylinder (taking and average of the two readings).
Specified Protrusion Measurement: 0.758-0.914mm
4. There are 3 different sizes of head gaskets, select the one that is equal to the largest projection measurements of each of the piston.

Average Projection	Gasket Thickness (mm)	Gasket Grade
0.758-0.813	1.50	A(1Notch)
0.813-0.859	1.55	B(2Notch)
0.859-0.914	1.60	C(3Notch)

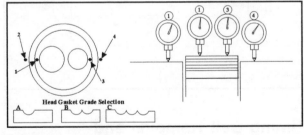

Head Gasket Grade Selection

Oil Pressure Check

1. Ensure that the engine oil level is correct, if not top up to suit.
2. Remove the oil pressure switch from the engine and install a pressure gauge to the engine block.
3. Start the engine and run to normal operating temperature and then record the oil pressure shown on the gauge.
Specified Oil Pressure: 390kpa @ 4000kpa
4. If the oil pressure is not as shown, repiar/replace as required.
Diagram is in the next column

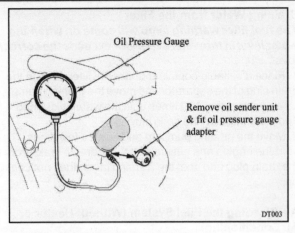

Oil Pressure Gauge

Remove oil sender unit & fit oil pressure gauge adapter

DT003

Cooling System Thermostat Check

1. Remove the thermostat from the engine and put into a suitable container of water.
2. Heat the water gradually and check the valve opening temperature and valve lift.

Valve Opening Temperature: 82°c (Gear Drive)
Valve Opening Temperature: 85°c (Belt Drive: Primary)
Valve Opening Temperature: 85°c (Belt Drive: Secondary)
Valve Lift: 8.0Nm (Gear Drive)
Valve Lift: 10.0Nm (Belt Drive)
If the operation is not as shown above replace the thermostat.
3. Check that the valve spring is tight when the thermostat is fully closed, if not replace the thermostat.

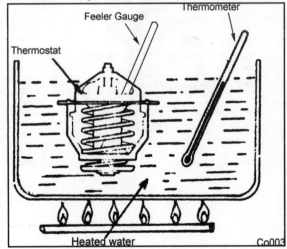

Feeler Gauge

Thermometer

Thermostat

Heated water

Co003

Fuel Filter Check and Replacement

1. Remove the fuel filter sensor (where fitted), drain the fuel and then remove the fuel filter.
2. Clean the fuel filter mounting bracket and then coat the fuel filter-sealing ring with some diesel fuel.
3. Screw the fuel filter on until a slight resistance is felt and then turn another 2/3 of a turn or until suitably tight.
4. Install the fuel filter sensor (if fitted) to the new filter and then bleed any air present from the system.

Draining Water from the Filter

The fuel filter warning lamp will come on when the water level in the water separator exceeds the correct level.

1. Place a suitable container under the filter, loosen the drain plug of the separator and move the priming pump up and down about 10 times until the water is drained and then retighten the drain plug.

2. Move the priming pump up and down a few times, start the engine and ensure that there are no leaks from the drain plug and that the warning lamp does not come on.

Air Bleeding the Fuel System (Without Heater or Air Conditioning)

1. Loosen the bleeder screw on the injection pump overflow valve.

2. Operate the priming pump until fuel mixed with the foam flows from the bleeder screw.

3. Retighten the bleeder screw, operate the priming pump several times and check for fuel leaks.

Air Bleeding the Fuel System (With Heater or Air Conditioning)

1. Operate the hand pump on the water separator to bleed the fuel system air into the injection pump.

2. Start the engine when it has finished bleeding and if the engine will not start within about 10 seconds repeat the process again.

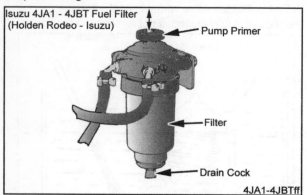

Isuzu 4JA1 - 4JBT Fuel Filter
(Holden Rodeo - Isuzu)
Pump Primer
Filter
Drain Cock
4JA1-4JBTff

Fuel Injector Nozzle Check

1. Fit the injector nozzle to an injector tester, pump the tester handle a few times and check both the opening nozzle pressure and the spray pattern.

Opening Pressure: 18,130kpa

If the pressure and/or the spray pattern are not as shown, adjust and/or repair/replace as required.

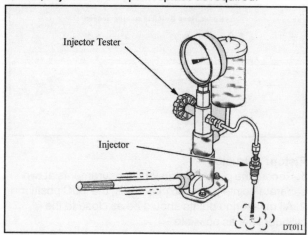

Injector Tester

Injector

DT011

Please Note: There are 41 different sizes of adjustment shims and are sized in 0.025mm increments from 0.5-1.5mm

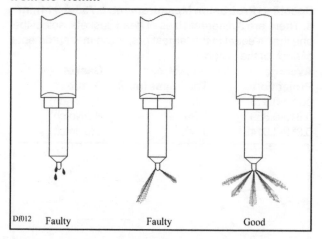

Df012   Faulty   Faulty   Good

Timing Belt Removal and Replacement (If Fitted)

Please Note: Some of these vehicles do not have a timing belt fitted to them and only have a gear set up.

Removal Procedures

Please Note: If the timing belt is being used again, before removing mark a direction arrow on the timing belt and place matchmarks on the pulleys and the belt.

1. Remove the crankshaft pulley and pulley housing covers A and B.

2. Refit the crankshaft pulley and then turn the engine in a clockwise direction until the No1 piston is at TDC on its compression stroke.

3. Check also that the timing mark on the crankshaft timing gear is lined up with the mark on the rear cover.

4. Remove the camshaft pulley and injection pump pulley flange, then remove the tension lever and tensioner.

5. Remove the timing belt from the engine.

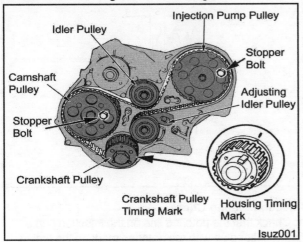

Isuz001

Replacement Procedures

Please Note: Before replacing the timing belt check the condition and/or operation of the timing belt pulleys, tensioners and/or pulleys, if faults are found repair/replace as required.

1. Ensure that the stopper bolts are properly installed to the camshaft and injection timing pulleys and then check that the timing marks on the crankshaft pulley lines up with the pointer on the front cover.

2. Fit the timing belt to the crankshaft pulley, camshaft pulley tensioner idler and injection pump pulley in this sequence and the adjust so as the slackness of the belt has been taken up by the tension pulley

3. Install the tensioner to the timing pulley housing and temporarily tighten the bolt.

4. Set the tensioner adjusting lever to the timing pulley housing, then remove the stopper bolts from the camshaft and injection timing pulleys.

5. Install a spring balance to the tensioner lever and adjust the timing belt tension by pulling straight down on the spring balancer with the specified force.

Specified Force: **98.1-117.7Nm**

Please Note: At this pint the belt must be adjusted and then the tensioner bolt tightened.

6. Turn the crankshaft 45° in an anti-clockwise direction and re-adjust the timing belt tension, removing ant slack left in the belt.

7. Tighten the tensioner bolts to 75.5±9.8Nm and then tighten the tension adjusting lever and bolt.

8. IInstall the flanges to the camshaft and injection timing pulleys.

9. Replace any more removed parts in the reverse order of removal

Timing Belt Warning Lamp Reset Procedures

1. Remove the tape from the KSW marked hole (B) on the back of the instrument cluster.

2. Remove the screw from the KSW marked hole (A) and replace the screw into the KSW marked hole (B) .

3. Fit a piece of new masking tape onto the KSW marked hole (A)

Timing Belt Replacement Torque's

Tensioner Idler:	75.54±9.8Nm
Crankshaft Pulley Bolt:	186.2±18.6Nm
Camshaft Gear Bolt:	63.7±4.9Nm
Injection Pump Drive Pulley Nut:	63.7±4.9Nm

Engine Tightening Torque's

Cylinder Head Tightening Torque Bolts: .... 49±4.9Nm (First Stage)

Cylinder Head Tightening Torque Bolts: .... Another 60-75° (Second Stage)

Cylinder Head Tightening Torque Bolts: .... Another 60-75° (Third Stage)

Rocker Shaft Bracket Bolts:	53.9±4.9Nm
Rocker Adjusting Screw Lock Nut:	14.7±4.9Nm
Exhaust Manifold Bolts and Nuts:	18.6±4.9Nm
Inlet Manifold Bolts and Nuts:	18.6±4.9Nm
Turbo Charger to Exhaust Manifold:	26.5±4.9Nm
Glow Plugs:	14Nm
Injection Nozzle:	37.2±4.9Nm
Injection Pump Drive Pulley Nut:	63.7±4.9Nm
Tensioner Idler:	75.54±9.8Nm
Flywheel Bolts:	117.6±4.9Nm

Connecting Rod Caps: .... 83.3±4.9 (Tighten in Two or Three Stages)

Main Bearings: 166.6±9.8Nm (Tighten in Three Stages)

Crankshaft Pulley Bolt:	186.2±18.6Nm
Camshaft Gear Bolt:	63.7±4.9Nm
Oil Pump Bolt:	18.6±4.9Nm
Oil Sump Bolt:	18.6±4.9Nm

System Adjustments

Idle Speed Check

1. Run the engine to normal operating temperatures and then disconnect the engine control cable from the control lever.

2. Install a tachometer to the engine, and then with the engine still running record the engine idle speed.

Specified Idle Speed: 770±20RPM.

3. If the idle speed is not as shown, loosen the idle set screw lock nut on the injection pump idle speed set bolt (on the injection pump), and turn until the setting is correct.

4. Re-tighten the lock nut, reconnect the engine control cable and adjust cable to suit.

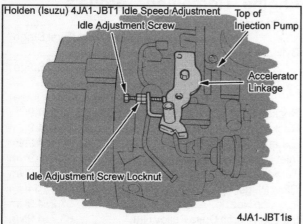

Holden (Isuzu) 4JA1-JBT1 Idle Speed Adjustment
Top of Injection Pump
Idle Adjustment Screw
Accelerator Linkage
Idle Adjustment Screw Locknut
4JA1-JBT1is

Fast Idle Speed Check

1. Run the engine to normal operating temperatures install a tachometer to the engine.

2. Disconnect the vacuum hose from the fast idle actuator on the injection pump, disconnect the other vacuum hose from the switching valve, connecting it to the fast idle actuator so as the vacuum line connects directly from the vacuum pump to the fast idle actuator.

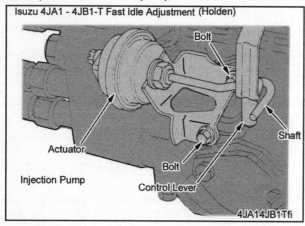

Isuzu 4JA1 - 4JB-T Fast Idle Adjustment (Holden)
Bolt
Actuator
Shaft
Injection Pump
Bolt
Control Lever
4JA14JB1Tfi

3. With the engine still running record the fast idle speed.

Specified Idle Speed: 850-950 RPM

4. If the fast idle speed is not as shown, loosen the fast idle actuator bracket bolts and adjust the idle speed by moving the actuator so as the clearance between the

actuator shaft and the control lever is between 1-2mm.

4. Retighten the bracket bolts.

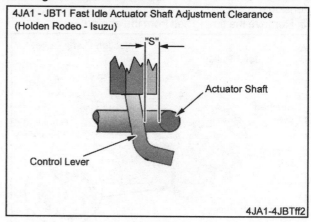

4JA1 - JBT1 Fast Idle Actuator Shaft Adjustment Clearance (Holden Rodeo - Isuzu)
"S"
Actuator Shaft
Control Lever
4JA1-4JBTff2

Injection Timing Check

1. Check that the notched line on the injection pump flange is lined up with the notched mark on the timing gear case.

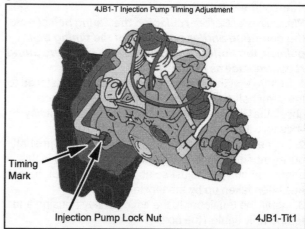

4JB1-T Injection Pump Timing Adjustment
Timing Mark
Injection Pump Lock Nut
4JB1-Tit1

2. Ensure that the No1 piston is at TDC on its compression stroke by checking that the push rods on the No1 valves are loose, and the marks on the crankshaft pulley and the front engine cover pointer are lined up.

3. Disconnect the injection pipe from the pump, remove the distributor head screw and install a static timing gauge.

4. Move the No1 piston to between 30-40° BTDC and

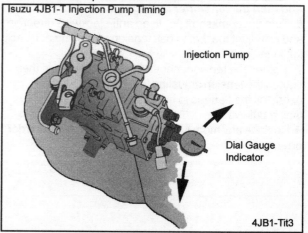

Isuzu 4JB1-T Injection Pump Timing
Injection Pump
Dial Gauge Indicator
4JB1-Tit3

then set the dial gauge to zero.

5. Turn the crankshaft in a clockwise direction and record a reading from the gauge when the timing marks (12°) on the crankshaft pulley lines up with its pointer on the front cover.

Specified Timing Setting: 0.5mm @ 12°BTDC

6. If the timing setting is not as shown, loosen the pump

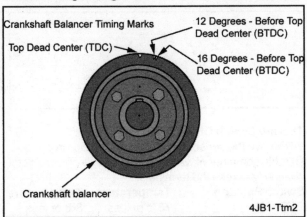

Crankshaft Balancer Timing Marks

12 Degrees - Before Top Dead Center (BTDC)

Top Dead Center (TDC)

16 Degrees - Before Top Dead Center (BTDC)

Crankshaft balancer

4JB1-Ttm2

fixing nuts and bracket bolts and adjust the timing to its correct setting.

7. If the timing setting is more than shown above adjust the timing by moving the pump away from the engine.(Belt Drive)

7. If the timing setting is more than shown above adjust the timing by moving the pump towards the engine.(Gear Drive)

8. If the timing setting is less than shown above adjust the timing by moving the pump towards the engine.(Belt Drive)

8. If the timing setting is less than shown above adjust the timing by moving the away from the engine.(Gear Drive)

9. After the adjustment has been done, retighten the pump and bracket nuts and bolts, remove the dial gauge and replace any removed parts in the reverse order of removal.

Pre Heating System Check.

System Inspection Check
1. Disconnect the thermo switch on the thermostat outlet pipe and turn the starter switch to the ON position.

2. If the system is operating correctly the glow relay will make a clicking sound about 15 seconds after the starter switch is turned on.

3. Record then glow plug terminal voltage with a circuit tester straight after the starter switch to the ON position.

Specified Glow Plug Terminal Voltage: 11v

System Circuit (Visual Check)
1. Check the condition and/or operation of the main fuses and/or glow indicator, if faults are found repair/replace as required.

Glow Plug Check
1. Check for continuity across the plug terminals and body.

2. If no continuity exists the heat wire is broken and should be replaced.

Glow Plug Specifications:
Normal System: 1.5 ohms
Glow Plug Specifications:
Quick ON Start System: 0.9ohms

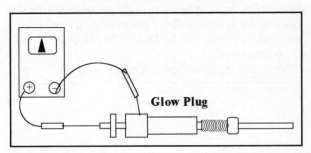

Glow Plug

Thermo Switch Check
1. Remove the sensor from the engine and place in a suitable container of water.

2. Heat the water gradually and make a continuity test across the terminal and body with a circuit tester.

Switch OFF>ON 7-13°c
Switch OFF>ON More than 3°c

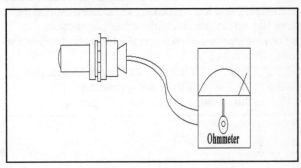

Ohmmeter

Fusible Link
1. Carry out continuity check across the fuse link terminal.

2. If the tester does not indicate continuity the fuse link has burned out and should be replaced.

Glow Plug Relay Check
1. Remove the glow relay (located near the fuse box in the engine compartment) and with an ohmmeter check the resistance between the No3 and No4 terminals.

Specified Resistance: **10-15ohms.**

2. If the resistance is not as shown, repair/replace as required.

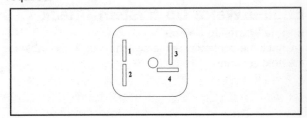

Glow Timer System Check
Glow Timer Operation Check
1-Disconnect the harness connector from the thermo sensor and connect a voltmeter between the glow plug and ground.
2-Turn the starter switch from OFF to ON (ensuring that the engine is OFF) and check the time that the glow indicator lamp is ON.
3-If the glow indicator lamp is ON for about 15 seconds (Normal Pre Heating System) or 3.5 seconds (Quick ON System) the system is OK. If the system operation is not as shown there may be faults in the glow timer and/or the glow relay.
4-Return the starter switch to the OFF position.

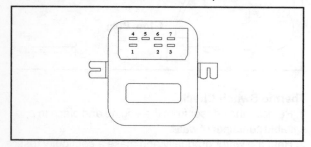

Glow Timer Output Check
1-Disconnect the lead wire from the starter switch, connect the (+) lead of the voltmeter to the No5 terminal on the timer and the (-) lead to the No6 terminal on the timer (do not disturb any of the other connections).
2-Turn the starter switch from OFF to ON and record the voltmeter reading.
3-If the voltmeter is reading 0v for approx 18 seconds before rising the glow timer delay is working OK.
4-Return the starter switch to the OFF position.

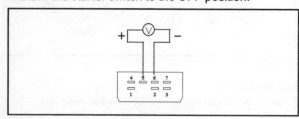

Terminal Configuration for the Glow Timer

Terminal No	Connected To
1	Starter Switch ON Position
2	
3	Thermo Switch
4	Starter Switch ST Position
5	Glow Relay
6	Ground
7	Glow Indicator Lamp

Engine Warm Up System Check
Engine Warm Up Switch
1-Check the continuity of the switch as as in the table in the next column.

Switch Position	Terminal Number 2	Terminal Number 3	Terminal Number
ON	Yes	Yes	Yes
OFF	Yes	Yes	

2-Ensure that the indicator lamp comes ON when the engine warning switch is ON with the engine running.

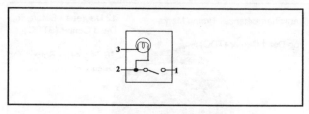

Thermo Switch Check
1-Remove the sensor from the engine, place in a suitable container of water, heat gradually and check for continuity across the terminals.

Switch Position	Temperature	Temperature
OFF>ON	73°c or less	8°c or less
ON>OFF	About 80°c	About 15°c

2-If the continuity is not as shown, repair/replace as required.
Use previous water thermo sensor diagrams

Throttle Switch (Half Throttle)
1-Install an ohmmeter across the switch connector terminals and check the continuity across the terminals.

	Switch Position	
	Free	Push
Throttle Switch	Continuity	No Continuity
Half Throttle Switch	No Continuity	Continuity

2-if the operation is not as shown, repair/replace as required.

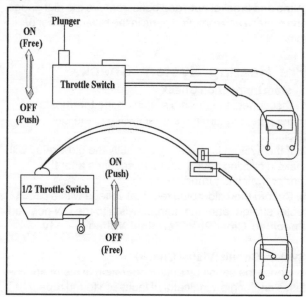

Vacuum Switch VSV Check

1. With an ohmmeter check the resistance across the VSV terminals.

Specified Resistance: **40ohms.**

2. If the resistance is not as shown, repair/replace as required.

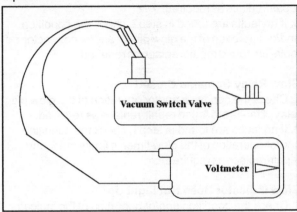

Vacuum Control Valve Check

1. Check the control valve pressure operating pressure by ensuring that the Port (X) is open to the atmosphere with no blockages.

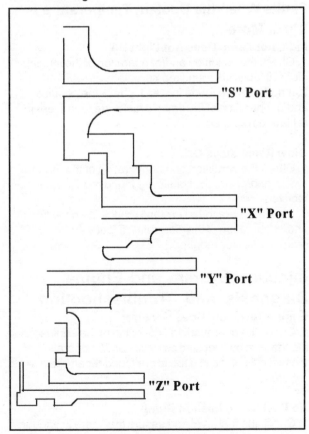

2. Apply a constant pressure of -500500mmhg to Port (Z).

3. Apply a pressure of -75mmhg to Port S and measure the operating pressure at port (Y).

Valve Operating Pressure: **0 to (-)50mmHg**

4. Apply a pressure of -155mmHg to port (S) and measure the operating pressure at port (Y).

Valve Operating Pressure: (-)400 to (-)500mmHg

5. If the operation is not as shown, repair/replace as required.

Vacuum Regulator Check

1. Check the regulator operating pressure by applying a pressure of (-)450mmHg to port(S) and recording the pressure at port (Z).

Regulator Operating Pressure:

                   (-)235 to (-) 265mmHg

2. If the operation is not as shown, repair/replace as required.

Intake Throttle Actuator Check

1. Apply a specified vacuum to the intake throttle actuator and check the actuator lift.

Vacuum (mmHg)	Actuator Lift
(-)150	1/4
(-)250	1/2
(-)340	3/4
(-)420	Fully Open

2. If the operation is not as shown, repair/replace as required.

Intake Throttle Valve Check

1. Check the valve shaft for wear and/or damage to the shaft and ensure that the shaft turns smoothly.

2. If the operation is not as shown, repair/replace as required.

Exhaust Throttle Actuator Check

1. Check the actuator for vacuum leakage by applying (-)500mmHg of vacuum to the actuator and check the amount of vacuum still left after 15 seconds.

Specified Vacuum Reading: (-)480mmHg

2. If the operation is not as shown, repair/replace as required.

Exhaust Throttle Valve Check

1. Check the valve shaft for wear and/or damage to the shaft and ensure that the shaft turns smoothly.

2. If the operation is not as shown, repair/replace as required.

Turbocharger

Wheel Shaft and End Play

1. Using a dial indicator to measure the wheel shaft end play, apply a force of 1.2kg alternately to the compressor wheel and the turbine wheel end and check the shaft play.

Standard	Limit
0.03-0.06	0.09

Wheel Shaft Bearing Clearance

1. Using a dial indicator to measure the wheel shaft and bearing clearance.

Standard	Limit
0.56-0.127	0.127

Turbo Pressure Check

1. Remove the pressure switch connecting hose and install a pressure gauge.
2. Start the engine and then gradually increase the engine speed (making sure that the vehicle is stationary with no load applied) and check that the turbo pressure rises to approximately 500mmHg.

Wastegate Operation Check

1. Remove the hose between the wastegate and the intake pipe and install a pressure gauge.
2. Ensure that the rod begins to move when a pressure of 665mmHg is applied to the wastegate.

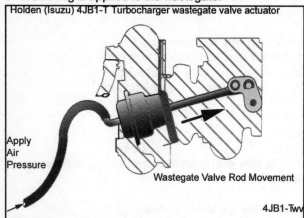

Holden (Isuzu) 4JB1-T Turbocharger wastegate valve actuator

Apply Air Pressure

Wastegate Valve Rod Movement

4JB1-Twv

Turbo Safety Valve Check

1. Operate the safety valve by hand and ensure that the operation is OK.
2. Check the condition and or operation if the val

Pre Heating System Trouble-Shooting and Diagnosis

Faults When the Coolant Temperature is 0°c or Less

Glow Plug Relay Will Not Close

1. Check for poor connections in the main fuse link wire, if faults are found repair/replace as required.
2. If no faults are found in step1, check for poor connections of the starter switch circuit, if faults are found repair/replace as required.
3. If no faults are found in step2, check for poor connections and/or condition of the No8 fuse and relevant circuits, if faults are found repair/replace as required.
4. If no faults are found in step3, check the condition and/or operation of the glow plug relay, if faults are found repair/replace as required.
5. If no faults are found in step4, check the condition and/or operation of the glow timer, timer connections and/or , timer circuits, if faults are found repair/replace as required.
6. If no faults are found in step5, check the condition and/or operation of the thermo switch and/or circuits, if faults are found repair/replace as required

Glow Relay Closes but Pre-Heating System Does Not Operate

1. Check for poor connections in the main fuse link wire, if faults are found repair/replace as required.
2. If no faults are found in step1, check the condition and/or operation of the glow plug relay, if faults are found repair/replace as required.
3. If no faults are found in step2, check the condition and/or operation of the glow plug/s and/or connectors, if faults are found repair/replace as required.

Glow Relay Remains Closed

1. Check the condition and/or operation of the glow plug relay, if faults are found repair/replace as required.
2. If no faults are found in step1, check the condition and/or operation of the glow timer, if faults are found repair/replace as required.

Glow Indicator Does Not Light Up

1. Check the condition and/or operation of the indicator globe, if faults are found repair/replace as required.
2. If no faults are found in step1 check the condition and/or operation of the glow timer, if faults are found repair/replace as required.

Faults When the Coolant Temperature is 0°c or More

Indicator Lamp Does Not Light Up

1. Check the condition and/or operation of the indicator globe, if faults are found repair/replace as required.
2. If no faults are found in step1, check the condition and/or operation of the timer, if faults are found repair/replace as required.

Glow Relay Stays ON

1. Check the condition and/or operation of the thermo switch and/or circuit, if faults are found repair/replace as required.
2. If no faults are found in step1, check the condition and/or operation of the glow relay, if faults are found repair/replace as required.

Injection System and Engine Diagnosis and Troubleshooting

Engine Turns But Does Not Start

1. Check the operation and condition of the engine stop mechanism by checking condition and/or operation of the fuel cut solenoid, if faults are found repair/replace as required.

No Fuel to the Injetion Pump

1. Check the fuel level and ensure that there is enough fuel in the tank to carry out this test, if not fill as required.
2. If the fuel level in step1 is OK, check the fuel lines for blockage and/or damage, if faults are found repair/replace as required.
3. If no faults are found in step2, check the condition

and/or operation of the fuel filter and/or overflow valve, if faults are found repair/replace as required.

4. If no faults are found in step3, check for air in the fuel system, if air is found bleed the system to suit.

5. If no air is found in the system in step4, check the condition and/or operation of the feed pump, if faults are found repair/replace as required.

Fuel is Being Delivered to the Injection Pump

1. Check the fuel in the tank and ensure that the correct fuel is being used and/or there is no water present in the fuel, if faults are found replace fuel as required.

2. If no faults are found in step1, check for air in the fuel injection pump, if air is found bleed the system to suit.

3. If no faults are found in step2, check the injection nozzles for sticking, wrong operating pressure and/or improper spray condition, if faults are found repair/replace as required.

4. If no faults are found in step3, check the injection pump and check for fuel drippage after fuel injection, if faults are found replace the fuel delivery valve.

5. If no faults are found in step4, check the condition and/or operation of the injection pump plunger, if faults are found repair/replace as required.

6. If no faults are found in step5, check the injection pump drive shaft for seizure and/or damage, if faults are found repair/replace the drive shaft as required.

7. If no faults are found in step6, check the injection pump govenor for being siezed, if faults are found repair/replace as required.

Unstable Idling

1. With the engine running, check the engine idle speed setting, if the setting is not correct adjust as required.

2. If no faults are found in step1, check the condition and/or operation of the fast idle speed control device, if faults are found adjust, repair/replace as required.

3. If no faults are found in step2, check the condition and/or operation of the throttle control system, if faults are found, adjust and/or replace as required.

4. If no faults are found in step3, check the fuel system for leaks and/or blockages, air or water in the fuel, and/or damaged or blocked fuel filter, if faults are found repair/replace as required.

5. If no faults are found in step4, check the condition and/or operation of the fuel feed pump, if faults are found repair/replace as required.

6. If no faults are found in step5, check the injection nozzles for sticking, poor starting pressure and/or poor spray condition, if faults are found repair/replace as required.

7. If no faults are found in step6, check the operation of the injection pump by checking the condition and/or operation of the fuel delivery valve, injection timing setting, poor injection volume and/or faults in the idle spring, if faults are found adjust and/or repair/replace as required.

8. If no faults are found in step7, check the injection pump for faults in the governor lever operation, incorrect

adjustment of the regulator valve, broken plunger spring, worn plunger and worn cam disc, if faults are found adjust/repair/replace as required.

9. If no faults are found in step8, check the engine valve clearance adjustment, if faults are found adjust as required.

10. If the valve clearances are OK in step9, carry out a compression test on the engine, if faults are found repair/replace as required.

Insufficient Power

1. Check the condition and/or operation of the air cleaner, if faults are found repair/replace as required.

2. If no faults are found in step1, check for water in the fuel, if faults are found, replace the fuel as required.

3. If the fuel is OK in step2, check the condition and/or operation of the fuel filter, if faults are found repair/replace as required.

4. If no faults are found in step3, check the condition and/or operation of the fuel feed pump, if faults are found repair/replace as required.

5. If no faults are found in step4, check the injection nozzle/s for sticking, poor starting pressure and/or poor spray condition, if faults are found repair/replace as required.

6. If no faults are found in step5, check the condition and/or operation of the fuel injection pipes, if faults are found repair/replace as required.

7. If no faults are found in step6, check the condition of the injection pump by checking the condition and/or operation of the regulating valve, fuel delivery valve, faulty timer, worn cam disc, faulty control lever operation, injection timing setting and/or faults in the governor spring, if faults are found adjust and/or repair/replace as required.

8. If no faults are found in step7, check the injection pump for a worn plunger and , worn cam disc, if faults are found repair/replace as required.

9. If no faults are found in step8, carry out a compression test on the engine, if faults are found repair/replace as required.

10. If no faults are found in step9, check the engine valve clearance adjustment, if faults are found adjust to suit.

11. If no faults are found in step10, check the condition and/operation of the engine valve springs, if faults are found repair/replace as required.

12. If no faults are found in step11, check the condition and/or operation of the exhaust system, if faults are found repair/replace as required.

13. If no faults are found in step12, check the condition and/or operation of the full load adjusting screw seal, if faults are found repair/replace as required.

Poor Fuel Consumption

1. Check the fuel system and related components for fuel leaks and/or damage, if faults are found repair/replace as required.

2. If no faults are found in step1, check the condition and/or operation of the air cleaner, if faults are found

repair/replace as required.

3. If no faults are found in step 2 and with the engine running, check and record the engine idle speed, if the idle speed is not correct adjust to suit.

4. If no faults are found in step3, check the injection nozzle/s for poor starting pressure and/or improper spray condition, if faults are found repair/replace as required.

5. If no faults are found in step4, check the fuel injection timing setting, if the setting is not correct adjust to suit.

6. If no faults are found in step5, check the operation of the injection pump delivery valve, if faults are found repair/replace as required.

7. If no faults are found in step6, check the engine valve clearances, if faults are found adjust to suit.

8. If no faults are found in step7, carry out a compression test on the engine, if the pressure is incorrect repair/replace faulty component/s as required.

9. If no faults are found in step8, check the condition and/or operation of the engine valve springs, if faults are found repair/replace as required.

Excessive Oil Consumption

1. Check the level of the engine oil and if the correct grade of oil is being used, if not correct fill or drain to the correct level.

2. If no faults are found in step1, check the engine for leaks from engine gaskets and/or seals, if faults are found repair/replace as required.

3. If no faults are found in step2, check the condition and/or operation of the air breather, if faults are found repair/replace as required.

4. If no faults are found in step3, check the inlet and exhaust valve stems and guides for wear and/or damage, if faults are found repair/replace as required.

Engine Overheating

1. Check the condition and/or level of the engine coolant in the radiator, if faults are found repair/replace as required.

2. If no faults are found check the condition of the fan coupling (if fitted), if faults are found repair/replace as required.

3. If no faults are found in step3, check the condition and/or operation of the fan belt, if faults are found repair/replace as required.

4. If no faults are found in step3, check the condition and/or operation of the radiator, if faults are found repair/replace as required.

5. If no faults are found in step4, check the condition and/or operation of the water pump, if faults are found repair/replace as required.

6. If no faults are found in step5, check the condition and/or operation of the cylinder head and cylinder body-sealing cap, if faults are found repair/replace as required.

7. If no faults are found in step6, check the condition and/or operation of the thermostat, if faults are found repair/replace as required.

8. If no faults are found in step7, check the cooling system operation and/or for blockages, if faults are found repair/replace as required.

9. If no faults are found in step8, check the injection timing setting, if faults are found adjust to suit.

White Smoke From The Exhaust

1. Check the fuel in the system for water contamination, if faults are found, replace as required.

2. If no faults are found in step1, check the fuel injection timing setting, if the setting is incorrect adjust to suit.

3. If no faults are found in step2, carry out a compression test on the engine, if the pressure is not correct repair/replace as required.

4. If no faults are found in step4, check the inlet and exhaust valve stems, oils seal and guides for wear and/or damage, if faults are found repair/replace as required.

Black Smoke From The Exhaust

1. Check the condition and/or operation of the air cleaner, if faults are found repair/replace as required.

2. If no faults are found in step1, check the condition of the injection nozzle/s for poor starting pressure and/or faulty spray pattern, if faults are found repair/replace as required.

3. If no faults are found in step2, check the fuel injection timing setting, if faults are found adjust to suit.

4. If no faults are found in step3, check the condition and/or operation of the injection pump for faults in the delivery valve and/or excessive injection volume, if faults are found adjust the injection volume and/or replace the delivery valve as required.

Oil Pressure Does Not Rise

1. Check the level and/or the quality of the engine oil, if faults are found replace or fill as required.

2. If no faults are found in step1, check the operation of the oil pressure gauge/switch and/or light, if faults are found repair/replace as required.

3. If no faults are found in step2, check the condition and/or operation of the oil filter, if faults are found repair/replace as required.

4. If no faults are found in step3, check the condition and/or operation of the relief valve and/or bypass valve, if faults are found repair/replace as required.

5. If no faults are found in step4, check the condition and/or operation of the oil pump and/or pump strainer, if faults are found repair/replace as required.

6. If no faults are found in step5, check the condition and/or operation of the rocker shaft, camshaft and bearings and crankshaft and bearings, if faults are found repair/replace as required.

Abnormal Engine Noise
Engine Knocking

1. Check the condition and/or operation of the fuel in the system, if faults are found, replace as required.

2. If no faults are found in step1, check the fuel injection timing setting, if faults are found adjust to suit.

3. If no faults are found in step2, check the condition of the injection nozzle/s for poor starting pressure and spray pattern, if faults are found repair/replace as required.

4. If no faults are found in step3, carry out a compression test on the engine, if the pressure is not correct repair/replace as required.

Abnormal Engine Noise
Gas Leaking

1. Check the exhaust system for leaks from the pipes and/or gaskets, if faults are found repair/replace as required.

2. If no faults are found in step2, check the condition and installation of the injectors, if faults are found re-tighten and/or replace as required.

3. If no faults are found in step2, check the condition and/or operation of the exhaust manifold, if faults are found repair/replace as required.

4. If no faults are found in step3, check the condition of the head gasket, if faults are found repair/replace as required.

Abnormal Engine Noise
Continuous Noise

1. Check the condition and/or operation of the fan belt, if faults are found repair/replace as required.

2. If no faults are found in step1, check the condition and/or operation of the cooling fan, if faults are found repair/replace as required.

3. If no faults are found in step2, check the condition and/or operation of the water pump, if faults are found repair/replace as required.

4. If no faults are found in step3, check the condition and/or operation of the alternator and/or vacuum pump, if faults are found repair/replace as required.

5. If no faults are found in step4, check the engine valve clearances, if faults are found adjust to suit.

Abnormal Engine Noise
Slapping Noise

1. Check the engine valve clearances, if faults are found adjust to suit.

2. If no faults are found in step1, check the condition and/or operation of the rocker arm/s, if faults are found repair/replace as required.

3. If no faults are found in step2, check the flywheel for loose bolts, if faults are found tighten to suit.

4. If no faults are found in step3, check for worn and/or damaged crankshaft and/or thrust bearings, if faults are found repair/replace as required.

5. If no faults are found in step4, check for worn and/or damaged crankshaft and/or con rod bearings, if faults are found repair/replace as required.

6. If no faults are found in step5, check for worn and/or damaged con rod bushes and/or piston pins, if faults are found repair/replace as required.

7. If no faults are found in step6, check for worn and/or damaged pistons and/or cylinder liners, if faults are found repair/replace as required.

VEHICLE SERVICE INFORMATION

Vehicle Filling Capacities

Engine Oil with Filter: .... 3.8 Litres (2WD)
Engine Oil without Filter: .... 4.5 Litres (2WD)
Engine Oil with Filter: .... 4.0 Litres (4WD)
Engine Oil without Filter: .... 4.5 Litres (4WD)
Cooling System: .... 9.5 Litres (2WD)
Cooling System: .... 10.3 Litres (4WD)
Manual Transmission: .... 1.55 Litres (2WD)
Manual Transmission: .... 2.95 Litres (4WD)
Transfer Case: .... 1.45 Litres (4WD)
Front Differential: .... 1.5 Litres (4WD)
Rear Differential: .... 1.5 Litres (2WD)
Rear Differential: .... 1.8 Litres (4WD)

Vehicle Component Service Interval Changes

Valve Clearance
    Check 12 months/20,000kms

Exhaust Manifold Nuts
    Tighten Every 6 months/10,000kms

Engine Oil
    Change Every 3 months/5,000kms

Engine Oil Filter
    Change @ 3 Months/5,000kms then Every 6 months/10,000kms

Air Cleaner
    Change Every 24 months/40,000kms

Fuel Filter
    Change Every 9 months/15,000kms

Engine Coolant
    Change Every 12 months/20,000kms

Brake Fluid
    Check Every 12 months/20,000kms

Manual Transmission Oil
    Change at 6Months/10,000kms then every 24 Months/40,000kms

Transfer Case Oil
    Change at 6Months/10,000kms then every 24 Months/40,000kms

Front /Rear Wheel Bearings
    Check @ 6Months/10,000kms then Every 12 Months/20,000kms

Front /Rear Wheel Bearings
    Repack Every Every 12 Months/20,000kms

Front Axle Oil
    Change at 6Months/10,000kms then every 24 Months 40,000kms

Rear Axle Oil
    Change at 6Months/10,000kms then every 24 Months 40,000kms

Timing Belt
    Change Every 60 Months/100,000kms

Mitsubishi Triton MF to MJ 4D56/4D56T Engine 1988-1996

Mitsubishi Triton MF-MJ 4D56/ 4D56T 1988-1996

Engine Checks

Valve Clearance Check

Please Note: Before carrying out the valve clearance check, ensure that the engine is warm and that the rocker arms have adjusting screws. If they do not, the valve clearances will not need adjusting.

1. Ensure that the ignition and injection timing is set correctly and then remove the breather hose, vacuum hose and the throttle cable.

2. Remove the rocker cover and check that the cylinder head bolts are all at the correct settings.

3. Remove the top timing cover, set the No1 piston to TDC on its compression stroke, and ensure that the timing marks on the sprockets are lined up.

4. Loosen the rocker arm nut, and while turning the adjusting screw , use a feeler gauge to adjust the valve clearance on the No1 and 3 exhaust, and No1 and No2 inlet valves to the correct setting.

Specified Valve Clearance: 0.25mm (Hot)

5. Secure the adjustment screw and then retighten the rocker arm nut.

6. Turn the crankshaft one full turn in a clockwise direction and set the No4 piston to TDC on its compression stroke, ensuring all of the timing marks are lined up.

7. Loosen the rocker arm nut, and while turning the adjusting screw, use a feeler gauge to adjust the valve clearance on the No2and 4exhaust and No3 and No4 inlet valves to the correct setting.

Specified Valve Clearance: 0.25mm (Hot)

8. Secure the adjustment screw and then retighten the rocker arm nut.

9. Run the engine to normal operating temperature and ensure that the valve clearances are ok, then replace the

removed components in the reverse order of removal.

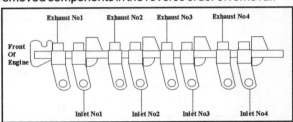

Compression Check

1. Run the engine too normal operating temperature.

2. Check each cylinder compression by loosening the nuts on the nozzle side of the injection pipes and disconnecting them from the nozzle holders.

3. Remove the glow plug plate and all 4 glow plugs, then attach a tachometer to the engine.

4. Install a pressure gauge to the No1 cylinder, and with the throttle fully open, record the compression pressure on each cylinder

Specified Compression Pressure: 2400 to 2700kpa
Minimum Pressure: 1,920kpa
Maximum variation Between Each Cylinder: 300kpa

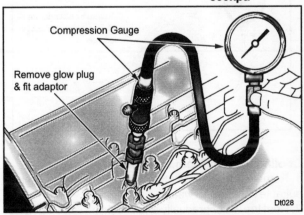

5. If the pressure is less than shown on one or more cylinders, pour a small amount of oil through the glow

plug hole and recheck the pressure. If the pressure is now OK, check the condition of the piston rings and/or cylinder bore. If the pressure is still low, check for a sticking valve and/or bad valve seating.

4. Replace any removed parts in the reverse order of removal.

Cylinder Head Tightening Procedures

1. With the cylinder head inplace, the bolts need to be tightened in three steps.

2. Apply a light coat of oil to each bolt thread, and using a torque wrench tighten the 18 bolts in three separate stages to a torque of **105 to 115Nm (Engine Cold)**

3. If any of the bolts do reach torque figures, break or deform, check the condition and/or length of the bolts and if faults are found repair/replace as required.

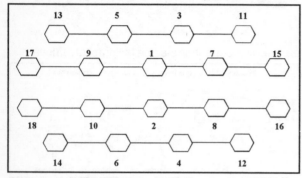

Oil Pressure Check

1. Remove the oil pressure switch from the block and install a pressure gauge in its place.

2. Run the engine to normal operating temperature and the check the engine oil pressure.

Specified Oil Pressure: 76kpa @ Idle

3. If the oil pressure is not as ahown, repair/replace as required.

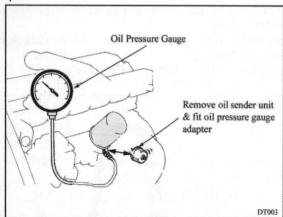

DT003

Cooling System Thermostat Check

1. Remove the thermostat from the engine and put into a suitable container of water.

2. Heat the water gradually and check the valve opening temperature and valve lift.

Valve Opening Temperature: **82°±1.5°c**

If the operation is not as shown above replace the thermostat.

3. Check that the valve spring is tight when the thermostat is fully closed, if not replace the thermostat.

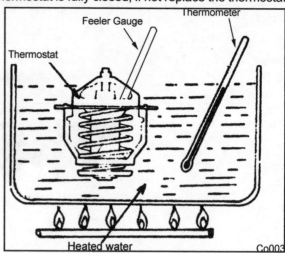

Co003

Fuel Filter Check and Replacement (All)

1. Disconnect the harness connector from the fuel filter water sensor (if fitted), place a suitable rag around the fuel filter to stop spillage of diesel fuel and disconnect the fuel hoses.

2. Remove the fuel filter assembly from the vehicle then remove the fuel filter canister from the assembly.

3. Refit the new filter to the filter assembly, replace the water sensor and then replace the assembly and other removed parts in the reverse order of removal.

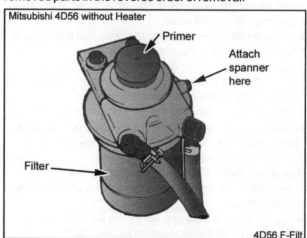

4D56 F-Filt

Fuel Sensor Check

1. Connect the water level sensor to the connector of the vehicle, and ensure that the warning lamp lights up when the starter key is in the ON position. If it does not, check the condition and/or operation of the warning lamp globe and/or diode.

2. Ensure that the warning lamp stops working when the engine starts up, if it does not move the float up and down and ensure that the light flashes on and off.

Diagram is on the next page.

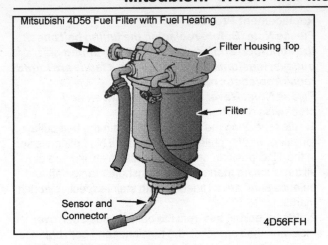

Mitsubishi 4D56 Fuel Filter with Fuel Heating

Filter Housing Top

Filter

Sensor and Connector

4D56FFH

Bleeding the Fuel System

1. Remove the small air plug fitted near the top of the fuel filter.

2. Place a suitable container under the filter to catch any spilt fuel and move the manual pump up and down until clear fuel comes out of the plughole.

3. Replace the plug into the top of the filter and pump the manual pump until a resistance is felt.

Draining Water from the Filter

1. When water becomes present in the fuel system, the warning lamp will light up on the dashboard.

2. To drain the water, loosen the drain plug on the bottom of the filter, operate the hand pump on the top of the filter until clean fuel comes out of the filter. When that happens retighten the drain plug.

Fuel Injector Nozzle Check

Please Note: When testing the leakage, spray pattern and breaking pressure an injection nozzle tester is required.

1. **Spray Testing**
    Isolate the gauge from the testers output and with short rapid strokes the spray pattern should be even, stop cleanly and not drip. If faults are found repair/replace as required.

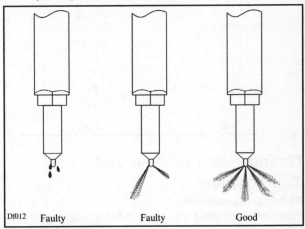

Df012   Faulty   Faulty   Good

2. **Noise Testing**
    Isolate the gauge from the testers output and with long slow strokes of the tester lever, ensure that a "pinging noise can be heard from the injector as fuel emerges. If any other sounds can be heard, replace the injector/s as required.

3. **Breaking Pressure Testing**
    With the gauge working and the tester lever moving slowly downwards, record the pressure when the injector starts to work.
    Specified Pressure: 12,000-13,000kpa
    If the pressure is not as shown, adjust and/or replace as required.
    A thicker adjusting shim will increase the breaking pressure, a thinner one will decrease the pressure.

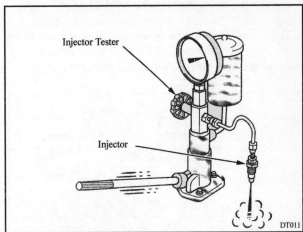

Injector Tester

Injector

DT011

4   **Leakage Check**
    With the gauge working, slowly press down the tester lever and hold in that position. With the lever in that position ensure that it maintains pressure at

about 10,787kpa for a period of about 10 seconds. In that time ensure that there are no fuel leaks and/ or drips from the injector nozzle/s, if there are, repair/replace as required.

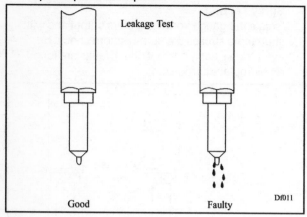

Leakage Test

Good   Faulty   Df011

Timing Belt Removal and Replacement

Removal Procedures

Please Note: If the timing belt is being used again, before removing, mark a direction arrow on the timing belt and place matchmarks on the pulleys and the belt.

1. Remove top radiator cowl, all of the engine drive belts (Fan Belt, A/C Belt and Power Steering Belt (If Fitted)), remove the fan clutch, water pump pulley, A/C compressor tensioner (if fitted), crankshaft pulley bolt and pulley, lower and upper front cover

2. Remove the rocker cover and while turning the crankshaft in a clockwise direction set the No1 piston in the TDC position on its compression stroke. This can be done by turning the crankshaft in a clockwise direction until the crankshaft pulley lines up with the mark on the front of the engine and the mark on the camshaft gear lines up with the mark on the front of the engine.

3. Loosen the timing belt tensioner adjuster bolt slightly and then slide the tensioner towards the water pump.

4. Temporarily tighten the tensioner in the same position so as the tensioner does not turn and then remove the balance shaft belt (Belt B) and the timing belt.

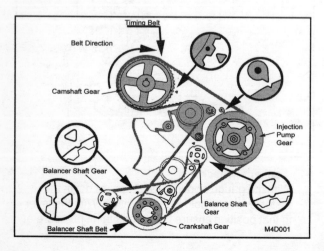

Timing Belt
Belt Direction
Camshaft Gear
Injection Pump Gear
Balancer Shaft Gear
Balance Shaft Gear
Balancer Shaft Belt
Crankshaft Gear
M4D001

Replacement Procedures

Please Note: Before replacing the timing belt check the condition and/or operation of the timing belt pulleys, tensioners and/or pulleys, if faults are found repair/replace as required.

Please Note: Never turn the engine in an anti clockwise direction.

1. After checking the condition of the timing belt pulleys, tensioner and/or pulley ensure that the No1 piston is set in the TDC position on its compression stroke and that all three timing marks on the camshaft, crankshaft and balance shaft are all lined up with their respective match marks.

2. After checking this, refit the balance shaft belt over the crankshaft sprocket, the tensioner and both balance shaft sprockets, ensuring that the tension side of the belt has no slack.

3. Ensure that all the timing marks are still lined up, release the tensioner so that only spring tension is applied to the timing belt.

4. Tighten the tension on the balance shaft tensioner mounting bolt and nut, ensuring that the nut is tightened first (other wise the tensioner will move in the same direction as the belt).

5. Press on the tension side of the belt and ensure that the deflection is between 4-5mm.

6. To replace the camshaft belt, move the tensioner as far as possible towards the water pump and tighten temporarily, ensure all of the timing marks are still lined up.

7. Replace the timing belt on the engine. While making sure that the tensioned side of the belt is not slack, replace the belt onto the crankshaft, injection pump and camshaft sprocket in this particular order.

8. Loosen the tensioner bolts slightly and then the tensioner will apply tension to the belt.

9. Turn the crankshaft in a clockwise direction through two teeth on the camshaft sprocket and hold in that position.

10. Retighten the tensioner mounting nuts and bolts, ensuring that the fulcrum side bolt is tightened first.

11. Turn the crankshaft in an anti-clockwise direction until the timing marks are lined up again, press down on the belt 1/2 way between the camshaft and injection pump sprocket and ensure that the deflection is between 4-5mm.

12. Replace the remaining removed parts in the reverse order of removal.

Timing Belt Replacement Torques

Timing Belt Cover: 10-12mm
Timing Belt Tensioner Bolts: 22-30Nm
Balance Shaft Belt Tensioner Bolts: 22-30Nm
Crankshaft Pulley Bolt: 170-190Nm
Camshaft Sprocket: 65-75Nm
Injection Pump Sprocket Nut: 79-88Nm

Engine Tightening Torques

Cylinder Head Bolts: ....
.... 105-110Nm Cold (Tighten in 2-3 Stages)
Camshaft Bearing Caps: 17-20Nm
Camshaft Sprocket Bolt: 65-75Nm
Rocker Cover Bolts: 5-7Nm
Crankshaft Pulley Bolt: 179-190Nm
Flywheel/DrivePlate Bolts: 128-137Nm
Big End Bearings: ..... 45-48Nm (Tighten in 2-3 Stages)
Main Bearings: .... 75-85Nm (Tighten in 2-3 Stages)
Front Cover Bolts: 10-12Nm
Sump to Engine Bolts: 7Nm
Exhaust Manifold Bolts: 15-19Nm
Inlet Manifold Bolts: 15-19Nm
Rocker Arm Bolts: 12-18Nm
Rocker Arm Shaft Bolts: 34-39Nm
Balance Shaft Sprocket Bolts: 34-39Nm
Timing Belt Tensioner Bolts: 22-30Nm
Balance Shaft Belt Tensioner Bolts: 22-30Nm
Injection Pump Sprocket Nut: 79-88Nm

System Adjustments

Idle Speed Check

1. Ensure that the handbrake is on, the transmission is in neutral, the engine is running at normal operating temperature and the A/C and all accessories are switched OFF.

2. Ensure that the valve clearances and injection timing setting is correct. Install a tachometer to the engine and while still running at normal operating temperature, check the engine idle speed.

Specified Engine Idle Speed: 720 to 780RPM

3. If the idle speed is not as shown, loosen the lock nut and turn the idle speed screw on the injection pump, adjust to the correct speed and then retighten the lock nut.

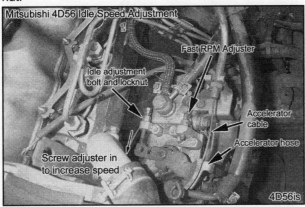
Mitsubishi 4D56 Idle Speed Adjustment
Fast RPM Adjuster
Idle adjustment bolt and locknut
Accelerator cable
Accelerator hose
Screw adjuster in to increase speed
4D56is

4. Run the engine and then recheck the idle speed.

Injection Timing Check

1. Remove the rocker cover and while turning the crankshaft in a clockwise direction set the No1 piston in the TDC position on its compression stroke. This can be done by removing the top front engine cover, turning the crankshaft in a clockwise direction until the crankshaft pulley lines up with the mark on the front of the engine and the mark on the camshaft gear lines up with the mark on the front of the engine.

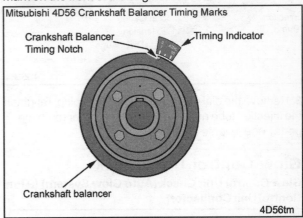
Mitsubishi 4D56 Crankshaft Balancer Timing Marks
Crankshaft Balancer Timing Notch
Timing Indicator
Crankshaft balancer
4D56tm

2. Loosen all of the injector pipe supply tubes on the injection pump side of the injection pump, and then loosen the bolts/nuts that hold the injection pump to the engine.

3. Remove the timing plug from the centre of the injection pump and install a dial gauge into the hole. Before installing, ensure that the tip of the dial gauge is protruding 10mm.

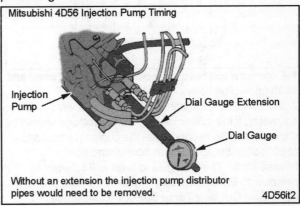
Mitsubishi 4D56 Injection Pump Timing
Injection Pump
Dial Gauge Extension
Dial Gauge
Without an extension the injection pump distributor pipes would need to be removed.
4D56it2

4. Turn the engine in a clockwise direction and set to a position of 30° BTDC, and then set the dial gauge to zero.

5. Turn the crankshaft slightly to the left and right side and ensure that the dial gauge needle does not move, if it does reset the BTDC position and check again.

6. Turn the engine in a clockwise direction until the timing notch lines up with the crankshaft pulley and record the plunger stroke measurement.

Specified Plunger Stroke: 0.97-1.03mm (7° ATDC)

7. If the plunger stroke is not as shown, move the injection pump to the LH or RH side until the setting is correct, and then retighten the pump fixing nuts and bolts.

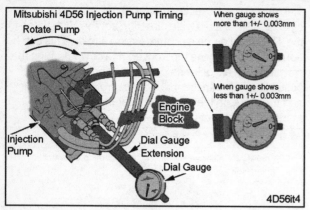

Mitsubishi 4D56 Injection Pump Timing

Rotate Pump

When gauge shows more than 1+/- 0.003mm

When gauge shows less than 1+/- 0.003mm

Engine Block

Injection Pump

Dial Gauge Extension

Dial Gauge

4D56it4

8. Remove the dial gauge and replace the plug, retighten the injection tube nuts and replace any other removed parts in the reverse order of removal.

Glow Control Unit Check

Glow Control Unit Check (Auto Glow System) (9 Pin Control Unit Connector)

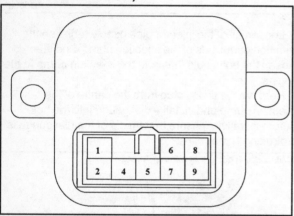

1. Connect a voltmeter between the glow plug plate and earth (glow plug body)

2. Switch ON the ignition and check the operation of the voltmeter. If the system is Ok, battery voltage should be shown within 36 seconds with the coolant temperature at 20°c after the ignition has been turned on.

Please Note: The energising time will change in relation to the engine coolant temperature.

Specified Coolant Temp Sensor Resistance:
3.25k/ohms @ 20°c

3. If the system operation is OK in step2, put the ignition key in the START position and ensure that battery voltage is indicated while the engine is being cranked and then carries on for about 6 seconds after the engine has started (Afterglow).

Please Note: The energising time will change in relation to the engine coolant temperature.

4. If the operations above do not show normal voltage and energising time, check the terminal voltage at the glow control unit and make on off vehicle inspection.

Glow Control Unit Voltage Check (A) (Auto Glow System) (9 Pin Control Unit Connector)

1. Check the glow control unit for terminal voltage and continuity with the harness connector connected.

Glow Control Unit Voltage Check (B) (Auto Glow System) (9 Pin Control Unit Connector)

1. Check the glow control unit for terminal voltage and continuity with the harness connector disconnected at the harness side connector

9 Pin Connector Harness Connected			
Between Terminals	Connected To	Condition	Specified Value (v)
2 and Earth	Glow Plug Relay	Ignition key Off>On, Coolant temp at 20°c	12v for about 36secs after the ignition key is turned to ON
2 and Earth	Glow Plug Relay	Engine cranking, coolant temp @ 20°c	Battery Voltage
2 and Earth	Glow Plug Relay	Engine idling	Battery Voltage is shown for about 6secs after the engine has started
6 and Earth	Pre Heat Indicator Lamp (Red)	Ignition key Off>On, Coolant temp at 20°c	0v is shown (pre heat lamp comes on) for about 6 seconds after the ignition key is turned to ON. Then 12v is shown and the lamp goes off.
7 and Earth	Start Indicator Lamp (Green)	Ignition key ON and the pre heat lamp lights up.	12v
7 and Earth	Start Indicator Lamp (Green)	Ignition key in the ON position and pre heat lamp goes out	0v is shown (start indicator lamp comes on) for about 30 secs after the pre heat indicator lamp has gone out
8 and Earth	Alternator L Terminal	Ignition Key ON	1-4v
8 and Earth	Alternator L Terminal	Engine Idling	14-15v

9 Pin Connector Harness Disconnected			
Between Terminals	Destination or Measured Part	Condition	Specified Value
1 and Earth	Ignition Switch (IG1 Power Supply)	Ignition key ON	12volts
2 and Earth	Glow Plug Relay Coil	All Times	Continuity is present
4 and Earth	Ignition Switch (ST Power Supply)	Ignition key (START)	12volts
5 and Earth	Earth	All Times	Continuity is present
6 and Earth	Pre Heat Indicator Lamp (Red)	Ignition key ON	12volts
7 and Earth	Start Indicator Lamp (Green)	Ignition key ON	12volts
9 and Earth	Water Temp Sensor	Coolant temp 0°c	8.6k/ohms
9 and Earth	Water Temp Sensor	Coolant temp 20°c	3.3k/ohms
9 and Earth	Water Temp Sensor	Coolant temp 40°c	1.5k/ohms
9 and Earth	Water Temp Sensor	Coolant temp 60°c	0.6k/ohms

Glow Control Unit Check (Quick Super Glow System) (13 Pin Control Unit Connector)

Please Note: Before carrying out this inspection ensure that the battery voltage is 12v, and the coolant temperature is less than 30°c

1. Connect a voltmeter between the glow plug plate and earth (glow plug body)

2. Switch ON the ignition and check the operation of the voltmeter. If the system is Ok, battery voltage is recorded for 3 seconds after the ignition switch has been put in the ON position (cold glow plug state).

Please Note: The energising time will change in relation to the engine coolant temperature.

3. If the system operation above is Ok, put the ignition key in the START position and ensure that there is battery voltage for about 30 seconds after starting the engine (afterglow)

4. If the operations above do not show normal voltage and energising time, check the terminal voltage at the glow control unit and make on off vehicle inspection.

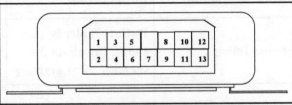

Glow Control Unit Voltage Check (A) (Super Quick Glow System) (13 Pin Control Unit Connector)

1. Check the glow control unit for terminal voltage and continuity with the harness connector connected at the harness side connector

Glow Control Unit Voltage Check (B) (Super Quick Glow System) (13 Pin Control Unit Connector)

1. Check the glow control unit for terminal voltage and continuity with the harness connector disconnected at the harness side connector

Mitsubishi Triton MF-MJ 4D56/4D56T 1988-1996

13 Pin Connector Harness Connected			
Between Terminals	**Destination or Measured Part**	**Condition**	**Specified Value**
2 and Earth	Glow Relay No1	Ignition key Off>On (Cold Glow Plug)	12volts is shown for about 3 seconds after turning the ignition key to ON.
4 and Earth	Glow Relay No2	Ignition key Off>On (Cold Glow Plug)	12volts is shown for about 3 seconds after turning the ignition key to ON.
4 and Earth	Glow Relay No2	Engine Cranking	Battery Volts
4 and Earth	Glow Relay No2	Engine Idling	Battery Volts is shown for about 30 seconds after starting
12 and Earth	Alternator L Terminal	Ignition Key ON	1-4v
12 and Earth	Alternator L Terminal	Engine Idling	14-15v

Mitsubishi Triton MF-MJ 4D56/4D56T 1988-1996

13 Pin Connector Harness Disconnected			
Between Terminals	Destination or Measured Part	Condition	Specified Value
1 and Earth	Ignition Switch (IG1 Power Supply)	Ignition key ON	12volts
2 and Earth	Glow Plug Relay No1 Coil	All Times	Continuity is present
3 and Earth	Ignition Switch (ST Power Supply)	Ignition Key (Start)	12v
4 and Earth	Glow Plug Relay No2 Coil	All Times	Continuity is present
5	Not Used		
6	Not Used		
7 and Earth	Glow Plug (For Terminal Voltage Measurement)	All Times	Continuity is present
8 and Earth	Glow Plug (For Terminal Voltage Measurement)	All Times	Continuity is present
9 and Earth	Glow Plug (For Terminal Voltage Measurement)	All Times	Continuity is present
10 and Earth	Glow Plug (For Terminal Voltage Measurement)	All Times	Continuity is present
11	Not Used		
12	Not Used		
13 and Earth	Water Temp Sensor	Coolant temp 0°c	8.6k/ohms
13 and Earth	Water Temp Sensor	Coolant temp 20°c	3.3k/ohms
13 and Earth	Water Temp Sensor	Coolant temp 40°c	1.5k/ohms
13 and Earth	Water Temp Sensor	Coolant temp 60°c	0.6k/ohms

Fuel Cut Solenoid Check

1-Switch off the ignition, switch back on the ignition and ensure an operating click can be heard from then solenoid.

2-If there is no operating sound in step1, disconnect the harness connector from the solenoid and apply battery volts to the solenoid. If no operating sound is heard, replace the solenoid.

3-If a sound is heard in step2, check the condition and/ or operation of the solenoid harness, if faults are found repair/replace as required.

Dropping Resistor Check

1-Disconnect the harness connector and check the resistance between terminals 1 and 2

Specified Resistance: **0.25 ohms**

2-If the resistance is not as shown, replace as required.

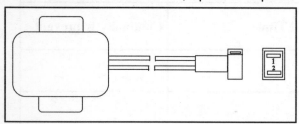

Glow Plug Check

1-Remove the glow plugs from the vehicle and check the resistance between the top tip of the glow plug and earth.

Specified Resistance:

        0.25 ohms (Auto Glow System)

Specified Resistance:

        0.23•2 ohms (Super Glow System)

2-If the resistance is not as shown, repair/replace as required.

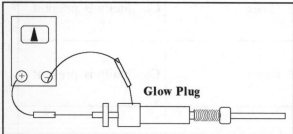

Water Temperature Sensor Check

1. Disconnect the water temperature sensor harness connector, remove the sensor from the engine and place in a suitable container of water.

2. Heat the water gradually and check the resistance between the sensor terminals at varying coolant temperatures.

Coolant Temperature (°c)	Resistance (k/ohms)
20	3-3.5

3. If the resistance is not as shown, repair/replace as required

Diagram is in the next column

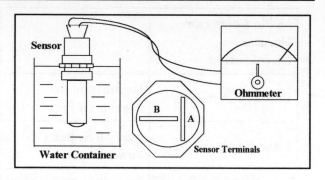

Glow Plug Relay Check (Auto Glow System)

1. Check for continuity between terminals while battery volts are being applied to terminal 2 and No1 connected to earth, and also while no battery voltage is being supplied..

Testing Condition	Between Terminals	Continuity
With Power	3 and 4	Yes
Without Power	1 and 2	Yes
Without Power	3 and 4	No

Specified Resistance: 0.25 ohms

2. If the resistance is not as shown, replace as required.

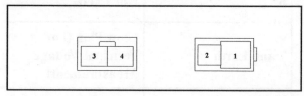

Glow Plug Relay Check (Super Quick Glow System)

1. Check for continuity between terminals while battery volts are being applied to terminal 1 and the bracket is connected to earth, and also while no battery voltage is being supplied..

Testing Condition	Between Terminals	Continuity
With Power	2 and 3	Yes
Without Power	1 and bracket	Yes
Without Power	2 and 3	No

2. If the relay operation is not as shown, repair/replace as required

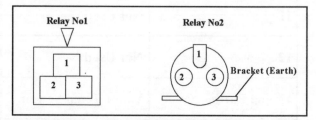

Turbocharger Check

1. When the turbocharger is running, check for any distinctive high pitched noises which may indicate an inlet air or exhaust leaks.

2. If there are any nosies coming from the exhaust turbine area, remove the turbocharger and check the condition of the turbine wheel.

3. With the engine turned off and the turbo has cooled down, reach inside the inlet turbine housing and ensure that the wheel moves freely, if it does not it may have been caused by sluging of the cooling and lubrication oil due to an overheating priblem.

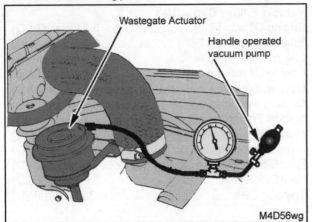

Wastegate Actuator

Handle operated vacuum pump

M4D56wg

4. Push in onto the inlet compressor/exhaust turbine wheels and ensure that they move freely, if they do not there could be problems with the bearings.
5. Check for cracks and/or damage to the exhaust system, also check for leaks and/or damage to the oil and coolant lines.
6. To carry out a boost check on the turbocharger, install a pressure gauge to the wastegate hose with a "T" piece. Ensure all of the connections are tight and check the boost pressure in a full throttle condition in low gear.
7. The maximum boost pressure of 85kpa should happen at 3000RPM.
8. If the boost is more than shown, there could be faults in the wastegate, if the boost is less than shown, there could be faults in the turbocharger system, problems with the engine, blockages in the intercooler, faults in the exhaust system, faults in the wastegate and/or faults in the turbocharger. If faults are found repair/replace as required.

Wastegate Check
1. Disconnect the small hose from the wastegate, install a hand vacuum/pressure pump to the wastegate.
2. Slowly apply pressure to the wastegate and check that the actuator begins to move.
Specified Pressure: **85kpa**
3. If the reading is to low, the engine will not produce enough pressure. If the wastegate operates at too higher pressure, engine damage could happen.

Injection System and Engine Diagnosis and Troubleshooting
Engine Does Not Start
1. If the engine will not start and there is no voltage at the fuel cut solenoid on the injection pump, check for voltage with a test lamp, if there is no voltage, replace relevant fuses and/or harness.

2. If no faults are found in step1, check for faulty installation of the fuel cut solenoid, if faults are found with the installation, check for an operating sound from the solenoid when the ignition is switched on. If faults are found repair/replace as required.
3. If no faults are found in step2, check for voltage at the glowplugs, if no voltage is found when the ignition switch is in the ON position, check the condition and/or operation of the glow plug relay and/or relevant harnesses, if faults are found repair/replace as required.
4. If no faults are found in step3, check the condition and/or operation of the glow plug/s, if faults are found repair/replace as required.
5. If no faults are found in step4, check for air being present in the system, if air is found bleed the system until all of the air is cleared.
6. If no faults are found in step5, loosen the injection pipe/s, crank the engine and ensure that fuel is being delivered to the injection pump, if it is not check the condition and/or operation of the timing belt and/or fuel supply from the fuel filter, if faults are found repair/replace as required.
7. If no faults are found in step6, check that the injection pipes are correctly installed, if not fix as required.
8. If no faults are found in step7, check the injection timing setting, if it is not correct, adjust to suit.
9. If no faults are found in step8, check the condition and/or operation of the fuel injection nozzles, if faults are found repair/replace as required.
10. If no faults are found in step9, substitute the original injection pump with another good one, try starting the engine, if it now starts replace the original injection pump.

Incorrect/Rough or Irregular Idle Speed
1. Start the engine and check the idle speed setting, if the setting is not correct, adjust to suit.
2. If no faults are found in step1, check the condition and/or operation of the throttle cable, if faults are found replace or adjust as required.
3. If no faults are found in step2, check the condition and/or installation of the fuel hose between the fuel filter and the injection pump, if faults are found repair/replace and/or bleed the fuel system as required.
4. If no faults are found in step3, check for air in the fuel system, if air is present in the system bleed the system as required.
5. If no faults are found in step4, check the system fuel hoses and pipes for poor installation, leaks, damage and/or blockages, if faults are found repair/replace as required.
6. If no faults are found in step5, check the condition and/or operation of the fuel injection nozzles, if faults are found repair/replace as required.
7. If no faults are found in step6, check the injection timing setting, if it is not correct, adjust to suit.'
8. If no faults are found in step7, substitute the original injection pump with another good one, try starting the engine, if it now starts replace the original injection pump.

Black/White or Blue Smoke From the Exhaust

1. With the engine running, check the maximum speed setting, if it is not correct and cannot be adjusted, replace the injection pump.

2. If no faults are found in step2, check the condition and/or operation of the fuel injection nozzles, if faults are found repair/replace as required.

3. If no faults are found in step3, check the injection timing setting, if it is not correct, adjust to suit.'

4. If no faults are found in step4, substitute the original injection pump with another good one, check the exhaust system for smoke from the exhaust, if there is now no smoke, replace the original injection pump.

Poor Power Output

1. If there is poor power output, check if the throttle lever is loose or not reaching the maximum speed adjusting screw. If the lever is loose check that the throttle pedal travel is not being restricted, if it is adjust the cable as required.

2. If there is no faults in step1, check the maximum speed setting, if it is not correct and cannot be adjusted, replace the injection pump.

3. If no faults are found in step2, check the system fuel filter, fuel hoses and pipes for poor installation, leaks, damage and/or blockages, if faults are found repair/replace as required.

4. If no faults are found in step3, check for air in the fuel system, if air is present in the system bleed the system as required.

5. If no faults are found in step4, check for ice and/or wax in the fuel lines. If any ice or wax is found in the fuel lines, move the vehicle to a warm garage, let the ice or wax melt and the bleed the fuel system.

6. If no faults are found in step5, check the condition and/or operation of the fuel injection nozzles, if faults are found repair/replace as required.

7. If no faults are found in step6, check the injection timing setting, if it is not correct, adjust to suit.'

8. If no faults are found in step7, substitute the original injection pump with another good one, check the acceleration and speed with the substitute pump and if required, replace the original injection pump.

Excessive Fuel Consumption

1. Check the condition and/or operation of the fuel system pipes, hoses and connections if faults are found repair/replace as required.

2. If no faults are found in step1, check for the return hose being blocked, if faults are found repair/replace as required.

3. If no faults are found in step2, check the idle speed and/or maximum speed for being to high, if faults are found adjust to suit.

4. If no faults are found in step3, check the condition and/or operation of the fuel injection nozzles, if faults are found repair/replace as required.

5. If no faults are found in step4, check the injection timing setting, if it is not correct, adjust to suit.

6. If no faults are found in step5, substitute the original

injection pump with another good one and then recheck the fuel consumption. If the consumption is now OK, replace the original injection pump.

VEHICLE SERVICE INFORMATION

Vehicle Filling Capacities

Engine Oil with Filter:	5.7 Litres (2WD)
Engine Oil without Filter :	6.2 Litres (2WD)
Engine Oil with Filter:	4.6 Litres (4WD)
Engine Oil without Filter :	5.0 Litres (4WD)
Cooling System:	7.3 Litres (2WD)
Cooling System:	8.4 Litres (4WD)
Manual Transmission:	2.3 Litres (2WD)
Manual Transmission:	2.5 Litres (4WD)
Front Differential:	1.1 Litres (4WD)
Rear Differential:	1.5 Litres (2WD)
Rear Differential:	2.6 Litres (4WD)
Transfer Case:	2.2 Litres (4WD)

Vehicle Component Service Interval Changes

Timing Belt Replacement
Change Every 100,000kms

Check Valve Clearance:
Check Every 20,000kms

Engine Coolant/Anti Freeze:
Change Every 24 Months or 40,000kms

Air Cleaner Element:
Change Every 40,000kms

Fuel Filter:
Change Every 20,000kms

Engine Oil:
Change Every 5000kms

Engine Oil Filter:
Change Every 10,000kms

Brake Fluid:
Change Every 24 Months/50,000kms

Manual Transmission Oil:
Change Every 80,000kms (2WD)

Manual Transmission Oil:
Change Every 40,000kms (4WD)

Front Differential Oil:
Change Every 40,000kms (4WD)

Transfer Case Oil
Change Every 40,000kms (4WD)

Rear Differential Oil
Change Every 80,000kms (2WD)

Rear Differential Oil
Change Every 40,000kms (4WD)

Rear Differential LSD Fluid
Change Every 40,000kms

Front Wheel Bearings
Check Every 30,000kms, Repack Every 60,000kms

Nissan Cabstar H40 BD30 Engine 1989 ON

CONTENTS   PAGE

CONTENTS   PAGE

1990 Cabstar

CABSTAR H40 BD30 1989ON

Engine Checks

Valve Clearance Check

Please Note: The adjustments need to be carried out when the engine not running.

1. Remove the rocker cover and ensure that the No1 piston is set at TDC on its compression stroke.

2. Adjust valve clearance of the No1, No2, No3, No6, valves as shown in the diagram.

Valve Clearance: **Inlet (1-3) and Exhaust (2-6)**
Valves: **0.35mm**

3. Set No4 piston to TDC on its compression stroke and adjust valve clearances on the No4, No5, No7, No8 as shown in the diagram.

Valve Clearance: Inlet (5-7) and Exhaust (4-8)
Valves: 0.35m

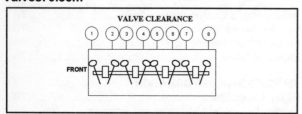

4. After the valve clearances have all been checked and/or adjusted, replace the rocker cover.

Compression Check

1. Run the engine to normal operating temperature, remove the injection tube on the nozzle side, spill tube assembly, nozzle assemblies and gaskets, and then install a compression gauge adapter to the cylinder head (ensuring that the bleeder of the gauge is closed).

2. Set the vehicle to 'No Fuel Injection Condition" by disconnecting the fuel cut solenoid harness (VE Pump), setting the control lever of the injection pump to zero setting (In Line Pump).

3. Crank the engine and record the compression pressure

Compression Pressure: 2,942 kpa (Standard)
Compression Pressure: 2,452kpa (Minimum)
Differential Limit Between Cylinders: 294kpa

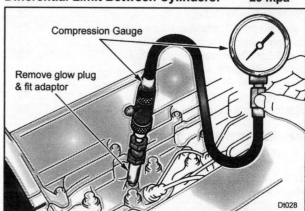

4. If the compression reading in step 3 on one or more cylinders is low, pour a small amount of oil into the faulty cylinders through the glow plug holes and retest the faulty cylinders.

5. If by adding oil in step 4 the pressure increases, there is a possibility that the piston rings are worn or damaged, if the pressure stays low, there may be sticking valves or the valves may not be seating correctly.

6. If the compression in any two adjacent cylinders are low and adding oil does not increase the pressure, there may be a leak past the gasket surface and could cause oil and water to be present in the combustion chambers.

7. Refit any removed parts in the reverse order of removal and bleed any air that may be present in the system.

Piston Protrusion Check

1. Set the No1 piston to TDC and record the clearance between the top of the piston and the cylinder block with a dial gauge (measure at the two positions shown in the diagram) and then select the correct grade of head gasket from the table shown below.

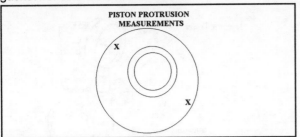

PISTON PROTRUSION
MEASUREMENTS

Average Piston Projection (mm) Values (mm)	Gasket Thickness	Gasket Grade No
Less than 0.44	1.35	1
044-0.49	1.4	2
More than 0.49 mm	1.45	3

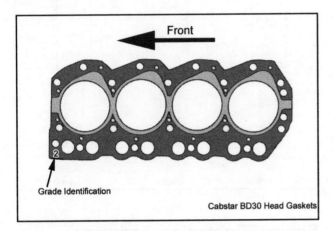

Front

2 Grade Identification

Cabstar BD30 Head Gaskets

Cylinder Head Tightening Procedures

1. Run the engine until normal operating temperature has been reached, remove the rocker cover and tighten the cylinder head bolts in the sequence shown in the diagram starting from the centre outwards.

Cylinder Head Bolts: 1st Stage: 39-49NM

Cylinder Head Bolts: 2st Stage: 54-59Nm

Cylinder Head Bolts: 3Rd Stage: **Mark the exhaust side of the cylinder head and bolts with paint and then turn all the bolts 90°±10° and ensure all of the paint marks line up facing the front of the vehicle.**

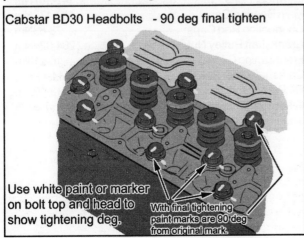

Cabstar BD30 Headbolts - 90 deg final tighten

Use white paint or marker on bolt top and head to show tightening deg.

With final tightening paint marks are 90 deg from original mark.

2. After tightening the bolts, replace the rocker cover.

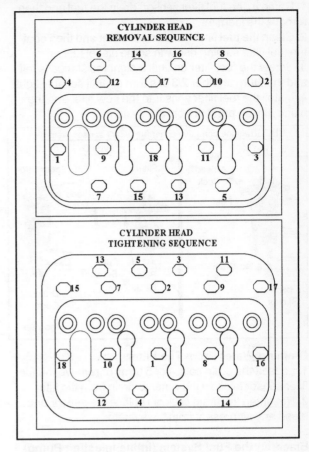

CYLINDER HEAD
REMOVAL SEQUENCE

CYLINDER HEAD
TIGHTENING SEQUENCE

Cooling System Thermostat Check

1. Remove the thermostat from the engine, place the thermostat into a suitable container of water and heat to normal operating temperature.

2. Check the valve opening temperature and maximum valve lift as shown below.

Valve Opening Temperature: 82°c

Maximum Valve Lift: More Than 8mm @ 95°c

3. If the specifications shown in step2 are Ok, ensure that the valve now closes at 5°c below the valve operating temperature.

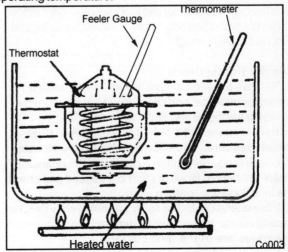

Feeler Gauge

Thermometer

Thermostat

Heated water

Co003

Fuel Filter Check and Replacement

1. Remove the fuel filter sensor, drain the fuel and then remove the fuel filter.
2. Clean the fuel filter mounting bracket and then coat the fuel filter sealing ring with some diesel fuel.
3. Screw the fuel filter on until a slght resistance is felt and then turn another 2/3 of a turn or until suitably tight.
4. Install the fuel filter sensor to the new filter and then bleed any air present from the system.

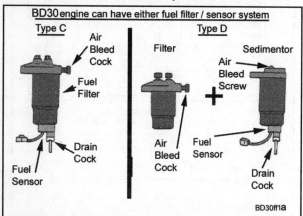

BD30ff1a

Draining Water From The Filter

1. Loosen the drain cock 4 or 5 turns or remove the fuel filter sensor to allow the water to drain from the filter.
2. Retighten the drain cock or replace the sensor and bleed any air present from the system.

Bleeding the Fuel System (Inline Injection Pump)

1. Loosen the air bleeder screw and move the priming pump up and down until no more air comes out of the air bleeder screw. While priming ensure that the fuel overflows from the vent screw hole.
2. Retighten the bleeder screw.

Bleeding the Fuel System (VE Type Injection Pump)

1. Loosen the air fuel flow overflow valve connector and fuel inlet valve connector. Move the priming pump up and down until no more air comes out of the fuel flow overflow valve connector and fuel inlet valve connector.
2. Retighten the fuel flow overflow valve connector and fuel inlet valve connector

Injector Nozzle Check

1. Remove the injector from the vehicle, connect up to the pressure tester and check the initial pressure by pumping the tester handle a few times.
Initial Pressure: 18,143-18,633kpa (Used Nozzle).
Initial Pressure: 18,633-19,614kpa (New Nozzle).
2. Check the spray pattern by pumping the pressure tester handle 4-6 times or more per second and check the injection spray pattern.
3. If the operation and/or spray pattern is not as shown, repair/replace the nozzle/s as required.
Diagrams are in the next column

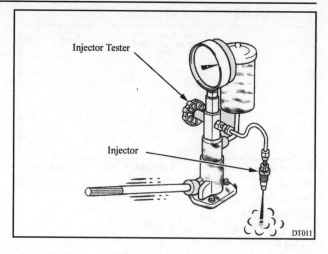

DT011

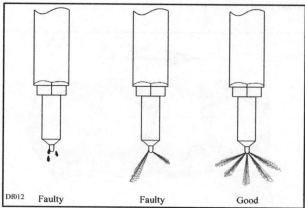

Df012   Faulty   Faulty   Good

Engine Tightening Torques

Cylinder Head Bolts: .... 1st Stage: 39-49NM
Cylinder Head Bolts: .... 2st Stage: 54-59Nm
Cylinder Head Bolts: .... 3Rd Stage: Mark the exhaust side of the cylinder head and bolts with paint and then turn all the bolts 90°±10° and ensure all of the paint marks line up facing the front of the vehicle.
Rocker Arm Shaft Bolt: 20-25Nm
Rocker Arm Lock Nut: 15-20Nm
Exhaust Manifold Bolts and Nuts: 25-29Nm
Inlet Manifold Bolts and Nuts: 15-20Nm
Flywheel Bolts: 147-167Nm
Main Bearing Caps: 167-177Nm
Connecting Rod Caps: 78-83Nm
Crankshaft Pulley Nut: 294-324Nm
Front Timing Cover: 16-21Nm
Camshaft Gear Bolt: 44-49Nm
Oil Pump Bolt: 13-19Nm
Oil Sump Bolt: 7-9Nm

System Adjustments

Idle Speed Check

1. Before carrying out this check ensure that the injection timing is correct, the injection nozzles are in good condition, there are no faults with the air cleaner, air heater system, engine oil and coolant levels are correct, the valve cleances are correct, there are no faults with the air intake system.

2. Put the shift lever into neutral, ensure that the handbrake is ON and that the air conditioner, headlamps and accessories are all off.

3. Run the engine until the normal operating temperature has been reached and then attach a tachometer pick up to the No1 injection pipe.

4. Run the engine at 2,000 RPM under no load and then let it run at normal idle speed for 60 seconds.

5. Record the idle speed shown on the tachometer.

Idle Speed Setting: 700±50RPM
Idle Speed Setting: 850±50RPM (A/C ON)
Idle Speed Setting: 950±50RPM (Exhaust Brake ON)

6. If the idle speed is not as shown in step5, adjust the idle speed as required by turning idle speed adjusting screw . After adjustment, race the engine a couple of times and ensure that the engine returns to normal idle speed.

Inline Pump

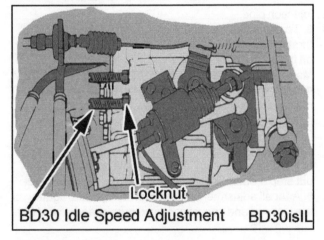

BD30 Idle Speed Adjustment — Locknut — BD30isIL

VE Pump

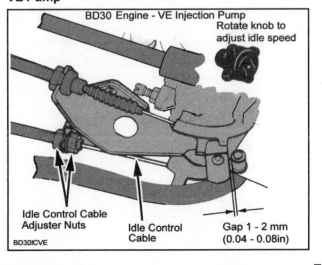

BD30 Engine - VE Injection Pump — Rotate knob to adjust idle speed — Idle Control Cable Adjuster Nuts — Idle Control Cable — Gap 1 - 2 mm (0.04 - 0.08in) — BD30ICVE

For Vehicles with Air Conditioning

1. Ensure that the clearance between the actuator idle control lever pin and injection pump control lever is between 1-2mm

2. Adjust the idle speed as required without the A/C ON and then check that the idle speed setting is correct with the A/C operating.

Idle Speed Setting: 850±50RPM

3. If the idle speed setting is not OK, adjust by turning the FICD actuator adjusting screw.

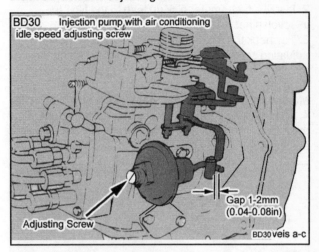

BD30 Injection pump with air conditioning idle speed adjusting screw — Adjusting Screw — Gap 1-2mm (0.04-0.08in) — BD30 veis a-c

Injection Timing Check (In Line Pump)

1. Turn the crankshaft in a clockwise direction, set the No1 piston to its applicable BTDC position by lining up the mark on the crankshaft pulley with the mark on the front cover.

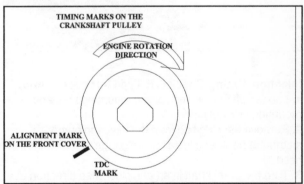

TIMING MARKS ON THE CRANKSHAFT PULLEY — ENGINE ROTATION DIRECTION — ALIGNMENT MARK ON THE FRONT COVER — TDC MARK

2. Remove all of the injection tubes.

3. Remove the No1 lock plate and delivery valve holder, pull out the delivery valve stopper (If Fitted) and the delivery valve spring.

4. Install the delivery valve holder without the spring and stopper, install a test pipe to the No1 delivery valve holder and then push the injection pump fully downwards towards the engine.

5. While feeding the system fuel by pressing the priming pump, slowly move the injection pump until the fuel flow from the No1 injection tube stops.

6. Fix the injection pump into the position where the fuel flow stopped and ensure that the timing marks on the injection pump and front plate lines up. If the marks do not line up stamp a new mark on the plate.

7. Remove the No1 injection test tube, replace any removed parts in the reverse order of removal and then bleed any air from the system that may be present.

Maximum Speed Adjustment (In Line Pump)
Please Note: The maximum speed adjusting screw is retained by sealing wire and under normal circumstances would not need adjustment.
1. Start the engine and let it run until normal operating temperature has been reached.
2. Install a tachometer pick up lead to the No1 fuel injection pipe.
3. To check the maximum speed reading, turn the adjusting screw in either direction while pressing the throttle down fully under no load and record the speed on the tachometer.
Maximum Engine Speed: 4300 (+50) or (- 150) RPM
4. After all adjustments have been completed, tighten up the lock not and secure the maximum speed screw with sealing wire.

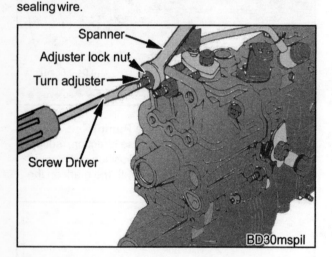

BD30mspil

Injection Timing Check (VE Type Injection Pump)
1. Loosen off the injection pump mounting nuts and mounting bracket bolts
2. Remove the plug bolt from the injection pump distributor head and install a dial gauge to the distributor head
3. Turn the crankshaft in an anti clockwise direction to a position of between 20-25° BTDC on the No1 piston.
4. With the dial gauge in a suitable rest position set the dial gauge to zero, turn the crankshaft in a clockwise direction until the No1 piston is set at TDC, and record the plunger lift measurement on the dial gauge.
Plunger Lift Measurement: 1.429±0.02mm
5. If the plunger lift measurement in step 4 is not as shown, turn the injection pump body until the reading is correct, then tighten the injection pump mounting bracket and bolts.
Please Note: If the measurement is smaller than shown, turn the injection pump body in an anti clockwise direction, if the measurement is more than shown, turn the injection pump body in a clockwise direction.

6. After all the adjustments have been carried out, remove the dial gauge and refit the plug with a new washer, reconnect the injection pipes and bleed any air from the system that may be present.

Maximum Speed Adjustment (VE Type Injection Pump)
Please Note: The maximum speed adjusting screw is retained by sealing wire and under normal circumstances would not need adjustment.
1. Start the engine and let it run until normal operating temperature has been reached.
2. Install a tachometer pick up lead to the No1 fuel

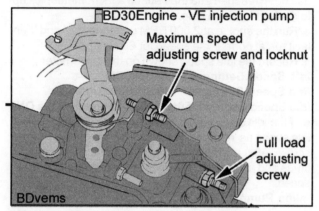

injection pipe.
3. To check the maximum speed reading, press the throttle down fully under no load and record the speed on the tachometer.
Maximum Engine Speed: 5100 (+50) or (- 150) RPM
4. If the speed is less than shown in step3, turn the maximum speed adjusting screw once or twice in an anti clockwise direction then press down the throttle fully and record the maximium speed shown on the tachometer.
5. If the speed shown in step 4 is still not correct, carry out step 4 operations until the speed setting is correct.
6. After all adjustments have been completed, tighten up the lock not and secure the maximum speed screw with sealing wire.

Fuel Heating System

Please Note: The fuel heater system will operate when the fuel temperature switch and oil pressure switch are ON.

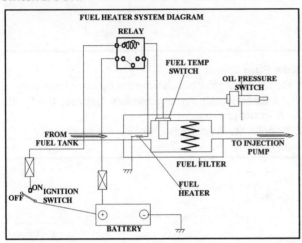

FUEL HEATER SYSTEM DIAGRAM

System Check

1. Install a jump wire between the terminals of the fuel temperature switch, run the engine at about 1000RPM and after a few minutes ensure that the feul heater is hot.

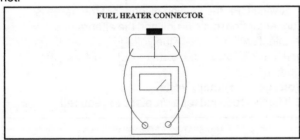

FUEL HEATER CONNECTOR

2. If the heater is not working, check for continuity of the fuel heater, if there is a fault replace the fuel filter bracket.

3. Run the engine at 1000RPM and check continuity of the oil pressure switch, if faults are found repair/replace the oil pressure switch.

4. Check the operation of the fuel heater relay by applying battery volts to the No1 and No2 terminals and check there is continuity between terminals 3 and 4, if faults are found repair/replace as required.

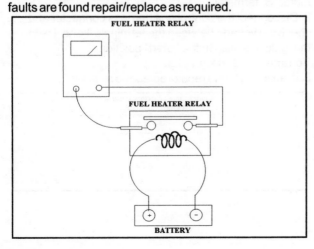

FUEL HEATER RELAY

Air Heater System Checks

Air Heater System Functional Checks

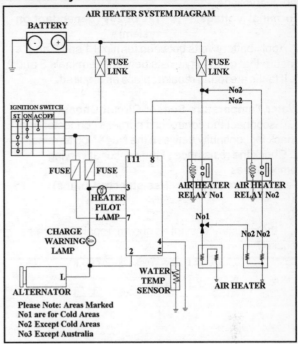

AIR HEATER SYSTEM DIAGRAM

Please Note: Areas Marked
No1 are for Cold Areas
No2 Except Cold Areas
No3 Except Australia

1. When the engine is cold, turn the ignition from OFF to ON to ensure that the pilot lamp comes ON.

2. When the ignition is ON, ensure that the air heater relay works for a short time *(operation correspond to the temperature of the engine coolant)*

3. Touch the air heater with your hand and ensure that the heater is warn.

Air Heater Check.

1. Switch ON the ignition and measure the air heater terminal voltage

Terminal Voltage: **12v or 24v (dependant on system)**

2. On the 12v system ensure that comtinuity exists between terminals A and B & C and D

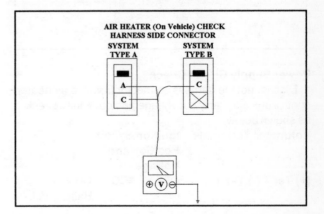

AIR HEATER (On Vehicle) CHECK
HARNESS SIDE CONNECTOR

Nissan Cabstar H40 BD30 Engine 1989 ON

Air Heater Relay Check
1. Switch ON the ignition and record the heater relay terminal voltage:

Terminal Voltage: **12v or 24v (dependant on system)**

2. Apply battery volts between terminal 1 and 2 and ensure that continuity exists between terminals 3 and 4.
3. If faults are found repair/replace as required.

Water Temperature Sensor Circuit Check
1. Disconnect the control unit harness connector and check for continuity between the No4&No5 terminals.
2. Check the resistance of the sensor at varying temperatures

Temperature (°c)	Resistance (K/ohms)
20	2.5
80	0.33

3. If the resistance is not as shown, repair/replace as required.

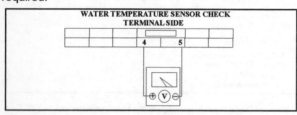

Water Temperature Sensor Check.
1. Disconnect the sensor harness connector and check the resistance between the sensor terminals at varying temperatures.

Temperature (°c)	Resistance (K/ohms)
20	2.5
80	0.33

2. If the resistance is not as shown, repair/replace as required.

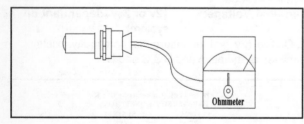

Power Supply Circuit Check
1. Disconnect the harness connector from the air heater control unit and carry out voltage and continuity check as shown below.

Voltmeter Terminals	Ignition Switch Position and Voltage		
	OFF	ACC	ON
(+) Ter 7 (-) Ter 4	0v	0v	Battery Volts

Ohmmeter Terminals	Ignition Switch OFF
(+) Ter 4 (-) Ter Ground	Continuity Exists

2. If the resistance is not as shown, repair/replace as required.

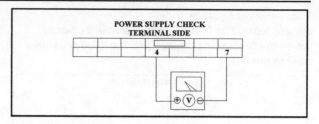

Glow Plug Check
1. Remove the glow plug/s from the cylinder head and check for continuity in the glow plugs between the tip of the plug and ground
2. If continuity is not found, replace the plug/s as required.

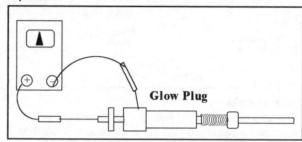

Alternator "L" Terminal Check
1. Switch OFF the ignition disconenct the harness connector from control unit and the alternator's "L" terminal and then check the voltage between the control unit harness connector terminals 2 and 4 with the ignition ON.

Voltage: Battery Volts.

2. If faults are found repair/replace as required.

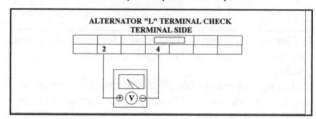

Start Signal Input Check
1. Switch OFF the ignition and disconnect the starter motor "S" terminal.
2. Disconnect the control unit harness connector and check the voltage between the terminals 1 and 4 with the ignition switch in the "Start" position.

Voltage: Battery Volts.

3. If faults are found repair/replace as required.

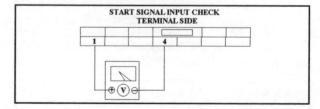

Heater Pilot Lamp Control Check

1. Switch OFF the ignition and leaving the control unit harness connector connected install a test lamp between the terminals 3 and 4.

2. Switch ON the ignition and ensure that the test lamp stays ON as shown below.

Test Lamp Stays ON: **1-20 seconds (12V)**
Test Lamp Stays ON: **1-18 seconds (24V)**
Please Note: Time will vary with coolant temperature

3. If faults are found repair/replace as required.

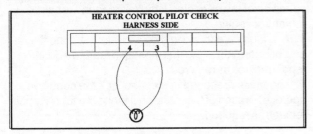

Pre Heating Control Check

1. Switch OFF the ignition and leaving the control unit harness connector connected install a test lamp between the terminals 8&4 .

2. Switch ON the ignition and check the test lamp stays ON time and voltage between terminals as shown below

Voltmeter Terminals	Time (secs)	Voltage (v)
(+) 8 (-) 4 (12v)	0-20	Battery
(+) 11 (-) 4 (12v)	0-20	Battery
(+) 11 (-) 4 (24v)	0-18	Battery

3-If the operation is not as shown, repair/replace as required

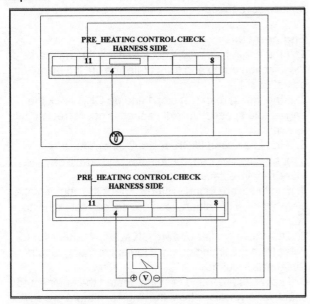

After Heating Control Check

1. Leaving the control unit harness connector connected install a test lamp between the terminals 11&4 .

2. Disconnect the harness connector from the starter motor "S" terminal and ensure that the test lamp comes on when the ignition switch is turned to the "Start" position.

3. Check the test lamp stays ON time and voltage between terminals as shown below when the ignition switch is turned to ON from Start

Voltmeter Terminals	Time (secs)	Voltage (v)
(+) 11 (-) 4 (12v)	0-180 Temp Less than 20°c	Battery
(+) 11 (-) 4 (24v)	0 Temp More than 20°c	Battery

4-If the voltage is not as shown, repair/replace as required.

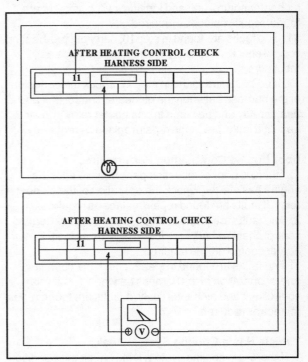

Air Heater System Fault Diagnosis

Engine Will Not Start or Hard to Start

1. Ensure that the fuel level is OK, the fuel supply system and starter system are all working OK, if faults are found, fill up, repair/replace as required.

2. If no faults are found check the condition and/or operation of the air heater harness and/or connectors, if faults are found repair/replace as required.

3. If no faults are found in step2, switch OFF the ingition for at least 10 seconds and check if the pilot lamp comes ON within a few seconds after turning on the ignition.

4. If the lamp does not come on in step3, check the condition of the pilot lamp globe, if faults are found

repair/replace as required.

5. If no faults are found in step4, carry out the 'Power Supply Circuit" check for the control unit. If faults are found check the condition of the harness between the fuse and heater control unit. If faults are found repair/replace as required.

6. If no faults are found in step5, carry out the heater pilot lamp control check, if faults are found repair/replace control unit as required.

7. If no faults are found in step6, check for short circuit on the harness between the ignition switch and heater pilot lamp, if faults are found repair/replace as required.

8. If the pilot lamp in step3 comes on OK, carry out the air heater check, if faults are found repair/replace air heater as required.

9. If no faults are found in step8, carry out air heater relay check, if faults are found repair/replace as required.

10. If no faults are found in step9, carry out start signal check, if faults are found check the harness between the air heater control unit and ignition switch, if faults are found, repair/replace as required.

11. If no faults are found in step10, carry out pre-heating control check, if faults are found repair/replace as required.

12. If no faults are found in step11, check the condition of the harness between the air heater control unit and air heater relay and between the air heater relay and air heater, if faults are found repair/replace as required.

Poor Engine Combustion Performance

1. If there is poor combustion performance after the engine has started, check the operation of the air heater relay, if faults are found repair/replace as required.

2. If no faults are found in step1, carry out after heating control check, if faults are found repair/replace the heater control unit as required.

3. If no faults are found in step2, check the condition and/or operation of the harness between the air relay control unit and air heater realy, if faults are found repair/replace as required.

Vehicle Has a Cooling System Leak

1. If there is a cooling system leak, check the condition and installation of the radiator drain plug, if faults are found repair/replace as required.

2. If no faults are found in step1, carry out a cooling system pressure test and check for leaks at the radiator, hoses and connections and heater core, if faults are found repair/replace as required.

3. If no faults are found in step2, check the condition and/or operation of the oil cooler, if faults are found repair/replace as required.

4. If no faults are found in step3, check the mating area between the cylinder head and cylinder block for leaks from the cylinder head, head gasket and/or cylinder block, if faults are found repair/replace as required.

5. If no faults are found in step4, check for leaks from the engine core plugs and/or water pump, if faults are

found repair/replace as required.

Vehicle Has an Engine Oil Leak

1. With the engine running check for leaks and/or damage around the rocker cover, if faults are found reapir/replace as required.

2. If no faults are found in step1, check the mating area between the cylinder head and cylinder block for leaks from the cylinder head, head gasket and/or cylinder block, if faults are found repair/replace as required.

3. If no faults are found in step2, check for leaks and/or condition of the oil cooler, if faults are found repair/replace as required

4. If no faults are found in step3, check the condition and/or operation of the thermostat, if faults are found repair/replace as required.

5. If no faults are found in step4, check the condition and/or operation of the radiator, if faults are found repair/replace as required.

Engine is Overheating.

1. If the engine is overherheating first check to see if the fan belt and/or adjustment is Ok, if not rectify as required.

2. If no faults are found in step1, check the cooling system for leaks *(Refer Vehicle Has a Cooling System Leak Information)* operations.

3. If no faults are found in step2, check the condition and level of the engine coolant, if the level is not OK, fill as required.

4. If no faults are found on step3, check the condition and/or operation of the thermostat, if faults are found repair/replace as required.

5. If no faults are found in step4, check the condition and/or operation of the radiator, if faults are found repair/replace as required.

Engine is Noisy

1. If the engine is noisy, check that the timimg marks on the injection pump and front plate line up, if they do not adjust to suit.

2. If the timing marks in step1 line up OK, check the engine idle speed, if the idle speed is not correct adjust to suit.

3. If the idle speed is OK in step2, check for any abnormal noises from the injection system, if any are found repair/replace as required.

4. If no faults are found in step3, check the engine valve clearances, if the clearances are not correct adjust to suit.

5. If the valve clearances are OK in step4, check for for noise from the timing gears, if faults are found repair/replace as required.

6. If no faults are found in step5, restart the engine and check for any noises from the engine, if there are still noises check for any noises from around the vacuum pump, if faults are found repair/replace as required.

7. If no faults are found in step6, check for any noise from the water pump, if noise is found repair/replace as required.

8. If no faults are found in step7, check for noise from big end and/or main bearings, damage to the con rods and/or crankshaft and/or warn tappets, if faults are found reapir/replace as required.

VEHICLE SERVICE INFORMATION

Vehicle Filling Capacities

Engine Oil with Filter: .... 8.2 Litres
Engine Oil without Filter: .... 7.5 Litres
Cooling System with Front Heater: .... 13.8 Litres
Cooling System with Front&Rear Heater: ..... 15.5 Litres
Cooling System without Heater: .... 12.9 Litres
Manual Transmission: .... 2.7 Litres (RS5W81A)
Steering Box: ...... 0.9 Litres (Manual Steering VRB70S)
Steering Box: ...... 0.7 Litres (Manual Steering VRB65K)
Steering Box: .... 2.0 Litres (Power Steering)
Rear Differential (H233B): .... 2.0 Litres
Rear Differential (C200): .... 1.3 Litres

Vehicle Component Service Interval Changes

Adjust Valve Clearance:
    Every 20,000kms
Engine Coolant/Anti Freeze:
    Change Every 24 Months/40,000kms
Air Cleaner Element:
    Change Every 24 Months/40,000kms
Pre-Air Cleaner Element:
    Change Every 24 Months/40,000kms (If Fitted)
Fuel Filter:
    Change Every 24 Months/40,000kms
Engine Oil:
    Change Every 3 Months/5,000kms
Engine Oil Filter:
    Change Every 6 Months/10,000kms
Brake Fluid:
    Change Every 24 Months/40,000kms
Manual Transmission Oil:
    Change Every 24 Months/40,000kms
Rear Differential Oil:
    Change Every 24 Months/40,000kms
Check/Repack Front Wheel Bearings:
    Every 24 Months/40,000kms

Nissan Cabstar ED33 Engine 1982-1986

CONTENTS   **PAGE**

CONTENTS   **PAGE**

Nissan Cabstar ED33 Engine 1982-1986

Engine Checks

Valve Clearance Check

Please Note: The adjustments need to be carried out when the engine not running.

1. Remove the rocker cover and ensure that the No1 piston is set at TDC on its compression stroke.

2. Adjust valve clearance of the No1, No2, No3, No6, valves as shown in the diagram.

Valve Clearance:	Inlet (1-3) and Exhaust (2-6)
Valves:	0.35mm

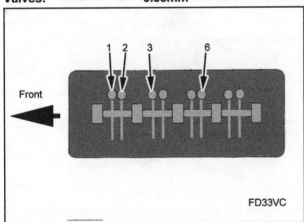

FD33VC

3. Set No4 piston to TDC on its compression stroke and adjust valve clearances on the No4, No5, No7, No8 as shown in the diagram.

Valve Clearance:	Inlet (5-7) and Exhaust (4-8)
Valves:	0.35m

Diagram is in the next column

4. After the valve clearances have all been checked and/or adjusted, replace the rocker cover.

FD33VC1

Compression Check

1. Run the engine to normal operating temperature, remove the injection tube on the nozzle side, spill tube assembly, nozzle assemblies and gaskets, and then install a compression gauge adapter to the cylinder head (ensuring that the bleeder of the gauge is closed).

2. Set the vehicle to 'No Fuel Injection Condition"

3. Crank the engine and record the compression pressure

Compression Pressure:	2,942 kpa (Standard)
Compression Pressure:	2,452kpa (Minimum)
Differential Limit Between Cylinders:	294kpa

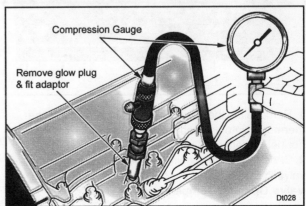

Compression Gauge

Remove glow plug & fit adaptor

Dt028

4. If the compression reading in step 3 on one or more cylinders is low, pour a small amount of oil into the faulty cylinders through the glow plug holes and retest the faulty cylinders.

5. If by adding oil in step 4 the pressure increases, there is a possibility that the piston rings are worn or damaged, if the pressure stays low, there may be sticking valves or the valves may not be seating correctly.

6. If the compression in any two adjacent cylinders are low and adding oil does not increase the pressure, there may be a leak past the gasket surface and could cause oil and water to be present in the combustion chambers.

7. Refit any removed parts in the reverse order of removal and bleed any air that may be present in the system.

Piston Protrusion Check

1. Set the No1 piston to TDC and record the clearance between the top of the piston and the cylinder block with a dial gauge (measure at the front and back of the piston)

Specified Clearance: -0.022-0.478 + 0.08mm

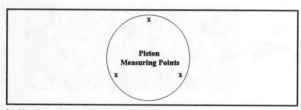

Cylinder Head Tightening Procedures

1. Run the engine until normal operating temperature has been reached, remove the rocker cover and tighten the cylinder head bolts in the sequence shown in the diagram starting from the centre outwards.

Cylinder Head Bolts: 1st Stage: 69-78NM
Cylinder Head Bolts: 2st Stage: 142-152Nm

2. After tightening the bolts, replace the rocker cover.

Cooling System Thermostat Check

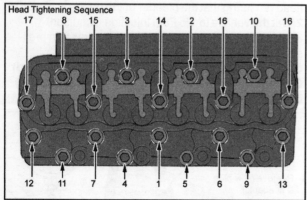

1. Remove the thermostat from the engine, place the thermostat into a suitable container of water and heat to normal operating temperature.

2. Check the valve opening temperature and maximum valve lift.ED33FBIL

Valve Opening Temperature: 82°c

Maximum Valve Lift: More Than 8mm @ 95°c

3. If the specifications shown in step2 are Ok, ensure that the valve now closes at 5°c below the valve operating temperature.

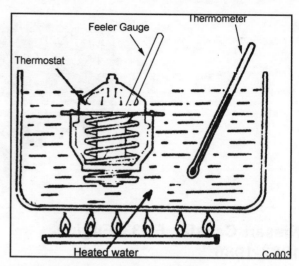

Fuel Filter Check and Replacement

1. Remove the fuel filter sensor, drain the fuel, then remove the fuel filter.

2. Clean the fuel filter mounting bracket and then coat the fuel filter sealing ring with some diesel fuel.

3. Screw the fuel filter on until a slght resistance is felt and then turn another 2/3 of a turn or until suitably tight.

4. Install the fuel filter sensor to the new filter and then bleed any air present from the system.

Draining Water From The Filter

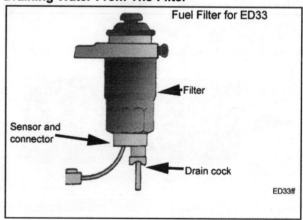

1. Loosen the drain cock 4 or 5 turns or remove the fuel filter sensor to allow the water to drain from the filter.

2. Retighten the drain cock or replace the sensor and bleed any air present from the system.

Bleeding the Fuel System (In Line Pump)

1. Remove the cap that covers the priming pump and then turn the pump anti clockwise.
2. Loosen the air vent screws and move the pump up and down until no more air comes out of the air vent screws.
3. Tighten the air vent screws, turn the priming pump clockwise and then fit the cap back onto the priming pump.

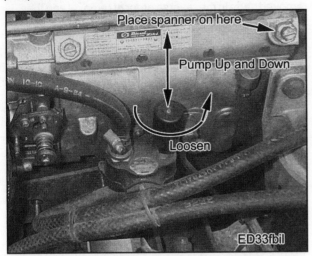

Bleeding the Fuel System (VE Type Injection Pump)

1. Loosen the air vent screw and while priming, ensure that the fuel overflows from the vent screw hole.
2. Tighten the vent screw, loosen the injection pump bleeder screw or disconnect the return hose and prime, ensuring that the fuel overflows at the bleeder screw tube end.
3. Retighten the bleeder screw and reconnect the hose

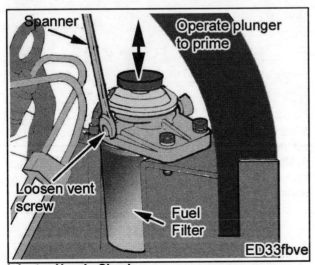

Injector Nozzle Check

1. Remove the injector from the vehicle, connect up to the pressure tester and check the initial pressure by pumping the tester handle a few times.

Initial Pressure: 9,807-10,297kpa (Used Nozzle)

Initial Pressure: 10,297-11287kpa (New Nozzle)

2. Check the spray pattern by pumping the pressure tester handle 4-6 times or more per second and check

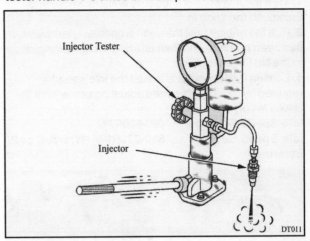

the injection spray pattern.
3. If the operation and/or spray pattern is not as shown, repair/replace the nozzle/s as required.

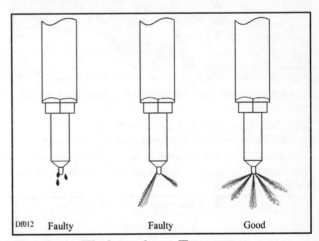

Engine Tightening Torques

Cylinder Head Bolts:	69-78Nm (1st Stage)
Cylinder Head Bolts:	142-152Nm (2nd Stage)
Rocker Arm Shaft Bolt:	34-44Nm
Rocker Arm Lock Nut:	20-25Nm
Exhaust Manifold Bolts and Nuts:	29-34Nm
Inlet Manifold Bolts and Nuts:	5-7Nm
Flywheel Bolts:	147-152Nm
Main Bearing Caps:	167-172Nm (Tighten in two or three stages from the centre outwards)
Connecting Rod Caps:	113-118Nm
Crankshaft Pulley Nut:	490-539Nm
Front Timing Cover:	8mm Bolts 10-13Nm
Camshaft Gear Bolt:	44-59Nm
Oil Pump Bolt:	10-13Nm
Oil Sump Bolt:	10-13Nm

System Adjustments

Idle Speed Check (Inline Pump System)

1. Turn the idle control knob fully anti-clockwise and then push the knob in.

2. Run the engine until the normal operating temperature has been reached and then attach a tachometer pick up to the No1 injection pipe.

3. Loosen the locknut and adjust the idle speed if required by turning idle speed adjusting screw until the speed is correct.

Idle Speed Setting:	**580-620RPM**
Idle Speed Setting:	**680-720RPM (With A/C or P/Steering)**

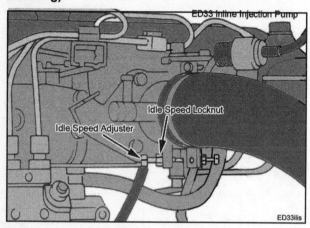

4. After adjusting the idle speed, re-tighten the lock nut.

Injection Timing Check (In Line Pump)

1. Turn the crankshaft in a clockwise direction, set the No1 piston to its applicable BTDC position by lining up the mark No1 on the crankshaft pulley with the mark on the front cover.

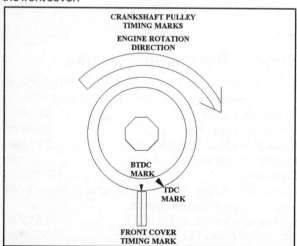

2. Remove all of the injection tubes.

3. Remove the No1 lock plate and delivery valve holder, pull out the delivery valve stopper and the delivery valve spring.

4. Install the delivery valve holder without the spring and stopper, install a test pipe to the No1 delivery valve holder and then push the injection pump fully downwards

towards the engine.

5. While feeding the system fuel by pressing the priming pump, slowly move the injection pump until the fuel flow from the No1 injection tube stops.

6. Fix the injection pump into the position where the fuel flow stopped and ensure that the timing marks on the injection pump and front plate lines up. If the marks do not line up stamp a new mark on the plate.

7. Remove the No1 injection test tube, replace any removed parts in the reverse order of removal and then bleed any air from the system that may be present.

Maximum Speed Adjustment (In Line Pump)

Please Note: The maximum speed adjusting screw is retained by sealing wire and under normal circumstances would not need adjustment.

1. Start the engine and let it run until normal operating temperature has been reached.

2. Install a tachometer pick up lead to the No1 fuel injection pipe.

3. To check the maximum speed reading, press the throttle down fully under no load and record the speed on the tachometer.

Maximum Engine Speed: 4000-4200RPM

4. If the speed is less than shown in step3, turn the maximum speed adjusting screw once or twice in an anti clockwise direction then press down the throttle fully and record the maximium speed shown on the tachometer.

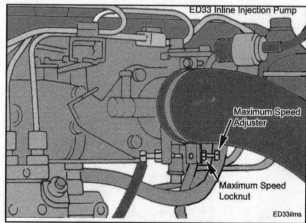

5. If the speed shown in step 4 is still not correct, carry out step 4 operation until the speed setting is correct.

6. After all adjustments have been completed, tighten up the lock nut and secure the maximum speed screw with sealing wire.

Exhaust Brake Switch

1. Loosen the adjustment screw lock nut and turn the adjusting screw in or out until the exhaust brake switch is pushed in 4-5mm when the control lever is in the idle position.

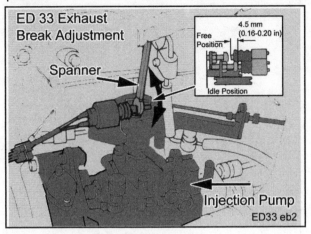

Intake Shutter (VE Type Pump)

1. Put the exhaust brake control lever to the ON position and start the engine.

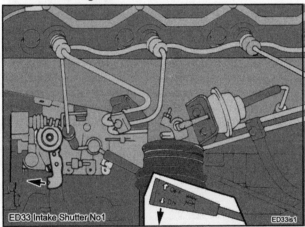

2. Turn on the pump lever and then release it , ensuring that the intake shutter moves.

Injection Timing Check (VE Type Injection Pump)

1. Loosen off the injection pump mounting nuts and mounting bracket bolts

2. Remove the plug bolt from the injection pump distributor head and install a dial gauge to the distributor head

3. Turn the crankshaft in an anti clockwise direction to a

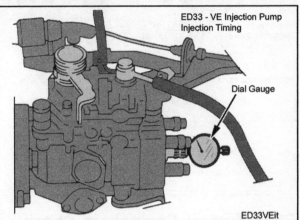

position of between 20-25° BTDC on the No1 piston.

4. With the dial gauge in a suitable rest position set the dial gauge to zero, turn the crankshaft in a clockwise direction until the No1 piston is set at TDC, and record the plunger lift measurement on the dial gauge.

Plunger Lift Measurement: 0.79±0.02mm

5. If the plunger lift measurement in step 4 is not as shown, turn the injection pump body until the reading is correct, then tighten the injection pump mounting bracket and bolts.

Please Note: If the measurement is smaller than shown, turn the injection pump body in an anti clockwise direction, if the measurement is more than shown, turn the injection pump body in a clockwise direction.

6. After all the adjustments have been carried out, remove the dial gauge and refit the plug with a new washer, reconnect the injection pipes and bleed any air from the system that may be present.

Maximum Speed Adjustment (VE Type Injection Pump)

Please Note: The maximum speed adjusting screw is retained by sealing wire and under normal circumstances would not need adjustment.

1. Start the engine and let it run until normal operating temperature has been reached.

2. Install a tachometer pick up lead to the No1 fuel injection pipe.

3. To check the maximum speed reading, press the throttle down fully under no load and record the speed on the tachometer.

Maximum Engine Speed: 4000-4200RPM

4. If the speed is less than shown in step3, turn the maximum speed adjusting screw once or twice in an anti clockwise direction then press down the throttle fully and record the maximium speed shown on the tachometer.

5. If the speed shown in step 4 is still not correct, carry out step 4 operation until the speed setting is correct.

6. After all adjustments have been completed, tighten up the lock not and secure the maximum speed screw with sealing wire.

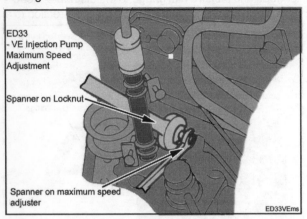

ED33
- VE Injection Pump
Maximum Speed
Adjustment

Spanner on Locknut

Spanner on maximum speed adjuster

ED33VEms

Glow System Component Check

Please Note: A Quick Glow system is fitted to this vehicle to shorten the time that it takes to pre-heat the glow plugs when the engine is cold as well as to aid smooth combustion. This vehicle is fitted with two different types of glow systems. The first system (Type A), is fitted with an after glow mechanism which allows current to flow through the glow plugs for a while after the engine has started. With the second system (Type B), the vehicle is fitted with an afterglow system which allows the current to flow through the glow plugs for a while after the engine has started.

With System Type A, when the ignition swith is turned on the relay No1 is turned on and the high level electric current flows through the glow plugs and heats them up quickly. After a set period the control unit turns off the pilot lamp but the relay No1 stays on. The No1 relay will turn off when the ignition switch returns from the "Start" to the "ON" position or 15 seconds after the ignition switch has turned "ON".

With System Type (B), When the ignition is switched ON, the relay No1 is switched ON and a high level electric current flows through the glow plugs and heats them up quickly, After a set time, the control unit will turn off the pilot lamp. The relay No1 automatically switches OFF after it has been ON for between 6-7 seconds.

With the Afterglow, when the coolant temperature is less than 50°c, the relay no2 turns on at the same time as the ignition is switched ON. It will stay ON for between 20-45 seconds (but time span will depend on the coolant temperature) and will allow low level current to flow through the glow plugs. This will improve the combustion performance of the engine after the engine has started. When the coolant temp is more than 50°c, the relay is only on when the engine is cranking.

Glow System Diagram 1982-1984

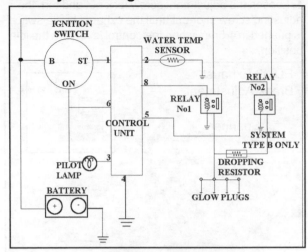

Glow System Diagram 1984 On

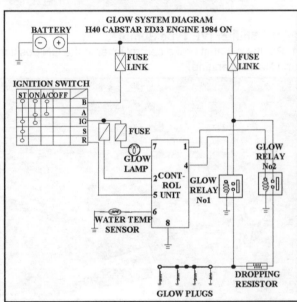

Glow Plug Check

1. Remove the glow plug/s from the cylinder head and check for continuity in the glow plugs between the tip of the plug and ground

2. If continuity is not found, replace the plug/s as required.

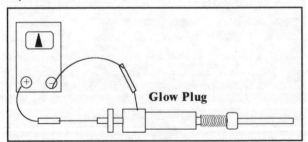

Glow Plug

Water Temperature Sensor Check

1. Remove the sensor from the engine, place into a suitable container of water and check the resistance at varying temperatures.

Sensor Temperature (°c)	Resistance (k/ohms)
0	5.1-6.1
20	2.5-2.75
40	1.1-1.3
60	0.55-0.67

2. If the resistance is not as shown above repair/replace as required.

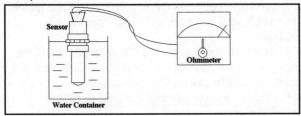

Glow Plug Relay Check

1. Apply battery volts between terminals 1 and ground and ensure that continuity exists between the terminals 3 and 4.

2. If continuity does not exist in step1, repair/replace as required.

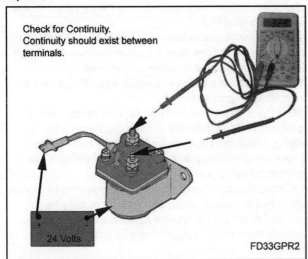

Check for Continuity. Continuity should exist between terminals.

24 Volts

FD33GPR2

Dropping Resistor

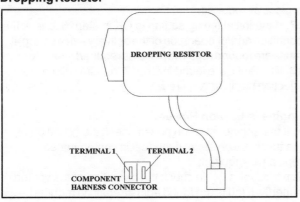

DROPPING RESISTOR

TERMINAL 1   TERMINAL 2

COMPONENT HARNESS CONNECTOR

1. Disconnect the harness connector and check the resistance between the No1 & 2 terminals.
Resistance: 0.5ohms.
2. If the resistance is not as shown, repair/replace as required.

Glow Control Unit Check
Type A System

1. Install jump leads and test lamps to the control unit as shown in the diagram, install resistors to terminal 2 and check that the test lamp goes out as shown below.

Resistor (k/ohms)	Test Lamp 1 Goes out in (secs)	Test Lamp 2 Goes out in (secs)
11.5	9.5-12.5	13-16
5.6	5.9-8.5	13-16
2.5	3.0-5.0	13-16
1.2	1.4-3.0	13-16
0.61	0.6-1.8	13-16

2. If the operation is not as shown, repair/replace as required.

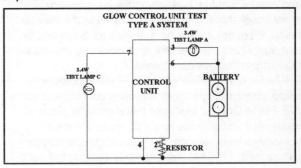

GLOW CONTROL UNIT TEST
TYPE A SYSTEM

TypeB System

1. Install jump leads and test lamps to the control unit as shown in the diagram, install resistors to terminal 2 and check that the test lamp goes out as shown below.

Resistor (k/ohms)	Test Lamp 1 Goes out in (secs)	Test Lamp 2 Goes out in (secs)	Test Lamp 3 Goes out in (secs)
19	4-6	5.5-6.5	38-55
11.5	4.5-6.3	5.5-6.5	33-49
5.6	3.5-5.1	5.5-6.5	25-39
3.7	2.9-4.3	5.5-6.5	20-31
1.2	0.3-0.7	6.0-8.0	15-25
0.61	0.3-0.7	6.0-8.0	0

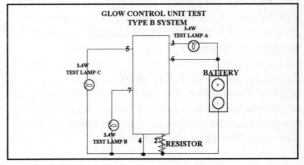

GLOW CONTROL UNIT TEST
TYPE B SYSTEM

2. If the operation is not as shown, repair/replace as required.

Injection System Diagnosis and Troubleshooting

Engine Will Not or is Difficult to Start

1. Ensure that the battery is fully charged and that there is sufficient fuel in the tank to carry out this test.

2. If there are no faults in step1, check that the starter motor will turn, the condition and/or operation of the relevant harness connections, ignition switch, starting circuit, starter motor, if faults are found repair/replace as required.

3. If no faults are found in step2, check the operation of the glow system, if faults are found repair/replace as required.

4. If no faults are found in step3, check the injection pump by ensuring that the timing marks on the front cover and injection pump line up, if they do not adjust to suit.

5. If the injection timing is OK in step4, crank the engine and ensure that fuel is reaching the injection nozzle, if it is not check that fuel is being delivered to the injection pump, if it is not, check the fuel lines for leaks and/or damage, check the fuel filter for blockages, if faults are found repair/replace as required.

6. If fuel is being delivered to the injection pump in step5, check the operation of the fuel cut solenoid valve (VE Pump Only), if faults are found repair/replace as required, if no faults are found check to see if the delivery valve is sticking, if it is sticking repair/replace as required, if it is not sticking repair/replace the injection pump as required.

7. If fuel does reach the injection nozzle in step 5, carry out a compression check on the engine, if the pressures are not correct repair/replace as required.

8. If the compression is OK in step7, check the valve clearances, if the clearances are not correct adjust as required.

9. If the valve clearances are OK in step8, check the condition and/or operation of the injection nozzles, if faults are found, adjust, repair/replace as required.

10. If the injection nozzles are OK in step9, check the injection timing setting, if the setting is not correct adjust to suit.

11. If the injection timing is OK in step10, check the condition and/or operation of the feed pump (In Line Pump), if faults are found reapir/replace as required.

12. If no faults are found in step11, check to see if the delivery valve is sticking, if it is sticking repair/replace as required, if it is not sticking repair/replace the injection pump as required.

Excessive White or Black Smoke

1. When the engine is running is the smoke coming out of the exhaust black or white, If the smoke is black, check the condition of the air cleaner element, if the filter is not OK, replace as required.

2. If the air cleaner element is OK in step1, check the injection timing marks on the front cover and injection pump line up, if the setting is not correct adjust to suit.

3. If the injection timing setting in step2 is Ok, carry out compression test on the engine, if the pressures are not correct repair/replace as required.

4. If the compression pressures are OK in step3, check the condition and/or operation of the injection nozzles, if faults are found repair/replace as required.

5. If the injection nozzles are OK in step4, check the injection timing setting is Ok, if it is not adjust to suit.

6. If the timing setting is OK in step5, check the initial timing setting, if faults are found repair/replace as required.

7. If the initial timing setting is OK in step6, check the condition and/or operation of the delivery valve spring, if faults are found repair/replace as required.

8. If no faults are found in step7, repair/replace the injection pump as required.

9. If white smoke is present in step1, check to see if oil or a similar material is present in the exhaust tail pipe.

10. If there is oil or a similar material present in the exhaust tail pipe in step9, check the oil level and if it is low carry out a compression test on the engine, if the pressures are not correct repair/replace as required.

11. If the compression pressures are OK in step10, check the initial timing setting, if faults are found repair/replace as required.

12. If the initial timing setting is OK in step11, check the condition and/or operation of the delivery valve spring, if faults are found repair/replace as required.

13. If no faults are found in step12, repair/replace the injection pump as required.

14. If the oil level in step10 is OK, and there is no oil or a similar material present in the exhaust tail pipe in step9, check the injection timing marks on the front cover and injection pump line up, if the setting is not correct adjust to suit.

15. If the injection timing marks line up in step14, purge air from the system, drain any water that may be present and then carry out a compression test on the engine, if the pressures are not correct repair/replace as required

16, If the compression pressures are OK in step15, check the initial timing setting, if faults are found repair/replace as required.

17. If the initial timing setting is OK in step16, check the condition and/or operation of the delivery valve spring, if faults are foound repair/replace as required.

18. If no faults are found in step17, repair/replace the injection pump as required.

Engine is Low on Power

1. If the engine is low on power check the condition of the fuel in the system, if the fuel is contaminated replace as required.

2. If the fuel is OK in check the operation of the venturi butterfly, if faults are found adjust/repair as required.

3. If the venturi operation in step2 is OK, check the the timing marks on the injection pump and front cover line up, if they do not adjust to suit.

4. If the timing marks line up in step3, check the condition and/or operation of the fuel lines and/or connections, if faults are found repair/replace as required.

5. If no faults are found in step4, purge any air from the system and then check the condition of the air cleaner element, if faults are found repair/replace as required.

6. If no faults are found in step5, carry out a compression test on the engine, if faults are found repair/replacae as required.

7. If the compression pressures are Ok in step6, check the valve clearances on the engine, if the clearances are not OK, adjust to suit.

8. If the clearances are OK in step7, check the condition of the injection nozzles, if faults are found repair/replace as required.

9. If the nozzles are Ok in step7, check the injection timing setting, if the setting is not correct adjust to suit.

10. If the injection timing is OK in step9, check the condition and/or operation of the feed pump, if faults are found repair/replace as required.

11. If the feed pump is oK in step10, check the condition and/or operation of the delivery valve, if faults are found repair/replace as required.

12. If no faults are found in step11, repair/replace the injection pump as required.

Vehicle Has a Cooling System Leak

1. If there is a cooling system leak, check the condition and installation of the radiator drain plug, if faults are found repair/replace as required.

2. If no faults are found in step1, carry out a cooling system pressure test and check for leaks at the radiator, hoses and connections and heater core, if faults are found repair/replace as required.

3. If no faults are found in step2, check the condition and/or operation of the oil cooler, if faults are found repair/replace as required.

4. If no faults are found in step3, check the mating area between the cylinder head and cylinder block for leaks from the cylinder head, head gasket and/or cylinder block, if faults are found repair/replace as required.

5. If no faults are found in step4, check for leaks from the engine core plugs and/or water pump, if faults are found repair/replace as required.

Vehicle Has an Engine Oil Leak

1. With the engine running check for leaks and/or damage around the rocker cover, if faults are found reapir/replace as required.

2. If no faults are found in step1, check the mating area between the cylinder head and cylinder block for leaks from the cylinder head, head gasket and/or cylinder block, if faults are found repair/replace as required.

3. If no faults are found in step2, check for leaks and/or condition of the oil cooler, if faults are found repair/replace as required

4. If no faults are found in step3, check the condition and/or operation of the system vacuum pump, if faults are found repair/replace as required.

5. If no faults are found in step3, check for oil leaks around the engine sump and/or front and rear engine oil seals, if faults are found repair/replace as required.

Engine is Overheating.

1. If the engine is overherheating first check to see if the fan belt and/or adjustment is Ok, if not rectify as required.

2. If no faults are found in step1, check the cooling system for leaks *(Refer Vehicle Has a Cooling System Leak Information)* operations.

3. If no faults are found in step2, check the condition and level of the engine coolant, if the level is not OK, fill as required.

4. If no faults are found on step3, check the condition and/or operation of the thermostat, if faults are found repair/replace as required.

5. If no faults are found in step4, check the condition and/or operation of the radiator, if faults are found repair/replace as required.

Engine Will Not Stop

1. If the engine will not stop, check the condition and/or operation of the fuel cut solenoid (VE Pump Only), if faults are found repair/replace as required.

2. If no faults are found in step, repair/replace the injection pump as required.

Engine is Noisy

1. If the engine is noisy, check that the timimg marks on the injection pump and front plate line up, if they do not adjust to suit.

2. If the timing marks in step1 line up OK, check the engine idle speed, if the idle speed is not correct adjust to suit.

3. If the idle speed is OK in step2, check for any abnormal noises from the injection system, if any are found repair/replace as required.

4. If no faults are found in step3, check the engine valve clearances, if the clearances are not correct adjust to suit.

5. If the valve clearances are OK in step4, check for for noise from the timing gears, if faults are found repair/replace as required.

6. If no faults are found in step5, restart the engine and check for any noises from the engine. If there are still noises check for any noises from around the vacuum pump, if faults are found repair/replace as required.

7. If no faults are found in step6, check for any noise from the water pump, if noise is found repair/replace as required.

8. If no faults are found in step7, check for noise from big end and/or main bearings, damage to the con rods and/or crankshaft and/or warn tappets, if faults are found reapir/replace as required.

VEHICLE SERVICE INFORMATION

Filling Capacities

Engine Oil with Filter: .... 10.0 Litres
Engine Oil without Filter: .... 8.0 Litres
Cooling System with Front Heater: .... 16.1 Litres
Cooling System with Front&Rear Heater: ..... 15.4 Litres
Cooling System without Heater: .... 14.6 Litres
Manual Transmission: 2.6 Litres (RS6R40A, RT5R41A)
Manual Transmission: .... 2.7 Litres (RS5W81A)
Manual Transmission: .... 2.6 Litres (RS5W71B)
Manual Transmission: .... 2.6 Litres (R4W71B)
Steering Box: ...... 0.7 Litres (Manual Steering VRB70L)
Steering Box: ...... 0.7 Litres (Manual Steering VRB65K)
Steering Box: .... 2.0 Litres (Power Steering)
Rear Differential (H290): .... 4.0 Litres
Rear Differential (H260): .... 2.8 Litres
Rear Differential (H233B): .... 2.0 Litres
Rear Differential (H190): .... 1.3 Litres
Rear Differential (C200): .... 1.3 Litres

Vehicle Component Service Interval Changes

Adjust Valve Clearance:
Every 20,000kms
Engine Coolant/Anti Freeze:
Change Every 24 Months/40,000kms
Air Cleaner Element:
Change Every 24 Months/40,000kms
Pre-Air Cleaner Element:
Change Every 24 Months/40,000kms (If Fitted)
Fuel Filter:
Change Every 12 Months/20,000kms
Engine Oil:
Change Every 3 Months/5,000kms
Engine Oil Filter:
Change Every 6 Months/10,000kms
Brake Fluid:
Change Every 12 Months/20,000kms
Manual Transmission Oil:
Change Every 24 Months/40,000kms
Rear Differential Oil:
Change Every 24 Months/40,000kms
Check/Repack Front Wheel Bearings:
Every 24 Months/40,000kms

Nissan Cabstar FD33/FD33T Engine 1983 ON

Nissan Cabstar FD33/FD33T Engine 1983 ON

Engine Checks

Valve Clearance Check
Please Note: The adjustments need to be carried out when the engine not running.

1. Remove the rocker cover and ensure that the No1 piston is set at TDC on its compression stroke.

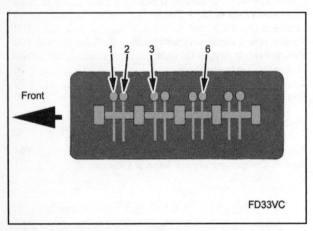

FD33VC

2. Adjust valve clearance of the No1, No2, No3, No6, valves as shown in the diagram.
Valve Clearance: Inlet and Exhaust Valves: 0.4mm
3. Set No4 piston to TDC on its compression stroke and adjust valve clearances on the No4, No5, No7, No8 as shown in the diagram.
Valve Clearance: Inlet and Exhaust Valves: 0.4mm
4. After the valve clearances have all been checked and/or adjusted, replace the rocker cover.
Diagram is on the next page

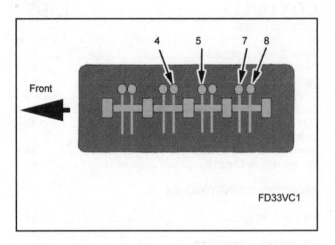

FD33VC1

Compression Check

1. Run the engine to normal operating temperature, remove the injection tube on the nozzle side, spill tube assembly, nozzle assemblies and gaskets, and then install a compression gauge adapter to the cylinder head (ensuring that the bleeder of the gauge is closed).

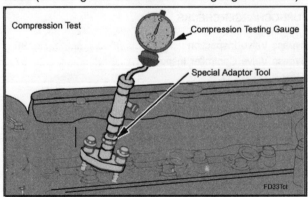

Compression Test
Compression Testing Gauge
Special Adaptor Tool
FD33Tct

2. Set the vehicle to 'No Fuel Injection Condition"
3. Crank the engine and record the compression pressure
Compression Pressure: 2,942 kpa (Standard)
Compression Pressure: 2,452kpa (Minimum)
Differential Limit Between Cylinders: 294kpa

4. If the compression reading in step 3 on one or more cylinders is low, pour a small amount of oil into the faulty cylinders through the glow plug holes and retest the faulty cylinders.

5. If by adding oil in step 4 the pressure increases, there is a possibility that the piston rings are worn or damaged, if the pressure stays low, there may be sticking valves or the valves may not be seating correctly.

6. If the compression in any two adjacent cylinders are low and adding oil does not increase the pressure, there may be a leak past the gasket surface and could cause oil and water to be present in the combustion chambers.

7. Refit any removed parts in the reverse order of removal and bled any air that may be present in the system.

Piston Protrusion Check

1. Set the No1 piston to TDC and record the clearance between the top of the piston and the cylinder block with a dial gauge (measure at the front and back of the piston)

Specified Clearance: -0.022-0.478 + 0.08mm

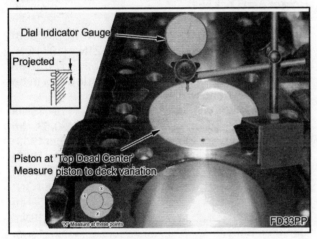

Cylinder Head Tightening Procedures

1. Run the engine until normal operating temperature has been reached, remove the rocker cover and tighten the cylinder head bolts in the sequence shown in the diagram starting from the centre outwards.

Cylinder Head Bolts: 1st Stage: 69-78NM
Cylinder Head Bolts: 2st Stage: 142-152Nm

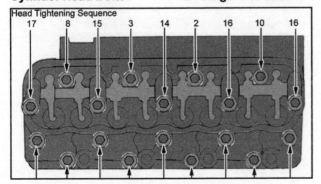

2. After tightening the bolts, replace the rocker cover.

Cooling System Thermostat Check

1. Remove the thermostat from the engine, place the thermostat into a suitable container of water and heat to normal operating temperature.

2. Check the valve opening temperature and maximum valve lift as shown below.

Valve Opening Temperature: 82°c
Maximum Valve Lift: More Than 10mm @ 95°c

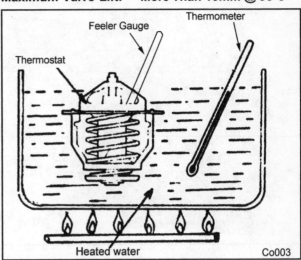

3. If the specifications shown in step2 are Ok, ensure that the valve now closes at 5°c below the valve operating temperature.

Fuel Filter Check and Replacement

1. Remove the fuel filter sensor, drain the fuel and then remove the fuel filter.

2. Clean the fuel filter mounting bracket and then coat the fuel filter sealing ring with some diesel fuel.

3. Screw the fuel filter on until a slght resistance is felt and then turn another 2/3 of a turn or until suitably tight.

4. Install the fuel filter sensor to the new filter and then bleed any air present from the system.

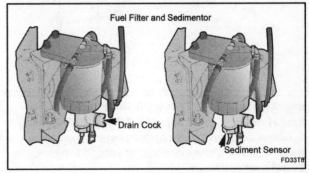

Draining Water From The Filter

1. Loosen the drain cock 4 or 5 turns or remove the fuel filter sensor to allow the water to drain from the filter.

2. Retighten the drain cock or replace the sensor and bleed any air present from the system.

Bleeding the Fuel System (In Line Pump)

1. Remove the cap that covers the priming pump and then turn the pump anti clockwise.

2. Loosen the air vent screws and move the pump up and down until no more air comes out of the air vent screws.

3. Tighten the air vent screws, turn the priming pump clockwise and then fit the cap back onto the priming pump.

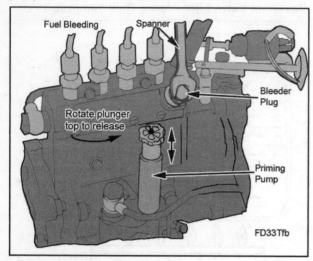

FD33Tfb

Injector Nozzle Check

1. Remove the injector from the vehicle, connect up to the pressure tester and check the initial pressure by pumping the tester handle a few times.

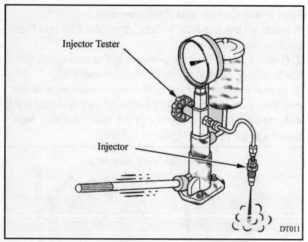

DT011

Initial Pressure: 19,614 to 20,104 kpa (FD33)
Initial Pressure: 21,575 to 22,066 kpa (FD33Turbo)

2. Check the spray pattern by pumping the pressure tester handle 4-6 times or more per second and check the injection spray pattern.

Diagram is in the next column

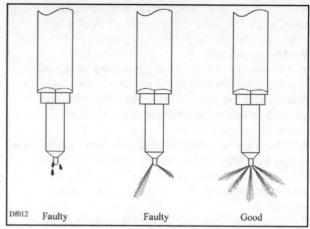

Df012   Faulty   Faulty   Good

3. If the operation and/or spray pattern is not as shown, repair/replace the nozzle/s as required.

Engine Tightening Torques

Cylinder Head Bolts: .... 69-78Nm (1st Stage)
Cylinder Head Bolts: .... 142-152Nm (2nd Stage)
Rocker Arm Shaft Bolt: 34-39Nm
Rocker Arm Lock Nut: 20-25Nm
Exhaust Manifold Bolts and Nuts: 29-34Nm
Inlet Manifold Bolts and Nuts: .... 8-11Nm (Upto 1983)
Inlet Manifold Bolts and Nuts: .... 16-21Nm (1984 ON)
Flywheel Bolts: 147-152Nm
Main Bearing Caps: 167-172Nm (Tighten in two or three stages from the centre outwards)
Connecting Rod Caps: 113-118Nm
Crankshaft Pulley Nut: 490-539Nm
Front Timing Cover: 10mm Bolts: 16-22Nm (Upto 1983)
Front Timing Cover: ... 8mm Bolts 10-13Nm (Upto 1983)
Front Timing Cover: .. 10mm Bolts: 32-42Nm (1984 ON)
Front Timing Cover: ..... 8mm Bolts 16-21Nm (1984 ON)
Camshaft Gear Bolt: 44-59Nm
Oil Pump Bolt: 13-19Nm
Oil Sump Bolt: 15Nm
Turbocharger: 34-44Nm

System Adjustments

Idle Speed Check (Inline Pump System)

1. Turn the idle control knob fully anti-clockwise and then push the knob in.
2. Run the engine until the normal operating temperature has been reached and then attach a tachometer pick up to the No1 injection pipe.
3. Loosen the locknut and adjust the idle speed if required by turning idle speed adjusting screw as required.

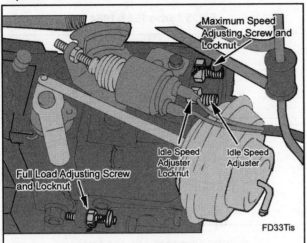

FD33Tis

Idle Speed Setting:	550-650RPM (Turbo Without A/C or P/Steering 1983)
Idle Speed Setting:	650-750RPM (Turbo With A/C or P/Steering 1983)
Idle Speed Setting:	580-620RPM (Turbo/Non Turbo Without A/C or P/Steering 1984 ON)
Idle Speed Setting:	680-720RPM (Turbo/Non Turbo With A/C or P/Steering 1984 ON)

4. After adjusting the idle speed, re-tighten the lock nut.

Injection Timing Check (In Line Pump)

1. Turn the crankshaft in a clockwise direction, set the No1 piston to its applicable BTDC position by lining up the mark No1 on the crankshaft pulley with the mark on the front cover. *(if there are only two marks on the crankshaft pulley, take the RH mark as the BTDC setting).*

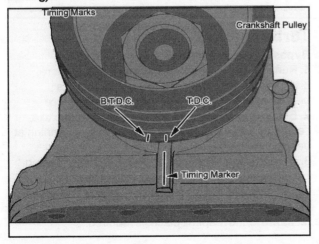

2. Remove all of the injection tubes.
3. Remove the No1 lock plate and delivery valve holder, pull out the delivery valve stopper and the delivery valve spring.
4. Install the delivery valve holder without the spring and stopper, install a test pipe to the No1 delivery valve holder and then push the injection pump fully downwards towards the engine.
5. While feeding the system fuel by pressing the priming pump, slowly move the injection pump until the fuel flow from the No1 injection tube stops.
6. Fix the injection pump into the position where the fuel flow stopped and ensure that the timing marks on the injection pump and front plate lines up. If the marks do not line up stamp a new mark on the plate.

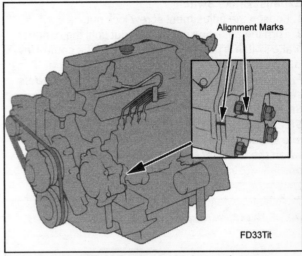

FD33Tit

7. Remove the No1 injection test tube, replace any removed parts in the reverse order of removal and then bleed any air from the system that may be present.

Maximum Speed Adjustment (In Line Pump)

Please Note: The maximum speed adjusting screw is retained by sealing wire and under normal circumstances would not need adjustment.

1. Start the engine and let it run until normal operating temperature has been reached.
2. Install a tachometer pick up lead to the No1 fuel injection pipe.
3. To check the maximum speed reading, press the throttle down fully under no load and record the speed on the tachometer.
Maximum Engine Speed: 4000-4200RPM
4. If the speed is less than shown in step3, turn the maximum speed adjusting screw once or twice in an anti clockwise direction, press down the throttle fully and record the maximium speed shown on the tachometer.
5. If the speed shown in step 4 is still not correct, carry out step 4 operation until the speed setting is correct.
6. After all adjustments have been completed, tighten up the lock nut and secure the maximum speed screw with sealing wire.

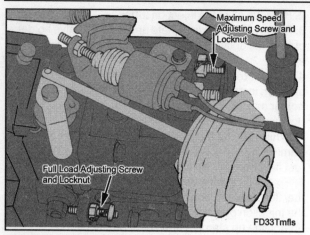

FD33Tmfls

Exhaust Brake Switch

1. Loosen the adjustment screw lock nut.

2. Turn the adjusting screw in or out until the exhaust brake switch is pushed in 4-5mm when the control lever is in the idle position.

Please Note: At this point for FD33 Engine models set the idle speed to 850±50 RPM (without Power Steering 1984 ON) or to 900±50RPM (With Power Steering 1984ON), For FD33T Engine models set the idle speed to between 900-1000 RPM (1983 ON) when the exhaust brake engine warm up switch is on.

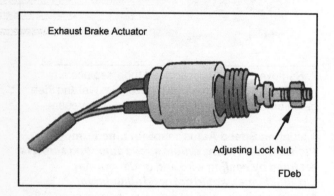

Exhaust Brake Actuator

Adjusting Lock Nut

FDeb

Intake Shutter

1. Remove the intake shutter from the vehicle and ensure that the clearance between the valve and inner wall is about 2.5±0.5mm (FD33 1984ON), 3.0mm (FD33T 1983), 3.0mm ±0.5mm (FD33T 1984ON)

2. Refit the shutter to the vehicle and put the exhaust brake control lever to the ON position and start the engine.

3. Turn on the pump lever and the release it ensuring that the intake shutter moves.

FD33 Turbo 1983-1984

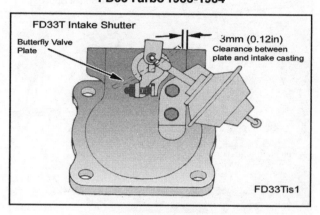

FD33T Intake Shutter

Butterfly Valve Plate

3mm (0.12in) Clearance between plate and intake casting

FD33Tis1

FD33/FD33 Turbo 1984 ON

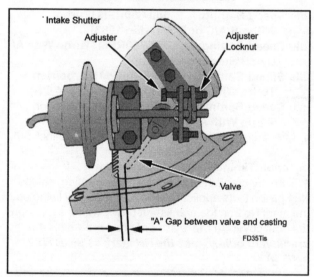

Intake Shutter

Adjuster

Adjuster Locknut

Valve

"A" Gap between valve and casting

FD35Tis

Turbocharger Checks

Bypass Valve Inspection

1. Run the engine to normal operating temperature, disconnect the by pass valve hose and install a pressure gauge via a 3 way connector in its place.

2. Ensure that the gauge needle does not move to a setting of more than 83.3kpa with the engine running at between 2500-3000RPM.

3. If the needle setting is outside the 83.3kpa reading, check the condition and/or operation of the intake and exhaust system (inc turbocharger) for any gas or oil leaks, and also check the intake relief valve foe leaks, if faults are found reapir/replace as required.

4. If the setting in step2 is more than 83.3kpa, check the condition and/or operation of the swing valve controler hose and/or operation of the swing controller, if faults are found repair/replace as required.

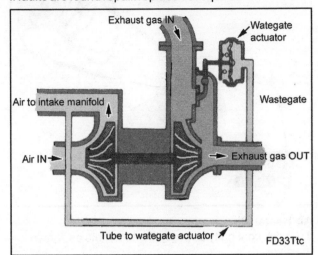

FD33Ttc

Bypass Valve Controller Inspection
1. Disconnect the hose at the end of the compressor housing running to the by pass valve controller.
2. Apply 98kpa of air with a hand vacuum pump through the opening of the hose to ensure that the by pass valve controller link activates.

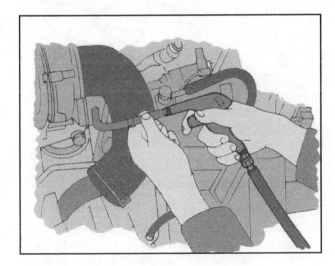

Quick Heat System Check
FD 33
FD33 *Turbo*
The Quick Heat System fitted to the FD33/33T engine, preheats the intake air and makes it easier

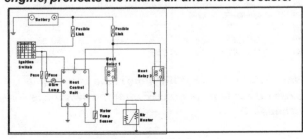

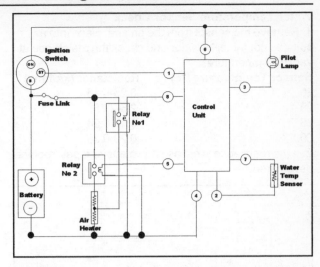

to start the engine. The After Heat System is used to stabilize the combustion after the engine has started.

Pre Heating System Operation
When the ignition switch is turned ON, the pilot lamp lights up. Current flows through the air heater via the relay No1 and No2. After a specified time period Relay No1 turns OFF and the pilot lamp goes out, but the current continues to flow through the air heater Relay No2.
Please Note:
1. After about 10 seconds after the pilot lamp has gone out,
2. Relay NO2 will turn OFF. Relay No2 will not activate when the temperature of the engine coolant temperature is more than 20°c
After Heating Operation
After the engine has started, current flows through the air heater via the Relay No2 for a specified length of time determined by the temperature of the engine coolant in order to stabilize the engine speed.
Please Note
Relay No2 will not activate when the temperature of the engine coolant temperature is more than 20°c

Glow Plug Check
1. Remove the glow plug/s from the cylinder head and check for continuity in the glow plugs between the tip of the plug and ground
2. If continuity is not found, replace the plug/s as required.

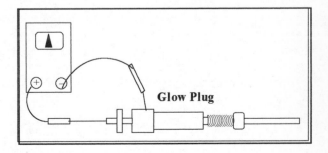

Glow Plug

Water Temperature Sensor Check

1. Remove the sensor from the engine, place into a suitable container of water and check the resistance at varying temperatures.

Sensor Temperature (°c)	Resistance (k/ohms)
10	3.25-4.15
20	2.5-2.75
50	074-0.94
80	0.29-0.36

2. If the resistance is not as shown above repair/replace as required.

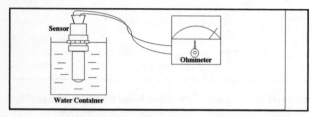

Glow Plug Relay Check

1. Apply battery volts between terminals as shown in diagram and ensure continuity exists.

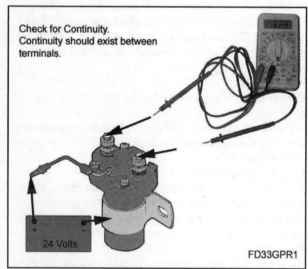

Check for Continuity.
Continuity should exist between terminals.

24 Volts

FD33GPR1

2. Apply battery volts between the terminals as shown in the diagram and ensure continuity exits.
Diagram is in the next column
3. If continuity is not as shown above repair/replace as required.

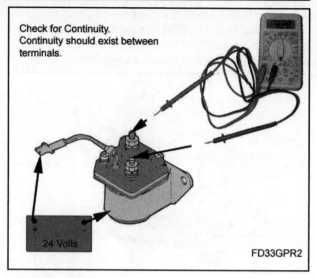

Check for Continuity.
Continuity should exist between terminals.

24 Volts

FD33GPR2

Air Heater Check

1. Check continuity between the terminals as shown in the diagram.

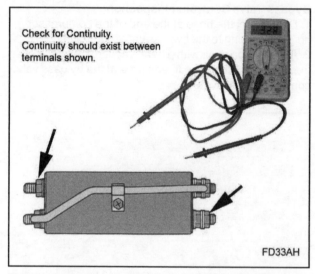

Check for Continuity.
Continuity should exist between terminals shown.

FD33AH

2. If continuity does not exist repair/replace as required.

Auto Glow Timer Check

1. Connect jump lead wires to the unit as shown in the diagram and then insert the resistors as shown below between terminals 2 and 7 and check the time it takes for the light to go out.

Switch1	Switch2	Resistor k/ohms	LampA Secs	LampB Secs	LampC Secs
ON	OFF	22.5	20-26	10.5-13.5	10-15
ON	OFF	12.5	10-17	6.0-12.0	10-15
ON	OFF	6.1	0.7-1.3	0.0	10-15
ON	ON/OFF	22.5			172-198
ON	ON/OFF	12.5			110-150
ON	ON/OFF	2.6			30-36
ON	ON/OFF	1.5			0.0

Please Note: The ON/OFF time is the time that it takes for the lamp to go OFF after the switch2 is turned OFF

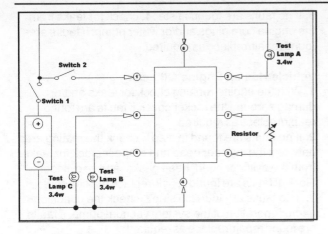

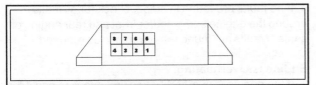

Injection System Diagnosis and Troubleshooting

Engine Will Not or is Difficult to Start

1. Ensure that the battery is fully charged and that there is sufficient fuel in the tank to carry out this test.

2. If there are no faults in step1, check that the starter motor will turn, the condition and/or operation of the relevant harness connections, ignition switch, starting circuit, starter motor, if faults are found repair/replace as required.

3. If no faults are found in step2, check the operation of the quick heat system, if faults are founf repair/replace as required.

4. If no faults are found in step3, check the injection pump by ensuring that the timing marks on the front cover and injection pump line up, if they do not adjust to suit.

5. If the injection timing is OK in step4, crank the engine and ensure that fuel is reaching the injection nozzle, if it is not check that fuel is being delivered to the injection pump, if it is not, check the fuel lines for leaks and/or damage, check the fuel filter for blockages, if faults are found repair/replace as required.

6. If fuel is being delivered to the injection pump in step5, check to see if the delivery valve is sticking, if it is sticking repair/replace as required, if it is not sticking repair/replace the injection pump as required.

7. If fuel does reach the injection nozzle in step 5, carry out a compression check on the engine, if the pressures are not correct repair/replace as required.

8. If the compression is OK in step7, check the valve clearances, if the clearances are not correct adjust as required.

9. If the valve clearances are OK in step8, check the condition and/or operation of the injection nozzles, if faults are found, adjust, repair/replace as required.

10. If the injection nozzles are OK in step9, check the injection timing setting, if the setting is not correct adjust to suit.

11. If the injection timing is OK in step10, check the condition and/or operation of the feed pump, if faults are found reapir/replace as required.

12. If no faults are found in step11, check to see if the delivery valve is sticking, if it is sticking repair/replace as required, if it is not sticking repair/replace the injection pump as required.

Excessive White or Black Smoke

1. When the engine is running, is the smoke coming out of the exhaust black or white, If the smoke is black, check the condition of the air cleaner element, if the filter is not OK, replace as required.

2. If the air cleaner element is OK in step1, check the injection timing marks on the front cover and injection pump line up, if the setting is not correct adjust to suit.

3. If the injection timing setting in step2 is Ok, carry out compression test on the engine, if the pressures are not correct repair/replace as required.

4. If the compression pressures are OK in step3, check the condition and/or operation of the injection nozzles, if faults are found repair/replace as required.

5. If the injection nozzles are OK in step4, check the injection timing setting is Ok, if it is not adjust to suit.

6. If the timing setting is OK in step5, check the initial timing setting, if faults are found repair/replace as required.

7. If the initial timing setting is OK in step6, check the condition and/or operation of the delivery valve spring, if faults are found repair/replace as required.

8. If no faults are found in step7, repair/replace the injection pump as required.

9. If white smoke is present in step1, check to see if oil or a similar material is present in the exhaust tail pipe.

10. If there is oil or a similar material present in the exhaust tail pipe in step9, check the oil level and if it is low carry out a compression test on the engine, if the pressures are not correct repair/replace as required.

11. If the compression pressures are OK in step10, check the initial timing setting, if faults are found repair/replace as required.

12. If the initial timing setting is OK in step11, check the condition and/or operation of the delivery valve spring, if faults are found repair/replace as required.

13. If no faults are found in step10, repair/replace the injection pump as required.

14. If the oil level in step10 is OK, and there is no oil or a similar material present in the exhaust tail pipe in step9, check the injection timing marks on the front cover and injection pump line up, if the setting is not correct adjust to suit.

15. If the injection timing marks line up in step14, purge air from the system, drain any water that may be present and then carry out a compression test on the engine, if the pressures are not correct repair/replace as required

16. If the compression pressures are OK in step15, check the initial timing setting, if faults are found repair/replace as required.

17. If the initial timing setting is OK in step16, check the condition and/or operation of the delivery valve spring, if faults are foound repair/replace as required.

18. If no faults are found in step17, repair/replace the injection pump as required.

Engine is Low on Power

1. If the engine is low on power check the condition of the fuel in the system, if the fuel is contaminated replace as required.

2. If the fuel is OK in step1, check the the timing marks on the injection pump and front cover line up, if they do not adjust to suit.

3. If the timing marks line up in step2, check the condition and/or operation of the fuel lines and/or connections, if faults are found repair/replace as required.

4. If no faults are found in step3, purge any air from the system and then check the condition of the air cleaner element, if faults are found repair/replace as required.

5. If no faults are found in step4, carry out a compression test on the engine, if faults are found repair/replacae as required.

6. If the compression pressures are Ok in step5, check the valve clearances on the engine, if the clearances are not OK, adjust to suit.

7. If the clearances are OK in step6, check the condition of the injection nozzles, if faults are found repair/replace as required.

8. If the nozzles are Ok in step7, check the injection timing setting, if the setting is not correct adjust to suit.

9. If the injection timing is OK in step8, check the condition and/or operation of the feed pump, if faults are found repair/replace as required.

10. If the feed pump is oK in step9, , check the condition and/or operation of the delivery valve, if faults are found repair/replace as required.

11. If no faults are found in step10, repair/replace the injection pump as required.

Vehicle Has a Cooling System Leak

1. If there is a cooling system leak, check the condition and installation of the radiator drain plug, if faults are found repair/replace as required.

2. If no faults are found in step1, carry out a cooling system pressure test and check for leaks at the radiator, hoses and connections and heater core, if faults are found repair/replace as required.

3. If no faults are found in step2, check the condition and/or operation of the oil cooler, if faults are found repair/replace as required.

4. If no faults are found in step3, check the mating area between the cylinder head and cylinder block for leaks from the cylinder head, head gasket and/or cylinder block, if faults are found repair/replace as required.

5. If no faults are found in step4, check for leaks from the engine core plugs and/or water pump, if faults are found repair/replace as required.

Vehicle Has an Engine Oil Leak

1. With the engine running check for leaks and/or damage around the rocker cover, if faults are found reapir/replace as required.

2. If no faults are found in step1, check the mating area between the cylinder head and cylinder block for leaks from the cylinder head, head gasket and/or cylinder block, if faults are found repair/replace as required.

3. If no faults are found in step2, check the condition and/or operation of the system vacuum pump, if faults are found repair/replace as required.

4. If no faults are found in step3, check for oil leaks around the engine sump and/or front and rear engine oil seals, if faults are found repair/replace as required.

Engine is Overheating.

1. If the engine is overherheating first check to see if the fan belt and/or adjustment is Ok, if not rectify as required.

2. If no faults are found in step1, check the cooling system for leaks *(Refer Vehicle Has a Cooling System Leak Information)* operations.

3. If no faults are found in step2, check the condition and level of the engine coolant, if the level is not OK, fill as required.

4. If no faults are found on step3, check the condition and/or operation of the thermostat, if faults are found repair/replace as required.

5. If no faults are found in step4, check the condition and/or operation of the radiator, if faults are found repair/replace as required.

Engine Will Not Stop

1. If the engine will not stop, check the condition and/or operation of the auto stop actuator, if faults are found repair/replace as required.

2. If no faults are found in step1, check the operation of the solenoid valve, if faults are found repair/replace as required.

3. If no faults are found in step2, repair/replace the injection pump as required.

Engine is Noisy

1. If the engine is noisy, check that the timimg marks on the injection pump and front plate line up, if they do not adjust to suit.

2. If the timing marks in step1 line up OK, check the engine idle speed, if the idle speed is not correct adjust to suit.

3. If the idle speed is OK in step2, check for any abnormal noises from the injection system, if any are found repair/replace as required.

4. If no faults are found in step3, check the engine valve clearances, if the clearances are not correct adjust to suit.

5. If the valve clearances are OK in step4, check for for noise from the timing gears, if faults are found repair/ replace as required.

6. If no faults are found in step5, restart the engine and check for any noises from the engine, if there are still noises check for any noises from around the vacuum pump, if faults are found repair/replace as required.

7. If no faults are found in step6, check for any noise from the water pump, if noise is found repair/replace as required.

8. If no faults arte found in step7, check for noise from big end and/or main bearings, damage to the con rods and/or crankshaft and/or warn tappets, if faults are found reapir/replace as required.

Vehicle Filling Capacities

Engine Oil with Filter: .... 8.7 Litres
Engine Oil without Filter: .... 8.0 Litres
Manual Transmission: .... 2.6 Litres

Vehicle Component Service Interval Changes

Adjust Valve Clearance:
Every 20,000kms
Engine Coolant/Anti Freeze:
Change Every 24 Months/40,000kms
Air Cleaner Element:
Change Every 24 Months/40,000kms
Pre-Air Cleaner Element: (If Fitted)
Change Every 24 Months/40,000kms
Fuel Filter:
Change Every 24 Months/40,000kms
Engine Oil:
Change Every 3 Months/5,000kms
Engine Oil Filter:
Change Every 6 Months/10,000kms
Brake Fluid:
Change Every 12 Months/20,000kms
Manual Transmission Oil:
Change Every 24 Months/40,000kms
Rear Differential Oil:
Change Every 24 Months/40,000kms
Repack Front Wheel Bearings:
Every 12 Months/20,000kms

Nissan Cabstar FD35/FD35T Engine 1987-1993

CONTENTS   PAGE

CONTENTS   PAGE

1987 Cabstar

Nissan Cabstar FD35-35T 1987-1993

Engine Checks

Valve Clearance Check

Please Note: The adjustments need to be carried out when the engine not running.

1-Remove the rocker cover and ensure that the No1 piston is set at TDC on its compression stroke.

2-Adjust valve clearance of the No1, No2, No3, No6, valves as shown in the diagram.

Valve Clearance: Inlet and Exhaust Valves:
0.40mm

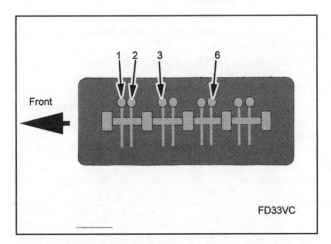

FD33VC

3-Set No4 piston to TDC on its compression stroke and adjust valve clearances on the No4, No5, No7, No8 as shown in the diagram.

Valve Clearance: Inlet and Exhaust Valves:
0.40mm

Diagram is in the next column

4-After the valve clearances have all been checked and/or adjusted, replace the rocker cover.

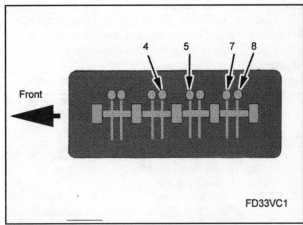

FD33VC1

Compression Check

1-Run the engine to normal operating temperature, remove the injection tube on the nozzle side, spill tube assembly, nozzle assemblies and gaskets, and then install a compression gauge adapter to the cylinder head (ensuring that the bleeder of the gauge is closed).

2-Set the vehicle to 'No Fuel Injection Condition"

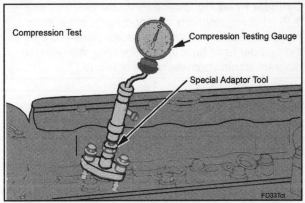

Compression Test

Compression Testing Gauge

Special Adaptor Tool

FD33Tct

3-Crank the engine and record the compression pressure

Compression Pressure: 2,942 kpa (Standard)
Compression Pressure: 2,452kpa (Minimum)
Differential Limit Between Cylinders: 294kpa

4-If the compression reading in step 3 on one or more cylinders is low, pour a small amount of oil into the faulty cylinders through the glow plug holes and retest the faulty cylinders.

5-If by adding oil in step 4 the pressure increases, there is a possibility that the piston rings are worn or damaged, if the pressure stays low, there may be sticking valves or the valves may not be seating correctly.

6-If the compression in any two adjacent cylinders are low and adding oil does not increase the pressure, there may be a leak past the gasket surface and could cause oil and water to be present in the combustion chambers.

7-Refit any removed parts in the reverse order of removal and bled any air that may be present in the system.

Piston Protrusion Check

1-Set the No1 piston to TDC and record the clearance between the top of the piston and the cylinder block with a dial gauge (measure at the three marks as per diagram)

Specified Clearance: -0.022-0.478 + 0.08mm

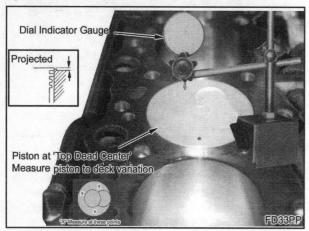

Cylinder Head Tightening Procedures

1-Run the engine until normal operating temperature has been reached, remove the rocker cover and tighten the cylinder head bolts in the sequence shown in the diagram starting from the centre outwards.

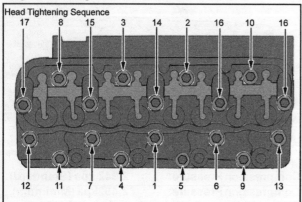

Cylinder Head Bolts: 1ˢᵗ Stage: 69-78NM

Cylinder Head Bolts: 2ˢᵗ Stage: 142-152Nm

2-After tightening the bolts, replace the rocker cover.

Cooling System Thermostat Check

1-Remove the thermostat from the engine, place the thermostat into a suitable container of water and heat to normal operating temperature.

2-Check the valve opening temperature and maximum valve lift

Valve Opening Temperature: 82°c

Maximum Valve Lift: More Than 10mm @ 95°c

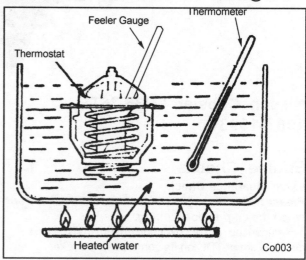

3-If the specifications shown in step2 are Ok, ensure that the valve now closes at 5°c below the valve operating temperature.

Fuel Filter Check and Replacement

1-Remove the fuel filter sensor, drain the fuel and then remove the fuel filter.

2-Clean the fuel filter mounting bracket and then coat the fuel filter sealing ring with some diesel fuel.

3-Screw the fuel filter on until a slght resistance is felt and then turn another 2/3 of a turn or until suitably tight.

4-Install the fuel filter sensor to the new filter and then bleed any air present from the system.

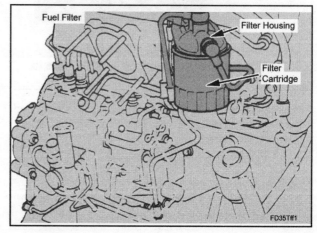

Draining Water From The Filter (Sedimentor Type)
Please Note: Sedimentor is located infront of the fuel tank)
1. Remove the screw from the sedimentor cover.
2. When the fuels drains out of the drain hole after loosening the screw, screw the scew back in to stop the fuel draining.

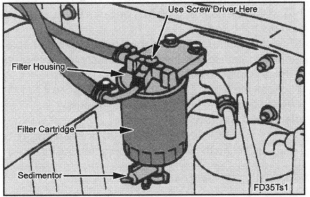

Draining Water From The Filter (Other Type of Filter)
1. Loosen the bleeder screw in the fuel filter cover.
2. When the fuel drains out of the drain cock, screw it back in to stop draining.

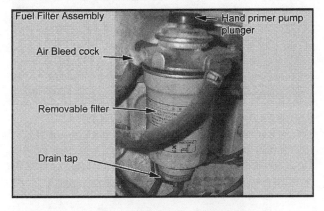

Bleeding the Fuel System (In Line Pump)
1-Tighten the bleeder screw on the sedimenter covver and then loosen the bleeder screw on the injection pump.

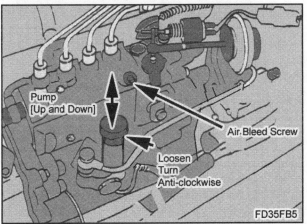

2-Prime the priming pump repeatedly by hand until no more air comes out of the air bleeder portion of the injection pump..
3-Tighten the air bleeder screws and priming pump.

Bleeding the Fuel System (VE Pump)
1. Tighten the air bleeder tap on the fuel filter cover .

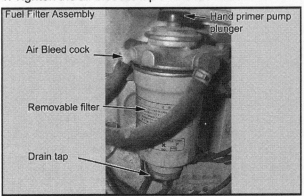

2. Loosen the overflow connector nut on the injection pump.

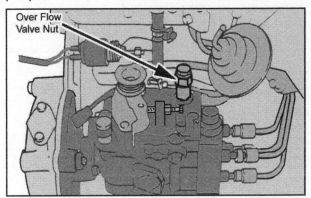

3. Manually operate the primimg pump until no air bubbles come out of the overflow pipe on the injection pump.

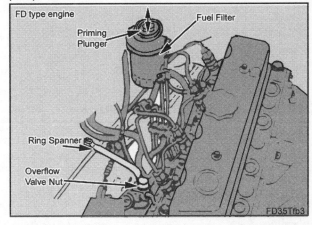

4. Retighten the connector bolt on the fuel injection pump overflow valve.

Injector Nozzle Check

1. Remove the injector from the vehicle, connect up to the pressure tester and check the initial pressure by pumping the tester handle a few times.

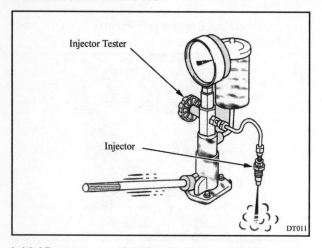

Initial Pressure: 19,614 to 20,104 kpa (FD35)
Initial Pressure: 21,575 to 22,066 kpa (FD35Turbo)

2. Check the spray pattern by pumping the pressure tester handle 4-6 times or more per second and check the injection spray pattern.

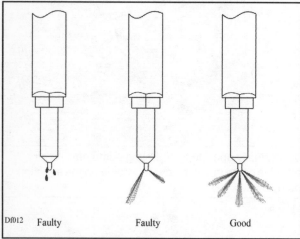

Df012 Faulty   Faulty   Good

3. If the operation and/or spray pattern is not as shown, repair/replace the nozzle/s as required.

Engine Tightening Torques

Cylinder Head Bolts: .... 69-78Nm (1st Stage)
Cylinder Head Bolts: .... 142-152Nm (2nd Stage)
Rocker Arm Shaft Bolt: 34-39Nm
Rocker Arm Lock Nut: 20-25Nm
Exhaust Manifold Bolts and Nuts: 34-44Nm
Inlet Manifold Bolts and Nuts: 7-10Nm
Flywheel Bolts: 147-152Nm
Main Bearing Caps:167-172Nm (Tighten in two or three stages from the centre outwards)
Connecting Rod Caps: 113-118Nm
Crankshaft Pulley Nut: 490-539Nm
Front Timing Cover: .... 10mm Bolts: 32-42Nm
Front Timing Cover: .... 8mm Bolts 16-21Nm

Camshaft Gear Bolt: 44-59Nm
Oil Pump Bolt: 13-19Nm
Oil Sump Bolt: 15Nm
Turbocharger: 34-44Nm

System Adjustments

Idle Speed Check (Inline Pump System)

1-Turn the idle control knob fully anti-clockwise and then push the knob in.

2-Run the engine until the normal operating temperature has been reached and then attach a tachometer pick up to the No1 injection pipe.

3-Loosen the locknut and adjust the idle speed if required by turning idle speed adjusting screw .

Idle Speed Setting:

680-720RPM (With A/C or P/Steering)

4-After adjusting the idle speed, re-tighten the lock nut.

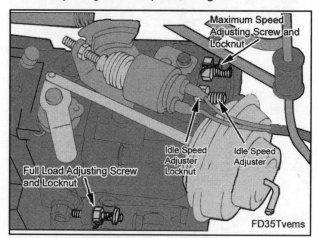

Injection Timing Check (In Line Pump)

1-Turn the crankshaft in a clockwise direction, set the No1 piston to its relevant BTDC timing mark lines on the crankshaft pulley

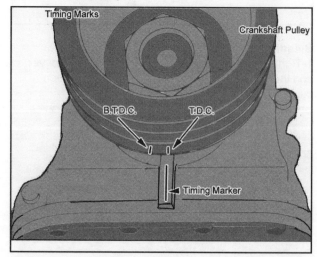

2-Remove all of the injection tubes.

3-Remove the No1 lock plate and delivery valve holder, pull out the delivery valve stopper and the delivery valve spring.

5-Install the delivery valve holder without the spring and stopper, install a test pipe to the No1 delivery valve holder and then push the injection pump fully downwards towards the engine.

6-While feeding the system fuel by pressing the priming pump, slowly move the injection pump until the fuel flow from the No1 injection tube stops.

7-Fix the injection pump into the position where the fuel flow stopped and ensure that the timing marks on the injection pump and front plate lines up. If the marks do not line up stamp a new mark on the plate.

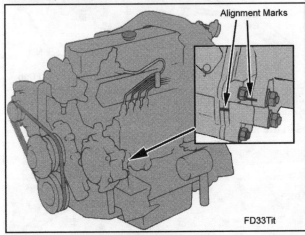

FD33Tit

8-Remove the No1 injection test tube, replace any removed parts in the reverse order of removal and then bleed any air from the system that may be present.

Maximum Speed Adjustment (In Line Pump)

Please Note: The maximum speed adjusting screw is retained by sealing wire and under normal circumstances would not need adjustment.

1-Start the engine and let it run until normal operating temperature has been reached.

2-Install a tachometer pick up lead to the No1 fuel injection pipe.

3-To check the maximum speed reading, press the throttle down fully under no load and record the speed on the tachometer.

Maximum Engine Speed: 4000-4200RPM

4-If the speed is less than shown in step3, turn the maximum speed adjusting screw once or twice in an anti clockwise direction then press down the throttle fully and record the maximium speed shown on the tachometer.

5-If the speed shown in step 4 is still incorrect, carry out step 4 operation until the speed setting is correct.

6-After all adjustments have been completed, tighten up the lock nut and secure the maximum speed screw with sealing wire.

Diagram is in the Next Column

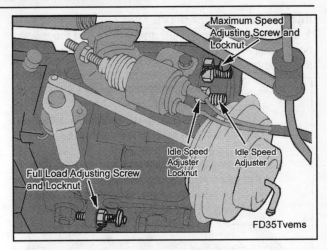

FD35Tvems

Idle Speed Check (VE Pump System)

1-Turn the idle control knob fully anti-clockwise and then push the knob in.

2-Run the engine until the normal operating temperature has been reached and then attach a tachometer pick up to the No1 injection pipe.

3-Loosen the locknut and adjust the idle speed if required by turning idle speed adjusting screw .

Idle Speed Setting:
   640-680RPM (Without A/C or P/Steering)
Idle Speed Setting:
   680-720RPM (With A/C or P/Steering)

4-After adjusting the idle speed, re-tighten the lock nut

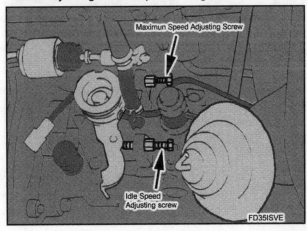

FD35ISVE

Injection Timing Check (VE Type Injection Pump)

1-Set the No1 piston to TDC and ensure that the marks on the crankshaft pulley line up with the mark on the timing cover.

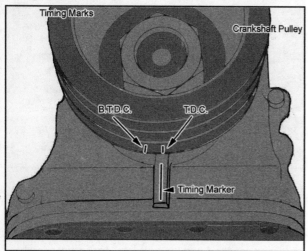

2-Remove the plug bolt from the injection pump and install a dial gauge

3-Turn the crankshaft in an anti clockwise direction to a position of between 20-25° BTDC on the No1 piston.

4-Turn the crankshaft in a clockwise direction until the No1 piston is set at TDC on its compression stroke and record the plunger lift measurement on the dial gauge.

Plunger Lift Measurement:

1.45±0.02mm (equivilant to 14° BTDC)

5-If the plunger lift measurement in step 4 is not as shown, turn the injection pump body until the reading is correct, then tighten the injection pump mounting bracket and bolts.

Please Note: If the measurement is smaller than shown, turn the injection pump body in an anti clockwise direction, if the measurement is more than shown, turn the injection pump body in a clockwise direction.

6-After all the adjustments have been carried out, remove the dial gauge and refit the plug with a new washer, reconnect the injection pipes and bleed any air from the system that may be present.

Exhaust Brake Switch

1-Loosen the adjustment screw lock nut.

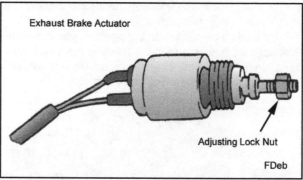

2. Turn the adjusting screw in or out until the exhaust brake switch is pushed in 4-5mm when the control lever is in the idle position.

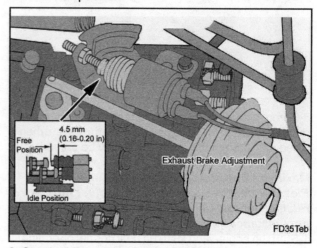

3. Set the idle speed to 900-100RPM when the exhaust switch is ON.

Intake Shutter

1-Remove the intake shutter from the vehicle and ensure that the clearance between the valve and inner wall is about 2.5±0.5mm (FD35), 3.0mm 3.0mm ±0.5mm (FD35T)

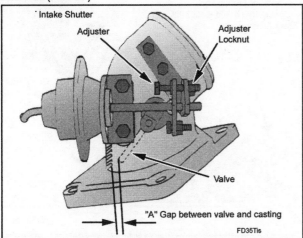

Intake Shutter
Adjuster
Adjuster Locknut
Valve
"A" Gap between valve and casting
FD35Tis

2-Refit the shutter to the vehicle and put the exhaust brake control lever to the ON position and start the engine.
3-Turn on the pump lever and then release it , ensuring that the intake shutter moves.

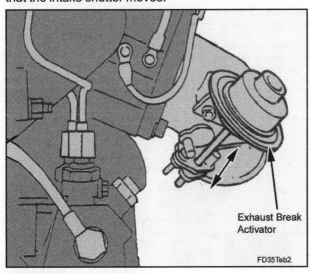

Exhaust Break Activator
FD35Teb2

Turbocharger Checks

Bypass Valve Inspection

1-Run the engine to normal operating temperature, disconnect the by pass valve hose and install a pressure gauge via a 3 way connector in its place.
2-Ensure that the gauge needle does not move to a setting of more than 90.6kpa with the engine running at between 2500-3000RPM.
4-If the needle setting is outside the 90.6kpa reading, check the condition and/or operation of the intake and exhaust system (inc turbocharger) for any gas or oil leaks, and also check the intake relief valve foe leaks, if faults are found reapir/replace as required.

5-If the setting in step2 is more than 90.6kpa, check the condition and/or operation of the swing valve controler hose and/or operation of the swing controller, if faults are found repair/replace as required.

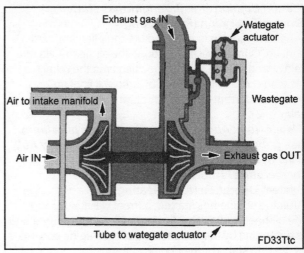

Exhaust gas IN
Wategate actuator
Air to intake manifold
Wastegate
Air IN
Exhaust gas OUT
Tube to wategate actuator
FD33Ttc

Bypass Valve Controller Inspection

1-Disconnect the hose at the end of the compressor housing running to the by pass valve controller.
2-Apply 98kpa of air with a hand vacuum pump through the opening of the hose to ensure that the by pass valve controller link activates.

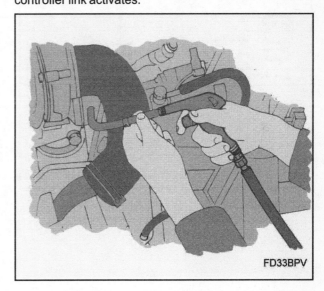

FD33BPV

Quick Heat System (FD35T Only)

Please Note: The quick heat system is used to pre heat the intake air and assist the engine in easier starting. An after heat system is aso used to stabilize the combustion after the engine has started.

System Operation (Pre-Heating)

When the ignition is switched on, the pilot lamp will light up. Current will flow through the air heater via the relay1 and relay2. After a specified time the relay No1 switches off and then the pilot lamp will light up (however current still flows through the air heater via the relay no2).

Please Note: About 10seconds after the pilot lamp has gone out, the relay No2 will turn off. Relay no2 will not activate when the engine coolant temperature is more than 30°c.

System Operation (After Heating)

After the engine has started, current will flow through the air haeter relay No2 for a specific length of time and is determind by the temperature of the engine coolant in order to stabilise the engine speed.

Please Note: Relay No2 will not activate when the temperature of the engine coolant is more than 30°c

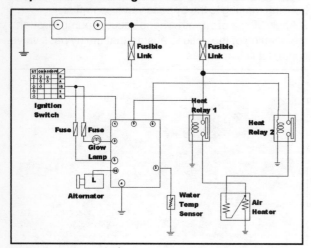

Air Heater Check

1-Install an ohmmeter to the No1 and 4 terminals (as per diagram) and ensure continuity exists.

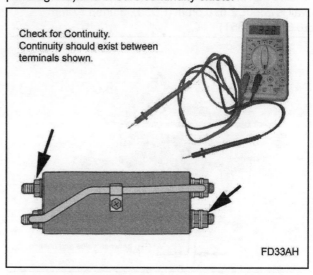

Check for Continuity.
Continuity should exist between terminals shown.

FD33AH

2-If continuity does not exist repair/replace as required.

Air Heater Relay Check

1-Apply battery voltage (24V) between the No1 and No2 terminals and check that continuity exists between the terminals 3 and 4

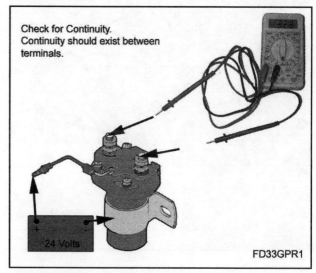

Check for Continuity.
Continuity should exist between terminals.

24 Volts

FD33GPR1

2-Apply battery volts between terminals 1 and ground and ensure continuity exists between 2 and 3
Diagram is on the next page
3-If continuity does not exist repair/replace as required.

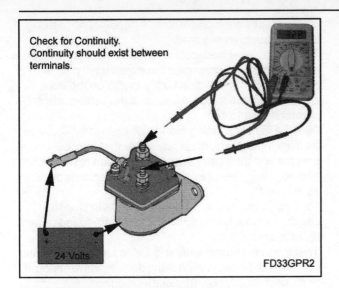

Check for Continuity.
Continuity should exist between terminals.

24 Volts

FD33GPR2

Water Temperature Sensor Check
1-Remove the sensor from the vehicle, place in a suitable container of water and check the resistance of the sensor at varying temperatures.

Temperature (°c)	Resistance (k/ohms)
10	3.25-4.15
20	2.25-2.75
50	0.74-0.94
80	0.29-0.36

2-If the resistance is not as shown, repair/replace as required.

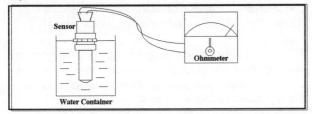

Sensor

Ohmmeter

Water Container

Air Heater Control Unit Check
1-The control unit is located on the dash side panel and should be checked by checking the voltages with a voltmeter as shown below.

+ Tester Probe Terminal Number	- Tester Probe Terminal Number	Ign Sw or Engine Condition	Voltage (V)
1	Earth	Ign Sw Start	Battery Volts
6	Earth	Engine @ Idle Speed	Battery Volts (Appearance Tiume Varies with Water Temp. Appx 2-180Secs)
7	3	Ignition Switch ON	Battery Volts (Appearance Time is Syncronised on the Heat Indicator Panel)
9	Earth	Ignition Switch ON	Battery Volts (Appearance Tiume Varies with Water Temp (Appx 0-12 Secs)
10	Earth	Engine @ Idle Speed	Battery Volts

CONNECTOR DIAGRAM

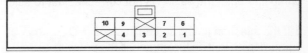

Injection System Diagnosis and Troubleshooting
Engine Will Not or is Difficult to Start
1-Ensure that the battery is fully charged and that there is sufficient fuel in the tank to carry out this test.
2-If there are no faults in step1, check that the starter motor will turn, the condition and/or operation of the relevant harness connections, ignition switch, starting circuit, starter motor, if faults are found repair/replace as required.
3-If no faults are found in step2, check the operation of the quick heat system, if faults are found repair/replace as required.
4-If no faults are found in step3, check the injection pump by ensuring that the timing marks on the front cover and injection pump line up, if they do not adjust to suit.
5-If the injection timing is OK in step4, crank the engine and ensure that fuel is reaching the injection nozzle, if it is not check that fuel is being delivered to the injection pump, if it is not, check the fuel lines for leaks and/or damage, check the fuel filter for blockages, if faults are found repair/replace as required.
6-If fuel is being delivered to the injection pump in step5, check to see if the delivery valve is sticking, if it

is sticking repair/replace as required, if it is not sticking repair/replace the injection pump as required.

7-If fuel does reach the injection nozzle in step 5, carry out a compression check on the engine, if the pressures are not correct repair/replace as required.

8-If the compression is OK in step7, check the valve clearances, if the clearances are not correct adjust as required.

9-If the valve clearances are OK in step8, check the condition and/or operation of the injection nozzles, if faults are found, adjust, repair/replace as required.

10-If the injection nozzles are OK in step9, check the injection timing setting, if the setting is not correct adjust to suit.

11-If the injection timing is OK in step10, check the condition and/or operation of the feed pump, if faults are found reapir/replace as required.

12-If no faults are found in step11, check to see if the delivery valve is sticking, if it is sticking repair/replace as required, if it is not sticking repair/replace the injection pump as required.

Excessive White or Black Smoke

1-When the engine is running, is the smoke coming out of the exhaust black or white, If the smoke is black, check the condition of the air cleaner element, if the filter is not OK, replace as required.

2-If the air cleaner element is OK in step1, check the injection timing marks on the front cover and injection pump line up, if the setting is not correct adjust to suit.

3-If the injection timing setting in step2 is Ok, carry out compression test on the engine, if the pressures are not correct repair/replace as required.

4-If the compression pressures are OK in step3, check the condition and/or operation of the injection nozzles, if faults are found repair/replace as required.

5-If the injection nozzles are OK in step4, check the injection timing setting is Ok, if it is not adjust to suit.

6-If the timing setting is OK in step5, check the initial timing setting, if faults are found repair/replace as required.

7-If the initial timing setting is OK in step6, check the condition and/or operation of the delivery valve spring, if faults are foound repair/replace as required.

8-If no faults are found in step7, repair/replace the injection pump as required.

9-If white smoke is present in step1, check to see if oil or a similar material is present in the exhaust tail pipe.

10-If there is oil or a similar material present in the exhaust tail pipe in step9, check the oil level and if it is low carry out a compression test on the engine, if the pressures are not correct repair/replace as required.

11-If the compression pressures are OK in step10, check the initial timing setting, if faults are found repair/replace as required.

12-If the initial timing setting is OK in step11, check the condition and/or operation of the delivery valve spring, if faults are foound repair/replace as required.

13-If no faults are found in step10, repair/replace the injection pump as required.

14-If the oil level in step10 is OK, and there is no oil or a similar material present in the exhaust tail pipe in step9, check the injection timing marks on the front cover and injection pump line up, if the setting is not correct adjust to suit.

15-If the injection timing marks line up in step14, purge air from the system, drain any water that may be present and then carry out a compression test on the engine, if the pressures are not correct repair/replace as required

16-If the compression pressures are OK in step15, check the initial timing setting, if faults are found repair/replace as required.

17-If the initial timing setting is OK in step16, check the condition and/or operation of the delivery valve spring, if faults are foound repair/replace as required.

18-If no faults are found in step17, repair/replace the injection pump as required.

Engine is Low on Power

1-If the engine is low on power check the condition of the fuel in the system, if the fuel is contaminated replace as required.

2-If the fuel is OK in step1, check that the timing marks on the injection pump and front cover line up, if they do not adjust to suit.

3-If the timing marks line up in step2, check the condition and/or operation of the fuel lines and/or connections, if faults are found repair/replace as required.

4-If no faults are found in step3, purge any air from the system and then check the condition of the air cleaner element, if faults are found repair/replace as required.

5-If no faults are found in step4, carry out a compression test on the engine, if faults are found repair/replacae as required.

6-If the compression pressures are Ok in step5, check the valve clearances on the engine, if the clearances are not OK, adjust to suit.

7-If the clearances are OK in step6, check the condition of the injection nozzles, if faults are found repair/replace as required.

8-If the nozzles are Ok in step7, check the injection timing setting, if the setting is not correct adjust to suit.

9-If the injection timing is OK in step8, check the condition and/or operation of the feed pump, if faults are found repair/replace as required.

10-If the feed pump is OK in step9, , check the condition and/or operation of the delivery valve, if faults are found repair/replace as required.

11-If no faults are found in step10, repair/replace the injection pump as required.

Vehicle Has a Cooling System Leak

1-If there is a cooling system leak, check the condition and installation of the radiator drain plug, if faults are found repair/replace as required.

2-If no faults are found in step1, carry out a cooling system pressure test and check for leaks at the radiator, hoses and connections and heater core, if faults are found repair/replace as required.

3-If no faults are found in step2, check the condition and/or operation of the oil cooler, if faults are found repair/replace as required.

4-If no faults are found in step3, check the mating area between the cylinder head and cylinder block for leaks from the cylinder head, head gasket and/or cylinder block, if faults are found repair/replace as required.

5-If no faults are found in step4, check for leaks from the engine core plugs and/or water pump, if faults are found repair/replace as required.

Vehicle Has an Engine Oil Leak

1-With the engine running check for leaks and/or damage around the rocker cover, if faults are found reapir/replace as required.

2- If no faults are found in step1, check the mating area between the cylinder head and cylinder block for leaks from the cylinder head, head gasket and/or cylinder block, if faults are found repair/replace as required.

3-If no faults are found in step2, check the condition and/or operation of the system vacuum pump, if faults are found repair/replace as required.

4-If no faults are found in step3, check for oil leaks around the engine sump and/or front and rear engine oil seals, if faults are found repair/replace as required.

Engine is Overheating.

1-If the engine is overherheating first check to see if the fan belt and/or adjustment is Ok, if not rectify as required.

2-If no faults are found in step1, check the cooling system for leaks *(Refer Vehicle Has a Cooling System Leak Information)* operations.

3-If no faults are found in step2, check the condition and level of the engine coolant, if the level is not OK, fill as required.

4-If no faults are found on step3, check the condition and/or operation of the thermostat, if faults are found repair/replace as required.

5-If no faults are found in step4, check the condition and/or operation of the radiator, if faults are found repair/replace as required.

Engine Will Not Stop

1-If the engine will not stop, check the condition and/or operation of the auto stop actuator or fuel cut solenoid, if faults are found repair/replace as required.

2-If no faults are found in step1, check the operation of the solenoid valve, if faults are found repair/replace as required.

3-If no faults are found in step2, repair/replace the injection pump as required.

Engine is Noisy

1-If the engine is noisy, check that the timimg marks on the injection pump and front plate line up, if they do not adjust to suit.

2-If the timing marks in step1 line up OK, check the engine idle speed, if the idle speed is not correct adjust to suit.

3-If the idle speed is OK in step2, check for any abnormal noises from the injection system, if any are found repair/replace as required.

4-If no faults are found in step3, check the engine valve clearances, if the clearances are not correct adjust to suit.

5-If the valve clearances are OK in step4, check for for noise from the timing gears, if faults are found repair/replace as required.

6-If no faults are found in step5, restart the engine and check for any noises from the engine, if there are still noises, check for any noises from around the vacuum pump, if faults are found repair/replace as required.

7-If no faults are found in step6, check for any noise from the water pump, if noise is found repair/replace as required.

8-If no faults arte found in step7, check for noise from big end and/or main bearings, damage to the con rods and/or crankshaft and/or warn tappets, if faults are found reapir/replace as required

Vehicle Filling Capacities

Engine Oil with Filter: .... 8.5 Litres
Engine Oil without Filter: .... 7.5 Litres
Cooling System with Heater: .... 15.3 Litres (FD35)
Cooling System with Heater: .... 15.8 Litres (FD35T)
Cooling System without Heater: ...... 14.5 Litres (FD35)
Cooling System without Heater: .... 15.0 Litres (FD35T)
Manual Transmission: .... 5.6 Litres (Standard)
Manual Transmission: .... 3.9 Litres (Long)
Steering Box: .... 0.7 Litres (Manual Steering)
Steering Box: .... 1.4 Litres (Power Steering)
Rear Differential (H290 LWB): .... 6.2 Litres
Rear Differential (H290 Standard): .... 8.3 Litres
Rear Differential (H260) : .... 4.3 Litres (SRW)
Rear Differential (H260) : .... 4.9 Litres (DRW)

Vehicle Component Service Interval Changes

Adjust Valve Clearance
Every 20,000kms
Engine Coolant/Anti Freeze
Change Every 24 Months/40,000kms
Air Cleaner Element
Change Every 24 Months/40,000kms
Pre-Air Cleaner Element
Change Every 24 Months/40,000kms
Fuel Filter
Change Every 24 Months/40,000kms
Engine Oil
Change Every 3 Months/5,000kms
Engine Oil Filter
Change Every 6 Months/10,000kms
Brake Fluid
Change Every 12 Months/20,000kms
Manual Transmission Oil
Change Every 24 Months/40,000kms
Transfer Case Oil
Change Every 24 Months/40,000kms
Front Differential Oil
Change Every 24 Months/40,000kms
Rear Differential Oil
Change Every 24 Months/40,000kms
Repack Front Wheel Bearings
Every 12 Months/20,000kms

Nissan Cabstar F22/H40
TD23 (2.3) & TD27 (2.7) 1987-1992

Cabstar 1988

Nissan Cabstar F22/H40 TD23 (2.3) & TD27 (2.7) 1987-1992

Engine Checks

Valve Clearance Check

Please Note: The adjustments need to be carried out when the engine is hot and with the engine not running.

1. Remove the rocker cover and ensure that the No1 piston is set at TDC on its compression stroke.
2. Adjust valve clearance of the No1, No2, No3 and No6 valves as shown in the diagram.

Valve Clearance:
    Inlet Valves No1, No3:   0.35mm
Valve Clearance:
    Exhaust Valves: No2, No6:   0.35mm

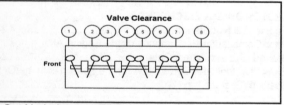

3. Set No4 piston to TDC on its compression stroke and adjust valve clearances on the No4, No5, No7 and No8 valves as shown in the diagram.

Valve Clearance:
    Inlet Valves No5, No7:   0.35mm
Valve Clearance:
    Exhaust Valves: No4, No8:   0.35mm

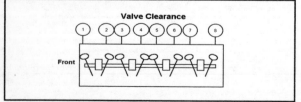

4. After the valve clearances have all been checked and/

or adjusted, replace the rocker cover.

Compression Check

1. Run the engine to normal operating temperature, then install a compression gauge adapter to the cylinder head.
2. Set the vehicle to 'No Fuel Injection Condition" by ensuring that the control lever of the injection pump is set to zero injection (In-Line Pump), or by disconnecting or removing the fuel cut solenoid wire (VE Type Pump)

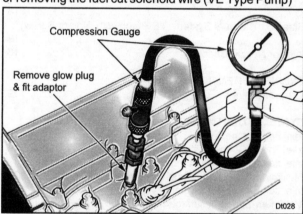

3. Press down the throttle fully, crank the engine and record the compression pressure

Compression Pressure: **2,942 kpa (Standard)**
Compression Pressure: **2,452kpa (Minimum)**
Differential Limit Between Cylinders: 294kpa

4. If the compression reading in step 3 on one or more cylinders is low, pour a small amount of oil into the faulty cylinders through the glow plug holes and retest the faulty cylinders.
5. If by adding oil in step 4 the pressure increases, there is a possibility that the piston rings are worn or damaged, if the pressure stays low, there may be sticking valves or the valves may not be seating correctly.
6. If the compression in any two adjacent cylinders are low and adding oil does not increase the pressure, there may be a leak past the gasket surface and could cause

116

oil and water to be present in the combustion chambers.

7. Refit any removed parts in the reverse order of removal and bleed any air that may be present in the system

Piston Protrusion Check

1. Set the No1 piston to TDC and record the clearance between the top of the piston and the cylinder block with a dial gauge (measure at the front and back of the piston)

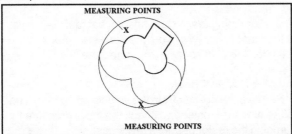

2. Calculate the average value of the two measurements, then check the protrusion of the other cylinders.

3. After checking all of the protrusions of the pistons, select a suitable headgasket which conforms to the largest amount of projections

Average Piston Projections	Gasket Thickness	Gasket Grade No
Less than 0.118mm	1.30mm	1
0.118-0.168mm	1.35mm	2
More than 0.168mm	1.4mm	3

Cylinder Head Tightening Procedures

1. Run the engine until normal operating temperature has been reached, remove the rocker cover and tighten the cylinder head bolts in the sequence shown in the diagram starting from the centre outwards.

2. Tighten the bolts in the following sequence, 1st stage is to tighten the bolts to between 39-44Nm, 2nd stage is to tighten the bolts to between 54-59Nm

3. 3rd stage is to mark the exhaust side of the cylinder head and cylinder head bolts with white pain and then turn all bolts 90±10° in a clockwise direction and check that the paint marks on each bolt are facing the front of the vehicle

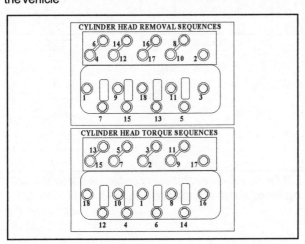

4. After tightening the bolts, replace the rocker cover.

Oil Pressure Check

1. Remove the oil pressure switch from the engine and install a pressure gauge to the engine block

2. Start the engine, let it run until normal operating temperature is reached and then record the oil pressure shown on the pressure gauge

Oil Pressure: More than 78kpa @ Idle Speed

Oil Pressure: 294-392kpa @ 3000RPM

3. If the pressure is not as shown, repair/replace as required

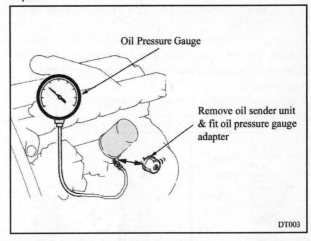

Cooling System Thermostat Check

1. Remove the thermostat from the engine, place the thermostat into a suitable container of water and heat to normal operating temperature.

2. Check the valve opening temperature and maximum valve lift as shown below.

Valve Opening Temperature: 82°c

Maximum Valve Lift: 8mm @ 95°c

3. If the specifications shown in step2 are Ok, ensure that the valve now closes at 5°c below the valve operating temperature.

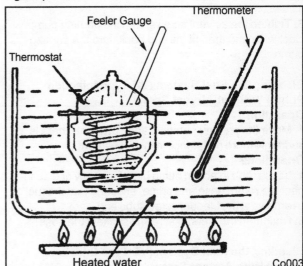

Fuel Filter Check and Replacement

1. Remove the fuel filter sensor (where fitted), drain the fuel, then remove the fuel filter.
2. Clean the fuel filter mounting bracket and then coat the fuel filter sealing ring with some diesel fuel.
3. Screw the fuel filter on until a slight resistance is felt and then turn another 2/3 of a turn or until suitably tight.
4. Install the fuel filter sensor (where fitted) to the new filter and then bleed any air present from the system.

Draining Water From The Filter

1. Loosen the air bleed cock on the fuel filter cover (Type X) or loosen the drain support screw from the sedimentor cover (Type Y).
2. Loosen the drain cock 4 or 5 turns to allow the water to drain from the filter (If the filter has not got an air bleed cock and the water does not drain, move the priming pump up and down)
3. Bleed air from the system if required.

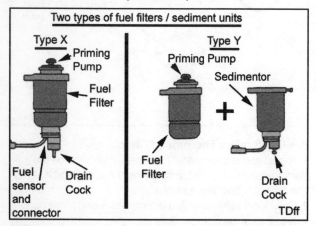

Two types of fuel filters / sediment units

Type X — Priming Pump, Fuel Filter, Fuel sensor and connector, Drain Cock

Type Y — Priming Pump, Sedimentor, Fuel Filter, Drain Cock

TDff

Bleeding the Fuel System (In Line Pump)

1. Remove the cap that covers the priming pump and then turn the pump anti clockwise.
2. Loosen the air vent screws and move the pump up and down until no more air comes out of the air vent screws.
3. Tighten the air vent screws, turn the priming pump clockwise and then fit the cap back onto the priming pump.

Bleeding the Fuel System (VE Type Injection Pump) Without Airvent Screw
Operation 1

1. Move the priming pump up and down until there is suddenly more resistance in the movement
Operation2
1. Loosen the injection pump bleeder screw or disconnect the return hose and prime, ensuring that the fuel overflows at the bleeder screw/tube end.
3. Retighten the bleeder screw/reconnect the hose.

Bleeding the Fuel System (VE Type Injection Pump) With Airvent Screw
Operation 1

1-Loosen the air vent screws and move the pump up and

down until no more air comes out of the air vent screws.
2. Tighten the air vent screws and move the pump up and down until there is suddenly more resistance in the movement.
Operation 2
1. Loosen the air vent screws and move the pump up and down until no more air comes out of the air vent screws.
2. Tighten the air vent screws and then loosen the injection pump bleeder screw or disconnect the return hose and prime
3. While priming the system ensure that fuel overflows at the bleeder screw or from the hose end, then retighten the vent screw or reconnect the hose.

Injector Nozzle Check

1. Remove the injector from the vehicle and connect up to the pressure tester and check the initial pressure by pumping the tester handle a few times.

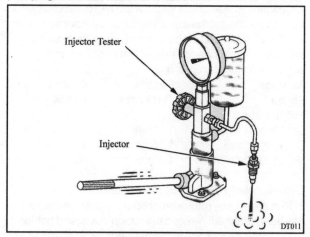

Injector Tester

Injector

DT011

Initial Pressure: 9,807 to 10,297kpa (Used Nozzle)
Initial Pressure: 10,297 to 11,278kpa (New Nozzle)
2. Check the spray pattern by pumping the pressure tester handle 4-6 times or more per second and check the injection spray pattern.

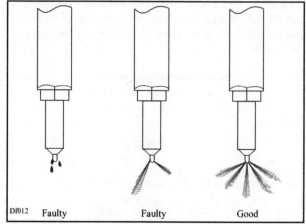

Df012   Faulty   Faulty   Good

3. If the operation and/or spray pattern is not as shown, repair/replace the nozzle/s as required.

Engine Tightening Torques

Cylinder Head Tightening Torque Main Bolts: .... (1st Stage: 39-44Nm)

Cylinder Head Tightening Torque Main Bolts: .... (2nd Stage: 54-59Nm)

Cylinder Head Tightening Torque Main Bolts: .... (3rd Stage 90°±10° Clockwise)

Rocker Shaft Bracket Bolts: 20-25Nm

Rocker Arm Lock Nut: 15-20Nm

Rocker Cover Screw: 1-2Nm

Exhaust Manifold Bolts and Nuts: .... 25.29Nm (Non Turbo Model)

Exhaust Manifold Bolts and Nuts: .... 29-34Nm (Turbo Model)

Inlet Manifold Bolts and Nuts: 15-20Nm

Turbocharger Nut: 17-23Nm

Injection Pump Nut: 20-25Nm

Injection Pump Drive Gear Nut: 59-69Nm

Injection Nozzle: 54-64Nm

EGR Valve Bolt: 16-21Nm

Main Bearing Caps: 167-177Nm

Connecting Rod Caps: 78-83Nm

Crankshaft Pulley Nut: 294-324Nm

Front Timing Cover: 16-21Nm

Camshaft Gear Bolt: 44-49Nm

Oil Sump Bolt: 7-9Nm

Oil Pump Bolt: 13-19Nm

System Adjustments

Idle Speed Check (Inline/VE Pump System)

Please Note: Before carrying out this check, ensure that the injection timing is correct, the injection nozzles are functioning correctly, the air cleaner is not blocked, the glow system is working OK, engine and coolant levels are correct, the valve clearances are correct, air intake system is functioning correctly, shift lever is in Neutral, hand brake is ON and that the air conditioning and all accessories are switched off.

1. Run the engine to normal operating temperature, ensure that all the accessories and air conditioning are switched off and fix a tachometer pick up lead to the No1 fuel injection tube.

2. With the engine running at about 2000RPM for at least two minutes under no load, let the engine run at idle for at least one minute before letting it idle and checking the idle speed recorded on the tachometer.

Idle Speed: **700±50RPM**

3. If the idle speed is not as shown, adjust the idle speed to suit by turning the idle speed adjusting screw until the idle speed setting is correct.

Diagrams are in the next column

4. After resetting the idle speed let the engine run at idle for at least one minute and check that the idle speed setting is still correct.

For Vehicles with Air Conditioning

1. Ensure that the clearance between the actuator control lever pin and the injection pump control lever is between 1-2mm.

2. Adjust the idle speed to the correct setting **750±50RPM** without the air-conditioning on and then with the engine still running switch on the air conditioning and check the idle speed setting.

Idle Speed Setting: **850±50RPM**

3. If the idle speed setting is not as shown, adjust by turning the FICD actuator stroke adjusting screw.

Inline Pump

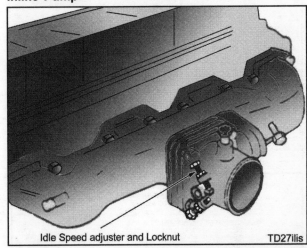

Idle Speed adjuster and Locknut   TD27ilis

VE Pump

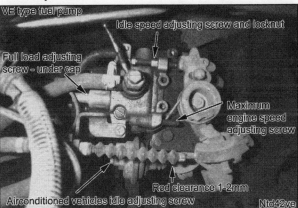

Injection Timing Check (In Line Pump)

1. Turn the crankshaft in a clockwise direction, set the No1 piston to its applicable BTDC position by lining up the relevant mark on the crankshaft pulley with the mark on the front cover. *(If there are only two marks on the crankshaft pulley, take the RH mark as the BTDC setting).*

2. Remove all of the injection tubes, governor hoses.

3. Remove the No1 lock plate and delivery valve holder, pull out the delivery valve stopper (if fitted) and the delivery valve spring.

4. Install the delivery valve holder without the spring, stopper and delivery valve.

5. Connect the test tube to the No1 delivery valve holder and then push the injection pump fully downwards towards the engine.

6. While feeding the system fuel by pressing the priming pump, slowly move the injection pump until the fuel flow from the No1 injection tube stops.

7. Fix the injection pump into the position where the fuel flow stopped and ensure that the timing marks on the injection pump and front plate lines up. If the marks do not line up stamp a new mark on the plate.

8. Remove the No1 injection test tube, replace any removed parts in the reverse order of removal and then bleed any air from the system that may be present.

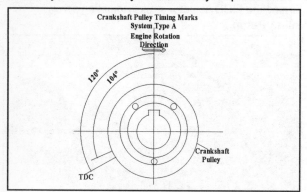

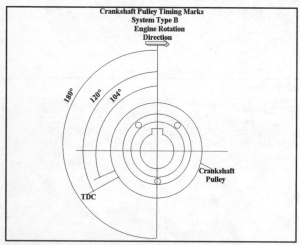

Maximum Speed Adjustment (In Line Pump)

Please Note: The maximum speed adjusting screw is retained by sealing wire and under normal circumstances would not need adjustment.

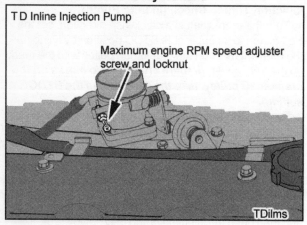

1. Start the engine and let it run until normal operating temperature has been reached.

2. Install a tachometer pick up lead to the No1 fuel injection pipe.

3. To obtain the maximum speed, turn the adjusting screw in either direction with the throttle pedal pressed down fully.

Maximum Engine Speed:

5100(+50RPM or -150RPM)

4. After carrying out the adjustment tighten the lock nut and replace the sealing wire.

Injection Timing Check (VE Type Injection Pump)

1. Loosen off the injection pump mounting nuts and mounting bracket bolts

2. Remove the plug bolt from the injection pump distributor head and install a dial gauge to the distributor head

3. Turn the crankshaft in an anti clockwise direction to a position of between 20-25° BTDC on the No1 piston.

4. With the dial gauge in a suitable rest position set the dial gauge to zero, turn the crankshaft in a clockwise direction until the No1 piston is set at TDC, and record the plunger lift measurement on the dial gauge.

Plunger Lift Measurement:

0.54±0.02mm (equivilant to 5° BTDC) TD23

Plunger Lift Measurement:

0.65±0.02mm (equivilant to 5° BTDC) TD27

5. If the plunger lift measurement in step 4 is not as shown, turn the injection pump body until the reading is correct, then tighten the injection pump mounting bracket and bolts.

Please Note: If the measurement is smaller than shown, turn the injection pump body in an anti clockwise direction, if the measurement is more than shown, turn the injection pump body in a clockwise direction.

6. After all the adjustments have been carried out, remove the dial gauge and refit the plug with a new washer, reconnect the injection pipes and bleed any air from the system that may be present.

Maximum Speed (Full Load) Adjustment (VE Type Injection Pump)

Please Note: The maximum speed (full load) adjusting screw is retained by sealing wire and under normal circumstances would not need adjustment. By disturbing the screw, this will cause the fuel flow to be changed and will cause incorrect adjustments on the engine. With this in mind, the injection pump timing will need to be adjusted again. If the maximum speed (full load) adjusting screw is turned in a direction that will increase the control lever angle, engine damage may occur

1. If adjustment is needed, start the engine, let it run until normal operating temperature is reached and connect a tachometer pick up to the No1 injection pipe.
2. Press down the throttle pedal fully and record the engine speed shown on the tachometer.

Maximum Engine Speed: 5,100 +50RPM or -150RPM

3. If the engine speed is lower than shown in step 2, turn the maximum speed (full load) adjusting screw anti-clockwise one or two full rotations, press down the throttle fully and record the engine speed.
4. If the engine speed is still lower than shown in step2, turn the maximum speed (full load) adjusting screw anticlockwise one or two full rotations, press down the throttle fully until the correct engine speed is reached.
5. After the adjustment has been done, tighten the adjustment screw lock nut and wind up again with sealing wire.
Refer to previous idle speed diagrams

Quick Glow System Check

This vehicle has two different systems and Type A System and a Type B System.

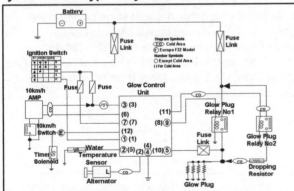

With the TypeA System: When the coolant temperature is less than 50°c the relay No1 and No2 are turned on at the same time that the ignition is switched on. From the time the ignition is switched on the high level current flows through the glow plugs and heats them up quickly. After between 2 and 6 seconds (time span varies with glow plug voltage and coolant temperature) the control unit will turn off the glow plug indicator. The relay No1 will automatically turn off after it has been on for between 3-11 seconds (time span varies with glow plug voltage or engine cranking time), whichever is the longest. The solenoid valve for the advance injection

timing is switched on at the time that the ignition switch is turned to the "Start" position. The relay No2 will stay on for 60-180 seconds (when the coolant is less than 50°c (time span will vary with coolant temperature) or 0 seconds if the coolant temperature is more than 50°c. The solenoid valve will stay on for 30 seconds (when the coolant temp is less than 10°c or 0°c), when the coolant temperature is more than 10°c) after the ignition switch is turned from "Start" to "ON". The Relay No2 allows low level current to flow through the glow plugs. The solenoid valve advances the injection timing, these functions will improve the combustion performance of the engine after is has started. When the coolant temperature is more than 50°c the relay No2 is turned on only during the engine cranking. When the coolant temperature is more than 10°c the solenoid valve is turned on only while the engine is being cranked. When the ignition switch is repeatedly turned "ON and OFF" the 3-11 seconds (time span varies with glow plug voltage) becomes shorter.

With the TypeB System: When the ignition switch is turned on, the relay No1 is turned on and the high level current flows through the glow plugs and heats them up quickly. After between 2-6 seconds (time span varies with coolant temperature) the control unit turns off the glow plug indicator but the relay No1 stays on. The relay No1 cuts off the current when the ignition switch turns from "ON" to "Start". The relay No1 has been cutting off for about 15 seconds after the ignition switch has returned from "Start" to "ON". When the engine is not cranking, the relay No1 cuts the electric current while 15 seconds and between 3-14 seconds (time span varies with glow plug voltage) after the ignition switch has been turned from "OFF:" to "ON". When the ignition switch is repeatedly turned "ON and OFF" the 3-14 seconds (time span varies with glow plug voltage) becomes shorter.

Control Unit Check (System TypeA)
Power Supply Circuit Check
Disconnect the harness connector from the glow control unit and carry out voltage and continuity checks as shown below.

1. With the (+) terminal of the voltmeter connected to terminal 7 and the (-) terminal connected to terminal 4 (Terminal Side) ensure that there is 0v when the ignition switch is on the OFF and ACC position and appx 12v when the ignition switch is on the ON position.
2. With the (+) terminal of the ohmmeter connected to terminal 7 and the (-) terminal connected to terminal ground ensure that continuity exists when the ignition switch is OFF.

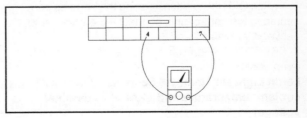

Water Temperature Sensor Circuit Check

1. With the harness connector disconnected check the continuity between terminals 5 (+) and 4 (Terminal Side) at varying temperatures.

Sensor Temperature (°)	Resistance (k/ohms)
-15	11.5
0	5.6
10	3.7
40	1.2

2. If the resistance is not as shown, repair/replace as required.

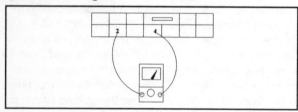

Alternator "L" Terminal Check

1. Switch OFF the ignition and disconnect the harness connector from the glow control unit.

2. Disconnect the harness connector from the "L" terminal on the alternator, and then check the terminal voltage between the 2 and 4 terminal (Terminal Side) when the ignition switch is turned ON.

Specified Voltage: **12V**

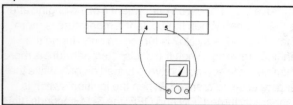

Start Signal Input Check

1. Switch OFF the ignition and disconnect the harness connector from the starter motor "S" terminal.

2. Check the terminal voltage between the No1 (+) and the No4(-)(Terminal Side) terminals when the ignition is in the START position.

Specified Voltage: **12V**

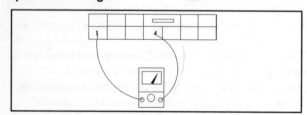

Glow Indicator Control Check

1. Switch OFF the ignition, leaving the harness connected to the control unit, connect a 3.4w test lamp between terminals 7 and 3.

2. Switch ON the ignition and record the time that the lamp stays lit.

Lamp Light Up Time: 2-6 Seconds (Varies with coolant temperature and glow plug terminal voltage)

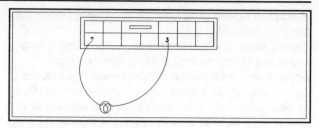

Pre Glow Control Check

1. Switch OFF the ignition, leaving the harness connected to the control unit, connect a 3.4w test lamp between terminals 4 and 8.

2. Switch ON the ignition and record the time that the lamp stays lit.

Lamp Light Up Time: 3-11 Seconds (Varies with glow plug terminal voltage).

Please Note: The time will be shortened if the ignition switch is OFF only a short time. Therefore when recording the time leave the ignition is switched OFF for more than 5 minutes and then put the ignition switch to the ON position

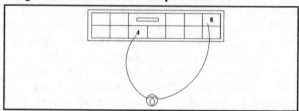

After Glow Control Check

1. Leaving the harness connected to the control unit, connect a 3.4w test lamp between terminals 11-4.

2. Disconnect the "S" terminal from the starter motor and ensure that the light comes on when the ignition switch is in the ON position.

3. Record the time that the light stays on when the ignition switch is moved from START to ON.

Lamp Light Up Time: **Less than 50°c (60-180 seconds dependant in coolant temperature)**

Lamp Light Up Time: **More than 50°c (0 seconds)**

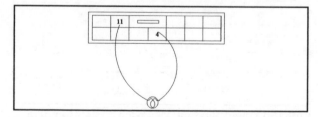

Solenoid Valve Control Check

1. Leaving the harness connected to the control unit, connect a 3.4w test lamp between terminals 12-4.

2. Disconnect the "S" terminal from the starter motor and ensure that the light comes on when the ignition switch is in the START position.

3. Record the time that the light stays on when the ignition switch is moved from START to ON.

Lamp Light Up Time:

        Less than 10°c (Approx 30 seconds)

Lamp Light Up Time:
More than 10°c (0 seconds)

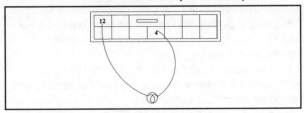

Control Unit Check (System Type B)
Power Supply Circuit Check

1. Disconnect the harness connector from the glow control unit and carry out voltage and continuity check as shown below.

2. With the voltmeter terminal (+) connected to terminal 7 and the (-) terminal connected to terminal (4) ensure that there is 0 voltage when the ignition switch is in the OFF and ACC position and that there is Approx 12v when the ignition is in the ON position.

3. With the (+) terminal of the ohmmeter connected to terminal4 and the (-) terminal connected to ground, ensure that continuity exists when the ignition switch is OFF.

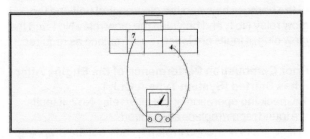

Water Temperature Sensor Circuit Check

1. With the harness connector disconnected check the continuity between terminals 2 (+) and 4 (Terminal Side) at varying temperatures.

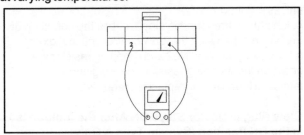

Sensor Temperature (°)	Resistence (k/ohms)
-15	11.5
1	5.6
11	3.7
41	1.2

2. If the resistance is not as shown, repair/replace as required.

Start Signal Input Check

1. Switch OFF the ignition and disconnect the harness connector from the starter motor "S" terminal.

2. Check the terminal voltage between the No1 (+) and the No4(-)(Terminal Side) terminals when the ignition is in the START position.

Specified Voltage: 12V

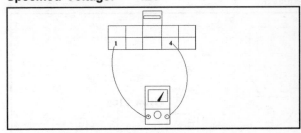

Glow Indicator Control Check

1. Switch OFF the ignition, leaving the harness connected to the control unit, connect a 3.4w test lamp between terminals 7 and 3.

2. Switch ON the ignition and record the time that the lamp stays lit.

Lamp Light Up Time: 2-6 Seconds (Varies with coolant temperature and glow plug terminal voltage)

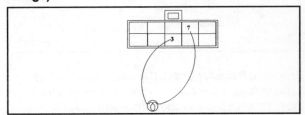

Glow Control Check

1. Switch OFF the ignition, leaving the harness connected to the control unit, connect a 3.4w test lamp between terminals 9 and 4.

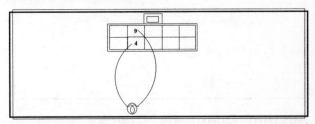

2. Switch ON the ignition and record the time that the lamp stays lit.

Lamp Light Up Time: 3-14 Seconds (Varies with glow plug terminal voltage).

Please Note: The time will be shortened if the ignition switch is OFF only a short time. Therefore when recording the time leave the ignition switched OFF for more than 1 minutes and then put the ignition switch to the ON position. This time the test lamp comes on and goes off between 1-3 times after which it should stay lit

3. When the ignition is turned to START and returned to ON, the test lamp comes on and goes off between 3-6 times.

Component Checks

Glow Plug Check

1. Remove the glow plug/s connecting plate and carry out continuity check between each glow plug and the cylinder head and ensure that continuity exists.

2. If there is no continuity replace the glow plug/s as required.

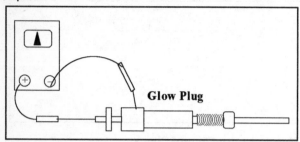

Glow Plug

Glow Relay Check.

1. Connect the ohmmeter and battery as shown in the diagram and carry out operation check.

The glow relay is normally open.

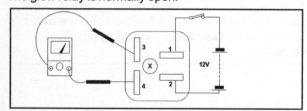

Dropping Resistor Check (System Type A Only)

1. Disconnect the resistor harness connector and check the resistance between the sensor terminals.

Resistance: 0.3ohms.

2. If the resistance is not as shown, replace as required.

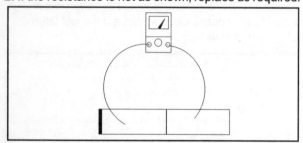

System Diagnosis Checks

Engine Will Not Start or is Hard to Start

1. Before carrying out this check ensure that the fuel level is OK, fuel supply system and starter motor operations are OK, if faults are found refil, repair/replace as required.

2. If no faults are found in step1, check the installation of the glow plugs, if faults are found repair/replace as required.

3. If no faults are found in step2, switch off the ignition for more than 10 seconds and see if the glow indicator comes on in a few seconds after the ignition is switched to the ON position, if it does not check the condition and/or operation of the warning lamp globe, if faults are

found repair/replace as required.

4. If there are no faults in step3, carry out the power supply circuit check for the glow control unit, if faults are found check the condition of the harness between the fuse and glow control unit, if faults are found repair/replace as required.

5. If no faults are found in step4, carry out the glow indicator control check, if faults are found repair/replace the glow control unit as required.

6. If no faults are found in step5, check for a short in the harness between the ignition switch and the glow indicator, if faults are found repair/replace as required.

7. If the glow indicator lamp does come on in step3, check the operation of the glow plugs, if faults are found repair/replace as required.

8. If no faults are found in step7, check the operation of the glow relay, if faults are found repair/replace as required.

9. If no faults are found in step8, carry out the "Start" signal input check, if faults are found repair/replace as required.

10. If no faults are found in step9, carry out the pre-glow control check, if faults are found replace the glow control unit as required.

11. If no faults are found in step10, check the condition of the harness between the glow control unit and the glow relay No1, and between the glow relay No1 and the glow plug, if faults are found repair/replace as required.

Poor Combustion Performance of the Engine After it has Started (System Type A Only)

1. Check the operation of the glow relay No2, if faults are found repair/replace as required.

2. If no faults are found in step1, carry out the dropping resistor check, if faults are found repair/replace as required.

3. If no faults are found in step2, carry out the after glow check, if faults are found repair/replace the glow control unit as required.

4. If no faults are found in step3, check the condition of the harness between the glow control unit and glow relay No2, glow relay No2 and dropping resistor and between the dropping resistor and the glow plugs, if faults are found repair/replace as required.

Glow Plug Indicator Stays ON After the Ignition is in the ON Position (System Type A Only)

1. Check the operation of the water temperature sensor, if faults are found repair/replace as required.

2. If no faults are found in step1, check the condition of the harness between the glow control unit and the water temperature sensor, if faults are found repair/replace as required.

3. If no faults are found in step2, carry out the glow indicator control check, if faults are found repair/replace the glow control unit as required.

4. If no faults are found in step3, check for a short circuit between the glow control unit and the glow indicator, if faults are found repair/replace as required.

VEHICLE SERVICE INFORMATION

Vehicle Filling Capacities

Engine Oil with Filter: .... 5.9 Litres
Engine Oil without Filter: .... 5.2 Litres
Cooling System: .... 12.6 Litres
(F22 (TD27) Model Front/Rear Heater)
Cooling System: .... 15.1 Litres
(H40 (TD27) Model Front/Rear Heater)
Cooling System: .... 11.8 Litres
F22 (TD27) Model Front Heater)
Cooling System: .... 14.3 Litres
(H40 (TD27) Model Front Heater)
Cooling System: .... 12.6 Litres
 (TD23) Model Front Heater)
Cooling System: .... 11.2 Litres
(F22 (TD27) Model Without Heater)
Cooling System: .... 13.4 Litres
(H40 (TD27) Model Without Heater)
Cooling System: .... 12.0 Litres
(TD23) Model Without Heater)
Manual Transmission: RT5R50A .... 5.6 Litres
Manual Transmission: RS5R50A .... 3.9 Litres
Manual Transmission: RS5W81A .... 2.7 Litres
Manual Transmission: RS5W71C .... 2.0 Litres
Manual Transmission: R4W71C .... 1.7 Litres
Rear Differential: H290 LWB .... 6.2 Litres
Rear Differential: H290 STD W/Base .... 8.3 Litres
Rear Differential: .... 4.3 Litres
H260 STD W/Base Single Tyre
Rear Differential: .... 4.9 Litres
H260 STD LWB Twin Rear Wheel
Rear Differential: H233B .... 2.0 Litres
Rear Differential: H190A .... 1.25 Litres
Rear Differential: C200 .... 1.3 Litres

Vehicle Component Service Interval Changes

Adjust Valve Clearance:
   Every 12 Months/20,000kms
Engine Coolant/Anti Freeze:
   Change Every 24 Months/40,000kms
Air Cleaner Element:
   Change Every 24 Months/40,000kms
Fuel Filter:
   Change Every 24 Months/40,000kms
Engine Oil:
   Change Every 3 Months/5,000kms
Engine Oil Filter:
   Change Every 6 Months/10,000kms
Brake Fluid:
   Change Every 24 Months/40,000kms
Manual Transmission Oil:
   Change Every 24 Months/40,000kms
Rear Differential Oil:
   Change Every 24 Months/40,000kms
Repack Front Wheel Bearings:
   Every 24 Months/40,000kms

Nissan Navara
TD25 (2.5) & TD27 (2.7) 1988-1997

Nissan Navara 1991

Nissan Navara TD25 (2.5) & TD27 (2.7) 1988-1997

Engine Checks

Valve Clearance Check

Please Note: The adjustments need to be carried out when the engine is hot and with the engine not running.

1. Remove the rocker cover and ensure that the No1 piston is set at TDC on its compression stroke.

2. Adjust valve clearance of the No1, No2, No3 and No6 valves as shown in the diagram.

Valve Clearance:

Inlet Valves No1, No3: 0.35mm

Valve Clearance:

Exhaust Valves: No2, No6: 0.35mm

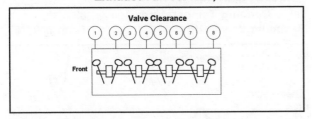

3. Set No4 piston to TDC on its compression stroke and adjust valve clearances on the No4, No5, No7 and No8 valves as shown in the diagram.

Valve Clearance:

Inlet Valves No5, No7: 0.35mm

Valve Clearance:

Exhaust Valves: No4, No8: 0.35mm

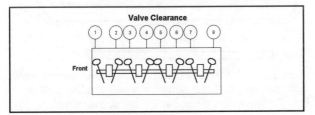

4. After the valve clearances have all been checked and/or adjusted, replace the rocker cover.

Compression Check

1. Run the engine to normal operating temperature, then install a compression gauge adapter to the cylinder head.

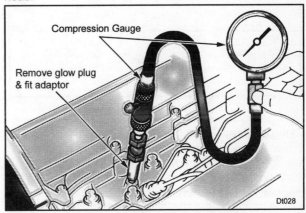

2. Set the vehicle to 'No Fuel Injection Condition" by ensuring that the control lever of the injection pump is set to zero injection (In-Line Pump), or by disconnecting or removing the fuel cut solenoid wire (VE Type Pump)

3. Press down the throttle fully, crank the engine and record the compression pressure

Compression Pressure: 2,942 kpa (Standard)

Compression Pressure: 2,452kpa (Minimum)

Differential Limit Between Cylinders: 294kpa

4. If the compression reading in step 3 on one or more cylinders is low, pour a small amount of oil into the faulty cylinders through the glow plug holes and retest the faulty cylinders.

5. If by adding oil in step 4 the pressure increases, there is a possibility that the piston rings are worn or damaged, if the pressure stays low, there may be sticking valves or the valves may not be seating correctly.

6. If the compression pressure in any two adjacent

cylinders is low and adding oil does not increase the pressure, there may be a leak past the gasket surface and could cause oil and water to be present in the combustion chambers.

7. Refit any removed parts in the reverse order of removal and bled any air that may be present in the system.

Piston Protrusion Check

1. Set the No1 piston to TDC and record the clearance between the top of the piston and the cylinder block with a dial gauge (measure at the front and back of the piston)

2. Calculate the average value of the two measurements, then check the protrusion of the other cylinders.

3. After checking all of the protrusions of the pistons, select a suitable headgasket which conforms to the largest amout of projections

Average Piston Projections	Gasket Thicknes	Grade No
Less than 0.118mm	1.30mm	1
0.118-0.168mm	1.35mm	2
More than 0.168mm	1.4mm	3

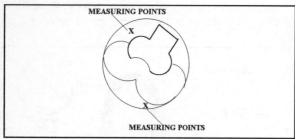

Cylinder Head Tightening Procedures

1. Run the engine until normal operating temperature has been reached, remove the rocker cover and tighten the cylinder head bolts in the sequence shown in the diagram starting from the centre outwards.

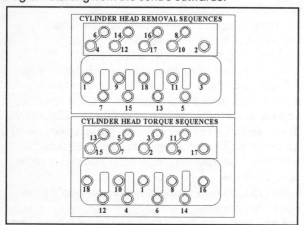

2. Tighten the bolts in the following sequence, 1st stage is to tighten the bolts to between 39-44Nm, 2nd stage is to tighten the bolts to between 54-59Nm

3. 3rd stage is to mark the exhaust side of the cylinder head and cylinder head bolts with white paint, turn all

bolts 90±10° in a clockwise direction and check that the paint marks on each bolt is facing the front of the vehicle

4. After tightening the bolts, replace the rocker cover.

Oil Pressure Check

1. Remove the oil pressure switch from the engien and install a pressure gauge to the engine block

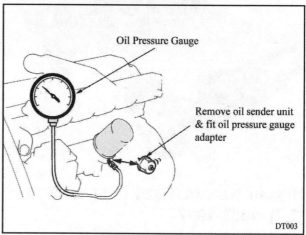

2. Start the engine and let it run until normal operating temperature is reached and then record the oil pressure shown on the pressure gauge.

Oil Pressure: More than 78kpa @ Idle Speed
Oil Pressure: 294-392kpa @ 3000RPM

3. if the pressure is not as shown, repair/replace as required.

Cooling System Thermostat Check

1. Remove the thermostat from the engine, place the thermostat into a suitable container of water and heat to normal operating temperature.

2. Check the valve opening temperature and maximum valve lift as shown below.

Valve Opening Temperature: 82°c
Maximum Valve Lift: 8mm @ 95°c

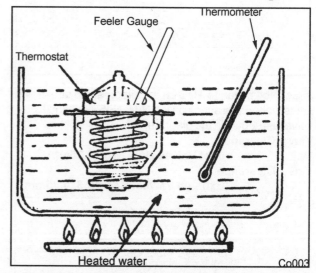

3. If the specifications shown in step2 are Ok, ensure that the valve now closes at 5°c below the valve

operating temperature.

Fuel Filter Check and Replacement

1. Remove the fuel filter sensor and drain the fuel, then remove the fuel filter.

2. Clean the fuel filter mounting bracket and then coat the fuel filter sealing rine with some diesel fuel.

3. Screw the fuel filter on until a slght resistance is felt and then turn another 2/3 of a turn or until suitably tight.

4. Install the fuel filter sensor to the new filter and then bleed any air present from the system.

Draining Water From The Filter

1. Loosen the drain cock 4 or 5 turns or remove the fuel filter sensor to allow the water to drain from the filter.

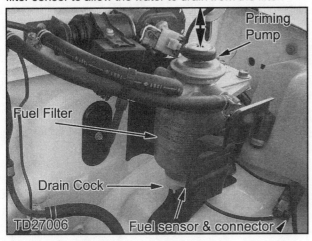

2. Retighten the drain cock or replace the sensor and bleed any air present from the system.

Injector Nozzle Check

1. Remove the injector from the vehicle, connect up to the pressure tester and check the initial pressure by pumping the tester handle a few times.

Initial Pressure: 9,807 to 10,297 (Used Nozzle).

Initial Pressure: 10,297 to 11,278kpa (New Nozzle).

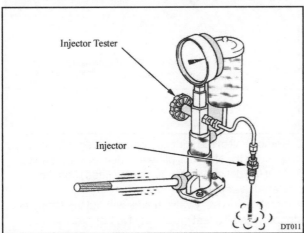

2. Check the spray pattern by pumping the pressure tester handle 4-6 times or more per second and check the injection spray pattern.

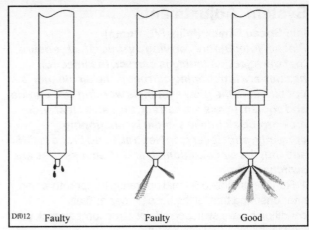

Df012   Faulty   Faulty   Good

3. If the operation and/or spray pattern is not as shown, repair/replace the nozzle/s as required

Engine Tightening Torques

Cylinder Head Tightening Torque:	
Main Bolts (1st Stage: 39-44Nm)	
Cylinder Head Tightening Torque:	
Main Bolts (2nd Stage: 54-59Nm)	
Cylinder Head Tightening Torque:	
Main Bolts (3rd Stage 90°±10° Clockwise)	
Rocker Shaft Bracket Bolts:	20-25Nm
Rocker Arm Lock Nut:	15-20Nm
Rocker Cover Screw:	1-2Nm
Exhaust Manifold Bolts and Nuts:	25.29Nm
Inlet Manifold Bolts and Nuts:	15-20Nm
Injection Pump Nut:	20-25Nm
Injection Pump Drive Gear Nut:	59-69Nm
Injection Nozzle:	54-64Nm
EGR Valve Bolt:	16-21Nm
Main Bearing Caps:	167-177Nm
Connecting Rod Caps:	78-83Nm
Crankshaft Pulley Nut:	294-324Nm
Front Timing Cover:	16-21Nm
Camshaft Gear Bolt:	44-49Nm
Oil Pump Bolt:	16-21Nm
Oil Sump Bolt:	7-9Nm

System Adjustments

Idle Speed Check (Inline/VE Pump)

Please Note: Before carrying out this check, ensure that the injection timing is correct, the injection nozzles are functioning correctly, the air cleaner is not blocked, the glow system is working OK, engine and coolant levels are correct, the valve clearances are correct, air intake system is functioning correctly, shift lever is in Neutral, hand brake is ON and that the air conditioning and all accessories are switched off.

1. Run the engine to normal operating temperature and after ensuring that all the accessories and air conditioning are switched off, fix a tachometer pick up lead to the No1 fuel ijection tube.

2. With the engine running at about 2000RPM for at least two minutes under no load, let the engine run at idle for at least one minute before letting it idle and checking the idle speed recorded on the tachometer.

Idle Speed: 700±50RPM

3. If the idle speed is not as shown, adjust the idle speed to suit by turning the idle speed adjusting screw until the idle speed setting is correct.

4. After reseting the idle speed let the engine run at idle for at least one minute and check that the idle speed setting is still correct.

Inline Pump

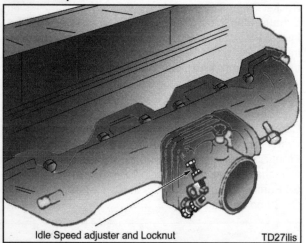

Idle Speed adjuster and Locknut   TD27ilis

VE Pump

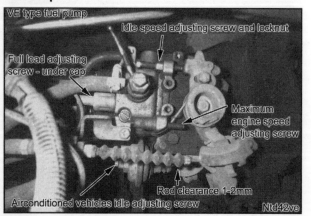

VE type fuel pump
Idle speed adjusting screw and locknut
Full load adjusting screw - under cap
Maximum engine speed adjusting screw
Rod clearance 1-2mm
Airconditioned vehicles idle adjusting screw   Ntd42ve

For Vehicles with Air Conditioning

1. Ensure that the clearance between the actuator control lever pin and the injection pump control lever is between 1-2mm.

2. Adjust the idle speed to the correct setting **750±50RPM** without the airconditioning on and then with the engine still running switch on the air conditioning and check the idle speed setting.

Idle Speed Setting: 850±50RPM

3. If the idle speed setting is not as shown, adjust by turning the FICD actuator stroke adjusting screw.

Diagram is in previous column

Injection Timing Check (In Line Pump)

1. Turn the crankshaft in a clockwise direction, set the No1 piston to its applicable BTDC position by lining up the relevant mark on the crankshaft pulley with the mark on the front cover. *(if there are only two marks on the crankshaft pulley, take the RH mark as the BTDC setting).*

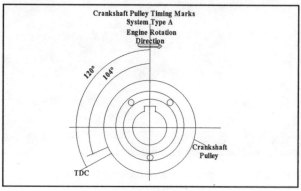

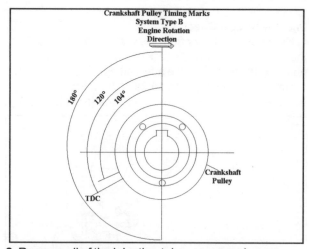

2. Remove all of the injection tubes, govenor hoses.

3. Remove the No1 lock plate and delivery valve holder, pull out the delivery valve stopper (if fitted) and the delivery valve spring.

4. Install the delivery valve holder without the spring and stopper, install a test pipe to the No1 delivery valve holder.

5. Connect the test tube to the No1 delivery valve holder and then push the injection pump fully downwards towards the engine.

6. While feeding the system fuel by pressing the priming pump, slowly move the injection pump until the fuel flow from the No1 injection tube stops.

7. Fix the injection pump into the position where the fuel flow stopped and ensure that the timing marks on the injection pump and front plate lines up. If the marks do not line up stamp a new mark on the plate.

8. Remove the No1 injection test tube, replace any removed parts in the reverse order of removal and then bleed any air from the system that may be present.

Maximum Speed Adjustment (In Line Pump)

Please Note: The maximum speed adjusting screw is retained by sealing wire and under normal circumstances would not need adjustment.

1. Start the engine and let it run until normal operating temperature has been reached.

2. Install a tachometer pick up lead to the No1 fuel injection pipe.

3. To obtain the maximum speed, turn the adjusting screw in either direction with the throttle pedal pressed down fully.

Maximum Engine Speed: 5100(+50RPM or -150RPM)

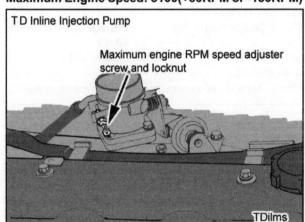

TD Inline Injection Pump

Maximum engine RPM speed adjuster screw and locknut

TDilms

4. After carrying out the adjustemnt tighten the lock nut and replace the sealing wire.

Bleeding the Fuel System (In Line Pump)

1. Remove the cap that covers the priming pump and then turn the pump anti clockwise.

2. Loosen the air vent screws and move the pump up and down until no more air comes out of the air vent screws.

3. Tighten the air vent screws, turn the priming pump clockwise and then fit the cap back onto the priming pump.

Injection Timing Check (VE Type Injection Pump)

1. Loosen off the injection pump mounting nuts and mounting bracket bolts

2. Remove the plug bolt from the injection pump distributor head and install a dial gauge to the distributor head

3. Turn the crankshaft in an anti clockwise direction to a position of between 20-25° BTDC on the No1 piston.

TDF27velT

4. With the dial gauge in a suitable rest position set the dial gauge to zero, turn the crankshaft in a clockwise direction until the No1 piston is set at TDC, and record the plunger lift measurement on the dial gauge.

Plunger Lift Measurement: 0.71±0.02mm (equivilant to 6° BTDC) TD25

Plunger Lift Measurement: 0.65±0.02mm (equivilant to 5° BTDC) TD27 (Except Navara Dual Cab)

Plunger Lift Measurement: 0.49±0.02mm (equivilant to 3° BTDC) TD27 (Navara Dual Cab)

5. If the plunger lift measurement in step 4 is not as shown, turn the injection pump body until the reading is correct, then tighten the injection pump mounting bracket and bolts.

Please Note: If the measurement is smaller than shown, turn the injection pump body in an anti clockwise direction, if the measurement is more than shown, turn the injection pump body in a clockwise direction.

6. After all the adjustments have been carried out, remove the dial gauge and refit the plug with a new washer, reconnect the injection pipes and bleed any air from the system that may be present.

Maximum Speed (Full Load) Adjustment (VE Type Injection Pump)

Please Note: The maximum speed (full load) adjusting screw is retained by sealing wire and under normal circumstances would not need adjustment. By disturbing the screw, this will cause the fuel flow to be changed and will cause incorrect adjustments on the engine. With this in mind, the injection pump timing will need to be adjusted again. If the maximum speed (full load) adjusting screw is turned in a direction that will increase the control lever angle, engine damage may occur

1. If adjustment is needed, start the engine, let it run until normal operating temperature is reached and connect a tachometer pick up to the No1 injection pipe.

2. Press down the throttle pedal fully and record the engine speed shown on the tachometer.

Maximum Engine Speed: 5,100 +50RPM or -150RPM

3. If the engine speed is lower than shown in step 2, turn the maximum speed (full load) adjusting screw anti-clockwise one or two full rotations, press down the throttle fully and record the engine speed.

4. If the engine speed is still lower than shown in step2, turn the maximum speed (full load) adjusting screw anti-clockwise one or two full rotations, press down the throttle fully until the correct engine speed is reached.

5. After the adjustment has been done, tighten the adjustment screw lock nut and wind up again with sealing wire.

Refer to previous VE Pump idle speed diagram

Bleeding the Fuel System (VE Type Injection Pump) Without Airvent Screw

Operation 1

1. Move the priming pump up and dowm until there is suddenly more resistance in the movement

Operation2

1. Loosen the injection pump bleeder screw or disconnect the return hose, prime and ensure that the fuel overflows at the bleeder screw/tube end.

2. Retighten the bleeder screw/reconnect the hose.

Bleeding the Fuel System (VE Type Injection Pump) With Airvent Screw

Operation 1

1. Loosen the air vent screws and move the pump up and down until no more air comes out of the air vent screws.

2. Tighten the air vent screws and move the pump up and down until there is suddenly more resistance in the movement.

Operation 2

1. Loosen the air vent screws and move the pump up and down until no more air comes out of the air vent screws.

2. Tighten the air vent screws and then loosen the injection pump bleeder screw or disconenct the return hose.

3. While priming the system ensure that fuel overflows at the bleeder screw or from the hose end, then retighten the vent screw or reconnect the hose.

EGR System Checks

System Checks

1. Check the condition and/or operation of the vacuum hoses, if faults are found repair/replace as required

2. If no faults are found in step1, run the engine to normal operating temperature and place your finger onto the EGR valve diaphram and ensure that the valve is functioning while the engine is running, if faults are found repair/replace as required.

Diagram is in the next column

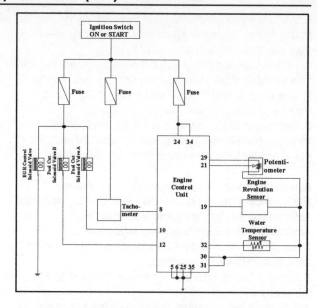

Control Unit Output Signal Check

1. Disconnect the control unit harness connector and check the voltage between terminal 10, 12 and ground as shown below.

Water Temperature(°c)	Voltage at Terminals 10, 12
Less than 60	Battery Volts
More than 60	0

If the voltage is not as shown, repair/replace as required.

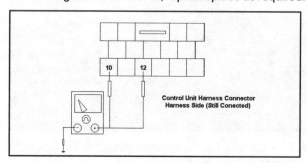

Control Unit Harness Connector
Harness Side (Still Conected)

EGR Control Valve Check

1. Install a hand vacuum pump to the EGR valve, place your finger onto the EGR valve diaphram and ensure that the diaphram moves up and down while the vacuum is being applied.

2. If the operation is not as shown in step1, repair/replace as required.

Throttle Chamber Control Valve Check

1. Ensure that the throttle chamber control valve is held shut at the stopper when a vacuum pressure of more than(-13.3kpa) is applied to the vacuum port.

2. With the valve held at the stopper, record the clearance between the valve and the body.

Clearance: 4±0.1mm

3. If the clearance is not as shown, repair/replace as required.

Diagram is on the next page

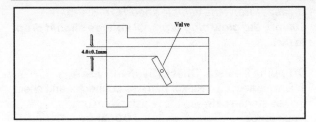

EGR Control Soleniud Valve/s Check

1. Disconnect the solenenoid valve vacuum hoses and harness connectors, and apply battery voltage between the solenoid valve ports A, B and C and shown below.

Solenoid Valve OFF:
          Continuity between ports A and C
Solenoid Valve ON: **Continuity between A and B**

2. If the operation is not as shown, repair/replace as required.

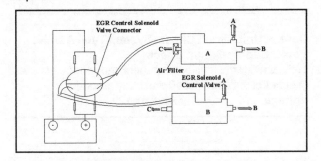

Potentiometer Check

1. Disconnect the potentiometer harness connector, install an ohmmeter between terminals 2 and 3 and ensure that the resistance changes when the control lever opening angle on the injection pump is changed.

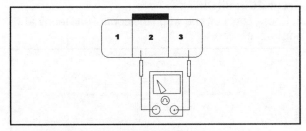

Engine Revolution Sensor Check

1. While the engine is idling, check the AC voltage across terminal B and body ground.

Voltage: **0.5v @ Idle**

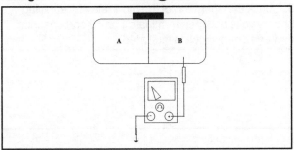

2. Race the engine and ensure that the AC voltage increases when the engine speed is increased.
3. If the voltage operation is not as shown above, install

an ohmmeter between terminals A and B and carry out a continuity test.
Resistance: 1.36-1.85k/ohms (continuity established)
4. If the operation is not as shown, repair/replace as required.

Water Temperature Sensor Check

1. Disconenct the sensor harness connector and check the resistance at the sensor terminals at varying temperatures.

Temperature(°c)	Resistance (K/ohms)
20	2.5
80	0.33

If the resistance is not as shown, repair/replace as required.

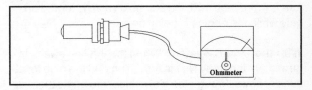

Quick Glow System Check

This vehicle has two different systems and Type A System and a Type B System.

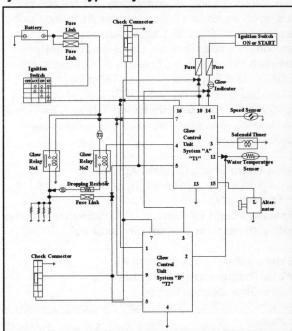

With the TypeA System: When the coolant temperature is less than 50°c the relay No1 and No2 are turned on at the same time that the ignition is switched on. From the time the ignition is switched on the high level current flows through the glow plugs and heats them up quickly. After between 2 and 6 seconds (time span varies with glow plug voltage and coolant temperature) the control unit will turn off the glow plug indicator. The relay No1 automatically turns off after it has been on for between 3-11 seconds (time span varies with glow plug voltage or engine cranking time), whichever is the longest. The solenoid valve for the advance injection timing is switched on at the time that the ignition switch is turned to the "Start" position. The relay No2 will stay on for 600 seconds (when the coolant is less than 50°c (time span will vary with coolant temperature) or 0 seconds if the coolant temperature is more than 50°c and the solenoid valve will stay on for 30 seconds (when the coolant tep is less than 10°c) or 0°c (when the coolant temperature is more than 10°c) after the ignition switch is turned from "Start" to "ON". The Relay No2 allows low level current to flow through the glow plugs. The solenoid valve advances the injection timing, these functions will improve the combustion performance of the engine after is has started. When the coolant temperature is more than 50°c the relay No2 is turned on only during the engine cranking. When the coolant temperature is more than 10°c the solenoid valve is turned on only while the engine is being cranked.

With the TypeB System: When the ignition switch is turned on, the relay No1 is turned on and the high level current flows through the glow plugs and heats them up quickly. After between 2-6 seconds (time span varies with coolant temperature) the control unit turns off the glow plug indicator but the relay No1 stays on. The relay No1 cuts off the current when the ignition switch turns from "ON" to "Start". When the relay No1 has been cutting off for about 15 seconds after the ignition switch is turned from "Start" to "ON". When the engine is not cranking, the relay No1 cuts the electric current for between 15 seconds and between 3-14 seconds (time span varies with glow plug voltage) after the ignition switch has been turned from "OFF:" to "ON". When the ignition switch is repeatedly turned "ON and OFF" the 3-14 seconds (time span varies with glow plug voltage) becomes shorter.

Glow Lamp Check (System A)
1. Switch ON the ingnitin and record the time that the lamp stays ON.
Specified Light Up Time: **1-10 Seconds (Varies with difference in coolant temperature)**

Glow Control Check (System A)
Water Temperature is Less than 10°c
1. Pre-Glow Control Check
Switch ON the ignition and record the glow plug terminal voltage.
Specified Voltage: **Battery Volts appears for 2-13 seconds and half that voltage after 30 seconds**
Please Note: This time will be shortened if the ignition switch is OFF for a short time. When measuring the time, leave OFF the ignition for more than 5 mins and then switch it ON.
2. After Glow Control Check
Put the ignition switch to the START position, run then run the engine and then record the glow plug terminal voltage.
Specified Voltage: **1/2 of the battery voltage should continue for 10 minutes.**

Please Note: If the vehicle speed is more than 20kmh, the glow plug terminal voltage should drop to 0v

Dropping Resistor Check (System Type A)
1. Disconnect the resistor harness connector and check the resistance between the resistor terminals
Resistance: 0.3ohms.
2. If the resistance is not as shown, repair/replace as required.

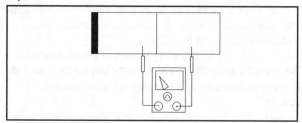

Control Unit Circuit Check (System Type A Only)
Power Supply Circuit Check
1. Switch ON the ignition and check the voltage between the control unit terminal 10 and body ground.
Voltage: Approx 12v.

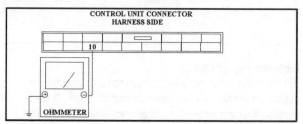

Ground Circuit Check
2. Check continuity between the control unit terminal 13 and body ground

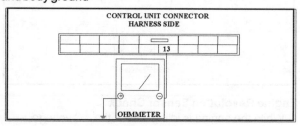

Glow Control Relay Check
3. Check the operation of the glow relay by applying battery volts between terminals 1 and 2 and ensuring that and open circuit is indicated.

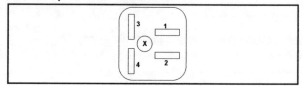

Water Temperature Sensor Check

1. Check the operation of the water temperature sensor by disconnecting the harness connector and checking the resistance between the terminals at varying temperatures.

Coolant Temperature (°c)	Resistance (k/ohms)
-25	19.0
0	5.6
20	2.5
40	1.2

2. If the resistance is not as shown, repair/replace as required.

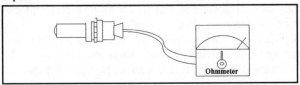

Input From the Alternator "L" Terminal Check (System Type A Only)

1. Switch OFF the ignition, disconnect the harness connector from the glow control unit, and then disconnect the harness connector from the alternator "L" terminal.

2. Install the (+) voltmeter terminal to terminal 15 and body ground check the voltage

Voltage: **More than 5v**

3. If the voltage is not as shown, repair/replace as required.

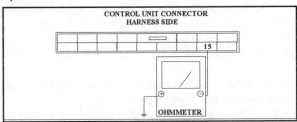

Speed Sensor Signal Check (System Type A Only)

1. When the engine is running check the voltage between the control unit terminal 11 and body ground is deflected.

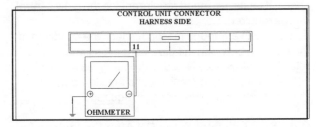

Solenoid Valve Control Check (System Type A Only)

1. Install a 3.4w test lamp to the control unit between the No3 and 13 terminals, disconnect the harness connector from the starter motor "S" terminal and ensure that the test lamp comes on when the ignition is turned ON (Austria Only)

1. Install a 3.4w test lamp to the control unit between the No3 and 13 terminals, disconnect the harness connector from the starter motor "S" terminal and ensure that the test lamp comes on when the ignition is turned to START (Except Austria)

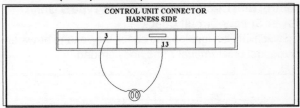

2. Record the time that the test lamp stays ON when the ignition switch is turned from "Start" to "ON".

Test Lamp ON Time Span: 30 seconds when the coolant temperature is less than 10°c.

Test Lamp ON Time Span: 0 seconds when the coolant temperature is more than 10°c.

3. If the operation is not as shown, repair/replace as required.

Start Signal Input Check (System Type A Only)

1. Switch OFF the ignition and then disconnect the harness connector from the starter motor "S" terminal.

2. Install the (+) voltmeter terminal to terminal 16 and the (-) terminal to terminal 13 and check the voltage when the ignition is in then "Start" position

Voltage: Approx 12v

3. If the voltage is not as shown, repair/replace as required.

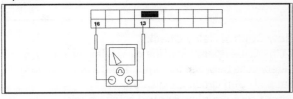

Glow Lamp Check (System Type B Only)

1. Switch ON the ingnitin and record the time that the lamp stays ON.

Specified Light Up Time: 2-7 Seconds (Varies with difference in coolant temperature)

Glow Control Check (System Type B Only)

Water Temperature is Less than 50°c

1. Pre-Glow Control Check

Switch ON the ignition and record the glow plug terminal voltage.

Specified Voltage: Battery Volts appears for 1-15 seconds and half that voltage after 30 seconds, and then battery voltage and 0v should alternately appear approx 2-8 times.

Please Note: This time will be shortened if the ignition switch os OFF for a short time. When measuring the time, leave OFF the ignition for more than 5 mins and then switch it ON.

2. After Glow Control Check

Put the ignition switch to the START position, run then run the engine and then record the glow plug terminal

voltage.
Specified Voltage: **Battery voltage and 0v should alternately appear approx 2-8 times.**

Control Unit Circuit Check (System Type B Only)
Power Supply Circuit Check
1. Switch ON the ignition and check the voltage between the control unit terminal 7 and body ground.

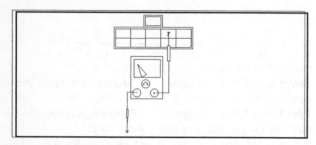

Ground Circuit Check
2. Check continuity between the control unit terminal 4 and body ground

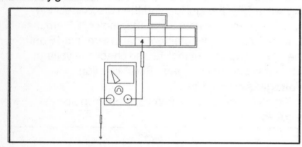

Glow Control Relay Check
3. Check the operation of the glow relay by applying battery volts between terminals 1 and 2 and ensuring that and open circuit is indicated.
Refer previous glow control relay check

Water Temperature Sensor Check
1. Check the operation of the water temperature sensor by disconnecting the harness connector and cheking the resistance between the terminals at varying temperatures.

Coolant Temperature (°c)	Resistance (k/ohms)
-25	19.0
0	5.6
20	2.5
40	1.2

2. If the resistance is not as shown, repair/replace as required.
Refer previous water temerature sensor diagrams

System Diagnosis Checks
Engine Will Not Start or is Hard to Start
1. Before carrying out this check ensure that the fuel level, fuel supply system and starter motor operations are OK, if faults are found repair/replace as required.
2. If no faults are found in step1, check the installation of the glow plugs, if faults are found repair/replace as required.

3. If no faults are found in step2, switch off the ignition for more than 10 seconds and see if the glow indicator comes on in a few seconds after the ignition is switched to the ON position, if it does not check the condition and/or operation of the warning lamp globe, if faults are found repair/replace as required.
4. If there are no faults in step3, carry out the power supply circuit check for the glow control unit, if faults are found check the condition of the harness between the fuse and glow control unit, if faults are found repair/replace as required.
5. If no faults are found in step4, carry out the glow indicator control check, if faults are found repair/replace the glow control unit as required.
6. If no faults are found in step5, check for a short in the harness between the ignition switch and the glow indicator, if faults are found repair/replace as required.
7. If the glow indicator lamp does come on in step3, check the operation of the glow plugs, if faults are found repair/replace as required.
8. If no faults are found in step7, check the operation of the glow relay, if faults are found repair/replace as required.
9. If no faults are found in step8, carry out the "Start" signal input check, if faults are found repair/replace as required.
10. If no faults are found in step9, carry out the pre-glow control check, if faults are found replace the glow control unit as required.
11. If no faults are found in step10, check the condition of the harness between the glow control unit and the glow relay No1, and between the glow relay No1 and the glow plug, if faults are found repair/replace as required.

Poor Combustion Performance of the Engine After it has Started (System Type A Only)
1. Check the operation of the glow relay No2, if faults are found repair/replace as required.
2. If no faults are found in step1, carry out the dropping resistor check, if faults are found repair/replace as required.
3. If no faults are found in step2, carry out the after glow check, if faults are found repair/replace the glow control unit as required.
4. If no faults are found in step3, check the condition of the harness between the glow control unit and glow relay No2, glow relay No2 and dropping resistor and between the dropping resistor and the glow plugs, if faults are found repair/replace as required.

Glow Plug Indicator Stays ON After the Ignition is in the ON Position (System Type A Only)
1. Check the operation of the water temperature sensor, if faults are found repair/replace as required.
2. If no faults are found in step1, check the condition of the harness between the glow control unit and the water temperature sensor, if faults are found repair/replace as required.
3. If no faults are found in step2, carry out the glow

indicator control check, if faults are found repair/replace the glow control unit as required.

4. If no faults are found in step3, check for a short circuit between the glow control unit and the glow indicator, if faults are found repair/replace as required.

VEHICLE SERVICE INFORMATION

Vehicle Filling Capacities

Engine Oil with Filter: .... 6.5 Litres
Engine Oil without Filter: .... 5.3 Litres
Cooling System: .... 10.4 Litres (2WD)
Cooling System: .... 12.2 Litres (4WD)
Manual Transmission: .... 1.9 Litres (2WD)
Manual Transmission: .... 4.0 Litres (4WD)
Transfer Case: .... 2.2 Litres (4WD)
Front Differential: .... 1.3 Litres (4WD)
Rear Differential: .... 1.25 Litres (2WD)
Rear Differential: .... 2.8 Litres (4WD)

Vehicle Component Service Interval Changes

Adjust Valve Clearance:
> Every 12 Months/20,000kms

Engine Coolant/Anti Freeze:
> Change Every 24 Months/40,000kms

Air Cleaner Element:
> Change Every 24 Months/40,000kms

Fuel Filter:
> Change Every 24 Months/40,000kms

Engine Oil:
> Change Every 3 Months/5,000kms

Engine Oil Filter:
> Change Every 6 Months/10,000kms

Brake Fluid:
> Change Every 24 Months/40,000kms

Manual Transmission Oil:
> Change Every 24 Months/40,000kms

Transfer Case Oil:
> Change Every 24 Months/40,000kms

Front Differential Oil:
> Change Every 24 Months/40,000kms

Rear Differential Oil:
> Change Every 24 Months/40,000kms

Repack Front Wheel Bearings:
> Every 24 Months/40,000kms

Nissan Patrol Y60
TD42 1988 ON

CONTENTS   PAGE

CONTENTS   PAGE

Nissan Patrol Y60

Nissan Patrol Y60 TD42 Engine 1988 ON

Engine Checks

Valve Clearance Check
Please Note: Valve clearance should only be made while the engine is warm but not running.
1. With the No1 cylinder set to TDC on the compression stroke adjust the valve clearances 1, 2, 4, 5, 8 and 9 With the No6 cylinder set to TDC on the compression stroke adjust the valve clearances 3, 6, 7, 10, 11 and 12
Intake valve clearances 1, 3, 5, 7, 9 and 11:
(0.35mm)
Exhaust valve clearances 2, 4, 6, 8, 10 and 12
(0.35mm)

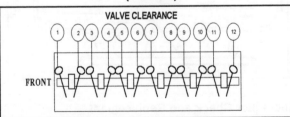

Compression Check
1. Run the engine to normal operating temperature, remove the glow plug or injector and the install a compression gauge adapter to the cylinder head.
2. Set the vehicle to 'No Fuel Injection Condition" by disconnecting the fuel cut solenoid wire (**VE Type Pump**) or by disconnecting the injection pump controller harness connector (**In Line Pump**).
3. Crank the engine and record the compression pressure *(Please Note: On vehicle with an In Line Pump, press the throttle down fully and then crank the engine)*
Compression Pressure: **2,942 kpa (Standard)**
Compression Pressure: **2,452kpa (Minimum)**
Differential Limit Between Cylinders: 294kpa

4. If the compression reading in step 3 on one or more cylinders is low, pour a small amount of oil into the faulty cylinders through the glow plug holes and retest the faulty cylinders.
5. If by adding oil in step 4 the pressure increases, there is a possibility that the piston rings are worn or damaged, if the pressure stays low, there may be sticking valves or the valves may not be seating correctly.
6. If the compression in any two adjacent cylinders are low and adding oil does not increase the pressure, there may be a leak past the gasket surface and could cause oil and water to be present in the combustion chambers.

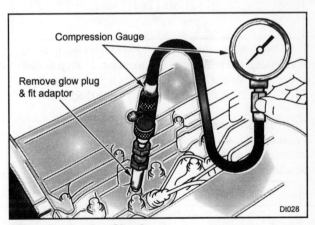

Piston Protrusion Check
1. Set each piston to TDC and with the piston set in that position record the measurement in each of the two positions shown. Calculate the average value of the two measurements and then check the protrusions on the other cylinders.
2. After calculating the measurements select the correct head gasket from the measurements shown below.

Average Piston Projection	Gasket Thickness (mm)	Gasket Grade Value (mm)
Less than 0.118	1.15	1
0.118-0.168	1.2	2
More than 0.168	1.25	3

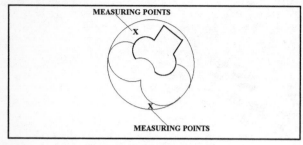

MEASURING POINTS

MEASURING POINTS

Cylinder Head Tightening Procedures

1. After selecting the correct grade of head gasket, apply oil to the thread of the head bolts and to the seat surface of the bolt.

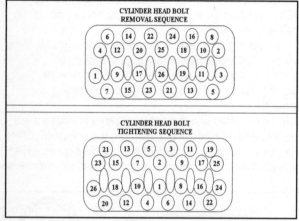

CYLINDER HEAD BOLT REMOVAL SEQUENCE

CYLINDER HEAD BOLT TIGHTENING SEQUENCE

2. Fit the gasket and cylinder head to the engine block and tighten the head bolts in two steps, 1st step tighten to between 49-59Nm, then 2nd stage tighten to between 98-108Nm in the sequence shown in the diagram.

Oil Pressure Check

Please Note: All oil pressure checks should be carried out with the transmission in the Neutral position.

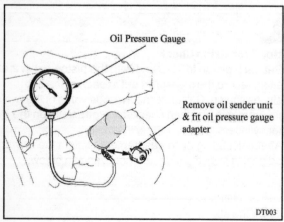

Oil Pressure Gauge

Remove oil sender unit & fit oil pressure gauge adapter

DT003

1. Check the oil level on the dipstick and if required fill as required. Remove the oil pressure switch and install a pressure gauge to the engine.
2. Start the engine, let it run until normal operating temperature has been reached and record the oil pressure shown on the gauge while the engine is running under no load.

Oil Pressure: 78kpa (engine at idle)
Oil Pressure: 294-392kpa (engine at 3000RPM)

3. If the oil pressure in step 2 has an extreme variance, check the oil passage and oil pump for leaks and/or damage, if faults are found repair/replace as required.

Cooling System Thermostat Check

1. Remove the thermostat from the engine, place the thermostat into a suitable container of water and heat to normal operating temperature.
2. Check the valve opening temperature and maximum valve lift as shown below.

Valve Opening Temperature: 82°c
Maximum Valve Lift: 8mm @ 95°c

3. If the specifications shown in step2 are Ok, ensure that the valve now closes at 5°c below the valve operating temperature.

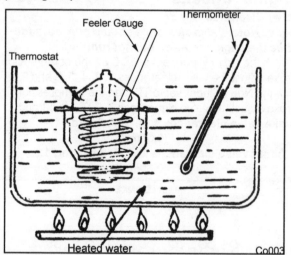

Feeler Gauge

Thermometer

Thermostat

Heated water

Co003

Fuel Filter Check and Replacement

1. Remove the fuel filter sensor, drain the fuel and then remove the fuel filter.
2. Clean the fuel filter mounting bracket and then coat the fuel filter sealing ring with some diesel fuel.
3. Screw the fuel filter on until a slght resistance is felt and then turn another 2/3 of a turn or until suitably tight.
4. Install the fuel filter sensor to the new filter and then bleed any air present from the system.

Draining Water From The Filter (VE Type Pump Only)

1. Loosen the drain cock 4 or 5 turns to allow the water to drain from the filter.
2. Retighten the drain cock and bleed any air present from the system
Diagram is on the next page

Bleeding the Fuel System (In Line Pump)

1. Remove the cap that covers the priming pump, turn the priming pump in an anti-clockwise direction and loosen the air vent screws.

2. Move the priming pump up and down until no more air-bleed comes out of the air vent screws.

3. Push and turn the priming pump in a clockwise direction, then refit the priming pump cap.

Bleeding the Fuel System (VE Type Injection Pump)

1. Loosen the air vent screw and move the priming pump up and down until no more air-bleed comes out of the air vent screws.

2. Re-tighten the air vent screws and then move the priming pump up and down until there is a sudden increase in the resistance when moving the priming pump up and down.

Engine Tightening Torques

Cylinder Head Tightening Torque: ... 1ˢᵗ Stage: 49-59Nm
Cylinder Head Tightening Torque: .. 2ˢᵗ Stage: 98-108Nm
Rocker Shaft Bracket Bolts: 20-25Nm
Rocker Shaft Lock Bolt: 10-13Nm
Rocker Arm Lock Bolt: 14-18Nm
Rocker Arm Lock Nut: 15-20Nm
Rocker Cover Bolts: 1-2Nm
Exhaust Manifold Bolts and Nuts: 15-20Nm
Inlet Manifold Bolts and Nuts: 25-29Nm
Exhaust Tube Nuts: 43-50Nm
Glow Plugs: 15-20Nm
Injection Nozzle: 54-64Nm
Flywheel: 147-167Nm
Main Bearing Caps: ....
167-167Nm (Tighten in two or three stages from the centre outwards)
Connecting Rod Caps: 78-83Nm
Crankshaft Pulley Bolt: 294–324Nm
Crankshaft Damper to Crankshaft Pulley Bolt: 26-30Nm
Front Timing Cover: 16-21Nm
Camshaft Gear Centre Bolt: 78-88Nm
Idler Gear Bolt: 25-35Nm
Oil Pump Bolt: 13-19Nm
Oil Pump Relief Valve: 16-21Nm
Wheel Bearing Lock Nuts: 167-196Nm

System Adjsutments

Idle Speed Check

Before checking the idle speed, ensure that the injection timing setting is correct, the injection nozzle's are in good condition, the air cleaner is not blocked, correct operation of the glow system, the engine oil and coolant levels are correct, valve clearances are correct, air intake system operation is correct.

1. Put the gear shift lever into Neutral, ensure that the parking brake is applied and then place wheel chocks on both the front and rear wheels.

2. Switch off the air conditioning and ensure all of the lights and accessories are switched off.

3. Run the engine to normal operating temperature, again ensure all the lights, heater fan and accessories are switched off and then fix a tachometer pick up to the No1 fuel injection tube.

4. With the engine still running, let it run at 2000RPM under no load for at least 2 minutes, let the engine run at normal idle speed for at least 1 minute **(Idle Speed: 700 +50 RPM)** and then recheck.

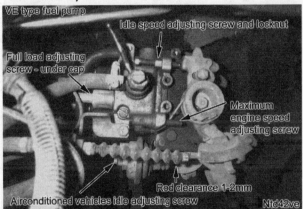

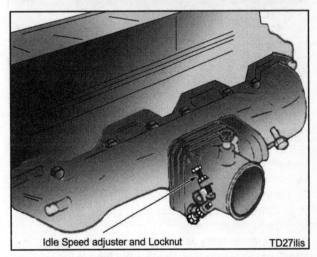

Idle Speed adjuster and Locknut   TD27ilis

5. If the idle speed is not as shown in step4, adjust by loosening the adjusting screw lock nut and setting to correct speed **(VE Type Pump)**, or by turning the idle speed adjusting screw **(In Line Pump)**.

6. Once the idle speed is correctly set, race the engine a few times and ensure that the idle speed is still correct after the engine returns to normal idle speed.

7. If the engine does not return to the correct idle speed in step6, check the condition and/or operation of the throttle linkages, if faults are found repair/replace as required.

For Vehicles with Air Conditioning

8. Ensure that the clearance between the actuator idle control lever pin and the injector pump control lever are correct **(1-2mm)**, adjust the idle speed setting to read **(850 -50Rpm)** without the air conditioning on, switch on the air conditioning and ensure that the idle speed setting is still correct

9. If the idle speed in step 8 is not correct, adjust the idle speed by turning the FICD actuator stroke adjusting screw.

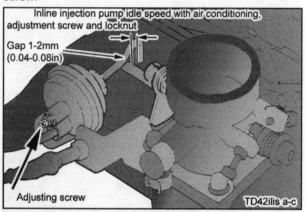

Inline injection pump idle speed with air conditioning, adjustment screw and locknut
Gap 1-2mm (0.04-0.08in)
Adjusting screw
TD42ilis a-c

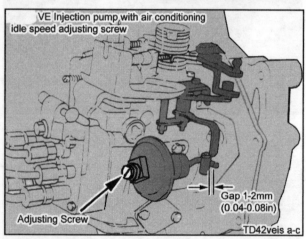

VE Injection pump with air conditioning idle speed adjusting screw
Adjusting Screw
Gap 1-2mm (0.04-0.08in)
TD42veis a-c

Injection Timing Check (In Line Pump)

1. Turn the crankshaft pulley in a clockwise direction and set the No1 piston to **16° BTDC**, remove all of the injection pipes and governor hoses.

2. Remove the No1 lockplate and delivery valve holder, pull out the delivery valve stopper (if fitted), delivery valve spring and delivery valve.

3. Install the delivery valve holder without the spring, valve and valve stopper, install a test tube to the No1 delivery valve holder and then push the injection pump assembly fully down towards the engine.

4. Feed the system fuel by using the priming pump, slowly move the injection pump until the fuel has stopped flowing from the No1 pipe and then tighten the

fixing bolts in the injection pump.

5. Check to see if the injection marks on the front plate and the injection pump are lined up, if they are not, stamp a new mark on the front plate.

6. Remove the No1 test tube and delivery valve holder and install the delivery valve spring, stopper, valve holder and valve.

7. Install injection tubes and governor hoses and then if required bleed any air that may be present from the system.

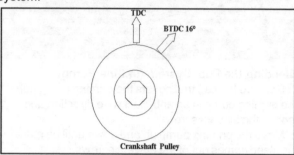

TDC
BTDC 16°
Crankshaft Pulley

Maximum Speed Adjustment (In Line Pump)

Please Note: The maximum speed adjusting screw is retained by sealing wire and under normal circumstances would not need adjustment.

1. If adjustment is needed, start the engine and let it run until normal operating temperature is reached then connect a tachometer pick up to the No1 injection pipe.

2. With the engine still running, turn the adjusting screw in either direction while the throttle is being pressed down fully.

Maximum Engine Speed:

4,600 ± 100 RPM (Under No Load)

3. After the adjustment has been done, tighten the adjustment screw lock nut and wind up again with sealing wire.

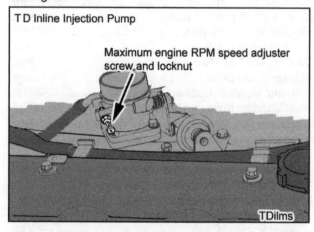

TD Inline Injection Pump
Maximum engine RPM speed adjuster screw and locknut
TDilms

Injection Timing Check (VE Type Injection Pump)

1. Remove the plug bolt from the injection pump distributor head and install a dial gauge to the distributor head.

2. Loosen off the injection pump mounting nuts and mounting bracket bolts.

3. Turn the crankshaft in an anti clockwise direction to a position of between 20-25° BTDC on the No1 piston.

4. With the dial gauge in a suitable rest position set the dial gauge to zero, turn the crankshaft in a clockwise direction until the No1 piston is set at TDC, and record the plunger lift measurement on the dial gauge.

Plunger Lift Measurement:
0.74±0.02mm (Equivalent to 6° BTDC)

TDF27velT

5. If the plunger lift measurement in step 4 is not as shown, turn the injection pump body until the reading is correct, then tighten the injection pump mounting bracket and bolts.

Please Note: If the measurement is smaller than shown, turn the injection pump body in an anti clockwise direction, if the measurement is more than shown, turn the injection pump body in a clockwise direction.

6. After all the adjustments have been carried out, remove the dial gauge and refit the plug with a new washer, reconnect the injection pipes and bleed any air from the system that may be present.

Maximum Speed (Full Load) Adjustment (VE Type Injection Pump)

Please Note: The maximum speed (full load) adjusting screw is retained by sealing wire and under normal circumstances would not need adjustment. By disturbing the screw, this will cause the fuel flow to be changed and will cause incorrect adjustments on the engine. With this in mind, the injection pump timing will need to be adjusted again. If the maximum speed (full load) adjusting screw is turned in a direction that will increase the control lever angle, engine damage may occur

1. If adjustment is needed, start the engine, let it run until normal operating temperature is reached and then connect a tachometer pick up to the No1 injection pipe.

2. With the engine still running, turn the adjusting screw in either direction while the throttle is being pressed down fully.

Maximum Engine Speed:
4,600 ± 100 RPM (Under No Load)

3. If the engine speed is lower than shown in step 2, turn the maximum speed (full load) adjusting screw anti-clockwise one or two full rotations, press down the throttle fully and record the engine speed.

4. If the engine speed is still lower than shown in step2, turn the maximum speed (full load) adjusting screw anti-clockwise one or two full rotations, press down the throttle fully until the correct engine speed is reached.

5. After the adjustment has been done, tighten the adjustment screw lock nut and wind up again with sealing wire.

Refer VE Idle Speed Diagrams

Injector Nozzle Check

1. Remove the injector from the vehicle and connect up to the pressure tester and check the initial pressure by pumping the tester handle a few times.

Initial Pressure: 9,807 to 10,297 (Used Nozzle).
Initial Pressure: 10,297 to 11,278kpa (New Nozzle).

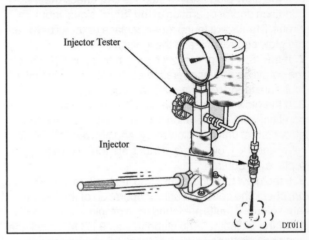

Injector Tester

Injector

DT011

2. Check the spray pattern by pumping the pressure tester handle 4-6 times or more per second and check the injection spray pattern.

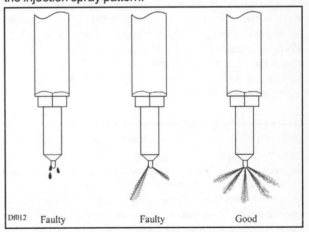

Df012   Faulty   Faulty   Good

3. If the operation and/or spray pattern is not as shown, repair/replace the nozzle/s as required.

Quick Glow System Check

1. If the engine fails to start or is hard top start, check the fuel level, condition and/or operation of the fuel supplying system, starter motor, if faults are found repair/replace as required.

2. If no faults are found in step1, check for correct installation of the glow plug connecting plate nuts, if faults are found repair/replace as required.

3. If no faults are found in step2, switch off the ignition for at least 10 seconds and then after switching on the ignition, check if the glow plug indicator lamp comes on a few seconds after the ignition is switched on.

4. If the lamp comes on in step3, check the condition and/or operation of the glow plugs, if faults are found repair/replace as required.

5. If the glow plugs in step4 are OK, check the condition and/or operation of the glow plug relay, if faults are found repair/replace as required.

6. If the glow plug relay in step5 is OK, check the condition and/or operation of the "Start" signal input circuit, if faults are found repair/replace harness between the glow control unit and the ignition switch.

7. If the "Start" signal input circuit in step6 is OK, check the condition and/or operation of the glow control unit, if faults are found repair/replace as required.

8. If the glow control unit in step7 is Ok, check the condition and/or operation of the harness between the glow control unit and glow relay, and between the glow relay and the glow plug/s, if faults are found repair/replace as required.

9. If the glow plug indicator lamp in step3 does not come on, check the condition and/or operation of the indicator lamp globe, if faults are found repair/replace as required.

10. If the indicator lamp globe in step 9 is OK, check the condition and/or operation of the power supply circuit between the fuse and glow control unit, if faults are found repair/replace as required.

11. If no faults are found in the power supply circuit in step10, check the condition and/or operation of the glow control unit, if faults are found repair/replace as required.

12. If no faults are found in the control unit in step11, check for a short in the harness between the ignition switch and the glow indicator lamp, if faults are found repair/replace as required.

Quick Glow System Component Tests

With this system, when the ignition is switched ON, the relay is turned on and a high level electric current flows through the glow plugs and heats them up quickly. After between 2-6 seconds (depends on coolant temperature), the control unit turns off the glow indicator but the relay stays on. The relay will chop the electric current when the ignition switch has turned from ON to Start. The relay will have been chopping for 15 seconds after the ignition switch has gone back the ON position from Start. When the engine is not being cranked the relay chops the electric current, while 15 seconds or between 3-14 seconds (varies with glow plug terminal voltage) after the ignition switch has been turned to ON from

OFF. *Please Note: When the ignition is repeatedly turned ON and OFF the 3-14 second time span will become shorter.*

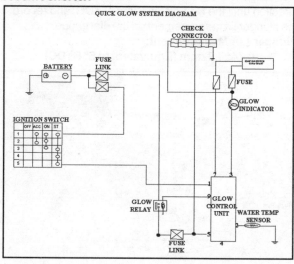

Glow Plug Check

1. Remove the glow plug connecting plate and check the continuity between each glow plug and the cylinder head.

2. If continuity exists the plug/s are OK, if no continuity exists repair/replace the plug/s as required.

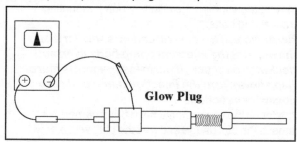

Water Temperature Sensor Check

1. Disconnect the sensor harness connector, install an ohmmeter to the sensor terminals and check the resistance at varying temperatures.

Coolant Temperature (°c)	Resistance (K/ohms)
-25	19.0
0	5.6
20	2.5
40	1.2

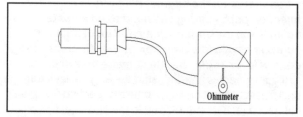

2. If the resistance is not as shown in step1, repair/replace sensor as required.

Quick Glow System Control Unit Check

1. Check the **"Power Supply Circuit"** by disconnecting the control unit harness connector, installing a voltmeter (+) lead to the harness connector terminal 7 and the (-) lead to terminal 4 and check the voltage with the ignition switch in the following position.

Ignition Switch Position OFF:	**Voltage 0v**
Ignition Switch Position ON:	**Voltage 0v**
Ignition Switch Position ACC:	**Approx. 12v**

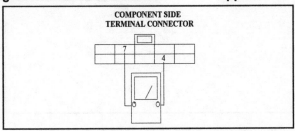

2. Disconnect the control unit harness connector, install an ohmmeter (+) lead to the harness connector terminal 4 and the (-) lead to body ground and check the continuity exists when the ignition switch is OFF.

3. If the voltage or resistance checks are not as shown, repair/replace as required.

4. Check the **"Water Temperature Sensor Circuit"** operation by disconnecting the control unit harness connector, installing an ohmmeter (+) lead to the harness connector terminal 2 and the (-) lead to terminal 4 and checking the resistance at varying temperatures.

Coolant Temperature (°c)	Resistance (K/ohms)
-25	19.0
1	5.6
20	2.5
40	1.2

5. If the resistance is not as shown in step4, repair/replace sensor, control unit and/or harness as required.

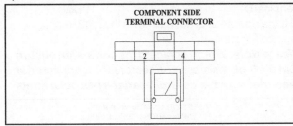

6. Check the **"Start" Signal Input Circuit** by disconnecting the harness from the starter motor "S" terminal, installing a voltmeter (+) lead to the No1 terminal and the (-) lead to the No4 terminal and checking the terminal voltage when the ignition switch is in the "START" position.

Voltage:	**Approx. 12v**

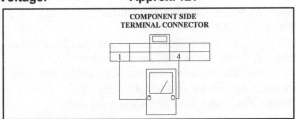

7. If the voltage in step6 is not as shown repair/replace as required

8. Check the **"Glow Indicator Control Circuit"** by switching off the ignition and leaving the harness connector connected to the control unit, installing a 3.4w test lamp between the No7 and No3 control unit harness connector terminals, switching on the ignition and recording the amount of time that the test lamp stays on.

Lamp Illumination Time Limit: **Between 2 and 6 seconds (varying with coolant temperature)**

9. If the time limit is not as shown in step8, repair/replace as required.

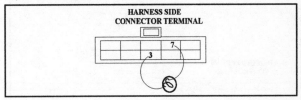

10. Check the **"Glow Control"** by switching off the ignition, leaving the harness connected to the control unit and installing a 3.4w test lamp to the No9 and No4 terminals, switching on the ignition and recording the amount of time that the indicator lamp stays on.

Indicator Lamp Time Limit: **Between 3 and 14 seconds (varies with glow plug terminal voltage)**

Please Note: The above time will be shortened if the ignition switch is only OFF for a short time. So when checking this reading, leave the ignition off for at least 60 seconds and then turn the ignition on.

When the ignition is turned to "START" and returned to the "ON" position, the test lamp will come on and off between 3 and 6 times.

11. If the operation is not as shown in step10, repair/replace as required.

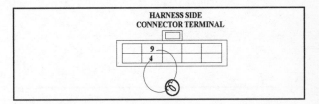

Injection Pump Control Lever Operation Check
Start Operation

1. Switch OFF the ignition, disconnect the harness connector from the starter motor "S" terminal.
2. Turn the ignition key to "Start" and ensure that the injection pump control lever moves to the start position.

Drive Operation

1. Switch OFF the ignition, disconnect the harness connector from the oil pressure switch.
2. Turn the ignition key to the "ON" position and ensure that the injection pump control lever moves to the drive position

Please Note: Diagram's are on the next page

Stop Operation

1. Switch OFF the ignition and ensure that the injection pump control lever moves to the stop position.

2. Start the engine, disconnect and ground the oil pressure switch connector and ensure that the injection pump control lever moves to the stop position

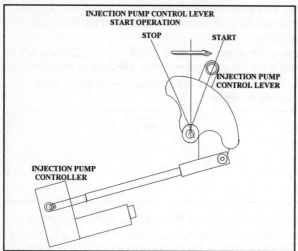

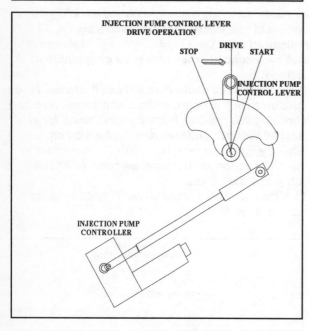

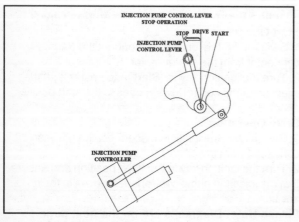

Injection Pump Controller Check
Motor Check

1. Switch OFF the ignition, disconnect the harness connector from the injection pump controller.

2. Apply battery voltage between the M (+) and M (-) terminals and ensure that the injector pump controller runs and that the control lever rotates.

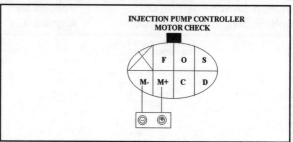

3. If the operation is not as shown in step2, repair/replace as required.

Please Note: When replacing the controller, ensure that the 6-pin harness connector is disconnected and reconnected from controller after it has been fitted.

Lever Position Check

1. Connect a lead from the (+) battery terminal to the harness connector terminal F, a lead from the (-) battery terminal to the harness connector terminal M (-)

2. Connect another lead (1) from the (+) battery terminal to the harness connector terminals O, S and D and check the control lever stops in the relevant position.

Terminal Lead (1) Connected To
Injection Pump Control

Harness Connector Terminal	Lever Position
Terminal O	Start
Terminal S	Stop
Terminal D	Drive

3. If the operation is not as shown in step2, repair/replace as required.

Please Note: When replacing the controller, ensure that the 6-pin harness connector is disconnected and reconnected from controller after it has been fitted.

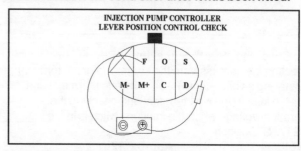

Injection Pump Control Unit Check
Preparation Check

1. Switch OFF the ignition, disconnect the "S" terminal from the starter motor, disconnect the 8 pin harness connector from the DPC module and install a test lamp between the M (+) and M (-) terminals.

Please Note: Diagram is on the next page

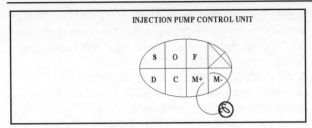

INJECTION PUMP CONTROL UNIT

Engine Stop Control Check

1. Carry out the **"Engine Stop Control Check"** by switching off the ignition, disconnecting the harness connector from the oil pressure switch and installing a jump wire between the DPC module 8 pin harness connector terminal S and C.

2. After the ignition switch is turned from OFF to ON, ensure that the test lamp comes ON and goes OFF in between 10-20 seconds. Disconnect the DPC module 6 pin harness connector and reconnect.

3. If the DPC moduleoperation is not as shown in step2, replace the DPC module.

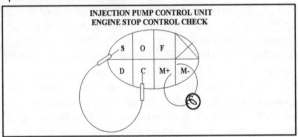

INJECTION PUMP CONTROL UNIT
ENGINE STOP CONTROL CHECK

Drive Position Control Check

1. Carry out the **"Drive Position Control Check"** by switching off the ignition, disconnecting the harness connector from the oil pressure switch and installing a jump wire between the DPC module 8 pin harness connector terminal D and C.

2. After the ignition switch is turned from Start to ON, ensure that the test lamp comes ON and goes OFF in between 10-20 seconds. Disconnect the DPC module 6 pin harness connector and reconnect.

3. If the DPC moduleoperation is not as shown in step2, replace the DPC module.

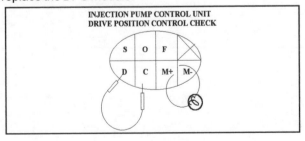

INJECTION PUMP CONTROL UNIT
DRIVE POSITION CONTROL CHECK

Fuel Excess Control Check

1. Carry out the **" Fuel Excess Control Check "** by switching off the ignition, disconnecting the harness connector from the oil pressure switch and grounding it with a suitable cable, installing a jump wire between the DPC module 8 pin harness connector terminal O and C.

2. After the ignition switch is turned to "Start", ensure that the test lamp comes ON and goes OFF in between 10-20 seconds. Disconnect the DPC module 6 pin harness connector and reconnect.

3. If the DPC moduleoperation is not as shown in step2, replace the DPC module.

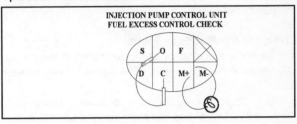

INJECTION PUMP CONTROL UNIT
FUEL EXCESS CONTROL CHECK

Anti Reverse Rotation Function Check

1. Carry out the **" Anti Reverse Rotation Function Check "** by switching off the ignition, disconnecting the harness connector from the oil pressure switch and grounding it with a suitable cable, installing a jump wire between the DPC module 8 pin harness connector terminal S and C.

2. After the ignition switch is turned from "Start to "On", ensure that the test lamp comes ON and goes OFF in between 10-20 seconds. Disconnect the DPC module 6 pin harness connector and reconnect.

3. If the DPC moduleoperation is not as shown in step2, replace the DPC module.

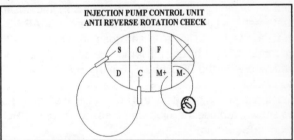

INJECTION PUMP CONTROL UNIT
ANTI REVERSE ROTATION CHECK

Injector Pump Control System Check

Engine Will Not Start

1. If the engine will not start, put the ignition switch into the "Start" position and ensure that the injection pump control lever moves to the "Start" position.

2. If the injection pump control lever in step1 does not move to the "Start" position, check and see if the connecting rod is disconnected, if it is reconnect it.

3. If the injection pump control lever rod is connected in step2, check the condition and/or operation of the injection pump controller, if faults are found repair/ replace as required.

4. If the fuel pump controller operation is OK in step3, check the operation of the injection pump control unit, if faults are found repair/replace the injection pump control unit (DPC module).

5. If the operation of the injection pump control unit in step4 is OK, check the operation of the oil pressure switch and/or the harness between the injection pump control unit and the oil pressure switch, if faults are found repair/replace as required.

6. If the injection pump control lever in step1 does move to the start position check the operation of the fuel system and/or the glow plugs, if faults are found repair/replace as required.

Engine Starts But Soon Stops

1. After the engine has been started (ignition switch ON), ensure that the injection pump control lever moves to the "Drive" position.

2. If the injection pump control lever in step1 does not move to the "Drive" position, with the ignition switch in the ON position disconnect the oil pressure switch harness connector and check if the injection pump control lever moves to the "Drive" position, if it does not check the condition and/or operation of the oil pressure lines and/or oil pressure switch, if faults are found repair/replace as required.

3. If the injection pump control lever in step2 does move to the "Drive" position, check the condition and/or operation of the injection pump controller, if faults are found repair/replace as required.

4. If the injection pump controller in step3 is OK, switch OFF the ignition, disconnect the oil pressure switch harness connector, install a jump wire between the D and C terminals and a test lamp between terminals M+ and M- on the 8 pin DPC harness connector, and ensure that when the ignition is switched to ON from START that then test lamp lights up and goes off in about 10-20 seconds. After checking the lamp operation disconnect and reconnect the DPC module 6-pin harness connector.

5. If the injection pump control unit check in step4 is not as shown, replace the injection pump control unit (DPC Module) as required.

6. If the injection pump control unit check in step4 is OK, check for a short in the harness between the injection pump control unit and the oil pressure switch, if faults are found repair/replace as required.

7. If the injection pump control lever in step1 does move to the drive position, check the condition of the fuel system components and/or venturi, if faults are found repair/replace as required.

Engine Runs On When the Ignition Switch is Turned Off

1. If the engine continues running when the ignition has been switched off, check whether the control lever rod is connected, if it is not, reconnect it.

2. If the connecting rod in step1 is connected, check the operation of the injection pump controller, if faults are found repair/replace as required.

3. If the injection pump controller in step 2 is OK, switch OFF the ignition, disconnect the harness from the oil pressure switch, install a jump wire between the S and C terminals on the 8 pin DPC module connector and when the ignition is switched to ON from the START

position ensure that the test lamp goes ON and OFF in between 10-20seconds. Disconnect and reconnect the DPC module 6 pin harness connector. If the operation is not as shown, replace the DPC module.

4. If the injection pump controller operation is not as shown in step3, check the condition and/or harness between the injection pump controller and the injection pump control unit, if faults are found repair/replace harness as required.

Engine Continues to Run in a Reverse Direction

1. If the engine continues to run in the reverse direction after the engine is turned off, carry out the test procedures shown above for the *Engine Runs On When the Ignition Switch is Turned Off*

2. If the engine does stop in step1, disconnect and ground the oil pressure switch connector with an earth lead and see if the engine stops, If the engine does stop, check the condition and/or operation of the oil pressure switch and/or oil pressure lines, if faults are found repair/replace as required.

3. If the engine does not stop in step2, switch OFF the ignition, disconnect the harness connector from the oil pressure switch and ground with a suitable wire, install a jump wire to the 8 pin DPC module connector terminals S and C, install a 3.4w test lamp to the 8 pin DPC module connector terminals M (+) and M (-), turn the ignition switch from "Start" to "On" and ensure that the test lamp comes on and then goes off in between 10-20 seconds, disconnect and reconnect the 6 pin DPC connector. If the operation is not as shown, replace the DPC module.

4. If the operation in step3 is OK, check the condition of the harness between the injection pump control unit (DPC Module) and the oil pressure switch, if faults are found repair/replace as required.

Vehicle Service Information

Vehicle Filling Capacities

Engine Oil with Filter: .... 9.2 Litres
Engine Oil without Filter: .... 8.0 Litres
Cooling System with Heater: .... 13.6 Litres
Cooling System without Heater: .... 12.8 Litres
Cooling System: .... 13.0 Litres
Manual Transmission: .... 3.9 Litres
Transfer Case: .... 2.2 Litres
Steering Box: .... 0.5 Litres
Front Differential (H233B): .... 5.4 Litres (Except Ute)
Front Differential (H233B): .... 4.3 Litres (Ute)
Rear Differential (H233B): .... 2.1 Litres
Rear Differential (H260): .... 4.7 Litres
Automatic Transmission: .... 8.5 Litres
Power Steering Fluid: .... 0.9-1.0 Litres

Vehicle Component Service Interval Changes

Adjust Valve Clearance:
Every 20,000kms
Engine Coolant/Anti Freeze:
Change Every 24 Months/40,000kms
Air Cleaner Element:
Change Every 24 Months/40,000kms
Pre-Air Cleaner Element:
Change Every 24 Months/40,000kms
Fuel Filter:
Change Every 24 Months/40,000kms
Engine Oil:
Change Every 3 Months/5,000kms
Engine Oil Filter:
Change Every 6 Months/10,000kms
Brake Fluid:
Change Every 24 Months/40,000kms
Manual Transmission Oil:
Change Every 24 Months/40,000kms
Transfer Case Oil:
Change Every 24 Months/40,000kms
Front Differential Oil:
Change Every 24 Months/40,000kms
Rear Differential Oil:
Change Every 24 Months/40,000kms
Repack Front Wheel Bearings:
Every 24 Months/40,000kms
Repack Front Axle Joint Grease:
Every 24 Months/40,000kms

Nissan Urvan (E24) 2.7L TD23-27 1987-1993

Nissan Urvan E24

Nissan Urvan (E24) 2.3 AND 2.7L
TD23-27 1987-1993

Engine Checks
Valve Clearance Check
Please Note: The adjustments need to be carried out when the engine is hot and with the engine not running.
1. Remove the rocker cover and ensure that the No1 piston is set at TDC on its compression stroke.
2. Adjust valve clearance of the No1, No2, No3 and No6 valves as shown in the diagram.
Valve Clearance: **Inlet No1, No3: 0.35mm**
Valve Clearance: **Exhaust No2, No6: 0.35mm**
3. Set No4 piston to TDC on its compression stroke and adjust valve clearances on the No4, No5, No7 and No8 valves as shown in the diagram.
Valve Clearance: Inlet No5, No7: 0.35mm
Valve Clearance: Exhaust No4, No8: 0.35mm
4. After the valve clearances have all been checked and/ or adjusted, replace the rocker cover.

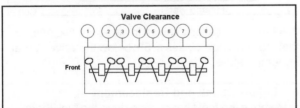

Valve Clearance

Compression Check
1. Run the engine to normal operating temperature, then install a compression gauge adapter to the cylinder head.
2. Set the vehicle to 'No Fuel Injection Condition" by ensuring that the control lever of the injection pump is set to zero injection (In-Line Pump), or by disconnecting or removing the fuel cut solenoid wire (VE Type Pump)
3. Press down the throttle fully, crank the engine and record the compression pressure

Compression Pressure:	**2,942 kpa (Standard)**
Compression Pressure:	**2,452kpa (Minimum)**
Differential Limit Between Cylinders:	**294kpa**

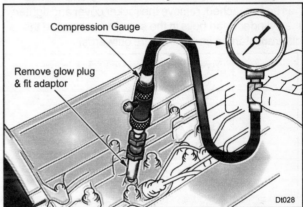

4. If the compression reading in step 3 on one or more cylinders is low, pour a small amount of oil into the faulty cylinders through the glow plug holes and retest the faulty cylinders.
5. If by adding oil in step 4 the pressure increases, there is a possibility that the piston rings are worn or damaged, if the pressure stays low, there may be sticking valves or the valves may not be seating correctly.
6. If the compression in any two adjacent cylinders are low and adding oil does not increase the pressure, there may be a leak past the gasket surface and could cause oil and water to be present in the combustion chambers.
7. Refit any removed parts in the reverse order of removal and blled any air that may be present in the system.

Piston Protrusion Check
1. Set the No1 piston to TDC and record the clearance between the top of the piston and the cylinder block with a dial gauge (measure at the front and back of the piston)
2. Calculate the average value of the two measurements,

151

then check the protrusion of the other cylinders.

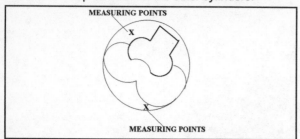

3. After checking all of the protrusions of the pistons, select a suitable headgasket which conforms to the largest amout of projections

Average Piston Projections	Gasket Thickness	Gasket Grade No
Less than 0.118mm	1.30mm	1
0.118-0.168mm	1.35mm	2
More than 0.168mm	1.4mm	3

Cylinder Head Tightening Procedures

1. Run the engine until normal operating temperature has been reached, remove the rocker cover and tighten the cylinder head bolts in the sequence shown in the diagram starting from the centre outwards.

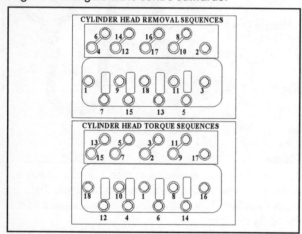

2. Tighten the bolts in the following sequence, 1st stage is to tighten the bolts to between 39-44Nm, 2nd stage is to tighten the bolts to between 54-59Nm
3. 3rd stage is to mark the exhaust side of the cylinder head and cylinder head bolts with white paint, turn all bolts 90±10° in a clockwise direction and check that the paint marks on each bolt is facing the front of the vehicle
4. After tightening the bolts, replace the rocker cover.

Oil Pressure Check

1. Remove the oil pressure switch from the engine and install a pressure gauge to the engine block
2. Start the engine and let it run until normal operating temperature is reached and then record the oil pressure shown on the pressure gauge.

Oil Pressure: More than 78kpa @ Idle Speed
Oil Pressure: 294-392kpa @ 3000RPM
Diagram is in the next column

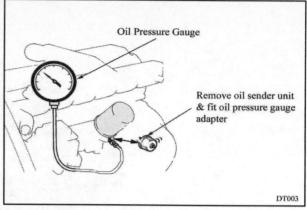

3. If the pressure is not as shown, repair/replace as required

Cooling System Thermostat Check

1. Remove the thermostat from the engine, place the thermostat into a suitable container of water and heat to normal operating temperature.
2. Check the valve opening temperature and maximum valve lift as shown below.

Valve Opening Temperature: 82°c
Maximum Valve Lift: 8mm @ 95°c

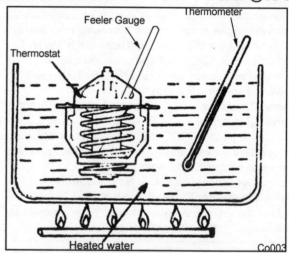

3. If the specifications shown in step2 are Ok, ensure that the valve now closes at 5°c below the valve operating temperature.

Fuel Filter Check and Replacement

1. Remove the fuel filter sensor, drain the fuel, then remove the fuel filter.
2. Clean the fuel filter mounting bracket and then coat the fuel filter sealing ring with some diesel fuel.
3. Screw the fuel filter on until a slght resistance is felt and then turn another 2/3 of a turn or until suitably tight.
4. Install the fuel filter sensor to the new filter and then bleed any air present from the system.
Diagram is on the Next Page

Two types of fuel filters / sediment units

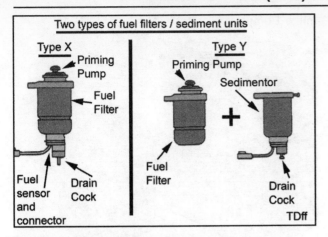

Type X
- Priming Pump
- Fuel Filter
- Fuel sensor and connector
- Drain Cock

Type Y
- Priming Pump
- Sedimentor
- Fuel Filter
- Drain Cock

TDff

Bleeding the Fuel System (In Line Pump)

1. Remove the cap that covers the priming pump and then turn the pump anti clockwise.

2. Loosen the air vent screws and move the pump up and down until no more air comes out of the air vent screws.

3. Tighten the air vent screws, turn the priming pump clockwise and then fit the cap back onto the priming pump

Bleeding the Fuel System (VE Type Injection Pump) Without Airvent Screw
Operation 1
1. Move the priming pump up and down until there is suddenly more resistance in the movement
Operation2
1. Loosen the injection pump bleeder screw or disconnect the return hose, prime and ensure that the fuel overflows at the bleeder screw/tube end.

2. Retighten the bleeder screw/reconnect the hose.

Bleeding the Fuel System (VE Type Injection Pump) With Airvent Screw
Operation 1
1. Loosen the air vent screws and move the pump up and down until no more air comes out of the air vent screws.

2. Tighten the air vent screws and move the pump up and down until there is suddenly more resistance in the movement.
Operation 2
1. Loosen the air vent screws and move the pump up and down until no more air comes out of the air vent screws.

2. Tighten the air vent screws and then loosen the injection pump bleeder screw or disconenct the return hose.

3. While priming the system ensure that fuel overflows at the bleeder screw or from the hose end, then retighten the vent screw or reconnect the hoses

Draining Water From The Filter
1-Loosen the drain cock 4 or 5 turns or remove the fuel filter sensor to allow the water to drain from the filter.
2-Retighten the drain cock or replace the sensor and bleed any air present from the system.

Injector Nozzle Check
1. Remove the injector from the vehicle, connect up to the pressure tester and check the initial pressure by pumping the tester handle a few times.
Initial Pressure: 9,807 to 10,297 (Used Nozzle).
Initial Pressure: 10,297 to 11,278kpa (New Nozzle).

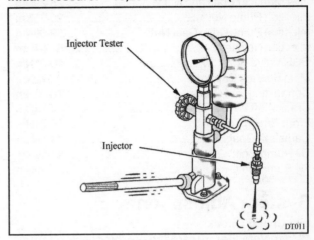

Injector Tester

Injector

DT011

2. Check the spray pattern by pumping the pressure tester handle 4-6 times or more per second and check the injection spray pattern.

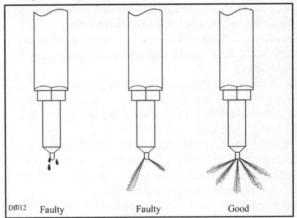

Df012   Faulty   Faulty   Good

3. If the operation and/or spray pattern is not as shown, repair/replace the nozzle/s as required

Engine Tightening Torques

Cylinder Head Tightening Torque Main Bolts: .... (1ˢᵗ Stage: 39-44Nm)
Cylinder Head Tightening Torque Main Bolts: .... (2ⁿᵈ Stage: 54-59Nm)
Cylinder Head Tightening Torque Main Bolts: .... (3ʳᵈ Stage 90°±10° Clockwise)
Rocker Shaft Bracket Bolts: 20-25Nm
Rocker Arm Lock Nut: 20-25Nm
Rocker Cover Screw: 1-2Nm
Exhaust Manifold Bolts and Nuts: 15-20Nm
Inlet Manifold Bolts and Nuts: 25-29Nm
Injection Pump Nut:: 20-25Nm
Injection Pump Drive Gear Nut: 59-69Nm
Injection Nozzle: 54-64Nm
EGR Valve Bolt: 16-21Nm
Main Bearing Caps: 147-167-172Nm
Connecting Rod Caps: 78-83Nm
Crankshaft Pulley Nut: 294-324Nm
Front Timing Cover: 16-21Nm
Camshaft Gear Bolt: 44-49Nm
Oil Pump Bolt: 13-19Nm
Oil Sump Bolt: 7-9Nm

System Adjustments

Idle Speed Check

Please Note: Before carrying out this check, ensure that the injection timing is correct, the injection nozzles are functioning correctly, the air cleaner is not blocked, the glow system is working OK, engine and coolant levels are correct, the valve clearances are correct, air intake system is functioning correctly, shift lever is in Neutral, hand brake is ON and that the air conditioning and all accessories are switched off.

1. Run the engine to normal operating temperature, ensure that all of the accessories and air conditioning are switched off. Fix a tachometer pick up lead to the No1 fuel ijection tube.
2. Run the engine at about 2000RPM for at least two minutes under no load. Let the engine run at idle for at least one minute before letting it idle and the check the idle speed recorded on the tachometer.

Idle Speed: **700±50RPM**

3. If the idle speed is not as shown, adjust the idle speed to suit by turning the idle speed adjusting screw until the idle speed setting is correct.
4. After reseting the idle speed let the engine run at idle for at least one minute and check that the idle speed setting is still correct.

Diagrams are in the next column

Inline Pump

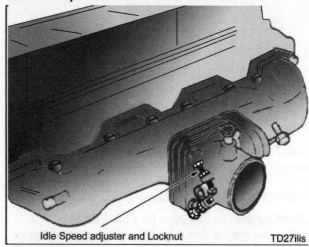

Idle Speed adjuster and Locknut   TD27ilis

VE Pump

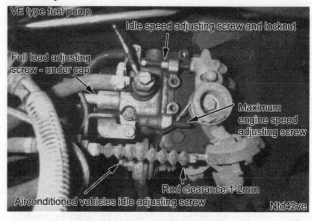

VE type fuel pump
Idle speed adjusting screw and locknut
Full load adjusting screw - under cap
Maximum engine speed adjusting screw
Rod clearance 1-2mm
Airconditioned vehicles idle adjusting screw   Ntd42ve

For Vehicles with Air Conditioning

1. Ensure that the clearance between the actuator control lever pin and the injection pump control lever is between 1-2mm.
2. Adjust the idle speed to the correct setting **750±50RPM** without the airconditioning on and then with the engine still ruinning switch on the air conditioning and check the idle speed setting.

Idle Speed Setting: 850±50RPM

3. If the idle speed setting is not as shown, adjust by turning the FICD actuator stroke adjusting screw.

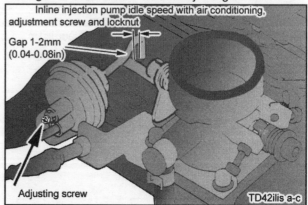

Inline injection pump idle speed with air conditioning, adjustment screw and locknut
Gap 1-2mm (0.04-0.08in)
Adjusting screw   TD42ilis a-c

Other diagram is in the next column

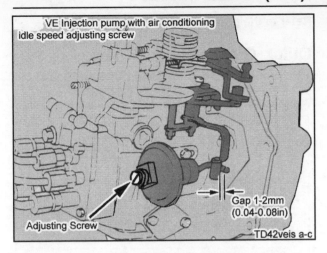

VE Injection pump with air conditioning idle speed adjusting screw

Adjusting Screw

Gap 1-2mm (0.04-0.08in)

TD42veis a-c

Injection Timing Check (In Line Pump)

1. Turn the crankshaft in a clockwise direction, set the No1 piston to its applicable BTDC position by lining up the relevant mark on the crankshaft pulley with the mark on the front cover. *(if there are only two marks on the crankshaft pulley, take the RH mark as the BTDC setting).*

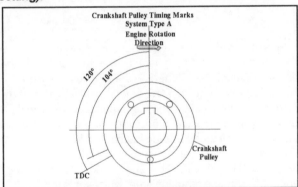

Crankshaft Pulley Timing Marks
System Type A
Engine Rotation
Direction

120° 104°

TDC

Crankshaft Pulley

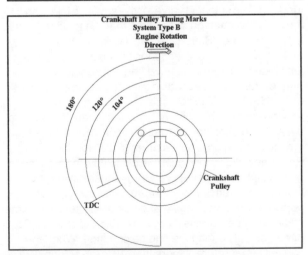

Crankshaft Pulley Timing Marks
System Type B
Engine Rotation
Direction

180° 120° 104°

TDC

Crankshaft Pulley

2. Remove all of the injection tubes, govenor hoses and the diesel pump control rod (if fitted).

3. Remove the No1 lock plate and delivery valve holder, pull out the delivery valve stopper (if fitted) and the delivery valve spring.

4. Install the delivery valve holder without the spring and stopper, install a test pipe to the No1 delivery valve

holder and then push the injection pump fully downwards towards the engine.

5. While feeding the system fuel by pressing the priming pump, slowly move the injection pump until the fuel flow from the No1 injection tube stops.

6. Fix the injection pump into the position where the fuel flow stopped and ensure that the timing marks on the injection pump and front plate lines up. If the marks do not line up stamp a new mark on the plate.

7. Remove the No1 injection test tube, replace any removed parts in the reverse order of removal and then bleed any air from the system that may be present.

Maximum Speed Adjustment (In Line Pump)

Please Note: The maximum speed adjusting screw is retained by sealing wire and under normal circumstances would not need adjustment.

1. Start the engine and let it run until normal operating temperature has been reached.

2. Install a tachometer pick up lead to the No1 fuel injection pipe.

3. To obtain the maximum speed, turn the adjusting screw in either direction with the throttle pedal pressed down fully.

Maximum Engine Speed: 5100(+50RPM or -150RPM)

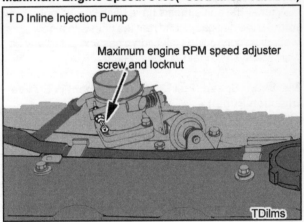

TD Inline Injection Pump

Maximum engine RPM speed adjuster screw and locknut

TDilms

4. After carrying out the adjusement, tighten the lock nut and replace the sealing wire.

Injection Timing Check (VE Type Injection Pump)

1. Loosen off the injection pump mounting nuts and mounting bracket bolts

2. Remove the plug bolt from the injection pump distributor head and install a dial gauge to the distributor head

3. Turn the crankshaft in an anti clockwise direction to a position of between 20-25° BTDC on the No1 piston.

4. With the dial gauge in a suitable rest position set the dial gauge to zero, turn the crankshaft in a clockwise direction until the No1 piston is set at TDC, and record the plunger lift measurement on the dial gauge.

Plunger Lift Measurement:
　　0.54±0.02mm (equivilant to 5° BTDC) TD23

Plunger Lift Measurement:
　　0.65±0.02mm (equivilant to 5° BTDC) TD27

5. If the plunger lift measurement in step 4 is not as

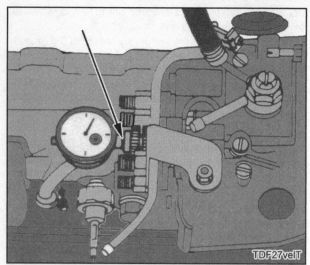

shown, turn the injection pump body until the reading is correct, then tighten the injection pump mounting bracket and bolts.

Please Note: If the measurement is smaller than shown, turn the injection pump body in an anti clockwise direction, if the measurement is more than shown, turn the injection pump body in a clockwise direction.

6. After all the adjustments have been carried out, remove the dial gauge and refit the plug with a new washer, reconnect the injection pipes and bleed any air from the system that may be present.

Maximum Speed (Full Load) Adjustment (VE Type Injection Pump)

Please Note: The maximum speed (full load) adjusting screw is retained by sealing wire and under normal circumstances would not need adjustment. By disturbing the screw, this will cause the fuel flow to be changed and will cause incorrect adjustments on the engine. With this in mind, the injection pump timing will need to be adjusted again. If the maximum speed (full load) adjusting screw is turned in a direction that will increase the control lever angle, engine damage may occur

1. If adjustment is needed, start the engine, let it run until normal operating temperature is reached and then connect a tachometer pick up to the No1 injection pipe.
2. Press down the throttle pedal fully and record the engine speed shown on the tachometer.

Maximum Engine Speed: 5,100 +50RPM or -150RPM

3. If the engine speed is lower than shown in step 2, turn the maximum speed (full load) adjusting screw anti-clockwise one or two full rotations, press down the throttle fully and record the engine speed.
4. If the engine speed is still lower than shown in step2, turn the maximum speed (full load) adjusting screw anti-clockwise one or two full rotations, press down the throttle fully until the correct engine speed is reached.
5. After the adjustment has been done, tighten the adjustment screw lock nut and wind up again with sealing wire.

Refer to the previous VE idle speed diagrams

Quick Glow System Check

This vehicle has two different systems and Type A System and a Type B System.

With the TypeA System, when the coolant temperature

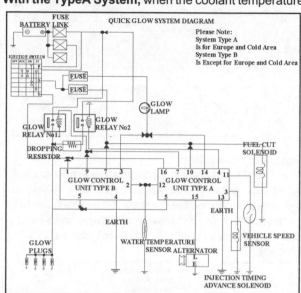

is less than 50°c the relay No1 and No2 are turned on at the same time that the ignition is switched on. From the time the ignition is switched on the high level current flows through the glow plugs and heats them up quickly. After between 2 and 6 seconds (time span varies with glow plug voltage and coolant temperature) the control unit will turn off the glow plug indicator. The relay No1 will automatically turns off after it has been on for between 3-11 seconds (time span varies with glow plug voltage or engine cranking time, whicever is the longest). The solenoid valve for the advance injection timing is switched on at the time that the ignition switch is turned to the "Start" position. The relay No2 will stay on for between 60-180 seconds (when the coolant is less than 50°c (time span will vary with coolant temperature) or 0 seconds if the coolant temperature is more than 50°c. The solenoid valve will stay on for 30 seconds (when the coolant tep is less than 10°c) or 0°c (when the coolant temperature is more than 10°c) after the ignition switch is turned from "Start" to "ON". The Relay No2 allows low level current to flow through the glow plugs. The solenoid valve advances the injection timing, these functions will improve the combustion performance of the engine after is has started. When the coolant temperature is more than 50°c the relay No2 is turned on only during the engine cranking. When the coolant temperature is more than 10°c the solenoid valve is turned on only while the engine is being cranked.

With the TypeB System, when the ignition switch is turned on, the relay No1 is turned on and the high level current flows through the glow plugs and heats them up quickly. After between 2-6 seconds (time span varies with coolant temperature) the control unit turns off the glow plug indicator but the relay No1 stays on. The relay No1 cuts off the current when the ignition switch turns from "ON" to "Start". When the relay No1 has been cutting off for about 15 seconds after the ignition switch is turned from "Start" to "ON". When the engine is not cranking, the relay No1 cuts the electric current for between 15 seconds and between 3-14 seconds (time span varies with glow plug voltage) after the ignition switch has been turned from "OFF:" to "ON". When the ignition switch is repeatedly turned "ON and OFF" the 3-14 seconds (time span varies with glow plug voltage) becomes shorter.

Glow Plug Check

1. Remove the glow plug/s from the cylinder head and check for continuity in the glow plugs between the tip of the plug and ground
2. If continuity is not found, replace the plug/s as required.

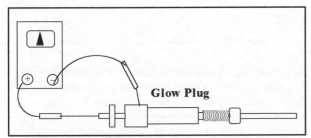

Glow Plug Relay Check

1. Apply battery volts between terminals 1 and 2 and ensure that continuity exists between terminals 3 and 4.
2. If the continuity does not exist in step1 repair/replace as required.

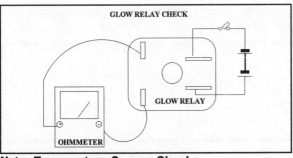

Water Temperature Sensor Check

1. Disconnect the water temperature sensor harness connector and check the resistance between the sensor terminals at varying coolant temperatures.

Coolant Temperature (°c)	Resistance(k/ohms)
-15	11.5
0	5.6
10	3.7
40	1.2

2. If the resistance is not as shown, repair/replace as required.
Diagram is in the next column

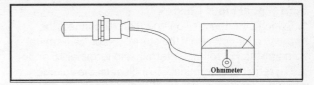

Dropping Resistor Check (System Type A)

1. Disconnect the resistor harness connector and check the resistance between the resistor terminals
Resistance: 0.3ohms.
2. If the resistance is not as shown, repair/replace as required

Control Unit Check (System Type A Only)
Power Supply Circuit Check

1. Disconnect the harness connector from the glow control unit and carry out voltage and continuity check as shown below.

Voltmeter Terminals	**Ignition Switch Position**		
(+) Ter No10 (-) Ter No13	**OFF**	**ACC**	**ON**
	0v	0v	Approx 12v

Ohmmeter Terminals	**Ignition Switch Position** (+)
No13 (-) Body Ground	**OFF**
	Continuity Exists

2. If the operation is not as shown, repair/replace as required

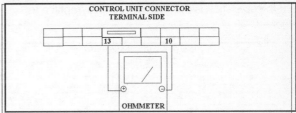

Input From the Alternator "L" Terminal Check

1. Switch OFF the ignition, disconnect the harness connector from the glow control unit, and then disconnect the harness connector from the alternator "L" terminal.
2. Install the (+) voltmeter terminal to terminal 15 and the (-) terminal to terminal 13 and check the voltage when the ignition is switched ON.
Voltage: **Approx 12v.**
3. If the voltage is not as shown, repair/replace as required.

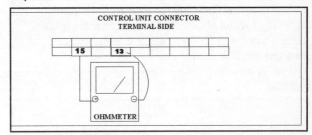

Start Signal Input Check

1. Switch OFF the ignition and then disconnect the harness connector from the starter motor "S" terminal.
2. Install the (+) voltmeter terminal to terminal 16 and the (-) terminal to terminal 13 and check the voltage when the ignition is in then "Start" position
Voltage: **Approx 12v**
3. If the voltage is not as shown, repair/replace as required.

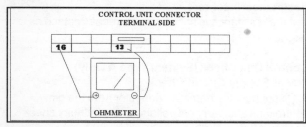

Glow Indicator Control Check

1. Switch OFF the ignition, and leaving the harness connected to the control unit install a 3.4w test lamp to the terminals 10 and 14.
2. Switch ON the ignition and check the amount of time that the test lamp stays on.
Test Lamp Light Up Time: **2-6 seconds (varies with coolant temperature and glow plug voltage)**
3. If the operation is not as shown, repair/replace as required.

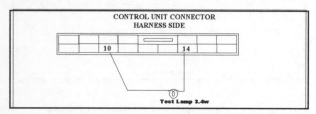

Pre-Glow Control Check

1. Switch OFF the ignition and leaving the harness connected to the glow control unit install a 3.4w test lamp to the No13 and No7 terminals.
2. Switch ON the ignition and check the amount of time that the test lamp stays on.
Test Lamp Light Up Time: **3-11 seconds (varies on glow plug voltage)**
Please Note: the time will be shortened if the ignition switch is turned off only for a short time. When carrying out the above test ensure that the ignition switch has been off for at least 5 minutes and then turn the ignition switch on.
3. If the operation is not as shown, repair/replace as required.

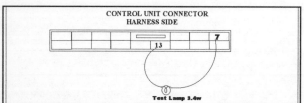

After Glow Control Check

1. Install a 3.4w test lamp to the terminals 4 and 13 on the control unit and then disconnect the "S" terminal from the starter motor.
2. Ensure that the test lamp comes on when the ignition switch is put to the "Start" position.
3. Record the time that the test lamp stays on when the ignition switch is turned to from the "Start" to "ON" position.
Test Lamp Light Up Time
Coolant Temperature Less Than 50°c 60-180 seconds (varies with coolant temperature)
Coolant Temperature Less Than 50°c 0 seconds
4. If the operation is not as shown above repair/replace as required.

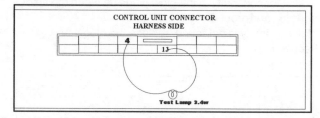

Injection Timing Advance Solenoid Control Check

1. Install a 3.4w test lamp to the control unit between the No3 and 13 terminals, disconnect the harness connector from the "S" terminal and ensure that the test lamnp comes on when the ignition is turned to "Start".
2. Record the time that the test lamp stays ON when the ignition switch is turned from "Start" to "ON".
Test Lamp ON Time Span: **30 seconds when the coolant temperature is less than 10°c.**
Test Lamp ON Time Span: **0 seconds when the coolant temperature is more than 10°c.**
3. If the operation is not as shown, repair/replace as required.

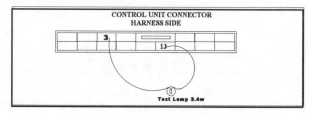

Power Supply Circuit Check (System Type B)

1. Disconnect the harness connector from the glow control unit and carry out voltage and continuity check as shown below.

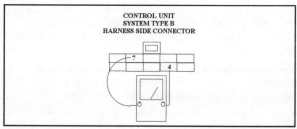

Voltmeter Terminals	Ignition Switch Position		
(+) Ter No7 (-) Ter No4	OFF	ACC	ON
	0v	0v	Approx 12v

Ohmmeter Terminals	Ignition Switch Position (+)
No4 (-) Body Ground	OFF
Continuity Exists	

2-If the operation is not as shown, repair/replace as required.

Start Signal Input Check

1. Switch OFF the ignition and then disconnect the harness connector from the starter motor "S" terminal.
2. Install the (+) voltmeter terminal to terminal 1 and the (-) terminal to terminal 4 and check the voltage when the ignition is in the "Start" position
Voltage: **Approx 12v**
3. If the voltage is not as shown, repair/replace as required.

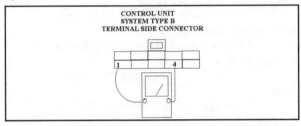

Glow Indicator Control Check

1. Switch OFF the ignition, and leaving the harness connected to the control unit install a 3.4w test lamp to the terminals 3 and 7.
2. Switch ON the ignition and check the amount of time that the test lamp stays on.
Test Lamp Light Up Time: **2-6 seconds (varies with coolant temperature)**
3. If the operation is not as shown, repair/replace as required.

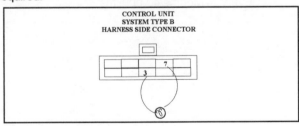

Glow Control Check

1. Switch off the engine, and leaving the control harness connected install a 3.4w test lamp to the control unit between the 4 and 9 terminals.
2. Switch ON the ignition and check the amount of time that the test lamp stays on.
Test Lamp Light Up Time: **3-14 seconds (varies with glow plug voltage)**
3. If the operation is not as shown, repair/replace as required.
Please Note: The time the lamp stays on will be shorter if the ignition switch is off for only a short time, so when carrying out this check ensure that

the ignition is off for more than 60 seconds before turning on the ignition.

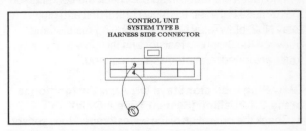

System Diagnosis Checks

Engine Will Not Start or is Hard to Start

1. Before carrying out this check ensure that the fuel level, fuel supply system and starter motor operations are OK, if faults are found repair/replace as required.
2. If no faults are found in step1, check the installation of the glow plugs, if faults are found repair/replace as required.
3. If no faults are found in step2, switch off the ignition for more than 10 seconds and see if the glow indicator comes on in a few seconds after the ignition is switched to the ON position, if it does not check the condition and/or operation of the warning lamp globe, if faults are found repair/replace as required.
4. If there are no faults in step3, carry out thew power supply circuit check for the glow control unit, if faults are found check the condition of the harness between the fuse and glow control unit, if faults are found repair/replace as required.
5. If no faults are found in step4, carry out the glow indicator control check, if faults are found repair/replace the glow control unit as required.
6. If no faults are found in step5, check for a short in the harness between the ignition switch and the glow indicator, if faults are found repair/replace aas required.
7. If the glow indicator lamp does come on in step3, check the operation of the glow plugs, if faults are found repair/replace as required.
8. If no faults are found in step7, carry out the "Start" signal input check, if faults are found repair/replace as required.
9. If no faults are found in step8, carry out the pre-glow control check, if faults are found replace the glow control unit as required.
10. If no faults are found in step9, check the condition of the harness between the glow control unit and the glow relay No1, and between the glow relay No1 and the glow plug, if faults are found repair/replace as required.

Poor Combustion Performance of the Engine After it has Started (System Type A Only)

1. Check the operation of the glow relay No2, if faults are found repair/replace as required.
2. If no faults are found in step1, carry out the dropping resistor check, if faults are found repair/replace as required.
3. If no faults are found in step2, carry out the after glow

check, if faults are found repair/replace the glow control unit as required.

4. If no faults are found in step3, check the condition of the harness between the glow control unit and glow relay No2, glow relay No2 and dropping resistor and between the dropping resistor and the glow plugs, if faults are found repair/replace as required.

Glow Plug Indicator Stays ON After the Ignition is in the ON Position (System Type A Only)

1. Check the operation of the water temperature sensor, if faults are found repair/replace as required.

2. If no faults are found in step1, check the condition of the harness between the glow control unit and the water temperature sensor, if faults are found repair/replace as required.

3. If no faults are found in step2, carry out the glow indicator control check, if faults are found repair/replace the glow control unit as required.

4. If no faults are found in step3, check for a short circuit between the glow control unit and the glow indicator, if faults are found repair/replace as required.

VEHICLE SERVICE INFORMATION

Vehicle Filling Capacities

Engine Oil with Filter: .... 5.9 Litres
Engine Oil without Filter: .... 5.2 Litres
Cooling System with Front Heater: .... 15.5 Litres
Cooling System without Heater: .... 12.0 Litres (TD23)
Cooling System without Heater: .... 14.5 Litres (TD27)
Cooling System: with front/rear Heater: .... 16.5 Litres
Manual Transmission: .... 1.7 Litres (4 Speed)
Manual Transmission: .... 2.0 Litres (5 Speed)
Automatic Transmission: .... 7.0 Litres
Rear Differential (H233B) : .... 2.8 Litres
Rear Differential (C200): .... 1.3 Litres

Vehicle Component Service Interval Changes

Adjust Valve Clearance:
  Every 20,000kms
Engine Coolant/Anti Freeze:
  Change Every 24 Months/40,000kms
Air Cleaner Element:
  Change Every 24 Months/40,000kms
Pre-Air Cleaner Element:
  Change Every 24 Months/40,000kms
Fuel Filter:
  Change Every 24 Months/40,000kms
Engine Oil:
  Change Every 6 Months/10,000kms
Engine Oil Filter:
  Change Every 6 Months/10,000kms
Brake Fluid:
  Change Every 24 Months/40,000kms
Manual Transmission Oil:
  Change Every 24 Months/40,000kms
Rear Differential Oil:
  Change Every 24 Months/40,000kms
Repack Front Wheel Bearings:
  Every 24 Months/40,000kms

Toyota Dyna LH80 Series 2L Engine (1985-1991)

Toyota Dyna LH80 Series 2L Engine (1985-1991)

Toyota Dyna LH80 Series
2L Engine (1985-1991)

Engine Checks

Valve Clearance Check (1985-1988)
Please Note: Before carrying out this check ensure that the engine is at normal operating temperature.
1. Remove the rocker cover, set the No1 piston to TDC on its compression stroke and ensure that the groove on the crankshaft pulley is lined up with the timing pointer on the front cover.
2. Ensure that the No1 cylinder rocker arms are loose and that the No4 cylinder rocker arms are tight (if they are not turn the engine on full turn (360°) and recheck).
3. Measure the valve clearances on the following valves 1&5 (Exhaust) and 2&4 (Inlet).

Inlet Valve Clearance:	**0.25mm**
Exhaust Valve Clearance:	**0.36mm**

If the clearances are not correct adjust to suit.

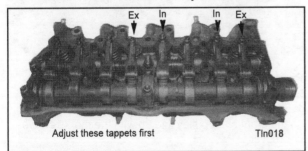

Adjust these tappets first   TIn018

4. Turn the crankshaft one full turn (360°) and ensure that the groove on the crankshaft pulley is lined up with the timing pointer on the front cover.
5. Measure the valve clearances on the following valves 3&7 (Exhaust) and 6&8 (Inlet).

Inlet Valve Clearance:	**0.25mm**
Exhaust Valve Clearance:	**0.36mm**

6. If the clearances are not correct adjust to suit, then replace the rocker cover and any other removed components

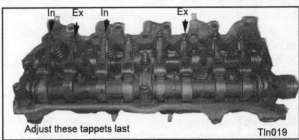

Adjust these tappets last   TIn019

Valve Clearance Check (1988 On)
Please Note: Before carrying out this check ensure that the engine is at normal operating temperature.
1. Remove the rocker cover, set the No1 piston to TDC on its compression stroke and ensure that the groove on the crankshaft pulley is lined up with the timing pointer on the front cover.
2. Ensure that the valve lifters on the No1 cylinder are loose and that the No4 valve lifters are tight (if they are not turn the engine on full turn (360°) and recheck).
3. Measure the valve clearances on the following valves 1&3 (Exhaust) and 1&2 (Inlet).

Inlet Valve Clearance:	**0.20-030mm (Cold)**
Exhaust Valve Clearance:	**0.40-0.50mm (Cold)**

If the clearances are not correct record the relevant readings to determine the adjusting shim required.

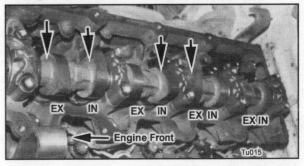

4. Turn the crankshaft one full turn (360°) and ensure that the groove on the crankshaft pulley is lined up with the timing pointer on the front cover.

5. Measure the valve clearances on the following valves 2&4 (Exhaust) and 3&4 (Inlet).

Inlet Valve Clearance: 0.20-030mm (Cold)
Exhaust Valve Clearance: 0.40-0.50mm (Cold)

If the clearances are not correct record the relevant readings to determine the adjusting shim required.

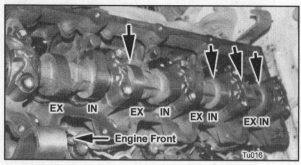

Compression Check (1985 On)

1. Run the engine to normal operating temperature, disconnect the fuel cut solenoid connector and remove all of the glow plugs from the engine.
2. Install and adaptor and compression gauge to the No1 cylinder, crank the engine and record the comperssion pressure on each cylinder.

Compression Pressure: 3138kpa
Minimum Pressure: 1961kpa
Difference Between Each Cylinder: 490kpa

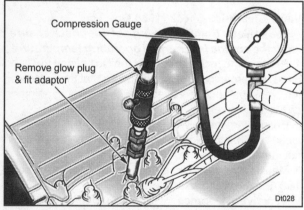

3. If the pressure on one or more cylinders is low, pour a small amount of oil into the cylinder through the glow plug hole and check the compression pressure again. If it helps the pressure there are possibly faults with the piston rings or cylinder bores, if the oil does not help there may be a valve sticking or not seated correctly and/or leaks past the gasket.

Cylinder Head Tightening Procedures (1985-1988)

1. After the cylinder head has been removed and the gasket replaced, apply a thin coat of oil to all of the cylinder head bolts. Install and gradually tighten each of the bolts to its correct torque in three stages in the sequence showed in the diagram
2. On the third stage ensure that the bolts are tourqed to its correct specification
Specified Torque Setting: 118Nm

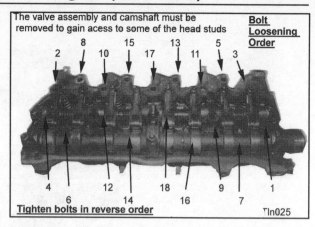

Cylinder Head Tightening Procedures (1988 On)

1. After the cylinder head has been removed and the gasket replaced, apply a thin coat of oil to all of the cylinder head bolts. Install and gradually tighten each of the bolts to its correct torque in three stages in the sequence showed in the diagram.
Specified Torque Setting: 78Nm
Please Note: If any of the bolts do not reach the correct torque, check the length of the bolts.
Short Bolt: 107mm
Long Bolt: 127mm
Replace any faulty bolts as required.
2. Mark the front of each bolt with some paint and the tighten the bolts a further 90°. After the sequence has been completed tighten the bolts a further 90° and now ensure that the paint mark is facing to the rear.

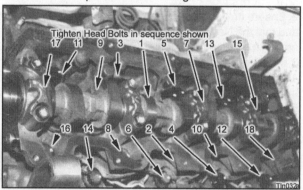

Piston Protrusion Height Check (1988 On)
No1 and 4 Piston Check
1. Rotate the engine and ensure that the timing marks on the crankshaft pulley line up with the marks on the front cover.
2. Fit a dial gauge to the engine block and set the gauge at the piston measuring point.
3. Find the point where the piston protrudes the most by turning the crankshaft in a clockwise and anti clockwise direction.
4. Set the dial gauge to zero and record the protrusion measurement from the block by sliding the dial gauge.
Protrusion Measurement: 0.68-0.97mm
Please Note: Record the measurement at two separate measuring points.

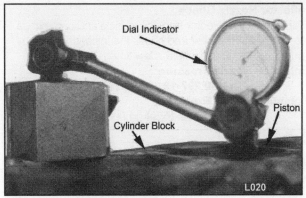

L020

No2 and No3 Piston Check

5. Turn the crankshaft 180° , Fit a dial gauge to the engine block and set the gauge at the piston measuring point.

6. Find the point where the piston protrudes the most by turning the crankshaft in a clockwise and anti clockwise direction.

7. Set the dial gauge to zero and record the protrusion measurement from the block by sliding the dial gauge.

Protrusion Measurement: 0.68-0.97mm

Please Note: Record the measurement at two separate measuring points.

8. When the measurment has been made, to select a new head gasket follow the procedures shown.

9. There are 3 different types of head gaskets marked either "B", "D" or "F", each of them different thicknesses.

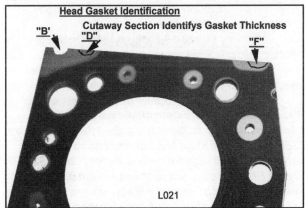

L021

Piston Protrusion Measurements	Gasket Thickness	Gasket Grade
0.68-0.77	1.4-1.5mm	B
0.78-0.87	1.5-1.6	D
0.88-0.97	1.6-1.7	F

Please Note: When selecting the gasket use the largest measurement of the 8 readings that are recorded.

Oil Pressure Check (1985-1988)

1. Ensure that the engine oil level is correct, if not top up to suit.

2. Remove the oil pressure switch from the engine and install a pressure gauge to the engine block.

3. Start the engine, run to normal operating temperature and then record the oil pressure shown on the gauge.

Specified Oil Pressure: 29kpa @ Idle
Specified Oil Pressure: 245-588kpa @ 3000RPM

4. If the oil pressure is not as shown, repair/replace as required.

Oil Pressure Check (1988 On)

1. Ensure that the engine oil level is correct, if not top up to suit.

2. Remove the oil pressure switch from the engine and install a pressure gauge to the engine block.

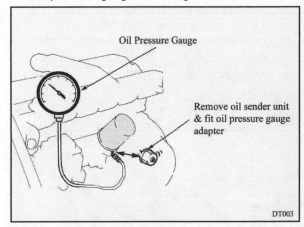

DT003

3. Start the engine, run to normal operating temperature and then record the oil pressure shown on the gauge.

Specified Oil Pressure: 29kpa @ Idle
Specified Oil Pressure: 294-539kpa @ 3000RPM

4. If the oil pressure is not as shown, repair/replace as required.

Cooling System Thermostat Check (1985 On)

1. Remove the thermostat from the engine and put into a suitable container of water.

2. Heat the water gradually and and check the valve opening temperature and valve lift.

Valve Opening Temperature: 86-90°c
Valve Lift: More than 8mm

If the operation is not as shown above replace the thermostat.

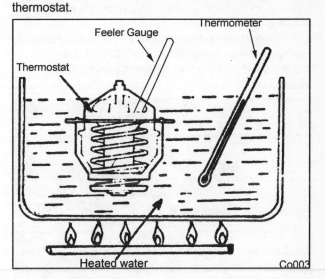

Co003

3. Check that the valve spring is tight when the thermostat is fully closed, if not replace the thermostat.

Fuel Filter Check and Replacement (1985 On)
1. Remove the fuel filter sensor, drain the fuel, then remove the fuel filter.
2. Clean the fuel filter mounting bracket and then coat the fuel filter sealing ring with some diesel fuel.
3. Screw the fuel filter on until a slght resistance is felt and then turn another 2/3 of a turn or until suitably tight.
4. Install the fuel filter sensor (if fitted) to the new filter and then bleed any air present from the system.

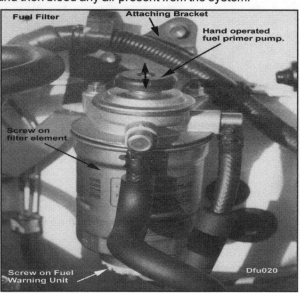

Draining Water Fron The Filter (1985 On)
1. Loosen the drain cock 4 or 5 turns or remove the fuel filter sensor to allow the water to drain from the filter.
2. Retighten the drain cock or replace the sensor and bleed any air present from the system.

Fuel Filter Warning Lamp Check (1985 On)
1. Remove the switch from the filter and check that there is continuity between the terminals when the warning switch is ON (Float Up)
2. Check that there is no continuity between the terminals when the warning switch is OFF (Float Down)
3. If the operation is not as shown, repair/replace as required.

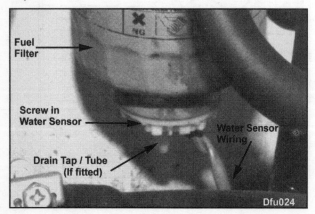

Injector Nozzle Check
1. Remove the injector from the vehicle and connect up to the pressure tester and check the initial pressure by pumping the tester handle a few times.
Injection Nozzle Pressure:
      10,297-12,258kpa (1985-88)
Injection Nozzle Pressure:
      14,200-1520kpa (1988-On)

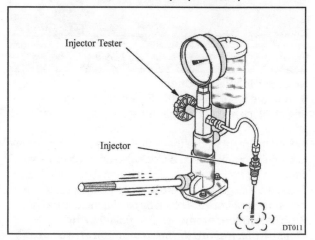

2. If the opening pressure is not as shown above, take the injector to pieces and change the adjusting shim on the top of the injector so as the correct pressure is recorded.
Injection Nozzle Pressure:
      10,297-12,258kpa (1985-88 Used)
Injection Nozzle Pressure:
      14,220-15,200kpa (1988-On Used)
Injection Nozzle Pressure:
      12,278-12,258kpa (1985-1988 New)
Injection Nozzle Pressure:
      14,808-15,593kpa (1988-On New)
Please Note: The adjusting shims vary in 0.05mm thicknesses, each 0.05mm will adjust the pressure by 628kpa. After the shim has been changed there should be no leakage from the injector (1985-1988).
Please Note: The adjusting shims vary in 0.025mm thicknesses, each 0.05mm will adjust the pressure by 341kpa. After the shim has been changed there should be no leakage from the injector (1988On)
3. Maintain the pressure between 981-1961kpa below the opening pressure and check that there is no leakage from the injector for a period of 10seconds.
4. Check the spray pattern by pumping the pressure tester handle 4-6 times or more per second and check the injection spray pattern.
4. If the operation and/or spray pattern is not as shown, repair/replace the nozzle/s as required.
Diagram is on the next page

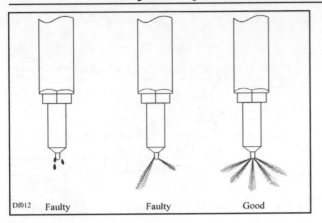

Df012   Faulty   Faulty   Good

Timing Belt Removal and Replacement (1985-1988)

Removal Procedures

1. Remove the drive belts, water pump pulley, crankshaft pulley and the front engine cover.

2. Remove the timing belt guide, the current sensor and the 4 glow plugs.

3. Set the No1 piston to TDC on its compression stroke by temporarily replacing the cranksahft pulley bolt and turning the crankshaft in a clockwise direction until the timimg mark on the camshaft gear lines up with the mark on top end of the cylinder head.

Please Note: If the timing belt is being used again, before removing, mark a direction arrow on the timing belt and place match marks on the pulleys and the belt.

4. Remove the timing belt tension spring, loosen the No1 pulley mount bolts and remove the timing belt from the engine.

Replacement Procedures

Please Note: Before replacing the timimg belt check the condition and/or operation of the timing belt pulleys, tensioners and/or pulleys, if faults are found repair/replace as required.

1. Check the tensioner spring free length

Spring Free Length: **39.7-40.7mm**

Check the tension of the spring at the specified free length

Installed Tension: **39Nm at 52mm**

2. Install the crankshaft pulley to the engine, replace any pulleys or idlers that may have been removed for checking.

3. Set the No1 piston to TDC on its compression stroke and ensure that the timing marks on each of the pulleys line up with their relevant matchmarks.

4. Fit the timing belt onto the camshaft pulley, line up the marks on the oil pump drive pulley and oil pump body and then fit the timing belt to it.

5. Fit the timing belt to the No2 idler pulley and the crankshaft timing pulley.

6. Install the timing belt tension spring and then loosen the idler pulley mount bolts to a point where the idler

pulley lightley moves with the tension spring force.

7. With the crankshaft pulley bolt installed turn the engine twice in a 360° rotation and ensure all of the timing marks on each of the pulleys line up with their relevant matchmarks again.

8. Retighten the No1 idler pulley bolts being careful not to move the pulley bracket.

9. Replace the remainder of the removed parts in the reverse order of removal.

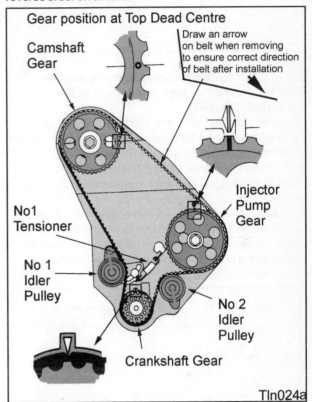

Gear position at Top Dead Centre

Draw an arrow on belt when removing to ensure correct direction of belt after installation

Camshaft Gear

Injector Pump Gear

No1 Tensioner

No 1 Idler Pulley

No 2 Idler Pulley

Crankshaft Gear

TIn024a

Timing Belt Replacement Torques

Injection Pump Drive Pulley Nut:	64Nm
No1 Idle Pulley:	19Nm
No2 Idle Pulley:	39Nm
Crankshaft Pulley Bolt:	137Nm
Camshaft Gear Bolt:	98Nm

Timing Belt Warning Lamp Reset Procedures (Rubber Plug in the Instrument Cluster Glass)

1. Remove the grommet from the speedometer and turn off the lamp by pushing the warning lamp reset switch, then replace the grommet.

2. Start the engine and ensure that the light stays off

Diagram is in the next column

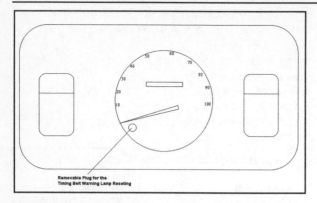

Removable Plug for the
Timing Belt Warning Lamp Reseting

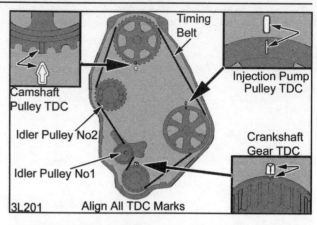

Timing Belt

Camshaft Pulley TDC

Idler Pulley No2

Idler Pulley No1

Injection Pump Pulley TDC

Crankshaft Gear TDC

3L201   Align All TDC Marks

Timing Belt Warning Lamp Reset Procedures (Change Screw Position on the Back of the Instrument Cluster)

1. Remove the instrument cluster from the vehicle, connect terminals A&B shown in the diagrams and then remove the CHARGE fuse from the vehicle.

2. Turn the ignition switch to ON and check that the warning lights light up, if not the check the condition and/or operation of the globe.

3. Check the condition and/or operation of the reset switches by checking that there is intermittent continuity between terminals A&B when the reset switch is pressed, if not repair/replace the speedometer/instrument cluster as required.

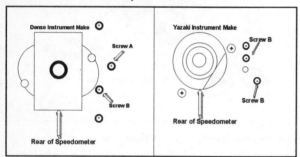

Denso Instrument Make

Screw A

Screw B

Rear of Speedometer

Yazaki Instrument Make

Screw B

Screw B

Rear of Speedometer

Timing Belt Removal and Replacement 1988-1991

Removal Procedures

1. Remove the drive belts, water pump pulley, glow plugs crankshaft pulley, and the No1 timing cover and timing belt guide.

2. Set the No1 piston to TDC on its compression stroke by turning the crankshaft in a clockwise direction until the timing mark on the camshaft gear lines up with the mark on the No2 timing cover.

Please Note: If the timing belt is being used again, before removing mark a direction arrow on the timing belt and place match marks on the pulleys and the belt.

3. Loosen the No1 Idler Pulley bolt, move the pulley as far to the LH side as possible and then re-tighten the bolt temporarily, relieve the tension from the timing belt and then remove the timing belt from the engine

Replacement Procedures

Please Note: Before replacing the timing belt check the condition and/or operation of the timing belt pulleys, tensioners and/or pulleys, if faults are found repair/replace as required.

1. Check the tensioner spring free length

Spring Free Length: **44.4-45.4mm**

Check the tension of the spring at the specified free length

Installed Tension: **53-59Nm @ 52.1mm**

2. Install the crankshaft pulley to the engine, replace any pulleys or idlers that may have been removed for checking.

3. Set the No1 piston to TDC on its compression stroke and ensure that the timing marks on each of the pulleys line up with their relevant match marks.

4. Fit the timing belt onto the crankshaft pulley and the No1 idler pulley. Slightly turn the injection pump drive pulley in a clockwise direction, hang the belt on the drive pulley and then line up the marks of the drive pulley and timing belt case.

5. Ensure that there is tension between the crankshaft timing and injection pump drive pulleys.

6. Slightly turn the camshaft timing pulley clockwise, hang the timing belt on the timing pulley and line up the marks on the timing pulley and timing belt case.

7. Ensure that there is tension between the injection pump drive and camshaft timing pulleys.

8. Check the valve timing by loosening the Idler Pulley "1" turning the crankshaft four full turns and ensure that all of the timing marks line up as shown in the diagram. If they do not line up, remove the timing belt and re-install as shown in the steps above.

9. Retighten the No1 idler pulley bolts being careful not to move the pulley bracket.

10. Replace the remainder of the removed parts in the reverse order of removal.

Timing Belt Warning Lamp Reset Procedures (Rubber Plug in the Instrument Cluster Glass) and (Change Screw Position on the Back of the Instrument Cluster)

See 1985-1988 section for information and diagrams

Timing Belt Replacement Tourqes

Injection Pump Drive Pulley Nut: 64Nm
No1 Idler Pulley Bolt: 44Nm
No2 Idle Pulley: 33Nm
Crankshaft Pulley Bolt: 167N
Camshaft Gear Bolt: 98Nm

Engine Tightening Torques (1985-1988)

Cylinder Head Tightening Torque Bolts: ....
.... 118Nm (In 3 Stages)
Rocker Shaft Bracket Bolts: 19Nm
Camshaft Carrier Retainer: 18Nm
Exhaust Manifold Bolts and Nuts: 39Nm
Inlet Manifold Bolts and Nuts: 24Nm
Glow Plugs: 13Nm
Injection Nozzle: 69Nm
Injection Pump Drive Pulley Nut: 64Nm
No1 Idle Pulley: 19Nm
No2 Idle Pulley: 39Nm
Flywheel Bolts: 123Nm
Drive Plate: 123Nm
Connecting Rod Caps: 59Nm (Tighten in Two or Three Stages)
Main Bearings: .... 103Nm (Tighten in Three Stages)
Crankshaft Pulley Bolt: 137Nm
Camshaft Gear Bolt: 98Nm
Oil Pump Bolt: 19Nm
Oil Sump Bolt: 8Nm
Oil Sump Pan Nuts: 17Nm

Engine Tightening Torques (1988 On)

Cylinder Head Tightening Torque Bolts: ....
.... 78Nm (1st Stage)
Cylinder Head Tightening Torque Bolts: .. 90° (2nd Stage)
Cylinder Head Tightening Torque Bolts: . 90° (3rd Stage)
Camshaft Bearing Cap: 25Nm
Exhaust Manifold Bolts and Nuts: 52Nm
Inlet Manifold Bolts and Nuts: 24Nm
Glow Plugs: 13Nm
Injection Nozzle: 64Nm
Injection Pump Drive Pulley Nut: 64Nm
No1 Idle Pulley (12mm Bolt): 19Nm
No1 Idle Pulley (14mm Bolt): 44Nm
No2 Idle Pulley: 33Nm
Flywheel Bolts: 123Nm
Drive Plate: 98Nm
Connecting Rod Caps: .... 54Nm (1st Stage)
Connecting Rod Caps: .... 90° (2nd Stage)
Main Bearings: 103Nm
Crankshaft Pulley Bolt: 167Nm
Camshaft Gear Bolt: 98Nm
Oil Pump to Timing Cover: 10Nm
Oil Pump to Block: 23Nm
Oil Pump to Injection Pump: 21Nm
Oil Sump Bolt: 18Nm

System Adjustments

Injection Timing Adjustment (1985-1988)

1. Remove the distributive head bolt, install a dial gauge to the plug hole and then set the No1 or No4 piston to 45° BTDC on its compression stroke.
2. Using a screwdriver turn the cold start lever anti clockwise about 20° and put a metal plate 8.5-10.0mm between the cold start lever and the thermo wax plunger.
3. Set the dial gauge to zero (mm) and then ensure it stays at zero (mm) while the crankshaft pulley is being moved right to left slightly.
4. Slowly turn the crankshaft pulley until the No1 or No4 piston is at TDC on its compression stroke and record the plunger stroke measurement.
Injection Plunger Stroke:
    1.06-1.22mm (2L Engine without ACSD Control)
Injection Plunger Stroke:
    0.82-0.98mm (2L Engine with ACSD Control)
5. If the plunger stroke measurment is not as shown, loosen the 4 injector pipe union nuts and inlet pipe union nuts on the injection pump side.
6. Loosen the 4 injection pump mounting nuts and adjust the plunger pump stroke by slightly tilting the injection pump body. If the stroke is less than shown tilt the pump towards the engine, if the plunger strike is more than shown tilt the pump away from the engine.
7. Retighten all of the fixing bolts and union nuts, recheck the plunger stroke and then remove the plate from the cold starting lever.
8. Remove the dial gauge, replace the plug bolt, retstart the engine and check for any leaks in the system.

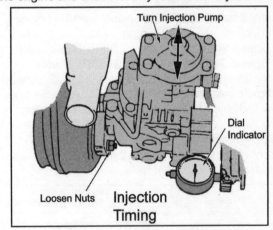

Injection Timing

Injection Timing Adjustment (1988 On)
Refer to Previous Diagram

1. Remove the distributive head bolt and install a special tool (SST09275-54010) plunger stroke measuring tool to the plug hole and then set the No1 or No4 piston to 25° BTDC on its compression stroke.
2. Please Note: (For vehicles with auto cold start device): Using a screwdriver turn the cold start lever anti clockwise about 20° and put a metal plate 8.5-10.0mm between the cold start lever and the thermo wax plunger.
3. Set the dial indicator to zero (mm) and then ensure it

stays at zero (mm) while the crankshaft pulley is being moved right to left slightly.

4. Slowly turn the crankshaft pulley until crankshaft pulley groove is lined up with the timing pointer and record the plunger movement.

Injection Plunger Stroke:
0.54-0.66 (With Auto Cold Start Device)
Injection Plunger Stroke:
0.84-0.96mm (Without Auto Cold Start Device)

5. If the plunger stroke measurment is not as shown, loosen the 4 injector pipe union nuts and inlet pipe union nuts on the injection pump side.

6. Loosen the 4 injection pump mounting nuts and adjust the plunger pump stroke by slightly tilting the injection pump body. If the stroke is less than shown tilt the pump towards the engine, if the plunger strike is more than shown tilt the pump away from the engine.

7. Retighten all of the fixing bolts and union nuts, recheck the plunger stroke and then remove the plate from the cold starting lever.

8. Remove the dial indicator gauge and replace the plug bolt. Restart the engine and check for any leaks in the system.

Idle Speed Check. (1985 On)

1. Ensure that the air cleaner is OK, the engine coolant temperature is at normal, the accessories are all switched off and that the transmission is in normal.

2. Ensure that the adjusting screw lever touches the idle speed adjusting screw when the throttle pedal is released, if it is not adjust to suit.

3. Install a tachometer to the engine, start the engine and check the idle speed setting.

Idle Speed Setting: **700RPM (Manual)**
Idle Speed Setting: **800RPM (Auto)**

4. If the idle speed is not as shown in step3, disconnect the throttle linkage, loosen the lock nut of the idle adjust screw and adjust by turning the idle speed adjusting screw, re-tighten the lock nut, reconnect the throttle linkage. Recheck the idle speed.

5. Remove the tachometer from the engine and replace any removed parts to the vehicle.

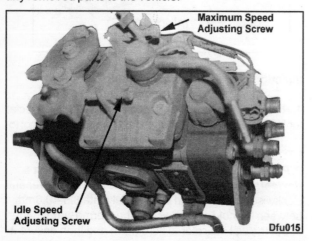

Maximum Speed Adjusting Screw

Idle Speed Adjusting Screw

Dfu015

Maximum Speed Adjustment Check (1985-1988)

1. Ensure that the adjusting lever touches the maximum speed adjusting screw when the throttle is pressed down all the way, if not adjust the stop bolt on the throttle pedal.

2. Install a tachometer to the engine, start the engine, press the throttle fully down and check the maximum speed.

Maximum Speed Setting:
4,900RPM, 2L Engine (Except LS Model Hong Kong/Singapore)
Maximum Speed Setting:
4,500RPM, 2L Engine (LS Model Hong Kong/Singapore)

3. If the maximum speed is not as shown, disconnect the throttle linkage, loosen the lock nut on the maximum speed adjusting screw and adjust by turning the adjusting screw.

4. Check the idle speed setting, then raise the engine speed and recheck the maximum speed.

5. Retighten the lock nut, reconnect the throttle linkage and recheck the throttle pedal stop bolt adjustment.

6. Remove the tachometer from the engine and replace any removed parts to the vehicle.

Refer to Idle Speed Diagram

Maximum Speed Adjustment Check (1988 On)

1. Ensure that the adjusting lever touches the maximum speed adjusting screw when the throttle is pressed down all the way, if not adjust the throttle linkages

2. Install a tachometer to the engine, start the engine, press the throttle fully down and check the maximum speed.

Maximum Speed Setting:
4700RPM (LH Except Australia)
4900RPM (LH Australia)
5100RPM (LH Europe)
5150RPM (Exc Europe)
4700RPM (Hong Kong/Malaysia)
4900RPM (Except Hong Kong/Malaysia)

3. If the maximum speed is not as shown, disconnect the throttle linkage, cut the seal wire on the adjusting screw, loosen the lock nut on the maximum speed adjusting screw and adjust by turning the adjusting screw.

4. Check the idle speed setting and then raise the engine speed and recheck the maximum speed.

5. Retighten the lock nut, re-seal the adjusting screw, reconnect the throttle linkage and recheck the throttle linkage adjustment.

6. Remove the tachometer from the engine and replace any removed parts to the vehicle.

Refer to Idle Speed Diagram

Fuel Heater System Check

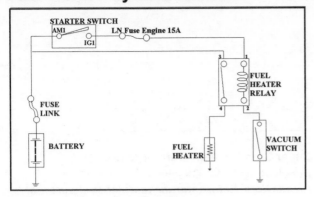

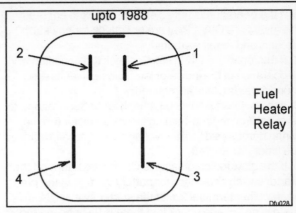

upto 1988

Fuel Heater Relay

Fuel Heater Check (1985-1988)

1. Check the fuel heater by recording the resistance between the connector terminals 1 and 2

Specified Resistance: 0.73±0.29ohms @ 20°c

If the resistance is not as showm, repair/replace as required.

Fuel Heater Check (1988 On)

1. Apply 38±6.7kpa or more to the vacuum switch port and with an ohmmeter record the resistance between terminal 1 and switch body

Specified Resistance: 0.7 ohms @ 20°c

If the resistance is not as shown, repair/replace as required.

Vacuum Switch Check (1985-1988)

1. With an ohmmeter check there is no continuity between the switch terminal and switch body.
2. Apply a vacuuum of 200±60mmHg or more to the vacuum switch and check that there is continuity between the switch terminal and body.
3. If the operation is not as shown, repair/replace as required.

Vacuum Switch Check (1988 On)

1. With an ohmmeter check there is no continuity between the switch terminal 1 and switch body.
If the resistance is not as shown, repair/replace as required.
2. Apply a vacuum of 38±6.7kpa or more to the vacuum port and check that there is continuity between the switch terminal 1 and body.
If the operation is not as shown, repair/replace as required.

Fuel Heater Relay (1985-1988)

1. Remove the relay (located in the engine bay relay box) and check for continuity between terminals 1-2 (ensure continuity exists), and between terminals 3-4 (ensure continuity does not exist).
2. Apply battery voltage between the 1-2 terminals and ensure continuity exists between the 3-4 terminals.'
If the operation is not as shown, repair/replace as required.

Fuel Heater Relay (1988 On)

1. Remove the relay (located under the instrument panel in the relay block and check for continuity between terminals 1-3 (ensure continuity exists), and between terminals 2-4 (ensure continuity does not exist).

2. Apply battery voltage between the 1-3 terminals and ensure continuity exists between the 2-4 terminals.'
If the operation is not as shown, repair/replace as required.

Pre-Heating System Checks

Super Glow System (Europe 1985-1988)

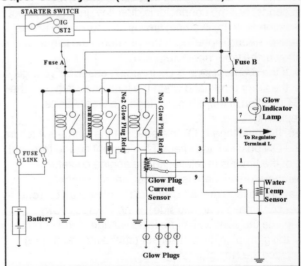

Pre-Heating Timer Check

Please Note: Before starting test please ensure that the battery is fully charged, the engine cranks normally and that all the fuse links are OK.
The timer unit is located Under the Instrument Panel Centre (LH Models)

1. Check if the glow indicator lamp lights up when the starter switch is ON, (Coolant Temp is 20°c and lamp lights up for 2 seconds).

2. If the operation is not as shown, check to ensure that the fuse/s are OK, if they are not check for any short circuit/s and repair as required.

3. If the fuses are OK in step2, check the condition and/ or operation of the indicator lamp globe, if faults are found repair/replace as required.

4. If the bulb is Ok in step3, check for battery voltage to terminal 7 on the pre-heating timer connector (on the wiring harness side), if the voltage is Ok, repair/replace the timer as required.

5. If the glow indicator lamp is OK in step1, turn off the starter switch and check for battery voltage at the pre-heater timer terminal 2 with the starter switch ON, if there is no voltage check that there is 0v between the terminals 3 and 9, if the voltage is OK, replace the timer, if the voltage is not OK, repair/replace the glow plug current sensor.

6. If the voltage in step5 is Ok, check the the voltage to the pre-heat timer terminal 2 is terminated, if it is not, start the engine and check for voltage present at terminal 4 of the pre heating timer, if the voltage is Ok, replace the timer, if the voltage is not Ok, repair fault/s in the vehicle charging system.

7. If the voltage is terminated in step6, turn off the starter switch, then turn on again and check for voltage to the glow plug (a few seconds later the the voltage should drop by about 1/2), if there is no voltage at all replace the timer.

8. If the pre heating time is a lot different from what was shown in step7, disconnect the water temperature sensor (situated at the LH Side Rear of the Engine), and check that the pre-heating duration is about 150 seconds, or if the connector is directley grounded about 3 seconds. If the pre-heat time is as shown, the water sensor needs replacing, if the pre heat time is not as shown, the timer needs replacing.

9. If the pre-heat time is Ok in step7, check for voltage at the timer terminal 8 when the ignition switch is in the ST position, if there is no voltage the timer needs replacing.

10. If the voltage is Ok in step9, put the starter switch in the ON position and check if the current flow to terminal 8 of the timer is in relation to the engine coolant temperature, if there is no voltage at all, check for battery voltage at the (+) side of the glow plug current sensor (intake manifold side), if the voltage is Ok replace the sensor. If there is no voltage at the (+) side of the glow plug current sensor (intake manifold side) replace the No1 glow plug relay.

11. If the voltage in step10 is OK to start with but then there is no 1/2 voltage after a short time, check for battery voltage at the (+) side of the resistor (intake manifold side), if the voltage is Ok, replace the resistor, if there is no voltage present at the (+) side of the resistor (intake manifold side) replace the No2 glow plug relay.

12. If the current flow is OK in step10, check the glow plug/s for continuity, if faults are found repair/replace as required.

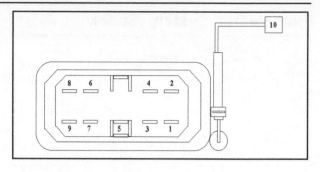

Super Glow System (Europe 1988 On)
Pre-Heating Timer Check
Please Note: Before starting test please ensure that the battery is fully charged, the engine cranks normally and that all the fuse links are OK.
The timer unit is located in under the instrument panel on the LH side (LH)

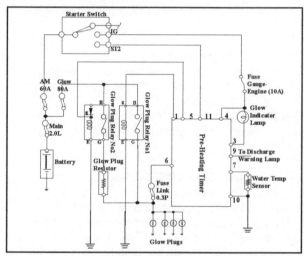

1. Check if the glow indicator lamp lights up when the starter switch is ON, (Coolant Temp is 20°c and lamp lights up for 2-3 seconds).

2. If the operation is not as shown, check to ensure that the fuse/s are OK, if they are not check for any short circuit/s and repair as required.

3. If the fuses are OK in step2, check the condition and/ or operation of the indicator lamp globe, if faults are found repair/replace as required.

4. If the bulb is Ok in step3, check for battery voltage to terminal 3 on the pre-heating timer connector (on the wiring harness side), if the voltage is Ok, repair/replace the timer as required.

5. If the glow indicator lamp is OK in step1, turn off the starter switch and check for battery voltage at the pre-heater timer terminal 1 with the starter switch ON, if there is no voltage check that there is 1v or less to terminal 9, if the voltage is OK, replace the timer.

6. If the voltage in step5 is Ok, check the the voltage to the pre-heat timer terminal 1 is terminated after the engine has started, if it is not, start the engine and check for voltage present at terminal 9 of the pre heating timer, if the voltage is Ok, replace the timer, if the voltage is not Ok, repair fault/s in the vehicle charging system.

7. If the voltage is terminated in step6, turn off the starter switch and then turn on again and check for current flow to terminal 5 of the timer in relation to the coolant temperature.

Current Flow: 16-26seconds @ less than 50°c

Current Flow: 1.7seconds @ more than 50°c

If there is no voltage at all replace the timer.

8. If the pre heating time is a lot different from what was shown in step7, the timer is faulty and should be replaced.

9. If the pre-heat time is Ok in step7, check for voltage at the timer terminal 8 when the ignition switch is in the ST position, if there is no voltage the timer needs replacing.

10. If the voltage is Ok in step9, put the starter switch in the ON position and check for voltage at the timer terminal 5 when the starter switch is at "Start", if there is no voltage at all replace the timer.

11. If the voltage in step10 is OK , switch off the ignition, switch ON the ignition and check for voltage to the glow plugs with coolant temperature a 50°c or less) a few seconds after (the voltage should drop by half). If there is no voltage at all, check for battery voltage at the (+) side of the glow plug resistor, if there is no voltage present at the (+) side of the resistor replace the No1 glow plug relay.

12. If the voltage in step11 remains at battery voltage or drops to 0v, check for battery voltage at the (+) side of the glow plug resistor, if the voltage is Ok, replace the resistor, if there is no voltage present at the (+) side of the resistor replace the No2 glow plug relay.

13. If the voltage is OK in step12, check the glow plug/s resistance, if the reading is infinity, repair/replace as required, if the reading is about 0ohms, the glow plugs are OK.

Pre Heating Timer Operation Check (1988 On)
The timer unit is located in under the instrument panel on the LH side (LH Models)

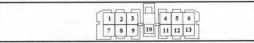

1. Disconnect the connector from the timer and check the connector harness as shown in the chart below.

Check For	Between Terminals	Condition	Specified Value
Continuity	1-ground	Continuity	
Voltage	3-ground	Starter Switch OFF	No volts
Voltage	3-ground	Starter Switch ON	Battery volts
Voltage	4-ground	Starter Switch OFF	No volts
Voltage	4-ground	Starter Switch ON	Battery volts
Continuity	5-ground	Continuity	
Continuity	6-ground	Continuity	
Continuity	7-ground	Continuity	
Continuity	10-ground	Continuity	
Voltage	11-ground	Starter Switch OFF	No volts
Voltage	11-ground	Starter Switch Start	Battery volts

No1 Glow Plug Relay Check (1985 On)
Please Note: The relay is located In the engine compartment on the LH side (LH Models).

1. With an ohmmeter check the continuity between the terminals 1-2 and ensure that it exists, check between terminals 3-4 and ensure that it does not exist.

2. Apply battery volts between terminals 1-2 and ensure that continuity exists between terminals 3-4

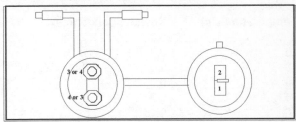

No2 Glow Plug Relay Check (1985 On)
Please Note: The relay is located Under the instrument panel on RH Side (LH Models).

1. With an ohmmeter check the continuity between the terminals 1-2 and ensure that it exists, check between terminals 3-4 and ensure that it does not exist.

2. Apply battery volts between terminals 1-2 and ensure that continuity exists between terminals 3-4

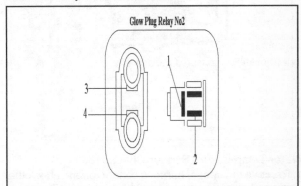

Glow Plug Check (1985 On)

1. With an ohmmeter check that there is continuity between the glow plug terminal and ground, if continuity does not exist, replace the faulty glow plug/s

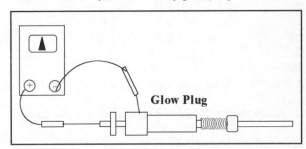

Glow Plug Sensor Check (1985 On)

1. With an ohmmeter check that there is continuity between the sensor terminals, if no continuity exists replace the sensor.

Glow Plug Resistor Check (1985-1988)

1. With an ohmmeter check that there is continuity between the resistor terminals, if no continuity exists replace the sensor.

Water Temperature Sensor Check (1985-1988)

1-Remove the sensor harness connector and check the resistance between the sensor terminals at varying temperatures

Temperature (°c)	Resistance (k/ohms)
0	5.0
20	2.3
40	1.0
60	0.55
80	0.3
100	0.18

2. If the resistance is not as shown, repair/replace as required.

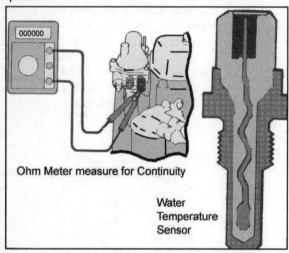

Ohm Meter measure for Continuity

Water Temperature Sensor

Water Temperature Sensor Check (1988 On)

1. Remove the sensor harness connector and check the resistance between the sensor terminals at varying temperatures.

Sensor Temperature (°c)	Sensor Resistance (k/ohms)
0	5.0
20	2.0
40	1.0
60	0.4
80	0.14
100	0.08

2. If the resistance is not as shown, repair/replace as required.

Refer to previous water temp sensor diagram

Main Relay Check (1985-1988)

Please Note: This relay is located under the instrument panel in the relay box (LH Models)

1. With an ohmmeter check the continuity between the terminals 1-3 and ensure that it exists, check between terminals 2-4 and ensure that it does not exist.

2. Apply battery volts between terminals 1-3 and ensure that continuity exists between terminals 2-4

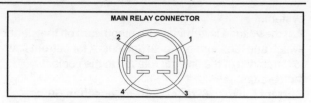

MAIN RELAY CONNECTOR

Pre-Heating System Checks
Variable Delay System

Pre-Heat Timer Check (1985-1988 Except Europe)
The timer unit is located Under the Instrument Panel Centre

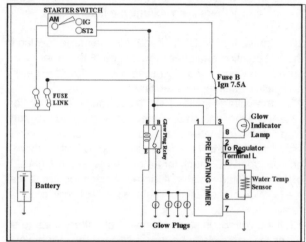

1. Put the starter switch to the ON position and record the lighting up time of the glow indicator lamp
Specified Glow Time: 9-15 seconds @ 20°c
2. Check that there is voltage at terminal 1 on the pre-heating timer when the starter switch is on the ON position.
3. If the operation is not as shown, repair/replace as required.

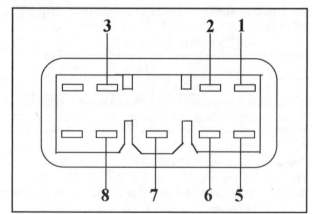

Pre-Heat Timer Check (Variable Delay System Australia 1988 ON)
The timer unit is located in under the instrument panel on the LH side

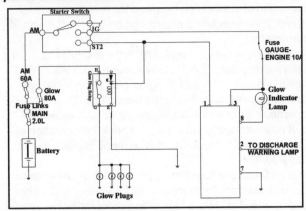

1. Disconnect the connector from the timer and check the connector harness as shown in the chart below.

Check For	Between Terminals	Condition	Specified Value
Voltage	1-ground	Starter Switch OFF	No volts
Voltage	1-ground	Starter Switch Start	Battery volts
Voltage	3-ground	Starter Switch OFF	No volts
Voltage	3-ground	Starter Switch ON	Battery volts
Continuity	7-ground		Continuity
Voltage	8-ground	Starter Switch OFF	No volts
Voltage	8-ground	Starter Switch Start	Battery volts

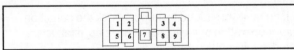

Glow Indicator Lamp Check (1988 On)
1. Turn the ignition switch to "Start" and check the lamp light up time.
Lamp Light Up Time: Approx 5 seconds

Glow Plug Relay
Please Note: The relay is located Under the Instrument Panel Centre (LH Models)
1. With an ohmmeter check the continuity between the terminals 3-4 and ensure that it exists, check between terminals 1-2 and ensure that it does not exist.
2. Apply battery volts between terminals 3-4 and ensure that continuity exists between terminals 1-2
Refer Previous Glow Plug Relay Connector Diagrams

Glow Plug Check
1. With an ohmmeter check that there is continuity between the glow plug terminal and ground, if continuity does not exist, replace the faulty glow plug/s
Refer Previous Glow Plug Diagrams

Water Temperature Sensor Check (1985-1988)
1. Remove the sensor harness connector and check the resistance between the sensor terminals at varying temperatures.

Sensor Temperature (°c)	Sensor Resistance (k/ohms)
0	5.0
20	2.3
40	1.0
60	0.55
80	0.3
100	0.18

2. If the resistance is not as shown, repair/replace as required.
Refer Previous Water Temp Sensor Diagrams

Pre-Heating System Checks Fixed Delay System

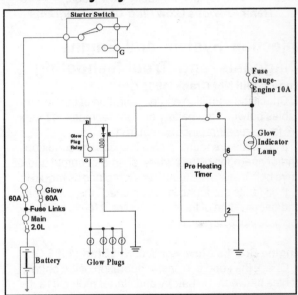

Pre-Heat Timer Check (Except Europe/Australia 1988 On)
The timer unit is located in under the instrument panel on the LH side
1. Disconnect the connector from the timer and check the connector harness as shown in the chart below

Check For	Between Terminals	Condition	Specified Value
Continuity	2-ground		Continuity
Voltage	5-ground	Starter Switch OFF	No volt
Voltage	5-ground	Starter Switch Glow	Battery volts
Voltage	6-ground	Starter Switch OFF	No volts
Voltage	6-ground	Starter Switch Glow	Battery volts

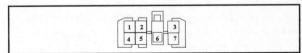

Glow Indicator Lamp Check (1988 On)
1. Turn the ignition switch to "Start" and check the lamp light up time.
Lamp Light Up Time: Approx 15.19.5seconds

Glow Plug Relay Check (LH Models 1988 On).
Please Note: The relay is located in the engine compartment on the rear side
1. With an ohmmeter check the continuity between the terminals 3-4 and ensure that it exists, check between terminals 1-2 and ensure that it does not exist.
2. Apply battery volts between terminals 3-4 and ensure that continuity exists between terminals 1-2
Refer Previous Glow Plug Relay Diagrams

Glow Plug Check (1988 On)
1. With an ohmmeter check that there is continuity between the glow plug terminal and ground, if continuity does not exist, replace the faulty glow plug/s
Refer Previous Glow Plug Check Diagrams

Injection System and Engine Diagnosis and Troubleshooting
Engine Will Not Crank (1985 On)
1. Check the condition and/or operation of the battery cables between the battery and starter motor, if faults are found repair/replace as required.
2. If no faults are found in step1, check the condition and/or operation of the battery, alternator output and/or drive belt, if faults are found repair/replace as required.
3. If no faults are found in step2, check the condition and/or operation of the starter motor, if faults are found repair/replace as required.

Engine Cranks Slowly or Will Not Start (1985 On)
1. Check the condition and/or operation of the battery cables between the battery and starter motor, if faults are found repair/replace as required.
2. If no faults are found in step1, check the condition and/or operation of the battery, alternator output and/or drive belt, if faults are found repair/replace as required.
3. If no faults are found in step2, check that the correct grade of engine oil is being used on the vehicle, if not draon and replace with the correct grade of oil.

Engine Cranks Normally But Does Not Start (1985-1988)
1. If the engine cranks normally but does not start, check and ensure that fuel is reaching the injection nozzles by loosening any of the injection pipes, cranking the engine and ensuring that fuel is coming out of the pipe.
2. If fuel is not coming out of the pipe in step1, check the operation of the fuel cut solenoid, if faults are found repair/replace as required.
3. If no faults are found in step3, check to ensure that fuel is getting to the injection pump by disconnecting the inlet hoses from the fuel filter, feeding clean fuel from a

separate container directly into the injection pump. If the engine now starts there may be blockages in the fuel filter and/or line between the fuel tank and fuel filter. If the engine does not start, check the condition and/or operation of the fuel line between the fuel filter and fuel pump. If the injection pump operation is normal it should be replaced.
4. If fuel is present in step1, check the pre-heating operation system operation by ensuring that after the ignition is turned on and the glow plug lamp lights up, that there are 6v applied to the glow plugs, if the operation is not as shown, repair/replace as required.
5. If no faults are found in step4, check the operation of the glow plug/s, if faults are found repair/replace as required.
6. If no faults are found in step5, check the fuel system pipes, hoses and/or components for leaks, cracks and/or damage, if faults are found repair/replace as required.
7. If no faults are found in step6, check the injection timing by setting either the No1 or No4 piston at TDC, releasing the cold start advance systen (where fitted) and checking the plunger stroke.
Injection Plunger Stroke:
   1.06-1.22mm (2L Engine without ACSD Control)
Injection Plunger Stroke:
   0.82-0.98mm (2L Engine with ACSD Control)
If the timing setting is not as shown, adjust to suit.
8. If no faults are found in step7, check the fast idle system operation, if faults are found repair/replace as required.
9. If no faults are found in step8, check the condition and/or operation of the injection nozzles, if faults are found repair/replace as required.

Engine Cranks Normally But Does Not Start (1988 On)
1. If the engine cranks normally but does not start, check and ensure that fuel is reaching the injection nozzles by loosening any of the injection pipes, cranking the engine and ensuring that fuel is coming out of the pipe.
2. If fuel is not coming out of the pipe in step1, check the operation of the fuel cut solenoid, if faults are found repair/replace as required.
3. If no faults are found in step3, check to ensure that fuel is getting to the injection pump by disconnecting the inlet hoses from the fuel filter, feeding clean fuel from a separate container directly into the injection pump. If the engine now starts there may be blockages in the fuel filter and/or line between the fuel tank and fuel filter. If the engine does not start, check the condition and/or operation of the fuel line between the fuel filter and fuel pump. If the injection pump operation is normal it should be replaced.
4. If fuel is present in step1, check the pre-heating operation system operation by ensuring that after the ignition is turned on, the glow plug lamp lights up and that there are 6v applied to the glow plugs, if the operation is not as shown, repair/replace as required.

5-If no faults are found in step4, check the operation of the glow plug/s, if faults are found repair/replace as required.

6-If no faults are found in step5, check the fuel system pipes, hoses and/or components for leaks, cracks and/or damage, if faults are found repair/replace as required.

7-If no faults are found in step6, check the injection timing by setting either the No1 or No4 piston at TDC, releasing the cold start advance systen (where fitted) and checking the plunger stroke.

Injection Plunger Stroke:
0.84-0.96mm (Without ACSD Control)
Injection Plunger Stroke:
0.54-0.66mm (With ACSD Control)

If the timing setting is not as shown, adjust to suit.

8-If no faults are found in step7, **(With ACSD Control Only),** check the cold start advance and fast idle system operation, if faults are found repair/replace as required.

9-If no faults are found in step7and/or 8, check the condition and/or operation of the injection nozzles, if faults are found repair/replace as required.

Idle Speed is Unstable When The Engine is Warm (1985-1988)

1-If the idle speed is unstable when the engine is warm, check the condition and/or operation of the throttle cable and/or linkages, if faults are found repair/replace as required.

2-If no faults are found in step1, check the engine idle speed setting.

Idle Speed:	**700RPM (Manual)**
Idle Speed:	**800RPM (Auto)**

3-If no faults are found in step2, check the fuel system components and/or lines for leaks and/or damage, if faults are found repair/replace as required.

4-If no faults are found in step3, check the injection timing by setting either the No1 or No4 piston at TDC, releasing the cold start advance systen (where fitted) and checking the plunger stroke.

Injection Plunger Stroke:
1.06-1.22mm (2L Engine without ACSD Control)
Injection Plunger Stroke:
0.82-0.98mm (2L Engine with ACSD Control)

If the timing setting is not as shown, adjust to suit.

5-If no faults are found in step4, check the operation of the injection nozzle/s and/or the delivery valve by letting the engine run at idle speed, loosening the union nuts on each of the cylinders in order and check if there is any change of idle speed. If there is no change at any of the cylinders this will indicate that a faulty cylinder/s is present. To fix the problem check the injection nozzle pressure.

Injection Nozzle Pressure: 10,297-12,258kpa

If the pressure is not as shown adjust pressure to suit. If the pressure is OK, the fault will be with the delivery valve and should be replaced.

6-If no faults are found in step5, check to ensure that fuel is getting to the injection pump by disconnecting the inlet hoses from the fuel filter, feeding clean fuel from a separate container directly into the injection pump. If the engine now starts there may be blockages in the fuel filter and/or line between the fuel tank and fuel filter. If the engine does not start, check the condition and/or operation of the fuel line between the fuel filter and fuel pump. If the injection pump operation is normal it should be replaced.

Idle Speed is Unstable When The Engine is Warm (1988 On)

1-If the idle speed is unstable when the engine is warm, check the condition and/or operation of the throttle cable and/or linkages, if faults are found repair/replace as required.

2-If no faults are found in step1, check the engine idle speed setting.

Idle Speed:	**700RPM (Manual)**
Idle Speed:	**800RPM (Auto)**

If the idle speed setting is not as shown, adjust to suit

3-If no faults are found in step2, check the fuel system components and/or lines for leaks and/or damage, if faults are found repair/replace as required.

4-If no faults are found in step3, check the injection timing by setting either the No1 or No4 piston at TDC, releasing the cold start advance systen (where fitted) and checking the plunger stroke.

Injection Plunger Stroke:
0.84-0.96mm (Without ACSD Control)
Injection Plunger Stroke:
0.54-0.66mm (With ACSD Control)

If the timing setting is not as shown, adjust to suit.

5-If no faults are found in step4, check the operation of the injection nozzle/s and/or the delivery valve by letting the engine run at idle speed, loosening the union nuts on each of the cylinders in order and check if there is any change of idle speed. If there is no change at any of the cylinders this will indicate that a faulty cylinder/s is present. To fix the problem check the injection nozzle pressure.

Injection Nozzle Pressure: 14,200-1520kpa

If the pressure is not as shown adjust pressure to suit. If the pressure is OK, the fault will be with the delivery valve and should be replaced.

Engine Suddenly Stops (1985-1988)

1- If the engine is running and then suddenly stops check and ensure that fuel is reaching the injection nozzles by loosening any of the injection pipes, cranking the engine and ensuring that fuel is coming out of the pipe.

2-If fuel is not coming out of the pipe in step1, check the operation of the fuel cut solenoid, if faults are found repair/replace as required.

3-If no faults are found in step3, check to ensure that fuel is getting to the injection pump by disconnecting the inlet hoses from the fuel filter, feeding clean fuel from a separate container directly into the injection pump. If the engine now starts there may be blockages in the fuel filter and/or line between the fuel tank and fuel filter. If the engine does not start, check the condition and/or operation of the fuel line between the fuel filter and fuel pump. If the injection pump operation is normal it should be replaced.

4-If fuel is present in step1, check the pre-heating operation system operation by ensuring that after the ignition is turned on and the glow plug lamp lights up that there are 6v applied to the glow plugs, if the operation is not as shown, repair/replace as required.

5-If no faults are found in step4, check the operation of then glow plug/s, if faults are found repair/replace as required.

6-If no faults are found in step5, check the fuel system pipes, hoses and/or components for leaks, cracks and/or damage, if faults are found repair/replace as required.

7-If no faults are found in step6, check the injection timing by setting either the No1 or No4 piston at TDC, releasing the cold start advance systen (where fitted) and checking the plunger stroke.

Injection Plunger Stroke:
        1.06-1.22mm (2L Engine without ACSD Control)
Injection Plunger Stroke:
        0.82-0.98mm (2L Engine with ACSD Control)

If the timing setting is not as shown, adjust to suit.

8-If no faults are found in step7, check the fast idle system operation, if faults are found repair/replace as required.

9-If no faults are found in step8, check the condition and/or operation of the injection nozzles, if faults are found repair/replace as required.

Engine Suddenly Stops (1988 On)

1- If the engine is running and then suddenly stops, switch off the ignition and try and start the engine, if it does not re-start, check and ensure that fuel is reaching the injection nozzles by loosening any of the injection pipes, cranking the engine and ensuring that fuel is coming out of the pipe.

2-If fuel is not coming out of the pipe in step1, check the operation of the fuel cut solenoid, if faults are found repair/replace as required.

3-If no faults are found in step3, check to ensure that fuel is getting to the injection pump by disconnecting the inlet hoses from the fuel filter, feeding clean fuel from a separate container directly into the injection pump. If the engine now starts there may be blockages in the fuel filter and/or line between the fuel tank and fuel filter. If the engine does not start, check the condition and/or operation of the fuel line between the fuel filter and fuel pump. If the injection pump operation is normal it should be replaced.

4-If fuel is present in step1, check the pre-heating operation system operation by ensuring that after the ignition is turned on, the glow plug lamp lights up and that there are 6v applied to the glow plugs, if the operation is not as shown, repair/replace as required.

5-If no faults are found in step4, check the operation of then glow plug/s, if faults are found repair/replace as

required.

6-If no faults are found in step5, check the fuel system pipes, hoses and/or components for leaks, cracks and/or damage, if faults are found repair/replace as required.

7-If no faults are found in step6, check the injection timing by setting either the No1 or No4 piston at TDC, releasing the cold start advance systen (where fitted) and checking the plunger stroke.

Injection Plunger Stroke:
        0.84-0.96mm (Without ACSD Control)
Injection Plunger Stroke:
        0.54-0.66mm (With ACSD Control)

If the timing setting is not as shown, adjust to suit.

8-If no faults are found in step7, **(With ACSD Control Only),** check the cold start advance and fast idle system operation, if faults are found repair/replace as required.

9-If no faults are found in step7and/or 8, check the condition and/or operation of the injection nozzles, if faults are found repair/replace as required.

Engine Has a Lack of Power (1985-1988)

1-If the engine has any lack of power, press down the throttle fully and ensure that the adjusting lever is in contact with the maximum speed adjusting screw, if it is not adjust to suit.

2-If no faults are found in step1, start the engine, press the throttle down to the floor and check that the no load maximum RPM is OK, if it is not, adjust using the maximum speed adjusting screw.

3-If no faults are found in step2, ensure that the interchange overflow screw (Out) and the inlet (No Mark) are fitted in the correct positions, if not refit in correct positions.

4-If no faults are found in step3, check the fuel system components and/or lines for leaks and/or damage, if faults are found repair/replace as required.

5-If no faults are found in step4, disconnect the inlet hoses from the fuel filter and pour diesel fuel directly into the injection pump, if the condition now improves replace the fuel filter. If the condition does not improve after the fuel filter has been replaced, check the condition and/or operation of the priming pump, if faults are found repair/replace as required.

6-If no faults are found in step5, check the injection timing by setting either the No1 or No4 piston at TDC, releasing the cold start advance systen (where fitted) and checking the plunger stroke.

Injection Plunger Stroke:
        1.06-1.22mm (2L Engine without ACSD Control)
Injection Plunger Stroke:
        0.82-0.98mm (2L Engine with ACSD Control)

If the timing setting is not as shown, adjust to suit

7-If no faults are found in step6, check the injection nozzle pressure.

Injection Nozzle Pressure: 10,297-12,258kpa

If the pressure is not as shown adjust pressure to suit, if the pressure cannot be adjusted replace the faulty injector nozzle/s as required.

Excessive Exhaust Smoke (1985-1988)

1-Check the condition and/or operation of the alr cleaner element, if faults are found repair/replace as required.

2-If no faults are found in step1, check the engine oil consumption, if faults are found repair/replace as required.

3-If the oil consumption is OK in step2, check the injection timing by setting either the No1 or No4 piston at TDC, releasing the cold start advance systen (where fitted) and checking the plunger stroke.

Injection Plunger Stroke:
   1.06-1.22mm (2L Engine without ACSD Control)
Injection Plunger Stroke:
   0.82-0.98mm (2L Engine with ACSD Control)
If the timing setting is not as shown, adjust to suit.
(Please Note: If the exhaust smoke is black it tends to indicate that the timing is advanced and if the smoke is white that the timing is retarded).

4- If no faults are found in step3, disconnect the inlet hoses from the fuel filter and pour diesel fuel directly into the injection pump, if the condition now improves replace the fuel filter. If the condition does not improve after the fuel filter has been replaced, check the condition and/or operation of the priming pump, if faults are found repair/replace as required. *(Please Note: At between 2000-3000RPM a blocked fuel filter tends to make the exhaust smoke white).*

5- If no faults are found in step4, check the injection nozzle pressure.

Injection Nozzle Pressure: **10,297-12,258kpa**
If the pressure is not as shown adjust pressure to suit, if the pressure cannot be adjusted replace the faulty injector nozzle/s as required. *(Please Note: Excessive exhaust smoke is normally caused when the nozzle pressure is to low)*

Excessive Exhaust Smoke (1988 On)

1-Check the condition and/or operation of the alr cleaner element, if faults are found repair/replace as required.

2-If no faults are found in step1, check the engine oil consumption, if faults are found repair/replace as required.

3-If the oil consumption is OK in step2, check the injection timing by setting either the No1 or No4 piston at TDC, releasing the cold start advance systen (where fitted) and checking the plunger stroke.

Injection Plunger Stroke:
      0.84-0.96mm (Without ACSD Control)
Injection Plunger Stroke:
      0.54-0.66mm (With ACSD Control)
If the timing setting is not as shown, adjust to suit.
(Please Note: If the exhaust smoke is black it tends to indicate that the timing is advanced and if the smoke is white that the timing is retarded).

4- If no faults are found in step3, disconnect the inlet hoses from the fuel filter and pour diesel fuel directly into the injection pump, if the condition now improves replace the fuel filter. If the condition does not improve after the fuel filter has been replaced, check the condition and/or operation of the priming pump, if faults are found repair/replace as required. *(Please Note: At between 2000-3000RPM a blocked fuel filter tends to make the exhaust smoke white).*

5- If no faults are found in step4, check the check the injection nozzle pressure.

Injection Nozzle Pressure: **14,200-1520kpa**
If the pressure is not as shown adjust pressure to suit, if the pressure cannot be adjusted, replace the faulty nozzle/s. *(Please Note: Excessive exhaust smoke is normally caused when the nozzle pressure is to low)*

Fuel Consumption is Poor (1985-1988)

1-If the fuel consumption is poor, check the fuel system components and/or lines for leaks and/or damage, if faults are found repair/replace as required.

2-If no faults are found in step1, check the engine idle speed setting is correct.

Idle Speed: **700RPM (Manual)**
Idle Speed: **800RPM (Auto)**
If the idle speed setting is not correct adjust to suit.

3-If the idle speed setting is OK in step2, check the no load maximum speed setting is OK by starting the engine, pressing down the throttle pedal to the floor and checking the no load maximum speed setting.

No Load Maximum Speed Setting:
      4,900RPM 2L Engine
         (Except LS Model Hong Kong/Singapore)
No Load Maximum Speed Setting:
      4,500RPM 2L Engine
         (LS Model Hong Kong/Singapore)
If the setting is not OK, adjust using the maximum speed adjusting screw.

4-If no faults are found in step3, check the injection timing by setting either the No1 or No4 piston at TDC, releasing the cold start advance systen (where fitted) and checking the plunger stroke.

Injection Plunger Stroke:
   1.06-1.22mm (2L Engine without ACSD Control)
Injection Plunger Stroke:
   0.82-0.98mm (2L Engine with ACSD Control)
If the timing setting is not as shown, adjust to suit.

5- If no faults are found in step4, check the injection nozzle pressure.

Injection Nozzle Pressure: **10,297-12,258kpa**
If the pressure is not as shown adjust pressure to suit, if the pressure cannot be adjusted replace the faulty injector nozzle/s as required.

Fuel Consumption is Poor (1988 On)

1-If the fuel consumption is poor, check the fuel system components and/or lines for leaks and/or damage, if faults are found repair/replace as required.

2-If no faults are found in step1, with the engine running check the idle speed setting.

Idle Speed: **700RPM (Manual)**
Idle Speed: **800RPM (Auto)**
                Refer Previous Idle Speed Diagram
If the idle speed setting is not as shown, adjust to suit

3-If the idle speed setting is OK in step2, check the no load maximum speed setting is OK by starting the engine, pressing down the throttle pedal to the floor and checking the no load maximum speed setting.

Maximum Speed Setting:
- 4700RPM (LH Except Australia)
- 4900RPM (LH Australia)
- 5100RPM (LH Europe)
- 5150RPM (Exc Europe)
- 4700RPM (Hong Kong/Malaysia)
- 4900RPM (Except Hong Kong/Malaysia)

If the setting is not OK, adjust using the maximum speed adjusting screw.

4-If no faults are found in step3, check the injection timing by setting either the No1 or No4 piston at TDC, releasing the cold start advance systen (where fitted) and checking the plunger stroke.

Injection Plunger Stroke:
0.84-0.96mm (Without ACSD Control)
Injection Plunger Stroke:
0.54-0.66mm (With ACSD Control)

If the timing setting is not as shown, adjust to suit.

5- If no faults are found in step4, check the check the injection nozzle pressure.

Injection Nozzle Pressure: 14,200-1520kpa

If the pressure is not as shown adjust pressure to suit, if the pressure cannot be adjusted, replace the faulty nozzle/s.

Noise When The Engine Is Warm (1985-1988)

1-If the engine is noisey when it is warm, first check the operation of the temperature gauge if that is Ok, check the operation of the thermostat if faults are found repair/replace as required.

2-If no faults are found in step1, check the injection timing by setting either the No1 or No4 piston at TDC, releasing the cold start advance systen (where fitted) and checking the plunger stroke.

Injection Plunger Stroke:
1.06-1.22mm (2L Engine without ACSD Control)
Injection Plunger Stroke:
0.82-0.98mm (2L Engine with ACSD Control)

If the timing setting is not as shown, adjust to suit.

3- If no faults are found in step2, check the injection nozzle pressure.

Injection Nozzle Pressure: 10,297-12,258kpa

If the pressure is not as shown adjust pressure to suit, if the pressure cannot be adjusted replace the faulty injector nozzle/s as required.

Noise When The Engine Is Warm (1988 On)

If the engine is noisey when it is warm, first check the operation of the temperature gauge if that is Ok, check the operation of the thermostat if faults are found repair/replace as required.

2-If no faults are found in step1, check the injection timing by setting either the No1 or No4 piston at TDC, releasing the cold start advance systen (where fitted) and checking the plunger stroke.

Injection Plunger Stroke: 0.84-0.96mm (Without ACSD Control)
Injection Plunger Stroke: 0.54-0.66mm (With ACSD Control)

If the timing setting is not as shown, adjust to suit.

3- If no faults are found in step2, check the check the injection nozzle pressure.

Injection Nozzle Pressure: 14,200-1520kpa

If the pressure is not as shown adjust pressure to suit, if the pressure cannot be adjusted, replace the faulty nozzle/s.

Engine Will Not Return to Idle (1985 On)

1-Operate the adjusting lever on top of the injection pump and ensure that the engine returns to normal idle speed, if it does the throttle cable is binding or not adjusted correctly and needs fixing.

2-If the engine does not return to idle in step1, the injection pump is faulty and needs replacing.

Engine Will Not Shut Off With The Key (1985 On)

1-Check the fuel cut solenoid operation by disconnecting the connector on top of the fuel cut solenoid and check if the engine stops, if it does the starter switch is faulty and needs repairing and/or replacing.

2-If the engine does not stop in step1, either the fuel cut solenoid is faulty or the solenoid is blocked, if required repair/replace as required.

Diesel System Electrical Diagnosis

Engine Will Not Start When Cold (1985-1988)
Please Note: Before starting test please ensure that the battery is fully charged, the engine cranks normally and that all the fuse links are OK.

1-Check if the glow indicator lamp lights up when the starter switch is ON, **(Coolant Temp is 20°c and lamp lights up for 2 seconds).**

2-If the operation is not as shown, check to ensure that the fuse/s are OK, if they are not check for any short circuit/s and repair as required.

3-If the fuses are OK in step2, check the condition and/or operation of the indicator lamp globe, if faults are found repair/replace as required.

4-If the bulb is Ok in step3, check for battery voltage to terminal 7 on the pre-heating timer connector (on the wiring harness side), if the voltage is Ok, repair/replace the timer as required.

5-If the glow indicator lamp is OK in step1, turn off the starter switch and check for battery voltage at the pre-heater timer terminal 2 with the starter switch ON, if there is no voltage check that there is 0v between the terminals 3 and 9, if the voltage is OK, replace the timer, if the voltage is not OK, repair/replace the glow plug current sensor.

6-If the voltage in step5 is Ok, check the the voltage to the pre-heat timer terminal 2 is terminated, if it is not, start the engine and check for voltage present at terminal 4 of the pre heating timer, if the voltage is Ok, replace the timer, if the voltage is not Ok, repair fault/s in the vehicle charging system.

7-If the voltage is terminated in step6, turn off the starter switch, turn on again and check for voltage to the glow plug (a few seconds later the the voltage should drop by about 1/2). If there is no voltage at all replace the timer.

8-If the pre heating time is a lot different from what was shown in step7, disconnect the water temperature sensor (situated at the LH Side Rear of the Engine), and check that the pre-heating duration is about 150 seconds or if the connector is directley grounded about 3 seconds, if the pre-heat time is as shown, the water sensor needs replacing, if the pre heat time is not as shown, the timer needs replacing.

9-If the pre-heat time is Ok in step7, check for voltage at the timer terminal 8 when the ignition switch is in the ST position, if there is no voltage the timer needs replacing.

10-If the voltage is Ok in step9, put the starter switch in the ON position and check if the current flow to terminal 8 of the timer is in relation to the engine coolant temperature, if there is no voltage at all, check for battery voltage at the (+) side of the glow plug current sensor (intake manifold side), if the voltage is Ok replace the sensor. If there is no voltage at the (+) side of the glow plug current sensor (intake manifold side) replace the No1 glow plug relay.

11-If the voltage in step10 is OK to start with but then there is no 1/2 voltage after a short time, check for battery voltage at the (+) side of the resistor (intake manifold side), if the voltage is Ok, replace the resistor, if there is no voltage present at the (+) side of the resistor (intake manifold side) replace the No2 glow plug relay.

12-If the current flow is OK in step10, check the glow plug/s for continuity, if faults are found repair/replace as required.

Engine Will Not Start When Cold
Super Glow System (LH Models for Europe 1988 On)

Please Note: Before starting test please ensure that the battery is fully charged, the engine cranks normally and that all the fuse links are OK.
The timer unit is located in under the instrument panel on the LH side (LH)

1-Check if the glow indicator lamp lights up when the starter switch is ON, **(Coolant Temp is 20°c and lamp lights up for 2-3 seconds).**

2-If the operation is not as shown, check to ensure that the fuse/s are OK, if they are not check for any short circuit/s and repair as required.

3-If the fuses are OK in step2, check the condition and/or operation of the indicator lamp globe, if faults are found repair/replace as required.

4-If the bulb is Ok in step3, check for battery voltage to terminal 3 on the pre-heating timer connector (on the wiring harness side), if the voltage is Ok, repair/replace the timer as required.

5-If the glow indicator lamp is OK in step1, turn off the starter switch and check for battery voltage at the pre-heater timer terminal 1 with the starter switch ON, if there is no voltage check that there is 1v or less to terminal 9, if the voltage is OK, replace the timer.

6-If the voltage in step5 is Ok, check the the voltage to the pre-heat timer terminal 1 is terminated after the engine has started, if it is not, start the engine and check for voltage present at terminal 9 of the pre heating timer, if the voltage is Ok, replace the timer, if the voltage is not Ok, repair fault/s in the vehicle charging system.

7-If the voltage is terminated in step6, turn off the starter switch and then turn on again and check for cuurent flow to terminal 5 of the timer in relation to the coolant temperature.

Current Flow: **16-26seconds @ less than 50°c**
Current Flow: **1.7seconds @ more than 50°c**

If there is no voltage at all replace the timer.

8-If the pre heating time is a lot different from what was shown in step7, the timer is faulty and should be replaced.

9-If the pre-heat time is Ok in step7, check for voltage at the timer terminal 8 when the ignition switch is in the ST position, if there is no voltage the timer needs replacing.

10-If the voltage is Ok in step9, put the starter switch in the ON position and check for voltage at the timer terminal 5 when the starter switch is at "Start", if there is no voltage at all replace the timer.

11-If the voltage in step10 is OK , switch off the ignition, switch ON the ignition and check for voltage to the glow plugs with coolant temperature a 50°c or less) a few seconds after (the voltage should drop by half). If there is no voltage at all, check for battery voltage at the (+) side of the glow plug resistor, if there is no voltage present at the (+) side of the resistor replace the No1 glow plug relay.

12-If the voltage in step11 remains at battery voltage or drops to 0v, check for battery voltage at the (+) side of the glow plug resistor, if the voltage is Ok, replace the resistor, if there is no voltage present at the (+) side of the resistor replace the No2 glow plug relay.

13-If the voltage is OK in step12, check the glow plug/s resistance, if the reading is infinity, repair/replace as required, if the reading is about 0ohms, the glow plugs are OK.

Fuel Cut Solenoid Operation Check (1985 On)

1-Put the starter switch into the ON position and check for an operating noise from the solenoid while repeatedly connecting and disconnecting the solenoid, if a noise is heard the solenoid is OK.

2-If the solenoid noise is not heard, check the condition and/or operation of the relevant fuse, if faults are found repair/replace as required.

3-If the fuse is OK in step2, apply battery volts to the solenoid and check for a noise, if a noise can be heard, check the condition of the harness between the fuse A and the fuel cut solenoid, if faults are found repair/replace as required.

4-If no noise can be heard in step3, replace the fuel cut solenoid.

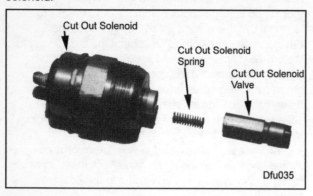

Dfu035

VEHICLE SERVICE INFORMATION
Vehicle Filling Capacities
Engine Oil with Filter: .... 5.8 Litres
Engine Oil without Filter: .... 4.8 Litres
Cooling System: .... 9.8 Litres (With Heater)
Manual Transmission: .... 2.2 Litres
Auto Transmission: .... 6.5Litres (Dry Fill)
Auto Transmission: .... 2.5Litres (Refill)
Rear Differential: .... 1.8 Litres

Vehicle Component Service Interval Changes
Check Valve Clearance:
>   Every 12Months/20,000kms

Engine Coolant/Anti Freeze:
>   Change Every 24 Months/40,000kms

Air Cleaner Element:
>   Change Every 60 Months/100,000kms

Fuel Filter:
>   Change Every 12 Months/20,000kms

Engine Oil:
>   Change Every 5,000kms

Engine Oil Filter:
>   Change Every 6 Months/10,000kms

Brake Fluid:
>   Change Every 24 Months/40,000kms

Manual Transmission Oil:
>   Change Every 18 Months/30,000kms

Auto Transmission Fluid:
>   Change Every 24 Months/40,000kms

Rear Differential Oil:
>   Change Every 18 Months/30,000kms

Front Wheel Bearings
>   Repack Every 12Months/20,000kms

Toyota Dyna LY61 Series 3L Engine 1988-1995

CONTENTS PAGE

CONTENTS PAGE

Toyota Dyna LY61Series
3L Engine 1988-1995

Engine Checks

Valve Clearance Check

Please Note: Before carrying out this check ensure that the engine is at normal operating temperature.

1. Remove the rocker cover, set the No1 piston to TDC on its compression stroke and ensure that the groove on the crankshaft pulley is lined up with the timing pointer on the front cover.

2. Ensure that the valve lifters on the No1 cylinder are loose and that the No4 valve lifters are tight (if they are not turn the engine on full turn (360°) and recheck).

3. Measure the valve clearances on the following valves 1&3 (Exhaust) and 1&2 (Inlet).

Inlet Valve Clearance:	**0.20-030mm (Cold)**
Exhaust Valve Clearance:	**0.40-0.50mm (Cold)**

If the clearances are not correct record the relevant readings to determine the adjusting shim required.

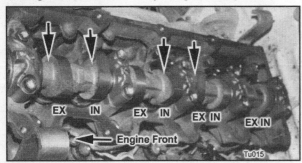

4. Turn the crankshaft one full turn (360°) and ensure that the groove on the crankshaft pulley is lined up with the timing pointer on the front cover.

5. Measure the valve clearances on the following valves 2&4 (Exhaust) and 3&4 (Inlet).

Inlet Valve Clearance:	**0.20-030mm (Cold)**
Exhaust Valve Clearance:	**0.40-0.50mm (Cold)**

If the clearances are not correct record the relevant readings to determine the adjusting shim required.

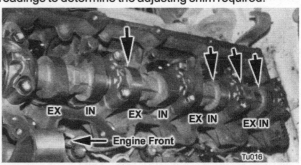

Compression Check

1. Run the engine to normal operating temperature, disconnect the fuel cut solenoid connector and remove all of the glow plugs from the engine.

2. Install and adapter and compression gauge to the No1 cylinder, fully open the throttle, crank the engine and record the compression pressure on each cylinder.

Compression Pressure:	**3138kpa**
Minimum Pressure:	**1961kpa**
Difference Between Each Cylinder:	**490kpa**

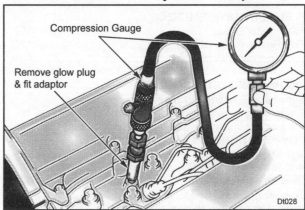

3. If the pressure on one or more cylinders is low, pour a small amount of oil into the cylinder through the glow plug hole and check the compression pressure again. If it helps the pressure there are possibly faults with the

piston rings or cylinder bores, if the oil does not help there may be a valve sticking or not seated correctly and/or leaks past the gasket.

Cylinder Head Tightening Procedures

1. After the cylinder head has been removed and the gasket replaced, apply a thin coat of oil to all of the cylinder head bolts. Install and gradually tighten each of the bolts to its correct torque in three stages in the sequence showed in the diagram.

Specified Torque Setting: **78Nm**
Please Note: If any of the bolts do not reach the correct torque, check the length of the bolts.

Short Bolt:	**107mm**
Long Bolt:	**127mm**

Replace any faulty bolts as required.

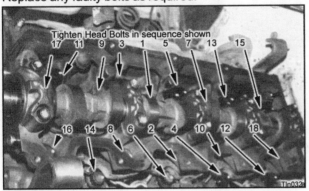

2. Mark the front of each bolt with some paint and then tighten the bolts a further 90°. After the sequence has been completed tighten the bolts a further 90° and now ensure that the paint mark is facing to the rear.

Piston Protrusion Height Check
No1 and 4 Piston Check

1. Rotate the engine and ensure that the timing marks on the crankshaft pulley line up with the marks on the front cover.
2. Fit a dial gauge to the engine block and set the gauge at the piston measuring point.
3. Find the point where the piston protrudes the most by turning the crankshaft in a clockwise and anti clockwise direction.

4. Set the dial gauge to zero and record the protrusion measurement from the block by sliding the dial gauge.

Protrusion Measurement: **0.68-0.97mm**
Please Note: Record the measurement at two separate measuring points.

No2 and No3 Piston Check

5. Turn the crankshaft 180° , Fit a dial gauge to the engine block and set the gauge at the piston measuring point.
6. Find the point where the piston protrudes the most by turning the crankshaft in a clockwise and anti clockwise direction.
7. Set the dial gauge to zero and record the protrusion measurement from the block by sliding the dial gauge.

Protrusion Measurement: **0.68-0.97mm**
Please Note: Record the measurement at two separate measuring points.

8. When the measurement has been made, to select a new head gasket follow the procedures shown.
9. There are 3 different types of head gaskets marked either "B", "D" or "F", each of them a different thickness.

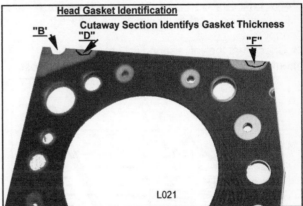

Piston Protrusion Measurements	Gasket Thickness	Gasket Grade
0.68-0.77	1.4-1.5mm	B
0.78-0.87	1.5-1.6	D
0.88-0.97	1.6-1.7	F

Please Note: When selecting the gasket use the largest measurement of the 8 readings that are recorded.

Oil Pressure Check
Test is on the next page

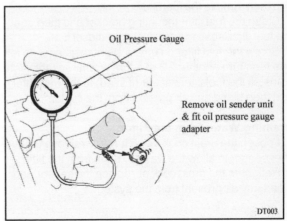

1. Ensure that the engine oil level is correct, if not top up to suit.

2. Remove the oil pressure switch from the engine and install a pressure gauge to the engine block.

3. Start the engine and run to normal operating temperature and then record the oil pressure shown on the gauge.

Specified Oil Pressure: **29kpa @ Idle**

Specified Oil Pressure: **294-539kpa @ 3000RPM**

4. If the oil pressure is not as shown, repair/replace as required.

Cooling System Thermostat Check

1. Remove the thermostat from the engine and put into a suitable container of water.

2. Heat the water gradually and check the valve opening temperature and valve lift.

Valve Opening Temperature: **86-90°c**

Valve Lift: **More than 8mm**

If the operation is not as shown above replace the thermostat.

3. Check that the valve spring is tight when the thermostat is fully closed, if not replace the thermostat.

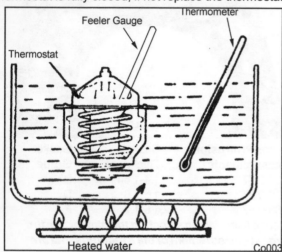

Co003

Fuel Filter Check and Replacement

1. Remove the fuel filter sensor (if fitted), drain the fuel and then remove the fuel filter.

2. Clean the fuel filter mounting bracket and then coat the fuel filter-sealing ring with some diesel fuel.

3. Screw the fuel filter on until a slight resistance is felt and then turn another 2/3 of a turn or until suitably tight.

4. Install the fuel filter sensor (if fitted) to the new filter and then bleed any air present from the system.

Draining Water from the Filter

1. Loosen the drain cock 4 or 5 turns or remove the fuel filter sensor to allow the water to drain from the filter.

2. Retighten the drain cock or replace the sensor and bleed any air present from the system.

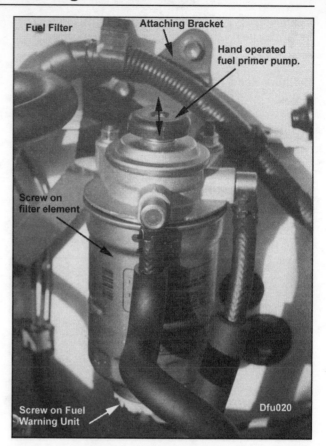

Dfu020

Fuel Filter Warning Lamp Check

1. Remove the switch from the filter and check that there is continuity between the terminals when the warning switch is ON (Float Up)

2. Check that there is no continuity between the terminals when the warning switch is OFF (Float Down)

3. If the operation is not as shown, repair/replace as required.

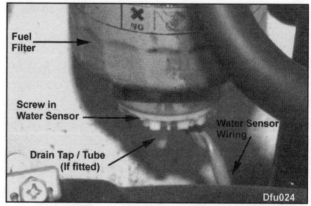

Dfu024

Injector Nozzle Check

1. Remove the injector from the vehicle, connect up to the pressure tester and check the initial pressure by pumping the tester handle a few times.

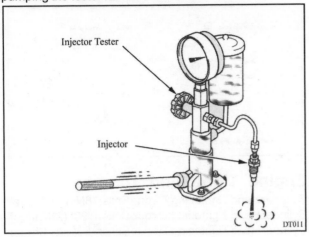

Initial Opening Pressure:
        14,220 to 15,593kpa (Used Nozzle)
 Initial Opening Pressure:
        14,808 to 15,593kpa (New Nozzle)

2. If the opening pressure is not as shown above, take the injector to pieces and change the adjusting shim on the top of the injector so as the correct pressure is recorded.

Adjusted Opening Pressure: 14,220-15,200kpa
Please Note: The adjusting shims vary in 0.025mm thicknesses, each 0.025mm will adjust the pressure by 341kpa. After the shim has been changed there should be no leakage from the injector (1988-1996) Please Note:

3. Maintain the pressure between 981-1961kpa below the opening pressure and check that there is no leakage from the injector for a period of 10seconds.

4. Check the spray pattern by pumping the pressure tester handle 4-6 times or more per second and check the injection spray pattern.

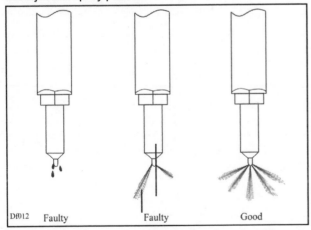

5. If the operation and/or spray pattern is not as shown, repair/replace the nozzle/s as required.

Timing Belt Removal and Replacement (1988-1995)

Removal Procedures

1. Remove the drive belts, water pump pulley, crankshaft pulley and the No1 timing cover.

2. Remove the timing belt guide, the current sensor and the 4 glow plugs.

3. Set the No1 piston to TDC on its compression stroke by temporarily replacing the crankshaft pulley bolt and turning the crankshaft in a clockwise direction until the timing mark on the camshaft gear lines up with the mark on the No2 timing belt cover.

Please Note: If the timing belt is being used again, before removing mark a direction arrow on the timing belt and place match marks on the pulleys and the belt.

4. Loosen the No1 idler pulley mount bolts and move to the left as far as it will go. Temporarily tighten the bolt, relieve the belt tension and remove the timing belt from the engine.

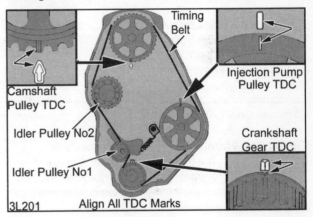

Replacement Procedures

Please Note: Before replacing the timing belt check the condition and/or operation of the timing belt pulleys, tensioner's and/or pulleys, if faults are found repair/replace as required.

1. Check the tensioner spring free length

Spring Free Length: 44.4-45.4mm

Check the tension of the spring at the specified free length

Installed Tension: 59Nm at 52.1mm

2. Install the crankshaft pulley to the engine, replace any pulleys or idlers that may have been removed for checking.

3. Set the No1 piston to TDC on its compression stroke and ensure that the timing marks on each of the pulleys line up with their relevant match marks.

4. Fit the timing belt onto the crankshaft pulley and No1 idler pulley, slightly turn the injection pulley in a clockwise direction, fit the timing belt onto the injection pulley and line up the marks on the injection pulley and timing belt case.

Please Note: Ensure that there is belt tension between the crankshaft timing pulley and injection pump drive pulleys.

5. Slightly turn the camshaft drive pulley in a clockwise direction, fit the timing belt onto the pulley and ensure that the marks on the pulley and timing belt case line up.

Please Note: Ensure that there is belt tension between the camshaft pulley and injection pump drive pulleys.

6. Install the timing belt to the No2 idler pulley.

7. Loosen the No1 idler pulley, stretch the timing belt and turn the crankshaft in a clockwise direction four full turns from TDC to TDC, ensuring that all of the timing marks on the drive pulleys line up with their respective match marks.

Please Note: If any of the marks do not line up, remove the belt and reinstall again.

8. Torque the No1 idler pulley bolt, refit the timing belt guide and replace any removed components in the reverse order of removal.

Timing Belt Replacement Torques

Injection Pump Drive Pulley Nut:	64Nm
No1 Idle Pulley (12mm Bolt):	19Nm
No1 Idle Pulley (14mm Bolt):	44Nm
No2 Idle Pulley:	33Nm
Crankshaft Pulley Bolt:	167Nm
Camshaft Gear Bolt:	98Nm

Timing Belt Warning Lamp Reset Procedures (Rubber Plug in the Instrument Cluster Glass)

1. Remove the grommet from the speedometer and turn off the lamp by pushing the warning lamp reset switch, then replace the grommet.

2. Start the engine and ensure that the light stays off.

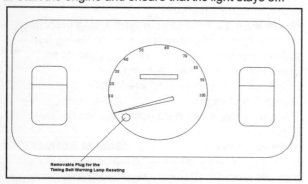

Timing Belt Warning Lamp Reset Procedures (Change Screw Position on the Back of the Instrument Cluster)

1. Remove the instrument cluster from the vehicle, connect terminals A&B shown in the diagrams and then remove the CHARGE fuse from the vehicle.

2. Turn the ignition switch to ON and check that the warning lights light up, if not the check the condition and/or operation of the globe.

3. Check the condition and/or operation of the reset

switches by checking that there is intermittent continuity between terminals A&B when the reset switch is pressed, if not repair/replace the speedometer/instrument cluster as required.

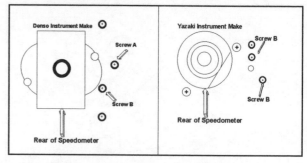

Engine Tightening Torques

Cylinder Head Tightening Torque Bolts:	78Nm (1st Stage)
Cylinder Head Tightening Torque Bolts:	.. 90° (2nd Stage)
Cylinder Head Tightening Torque Bolts:	. 90° (3rd Stage)
Camshaft Bearing Cap:	25Nm
Exhaust Manifold Bolts and Nuts:	52Nm
Inlet Manifold Bolts and Nuts:	24Nm
Glow Plugs:	13Nm
Injection Nozzle:	64Nm
Injection Pump Drive Pulley Nut:	64Nm
No1 Idle Pulley (12mm Bolt):	19Nm
No1 Idle Pulley (14mm Bolt):	44Nm
No2 Idle Pulley:	33Nm
Flywheel Bolts:	123Nm
Drive Plate:	98Nm
Connecting Rod Caps:	54Nm (1st Stage)
Connecting Rod Caps:	90° (2nd Stage)
Main Bearings:	103Nm
Crankshaft Pulley Bolt:	235Nm
Camshaft Gear Bolt:	98Nm
Oil Pump to Block:	23Nm
Oil Pump to Injection Pump:	21Nm
Oil Sump Bolt:	18Nm

System Adjustments

Injection Timing Adjustment

1. Remove the distributive head bolt, install a special tool (SST09275-54010 plunger stroke measuring tool) to

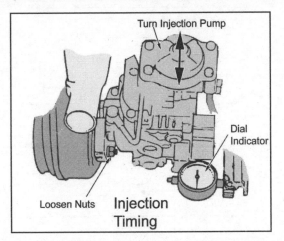

Turn Injection Pump

Dial Indicator

Loosen Nuts — **Injection Timing**

the plug hole and then set the No1 or No4 piston to 25° BTDC on its compression stroke.

2. *Please Note: (For vehicles with auto cold start device):* Using a screwdriver turn the cold start lever anti clockwise about 20° and put a metal plate 8.5-10.0mm between the cold start lever and the thermo wax plunger.

3. Set the dial indicator to zero (mm) and then ensure it stays at zero (mm) while the crankshaft pulley is being moved right to left slightly.

4. Slowly turn the crankshaft pulley until crankshaft pulley groove is lined up with the timing pointer and record the plunger movement.

Injection Plunger Stroke:
   0.54-0.66 (With Auto Cold Start Device)
Injection Plunger Stroke:
   0.84-0.96mm (Without Auto Cold Start Device)

5. If the plunger stroke measurement is not as shown, loosen the 4 injector pipe union nuts and inlet pipe union nuts on the injection pump side.

6. Loosen the 4 injection pump mounting nuts and adjust the plunger pump stroke by slightly tilting the injection pump body. If the stroke is less than shown tilt the pump towards the engine, if the plunger strike is more than shown tilt the pump away from the engine.

7. Retighten all of the fixing bolts and union nuts, recheck the plunger stroke and then remove the plate from the cold starting lever.

8. Remove the dial indicator gauge and replace the plug bolt. Restart the engine and check for any leaks in the system.

Idle Speed Check

1. Ensure that the air cleaner is OK, the engine coolant temperature is at normal, the accessories are all switched off and that the transmission is in neutral.

2. Ensure that the adjusting screw lever touches the idle speed adjusting screw when the throttle pedal is released, if it is not adjust to suit.

3. Install a tachometer to the engine, start the engine

and check the idle speed setting.

Idle Speed Setting: **700RPM (Manual)**
Idle Speed Setting: **800RPM (Auto)**

4. If the idle speed is not as shown in step3, disconnect the throttle linkage, loosen the lock nut of the idle adjust screw and adjust by turning the idle speed adjusting screw, re-tighten the lock nut and reconnect the throttle linkage. Recheck the idle speed.

5. Remove the tachometer from the engine and replace

Maximum Speed Adjusting Screw

Idle Speed Adjusting Screw

Dfu015

any removed parts to the vehicle.

Maximum Speed Adjustment Check

1. Ensure that the adjusting lever touches the maximum speed adjusting screw when the throttle is pressed down all the way, if not adjust the throttle linkages

2. Install a tachometer to the engine, start the engine, press the throttle fully down and check the maximum speed.

Maximum Speed Setting:
   4400RPM (LY Except Australia)
   4600RPM (LY Australia/Portugal)
   4900RPM (LY Europe Except Portugal).

3. If the maximum speed is not as shown, disconnect the throttle linkage, cut the seal wire on the adjusting screw, loosen the lock nut on the maximum speed adjusting screw and adjust by turning the adjusting screw.

4. Check the idle speed setting, then raise the engine speed and recheck the maximum speed.

5. Retighten the lock nut, re-seal the adjusting screw, reconnect the throttle linkage and recheck the throttle linkage adjustment.

6. Remove the tachometer from the engine and replace any removed parts to the vehicle.

Refer Previous Idle Speed Diagrams

Fuel Heater System Check

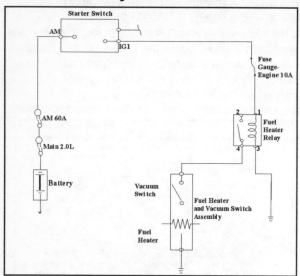

Fuel Heater Check

1. Apply 38±6.7kpa or more to the vacuum switch port and with an ohmmeter record the resistance between terminal 1 and switch body

Specified Resistance: **0.7 ohms @ 20°c**

If the resistance is not as shown, repair/replace as required.

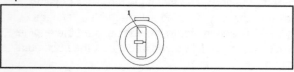

Fuel Heater Relay

1. Remove the relay (located under the instrument panel in the relay block (LY) and check for continuity between terminals 1-3 (ensure continuity exists), and between terminals 2-4 (ensure continuity does not exist).

2. Apply battery voltage between the 1-3 terminals and ensure continuity exists between the 2-4 terminals.

3. If the operation is not as shown, repair/replace as required.

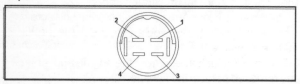

Vacuum Switch Check

1. With an ohmmeter check there is no continuity between the switch terminal 1 and switch body.
If the resistance is not as shown, repair/replace as required.

2. Apply a vacuum of 38±6.7kpa or more to the vacuum port and check that there is continuity between the switch terminal 1 and body.
If the operation is not as shown, repair/replace as required.

Refer to Fuel Heater Diagram

Pre-Heating System Checks

Super Glow System (Models for Europe) 1988-1995

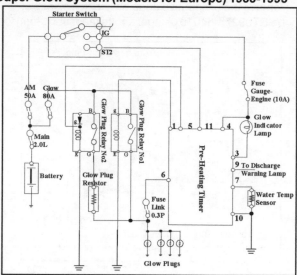

Pre-Heating Timer Check

Please Note: Before starting test please ensure that the battery is fully charged, the engine cranks normally and that all the fuse links are OK.

The timer unit is located in under the instrument panel on the LH side (LY)

1. Check if the glow indicator lamp lights up when the starter switch is ON, (Coolant Temp is 20°c and lamp lights up for 2-3 seconds).

2. If the operation is not as shown, check to ensure that the fuse/s are OK, if they are not check for any short circuit/s and repair as required.

3. If the fuses are OK in step2, check the condition and/or operation of the indicator lamp globe, if faults are found repair/replace as required.

4. If the bulb is Ok in step3, check for battery voltage to terminal 3 on the pre-heating timer connector (on the wiring harness side), if the voltage is Ok, repair/replace the timer as required.

5. If the glow indicator lamp is OK in step1, turn off the starter switch and check for battery voltage at the pre-heater timer terminal 1 with the starter switch ON, if there is no voltage check that there is 1v or less to terminal 9, if the voltage is OK, replace the timer.

6. If the voltage in step5 is Ok, check the voltage to the pre-heat timer terminal 1 is terminated after the engine has started, if it is not, start the engine and check for voltage present at terminal 9 of the pre heating timer, if the voltage is Ok, replace the timer, if the voltage is not Ok, repair fault/s in the vehicle charging system.

7. If the voltage is terminated in step6, turn off the starter switch, turn on again and check for current flow to terminal 5 of the timer in relation to the coolant temperature.

Current Flow: **16-26seconds @ less than 50°c**
Current Flow: **1.7seconds @ more than 50°c**

If there is no voltage at all replace the timer.

8. If the pre heating time is a lot different from what was shown in step7, the timer is faulty and should be replaced.

9. If the pre-heat time is Ok in step7, check for voltage at the timer terminal 8 when the ignition switch is in the ST position, if there is no voltage the timer needs replacing.

10. If the voltage is Ok in step9, put the starter switch in the ON position and check for voltage at the timer terminal 5 when the starter switch is at "Start", if there is no voltage at all replace the timer.

11. If the voltage in step10 is OK , switch off the ignition, switch ON the ignition and check for voltage to the glow plugs with coolant temperature a 50°c or less) a few seconds after (the voltage should drop by half), if there is no voltage at all, check for battery voltage at the (+) side of the glow plug resistor, if there is no voltage present at the (+) side of the resistor replace the No1 glow plug relay.

12. If the voltage in step11 remains at battery voltage or drops to 0v, check for battery voltage at the (+) side of the glow plug resistor, if the voltage is Ok, replace the resistor, if there is no voltage present at the (+) side of the resistor replace the No2 glow plug relay.

13. If the voltage is OK in step12, check the glow plug/s resistance, if the reading is infinity, repair/replace as required, if the reading is about 0ohms, the glow plugs are OK.

Pre Heating Timer Operation Check
The timer unit is located in under the instrument panel on the LH side (LY).

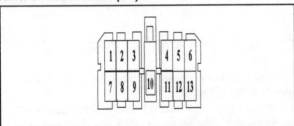

1. Disconnect the connector from the timer and check the connector harness as shown in the chart below.

Check For	Between Terminals	Condition	Specified Value
Continuity	1-ground		Continuity
Voltage	3-ground Starter	Switch OFF	No volts
Voltage	3-ground Starter	Switch ON	Battery volts
Voltage	4-ground Starter	Switch OFF	No volts
Voltage	4-ground Starter	Switch ON	Battery volts
Continuity	5-ground		Continuity
Continuity	6-ground		Continuity
Continuity	7-ground		Continuity
Continuity	10-ground		Continuity
Voltage	11-ground Starter	Switch OFF	No volts
Voltage	11-ground Starter	Switch Start	Battery volts

No1 Glow Plug Relay Check
Please Note: The relay is located in the LH engine compartment on the rear side

1. With an ohmmeter check the continuity between the terminals 1-2 and ensure that it exists, check between terminals 3-4 and ensure that it does not exist.

2. Apply battery volts between terminals 1-2 and ensure that continuity exists between terminals 3-4

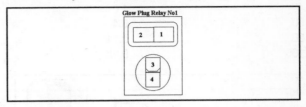

No2 Glow Plug Relay Check
Please Note: The relay is located Under the instrument panel on LH Side

1. With an ohmmeter check the continuity between the terminals 1-2 and ensure that it exists, check between terminals 3-4 and ensure that it does not exist.

2. Apply battery volts between terminals 1-2 and ensure that continuity exists between terminals 3-4

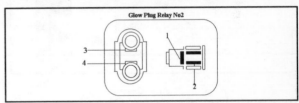

Glow Plug Check
1. With an ohmmeter check that there is continuity between the glow plug terminal and ground, if continuity does not exist, replace the faulty glow plug/s

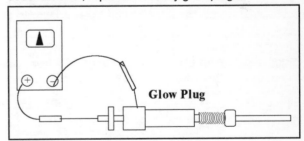

Glow Plug Sensor Check
1. With an ohmmeter check that there is continuity between the sensor terminals, if no continuity exists replace the sensor.

2. If the resistance is not as shown, repair/replace as required.

Water Temperature Sensor Check 1988 On

1. Remove the sensor harness connector and check the resistance between the sensor terminals at varying temperatures.

Sensor Temperature (°c)	Sensor Resistance (k/ohms)
0	5.0
20	2.0
40	1.0
60	0.4
80	0.14
100	0.08

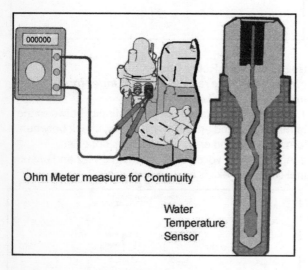

Ohm Meter measure for Continuity

Water Temperature Sensor

Pre-Heating System Checks Variable Delay System

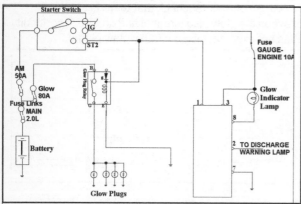

Glow Plugs

Pre-Heat Timer Check (LY Models Australia)
The timer unit is located in under the instrument panel on the LH side)

1. Disconnect the connector from the timer and check the connector harness as shown in the chart below.

Check For	Between Terminals	Condition	Specified Value
Voltage	1-ground	Starter Switch OFF	No volts
Voltage	1-ground	Starter Switch Start	Battery volts
Voltage	3-ground	Starter Switch OFF	No volts
Voltage	3-ground	Starter Switch ON	Battery volts
Continuity	7-ground		Continuity

Voltage	8-ground	Starter Switch OFF	No volt
Voltage	8-ground	Starter Switch Start	Battery Volts

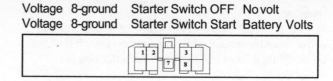

Glow Indicator Lamp Check 1988-1995

1. Turn the ignition switch to "Start" and check the lamp light up time.

Lamp Light Up Time: Approx 5 Seconds

Pre-Heating System Checks Fixed Delay System

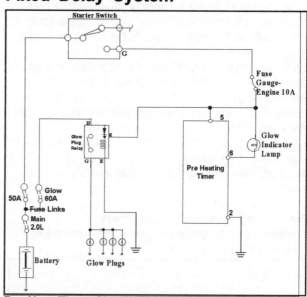

Pre-Heat Timer Check (Models Except Europe/Australia)
The timer unit is located in under the instrument panel on the LH side

1. Disconnect the connector from the timer and check the connector harness as shown in the chart below.

Check For	Between Terminals	Condition	Specified Value
Continuity	2-ground		Continuity
Voltage	5-ground	Starter Switch OFF	No volts
Voltage	5-ground	Starter Switch Glow	Battery volts
Voltage	6-ground	Starter Switch OFF	No volts
Voltage	6-ground	Starter Switch Glow	Battery volts

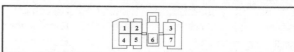

Glow Plug Relay Check
Please Note: The relay is located in the engine compartment on the rear side
1. With an ohmmeter check the continuity between the terminals 1-2 and ensure that it exists, check between terminals 3-4 and ensure that it does not exist.
2. Apply battery volts between terminals 1-2 and ensure that continuity exists between terminals 3-4
Refer No2 Glow Plug Relay Diagram in the Superglow System

Glow Plug Check 1988-1996
1. With an ohmmeter check that there is continuity between the glow plug terminal and ground, if continuity does not exist, replace the faulty glow plug/s
Refer Previous Glow Plug Check Diagrams

Glow Plug Light Up Time Check 1988-1996
1. Switch ON the ignition and check the indicator lamp light up time.
Light Up Time: 15-19.5 Seconds

Injection System and Engine Diagnosis and Troubleshooting
Engine Will Not Crank
1. Check the condition and/or operation of the battery cables between the battery and starter motor, if faults are found repair/replace as required.
2. If no faults are found in step1, check the condition and/or operation of the battery, alternator output and/or drive belt, if faults are found repair/replace as required.
3. If no faults are found in step2, check the condition and/or operation of the starter motor, if faults are found repair/replace as required.

Engine Cranks Slowly or Will Not Start
1. Check the condition and/or operation of the battery cables between the battery and starter motor, if faults are found repair/replace as required.
2. If no faults are found in step1, check the condition and/or operation of the battery, alternator output and/or drive belt, if faults are found repair/replace as required.
3. If no faults are found in step2, check that the correct grade of engine oil is being used on the vehicle, if not drain and replace with the correct grade of oil.

Engine Cranks Normally But Does Not Start
1. If the engine cranks normally but does not start, check and ensure that fuel is reaching the injection nozzles by loosening any of the injection pipes, cranking the engine and ensuring that fuel is coming out of the pipe.
2. If fuel is not coming out of the pipe in step1, check the operation of the fuel cut solenoid, if faults are found repair/replace as required.
3. If no faults are found in step3, check to ensure that fuel is getting to the injection pump by disconnecting the inlet hoses from the fuel filter, feeding clean fuel from a separate container directly into the injection pump. If the

engine now starts there may be blockages in the fuel filter and/or line between the fuel tank and fuel filter. If the engine does not start, check the condition and/or operation of the fuel line between the fuel filter and fuel pump. If the injection pump operation is normal it should be replaced.
4. If fuel is present in step1, check the pre-heating operation system operation by ensuring that after the ignition is turned on, the glow plug lamp lights up and that there are 6v applied to the glow plugs, if the operation is not as shown, repair/replace as required.
5. If no faults are found in step4, check the operation of then glow plug/s, if faults are found repair/replace as required.
6. If no faults are found in step5, check the fuel system pipes, hoses and/or components for leaks, cracks and/or damage, if faults are found repair/replace as required.
7. If no faults are found in step6, check the injection timing by setting either the No1 or No4 piston at TDC, releasing the cold start advance system (where fitted) and checking the plunger stroke.
Injection Plunger Stroke:
    0.84-0.96mm (Without ACSD Control)
Injection Plunger Stroke:
    0.54-0.66mm (With ACSD Control)
If the timing setting is not as shown, adjust to suit.
8. If no faults are found in step7, **(With ACSD Control Only),** check the cold start advance and fast idle system operation, if faults are found repair/replace as required.
9. If no faults are found in step7and/or 8, check the condition and/or operation of the injection nozzles, if faults are found repair/replace as required.

Idle Speed is Unstable When The Engine is Warm
1. If the idle speed is unstable when the engine is warm, check the condition and/or operation of the throttle cable and/or linkages, if faults are found repair/replace as required.
2. If no faults are found in step1, check the engine idle speed setting.
Idle Speed: 700RPM (Manual)
Idle Speed: 800RPM (Auto)
If the idle speed setting is not as shown, adjust to suit
3. If no faults are found in step2, check the fuel system components and/or lines for leaks and/or damage, if faults are found repair/replace as required.
4. If no faults are found in step3, check the injection timing by setting either the No1 or No4 piston at TDC, releasing the cold start advance system (where fitted) and checking the plunger stroke.
Injection Plunger Stroke:
    0.84-0.96mm (Without ACSD Control)
Injection Plunger Stroke:
    0.54-0.66mm (With ACSD Control)
If the timing setting is not as shown, adjust to suit.
5. If no faults are found in step4, check the operation of the injection nozzle/s and/or the delivery valve by letting the engine run at idle speed, loosening the union nuts on each of the cylinders in order and check if there is

any change of idle speed. If there is no change at any of the cylinders this will indicate that a faulty cylinder/s is present. To fix the problem check the injection nozzle pressure.

Injection Nozzle Pressure: 14,200-1520kpa

If the pressure is not as shown adjust pressure to suit. If the pressure is OK, the fault will be with the delivery valve and should be replaced.

Rough Idle When the Engine is Warm

1. If the engine idle is rough when the engine is warm, check the throttle linkages and/or cable for correct operation and/or adjustment, if faults are found repair/replace as required.

2. If no faults are found in step1, with the engine running check the idle speed setting.

Idle Speed: 700RPM (Manual)
Idle Speed: 800RPM (Auto)

If the idle speed setting is not as shown, adjust to suit

3. If no faults are found in step2, check the fuel system pipes, hoses and/or components for leaks, cracks and/or damage, if faults are found repair/replace as required.

4. If no faults are found in step3, check the injection timing by setting either the No1 or No4 piston at TDC, releasing the cold start advance system (where fitted) and checking the plunger stroke.

Injection Plunger Stroke:
0.84-0.96mm (Without ACSD Control)
Injection Plunger Stroke:
0.54-0.66mm (With ACSD Control)

If the timing setting is not as shown, adjust to suit.

5. If no faults are found in step4 check the check the injection nozzle pressure.

Injection Nozzle Pressure: 14,200-1520kpa

If the pressure is not as shown adjust pressure to suit, if the pressure cannot be adjusted, replace the faulty nozzle/s

Engine Suddenly Stops

1. If the engine is running and then suddenly stops, switch off the ignition and try and start the engine, if it does not re-start, check and ensure that fuel is reaching the injection nozzles by loosening any of the injection pipes, cranking the engine and ensuring that fuel is coming out of the pipe.

2. If fuel is not coming out of the pipe in step1, check the operation of the fuel cut solenoid, if faults are found repair/replace as required.

3. If no faults are found in step3, check to ensure that fuel is getting to the injection pump by disconnecting the inlet hoses from the fuel filter, feeding clean fuel from a separate container directly into the injection pump. If the engine now starts there may be blockages in the fuel filter and/or line between the fuel tank and fuel filter. If the engine does not start, check the condition and/or operation of the fuel line between the fuel filter and fuel pump. If the injection pump operation is normal it should be replaced.

4. If fuel is present in step1, check the pre-heating operation system operation by ensuring that after the

ignition is turned on, the glow plug lamp lights up and that there are 6v applied to the glow plugs, if the operation is not as shown, repair/replace as required.

5. If no faults are found in step4, check the operation of the glow plug/s, if faults are found repair/replace as required.

6. If no faults are found in step5, check the fuel system pipes, hoses and/or components for leaks, cracks and/or damage, if faults are found repair/replace as required.

7. If no faults are found in step6, check the injection timing by setting either the No1 or No4 piston at TDC, releasing the cold start advance system (where fitted) and checking the plunger stroke.

Injection Plunger Stroke:
0.84-0.96mm (Without ACSD Control)
Injection Plunger Stroke:
0.54-0.66mm (With ACSD Control)

If the timing setting is not as shown, adjust to suit.

8. If no faults are found in step7, **(With ACSD Control Only),** check the cold start advance and fast idle system operation, if faults are found repair/replace as required.

9. If no faults are found in step7and/or 8, check the condition and/or operation of the injection nozzles, if faults are found repair/replace as required.

Engine Has a Lack of Power

1. If the engine has any lack of power, check the maximum speed operation by ensuring that the adjusting lever touches the maximum speed adjusting screw when the throttle is pressed down all the way, if not adjust the throttle linkages

2. Install a tachometer to the engine, start the engine, press the throttle fully down and check the maximum speed.

Maximum Speed Setting:
4400RPM (Except Australia)
4600RPM (Australia/Portugal)
4900RPM (Europe Except Portugal).

3. If the maximum speed is not as shown, disconnect the throttle linkage, cut the seal wire on the adjusting screw, loosen the lock nut on the maximum speed adjusting screw and adjust by turning the adjusting screw.

4. Check the idle speed setting, raise the engine speed and recheck the maximum speed.

5. Retighten the lock nut, re-seal the adjusting screw, reconnect the throttle linkage and recheck the throttle linkage adjustment.

6. Remove the tachometer from the engine and replace any removed parts to the vehicle.

7. If the maximum speed in step2 is OK, check the interchanged overflow screw (out) and inlet (no marking) are fitted into the correct positions (the screw marked out has an inner jet) and cannot be interchanged.

8. If no faults are found in step7, check the fuel system pipes, hoses and/or components for leaks, cracks and/or damage, if faults are found repair/replace as required.

9. If no faults are found in step8, disconnect the inlet hoses from the fuel filter and pour diesel fuel directly into the injection pump, if the condition now improves replace the fuel filter. If the condition does not improve after the fuel filter has been replaced, check the condition and/or operation of the priming pump, if faults are found repair/replace as required.

10. If no faults are found in step9, check the injection timing by setting either the No1 or No4 piston at TDC, releasing the cold start advance system (where fitted) and checking the plunger stroke.

Injection Plunger Stroke:
         0.84-0.96mm (Without ACSD Control)
Injection Plunger Stroke:
         0.54-0.66mm (With ACSD Control)
If the timing setting is not as shown, adjust to suit.

11. If no faults are found in step10, check the check the injection nozzle pressure.

Injection Nozzle Pressure: 14,200-1520kpa
If the pressure is not as shown adjust pressure to suit, if the pressure cannot be adjusted, replace faulty nozzle/s

Excessive Exhaust Smoke

1. Check the condition and/or operation of the air cleaner element, if faults are found repair/replace as required.

2. If no faults are found in step1, check the engine oil consumption, if faults are found repair/replace as required.

3. If the oil consumption is OK in step2, check the injection timing by setting either the No1 or No4 piston at TDC, releasing the cold start advance system (where fitted) and checking the plunger stroke.

Injection Plunger Stroke:
         0.84-0.96mm (Without ACSD Control)
Injection Plunger Stroke:
         0.54-0.66mm (With ACSD Control)
If the timing setting is not as shown, adjust to suit.
(Please Note: If the exhaust smoke is black it tends to indicate that the timing is advanced and if the smoke is white that the timing is retarded).

4. If no faults are found in step3, disconnect the inlet hoses from the fuel filter and pour diesel fuel directly into the injection pump, if the condition now improves replace the fuel filter. If the condition does not improve after the fuel filter has been replaced, check the condition and/or operation of the priming pump, if faults are found repair/replace as required. *(Please Note: At between 2000-3000RPM a blocked fuel filter tends to make the exhaust smoke white).*

5. If no faults are found in step4, check the check the injection nozzle pressure.

Injection Nozzle Pressure: 14,200-1520kpa
If the pressure is not as shown adjust pressure to suit, if the pressure cannot be adjusted, replace the faulty nozzle/s. *(Please Note: Excessive exhaust smoke is normally caused when the nozzle pressure is to low)*

Fuel Consumption is Poor

1. If the fuel consumption is poor, check the fuel system components and/or lines for leaks and/or damage, if faults are found repair/replace as required.

2. If no faults are found in step1, with the engine running check the idle speed setting.

Idle Speed: 700RPM (Manual)
Idle Speed: 800RPM (Auto)
If the idle speed setting is not as shown, adjust to suit

3. If the idle speed setting is OK in step2, check the no load maximum speed setting is OK by starting the engine, pressing down the throttle pedal to the floor and checking the no load maximum speed setting.

Maximum Speed Setting:
         4400RPM (LY Except Australia)
         4600RPM (LY Australia/Portugal)
         4900RPM (LY Europe Except Portugal).
If the setting is not OK, adjust using the maximum speed adjusting screw.

4. If no faults are found in step3, check the injection timing by setting either the No1 or No4 piston at TDC, releasing the cold start advance system (where fitted) and checking the plunger stroke.

Injection Plunger Stroke:
         0.84-0.96mm (Without ACSD Control)
Injection Plunger Stroke:
         0.54-0.66mm (With ACSD Control)
If the timing setting is not as shown, adjust to suit.

5. If no faults are found in step4, check the check the injection nozzle pressure.

Injection Nozzle Pressure: 14,200-1520kpa
If the pressure is not as shown adjust pressure to suit, if the pressure cannot be adjusted, replace the faulty nozzle/s.

Noise When The Engine Is Warm

1. If the engine is noisy when it is warm, first check the operation of the temperature gauge if that is Ok, check the operation of the thermostat if faults are found repair/replace as required.

2. If no faults are found in step1, check the injection timing by setting either the No1 or No4 piston at TDC, releasing the cold start advance system (where fitted) and checking the plunger stroke.

Injection Plunger Stroke:
         0.84-0.96mm (Without ACSD Control)
Injection Plunger Stroke:
         0.54-0.66mm (With ACSD Control)
If the timing setting is not as shown, adjust to suit.

3. If no faults are found in step2, check the check the injection nozzle pressure.

Injection Nozzle Pressure: 14,200-1520kpa
If the pressure is not as shown adjust pressure to suit, if the pressure cannot be adjusted, replace the faulty nozzle/s.

Engine Will Not Return to Idle

1. Operate the adjusting lever on top of the injection pump and ensure that the engine returns to normal idle speed, if it does the throttle cable is binding or not adjusted correctly and needs fixing.

2. If the engine does not return to idle in step1, the injection pump is faulty and needs replacing.

Engine Will Not Shut Off With The Key

1. Check the fuel cut solenoid operation by disconnecting the connector on top of the fuel cut solenoid and check if the engine stops, if it does the starter switch is faulty and needs repairing and/or replacing.

2. If the engine does not stop in step1, either the fuel cut solenoid is faulty or the solenoid is blocked, if required repair/replace as required.

Diesel System Electrical Diagnosis

Engine Will Not Start When Cold

Super Glow System (Models for Europe)

Please Note: Before starting test please ensure that the battery is fully charged, the engine cranks normally and that all the fuse links are OK.
The timer unit is located in under the instrument panel on the LH side (LY)

1. Check if the glow indicator lamp lights up when the starter switch is ON, (Coolant Temp is 20°c and lamp lights up for 2-3 seconds).

2. If the operation is not as shown, check to ensure that the fuse/s are OK, if they are not check for any short circuit/s and repair as required.

3. If the fuses are OK in step2, check the condition and/or operation of the indicator lamp globe, if faults are found repair/replace as required.

4. If the bulb is Ok in step3, check for battery voltage to terminal 3 on the pre-heating timer connector (on the wiring harness side), if the voltage is Ok, repair/replace the timer as required.

5. If the glow indicator lamp is OK in step1, turn off the starter switch and check for battery voltage at the pre-heater timer terminal 1 with the starter switch ON, if there is no voltage check that there is 1v or less to terminal 9, if the voltage is OK, replace the timer.

6. If the voltage in step5 is Ok, check the voltage to the pre-heat timer terminal 1 is terminated after the engine has started, if it is not, start the engine and check for voltage present at terminal 9 of the pre heating timer, if the voltage is Ok, replace the timer, if the voltage is not Ok, repair fault/s in the vehicle charging system.

7. If the voltage is terminated in step6, turn off the starter switch and then turn on again and check for current flow to terminal 5 of the timer in relation to the coolant temperature.

Current Flow: 16-26seconds @ less than 50°c
Current Flow: 1.7seconds @ more than 50°c
If there is no voltage at all replace the timer.

8. If the pre heating time is a lot different from what was shown in step7, the timer is faulty and should be replaced.

9. If the pre-heat time is Ok in step7, check for voltage at the timer terminal 8 when the ignition switch is in the ST position, if there is no voltage the timer needs replacing.

10. If the voltage is Ok in step9, put the starter switch in the ON position and check for voltage at the timer terminal 5 when the starter switch is at "Start", if there is no voltage at all replace the timer.

11. If the voltage in step10 is OK , switch of the ignition, switch ON the ignition and check for voltage to the glow plugs with coolant temperature a 50°c or less) a few seconds after (the voltage should drop by half), if there is no voltage at all, check for battery voltage at the (+) side of the glow plug resistor, if there is no voltage present at the (+) side of the resistor replace the No1 glow plug relay.

12. If the voltage in step11 remains at battery voltage or drops to 0v, check for battery voltage at the (+) side of the glow plug resistor, if the voltage is Ok, replace the resistor, if there is no voltage present at the (+) side of the resistor replace the No2 glow plug relay.

13. If the voltage is OK in step12, check the glow plug/s resistance, if the reading is infinity, repair/replace as required, if the reading is about 0ohms, the glow plugs are OK.

Fuel Cut Solenoid Operation Check

1. Put the starter switch into the ON position and check for an operating noise from the solenoid while repeatedly connecting and disconnecting the solenoid, if a noise is heard the solenoid is OK.

2. If the solenoid noise is not heard, check the condition and/or operation of the relevant fuse, if faults are found repair/replace as required.

3. If the fuse is OK in step2, apply battery volts to the solenoid and check for a noise, if a noise can be heard, check the condition of the harness between the fuse A and the fuel cut solenoid, if faults are found repair/ replace as required.

4. If no noise can be heard in step3, replace the fuel cut solenoid.

VEHICLE SERVICE INFORMATION

Vehicle Filling Capacities
Engine Oil with Filter: ....5.9 Litres (Europe)
Engine Oil without Filter: ....5.0 Litres (Europe)
Engine Oil dry fill : ....6.4 Litres (Europe)
Engine Oil with Filter: .... 6.0 Litres (Except Europe)
Engine Oil without Filter: ..... 5.0 Litres (Except Europe)
Engine Oil dry fill : .... 6.5 Litres (Except Europe)
Cooling System: .... 9.3 Litres (With Heater)
Manual Transmission: .... 2.2 Litres
Rear Differential: .... 1.8 Litres
Cooling System: .... 10.8 Litres (Europe With Heater)
Cooling System: .... 9.9 Litres (Without Heater)
Cooling System: .... 11.1Litres (Australia)
Cooling System: .... 10.2 Litres (Others)
Manual Transmission: .... 2.4 Litres
Rear Differential: .... 2.5 Litres

Vehicle Component Service Interval Changes
Timing Belt Replacement
Every 100,000kms
Check Valve Clearance:
Every 20,000kms
Engine Coolant/Anti Freeze
Change Every 12 Months/20,000kms
Air Cleaner Element:
Change Every 24 Months/40,000kms
Fuel Filter:
Change Every 12 Months/20,000kms
Engine Oil:
Change Every 5000kms
Engine Oil Filter:
Change Every 6 Months/10,000kms
Brake Fluid:
Change Every 24 Months/40,000kms
Manual Transmission Oil:
Change Every 18 Months/30,000kms
Auto Transmission Fluid
Change Every 24 Months/40,000kms
Rear Differential Oil:
Change Every 18 Months/30,000kms
Front Wheel Bearings
Repack Every 20,000kms

Toyota Dyna LY211 Series
3L Engine 1995 ON

CONTENTS   PAGE

CONTENTS   PAGE

Toyota Dyna LY211 Series
3L Engine 1995 ON

Engine Checks

Valve Clearance Check

Please Note: Before carrying out this check ensure that the engine is at normal operating temperature.

1. Remove the rocker cover, set the No1 piston to TDC on its compression stroke and ensure that the groove on the crankshaft pulley is lined up with the timing pointer on the front cover.

2. Ensure that the valve lifters on the No1 cylinder are loose and that the No4 valve lifters are tight (if they are not turn the engine on full turn (360°) and recheck).

3. Measure the valve clearances on the following valves 1&3 (Exhaust) and 1&2 (Inlet).

Inlet Valve Clearance: 0.20-030mm (Cold)
Exhaust Valve Clearance: 0.40-0.50mm (Cold)

If the clearances are not correct record the relevant readings to determine the adjusting shim required.

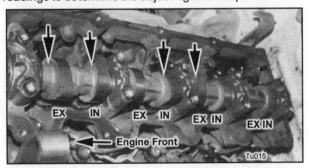

4. Turn the crankshaft one full turn (360°) and ensure that the groove on the crankshaft pulley is lined up with the timing pointer on the front cover.

5. Measure the valve clearances on the following valves 2&4 (Exhaust) and 3&4 (Inlet).

Inlet Valve Clearance: 0.20-030mm (Cold)
Exhaust Valve Clearance: 0.40-0.50mm (Cold)

If the clearances are not correct record the relevant

readings to determine the adjusting shim required.

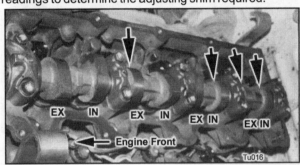

Compression Check

1. Run the engine to normal operating temperature, disconnect the fuel cut solenoid connector and remove all of the glow plugs from the engine.

2. Install and adapter and compression gauge to the No1 cylinder, fully open the throttle, crank the engine and record the compression pressure on each cylinder.

Compression Pressure: 3138kpa
Minimum Pressure: 1961kpa
Difference Between Each Cylinder: 490kpa

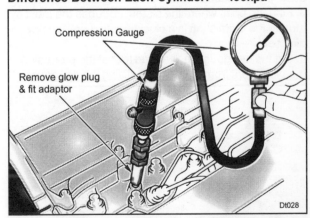

3. If the pressure on one or more cylinders is low, pour a small amount of oil into the cylinder through the glow plug hole and check the compression pressure again. If it helps the pressure there are possibly faults with the

piston rings or cylinder bores, if the oil does not help there may be a valve sticking or not seated correctly and/or leaks past the gasket.

Cylinder Head Tightening Procedures

1. After the cylinder head has been removed and the gasket replaced, apply a thin coat of oil to all of the cylinder head bolts. Install and gradually tighten each of the bolts to its correct torque in three stages in the sequence showed in the diagram.

Specified Torque Setting: **118Nm**

Please Note: If any of the bolts do not reach the correct torque, check the length of the bolts.

Short Bolt: **107mm**

Long Bolt: **127mm**

Replace any faulty bolts as required.

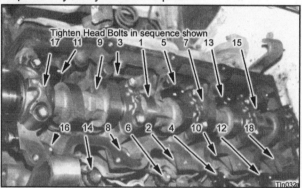

2. Mark the front of each bolt with some paint and then tighten the bolts a further 90°. After the sequence has been completed tighten the bolts a further 90° and now ensure that the paint mark is facing to the rear.

Piston Protrusion Height Check
No1 and 4 Piston Check

1. Rotate the engine and ensure that the timing marks on the crankshaft pulley line up with the marks on the front cover.

2. Fit a dial gauge to the engine block and set the gauge at the piston measuring point.

3. Find the point where the piston protrudes the most by turning the crankshaft in a clockwise and anti clockwise direction.

4. Set the dial gauge to zero and record the protrusion measurement from the block by sliding the dial gauge.

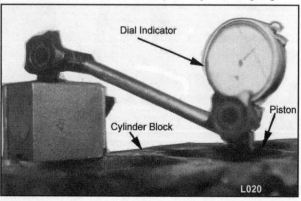

Protrusion Measurement: **0.68-0.97mm**

Please Note: Record the measurement at two separate measuring points.

No2 and No3 Piston Check

5. Turn the crankshaft 180°, Fit a dial gauge to the engine block and set the gauge at the piston measuring point.

6. Find the point where the piston protrudes the most by turning the crankshaft in a clockwise and anti clockwise direction.

7. Set the dial gauge to zero and record the protrusion measurement from the block by sliding the dial gauge.

Protrusion Measurement: **0.68-0.97mm**

Please Note: Record the measurement at two separate measuring points.

8. When the measurement has been made, to select a new head gasket follow the procedures shown.

9. There are 3 different types of head gaskets marked either "B", "D" or "F", each of them a different thickness.

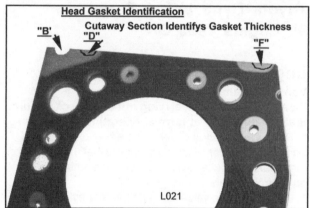

Piston Protrusion Measurements	Gasket Thickness	Gasket Grade
0.68-0.77	1.4-1.5mm	B
0.78-0.87	1.5-1.6	D
0.88-0.97	1.6-1.7	F

Please Note: When selecting the gasket use the largest measurement of the 8 readings that are recorded.

Oil Pressure Check
Test is on the next page

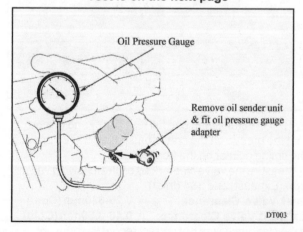

1. Ensure that the engine oil level is correct, if not top up to suit.

2. Remove the oil pressure switch from the engine and install a pressure gauge to the engine block.

3. Start the engine, run to normal operating temperature and then record the oil pressure shown on the gauge.

Specified Oil Pressure: **29kpa @ Idle**

Specified Oil Pressure: **294-539kpa @ 3000RPM**

4. If the oil pressure is not as shown, repair/replace as required.

Cooling System Thermostat Check

1. Remove the thermostat from the engine and put into a suitable container of water.

2. Heat the water gradually and check the valve opening temperature and valve lift.

Valve Opening Temperature: **86-90°c**

Valve Lift: **More than 8mm**

If the operation is not as shown above replace the thermostat.

3. Check that the valve spring is tight when the thermostat is fully closed, if not replace the thermostat.

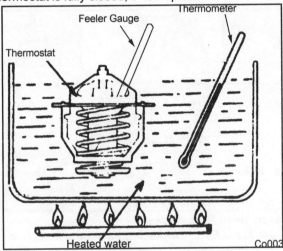

Fuel Filter Check and Replacement

1. Remove the fuel filter sensor (if fitted) and drain the fuel, then remove the fuel filter.

2. Clean the fuel filter mounting bracket and then coat the fuel filter-sealing ring with some diesel fuel.

3. Screw the fuel filter on until a slight resistance is felt and then turn another 2/3 of a turn or until suitably tight.

4. Install the fuel filter sensor (if fitted) to the new filter and then bleed any air present from the system.

Draining Water from the Filter

1. Loosen the drain cock 4 or 5 turns or remove the fuel filter sensor to allow the water to drain from the filter.

2. Retighten the drain cock or replace the sensor and bleed any air present from the system.

Fuel Filter Warning Lamp Check

1. Remove the switch from the filter and check that there is continuity between the terminals when the warning switch is ON (Float Up)

2. Check that there is no continuity between the terminals when the warning switch is OFF (Float Down)

3. If the operation is not as shown, repair/replace as required

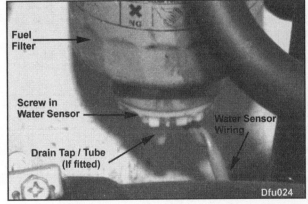

Injector Nozzle Check

1. Remove the injector from the vehicle, connect up to the pressure tester and check the initial pressure by pumping the tester handle a few times.

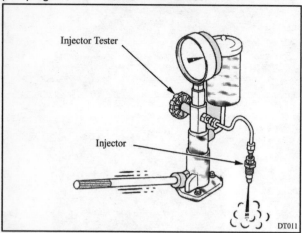

Initial Opening Pressure:

13,729 to 15,690kpa (Used Nozzle)

Initial Opening Pressure:

14,810 to 15,590kpa (New Nozzle)

2. If the opening pressure is not as shown above, take the injector to pieces and change the adjusting shim on the top of the injector so as the correct pressure is recorded.

Adjusted Opening Pressure: 13,279-15,690kpa

Please Note: The adjusting shims vary in 0.025mm thicknesses, each 0.025mm will adjust the pressure by 341kpa. After the shim has been changed there should be no leakage from the injector (upto 1996)

Please Note: The adjusting shims vary in 0.05mm thicknesses, each 0.05mm will adjust the pressure by 628kpa. After the shim has been changed there should be no leakage from the injector (1996On)

3. Maintain the pressure between 981-1961kpa below the opening pressure and check that there is no leakage from the injector for a period of 10seconds.

4. Check the spray pattern by pumping the pressure tester handle 4-6 times or more per second and check the injection spray pattern.

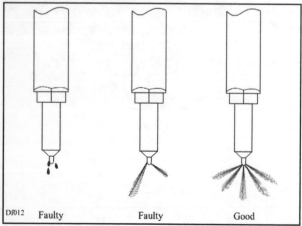

Faulty   Faulty   Good

5. If the operation and/or spray pattern is not as shown, repair/replace the nozzle/s as required.

Timing Belt Removal and Replacement

1. Remove the glow plugs, drive belts, water pump pulley, crankshaft pulley and the No1 timing cover.

2. Remove the timing belt guide.

3. Set the No1 piston to TDC on its compression stroke by temporarily replacing the crankshaft pulley bolt and turning the crankshaft in a clockwise direction until the timing mark on the camshaft gear lines up with the mark on the No2 timing belt cover.

Please Note: If the timing belt is being used again, before removing, mark a direction arrow on the timing belt and place match marks on the pulleys and the belt.

4. Turn the engine 90° in an anti clockwise direction and ensure that the timing mark on the crankshaft pulley lines up with the protrusion on the timing case.

5. Loosen the No1 idler pulley mount bolts and move to the left as far as it will go. Temporarily tighten the bolt, relieve the belt tension and remove the timing belt from the engine.

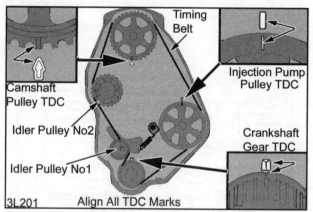

Camshaft Pulley TDC

Timing Belt

Injection Pump Pulley TDC

Idler Pulley No2

Crankshaft Gear TDC

Idler Pulley No1

3L201   Align All TDC Marks

Replacement Procedures

Please Note: Before replacing the timing belt check the condition and/or operation of the timing belt pulleys, tensioner's and/or pulleys, if faults are found repair/replace as required.

1. Check the tensioner spring free length

Spring Free Length: **44.4-45.4mm**

Check the tension of the spring at the specified free length

Installed Tension: **53-59Nm at 52.1mm**

2. Install the crankshaft pulley to the engine, replace any pulleys or idlers that may have been removed for checking.

3. Set the No1 piston to TDC on its compression stroke and ensure that the timing marks on each of the pulleys line up with their relevant match marks.

4. Fit the timing belt onto the crankshaft pulley and No1 idler pulley, slightly turn the injection pulley in a clockwise direction, fit the timing belt onto the injection pulley and line up the marks on the injection pulley and timing belt case.

5. Slightly turn the camshaft drive pulley in a clockwise direction, fit the timing belt onto the pulley and ensure that the marks on the pulley and timing belt case line up.

Please Note: Ensure that there is belt tension between the camshaft pulley and injection pump drive pulleys.

6. Install the timing belt to the No2 idler pulley.

7. Loosen the No1 idler pulley, stretch the timing belt and turn the crankshaft in a clockwise direction two full turns from TDC to TDC, ensuring that all of the timing marks on the drive pulleys line up with their respective match marks.

Please Note: If any of the marks do not line up, remove the belt and reinstall again.

8. Tighten the No1 idler pulley bolt, refit the timing belt guide and replace any removed components in the reverse order of removal.

Timing Belt Replacement Torques

Injection Pump Drive Pulley:	64Nm
No1 Idle Pulley (12mm Bolt):	19Nm
No1 Idle Pulley (14mm Bolt):	44Nm
No2 Idle Pulley:	33Nm
Crankshaft Pulley Bolt:	235Nm
Camshaft Gear Bolt:	98Nm

Timing Belt Warning Lamp Reset Procedures (Rubber Plug in the Instrument Cluster Glass)

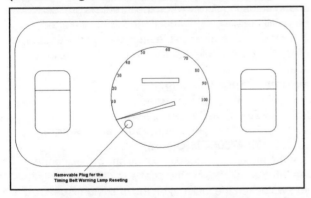

Removable Plug for the
Timing Belt Warning Lamp Reseting

1. Remove the grommet from the speedometer and turn off the lamp by pushing the warning lamp reset switch, then replace the grommet.

2. Start the engine and ensure that the light stays off.

Timing Belt Warning Lamp Reset Procedures (Change Screw Position on the Back of the Instrument Cluster)

1. Remove the instrument cluster from the vehicle, connect terminals A&B shown in the diagrams and then remove the CHARGE fuse from the vehicle.

2. Turn the ignition switch to ON and check that the warning lights light up. If not, check the condition and/or operation of the globe.

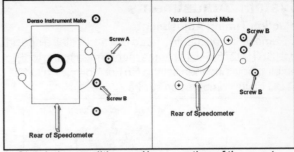

3. Check the condition and/or operation of the reset switches by checking that there is intermittent continuity between terminals A&B when the reset switch is pressed, if not repair/replace the speedometer/instrument cluster as required.

Engine Tightening Torques

Cylinder Head Tightening Torque Bolts:	78Nm (1st Stage)
Cylinder Head Tightening Torque Bolts:	90° (2nd Stage)
Cylinder Head Tightening Torque Bolts:	90° (3rd Stage)
Camshaft Bearing Cap:	25Nm
Exhaust Manifold Bolts and Nuts:	52Nm
Inlet Manifold Bolts and Nuts:	24Nm
Glow Plugs:	13Nm
Injection Nozzle:	64Nm
Injection Pump Drive Pulley Nut:	64Nm
No1 Idle Pulley (12mm Bolt):	19Nm
No1 Idle Pulley (14mm Bolt):	44Nm
No2 Idle Pulley:	33Nm
Flywheel Bolts:	123Nm
Drive Plate:	98Nm
Connecting Rod Caps:	54Nm (1st Stage)
Connecting Rod Caps:	90° (2nd Stage)
Main Bearings:	103Nm
Crankshaft Pulley Bolt:	167Nm
Camshaft Gear Bolt:	98Nm
Oil Pump to Timing Cover:	10Nm
Oil Pump to Block:	23Nm
Oil Pump to Injection Pump:	21Nm
Oil Sump Bolt:	18Nm

Toyota Dyna LY211 Series 3L Engine 1995 ON

System Adjustments

Injection Timing Adjustment

1. Remove the distributive head bolt and install a special tool (SST09275-54011 plunger stroke measuring tool) to the plug hole and then set the No1 or No4 piston to 25° BTDC on its compression stroke.

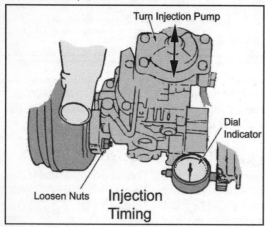

2. Please Note: (For vehicles with auto cold start device): Using a screwdriver turn the cold start lever anti clockwise about 20° and put a metal plate 8.5-10.0mm between the cold start lever and the thermo wax plunger.

3. Turn the crankshaft pulley in a clockwise direction until it is between 25-30° BTDC, set the dial indicator to zero (mm).Slowly turn the crankshaft pulley until crankshaft pulley groove is lined up with the timing pointer and record the plunger movement.

Injection Plunger Stroke:

> 0.54-0.66 (Europe and others With Auto
> Cold Start Device)

Injection Plunger Stroke:

> 0.84-0.96mm (Without Auto Cold Start
> Device)

4. If the plunger stroke measurement is not as shown, loosen the 4 injector pipe union nuts and inlet pipe union nuts on the injection pump side.

5. Loosen the 4 injection pump mounting nuts and adjust the plunger pump stroke by slightly tilting the injection pump body. If the stroke is less than shown tilt the pump towards the engine, if the plunger strike is more than shown tilt the pump away from the engine.

6. Retighten all of the fixing bolts and union nuts, recheck the plunger stroke and then remove the plate from the cold starting lever.

7. Remove the dial indicator gauge and replace the plug bolt. Restart the engine and check for any leaks in the system.

Idle Speed Check.

1. Ensure that the air cleaner is OK, the engine coolant temperature is at normal, the accessories are all switched off and that the transmission is in neutral.

2. Ensure that the adjusting screw lever touches the idle speed adjusting screw when the throttle pedal is released, if it is not adjust to suit.

3. Install a tachometer to the engine, start the engine

and check the idle speed setting.

Idle Speed Setting: 650-750RPM (Manual)
Idle Speed Setting: 750-850RPM (Auto)

4. If the idle speed is not as shown in step3, disconnect the throttle linkage, loosen the lock nut of the idle adjust screw and adjust by turning the idle speed adjusting screw, re-tighten the lock nut, and reconnect the throttle linkage. Recheck the idle speed.

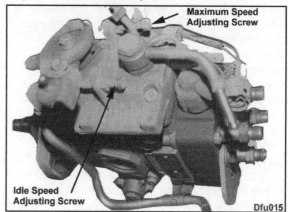

5. Remove the tachometer from the engine and replace any removed parts to the vehicle.

Maximum Speed Adjustment Check

1. Ensure that the adjusting lever touches the maximum speed adjusting screw when the throttle is pressed down all the way, if not adjust the throttle linkages

2. Install a tachometer to the engine, start the engine, press the throttle fully down and check the maximum speed.

Maximum Speed Setting:

> 4670-4930RPM (Europe)
> 4270-4530RPM (Hong Kong
>   /Malaysia, Singapore and General)
> 4470-4730RPM (Others)

3. If the maximum speed is not as shown, disconnect the throttle linkage, cut the seal wire on the adjusting screw, loosen the lock nut on the maximum speed adjusting screw and adjust by turning the adjusting screw.

4. Check the idle speed setting, raise the engine speed and recheck the maximum speed.

5. Retighten the lock nut, re-seal the adjusting screw, reconnect the throttle linkage and recheck the throttle linkage adjustment.

6. Remove the tachometer from the engine and replace any removed parts to the vehicle

See Idle Speed Diagram

Fuel Heater System Check

Fuel Heater Check

1. Remove the fuel heater from the fuel filter cap and apply 34.7±5.3kpa or more to the vacuum switch port and with an ohmmeter record the resistance between terminal 1 and switch body

Specified Resistance: 0.5-2.0ohms @20°c

2. If the resistance is not as shown, repair/replace as required.

Refer to vacuum switch diagram for connector diagram

Vacuum Switch Check

1. With an ohmmeter check there is no continuity between the switch terminal 1 and switch body.
If the resistance is not as shown, repair/replace as required.

2. Apply a vacuum of 34.7±5.3kpa or more to the vacuum port and check that there is continuity between the switch terminal 1 and body.

3. If the operation is not as shown, repair/replace as required

Pre-Heating System Checks

Super Glow System With Resistor
Pre-Heating Timer Check

Please Note: Before starting test please ensure that the battery is fully charged, the engine cranks normally and that all the fuse links are OK.

1. Disconnect the water temperature sensor and check if the glow indicator lamp lights up when the starter switch is ON

Lamp Light Up Time: 6 Seconds

2. If the operation is not as shown, check to ensure that the fuse/s are OK, if they are not check for any short circuit/s and repair as required.

3. If the fuses are OK in step2, check the condition and/or operation of the indicator lamp globe, if faults are found repair/replace as required.

4. If the bulb is Ok in step3, check for battery voltage to terminal 3 on the pre-heating timer connector (on the wiring harness side), if the voltage is Ok, repair/replace the timer as required.

5. If the glow indicator lamp is OK in step1, turn off the starter switch and check for battery voltage at the pre-heater timer terminal 5 with the starter switch ON, if there is no voltage check that there is 1v or less to terminal 10, if the voltage is OK, replace the timer.

6. If the voltage in step5 is Ok, check the voltage to the pre-heat timer terminal 5 is terminated after the engine has started, if it is not, start the engine and check for voltage present at terminal 10 of the pre heating timer, if the voltage is Ok, replace the timer, if the voltage is not Ok, repair fault/s in the vehicle charging system.

7. If the voltage is terminated in step6, turn off the starter switch and then turn on again and check for current flow to terminal 1 of the timer in relation to the coolant temperature.

Current Flow: 22.5seconds

If there is no voltage at all replace the timer.

8. If the pre heating time is a lot different from what was shown in step7, the timer is faulty and should be replaced.

9. If the pre-heat time is Ok in step7, check for voltage at the timer terminal 1 when the ignition switch is in the ST position, if there is no voltage the timer needs replacing.

10. If the voltage is Ok in step9, put the starter switch in the OFF position, turn back on the ignition and check for voltage to the glow plugs, (a few seconds after the voltage should drop by half), if there is no voltage at all replace the NO1 and No2 glow plug relays.

11. If the voltage in step10 stays at battery voltage or at 1/2 voltage for 32 seconds replace the No1 glow plug relay.

12. If the voltage is OK in step11, check the glow plug/s resistance, if the reading is infinity, repair/replace as required, if the reading is about 0ohms, the glow plugs are OK.

Pre Heating Timer Operation Check
Super Glow System With Resistor

1. Disconnect the connector from the timer and check the connector harness as shown in the chart below.

Check For	Between Terminals	Condition	Specified Value
Voltage	4-ground Starter	Switch OFF	No volts
Voltage	4-ground Starter	Switch ON	Battery volts
Voltage	2-ground Starter	Switch OFF	No volts
Voltage	2-ground Starter	Switch ON	Battery volts
Voltage	7-ground Starter	Switch OFF	No volts
Voltage	7-ground Starter	Switch ON	Battery volts
Continuity	1/5-ground		Continuity
Continuity	6-ground		Continuity
Continuity	12-ground		Continuity
Continuity	9-ground		Continuity
Continuity	11-ground		Continuity

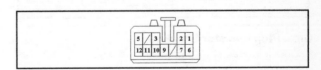

No1 Glow Plug Relay Check

1. With an ohmmeter check the continuity between the terminals 1-2 and ensure that it exists
If there is no continuity replace the relay
2. Check for continuity between terminals 3 and 4 and ensure that it does not exist
If there is continuity replace the relay.
3. Apply battery volts between terminals 1-2 and ensure that continuity exists between terminals 3-4
If there is no continuity replace the relay

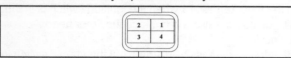

No2 Glow Plug Relay Check

1. With an ohmmeter check the continuity between the terminals 1-2 and ensure that it exists
If there is no continuity replace the relay
2. Check for continuity between terminals 3 and 4 and ensure that it does not exist
If there is continuity replace the relay.

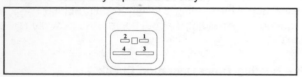

3. Apply battery volts between terminals 3-4 and ensure that continuity exists between terminals 1-2
If there is no continuity replace the relay

Glow Plug Check

1. With an ohmmeter check that there is continuity between the glow plug terminal and ground
Specified Resistance: 0.65ohms @ 20°c
If continuity does not exist, replace the faulty glow plugs

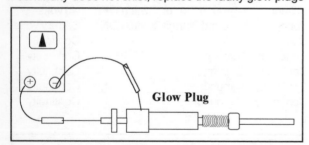

Glow Plug

Glow Plug Resistor Check

1. Check the resistance between the resistor terminals with an ohmmeter
Specified Resistance: 0.17ohms @ 20°c
If the resistance is not as shown, replace the resistor

Water Temperature Sensor Check

1. Remove the sensor harness connector and check the resistance between the sensor terminals at varying temperatures.

Sensor Temperature (°c)	Sensor Resistance (k/ohms)
0	5.0
20	2.0
40	1.0
60	0.4
80	0.14
100	0.08

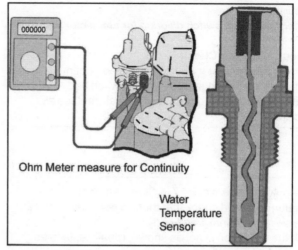

Ohm Meter measure for Continuity

Water Temperature Sensor

2. If the resistance is not as shown, repair/replace as required.

Pre-Heating System Checks

Super Glow System Without Resistor
Pre-Heating Timer Check
Please Note: Before starting test please ensure that the battery is fully charged, the engine cranks normally and that all the fuse links are OK.
1. Disconnect the water temperature sensor and check if the glow indicator lamp lights up when the starter switch is ON
Lamp Light Up Time: 6 Seconds
2. If the operation is not as shown, check to ensure that the fuse/s are OK, if they are not check for any short circuit/s and repair as required.
3. If the fuses are OK in step2, check the condition and/ or operation of the indicator lamp globe, if faults are found repair/replace as required.
4. If the bulb is Ok in step3, check for battery voltage to terminal 3 (wire harness side) on the pre-heating timer connector. If the voltage is Ok, repair/replace the timer as required.
5. If the glow indicator lamp is OK in step1, turn off the starter switch and check for battery voltage at the pre-heater timer terminal 1 with the starter switch ON, if there is no voltage check that there is 1v or less to terminal 10, if the voltage is OK, replace the timer.
6. If the voltage in step5 is Ok, check the voltage to the pre-heat timer terminal 1 is terminated after the engine has started, if it is not, start the engine and check for voltage present at terminal 10 of the pre heating timer, if the voltage is Ok, replace the timer, if the voltage is not Ok, repair fault/s in the vehicle charging system.

7. If the voltage is terminated in step6, turn off the starter switch, turn on again and check for current flow to terminal 1 of the timer in relation to the coolant temperature.

Current Flow: 120.0seconds

If there is no voltage at all replace the timer.

8. If the pre heating time is a lot different from what was shown in step7, the timer is faulty and should be replaced.

9. If the pre-heat time is Ok in step7, check for voltage at the timer terminal 1 when the ignition switch is in the START position, if there is no voltage the timer needs replacing.

10. If the voltage is Ok in step9, put the starter switch in the OFF position, turn back on the ignition and check for voltage to the glow plugs, if there is no voltage check the operation of then glow plug relay/s and/or the glow plugs, if faults are found repair/replace as required.

11. If the voltage in step10 is OK, reconnect the coolant temperature sensor.

Pre Heating Timer Operation Check
Super Glow System Without Resistor

1. Disconnect the connector from the timer and check the connector harness as shown in the chart below.

Check For	Between Terminals	Condition	Specified Value
Voltage	3-ground	Starter Switch OFF	No volts
Voltage	3-ground	Starter Switch ON	Battery volts
Voltage	2-ground	Starter Switch OFF	No volts
Voltage	2-ground	Starter Switch ON	Battery volts
Voltage	7-ground	Starter Switch OFF	No volts
Voltage	7-ground	Starter Switch ON	Battery volts
Continuity	1-ground		Continuity
Continuity	12-ground		Continuity
Continuity	9-ground		Continuity
Continuity	11-ground		Continuity

Glow Plug Relay Check

1. With an ohmmeter check the continuity between the terminals 1-2 and ensure that it exists
If there is no continuity replace the relay
2. Check for continuity between terminals 3-4 and ensure that it does not exist
If there is continuity replace the relay.
3. Apply battery volts between terminals 1-2 and ensure that continuity exists between terminals 3-4
If there is no continuity replace the relay
    Refer No2 Glow Plug Relay in Previous System

Glow Plug Check

1. With an ohmmeter check that there is continuity between the glow plug terminal and ground
Specified Resistance: 0.65ohms @ 20°c
If continuity does not exist, replace the faulty glow plug/plugs.

    Refer Previous Diagrams

Water Temperature Sensor Check

1. Remove the sensor harness connector and check the resistance between the sensor terminals at varying temperatures.

Sensor Temperature (°c)	Sensor Resistance (k/ohms)
0	5.0
20	2.0
40	1.0
60	0.4
80	0.14
100	0.08

2. If the resistance is not as shown, repair/replace as required.
    Refer Previous Diagrams

Pre-Heating System Checks
Variable Delay System
Pre-Heat Timer Check

1. Disconnect the connector from the timer and check the connector harness as shown in the chart below.

Check For	Between Terminals	Condition	Specified Value
Voltage	4-ground	Starter Switch OFF	No volts
Voltage	4-ground	Starter Switch ON	Battery volts
Voltage	1-ground	Starter Switch OFF	No volts
Voltage	1-ground	Starter Switch ON	Battery volts
Continuity	3-ground		Continuity
Continuity	5-ground		Continuity

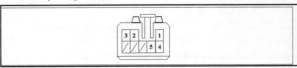

After Glow Time Check

1. Turn the ignition to START and record the time battery voltage is applied to terminal 1.
After Glow Time: **18 Seconds**

Glow Plug Relay Check

1. With an ohmmeter check the continuity between the terminals 1-2 and ensure that it exists
If there is no continuity replace the relay
2. Check for continuity between terminals 3-4 and ensure that it does not exist
If there is continuity replace the relay.
3. Apply battery volts between terminals 3-4 and ensure that continuity exists between terminals 1-2
If there is no continuity replace the relay
Refer Previous Glow Plug Relay Diagrams

Glow Plug Check

1. With an ohmmeter check that there is continuity between the glow plug terminal and ground
Specified Resistance: 0.65ohms @ 20°c
If continuity does not exist, replace the faulty glow plug/plugs
    Refer Previous Glow Plug Check Diagrams

Pre-Heating System Checks Fixed Delay System

Pre-Heat Timer Check

1. Disconnect the connector from the timer and check the connector harness as shown in the chart below.

Check For	Between Terminals	Condition	Specified Value
Voltage	5-ground	Ignition Switch OFF	No volts
Voltage	5-ground	Ignition Switch ON	Battery volts
Voltage	6-ground	Ignition Switch OFF	No volts
Voltage	6-ground	Ignition Switch ON	Battery volts
Continuity	2-ground		Continuity

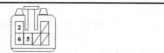

Glow Plug Relay Check

1. With an ohmmeter check the continuity between the terminals 1-2 and ensure that it exists
If there is no continuity replace the relay
2. Check for continuity between terminals 1-2 and ensure that it does not exist
If there is continuity replace the relay.
3. Apply battery volts between terminals 3-4 and ensure that continuity exists between terminals 1-2
If there is no continuity replace the relay
Refer to previous glow plug relay diagrams

Glow Plug Check 1996 On

1. With an ohmmeter check that there is continuity between the glow plug terminal and ground
Specified Resistance: 0.65ohms @ 20°c
If continuity does not exist, replace the faulty glow plug/plugs
Refer to previous glow plug check diagrams

Glow Plug Light Up Time Check 1996 On

1. Switch ON the ignition and check the indicator lamp light up time.
Light Up Time: 5 Seconds

Injection System and Engine Diagnosis and Troubleshooting

Engine Will Not Crank

1. Check the condition and/or operation of the battery cables between the battery and starter motor, if faults are found repair/replace as required.
2. If no faults are found in step1, check the condition and/or operation of the battery, alternator output and/or drive belt, if faults are found repair/replace as required.
3. If no faults are found in step2, check the condition and/or operation of the starter motor, if faults are found repair/replace as required.

Engine Cranks Slowly or Will Not Start

1. Check the condition and/or operation of the battery cables between the battery and starter motor, if faults are found repair/replace as required.
2. If no faults are found in step1, check the condition and/or operation of the battery, alternator output and/or drive belt, if faults are found repair/replace as required.
3. If no faults are found in step2, check that the correct grade of engine oil is being used on the vehicle, if not drain and replace with the correct grade of oil.

Engine Cranks Normally But Does Not Start

1. If the engine cranks normally but does not start, check and ensure that fuel is reaching the injection nozzles by loosening any of the injection pipes, cranking the engine and ensuring that fuel is coming out of the pipe.
2. If fuel is not coming out of the pipe in step1, check the operation of the fuel cut solenoid, if faults are found repair/replace as required.
3. If no faults are found in step3, check to ensure that fuel is getting to the injection pump by disconnecting the inlet hoses from the fuel filter, feeding clean fuel from a separate container directly into the injection pump. If the engine now starts there may be blockages in the fuel filter and/or line between the fuel tank and fuel filter. If the engine does not start, check the condition and/or operation of the fuel line between the fuel filter and fuel pump. If the injection pump operation is normal it should be replaced.
4. If fuel is present in step1, check the pre-heating operation system operation by ensuring that after the ignition is turned on, the glow plug lamp lights up and that there are 6v applied to the glow plugs, if the operation is not as shown, repair/replace as required.
5. If no faults are found in step4, check the operation of the glow plug/s, if faults are found repair/replace as required.
6. If no faults are found in step5, check the fuel system pipes, hoses and/or components for leaks, cracks and/or damage, if faults are found repair/replace as required.
7. If no faults are found in step6, check the injection timing by setting either the No1 or No4 piston at TDC, releasing the cold start advance system (where fitted) and checking the plunger stroke.

Injection Plunger Stroke:

    0.54-0.66 (Europe and others With Auto Cold Start Device)

Injection Plunger Stroke:

    0.84-0.96mm (Without Auto Cold Start Device)

If the timing setting is not as shown, adjust to suit.

8. If no faults are found in step7, **(Auto Cold Start Device Only),** check the cold start advance and fast idle system operation, if faults are found repair/replace as required.

9. If no faults are found in step7and/or 8, check the condition and/or operation of the injection nozzles, if faults are found repair/replace as required.

Idle Speed is Unstable When The Engine is Warm

1. If the idle speed is unstable when the engine is warm, check the condition and/or operation of the throttle cable and/or linkages, if faults are found repair/replace as required.

2. If no faults are found in step1, check the engine idle speed setting.

Idle Speed Setting: **650-750RPM (Manual)**

Idle Speed Setting: **750-850RPM (Auto)**

If the idle speed setting is not as shown, adjust to suit

3. If no faults are found in step2, check the fuel system components and/or lines for leaks and/or damage, if faults are found repair/replace as required.

4. If no faults are found in step3, check the injection timing by setting either the No1 or No4 piston at TDC, releasing the cold start advance system (where fitted) and checking the plunger stroke.

Injection Plunger Stroke:

    0.54-0.66 (Europe and others With Auto Cold Start Device)

Injection Plunger Stroke:

    0.84-0.96mm (Without Auto Cold Start Device

If the timing setting is not as shown, adjust to suit.

5. If no faults are found in step4, check the operation of the injection nozzle/s and/or the delivery valve by letting the engine run at idle speed, loosening the union nuts on each of the cylinders in order and check if there is any change of idle speed. If there is no change at any of the cylinders this will indicate that a faulty cylinder/s is present. To fix the problem check the injection nozzle pressure.

Injection Nozzle Pressure:

    13,729-15,690kpa (New Nozzle)

Injection Nozzle Pressure:

    14,810-15,950kpa (Reused Nozzle)

6. If the pressure is not as shown adjust pressure to suit. If the pressure is OK, the fault will be with the delivery valve and should be replaced.

Rough Idle When the Engine is Warm

1. If the engine idle is rough when the engine is warm, check the throttle linkages and/or cable for correct operation and/or adjustment, if faults are found repair/replace as required.

2. If no faults are found in step1, with the engine running check the idle speed setting.

Idle Speed Setting: **650-750RPM (Manual)**

Idle Speed Setting: **750-850RPM (Auto)**

If the idle speed setting is not as shown, adjust to suit

3. If no faults are found in step2, check the fuel system pipes, hoses and/or components for leaks, cracks and/or damage, if faults are found repair/replace as required.

4. If no faults are found in step3, check the injection timing by setting either the No1 or No4 piston at TDC, releasing the cold start advance system (where fitted) and checking the plunger stroke.

Injection Plunger Stroke:

    0.54-0.66 (Europe and others With Auto Cold Start Device)

Injection Plunger Stroke:

    0.84-0.96mm (Without Auto Cold Start Device

If the timing setting is not as shown, adjust to suit.

5. If no faults are found in step4 check the check the injection nozzle pressure.

Injection Nozzle Pressure:

    13,729-15,690kpa (New Nozzle)

Injection Nozzle Pressure:

    14,810-15,950kpa (Reused Nozzle)

6. If the pressure is not as shown adjust pressure to suit, if the pressure cannot be adjusted, replace the faulty nozzle/s

Engine Suddenly Stops

1. If the engine is running and then suddenly stops, switch off the ignition and try and start the engine, if it does not re-start, check and ensure that fuel is reaching the injection nozzles by loosening any of the injection pipes, cranking the engine and ensuring that fuel is coming out of the pipe.

2. If fuel is not coming out of the pipe in step1, check the operation of the fuel cut solenoid, if faults are found repair/replace as required.

3. If no faults are found in step3, check to ensure that fuel is getting to the injection pump by disconnecting the inlet hoses from the fuel filter, feeding clean fuel from a separate container directly into the injection pump. If the engine now starts there may be blockages in the fuel filter and/or line between the fuel tank and fuel filter. If the engine does not start, check the condition and/or operation of the fuel line between the fuel filter and fuel pump. If the injection pump operation is normal it should be replaced.

4. If fuel is present in step1, check the pre-heating operation system operation by ensuring that after the ignition is turned on, the glow plug lamp lights up and that there are 6v applied to the glow plugs, if the operation is not as shown, repair/replace as required.

5. If no faults are found in step4, check the operation of the glow plug/s, if faults are found repair/replace as required.

6. If no faults are found in step5, check the fuel system pipes, hoses and/or components for leaks, cracks and/or damage, if faults are found repair/replace as required.

7. If no faults are found in step6, check the injection timing by setting either the No1 or No4 piston at TDC, releasing the cold start advance system (where fitted)

and checking the plunger stroke.

Injection Plunger Stroke:

    0.54-0.66 (Europe and others With Auto Cold
    Start Device)

Injection Plunger Stroke:

    0.84-0.96mm (Without Auto Cold Start Device

If the timing setting is not as shown, adjust to suit.

8. If no faults are found in step7, **(With Auto Cold Start Device Only),** check the cold start advance and fast idle system operation, if faults are found repair/replace as required.

9. If no faults are found in step7and/or 8, check the condition and/or operation of the injection nozzles, if faults are found repair/replace as required.

Engine Has a Lack of Power

1. If the engine has any lack of power, check the maximum speed operation by ensuring that the adjusting lever touches the maximum speed adjusting screw when the throttle is pressed down all the way, if not adjust the throttle linkages

2. Install a tachometer to the engine, start the engine, press the throttle fully down and check the maximum speed.

Maximum Speed Setting:

    4670-4930RPM (Europe)

    4270-4530RPM (Hong Kong/Malaysia,
        Singapore and LY General)

    4470-4730RPM (Others)

3. If the maximum speed is not as shown, disconnect the throttle linkage, cut the seal wire on the adjusting screw, loosen the lock nut on the maximum speed adjusting screw and adjust by turning the adjusting screw.

4. Check the idle speed setting, raise the engine speed and recheck the maximum speed.

5. Retighten the lock nut, re-seal the adjusting screw, reconnect the throttle linkage and recheck the throttle linkage adjustment.

6. Remove the tachometer from the engine and replace any removed parts to the vehicle.

7. If the maximum speed in step2 is OK, check the interchanged overflow screw (out) and inlet (no marking) are fitted into the correct positions (the screw marked out has an inner jet) and cannot be interchanged.

8. If no faults are found in step7, check the fuel system pipes, hoses and/or components for leaks, cracks and/or damage, if faults are found repair/replace as required.

9. If no faults are found in step8, disconnect the inlet hoses from the fuel filter and pour diesel fuel directly into the injection pump, if the condition now improves replace the fuel filter. If the condition does not improve after the fuel filter has been replaced, check the condition and/or operation of the priming pump, if faults are found repair/replace as required.

10. If no faults are found in step9, check the injection timing by setting either the No1 or No4 piston at TDC, releasing the cold start advance system (where fitted) and checking the plunger stroke.

Injection Plunger Stroke:

    0.54-0.66 (Europe and others With Auto Cold
    Start Device)

Injection Plunger Stroke:

    0.84-0.96mm (Without Auto Cold Start Device

If the timing setting is not as shown, adjust to suit.

11. If no faults are found in step10, check the check the injection nozzle pressure.

Injection Nozzle Pressure:

    13,729-15,690kpa (New Nozzle)

Injection Nozzle Pressure:

    14,810-15,950kpa (Reused Nozzle)

12. If the pressure is not as shown adjust pressure to suit, if the pressure cannot be adjusted, replace the faulty nozzle/s

Excessive Exhaust Smoke

1. Check the condition and/or operation of the air cleaner element, if faults are found repair/replace as required.

2. If no faults are found in step1, check the engine oil consumption, if faults are found repair/replace as required.

3. If the oil consumption is OK in step2, check the injection timing by setting either the No1 or No4 piston at TDC, releasing the cold start advance system (where fitted) and checking the plunger stroke.

Injection Plunger Stroke:

    0.54-0.66 (Europe and others With Auto Cold
    Start Device)

Injection Plunger Stroke:

    0.84-0.96mm (Without Auto Cold Start Device

If the timing setting is not as shown, adjust to suit.

(Please Note: If the exhaust smoke is black it tends to indicate that the timing is advanced and if the smoke is white that the timing is retarded).

4. If no faults are found in step3, disconnect the inlet hoses from the fuel filter and pour diesel fuel directly into the injection pump, if the condition now improves replace the fuel filter. If the condition does not improve after the fuel filter has been replaced, check the condition and/or operation of the priming pump, if faults are found repair/replace as required. *(Please Note: At between 2000-3000RPM a blocked fuel filter tends to make the exhaust smoke white).*

5. If no faults are found in step4, check the check the injection nozzle pressure.

Injection Nozzle Pressure:

    13,729-15,690kpa (New Nozzle)

Injection Nozzle Pressure:

    14,810-15,950kpa (Reused Nozzle)

6. If the pressure is not as shown adjust pressure to suit, if the pressure cannot be adjusted, replace the faulty nozzle/s. *(Please Note: Excessive exhaust smoke is normally caused when the nozzle pressure is to low)*

Fuel Consumption is Poor 1996 On

1. If the fuel consumption is poor, check the fuel system components and/or lines for leaks and/or damage, if faults are found repair/replace as required.

2. If no faults are found in step1, with the engine running check the idle speed setting.

Idle Speed Setting:	**650-750RPM (Manual)**
Idle Speed Setting:	**750-850RPM (Auto)**

If the idle speed setting is not as shown, adjust to suit

3. If the idle speed setting is OK in step2, check the no load maximum speed setting is OK by starting the engine, pressing down the throttle pedal to the floor and checking the no load maximum speed setting.

Maximum Speed Setting:
   4670-4930RPM (Europe)
   4270-4530RPM (Hong Kong/
      Malaysia, Singapore and LY General)
   4470-4730RPM (Others)

If the setting is not OK, adjust using the maximum speed adjusting screw.

4. If no faults are found in step3, check the injection timing by setting either the No1 or No4 piston at TDC, releasing the cold start advance system (where fitted) and checking the plunger stroke.

Injection Plunger Stroke:
   0.54-0.66 (3L Europe and others With Auto
      Cold Start Device)

Injection Plunger Stroke:
   0.84-0.96mm (Without Auto Cold Start Service

If the timing setting is not as shown, adjust to suit.

5. If no faults are found in step4, check the check the injection nozzle pressure.

Injection Nozzle Pressure:
   13,729-15,690kpa (New Nozzle)
Injection Nozzle Pressure:
   14,810-15,950kpa (Reused Nozzle)

6. If the pressure is not as shown adjust pressure to suit, if the pressure cannot be adjusted, replace the faulty nozzle/s.

Noise When The Engine Is Warm

1. If the engine is noisy when it is warm, first check the operation of the temperature gauge if that is Ok, check the operation of the thermostat if faults are found repair/replace as required.

2. If no faults are found in step1, check the injection timing by setting either the No1 or No4 piston at TDC, releasing the cold start advance system (where fitted) and checking the plunger stroke.

Injection Plunger Stroke:
   0.54-0.66 (Europe and others With Auto Cold
      Start Device)

Injection Plunger Stroke:
   0.84-0.96mm (Without Auto Cold Start Device

If the timing setting is not as shown, adjust to suit.

3. If no faults are found in step2, check the check the injection nozzle pressure.

Injection Nozzle Pressure:
   13,729-15,690kpa (New Nozzle)
Injection Nozzle Pressure:
   14,810-15,950kpa (Reused Nozzle)

4. If the pressure is not as shown adjust pressure to suit, if the pressure cannot be adjusted, replace the faulty nozzle/s.

Engine Will Not Return to Idle

1. Operate the adjusting lever on top of the injection pump and ensure that the engine returns to normal idle speed, if it does the throttle cable is binding or not adjusted correctly and needs fixing.

2. If the engine does not return to idle in step1, the injection pump is faulty and needs replacing.

Engine Will Not Shut Off With The Key

1. Check the fuel cut solenoid operation by disconnecting the connector on top of the fuel cut solenoid and check if the engine stops, if it does the starter switch is faulty and needs repairing and/or replacing.

2. If the engine does not stop in step1, either the fuel cut solenoid is faulty or the solenoid is blocked, if required repair/replace as required.

Diesel System Electrical Diagnosis

Engine Will Not Start When Cold

Super Glow System (With Resistor)

Please Note: Before starting test please ensure that the battery is fully charged, the engine cranks normally and that all the fuse links are OK.

1. If the engine will not start when cold, disconnect the water temperature sensor and check if the glow indicator lamp lights up when the starter switch is ON

Lamp Light Up Time: 6 Seconds

2. If the operation is not as shown in step1, check to ensure that the fuse/s are OK, if they are not check for any short circuit/s and repair as required.

3. If the fuses are OK in step2, check the condition and/or operation of the indicator lamp globe, if faults are found repair/replace as required.

4. If the bulb is Ok in step3, check for battery voltage to terminal 3 on the pre-heating timer connector (on the wiring harness side), if the voltage is Ok, repair/replace the timer as required.

5. If the glow indicator lamp is OK in step1, turn off the starter switch and check for battery voltage at the pre-heater timer terminal 5 with the starter switch ON, if there is no voltage check that there is 1v or less to terminal 10, if the voltage is OK, replace the timer.

6. If the voltage in step5 is Ok, check the voltage to the pre-heat timer terminal 5 is terminated after the engine has started, if it is not, start the engine and check for voltage present at terminal 10 of the pre heating timer, if the voltage is Ok, replace the timer, if the voltage is not Ok, repair fault/s in the vehicle charging system.

7. If the voltage is terminated in step6, turn off the starter switch, turn on again and check for current flow to

terminal 1 of the timer in relation to the coolant temperature.

Current Flow: **22.5seconds**

If there is no voltage at all replace the timer.

8. If the pre heating time is a lot different from what was shown in step7, the timer is faulty and should be replaced.

9. If the pre-heat time is Ok in step7, check for voltage at the timer terminal 1 when the ignition switch is in the ST position, if there is no voltage the timer needs replacing.

10. If the voltage is Ok in step9, put the starter switch in the OFF position, turn back on the ignition and check for voltage to the glow plugs, (a few seconds after the voltage should drop by half). If there is no voltage at all replace the NO1 and No2 glow plug relays.

11. If the voltage in step10 stays at battery voltage or at 1/2 voltage for 32 seconds replace the No1 glow plug relay.

12. If the voltage is OK in step11, check the glow plug/s resistance, if the reading is infinity, repair/replace as required, if the reading is about 0ohms, the glow plugs are OK.

Engine Will Not Start When Cold
Super Glow System (Without Resistor)

1. If the engine will not start when it is cold, disconnect the water temperature sensor and check if the glow indicator lamp lights up when the starter switch is ON

Lamp Light Up Time: 6 Seconds

2. If the operation is not as shown in step1, check to ensure that the fuse/s are OK, if they are not check for any short circuit/s and repair as required.

3. If the fuses are OK in step2, check the condition and/or operation of the indicator lamp globe, if faults are found repair/replace as required.

4. If the bulb is Ok in step3, check for battery voltage to terminal 3(wire harness side) on the pre-heating timer connector. If the voltage is Ok, repair/replace the timer as required.

5. If the glow indicator lamp is OK in step1, turn off the starter switch and check for battery voltage at the pre-heater timer terminal 1 with the starter switch ON, if there is no voltage check that there is 1v or less to terminal 10, if the voltage is OK, replace the timer.

6. If the voltage in step5 is Ok, check the voltage to the pre-heat timer terminal 1 is terminated after the engine has started, if it is not, start the engine and check for voltage present at terminal 10 of the pre heating timer, if the voltage is Ok, replace the timer, if the voltage is not Ok, repair fault/s in the vehicle charging system.

7. If the voltage is terminated in step6, turn off the starter switch and then turn on again and check for current flow to terminal 1 of the timer in relation to the coolant temperature.

Current Flow: **120.0seconds**

If there is no voltage at all replace the timer.

8. If the pre heating time is a lot different from what was shown in step7, the timer is faulty and should be

replaced.

9. If the pre-heat time is Ok in step7, check for voltage at the timer terminal 1 when the ignition switch is in the START position, if there is no voltage the timer needs replacing.

10. If the voltage is Ok in step9, put the starter switch in the OFF position, turn back on the ignition and check for voltage to the glow plugs, if there is no voltage check the operation of the glow plug relay/s and/or the glow plugs, if faults are found repair/replace as required.

11. If the voltage in step10 is OK, reconnect the coolant temperature sensor.

Fuel Cut Solenoid Operation Check

1. Put the starter switch into the ON position and check for an operating noise from the solenoid while repeatedly connecting and disconnecting the solenoid, if a noise is heard the solenoid is OK.

2. If the solenoid noise is not heard, check the condition and/or operation of the relevant fuse, if faults are found repair/replace as required.

3. If the fuse is OK in step2, apply battery volts to the solenoid and check for a noise, if a noise can be heard, check the condition of the harness between the fuse A and the fuel cut solenoid, if faults are found repair/replace as required.

4. If no noise can be heard in step3, replace the fuel cut solenoid.

VEHICLE SERVICE INFORMATION

Vehicle Filling Capacities
Engine Oil dry fill : .... 6.5 Litres
Engine Oil with Filter: .... 6.0 Litres
Engine Oil without Filter: .... 5.0 Litres
Cooling System: .... 10.8 Litres (Europe With Heater)
Cooling System: .... 9.9 Litres (Without Heater)
Cooling System: .... 11.1Litres (Australia)
Cooling System: .... 10.2 Litres (Others)
Manual Transmission: .... 2.4 Litres
Rear Differential: .... 2.5 Litres

Vehicle Component Service Interval Changes
Timing Belt Replacement
Every 100,000kms
Check Valve Clearance:
Every 20,000kms
Engine Coolant/Anti Freeze
Change Every 24 Months/40,000kms
Air Cleaner Element:
Change Every 24 Months/40,000kms
Fuel Filter:
Change Every 12 Months/20,000kms
Engine Oil:
Change Every 5000kms
Engine Oil Filter:
Change Every 6 Months/10,000kms
Brake Fluid:
Change Every 24 Months/40,000kms
Manual Transmission Oil:
Change Every 18 Months/30,000kms
Auto Transmission Fluid
Change Every 24 Months/40,000kms
Rear Differential Oil:
Change Every 18 Months/30,000kms
Front Wheel Bearings
Repack Every 20,000kms

Toyota Hiace 3L Engine 1988-1996 LH103-113-125

CONTENTS   PAGE

214

Toyota Hiace 3L Engine 1988-1996 LH103-113-125

Engine Checks

Valve Clearance Check

Please Note: Before carrying out this check ensure that the engine is at normal operating temperature.

1. Remove the rocker cover, set the No1 piston to TDC on its compression stroke and ensure that the groove on the crankshaft pulley is lined up with the timing pointer on the front cover.

2. Ensure that the valve lifters on the No1 cylinder are loose and that the No4 valve lifters are tight (if they are not turn the engine on full turn (360°) and recheck).

3. Measure the valve clearances on the following valves 1&3 (Exhaust) and 1&2 (Inlet).

Inlet Valve Clearance: 0.20-030mm (Cold)
Exhaust Valve Clearance: 0.40-0.50mm (Cold)

If the clearances are not correct record the relevant readings to determine the adjusting shim required.

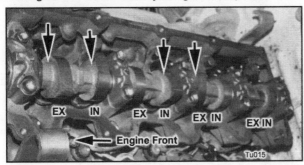

4. Turn the crankshaft one full turn (360°) and ensure that the groove on the crankshaft pulley is lined up with the timing pointer on the front cover.

5. Measure the valve clearances on the following valves 2&4 (Exhaust) and 3&4 (Inlet).

Inlet Valve Clearance: 0.20-030mm (Cold)
Exhaust Valve Clearance: 0.40-0.50mm (Cold)

6. If the clearances are not correct record the relevant readings to determine the adjusting shim required.

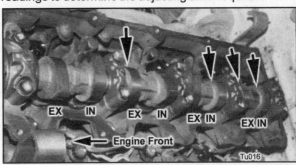

Compression Check

1. Run the engine to normal operating temperature, disconnect the fuel cut solenoid connector and remove all of the glow plugs from the engine.

2. Install an adaptor and compression gauge to the No1 cylinder, fully open the throttle, crank the engine and record the comprerssion pressure on each cylinder.

Compression Pressure: 3138kpa
Minimum Pressure: 1961kpa
Difference Between Each Cylinder: 490kpa

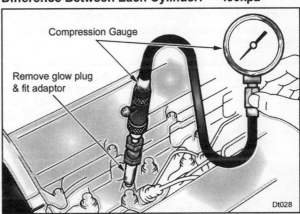

3. If the pressure on one or more cylinders is low, pour a small amount of oil into the cylinder through the glow plug hole and check the compression pressure again. If

it helps the pressure there are possibly faults with the piston rings or cylinder bores, if the oil does not help there may be a valve sticking or not seated correctly and/or leaks past the gasket.

Cylinder Head Tightening Procedures

1. After the cylinder head has been removed and the gasket replaced, apply a thin coat of oil to all of the cylinder head bolts. Install and gradually tighten each of the bolts to its correct torque in three stages in the sequence showed in the diagram.

Specified Torque Setting: 78Nm

Please Note: If any of the bolts do not reach the correct torque, check the length of the bolts.

Short Bolt:	**107mm**
Long Bolt:	**127mm**

Replace any faulty bolts as required.

2. Mark the front of each bolt with some paint and the tighten the bolts a further 90°. After the sequence has been completed tighten the bolts a further 90° and now ensure that the paint mark is facing to the rear.

Tighten Head Bolts in sequence shown

TIn032a

Piston Protrusion Height Check
No1 and 4 Piston Check

1. Rotate the engine and ensure that the timing marks on the crankshaft pulley line up with the marks on the front cover.

2. Fit a dial gauge to the engine block and set the gauge at the piston measuring point.

3. Find the point where the piston protrudes the most by turning the crankshaft in a clockwise and anti clockwise direction.

4. Set the dial gauge to zero and record the protrusion measurement from the block by sliding the dial gauge.

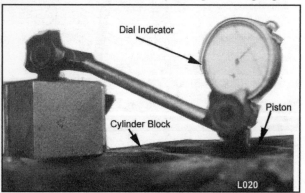

Dial Indicator

Cylinder Block

Piston

L020

Protrusion Measurement: 0.68-0.97mm

Please Note: Record the measurement at two separate measuring points.

No2 and No3 Piston Check

5. Turn the crankshaft 180° , Fit a dial gauge to the engine block and set the gauge at the piston measuring point.

6. Find the point where the piston protrudes the most by turning the crankshaft in a clockwise and anti clockwise direction.

7. Set the dial gauge to zero and record the protrusion measurement from the block by sliding the dial gauge.

Protrusion Measurement: 0.68-0.97mm

Please Note: Record the measurement at two separate measuring points.

8. When the measurment has been made, to select a new head gasket follow the procedures shown.

9. There are 3 different types of head gaskets marked either "B", "D" or "F", each of them different thicknesses.

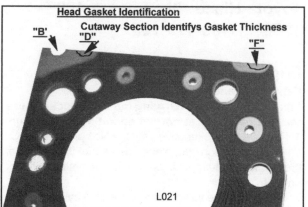

Head Gasket Identification

Cutaway Section Identifys Gasket Thickness

"B"   "D"   "F"

L021

Piston Protrusion Measurements	Gasket Thickness	Gasket Grade
0.68-0.77	1.4-1.5mm	B
0.78-0.87	1.5-1.6	D
0.88-0.97	1.6-1.7	F

Please Note: When selecting the gasket use the largest measurement of the 8 readings that are recorded.

Oil Pressure Check

1. Ensure that the engine oil level is correct, if not top up to suit.

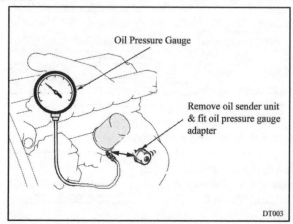

Oil Pressure Gauge

Remove oil sender unit & fit oil pressure gauge adapter

DT003

2. Remove the oil pressure switch from the engine and install a pressure gauge to the engine block.
3. Start the engine and run to normal operating temperature and then record the oil pressure shown on the gauge.
Specified Oil Pressure: 29kpa @ Idle
Specified Oil Pressure: 294-539kpa @ 3000RPM
4. If the oil pressure is not as shown, repair/replace as required.

Cooling System Thermostat Check
1. Remove the thermostat from the engine and put into a suitable container of water.
2. Heat the water gradually and and check the valve opening temperature and valve lift.
Valve Opening Temperature: 86-90°c
Valve Lift: More than 8mm
If the operation is not as shown above replace the thermostat.
3. Check that the valve spring is tight when the thermostat is fully closed, if not replace the thermostat.

Fuel Filter Check and Replacement

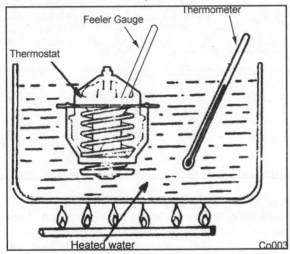

1. Remove the fuel filter sensor (if fitted) and drain the fuel, then remove the fuel filter.
2. Clean the fuel filter mounting bracket and then coat the fuel filter sealing rine with some diesel fuel.
3. Screw the fuel filter on until a slght resistance is felt and then turn another 2/3 of a turn or until suitably tight.
4. Install the fuel filter sensor (if fitted) to the new filter and then bleed any air present from the system.

Draining Water From The Filter
1. Loosen the drain cock 4 or 5 turns or remove the fuel filter sensor to allow the water to drain from the filter.
2. Retighten the drain cock or replace the sensor and bleed any air present from the system.
Diagram is in the next column

Fuel Filter Warning Lamp Check
1. Remove the switch from the filter and check that there is continuity between the terminals when the warning switch is ON (Float Up)
2. Check that there is no continuity between the terminals when the warning switch is OFF (Float Down)
3. If the operation is not as shown, repair/replace as required

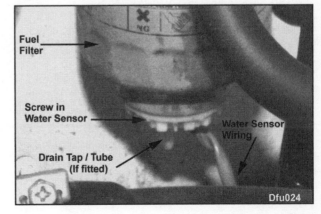

Injector Nozzle Check

1. Remove the injector from the vehicle, connect up to the pressure tester and check the initial pressure by pumping the tester handle a few times.

Initial Opening Pressure:
14,808-15,593-12,258kpa (New)

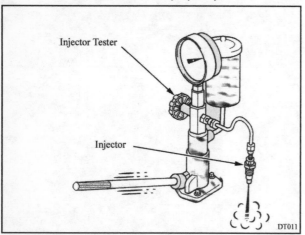

2. If the opening pressure is not as shown above, take the injector to pieces and change the adjusting shim on the top of the injector so as the correct pressure is recorded.

Adjusted Opening Pressure: 14,220-15,220kpa
Please Note: The adjusting shims vary in 0.025mm thicknesses, each 0.025mm will adjust the pressure by 341kpa. After the shim has been changed there should be no leakage from the injector (1988-1996)
Please Note: The adjusting shims vary in 0.05mm thicknesses, each 0.05mm will adjust the pressure by 628kpa. After the shim has been changed there should be no leakage from the injector(1996On)

3. Maintain the pressure between 981-1961kpa below the opening pressure and check that there is no leakage from the injector for a period of 10seconds.

4. Check the spray pattern by pumping the pressure tester handle 4-6 times or more per second and check the injection spray pattern.

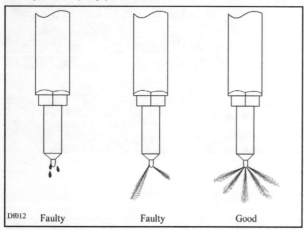

Faulty   Faulty   Good

5. If the operation and/or spray pattern is not as shown, repair/replace the nozzle/s as required.

Timing Belt Removal and Replacement

Removal Procedures

1. Remove the drive belts, water pump pulley, crankshaft pulley and the No1 timing cover.

2. Remove the timing belt guide, the current sensor and the 4 glow plugs.

3. Set the No1 piston to TDC on its compression stroke by temporarily replacing the cranksahft pulley bolt and turning the crankshaft in a clockwise direction until the timimg mark on the camshaft gear lines up with the mark on the No2 timing belt cover.

Please Note: If the timing belt is being used again, before removing, mark a direction arrow on the timing belt and place match,arks on the pulleys and the belt.

4. Loosen the No1 idler pulley mount bolts and move to the left as far as it will go. Temporarily tighten the bolt, relieve the belt tension and remove the timing belt from the engine.

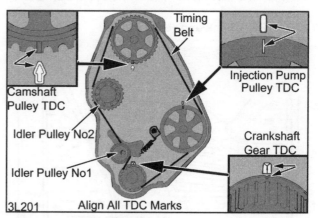

Replacement Procedures

Please Note: Before replacing the timimg belt check the condition and/or operation of the timing belt pulleys, tensioners and/or pulleys, if faults are found repair/replace as required.

1. Check the tensioner spring free length

Spring Free Length: 44.4-45.4mm

Check the tension of the spring at the specified free length

Installed Tension: 59Nm at 52.1mm

2. Install the crankshaft pulley to the engine, replace any pulleys or idlers that may have been removed for checking.

3. Set the No1 piston to TDC on its compression stroke and ensure that the timing marks on each of the pulleys line up with their relevant matchmarks.

4. Fit the timing belt onto the crankshaft pulley and No1 idler pulley, slightly turn the injection pulley in a clockwise direction, fit the timing belt onto the injection pulley and line up the marks on the injection pulley and timing belt case. ***Please Note: Ensure that there is belt tension between the crankshaft timing pulley and injection pump drive pulleys.***

5. Slightly turn the camshaft drive pulley in a clockwise direction, fit the timing belt onto the pulley and ensure that the marks on the pulley and timing belt case line up.

Please Note: Ensure that there is belt tension between the camshaft pulley and injection pump drive pulleys.

6. Install the timing belt to the No2 idler pulley.

7. Loosen the No1 idler pulley, stretch the timing belt and turn the crankshaft in a clockwise direction four full turns from TDC to TDC, ensuring that all of the timing marks on the drive pulleys line up with their respective match marks.

Please Note: If any of the marks do not line up, remove the belt and reinstall again.

8. Torque the No1 idler pulley bolt, refit the timimg belt guide and replace any removed components in the reverse order of removal.

Timing Belt Replacement Torques

Injection Pump Drive Pulley Nut: 64Nm
No1 Idle Pulley (12mm Bolt): 19Nm
No1 Idle Pulley (14mm Bolt): 44Nm
No2 Idle Pulley: 33Nm
Crankshaft Pulley Bolt: 167Nm
Camshaft Gear Bolt: 98Nm

Timing Belt Warning Lamp Reset Procedures (Rubber Plug in the Instrument Cluster Glass)

1. Remove the grommet from the speedometer and turn off the lamp by pushing the warning lamp reset switch, then replace the grommet.

2. Start the engine and ensure that the light stays off.

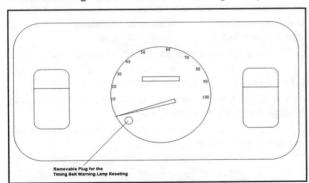

Removable Plug for the
Timing Belt Warning Lamp Reseting

Timing Belt Warning Lamp Reset Procedures (Change Screw Position on the Back of the Instrument Cluster)

1. Remove the instrument cluster from the vehicle, connect terminals A&B shown in the diagrams and then remove the CHARGE fuse from the vehicle.

2. Turn the ignition switch to ON and check that the warning lights light up, if not the check the condition and/or operation of the globe.

3. Check the condition and/or operation of the reset switches by checking that there is intermittent continuity between terminals A&B when the reset switch is pressed, if not repair/replace the speedometer/instru-

ment cluster as required.

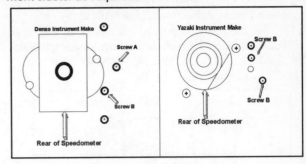

Engine Tightening Torques

Cylinder Head Tightening Torque Bolts: ....
.... 78Nm (1st Stage)
Cylinder Head Tightening Torque Bolts: ....
.... 90° (2nd Stage)
Cylinder Head Tightening Torque Bolts: ....
.... 90° (3rd Stage)
Camshaft Bearing Cap: 25Nm
Exhaust Manifold Bolts and Nuts: 52Nm
Inlet Manifold Bolts and Nuts: 24Nm
Glow Plugs: 13Nm
Injection Nozzle: 64Nm
Injection Pump Drive Pulley Nut: 64Nm
No1 Idle Pulley (12mm Bolt): 19Nm
No1 Idle Pulley (14mm Bolt): 44Nm
No2 Idle Pulley: 33Nm
Flywheel Bolts: 123Nm
Drive Plate: 98Nm
Connecting Rod Caps: .... 54Nm (1st Stage)
Connecting Rod Caps: .... 90° (2nd Stage)
Main Bearings: 103Nm
Crankshaft Pulley Bolt: 167Nm
Camshaft Gear Bolt: 98Nm
Oil Pump to Timing Cover: 10Nm
Oil Pump to Block: 23Nm
Oil Pump to Injection Pump: 21Nm
Oil Sump Bolt: 18Nm

System Adjustments

Injection Timing Adjustment (1988-1989)

1. Remove the distributive head bolt and install a special tool (SST09275-54010 plunger stroke measuring tool) to the plug hole and then set the No1 or No4 piston to 25° BTDC on its compression stroke.

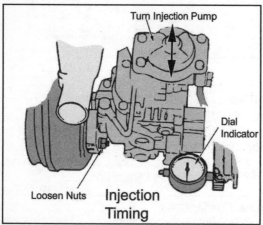

Turn Injection Pump

Dial Indicator

Loosen Nuts

Injection Timing

2. Please Note: (For vehicles with auto cold start device): Using a screwdriver turn the cold start lever anti clockwise about 20° and put a metal plate 8.5-10.0mm between the cold start lever and the thermo wax plunger.

3. Set the dial indicator to zero (mm) and then ensure it stays at zero (mm) while the crankshaft pulley is being moved right to left slightly.

4. Slowly turn the crankshaft pulley until crankshaft pulley groove is lined up with the timing pointer and record the plunger movement.

Injection Plunger Stroke:
0.54-0.66 (With Auto Cold Start Device)
Injection Plunger Stroke:
0.84-0.96mm (W/Out Auto Cold Start Device)

5. If the plunger stroke measurment is not as shown, loosen the 4 injector pipe union nuts and inlet pipe union nuts on the injection pump side.

6. Loosen the 4 injection pump mounting nuts and adjust the plunger pump stroke by slightly tilting the injection pump body. If the stroke is less than shown tilt the pump towards the engine, if the plunger strike is more than shown tilt the pump away from the engine.

7. Retighten all of the fixing bolts and union nuts, recheck the plunger stroke and then remove the plate from the cold starting lever.

8. Remove the dial indicator gauge and replace the plug bolt. Restart the engine and check for any leaks in the system.

Injection Timing Adjustment (1989-1996)

1. Remove the distributive head bolt and install a special tool (SST09275-54011 plunger stroke measuring tool) to the plug hole and then set the No1 or No4 piston to 25° BTDC on its compression stroke.

2. Please Note: (For vehicles with auto cold start device): Using a screwdriver turn the cold start lever anti clockwise about 20° and put a metal plate 8.5-10.0mm between the cold start lever and the thermo wax plunger.

3. Turn the crankshaft pulley in a clockwise direction until it is between 25-30° BTDC, set the dial indicator to zero (mm).Slowly turn the crankshaft pulley until crankshaft pulley groove is lined up with the timing pointer and record the plunger movement.

Injection Plunger Stroke: 0.54-0.66 (Europe
and others With Auto Cold Start Device)
Injection Plunger Stroke: 0.84-0.96mm
(Without Auto Cold Start Device)

4. If the plunger stroke measurment is not as shown, loosen the 4 injector pipe union nuts and inlet pipe union nuts on the injection pump side.

5. Loosen the 4 injection pump mounting nuts and adjust the plunger pump stroke by slightly tilting the injection pump body. If the stroke is less than shown tilt the pump towards the engine, if the plunger strike is more than shown tilt the pump away from the engine.

6. Retighten all of the fixing bolts and union nuts, recheck the plunger stroke and then remove the plate from the cold starting lever.

7. Remove the dial indicator gauge and replace the plug bolt. Restart the engine and check for any leaks in the system.

Refer Previous Injection Timing Diagram

Idle Speed Check

1. Ensure that the air cleaner is OK, the engine coolant temperature is at normal, the accessories are all switched off and that the transmission is in neutral.

2. Ensure that the adjusting screw lever touches the idle speed adjusting screw when the throttle pedal is released, if it is not adjust to suit.

3. Install a tachometer to the engine, start the engine and check the idle speed setting.

Idle Speed Setting: 700RPM (Manual)
Idle Speed Setting: 800RPM (Auto)

4. If the idle speed is not as shown in step3, disconnect the throttle linkage, loosen the lock nut of the idle adjust screw and adjust by turning the idle speed adjusting screw, re-tighten the lock nut, and reconnect the throttle linkage. Recheck the idle speed.

5- Remove the tachometer from the engine and replace any removed parts to the vehicle.

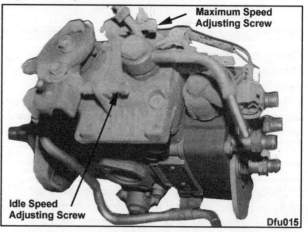

Maximum Speed Adjusting Screw

Idle Speed Adjusting Screw

Dfu015

Maximum Speed Adjustment Check (1988-1989)

1. Ensure that the adjusting lever touches the maximum speed adjusting screw when the throttle is pressed down all the way, if not adjust the throttle linkages
2. Install a tachometer to the engine, start the engine, press the throttle fully down and check the maximum speed.

Maximum Speed Setting:

4700RPM (LH Except Australia)
4900RPM (LH Australia)
5100RPM (LH Europe),

3. If the maximum speed is not as shown, disconnect the throttle linkage, cut the seal wire on the adjusting screw, loosen the lock nut on the maximum speed adjusting screw and adjust by turning the adjusting screw.
4. Check the idle speed setting, raise the engine speed and recheck the maximum speed.
5. Retighten the lock nut, re-seal the adjusting screw, reconnect the throttle linkage and recheck the throttle linkage adjustment.
6. Remove the tachometer from the engine and replace any removed parts to the vehicle.

Refer Previous Idle Speed Diagrams

Maximum Speed Adjustment Check (1989-1996)

1. Ensure that the adjusting lever touches the maximum speed adjusting screw when the throttle is pressed down all the way, if not adjust the throttle linkages
2. Install a tachometer to the engine, start the engine, press the throttle fully down and check the maximum speed.

Maximum Speed Setting:

4400RPM
(Hong Kong/Singapore Malaysia)
4600RPM
(Ex Hong Kong/Singapore Malaysia)

3. If the maximum speed is not as shown, disconnect the throttle linkage, cut the seal wire on the adjusting screw, loosen the lock nut on the maximum speed adjusting screw and adjust by turning the adjusting screw.
4. Check the idle speed setting, raise the engine speed and recheck the maximum speed.
5. Retighten the lock nut, re-seal the adjusting screw, reconnect the throttle linkage and recheck the throttle linkage adjustment.
6. Remove the tachometer from the engine and replace any removed parts to the vehicle.

Refer Previous Idle Speed Diagrams

Fuel Heater System Check

Fuel Heater Check (LH Models 1988-1989)

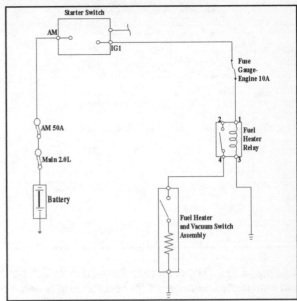

1. Apply 38±6.7kpa or more to the vacuum switch port and with an ohmmete record the resistance between terminal 1 and switch body

Specified Resistance: **0.7 ohms @ 20°c**

If the resistance is not as shown, repair/replace as required.

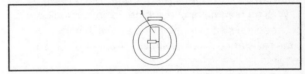

Vacuum Switch Check (LH Models 1988-1989)

1. With an ohmmeter check there is no continuity between the switch terminal 1 and switch body.
If the resistance is not as shown, repair/replace as required.
2. Apply a vacuum of 38±6.7kpa or more to the vacuum port and check that there is continuity between the switch terminal 1 and body.
3. If the operation is not as shown, repair/replace as required.

Refer to Fuel Heater Connector Diagram

Fuel Heater Check (LH Models 1989-1996)

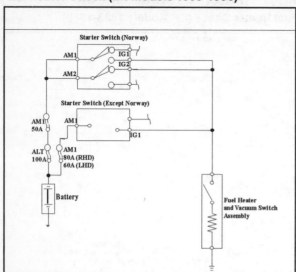

1. Apply 46.7±6.7kpa or more to the vacuum switch port and with an ohmmeter record the resistance between terminal 1 and switch body

Specified Resistance: 0.5-2.0ohms @ 20°c

2. If the resistance is not as shown, repair/replace as required

Refer to Previous Fuel Heater Connector Diagram

Vacuum Switch Check (LH Models 1989-1996)

1. With an ohmmeter check there is no continuity between the switch terminal 1 and switch body.
If the resistance is not as shown, repair/replace as required.

2. Apply a vacuum of 46.7±6.7kpa or more to the vacuum port and check that there is continuity between the switch terminal 1 and body.

3. If the operation is not as shown, repair/replace as required.

Refer to Previous Fuel Heater Connector Diagram

Fuel Heater Relay

1. Remove the relay (located under the instrument panel in the relay block (LH) and check for continuity between terminals 1-3 (ensure continuity exists), and between terminals 3-4 (ensure continuity does not exist).

2. Apply battery voltage between the 1-3 terminals and ensure continuity exists between the 2-4 terminals.'
If the operation is not as shown, repair/replace as required.

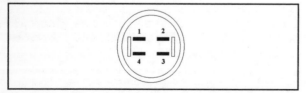

Pre-Heating System Checks
Super Glow System (LH Models for Europe (1988-1996)
System Diagram 1988-1989

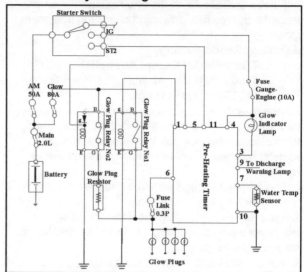

System Diagram 1989-1996

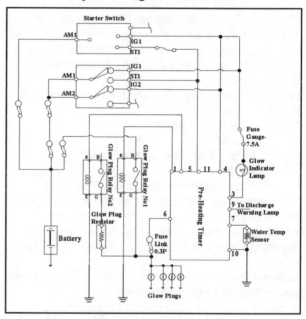

Pre-Heating Timer Check

Please Note: Before starting test please ensure that the battery is fully charged, the engine cranks normally and that all the fuse links are OK.
The timer unit is located in under the instrument panel on the LH side

1. Check if the glow indicator lamp lights up when the starter switch is ON, (Coolant Temp is 20°c and lamp lights up for 2-3 seconds).

2. If the operation is not as shown, check to ensure that the fuse/s are OK, if they are not check for any short circuit/s and repair as required.

3. If the fuses are OK in step2, check the condition and/or operation of the indicator lamp globe, if faults are found repair/replace as required.

4. If the bulb is Ok in step3, check for battery voltage to terminal 3 on the pre-heating timer connector (on the wiring harness side), if the voltage is Ok, repair/replace the timer as required.

5. If the glow indicator lamp is OK in step1, turn off the starter switch and check for battery voltage at the pre-heater timer terminal 1 with the starter switch ON, if there is no voltage check that there is 1v or less to terminal 9, if the voltage is OK, replace the timer.

6. If the voltage in step5 is Ok, check the the voltage to the pre-heat timer terminal 1 is terminated after the engine has started, if it is not, start the engine and check for voltage present at terminal 9 of the pre heating timer, if the voltage is Ok, replace the timer, if the voltage is not Ok, repair fault/s in the vehicle charging system.

7. If the voltage is terminated in step6, turn off the starter switch, turn on again and check for current flow to terminal 5 of the timer in relation to the coolant temperature.

Current Flow: 16-26seconds @ less than 50°c
Current Flow: 1.7seconds @ more than 50°c
If there is no voltage at all replace the timer.

8. If the pre heating time is a lot different from what was shown in step7, the timer is faulty and should be replaced.

9. If the pre-heat time is Ok in step7, check for voltage at the timer terminal 8 when the ignition switch is in the ST position, if there is no voltage the timer needs replacing.

10. If the voltage is Ok in step9, put the starter switch in the ON position and check for voltage at the timer terminal 5 when the starter switch is at "Start", if there is no voltage at all replace the timer.

11. If the voltage in step10 is OK , switch off the ignition, switch ON the ignition and check for voltage to the glow plugs with coolant temperature a 50°c or less, (a few seconds after the voltage should drop by half). If there is no voltage at all, check for battery voltage at the (+) side of the glow plug resistor, if there is no voltage present at the (+) side of the resistor replace the No1 glow plug relay.

12. If the voltage in step11 remains at battery voltage or drops to 0v, check for battery voltage at the (+) side of the glow plug resistor, if the voltage is Ok, replace the resistor, if there is no voltage present at the (+) side of the resistor replace the No2 glow plug relay.

13. If the voltage is OK in step12, check the glow plug/s resistance, if the reading is infinity, repair/replace as required, if the reading is about 0ohms, the glow plugs are OK.

Pre Heating Time Unit Voltage Check
The timer unit is located in under the instrument panel on the LH side (LH 1988-1989), The timer unit is located in LH Side Centre Pillar (1989 On)

1. Disconnect the connector from the timer and check the connector harness as shown in the chart below.

Check For	Between Terminals	Condition	Specified Value
Continuity	1-ground		Continuity
Voltage	3-ground	Starter Switch OFF	No volts
Voltage	3-ground	Starter Switch ON	Battery volts
Voltage	4-ground	Starter Switch OFF	No volts
Voltage	4-ground	Starter Switch ON	Battery volts
Continuity	5-ground		Continuity
Continuity	6-ground		Continuity
Continuity	7-ground		Continuity
Continuity	10-ground		Continuity
Voltage	11-ground	Starter Switch OFF	No volts
Voltage	11-ground	Starter Switch Start	Battery volts

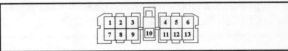

No1 Glow Plug Relay Check. (LH Europe Models 1988 On)
Please Note: The relay is located in the engine compartment on the LH side

1. With an ohmmeter check the continuity between the terminals 1-2 and ensure that it exists, check between terminals 3-4 and ensure that it does not exist.

2. Apply battery volts between terminals 1-2 and ensure that continuity exists between terminals 3-4

No1 Glow Plug Relay Connector 1988-1989

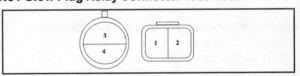

No1 Glow Plug Relay Connector 1989-1996

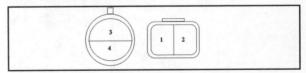

No2 Glow Plug Relay Check (LH Europe Models 1988 On)
Please Note: The relay is located Under the instrument panel on LH Side

1. With an ohmmeter check the continuity between the terminals 1-2 and ensure that it exists, check between terminals 3-4 and ensure that it does not exist.

2. Apply battery volts between terminals 1-2 and ensure that continuity exists between terminals 3-4
Diagrams on the next page

No2 Glow Plug Relay Connector 1988-1989

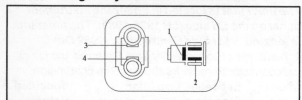

No2 Glow Plug Relay Connector 1989-1996

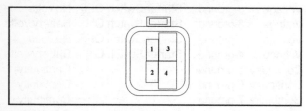

Glow Plug Check

1. With an ohmmeter check that there is continuity between the glow plug terminal and ground, if continuity does not exist, replace the faulty glow plug/s

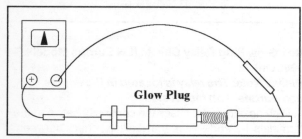

Glow Plug

Glow Plug Sensor Check

1. With an ohmmeter check that there is continuity between the sensor terminals, if no continuity exists replace the sensor.

Water Temperature Sensor Check (1988-1989)

1. Remove the sensor harness connector and check the resistance between the sensor terminals at varying temperatures.

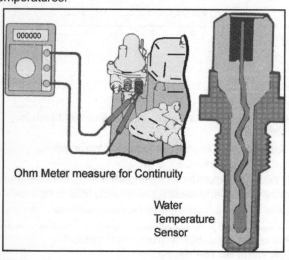

Ohm Meter measure for Continuity

Water Temperature Sensor

Temperature (°c)	Resistance (k/ohms)
0	5.0
20	2.0
40	1.0
60	0.4
80	0.14
100	0.08

2. If the resistance is not as shown, repair/replace as required.

Water Temperature Sensor Check (1989-1996)

1. Remove the sensor from the engine and place in a suitable container of water. Heat the water gradually and check the resistance between the sensor terminals at varying temperatures.

Sensor Temperature (°c)	Sensor Resistance (k/ohms)
0	5.0
20	2.0
40	1.0
60	0.4
80	0.14
100	0.08

2. If the resistance is not as shown, repair/replace as required

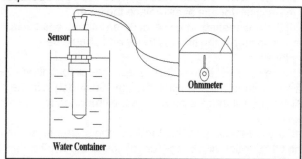

Sensor

Ohmmeter

Water Container

Main Relay Check (1988-1989)

Please Note: This relay is located under the instrument panel in the relay box (LH Models)

1. With an ohmmeter check the continuity between the terminals 1-3 and ensure that it exists, check between terminals 2-4 and ensure that it does not exist.

2. Apply battery volts between terminals 1-3 and ensure that continuity exists between terminals 2-4

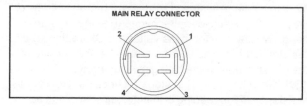

MAIN RELAY CONNECTOR

Pre-Heating System Checks Variable Delay System

Pre-Heat Timer Check ((LH 103/112/125 Models Australia 1988-1989)

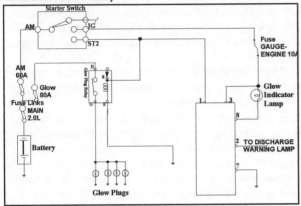

The timer unit is located in under the instrument panel on the LH side (LH)

1. Disconnect the connector from the timer and check the connector harness as shown in the chart below.

Check For	Between Terminals	Condition	Specified Value
Voltage	1-ground	Starter Switch OFF	No volts
Voltage	1-ground	Starter Switch Start	Battery volts
Voltage	3-ground	Starter Switch OFF	No volts
Voltage	3-ground	Starter Switch ON	Battery volts
Continuity	7-ground		Continuity
Voltage	8-ground	Starter Switch OFF	No volts
Voltage	8-ground	Starter Switch Start	Battery volts

Pre-Heat Timer Check (LH 103/112/125 Models 1989-1996)
The timer unit is located in the LH Side centre pillar (LH)

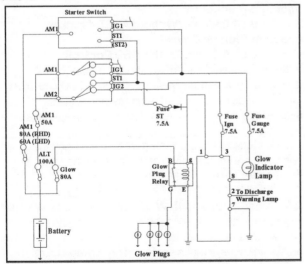

1. Disconnect the connector from the timer and check the connector harness as shown in the chart in the next column.

Check For	Between Terminals	Condition	Specified Value
Voltage	1-ground	Starter Switch OFF	No volts
Voltage	1-ground	Starter Switch Start	Battery volts
Voltage	3-ground	Starter Switch OFF	No volts
Voltage	3-ground	Starter Switch ON	Battery volts
Continuity	7-ground		Continuity
Voltage	8-ground	Starter Switch OFF	No volts
Voltage	8-ground	Starter Switch Start	Battery volts

Glow Indicator Lamp Check
1. Turn the ignition switch to "Start" and check the lamp light up time.
Lamp Light Up Time: Approx 5 Seconds

Glow Plug Relay Check (LH 103/112/125 Models 1988-1989).
Please Note: The relay is located Under the instrument panel on LH Side
1. With an ohmmeter check the continuity between the terminals 1-2 and ensure that it exists, check between terminals 3-4 and ensure that it does not exist.
2. Apply battery volts between terminals 1-2 and ensure that continuity exists between terminals 3-4
Refer Glow Plug Relay No2 Diagram in Superglow System

Glow Plug Check
1. With an ohmmeter check that there is continuity between the glow plug terminal and ground, if continuity does not exist, replace the faulty glow plug/s
Refer previous glow plug check diagrams

Pre-Heating System Checks Fixed Delay System
Pre-Heat Timer Check (LH Models Except Europe/Australia 1988-1996)

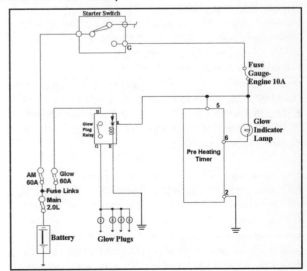

The timer unit is located in under the instrument panel on the LH side

1. Disconnect the connector from the timer and check the connector harness as shown in the chart below.

Check For	Between Terminals	Condition	Specified Value
Continuity	2-ground		Continuity
Voltage	5-ground	Starter Switch OFF	No volts
Voltage	5-ground	Starter Switch Glow	Battery volts
Voltage	6-ground	Starter Switch OFF	No volts
Voltage	6-ground	Starter Switch Glow	Battery volts

Glow Indicator Lamp Check

1. Turn the ignition switch to "Start" and check the lamp light up time.

Lamp Light Up Time: Approx 15-19.5 Seconds

Glow Plug Relay Check.

Please Note: The relay is located in the engine compartment on the rear side

1. With an ohmmeter check the continuity between the terminals 1-2 and ensure that it exists, check between terminals 3-4 and ensure that it does not exist.

2. Apply battery volts between terminals 1-2 and ensure that continuity exists between terminals 3-4

Refer Glow Plug Relay No2 Diagram in Superglow System

Glow Plug Check

1. With an ohmmeter check that there is continuity between the glow plug terminal and ground, if continuity does not exist, replace the faulty glow plug/s

Refer Previous Glow Plug Check Diagrams

Injection System and Engine Diagnosis and Troubleshooting

Engine Will Not Crank

1. Check the condition and/or operation of the battery cables between the battery and starter motor, if faults are found repair/replace as required.

2. If no faults are found in step1, check the condition and/or operation of the battery, alternator output and/or drive belt, if faults are found repair/replace as required.

3. If no faults are found in step2, check the condition and/or operation of the starter motor, if faults are found repair/replace as required.

Engine Cranks Slowly or Will Not Start

1. Check the condition and/or operation of the battery cables between the battery and starter motor, if faults are found repair/replace as required.

2. If no faults are found in step1, check the condition and/or operation of the battery, alternator output and/or drive belt, if faults are found repair/replace as required.

3. If no faults are found in step2, check that the correct grade of engine oil is being used on the vehicle, if not drain and replace with the correct grade of oil.

Engine Cranks Normally But Does Not Start

1. If the engine cranks normally but does not start, check and ensure that fuel is reaching the injection nozzles by loosening any of the injection pipes, cranking the engine and ensuring that fuel is coming out of the pipe.

2. If fuel is not coming out of the pipe in step1, check the operation of the fuel cut solenoid, if faults are found repair/replace as required.

3. If no faults are found in step3, check to ensure that fuel is getting to the injection pump by disconnecting the inlet hoses from the fuel filter, feeding clean fuel from a separate container directly into the injection pump. If the engine now starts there may be blockages in the fuel filter and/or line between the fuel tank and fuel filter. If the engine does not start, check the condition and/or operation of the fuel line between the fuel filter and fuel pump. If the injection pump operation is normal it should be replaced.

4. If fuel is present in step1, check the pre-heating operation system operation by ensuring that after the ignition is turned on, the glow plug lamp lights up and that there are 6v applied to the glow plugs, if the operation is not as shown, repair/replace as required.

5. If no faults are found in step4, check the operation of the glow plug/s, if faults are found repair/replace as required.

6. If no faults are found in step5, check the fuel system pipes, hoses and/or components for leaks, cracks and/or damage, if faults are found repair/replace as required.

7. If no faults are found in step6, check the injection timing by setting either the No1 or No4 piston at TDC, releasing the cold start advance systen (where fitted) and checking the plunger stroke.

Injection Plunger Stroke:
**   0.84-0.96mm (Without ACSD Control)**
Injection Plunger Stroke:
**   0.54-0.66mm (With ACSD Control)**

If the timing setting is not as shown, adjust to suit.

8. If no faults are found in step7, **(With ACSD Control Only),** check the cold start advance and fast idle system operation, if faults are found repair/replace as required.

9. If no faults are found in step7and/or 8, check the condition and/or operation of the injection nozzles, if faults are found repair/replace as required.

Idle Speed is Unstable When The Engine is Warm

1. If the idle speed is unstable when the engine is warm, check the condition and/or operation of the throttle cable and/or linkages, if faults are found repair/replace as required.

2. If no faults are found in step1, check the engine idle speed setting.

Idle Speed: 700RPM (Manual)
Idle Speed: 800RPM (Auto)

If the idle speed setting is not as shown, adjust to suit

3. If no faults are found in step2, check the fuel system components and/or lines for leaks and/or damage, if faults are found repair/replace as required.

4. If no faults are found in step3, check the injection timing by setting either the No1 or No4 piston at TDC, releasing the cold start advance systen (where fitted) and checking the plunger stroke.

Injection Plunger Stroke:

0.84-0.96mm (Without ACSD Control)

Injection Plunger Stroke:

0.54-0.66mm (With ACSD Control)

If the timing setting is not as shown, adjust to suit.

5. If no faults are found in step4, check the operation of the injection nozzle/s and/or the delivery valve by letting the engine run at idle speed, loosening the union nuts on each of the cylinders in order and check if there is any change of idle speed. If there is no change at any of the cylinders this will indicate that a faulty cylinder/s is present. To fix the problem check the injection nozzle pressure.

Injection Nozzle Pressure: 14,200-1520kpa

6. If the pressure is not as shown adjust pressure to suit. If the pressure is OK, the fault will be with the delivery valve and should be replaced.

Rough Idle When the Engine is Warm

1. If the engine idle is rough when the engine is warm, check the throttle linkages and/or cable for correct operation and/or adjustment, if faults are found repair/replace as required.

2. If no faults are found in step1, with the engine running check the idle speed setting.

Idle Speed: 700RPM (Manual)

Idle Speed: 800RPM (Auto)

If the idle speed setting is not as shown, adjust to suit

3. If no faults are found in step2, check the fuel system pipes, hoses and/or components for leaks, cracks and/or damage, if faults are found repair/replace as required.

4. If no faults are found in step3, check the injection timing by setting either the No1 or No4 piston at TDC, releasing the cold start advance systen (where fitted) and checking the plunger stroke.

Injection Plunger Stroke:

0.84-0.96mm (Without ACSD Control)

Injection Plunger Stroke:

0.54-0.66mm (With ACSD Control)

If the timing setting is not as shown, adjust to suit.

5. If no faults are found in step4 check the check the injection nozzle pressure.

Injection Nozzle Pressure: 14,200-1520kpa

6. If the pressure is not as shown adjust pressure to suit, if the pressure cannot be adjusted, replace the faulty nozzle/s

Engine Suddenly Stops

1. If the engine is running and then suddenly stops, switch off the ignition and try and start the engine, if it does not re-start, check and ensure that fuel is reaching the injection nozzles by loosening any of the injection pipes, cranking the engine and ensuring that fuel is coming out of the pipe.

2. If fuel is not coming out of the pipe in step1, check the operation of the fuel cut solenoid, if faults are found repair/replace as required.

3. If no faults are found in step3, check to ensure that fuel is getting to the injection pump by disconnecting the inlet hoses from the fuel filter, feeding clean fuel from a separate container directly into the injection pump. If the engine now starts there may be blockages in the fuel filter and/or line between the fuel tank and fuel filter. If the engine does not start, check the condition and/or operation of the fuel line between the fuel filter and fuel pump. If the injection pump operation is normal it should be replaced.

4. If fuel is present in step1, check the pre-heating operation system operation by ensuring that after the ignition is turned on, the glow plug lamp lights up and that there are 6v applied to the glow plugs, if the operation is not as shown, repair/replace as required.

5. If no faults are found in step4, check the operation of the glow plug/s, if faults are found repair/replace as required.

6. If no faults are found in step5, check the fuel system pipes, hoses and/or components for leaks, cracks and/or damage, if faults are found repair/replace as required.

7. If no faults are found in step6, check the injection timing by setting either the No1 or No4 piston at TDC, releasing the cold start advance systen (where fitted) and checking the plunger stroke.

Injection Plunger Stroke:

0.84-0.96mm (Without ACSD Control)

Injection Plunger Stroke:

0.54-0.66mm (With ACSD Control)

If the timing setting is not as shown, adjust to suit.

8. If no faults are found in step7, **(With Cruise ACSD Control),** check the cold start advance and fast idle system operation, if faults are found repair/replace as required.

9. If no faults are found in step7and/or 8, check the condition and/or operation of the injection nozzles, if faults are found repair/replace as required.

Engine Has a Lack of Power (1988-1989)

1. If the engine has any lack of power, check the maximum speed operation by ensuring that the adjusting lever touches the maximum speed adjusting screw when the throttle is pressed down all the way, if not adjust the throttle linkages

2. Install a tachometer to the engine, start the engine, press the throttle fully down and check the maximum speed.

Maximum Speed Setting:

4700RPM (LH Except Australia)

4900RPM (LH Australia)

5100RPM (LH Europe)

4400RPM (Hong Kong/Malaysia)

4600RPM (Except Hong Kong/Malaysia)

3. If the maximum speed is not as shown, disconnect the throttle linkage, cut the seal wire on adjusting screw, loosen the lock nut on the maximum speed adjusting screw and adjust by turning the adjusting screw.

4. Check the idle speed setting, raise the engine speed and recheck the maximum speed.

5. Retighten the lock nut, re-seal the adjusting screw, reconnect the throttle linkage and recheck the throttle linkage adjustment.

6. Remove the tachometer from the engine and replace any removed parts to the vehicle.

7. If the maximum speed in step2 is OK, check the interchanged overflow screw (out) and inlet (no marking) are fitted into the correct positions (the screw marked out has an inner jet) and cannot be intercahnged.

8. If no faults are found in step7, check the fuel system pipes, hoses and/or components for leaks, cracks and/or damage, if faults are found repair/replace as required.

9. If no faults are found in step8, disconnect the inlet hoses from the fuel filter and pour diesel fuel directly into the injection pump, if the condition now improves replace the fuel filter. If the condition does not improve after the fuel filter has been replaced, check the condition and/or operation of the priming pump, if faults are found repair/replace as required.

10. If no faults are found in step9, check the injection timing by setting either the No1 or No4 piston at TDC, releasing the cold start advance systen (where fitted) and checking the plunger stroke.

Injection Plunger Stroke:
0.84-0.96mm (Without ACSD Control)
Injection Plunger Stroke:
0.54-0.66mm (With ACSD Control)
If the timing setting is not as shown, adjust to suit.

11. If no faults are found in step10, check the check the injection nozzle pressure.

Injection Nozzle Pressure: **14,200-1520kpa**

12. If the pressure is not as shown adjust pressure to suit, if the pressure cannot be adjusted, replace the faulty nozzle/s

Engine Has a Lack of Power (1989-1996)
Please Note: Before carrying out this test, ensure that the air cleaner is not blocked and the engine is not overheating

1. If the engine has any lack of power, check the maximum speed operation by ensuring that the adjusting lever touches the maximum speed adjusting screw when the throttle is pressed down all the way, if not adjust the throttle linkages

2. Install a tachometer to the engine, start the engine, press the throttle fully down and check the maximum speed.

Maximum Speed Setting:
4400RPM (Hong Kong/Singapore Malaysia)
4600RPM (Ex Hong Kong/Singapore and Malaysia)

3. If the maximum speed is not as shown, disconnect the throttle linkage, cut the seal wire on the adjusting screw, loosen the lock nut on the maximum speed adjusting screw and adjust by turning the adjusting screw.

4. Check the idle speed setting, raise the engine speed and recheck the maximum speed.

5. Retighten the lock nut, re-seal the adjusting screw, reconnect the throttle linkage and recheck the throttle linkage adjustment.

6. Remove the tachometer from the engine and replace any removed parts to the vehicle.

7. If the maximum speed in step2 is OK, check the interchanged overflow screw (out) and inlet (no marking) are fitted into the correct positions (the screw marked out has an inner jet) and cannot be intercahnged.

8. If no faults are found in step7, check the fuel system pipes, hoses and/or components for leaks, cracks and/or damage, if faults are found repair/replace as required.

9. If no faults are found in step8, disconnect the inlet hoses from the fuel filter and pour diesel fuel directly into the injection pump, if the condition now improves replace the fuel filter. If the condition does not improve after the fuel filter has been replaced, check the condition and/or operation of the priming pump, if faults are found repair/replace as required.

10. If no faults are found in step9, check the injection timing by setting either the No1 or No4 piston at TDC, releasing the cold start advance systen (where fitted) and checking the plunger stroke.

Injection Plunger Stroke:
0.84-0.96mm (Without ACSD Control)
Injection Plunger Stroke:
0.54-0.66mm (With ACSD Control)
If the timing setting is not as shown, adjust to suit.

11. If no faults are found in step10, check the check the injection nozzle pressure.

Injection Nozzle Pressure:
13,729-15,690kpa (New Nozzle)
Injection Nozzle Pressure:
14,810-15,950kpa (Reused Nozzle)

12. If the pressure is not as shown adjust pressure to suit, if the pressure cannot be adjusted, replace the faulty nozzle/s

Rough Idle When the Engine is Warm

1. If the engine idle is rough when the engine is warm, check the throttle linkages and/or cable for correct operation and/or adjustment, if faults are found repair/replace as required.

2. If no faults are found in step1, with the engine running check the idle speed setting.

Idle Speed: **700RPM (Manual)**
Idle Speed: **800RPM (Auto)**
If the idle speed setting is not as shown, adjust to suit

3. If no faults are found in step2, check the fuel system pipes, hoses and/or components for leaks, cracks and/or damage, if faults are found repair/replace as required.

Excessive Exhaust Smoke

1. Check the condition and/or operation of the alr cleaner element, if faults are found repair/replace as required.

2. If no faults are found in step1, check the engine oil consumption, if faults are found repair/replace as required.

3. If the oil consumption is OK in step2, check the injection timing by setting either the No1 or No4 piston at TDC, releasing the cold start advance systen (where fitted) and checking the plunger stroke.

Injection Plunger Stroke:

0.84-0.96mm (Without ACSD Control)

Injection Plunger Stroke:

0.54-0.66mm (With ACSD Control)

If the timing setting is not as shown, adjust to suit.

(Please Note: If the exhaust smoke is black it tends to indicate that the timing is advanced and if the smoke is white that the timing is retarded).

4. If no faults are found in step3, disconnect the inlet hoses from the fuel filter and pour diesel fuel directly into the injection pump, if the condition now improves replace the fuel filter. If the condition does not improve after the fuel filter has been replaced, check the condition and/or operation of the priming pump, if faults are found repair/replace as required. *(Please Note: At between 2000-3000RPM a blocked fuel filter tends to make the exhaust smoke white).*

5. If no faults are found in step4, check the check the injection nozzle pressure.

Injection Nozzle Pressure: **14,200-1520kpa**

6. If the pressure is not as shown adjust pressure to suit, if the pressure cannot be adjusted, replace the faulty nozzle/s. *(Please Note: Excessive exhaust smoke is normally caused when the nozzle pressure is to low)*

Fuel Consumption is Poor

1. If the fuel consumption is poor, check the fuel system components and/or lines for leaks and/or damage, if faults are found repair/replace as required.

2. If no faults are found in step1, with the engine running check the idle speed setting.

Idle Speed: **700RPM (Manual)**

Idle Speed: **800RPM (Auto)**

If the idle speed setting is not as shown, adjust to suit

3. If the idle speed setting is OK in step2, check the no load maximum speed setting is OK by starting the engine, pressing down the throttle pedal to the floor and cheking the no load maximum speed setting.

Maximum Speed Setting:

4700RPM (Except Australia)

4900RPM (Australia)

5100RPM (Europe)

4400RPM (Hong Kong/Malaysia)

4600RPM (Except Hong Kong/Malaysia)

If the setting is not OK, adjust using the maximum speed adjusting screw.

4. If no faults are found in step3, check the injection timing by setting either the No1 or No4 piston at TDC, releasing the cold start advance systen (where fitted) and checking the plunger stroke.

Injection Plunger Stroke:

0.84-0.96mm (Without ACSD Control)

njection Plunger Stroke:

0.54-0.66mm (With ACSD Control)

If the timing setting is not as shown, adjust to suit.

5. If no faults are found in step4, check the check the injection nozzle pressure.

Injection Nozzle Pressure: **14,200-1520kpa**

6. If the pressure is not as shown adjust pressure to suit, if the pressure cannot be adjusted, replace the faulty nozzle/s.

Excessive Fuel Consumption

1. If the fuel consumption is poor, check the fuel system components and/or lines for leaks and/or damage, if faults are found repair/replace as required.

2. If no faults are found in step1, with the engine running check the idle speed setting.

Idle Speed: **700RPM (Manual)**

Idle Speed: **800RPM (Auto)**

If the idle speed setting is not as shown, adjust to suit

3. If the idle speed setting is OK in step2, check the no load maximum speed setting is OK by starting the engine, pressing down the throttle pedal to the floor and cheking the no load maximum speed setting.

Maximum Speed Setting:

4400RPM

(Hong Kong/Singapore Malaysia)

4600RPM

(Exc Hong Kong/Singapore Malaysia)

If the setting is not OK, adjust using the maximum speed adjusting screw.

4. If no faults are found in step3, check the injection timing by setting either the No1 or No4 piston at TDC, releasing the cold start advance systen (where fitted) and checking the plunger stroke.

Injection Plunger Stroke:

0.84-0.96mm (W/Out Auto Cold Start Device)

Injection Plunger Stroke:

0.54-0.66mm (With Auto Cold Start Device)

If the timing setting is not as shown, adjust to suit.

5. If no faults are found in step4, check the check the injection nozzle pressure.

Injection Nozzle Pressure:

14,808-15,593kpa (New Nozzle)

Injection Nozzle Pressure:

14,200-15200kpa (Reused Nozzle)

6. If the pressure is not as shown adjust pressure to suit, if the pressure cannot be adjusted, replace the faulty nozzle/s.

Noise When The Engine Is Warm

1. If the engine is noisey when it is warm, first check the operation of the temperature gauge if that is Ok, check the operation of the thermostat if faults are found repair/replace as required.

2. If no faults are found in step1, check the injection timing by setting either the No1 or No4 piston at TDC, releasing the cold start advance systen (where fitted) and checking the plunger stroke.

Injection Plunger Stroke:

0.84-0.96mm (Without ACSD Control)

Injection Plunger Stroke:

0.54-0.66mm (With ACSD Control)

If the timing setting is not as shown, adjust to suit.

3. If no faults are found in step2, check the check the injection nozzle pressure.

Injection Nozzle Pressure: 14,200-1520kpa

4. If the pressure is not as shown adjust pressure to suit, if the pressure cannot be adjusted, replace the faulty nozzle/s.

Engine Will Not Return to Idle

1. Operate the adjusting lever on top of the injection pump and ensure that the engine returns to normal idle speed, if it does the throttle cable is binding or not adjusted correctly and needs fixing.

2. If the engine does not return to idle in step1, the injection pump is faulty and needs replacing.

Engine Will Not Shut Off With The Key.

1. Check the fuel cut solenoid operation by disconnecting the connector on top of the fuel cut solenoid and check if the engine stops, if it does the starter switch is faulty and needs repairing and/or replacing.

2. If the engine does not stop in step1, either the fuel cut solenoid is faulty or the solenoid is blocked, if required repair/replace as required.

Diesel System Electrical Diagnosis

Engine Will Not Start When Cold

Super Glow System (Models for Europe 1988-1996)

Please Note: Before starting test please ensure that the battery is fully charged, the engine cranks normally and that all the fuse links are OK.
The timer unit is located in under the instrument panel on the LH side (LH)

1. Check if the glow indicator lamp lights up when the starter switch is ON, (Coolant Temp is 20°c and lamp lights up for 2-3 seconds).

2. If the operation is not as shown, check to ensure that the fuse/s are OK, if they are not check for any short circuit/s and repair as required.

3. If the fuses are OK in step2, check the condition and/or operation of the indicator lamp globe, if faults are found repair/replace as required.

4. If the bulb is OK, in step3, check for battery voltage to terminal 3 on the pre-heating timer connector (on the wiring harness side), if the voltage is Ok, repair/replace the timer as required.

5. If the glow indicator lamp is OK in step1, turn off the starter switch and check for battery voltage at the pre-heater timer terminal 1 with the starter switch ON, if there is no voltage check that there is 1v or less to terminal 9, if the voltage is OK, replace the timer.

6. If the voltage in step5 is Ok, check the the voltage to the pre-heat timer terminal 1 is terminated after the engine has started, if it is not, start the engine and check for voltage present at terminal 9 of the pre heating timer, if the voltage is Ok, replace the timer, if the voltage is not Ok, repair fault/s in the vehicle charging system.

7. If the voltage is terminated in step6, turn off the starter switch, turn on again and check for cuurent flow to terminal 5 of the timer in relation to the coolant temperature.

Current Flow: 16-26seconds @ less than 50°c
Current Flow: 1.7seconds @ more than 50°c

If there is no voltage at all replace the timer.

8. If the pre heating time is a lot different from what was shown in step7, the timer is faulty and should be replaced.

9. If the pre-heat time is Ok in step7, check for voltage at the timer terminal 8 when the ignition switch is in the ST position, if there is no voltage the timer needs replacing.

10. If the voltage is Ok in step9, put the starter switch in the ON position and check for voltage at the timer terminal 5 when the starter switch is at "Start", if there is no voltage at all replace the timer.

11. If the voltage in step10 is OK , switch off the ignition, switch ON the ignition and check for voltage to the glow plugs with coolant temperature a 50°c or less, (a few seconds after the voltage should drop by half). If there is no voltage at all, check for battery voltage at the (+) side of the glow plug resistor, if there is no voltage present at the (+) side of the resistor replace the No1 glow plug relay.

12. If the voltage in step11 remains at battery voltage or drops to 0v, check for battery voltage at the (+) side of the glow plug resistor, if the voltage is Ok, replace the resistor, if there is no voltage present at the (+) side of the resistor replace the No2 glow plug relay.

13. If the voltage is OK in step12, check the glow plug/s resistance, if the reading is infinity, repair/replace as required, if the reading is about 0ohms, the glow plugs are OK.

Fuel Cut Solenoid Operation Check

1. Put the starter switch into the ON position and check for an operating noise from the solenoid while repeatedly connecting and disconnecting the solenoid, if a noise is heard the solenoid is OK.

2. If the solenoid noise is not heard, check the condition and/or operation of the relevant fuse, if faults are found repair/replace as required.

3. If the fuse is OK in step2, apply battery volts to the solenoid and check for a noise, if a noise can be heard, check the condition of the harness between the fuse A and the fuel cut solenoid, if faults are found repair/replace as required.

4. If no noise can be heard in step3, replace the fuel cut solenoid.

VEHICLE SERVICE INFORMATION

Vehicle Filling Capacities

Engine Oil with Filter: .... 5.9 Litres (Europe)

Engine Oil without Filter: .... 5.0 Litres (Europe)

Engine Oil dry fill : .... 6.4 Litres (Europe)

Engine Oil with Filter: .... 6.0 Litres (Except Europe)

Engine Oil without Filter: .... 5.0 Litres (Except Europe)

Engine Oil dry fill : .... 6.5 Litres (Except Europe)

Cooling System: .... 9.5 Litres (With Heater)

Cooling System: .... 11.0 Litres (With Front/Rear Heater)

Manual Transmission: .... 2.2 Litres

Auto Transmission: 6.5 Litres (Dry Fill), 2.4 Litres (Refill)

Rear Differential: .... 2.2 Litres

Vehicle Component Service Interval Changes

Timing Belt Replacement

Change Every 100,000kms

Check Valve Clearance:

Check Every 40,000kms

Engine Coolant/Anti Freeze:

Change Every 24 Months/40,000kms

Air Cleaner Element:

Change Every 24 Months/40,000kms

Fuel Filter:

Change Every 12 Months/24,000kms

Engine Oil:

Change Every 5,000kms

Engine Oil Filter:

Change Every 6 Months/10,000kms

Brake Fluid:

Change Every 24 Months/40,000kms

Manual Transmission Oil:

Change Every 24 Months/40,000kms

Auto Transmission Fluid

Change Every 24 Months/40,000kms

Rear Differential Oil:

Change Every 24 Months/40,000kms

Front Wheel Bearings

Repack Every 40,000kms

Toyota Hiace LH103-113-125
3L Engine 1996 ON

CONTENTS   PAGE

CONTENTS   PAGE

Toyota Hiace

Hiace

Toyota Hiace LH103-113-125 3L Engine 1996 ON

Engine Checks

Valve Clearance Check

Please Note: Before carrying out this check ensure that the engine is at normal operating temperature.

1. Remove the rocker cover, set the No1 piston to TDC on its compression stroke and ensure that the groove on the crankshaft pulley is lined up with the timing pointer on the front cover.

2. Ensure that the valve lifters on the No1 cylinder are loose and that the No4 valve lifters are tight (if they are not turn the engine on full turn (360°) and recheck).

3. Measure the valve clearances on the following valves 1&3 (Exhaust) and 1&2 (Inlet).

Inlet Valve Clearance:	**0.20-030mm (Cold)**
Exhaust Valve Clearance:	**0.40-0.50mm (Cold)**

If the clearances are not correct record the relevant readings to determine the adjusting shim required.

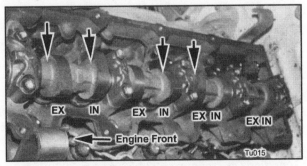

4. Turn the crankshaft one full turn (360°) and ensure that the groove on the crankshaft pulley is lined up with the timing pointer on the front cover.

5. Measure the valve clearances on the following valves 2&4 (Exhaust) and 3&4 (Inlet).

Inlet Valve Clearance:	**0.20-030mm (Cold)**
Exhaust Valve Clearance:	**0.40-0.50mm (Cold)**

6. If the clearances are not correct record the relevant readings to determine the adjusting shim required.

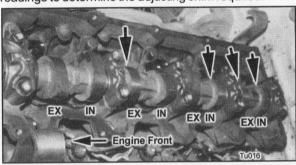

Compression Check

1. Run the engine to normal operating temperature, disconnect the fuel cut solenoid connector and remove all of the glow plugs from the engine.

2. Install an adaptor and compression gauge to the No1 cylinder, fully open the throttle, crank the engine and record the comprerssion pressure on each cylinder.

Compression Pressure:	**3138kpa**
Minimum Pressure:	**1961kpa**
Difference Between Each Cylinder:	**490kpa**

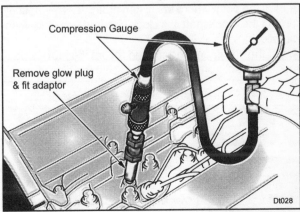

3. If the pressure on one or more cylinders is low, pour a small amount of oil into the cylinder through the glow plug hole and check the compression pressure again. If

it helps the pressure there are possibly faults withy the piston rings or cylinder bores, if the oil does not help there may be a valve sticking or not seated correctly and/or leaks past the gasket.

Cylinder Head Tightening Procedures

1. After the cylinder head has been removed and the gasket replaced, apply a thin coat of oil to all of the cylinder head bolts. Install and gradually tighten each of the bolts to its correct torque in three stages in the sequence showed in the diagram.

Specified Torque Setting: **78Nm**

Please Note: If any of the bolts do not reach the correct torque, check the length of the bolts.

Short Bolt: **107mm**

Long Bolt: **127mm**

Replace any faulty bolts as required.

2. Mark the front of each bolt with some paint and the tighten the bolts a further 90°. After the sequence has been completed tighten the bolts a further 90° and now ensure that the paint mark is facing to the rear.

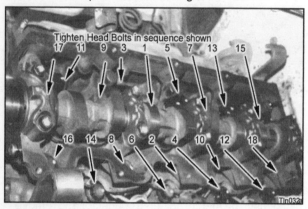

Piston Protrusion Height Check
No1 and 4 Piston Check

1. Rotate the engine and ensure that the timing marks on the crankshaft pulley line up with the marks on the front cover.

2. Fit a dial gauge to the engine block and set the gauge at the piston measuring point.

3. Find the point where the piston protrudes the most by turning the crankshaft in a clockwise and anti clockwise direction.

4. Set the dial gauge to zero and record the protrusion measurement from the block by sliding the dial gauge.

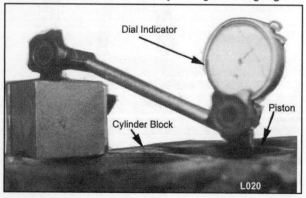

Protrusion Measurement: **0.68-0.97mm**

Please Note: Record the measurement at two separate measuring points.

No2 and No3 Piston Check

5. Turn the crankshaft 180° , fit a dial gauge to the engine block and set the gauge at the piston measuring point.

6. Find the point where the piston protrudes the most by turning the crankshaft in a clockwise and anti clockwise direction.

7. Set the dial gauge to zero and record the protrusion measurement from the block by sliding the dial gauge.

Protrusion Measurement: **0.68-0.97mm**

Please Note: Record the measurement at two separate measuring points.

8. When the measurment has been made, to select a new head gasket follow the procedures shown.

9. There are 3 different types of head gaskets marked either "B", "D" or "F", each of them different thicknesses.

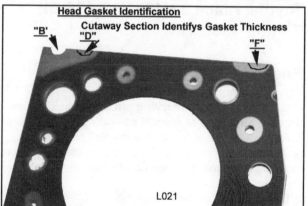

Piston Protrusion Measurements	Gasket Thickness	Gasket Grade
0.68-0.77	1.4-1.5mm	B
0.78-0.87	1.5-1.6	D
0.88-0.97	1.6-1.7	F

Please Note: When selecting the gasket use the largest measurement of the 8 readings that are recorded.

Oil Pressure Check

1. Ensure that the engine oil level is correct, if not top up to suit.

2. Remove the oil pressure switch from the engine and install a pressure gauge to the engine block.

3. Start the engine and run to normal operating temperature and then record the oil pressure shown on the gauge.

Specified Oil Pressure: **29kpa @ Idle**

Specified Oil Pressure: 294-539kpa @ 3000RPM

4. If the oil pressure is not as shown, repair/replace as required.

Diagram is on the next page

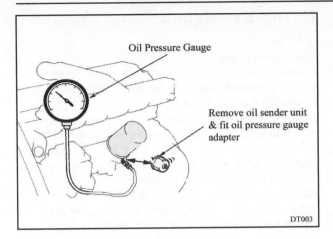

DT003

Cooling System Thermostat Check

1. Remove the thermostat from the engine and put into a suitable container of water.

2. Heat the water gradually and and check the valve opening temperature and valve lift.

Valve Opening Temperature: **86-90°c**

Valve Lift: **More than 8mm**

If the operation is not as shown above replace the thermostat.

3. Check that the valve spring is tight when the thermostat is fully closed, if not replace the thermostat.

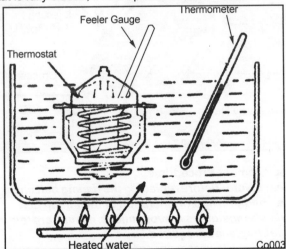

Co003

Fuel Filter Check and Replacement

1. Remove the fuel filter sensor (if fitted) and drain the fuel, then remove the fuel filter.

2. Clean the fuel filter mounting bracket and then coat the fuel filter sealing rine with some diesel fuel.

3. Screw the fuel filter on until a slght resistance is felt and then turn another 2/3 of a turn or until suitably tight.

4. Install the fuel filter sensor (if fitted) to the new filter and then bleed any air present from the system.

Draining Water From The Filter

1. Loosen the drain cock 4 or 5 turns or remove the fuel filter sensor to allow the water to drain from the filter.

2. Retighten the drain cock or replace the sensor and bleed any air present from the system.

Dfu020

Fuel Filter Warning Lamp Check

1. Remove the switch from the filter and check that there is continuity between the terminals when the warning switch is ON (Float Up)

2. Check that there is no continuity between the terminals when the warning switch is OFF (Float Down)

3. If the operation is not as shown, repair/replace as required

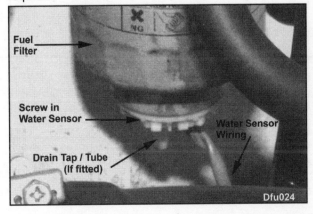

Dfu024

Injector Nozzle Check

1. Remove the injector from the vehicle, connect up to the pressure tester and check the initial pressure by pumping the tester handle a few times.

Initial Opening Pressure: **14,810-15,590kpa**

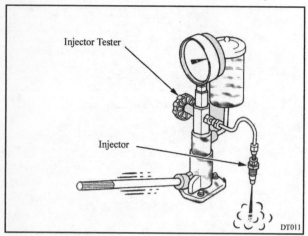

2. If the opening pressure is not as shown above, take the injector to pieces and change the adjusting shim on the top of the injector so as the correct pressure is recorded.

Adjusted Opening Pressure: **13,278-15,690kpa**

Please Note: The adjusting shims vary in 0.05mm thicknesses, each 0.05mm will adjust the pressure by 628kpa. After the shim has been changed there should be no leakage from the injector

3. Maintain the pressure between 981-1961kpa below the opening pressure and check that there is no leakage from the injector for a period of 10seconds.

4. Check the spray pattern by pumping the pressure tester handle 4-6 times or more per second and check the injection spray pattern.

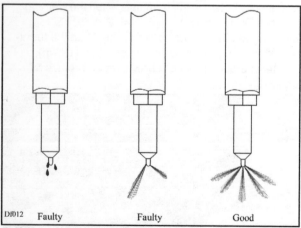

Df012   Faulty   Faulty   Good

5. If the operation and/or spray pattern is not as shown, repair/replace the nozzle/s as required.

Timing Belt Removal and Replacement

Removal Procedures

1. Remove the glow plugs, drive belts, water pump pulley, crankshaft pulley and the No1 timing cover.

2. Remove the timing belt guide.

3. Set the No1 piston to TDC on its compression stroke by temporarily replacing the crankshaft pulley bolt and turning the crankshaft in a clockwise direction until the timimg mark on the camshaft gear lines up with the mark on the No2 timing belt cover.

Please Note: If the timing belt is being used again, before removing, mark a direction arrow on the timing belt and place match,arks on the pulleys and the belt.

4. Turn the engine 90° in an anti clockwise direction and ensure that the timing mark on the crankshaft pulley lines up with the protrusion on the timing case.

5. Loosen the No1 idler pulley mount bolts and move to the left as far as it will go. Temporarily tighten the bolt, relieve the belt tension and remove the timing belt from the engine.

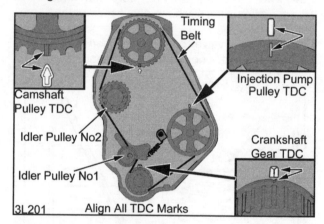

3L201   Align All TDC Marks

Replacement Procedures

Please Note: Before replacing the timimg belt check the condition and/or operation of the timing belt pulleys, tensioners and/or pulleys, if faults are found repair/replace as required.

1. Check the tensioner spring free length

Spring Free Length: **44.4-45.4mm**

Check the tension of the spring at the specified free length

Installed Tension: **53-59Nm at 52.1mm**

2. Install the crankshaft pulley to the engine, replace any pulleys or idlers that may have been removed for checking.

3. Set the No1 piston to TDC on its compression stroke and ensure that the timing marks on each of the pulleys line up with their relevant matchmarks.

4. Fit the timing belt onto the crankshaft pulley and No1 idler pulley, slightly turn the injection pulley in a clockwise direction, fit the timing belt onto the injection pulley and line up the marks on the injection pulley and timing belt case.

5. Slightly turn the camshaft drive pulley in a clockwise direction, fit the timing belt onto the pulley and ensure that the marks on the pulley and timing belt case line up.

Please Note: Ensure that there is belt tension between the camshaft pulley and injection pump drive pulleys.

6. Install the timing belt to the No2 idler pulley.

7. Loosen the No1 idler pulley, stretch the timing belt and turn the crankshaft in a clockwise direction two full turns from TDC to TDC, ensuring that all of the timing marks on the drive pulleys line up with their respective match marks.

Please Note: If any of the marks do not line up, remove the belt and reinstall again.

8. Tighten the No1 idler pulley bolt, refit the timimg belt guide and replace any removed components in the reverse order of removal.

Timing Belt Replacement Torques

Injection Pump Drive Pulley:	64Nm
No1 Idle Pulley (12mm Bolt):	19Nm
No1 Idle Pulley (14mm Bolt):	44Nm
No2 Idle Pulley:	33Nm
Crankshaft Pulley Bolt:	235Nm
Camshaft Gear Bolt:	98Nm

Timing Belt Warning Lamp Reset Procedures (Rubber Plug in the Instrument Cluster Glass)

1. Remove the grommet from the speedometer and turn off the lamp by pushing the warning lamp reset switch, then replace the grommet.

2. Start the engine and ensure that the light stays off.

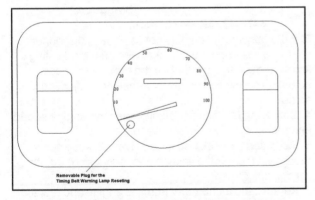

Removable Plug for the
Timing Belt Warning Lamp Reseting

Timing Belt Warning Lamp Reset Procedures (Change Screw Position on the Back of the Instrument Cluster)

1. Remove the instrument cluster from the vehicle, connect terminals A&B shown in the diagrams and then remove the CHARGE fuse from the vehicle.

2. Turn the ignition switch to ON and check that the warning lights light up, if not the check the condition and/or operation of the globe.

3. Check the condition and/or operation of the reset switches by checking that there is intermittent continuity between terminals A&B when the reset switch is pressed, if not repair/replace the speedometer/instrument cluster as required.

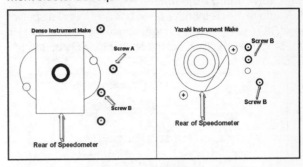

Engine Tightening Torques

Cylinder Head Tightening Torque Bolts:	78Nm (1st Stage)
Cylinder Head Tightening Torque Bolts:	90° (2nd Stage)
Cylinder Head Tightening Torque Bolts:	90° (3rd Stage)
Camshaft Bearing Cap:	25Nm
Exhaust Manifold Bolts and Nuts:	52Nm
Inlet Manifold Bolts and Nuts:	24Nm
Glow Plugs:	13Nm
Injection Nozzle:	64Nm
Injection Pump Drive Pulley Nut:	64Nm
No1 Idle Pulley (12mm Bolt):	19Nm
No1 Idle Pulley (14mm Bolt):	44Nm
No2 Idle Pulley:	33Nm
Flywheel Bolts:	123Nm
Drive Plate:	98Nm
Connecting Rod Caps:	54Nm (1st Stage)
Connecting Rod Caps:	90° (2nd Stage)
Main Bearings:	103Nm
Crankshaft Pulley Bolt:	235Nm
Camshaft Gear Bolt:	98Nm
Oil Pump to Block:	23Nm
Oil Pump to Injection Pump:	21Nm
Oil Sump Bolt:	18Nm

System Adjustments

Injection Timing Adjustment

1. Remove the distributive head bolt and install a special tool (SST09275-54011 plunger stroke measuring tool) to the plug hole and then set the No1 or No4 piston to 25° BTDC on its compression stroke.

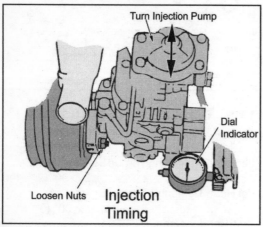

Turn Injection Pump

Dial Indicator

Loosen Nuts   Injection Timing

2. Please Note: (For vehicles with auto cold start device): Using a screwdriver turn the cold start lever anti clockwise about 20° and put a metal plate 8.5-10.0mm between the cold start lever and the thermo wax plunger.
3. Turn the crankshaft pulley in a clockwise direction until it is between 25-30° BTDC, set the dial indicator to zero (mm).Slowly turn the crankshaft pulley until crankshaft pulley groove is lined up with the timing pointer and record the plunger movement.

Injection Plunger Stroke: 0.54-0.66 (3L Europe and others With Auto Cold Start Device)
Injection Plunger Stroke: 0.84-0.96mm (Without Auto Cold Start Device)

4. If the plunger stroke measurment is not as shown, loosen the 4 injector pipe union nuts and inlet pipe union nuts on the injection pump side.
5. Loosen the 4 injection pump mounting nuts and adjust the plunger pump stroke by slightly tilting the injection pump body. If the stroke is less than shown tilt the pump towards the engine, if the plunger strike is more than shown tilt the pump away from the engine.
6. Retighten all of the fixing bolts and union nuts, recheck the plunger stroke and then remove the plate from the cold starting lever.
7. Remove the dial indicator gauge and replace the plug bolt. Restart the engine and check for any leaks in the system.

Idle Speed Check

1. Ensure that the air cleaner is OK, the engine coolant temperature is at normal, the accessories are all switched off and that the transmission is in neutral.
2. Ensure that the adjusting screw lever touches the idle speed adjusting screw when the throttle pedal is released, if it is not adjust to suit.
3. Install a tachometer to the engine, start the engine and check the idle speed setting.
Idle Speed Setting: 650-750RPM (Manual)

Idle Speed Setting: 750-850RPM (Auto)
4. If the idle speed is not as shown in step3, disconnect the throttle linkage, loosen the lock nut of the idle adjust screw and adjust by turning the idle speed adjusting screw, re-tighten the lock nut and reconnect the throttle linkage. Recheck the idle speed.

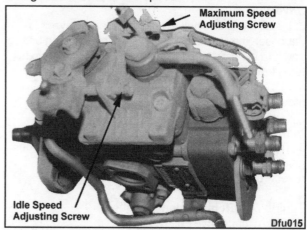

Maximum Speed Adjusting Screw

Idle Speed Adjusting Screw

Dfu015

5. Remove the tachometer from the engine and replace any removed parts to the vehicle.

Maximum Speed Adjustment Check

1. Ensure that the adjusting lever touches the maximum speed adjusting screw when the throttle is pressed down all the way, if not adjust the throttle linkages
2. Install a tachometer to the engine, start the engine, press the throttle fully down and check the maximum speed.
Maximum Speed Setting:
      4670-4930RPM (Europe)
      4270-4530RPM (Hong Kong/Malaysia, Singapore)
      4470-4730RPM (Others)
3. If the maximum speed is not as shown, disconnect the throttle linkage, cut the seal wire on the adjusting screw, loosen the lock nut on the maximum speed adjusting screw and adjust by turning the adjusting screw.
4. Check the idle speed setting, raise the engine speed and recheck the maximum speed.
5. Retighten the lock nut, re-seal the adjusting screw, reconnect the throttle linkage and recheck the throttle linkage adjustment.
6. Remove the tachometer from the engine and replace any removed parts to the vehicle.
                Refer Idle Speed Diagrams

Fuel Heater System Check

Fuel Heater Check

1. Remove the fuel heater from the fuel filter cap and apply 34.7±5.3kpa or more to the vacuum switch port and with an ohmmeter, record the resistance between terminal 1 and switch body

Specified Resistance: **0.5-2.0ohms @ 20°c**

If the resistance is not as shown, repair/replace as required.

Vacuum Switch Check

1. With an ohmmeter check there is no continuity between the switch terminal 1 and switch body.
If the resistance is not as shown, repair/replace as required.

2. Apply a vacuum of 34.7±5.3kpa or more to the vacuum port and check that there is continuity between the switch terminal 1 and body.
If the operation is not as shown, repair/replace as required

Refer to Fuel Heater Connector Diagram

Pre-Heating System Checks

Super Glow System With Resistor
Pre-Heating Timer Check

Please Note: Before starting test please ensure that the battery is fully charged, the engine cranks normally and that all the fuse links are OK.

1. Disconnect the water temperature sensor and check if the glow indicator lamp lights up when the starter switch is ON

Lamp Light Up Time: 6 Seconds

2. If the operation is not as shown, check to ensure that the fuse/s are OK, if they are not check for any short circuit/s and repair as required.

3. If the fuses are OK in step2, check the condition and/or operation of the indicator lamp globe, if faults are found repair/replace as required.

4. If the bulb is Ok in step3, check for battery voltage to terminal 3 on the pre-heating timer connector (on the wiring harness side), if the voltage is Ok, repair/replace the timer as required.

5. If the glow indicator lamp is OK in step1, turn off the starter switch and check for battery voltage at the pre-heater timer terminal 5 with the starter switch ON, if there is no voltage check that there is 1v or less to terminal 10, if the voltage is OK, replace the timer.

6. If the voltage in step5 is Ok, check the the voltage to the pre-heat timer terminal 5 is terminated after the engine has started, if it is not, start the engine and check for voltage present at terminal 10 of the pre heating timer, if the voltage is Ok, replace the timer, if the voltage is not Ok, repair fault/s in the vehicle charging system.

7. If the voltage is terminated in step6, turn off the starter switch, turn on again and check for current flow to terminal 1 of the timer in relation to the coolant temperature.

Current Flow: **22.5seconds**

If there is no voltage at all replace the timer.

8. If the pre heating time is a lot different from what was shown in step7, the timer is faulty and should be replaced.

9. If the pre-heat time is Ok in step7, check for voltage at the timer terminal 1 when the ignition switch is in the ST position, if there is no voltage the timer needs replacing.

10. If the voltage is Ok in step9, put the starter switch in the OFF position, turn back on the ignition and check for voltage to the glow plugs (a few seconds after the voltage should drop by half). If there is no voltage at all replace the NO1 and No2 glow plug relays.

11. If the voltage in step10 stays at battery voltage or at 1/2 voltage for 32 seconds replace the No1 glow plug relay.

12. If the voltage is OK in step11, check the glow plug/s resistance, if the reading is infinity, repair/replace as required, if the reading is about 0ohms, the glow plugs are OK.

Pre Heating Timer Operation Check
Super Glow System

1. Disconnect the connector from the timer and check the connector harness as shown in the chart below.

Check For	Between Terminals	Condition	Specified Value
Voltage	4-ground	Starter Switch OFF	No volts
Voltage	4-ground	Starter Switch ON	Battery volts
Voltage	2-ground	Starter Switch OFF	No volts
Voltage	2-ground	Starter Switch ON	Battery volts
Voltage	7-ground	Starter Switch OFF	No volts
Voltage	7-ground	Starter Switch ON	Battery volts
Continuity	1/5-ground		Continuity
Continuity	6-ground		Continuity
Continuity	12-ground		Continuity
Continuity	9-ground		Continuity
Continuity	11-ground		Continuity

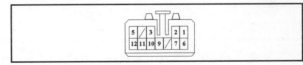

No1 Glow Plug Relay Check.

1. With an ohmmeter check the continuity between the terminals 1 and 2 of the No1 connector and ensure that it exists
If there is no continuity replace the relay
2. Check between terminals 3 and 4 of the No2 connector ensure that it does not exist.
If there is continuity replace the relay
3. Apply battery volts between terminals 1 and 2 of the No1 and ensure that continuity exists between terminals 3 and 4 of the No2 connector.

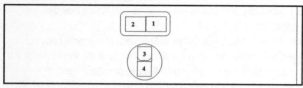

4. If there is no continuity replace the relay

No2 Glow Plug Relay Check

1. With an ohmmeter check the continuity between the terminals 1-2 and ensure that it exists
If there is no continuity replace the relay
2. Check for continuity between terminals 3-4 and ensure that it does not exist
If there is continuity replace the relay.
3. Apply battery volts between terminals 1-2 and ensure that continuity exists between terminals 3-4

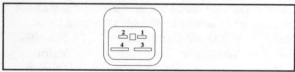

4. If there is no continuity replace the relay

Glow Plug Check

1. With an ohmmeter check that there is continuity between the glow plug terminal and ground
Specified Resistance: 0.65ohms @20°c
If continuity does not exist, replace the faulty glow plug/s

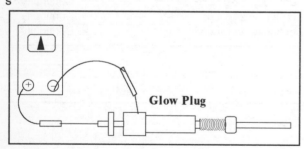

Glow Plug

Glow Plug Resistor Check

1. Check the resistance between the resistor terminals with an ohmmeter
Specified Resistance: 0.17ohms @20°c
If the resistance is not as shown, replace the resistor

Water Temperature Sensor Check

1. Remove the sensor harness connector and check the resistance between the sensor terminals at varying temperatures.

Sensor Temperature (°c)	Sensor Resistance (k/ohms)
0	5.0
20	2.0
40	1.0
60	0.4
80	0.14
100	0.08

2. If the resistance is not as shown, repair/replace as required.

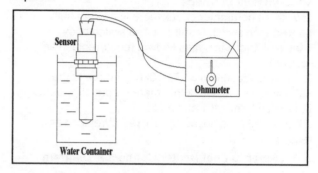

Sensor / Ohmmeter / Water Container

Pre-Heating System Checks

Super Glow System Without Resistor
Pre-Heating Timer Check
Please Note: Before starting test please ensure that the battery is fully charged, the engine cranks normally and that all the fuse links are OK.
1. Disconnect the water temperature sensor and check if the glow indicator lamp lights up when the starter switch is ON
Lamp Light Up Time: 6 Seconds
2. If the operation is not as shown, check to ensure that the fuse/s are OK, if they are not check for any short circuit/s and repair as required.
3. If the fuses are OK in step2, check the condition and/or operation of the indicator lamp globe, if faults are found repair/replace as required.
4. If the bulb is Ok in step3, check for battery voltage to terminal 3 (wire harness side) on the pre-heating timer connector, if the voltage is Ok, repair/replace the timer as required.
5. If the glow indicator lamp is OK in step1, turn off the starter switch and check for battery voltage at the pre-heater timer terminal 1 with the starter switch ON, if there is no voltage check that there is 1v or less to terminal 10, if the voltage is OK, replace the timer.
6. If the voltage in step5 is Ok, check the the voltage to the pre-heat timer terminal 1 is terminated after the engine has started, if it is not, start the engine and check for voltage present at terminal 10 of the pre heating timer, if the voltage is Ok, replace the timer, if the voltage is not Ok, repair fault/s in the vehicle charging system.
7. If the voltage is terminated in step6, turn off the starter

switch, turn on again and check for currrent flow to terminal 1 of the timer in relation to the coolant temperature.

Current Flow: 120.0seconds

If there is no voltage at all replace the timer.

8. If the pre heating time is a lot different from what was shown in step7, the timer is faulty and should be replaced.

9. If the pre-heat time is Ok in step7, check for voltage at the timer terminal 1 when the ignition switch is in the START position, if there is no voltage the timer needs replacing.

10. If the voltage is Ok in step9, put the starter switch in the OFF position, turn back on the ignition and check for voltage to the glow plugs, if there is no voltage check the operation of the glow plug relay/s and/or the glow plugs, if faults are found repair/replace as required.

11. If the voltage in step10 is OK, reconnect the coolant temperature sensor.

Pre Heating Timer Operation Check
Super Glow System

1. Disconnect the connector from the timer and check the connector harness as shown in the chart below.

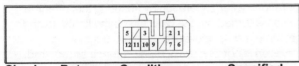

Check For	Between Terminals	Condition	Specified Value
Voltage	3-ground	Starter Switch OFF	No volts
Voltage	3-ground	Starter Switch ON	Battery volts
Voltage	2-ground	Starter Switch OFF	No volts
Voltage	2-ground	Starter Switch ON	Battery volts
Voltage	7-ground	Starter Switch OFF	No volts
Voltage	7-ground	Starter Switch ON	Battery volts
Continuity	1-ground		Continuity
Continuity	12-ground		Continuity
Continuity	9-ground		Continuity
Continuity	11-ground		Continuity

Glow Plug Relay Check

1. With an ohmmeter check the continuity between the terminals 1-2 and ensure that it exists
If there is no continuity replace the relay
2. Check for continuity between terminals 3-4 and ensure that it does not exist
If there is continuity replace the relay.
3. Apply battery volts between terminals 1-2 and ensure that continuity exists between terminals 3-4
If there is no continuity replace the relay
Refer to No2 Glow Plug Relay in the with resistor system

Glow Plug Check

1. With an ohmmeter check that there is continuity between the glow plug terminal and ground
Specified Resistance: 0.65ohms @ 20°c
If continuity does not exist, replace the faulty glow plug/plugs.**Refer Previous Glow Plug Check Diagrams**

Water Temperature Sensor Check

1. Remove the sensor harness connector and check the resistance between the sensor terminals at varying temperatures.

Temperature (°c)	Resistance (k/ohms)
0	5.0
20	2.0
40	1.0
60	0.4
80	0.14
100	0.08

2. If the resistance is not as shown, repair/replace as required.

Refer Previous Water Temp Sensor Diagrams

Pre-Heating System Checks
Variable Delay System

Pre-Heat Timer Check:

1. Disconnect the connector from the timer and check the connector harness as shown in the chart below

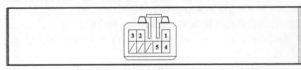

Check For	Between Terminals	Condition	Specified Value
Voltage	4-ground	Starter Switch OFF	No volts
Voltage	4-ground	Starter Switch ON	Battery volt
Voltage	1-ground	Starter Switch OFF	No volts
Voltage	1-ground	Starter Switch ON	Battery volts
Continuity	3-ground		Continuity
Continuity	5-ground		Continuity

After Glow Time Check:

1. Turn the ignition switch to "Start" and record the time battery voltage is applied to the terminal 1 on the timer
After Glow Time: 18 Seconds

Glow Plug Relay Check:

1. With an ohmmeter check the continuity between the terminals 1-2 and ensure that it exists
If there is no continuity replace the relay
2. Check for continuity between terminals 3-4 and ensure that it does not exist
If there is continuity replace the relay.
3. Apply battery volts between terminals 1-2 and ensure that continuity exists between terminals 3-4
If there is no continuity replace the relay

Refer Glow Plug Relay No2 Diagram in the Superglow System with Resistor

Glow Plug Check

1. With an ohmmeter check that there is continuity between the glow plug terminal and ground

Specified Resistance: 0.65ohms @ 20°c

If continuity does not exist, replace the faulty glow plug/plugs

Refer previous glow plug check diagrams

Pre-Heating System Checks Fixed Delay System

Pre-Heat Timer Check

1. Disconnect the connector from the timer and check the connector harness as shown in the chart below.

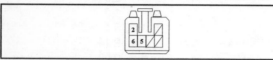

Check For	Between Terminals	Condition	Specified Value
Voltage	5-ground	Ignition Switch OFF	No volts
Voltage	5-ground	Ignition Switch ON	Battery volts
Voltage	6-ground	Ignition Switch OFF	No volts
Voltage	6-ground	Ignition Switch ON	Battery volts
Continuity	2-Ground		Continuity

Glow Plug Check

1. With an ohmmeter check that there is continuity between the glow plug terminal and ground

Specified Resistance: 0.65ohms @ 20°c

If continuity does not exist, replace the faulty glow plug/plugs

Refer previous glow plug check diagram

Glow Plug Light Up Time Check

1. Switch ON the ignition and check the indicator lamp light up time.   **Light Up Time: 5 Seconds**

Injection System and Engine Diagnosis and Troubleshooting

Engine Will Not Crank

1. Check the condition and/or operation of the battery cables between the battery and starter motor, if faults are found repair/replace as required.

2. If no faults are found in step1, check the condition and/or operation of the battery, alternator output and/or drive belt, if faults are found repair/replace as required.

3. If no faults are found in step2, check the condition and/or operation of the starter motor, if faults are found repair/replace as required.

Engine Cranks Slowly or Will Not Start

1. Check the condition and/or operation of the battery cables between the battery and starter motor, if faults are found repair/replace as required.

2. If no faults are found in step1, check the condition and/or operation of the battery, alternator output and/or drive belt, if faults are found repair/replace as required.

3. If no faults are found in step2, check that the correct grade of engine oil is being used on the vehicle, if not drain and replace with the correct grade of oil.

Engine Cranks Normally But Does Not Start

1. If the engine cranks normally but does not start, check and ensure that fuel is reaching the injection nozzles by loosening any of the injection pipes, cranking the engine and ensuring that fuel is coming out of the pipe.

2. If fuel is not coming out of the pipe in step1, check the operation of the fuel cut solenoid, if faults are found repair/replace as required.

3. If no faults are found in step3, check to ensure that fuel is getting to the injection pump by disconnecting the inlet hoses from the fuel filter, feeding clean fuel from a separate container directly into the injection pump. If the engine now starts there may be blockages in the fuel filter and/or line between the fuel tank and fuel filter. If the engine does not start, check the condition and/or operation of the fuel line between the fuel filter and fuel pump. If the injection pump operation is normal it should be replaced.

4. If fuel is present in step1, check the pre-heating operation system operation by ensuring that after the ignition is turned on, the glow plug lamp lights up and that there are 6v applied to the glow plugs, if the operation is not as shown, repair/replace as required.

5. If no faults are found in step4, check the operation of the glow plug/s, if faults are found repair/replace as required.

6. If no faults are found in step5, check the fuel system pipes, hoses and/or components for leaks, cracks and/or damage, if faults are found repair/replace as required.

7. If no faults are found in step6, check the injection timing by setting either the No1 or No4 piston at TDC, releasing the cold start advance systen (where fitted) and checking the plunger stroke.

Injection Plunger Stroke: 0.54-0.66 (Europe and others With Auto Cold Start Device)

Injection Plunger Stroke: 0.84-0.96mm (Without Auto Cold Start Device)

If the timing setting is not as shown, adjust to suit.

8. If no faults are found in step7, **(Auto Cold Start Device Only),** check the cold start advance and fast idle system operation, if faults are found repair/replace as required.

9. If no faults are found in step7and/or 8, check the condition and/or operation of the injection nozzles, if faults are found repair/replace as required.

Idle Speed is Unstable When The Engine is Warm

1. If the idle speed is unstable when the engine is warm, check the condition and/or operation of the throttle cable and/or linkages, if faults are found repair/replace as required.

2. If no faults are found in step1, check the engine idle speed setting.

Idle Speed Setting: 650-750RPM (Manual)

Idle Speed Setting: 750-850RPM (Auto)

If the idle speed setting is not as shown, adjust to suit

3. If no faults are found in step2, check the fuel system components and/or lines for leaks and/or damage, if faults are found repair/replace as required.

4. If no faults are found in step3, check the injection timing by setting either the No1 or No4 piston at TDC, releasing the cold start advance systen (where fitted) and checking the plunger stroke.

Injection Plunger Stroke: 0.54-0.66 (Europe and others With Auto Cold Start Device)

Injection Plunger Stroke: 0.84-0.96mm (Without Auto Cold Start Device

If the timing setting is not as shown, adjust to suit.

5. If no faults are found in step4, check the operation of the injection nozzle/s and/or the delivery valve by letting the engine run at idle speed, loosening the union nuts on each of the cylinders in order and check if there is any change of idle speed. If there is no change at any of the cylinders this will indicate that a faulty cylinder/s is present. To fix the problem check the injection nozzle pressure.

Injection Nozzle Pressure: 13,729-15,690kpa (New Nozzle)

Injection Nozzle Pressure: 14,810-15,950kpa (Reused Nozzle)

6. If the pressure is not as shown adjust pressure to suit. If the pressure is OK, the fault will be with the delivery valve and should be replaced.

Rough Idle When the Engine is Warm

1. If the engine idle is rough when the engine is warm, check the throttle linkages and/or cable for correct operation and/or adjustment, if faults are found repair/replace as required.

2. If no faults are found in step1, with the engine running check the idle speed setting.

Idle Speed Setting: 650-750RPM (Manual)

Idle Speed Setting: 750-850RPM (Auto)

If the idle speed setting is not as shown, adjust to suit

3. If no faults are found in step2, check the fuel system pipes, hoses and/or components for leaks, cracks and/or damage, if faults are found repair/replace as required.

4. If no faults are found in step3, check the injection timing by setting either the No1 or No4 piston at TDC, releasing the cold start advance systen (where fitted) and checking the plunger stroke.

Injection Plunger Stroke: 0.54-0.66 (3L Europe and others With Auto Cold Start Device)

Injection Plunger Stroke: 0.84-0.96mm (Without Auto Cold Start Device)

If the timing setting is not as shown, adjust to suit.

5. If no faults are found in step4 check the check the injection nozzle pressure.

Injection Nozzle Pressure: 13,729-15,690kpa (New Nozzle)

Injection Nozzle Pressure: 14,810-15,950kpa (Reused Nozzle)

6. If the pressure is not as shown adjust pressure to suit, if the pressure cannot be adjusted, replace the faulty nozzle/s

Engine Suddenly Stops

1. If the engine is running and then suddenly stops, switch off the ignition and try and start the engine, if it does not re-start, check and ensure that fuel is reaching the injection nozzles by loosening any of the injection pipes, cranking the engine and ensuring that fuel is coming out of the pipe.

2. If fuel is not coming out of the pipe in step1, check the operation of the fuel cut solenoid, if faults are found repair/replace as required.

3. If no faults are found in step3, check to ensure that fuel is getting to the injection pump by disconnecting the inlet hoses from the fuel filter, feeding clean fuel from a separate container directly into the injection pump. If the engine now starts there may be blockages in the fuel filter and/or line between the fuel tank and fuel filter. If the engine does not start, check the condition and/or operation of the fuel line between the fuel filter and fuel pump. If the injection pump operation is normal it should be replaced.

4. If fuel is present in step1, check the pre-heating operation system operation by ensuring that after the ignition is turned on, the glow plug lamp lights up and that there are 6v applied to the glow plugs, if the operation is not as shown, repair/replace as required.

5. If no faults are found in step4, check the operation of the glow plug/s, if faults are found repair/replace as required.

6. If no faults are found in step5, check the fuel system pipes, hoses and/or components for leaks, cracks and/or damage, if faults are found repair/replace as required.

7. If no faults are found in step6, check the injection timing by setting either the No1 or No4 piston at TDC, releasing the cold start advance systen (where fitted) and checking the plunger stroke.

Injection Plunger Stroke: 0.54-0.66 (Europe and others With Auto Cold Start Device)

Injection Plunger Stroke: 0.84-0.96mm (Without Auto Cold Start Device)

If the timing setting is not as shown, adjust to suit.

8. If no faults are found in step7, **(With Auto Cold Start Device Only),** check the cold start advance and fast idle system operation, if faults are found repair/replace as required.

9. If no faults are found in step7 and/or 8, check the condition and/or operation of the injection nozzles, if faults are found repair/replace as required.

Excessive Exhaust Smoke

1. Check the condition and/or operation of the alr cleaner element, if faults are found repair/replace as required.

2. If no faults are found in step1, check the engine oil consumption, if faults are found repair/replace as required.

3. If the oil consumption is OK in step2, check the

injection timing by setting either the No1 or No4 piston at TDC, releasing the cold start advance systen (where fitted) and checking the plunger stroke.

Injection Plunger Stroke: 0.54-0.66 (Europe and others With Auto Cold Start Device)

Injection Plunger Stroke: 0.84-0.96mm (Without Auto Cold Start Device)

If the timing setting is not as shown, adjust to suit.

(Please Note: If the exhaust smoke is black it tends to indicate that the timing is advanced and if the smoke is white that the timing is retarded).

4. If no faults are found in step3, disconnect the inlet hoses from the fuel filter and pour diesel fuel directly into the injection pump, if the condition now improves replace the fuel filter. If the condition does not improve after the fuel filter has been replaced, check the condition and/or operation of the priming pump, if faults are found repair/replace as required. *(Please Note: At between 2000-3000RPM a blocked fuel filter tends to make the exhaust smoke white).*

5. If no faults are found in step4, check the check the injection nozzle pressure.

Injection Nozzle Pressure: 13,729-15,690kpa (New Nozzle)

Injection Nozzle Pressure: 14,810-15,950kpa (Reused Nozzle)

6. If the pressure is not as shown adjust pressure to suit, if the pressure cannot be adjusted, replace the faulty nozzle/s. *(Please Note: Excessive exhaust smoke is normally caused when the nozzle pressure is to low)*

Fuel Consumption is Poor

1. If the fuel consumption is poor, check the fuel system components and/or lines for leaks and/or damage, if faults are found repair/replace as required.

2. If no faults are found in step1, with the engine running check the idle speed setting.

Idle Speed Setting: 650-750RPM (Manual)
Idle Speed Setting: 750-850RPM (Auto)

If the idle speed setting is not as shown, adjust to suit

3. If the idle speed setting is OK in step2, check the no load maximum speed setting is OK by starting the engine, pressing down the throttle pedal to the floor and cheking the no load maximum speed setting.

Maximum Speed Setting:
4670-4930RPM (Europe)
4270-4530RPM (Hong Kong/Malaysia, Singapore and LY General)
4470-4730RPM (Others)

If the setting is not OK, adjust using the maximum speed adjusting screw.

4. If no faults are found in step3, check the injection timing by setting either the No1 or No4 piston at TDC, releasing the cold start advance systen (where fitted) and checking the plunger stroke.

Injection Plunger Stroke: 0.54-0.66 (Europe and others With Auto Cold Start Device)

Injection Plunger Stroke: 0.84-0.96mm (With out Auto Cold Start Device

If the timing setting is not as shown, adjust to suit.

5. If no faults are found in step4, check the check the injection nozzle pressure.

Injection Nozzle Pressure: 13,729-15,690kpa (New Nozzle)

Injection Nozzle Pressure: 14,810-15,950kpa (Reused Nozzle)

6. If the pressure is not as shown adjust pressure to suit, if the pressure cannot be adjusted, replace the faulty nozzle/s.

Noise When The Engine Is Warm

1. If the engine is noisey when it is warm, first check the operation of the temperature gauge if that is Ok, check the operation of the thermostat if faults are found repair/replace as required.

2. If no faults are found in step1, check the injection timing by setting either the No1 or No4 piston at TDC, releasing the cold start advance systen (where fitted) and checking the plunger stroke.

Injection Plunger Stroke: 0.54-0.66 (Europe & others With Auto Cold Start Device)

Injection Plunger Stroke: 0.84-0.96mm (W/Out Auto Cold Start Device)

If the timing setting is not as shown, adjust to suit.

3. If no faults are found in step2, check the check the injection nozzle pressure.

Injection Nozzle Pressure: 13,729-15,690kpa (New Nozzle)

Injection Nozzle Pressure: 14,810-15,950kpa (Reused Nozzle)

4. If the pressure is not as shown adjust pressure to suit, if the pressure cannot be adjusted, replace the faulty nozzle/s.

Engine Will Not Return to Idle

1. Operate the adjusting lever on top of the injection pump and ensure that the engine returns to normal idle speed, if it does the throttle cable is binding or not adjusted correctly and needs fixing.

2. If the engine does not return to idle in step1, the injection pump is faulty and needs replacing.

Engine Will Not Shut Off With The Key.

1. Check the fuel cut solenoid operation by disconnecting the connector on top of the fuel cut solenoid and check if the engine stops, if it does the starter switch is faulty and needs repairing and/or replacing.

2. If the engine does not stop in step1, either the fuel cut solenoid is faulty or the solenoid is blocked, if required repair/replace as required.

Diesel System Electrical Diagnosis

Engine Will Not Start When Cold

Super Glow System (With Resistor)

Please Note: Before starting test please ensure that the battery is fully charged, the engine cranks normally and that all the fuse links are OK.

1. If the engine will not start when cold, disconnect the water temperature sensor and check if the glow indicator lamp lights up when the starter switch is ON

Lamp Light Up Time: 6 Seconds

2. If the operation is not as shown in step1, check to ensure that the fuse/s are OK, if they are not check for any short circuit/s and repair as required.

3. If the fuses are OK in step2, check the condition and/or operation of the indicator lamp globe, if faults are found repair/replace as required.

4. If the bulb is Ok in step3, check for battery voltage to terminal 3 on the pre-heating timer connector (on the wiring harness side), if the voltage is Ok, repair/replace the timer as required.

5. If the glow indicator lamp is OK in step1, turn off the starter switch and check for battery voltage at the pre-heater timer terminal 5 with the starter switch ON, if there is no voltage check that there is 1v or less to terminal 10, if the voltage is OK, replace the timer.

6. If the voltage in step5 is Ok, check the voltage to the pre-heat timer terminal 5 is terminated after the engine has started, if it is not, start the engine and check for voltage present at terminal 10 of the pre heating timer, if the voltage is Ok, replace the timer, if the voltage is not Ok, repair fault/s in the vehicle charging system.

7. If the voltage is terminated in step6, turn off the starter switch, turn on again and check for cuurent flow to terminal 1 of the timer in relation to the coolant temperature.

Current Flow: 22.5seconds

If there is no voltage at all replace the timer.

8. If the pre heating time is a lot different from what was shown in step7, the timer is faulty and should be replaced.

9. If the pre-heat time is Ok in step7, check for voltage at the timer terminal 1 when the ignition switch is in the ST position, if there is no voltage the timer needs replacing.

10. If the voltage is Ok in step9, put the starter switch in the OFF position, turn back on the ignition and check for voltage to the glow plugs (a few seconds after the voltage should drop by half), if there is no voltage at all replace the NO1 and No2 glow plug relays.

11. If the voltage in step10 stays at battery voltage or at 1/2 voltage for 32 seconds replace the No1 glow plug relay.

12. If the voltage is OK in step11, check the glow plug/s resistance, if the reading is infinity, repair/replace as required, if the reading is about 0ohms, the glow plugs are OK.

Engine Will Not Start When Cold

Super Glow System (Without Resistor)

1. If the engine will not start when it is cold, disconnect the water temperature sensor and check if the glow indicator lamp lights up when the starter switch is ON

Lamp Light Up Time: 6 Seconds

2. If the operation is not as shown in step1, check to ensure that the fuse/s are OK, if they are not check for any short circuit/s and repair as required.

3. If the fuses are OK in step2, check the condition and/or operation of the indicator lamp globe, if faults are found repair/replace as required.

4. If the bulb is Ok in step3, check for battery voltage to terminal 3(wire harness side) on the pre-heating timer connector, if the voltage is Ok, repair/replace the timer as required.

5. If the glow indicator lamp is OK in step1, turn off the starter switch and check for battery voltage at the pre-heater timer terminal 1 with the starter switch ON, if there is no voltage check that there is 1v or less to terminal 10, if the voltage is OK, replace the timer.

6. If the voltage in step5 is Ok, check the voltage to the pre-heat timer terminal 1 is terminated after the engine has started, if it is not, start the engine and check for voltage present at terminal 10 of the pre heating timer, if the voltage is Ok, replace the timer, if the voltage is not Ok, repair fault/s in the vehicle charging system.

7. If the voltage is terminated in step6, turn off the starter switch, turn on again and check for current flow to terminal 1 of the timer in relation to the coolant temperature.

Current Flow: **120.0seconds**

If there is no voltage at all replace the timer.

8. If the pre heating time is a lot different from what was shown in step7, the timer is faulty and should be replaced.

9. If the pre-heat time is Ok in step7, check for voltage at the timer terminal 1 when the ignition switch is in the START position, if there is no voltage the timer needs replacing.

10. If the voltage is Ok in step9, put the starter switch in the OFF position, turn back on the ignition and check for voltage to the glow plugs, if there is no voltage check the operation of the glow plug relay/s and/or the glow plugs, if faults are found repair/replace as required.

11. If the voltage in step10 is OK, reconnect the coolant temperature sensor.

Fuel Cut Solenoid Operation Check

1. Put the starter switch into the ON position and check for an operating noise from the solenoid while repeatedly connecting and disconnecting the solenoid, if a noise is heard the solenoid is OK.

2. If the solenoid noise is not heard, check the condition and/or operation of the relevant fuse, if faults are found repair/replace as required.

3. If the fuse is OK in step2, apply battery volts to the solenoid and check for a noise, if a noise can be heard, check the condition of the harness between the fuse A

and the fuel cut solenoid, if faults are found repair/
replace as required.
4. If no noise can be heard in step3, replace the fuel cut
solenoid.

VEHICLE SERVICE INFORMATION

Vehicle Filling Capacities

Engine Oil with Filter: .... 5.8 Litres
Engine Oil without Filter: .... 4.8 Litres
Engine Oil dry fill : .... 6.5 Litres
Cooling System: .... 9.3 Litres (Without Heater)
Cooling System: .... 11.0 Litres (With Front/Rear Heater)
Cooling System: .... 9.5 Litres (With Front Heater)
Manual Transmission: .... 2.2 Litres
Auto Transmission: 6.5Litres (Dry Fill), 2.4 Litres (Refill)
Rear Differential .... 2.2 Litres

Vehicle Component Service Interval Changes

Timing Belt Replacement
Every 100,000kms

Check Valve Clearance:
Every 40,000kms

Engine Coolant/Anti Freeze:
Change Every 24 Months/40,000kms

Air Cleaner Element:
Change Every 24 Months/40,000kms

Fuel Filter:
Change Every 12 Months/24,000kms

Engine Oil:
Change Every 5,000kms

Engine Oil Filter:
Change Every 6 Months/10,000kms

Brake Fluid:
Change Every 24 Months/40,000kms

Manual Transmission Oil:
Change Every 24 Months/40,000kms

Auto Transmission Fluid
Change Every 24 Months/40,000kms

Rear Differential Oil:
Change Every 24 Months/40,000kms

Front Wheel Bearings
Repack Every 40,000kms

Toyota Hiace LH103-113-125
5L Engine 1998 On

Toyota Hiace

Hiace

Toyota 5L Engine 1998 On
Hiace LH103-113-125

Engine Checks

Valve Clearance Check

Please Note: Before carrying out this check ensure that the engine is at normal operating temperature.

1. Remove the rocker cover, set the No1 piston to TDC on its compression stroke and ensure that the groove on the crankshaft pulley is lined up with the timing pointer on the front cover.

2. Ensure that the valve lifters on the No1 cylinder are loose and that the No4 valve lifters are tight (if they are not turn the engine on full turn (360°) and recheck).

3. Measure the valve clearances on the following valves 1&3 (Exhaust) and 1&2 (Inlet).

Inlet Valve Clearance: 0.20-030mm (Cold)
Exhaust Valve Clearance: 0.40-0.50mm (Cold)

If the clearances are not correct record the relevant readings to determine the adjusting shim required.

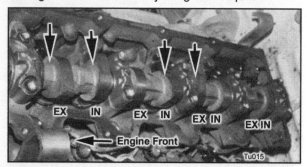

EX   IN   EX   IN   EX IN   EX IN

← Engine Front

Tu015

4. Turn the crankshaft one full turn (360°) and ensure that the groove on the crankshaft pulley is lined up with the timing pointer on the front cover.

5. Measure the valve clearances on the following valves 2&4 (Exhaust) and 3&4 (Inlet).

Inlet Valve Clearance: 0.20-030mm (Cold)
Exhaust Valve Clearance: 0.40-0.50mm (Cold)

If the clearances are not correct record the relevant

readings to determine the adjusting shim required.

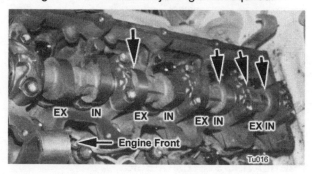

EX   IN   EX   IN   EX IN   EX IN

← Engine Front

Tu016

Compression Check

1. Run the engine to normal operating temperature, disconnect the fuel cut solenoid connector and remove all of the glow plugs from the engine.

2. Install an adaptor and compression gauge to the No1 cylinder, fully open the throttle, crank the engine and record the comprerssion pressure on each cylinder.

Compression Pressure: 3138kpa
Minimum Pressure: 1961kpa
Difference Between Each Cylinder: 490kpa

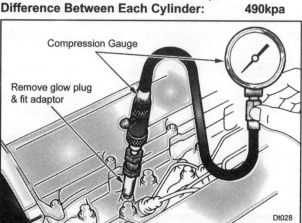

Compression Gauge

Remove glow plug & fit adaptor

Dt028

3. If the pressure on one or more cylinders is low, pour a small amount of oil into the cylinder through the glow plug hole and check the compression pressure again. If

it helps the pressure there are possibly faults withy the piston rings or cylinder bores, if the oil does not help there may be a valve sticking or not seated correctly and/or leaks past the gasket.

Cylinder Head Tightening Procedures

1. After the cylinder head has been removed and the gasket replaced, apply a thin coat of oil to all of the cylinder head bolts. Install and gradually tighten each of the bolts to its correct torque in three stages in the sequence showed in the diagram.

Specified Torque Setting: 78Nm

Please Note: If any of the bolts do not reach the correct torque, check the length of the bolts.

Short Bolt: 107mm

Long Bolt: 127mm

Replace any faulty bolts as required.

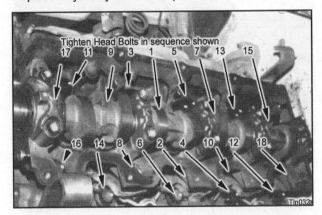

2. Mark the front of each bolt with some paint and the tighten the bolts a further 90°. After the sequence has been completed tighten the bolts a further 90° and now ensure that the paint mark is facing to the rear.

Piston Protrusion Height Check
No1 and 4 Piston Check

1. Rotate the engine and ensure that the timing marks on the crankshaft pulley line up with the marks on the front cover.

2. Fit a dial gauge to the engine block and set the gauge at the piston measuring point.

3. Find the point where the piston protrudes the most by turning the crankshaft in a clockwise and anti clockwise direction.

4. Set the dial gauge to zero and record the protrusion measurement from the block by sliding the dial gauge.

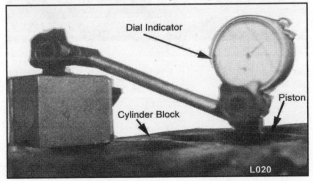

Protrusion Measurement: 0.68-0.97mm

Please Note: Record the measurement at two separate measuring points.

No2 and No3 Piston Check

5. Turn the crankshaft 180°, fit a dial gauge to the engine block and set the gauge at the piston measuring point.

6. Find the point where the piston protrudes the most by turning the crankshaft in a clockwise and anti clockwise direction.

7. Set the dial gauge to zero and record the protrusion measurement from the block by sliding the dial gauge.

Protrusion Measurement: 0.68-0.97mm

Please Note: Record the measurement at two separate measuring points.

8. When the measurment has been made, to select a new head gasket follow the procedures shown.

9. There are 3 different types of head gaskets marked either "B", "D" or "F", each of them different thicknesses.

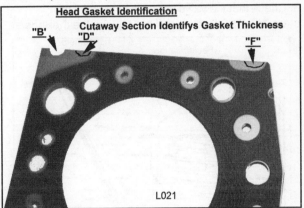

Piston Protrusion Measurements	Gasket Thickness	Gasket Grade
0.68-0.77	1.4-1.5mm	B
0.78-0.87	1.5-1.6	D
0.88-0.97	1.6-1.7	F

Please Note: When selecting the gasket use the largest measurement of the 8 readings that are recorded.

Oil Pressure Check (test is on the next page)

1. Ensure that the engine oil level is correct, if not top up to suit.

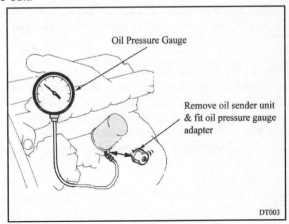

2. Remove the oil pressure switch from the engine and install a pressure gauge to the engine block.

3. Start the engine and run to normal operating temperature and then record the oil pressure shown on the gauge.

Specified Oil Pressure: 29kpa @ Idle
Specified Oil Pressure: 294-539kpa @ 3000RPM

4. If the oil pressure is not as shown, repair/ replace as required.

Cooling System Thermostat Check

1. Remove the thermostat from the engine and put into a suitable container of water.

2. Heat the water gradually and and check the valve opening temperature and valve lift.

Valve Opening Temperature: 86-90°c
Valve Lift: More than 8mm

If the operation is not as shown above replace the thermostat.

3. Check that the valve spring is tight when the thermostat is fully closed, if not replace the thermostat.

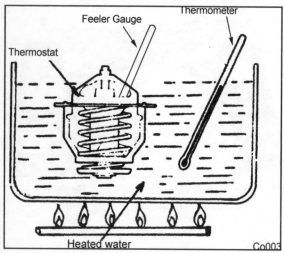

Fuel Filter Check and Replacement

1. Remove the fuel filter sensor (if fitted), drain the fuel, then remove the fuel filter.

2. Clean the fuel filter mounting bracket, and then coat the fuel filter sealing ring with some diesel fuel.

3. Screw the fuel filter on until a slght resistance is felt and then turn another 2/3 of a turn or until suitably tight.

4. Install the fuel filter sensor (if fitted) to the new filter and then bleed any air present from the system.

Draining Water From The Filter

1. Loosen the drain cock 4 or 5 turns or remove the fuel filter sensor to allow the water to drain from the filter.

2. Retighten the drain cock or replace the sensor and bleed any air present from the system.

Diagram is in the next column

Fuel Filter Warning Lamp Check

1. Remove the switch from the filter and check that there is continuity between the terminals when the warning switch is ON (Float Up)

2. Check that there is no continuity between the terminals when the warning switch is OFF (Float Down)

3. If the operation is not as shown, repair/replace as required.

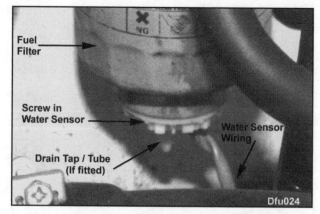

Injector Nozzle Check

1. Remove the injector from the vehicle, connect up to the pressure tester and check the initial pressure by pumping the tester handle a few times.

Initial Opening Pressure:
        15,581-16,781kpa (New Nozzle)
Initial Opening Pressure:
        15,090-16,290kpa (Used Nozzle).

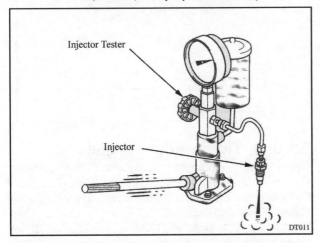

2. If the opening pressure is not as shown above, take the injector to pieces and change the adjusting shim on the top of the injector so as the correct pressure is recorded.

Adjusted Opening Pressure: 14,220-15,220kpa

3. Maintain the pressure between 981-1961kpa below the opening pressure and check that there is no leakage from the injector for a period of 10seconds.

4. Check the spray pattern by pumping the pressure tester handle 4-6 times or more per second and check the injection spray pattern.

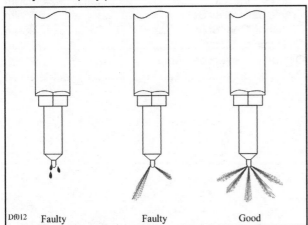

| Faulty | Faulty | Good |

5. If the operation and/or spray pattern is not as shown, repair/replace the nozzle/s as required.

Timing Belt Removal and Replacement

Removal Procedures

1. Remove the glow plugs, drive belts, water pump pulley, crankshaft pulley and the No1 timing cover.
2. Remove the timing belt guide.
3. Set the No1 piston to TDC on its compression stroke by temporarily replacing the crankshaft pulley bolt and turning the crankshaft in a clockwise direction until the timing mark on the camshaft gear lines up with the mark on the No2 timing belt cover.

Please Note: If the timing belt is being used again, before removing, mark a direction arrow on the timing belt and place match marks on the pulleys and the belt.

4. Turn the engine 90° in an anti clockwise direction and ensure that the timing mark on the crankshaft pulley lines up with the protrusion on the timing case.
5. Loosen the No1 idler pulley mount bolts and move to the left as far as it will go. Temporarily tighten the bolt, relieve the belt tension and remove the timing belt from the engine.

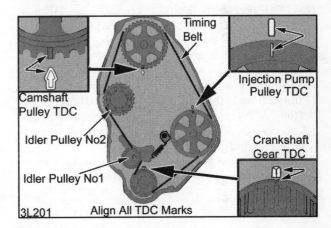

Replacement Procedures

Please Note: Before replacing the timimg belt check the condition and/or operation of the timing belt pulleys, tensioners and/or pulleys, if faults are found repair/replace as required.

1. Check the tensioner spring free length
Spring Free Length: **44.4-45.4mm**
Check the tension of the spring at the specified free length
Installed Tension: **53-59Nm at 52.1mm**
2. Install the crankshaft pulley to the engine, replace any pulleys or idlers that may have been removed for checking.
3. Set the No1 piston to TDC on its compression stroke and ensure that the timing marks on each of the pulleys line up with their relevant matchmarks.
4. Fit the timing belt onto the crankshaft pulley and No1 idler pulley, slightly turn the injection pulley in a clockwise direction, fit the timing belt onto the injection pulley and line up the marks on the injection pulley and

timing belt case.

5. Slightly turn the camshaft drive pulley in a clockwise direction, fit the timing belt onto the pulley and ensure that the marks on the pulley and timing belt case line up.

Please Note: Ensure that there is belt tension between the camshaft pulley and injection pump drive pulleys.

6. Install the timing belt to the No2 idler pulley.

7. Loosen the No1 idler pulley, stretch the timing belt and turn the crankshaft in a clockwise direction two full turns from TDC to TDC, ensuring that all of the timing marks on the drive pulleys line up with their respective match marks.

Please Note: If any of the marks do not line up, remove the belt and reinstall again.

8. Tighten the No1 idler pulley bolt, refit the timimg belt guide and replace any removed components in the reverse order of removal.

Timing Belt Replacement Torques

Injection Pump Drive Pulley:	64Nm
No1 Idle Pulley (12mm Bolt):	19Nm
No1 Idle Pulley (14mm Bolt):	44Nm
No2 Idle Pulley:	33Nm
Crankshaft Pulley Bolt:	235Nm
Camshaft Gear Bolt:	98Nm

Timing Belt Warning Lamp Reset Procedures (Rubber Plug in the Instrument Cluster Glass)

1. Remove the grommet from the speedometer and turn off the lamp by pushing the warning lamp reset switch, then replace the grommet.

2. Start the engine and ensure that the light stays off.

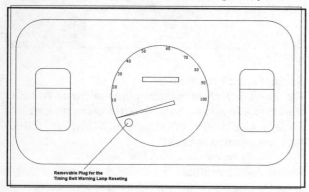

Removable Plug for the
Timing Belt Warning Lamp Reseting

Timing Belt Warning Lamp Reset Procedures (Change Screw Position on the Back of the Instrument Cluster)

1. Remove the instrument cluster from the vehicle, connect terminals A&B shown in the diagrams and then remove the CHARGE fuse from the vehicle.

2. Turn the ignition switch to ON and check that the warning lights light up, if not the check the condition and/or operation of the globe.

3. Check the condition and/or operation of the reset switches by checking that there is intermittent continu-

ity between terminals A&B when the reset switch is pressed, if not repair/replace the speedometer/instrument cluster as required.

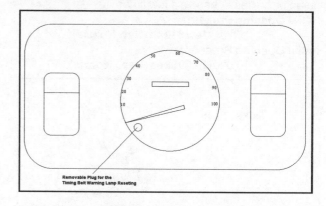

Removable Plug for the
Timing Belt Warning Lamp Reseting

Engine Tightening Torques

Cylinder Head Tightening Torque Bolts:	78Nm (1st Stage)
Cylinder Head Tightening Torque Bolts:	... 90° (2nd Stage)
Cylinder Head Tightening Torque Bolts:	.. 90° (3rd Stage)
Camshaft Bearing Cap:	25Nm
Exhaust Manifold Bolts and Nuts:	52Nm
Inlet Manifold Bolts and Nuts:	24Nm
Glow Plugs:	13Nm
Injection Nozzle:	64Nm
Injection Pump Drive Pulley Nut:	64Nm
No1 Idle Pulley (12mm Bolt):	19Nm
No1 Idle Pulley (14mm Bolt):	44Nm
No2 Idle Pulley:	33Nm
Flywheel Bolts:	123Nm
Drive Plate:	98Nm
Connecting Rod Caps:	54Nm (1st Stage)
Connecting Rod Caps:	90° (2nd Stage)
Main Bearings:	105Nm
Crankshaft Pulley Bolt:	235Nm
Camshaft Gear Bolt:	98Nm
Oil Pump to Block:	23Nm
Oil Pump to Injection Pump:	21Nm
Oil Sump Bolt:	18Nm

System Adjustments

Injection Timing Adjustment

1. Remove the distributive head bolt and install a special tool (SST09275-54011 plunger stroke measuring tool) to the plug hole and then set the No1 or No4 piston to between 25-30° BTDC on its compression stroke.

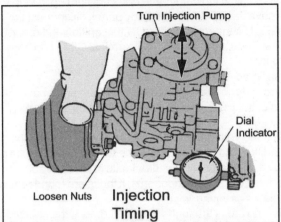

Turn Injection Pump

Dial Indicator

Loosen Nuts   Injection Timing

2. Please Note: (For vehicles with auto cold start device): Using a screwdriver turn the cold start lever anti clockwise about 20° and put a metal plate 8.5-10.0mm between the cold start lever and the thermo wax plunger.

3. Turn the crankshaft pulley in a clockwise direction until it is between 25-30° BTDC, set the dial indicator to zero (mm).Slowly turn the crankshaft pulley until crankshaft pulley groove is lined up with the timing pointer and record the plunger movement.

Injection Plunger Stroke: **0.44-0.56 (With Auto Cold Start Device)**

Injection Plunger Stroke: **0.64-0.76mm (W/out Auto Cold Start Device)**

4. If the plunger stroke measurment is not as shown, loosen the 4 injector pipe union nuts and inlet pipe union nuts on the injection pump side.

5. Loosen the 4 injection pump mounting nuts and adjust the plunger pump stroke by slightly tilting the injection pump body. If the stroke is less than shown tilt the pump towards the engine, if the plunger strike is more than shown tilt the pump away from the engine.

6. Retighten all of the fixing bolts and union nuts, recheck the plunger stroke and then remove the plate from the cold starting lever.

7. Remove the dial indicator gauge and replace the plug bolt. Restart the engine and check for any leaks in the system.

Idle Speed Check

1. Ensure that the air cleaner is OK, the engine coolant temperature is at normal, the accessories are all switched off and that the transmission is in neutral.

2. Ensure that the adjusting screw lever touches the idle speed adjusting screw when the throttle pedal is released, if it is not adjust to suit.

3. Install a tachometer to the engine, start the engine and check the idle speed setting.

Idle Speed Setting: **650-750RPM**

4. If the idle speed is not as shown in step3, disconnect the throttle linkage, loosen the lock nut of the idle adjust screw and adjust by turning the idle speed adjusting screw, re-tighten the lock nut, and reconnect the throttle linkage. Recheck the idle speed.

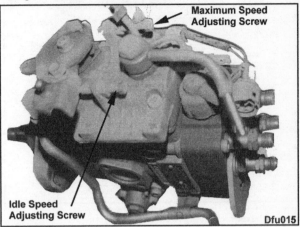

Maximum Speed Adjusting Screw

Idle Speed Adjusting Screw

Dfu015

5. Remove the tachometer from the engine and replace any removed parts to the vehicle.

Maximum Speed Adjustment Check

1. Ensure that the adjusting lever touches the maximum speed adjusting screw when the throttle is pressed down all the way, if not adjust the throttle linkages

2. Install a tachometer to the engine, start the engine, press the throttle fully down and check the maximum speed.

Maximum Speed Setting: **4770-5030RPM**

3. If the maximum speed is not as shown, disconnect the throttle linkage, cut the seal wire on the adjusting screw, loosen the lock nut on the maximum speed adjusting screw and adjust by turning the adjusting screw.

4. Check the idle speed setting, raise the engine speed and recheck the maximum speed.

5. Retighten the lock nut, re-seal the adjusting screw, reconnect the throttle linkage and recheck the throttle linkage adjustment.

6. Remove the tachometer from the engine and replace any removed parts to the vehicle.

Refer to Idle Speed Diagram

Pre Heat System Checks

Pre Heat System Circuit Check

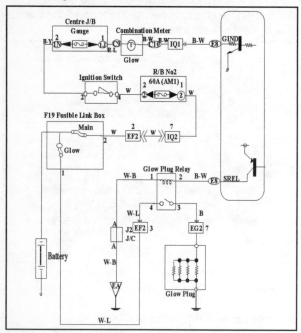

1. Switch ON the ignition and ensure that the glow indicator lamp lights up, if it does, check the glow lighting and afterglow light up times.

Lamp Light Up Time: Approx 3.5 Secs
After Glow Time: Approx 6.0 secs.

If the times are not OK, check the condition and/or operation of the ECU, if faults are found repair/replace as required.

2. If the light up times and afterglow times are Ok, carry out self diagnosis test and check for any codes present in the system, if codes are found repair faults as required.

3. If no codes are present in step2, check the operation of the glow plug relay, if faults are found repair/replace as required.

4. If no faults are found in step3, remove the ECU from the body panel, disconnect the 26 pin ECU connector, put the ignition switch into the STA position and check the voltage between the SREL and body ground while the engine is cranking.

Specified Voltage: 9-14v

If the voltage is not as shown, check the condition and/or operation of the ECU, if faults are found repair/replace as required.

5. If the voltage is OK in step 4, check for open and short in the harness and connector between the glow plug relay and ECU, and between the glow plug relay and body ground, if faults are found repair/replace as required.

6. If no faults are found in step5, check the resistance of the glow plug/s.

Specified Resistance: 0.72ohms @ 20°c

If the resistance is not as shown, repair/replace as required

7. If no faults are found in step6, check the installation of the glow plug/s, if faults are found repair/replace as required.

8. If no faults are found in step7, check for open in the harness and connector between the glow plug relay and glow plug, if faults are found repair/replace as required.

9. If the glow indicator lamp does not light up in step1, remove the ECU from the body panel, disconnect the 16 pin ECU connector, switch ON the ignition and record the voltage between the ECU terminal GIND and body ground.

Specified Voltage: 9-14v

If the voltage is OK, check the condition and/or operation of the ECU, if faults are found repair/replace as required.

10. If the voltage is not as shown in step9, check the condition and/or operation of the Gauge fuse, if faults are found, check for short and/or faults in the relevant harness/s and/or components, if faults are found repair/replace as required.

11. If no faults are found in step10, check the condition and/or operation of the glow indicator lamp globe, if faults are found repair/replace as required.

12. If no faults are found in step11, check for open in the harness and connector between the combination meter and ECU, and between the combination meter and gauge fuse, if faults are found repair/replace as required.

Pre Heat System
Glow Indicator Lamp Check

1. Switch ON the ingition and check the glow indicator light up time.

Lamp Light Up Time: Approx 3.5 Secs

2. Start the engine and record the time that the lamp lights up when battery volts are applied to terminal 9 of the 16 pin ECU connector.

After Glow Time: Approx 6.0 secs.

3. If the operation is not as shown, check the condition and/or operation of the ECU.

Glow Plug Relay Check

1. With an ohmmeter check the continuity between the terminals 1-2 and ensure that it exists
If there is no continuity replace the relay

2. Check for continuity between terminals 3-4 and ensure that it does not exist
If there is continuity replace the relay.

3. Apply battery volts between terminals 1-2 and ensure that continuity exists between terminals 3-4
If there is no continuity replace the relay

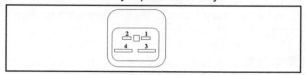

Glow Plug Check

1. With an ohmmeter check that there is continuity between the glow plug terminal and ground
Specified Resistance: 0.72ohms @ 20°c
If continuity does not exist, replace the faulty glow plug/plugs

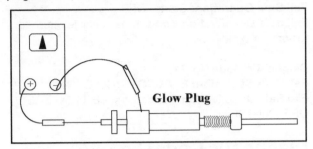

Glow Plug

Water Temperature Sensor Check

1. Remove the sensor harness connector and check the resistance between the sensor terminals at varying temperatures.

Sensor Temperature (°c)	Sensor Resistance (k/ohms)
0	4.8
20	2.0
40	0.8
60	0.45
80	0.20
100	0.12

2. If the resistance is not as shown, repair/replace as required.

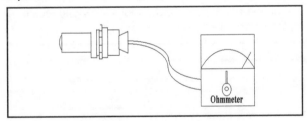

Ohmmeter

Diesel Self Diagnosis System Checks

Self Diagnosis Test
Glow Indicator Lamp Check

1. Switch on the ingition (don't start the engine) and check that the Glow Indicator Lamp on the instrument cluster lights up, if it does not check the condition of the indicator lamp globe and/or relevant harness/s.
2. Start the engine and ensure that the light goes out after a few seconds. If the lamp stays on it will indicate that there are faults present in the system and the diagnostic codes need to be extracted.

How to Extract Diagnostic Codes

1. Switch on the ignition and install a jump wire between the TE1 and E1 connectors on the diagnostic connector. Read the codes that are being output through the Glow Indicator Lamp on the dash panel.

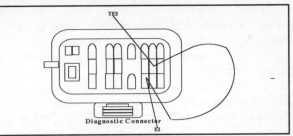

Diagnostic Connector

How to Read Diagnostic Codes.

1. If no fault codes are present in the system the Glow Indicator Lamp will flash continuously at 0.26 second intervals. If faults codes are present (For Example Code 13), in the system there will at first be a 4.5 second pause, there will then be a 0.52 second flash, a 1.5 second pause and then 3 more 0.52 second flashes on the Glow Indicator Lamp.

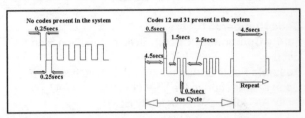

2. If more than one code is present in the system the codes are output in numerical sequence lowest to highest.
3. The codes will continue to be output until the jump wire has been removed from the diagnostic connector.
4. All codes that appear in the code list below will light up the Glow Indicator Lamp and will be stored in the ECU memory.

How to Clear Diagnostic Codes

1. After all of the codes have been output, clear all codes from the system by disconnecting the jump wire from the diagnostic connector and switching off the ignition. It is advisable to now roadtest the vehicle and then carry out the self diagnosis test again to ensure all codes have been cleared from the system and that there are no intermittent faults in the system

Diagnostic Code List
Code Number: 13
Faulty Component/Circuit: Engine Speed Sensor
Possible Fault Causes: Open and/or short in the pick up sensor circuit, faulty pick up sensor or faulty ECU.

Code Number: 22
Faulty Component/Circuit: Water Temperature Sensor
Possible Fault Causes: Open and/or short in the water temperature sensor circuit, faulty water temperature sensor or faulty ECU.

Code Number: 31
Faulty Component/Circuit: Vacuum Sensor
Possible Fault Causes: Open and/or short in the vacuum sensor circuit, faulty vacuum sensor or faulty ECU.

Code Number: 41
Faulty Component/Circuit: Throttle Position Sensor
Possible Fault Causes: Open and/or short in the throttle position sensor circuit, faulty throttle position sensor or faulty ECU.

Code Number: 42
Faulty Component/Circuit: Vehicle Speed Sensor Signal
Possible Fault Causes: Open and/or short in the vehicle speed sensor circuit, faulty vehicle speed sensor, faulty instrument cluster or faulty ECU.

Code Number: 43
Faulty Component/Circuit: Starter Signal Circuit
Possible Fault Causes: Open and/or short in the starter signal circuit or faulty ECU.

Code Number: 51
Faulty Component/Circuit: Switch Condition Signal Circuit
Possible Fault Causes: Faulty A/C switch system, Open and/or short in the VSV circuit for the A/C idle up, faulty A/C Idle Up VSV or faulty ECU.

Code Number: 71
Faulty Component/Circuit: EGR System
Possible Fault Causes: Blocked and/or damaged sensing pipe, faulty vacuum pump, EGR valve, E-VRV, open or short in the E-VRV circuit for the EGR and/or faulty ECU.

Fail Safe Mode
1-If any of the following codes DTC13, 22, 31, 41, 42, 43 and/or 71 are recorded the ECU will automatically be placed into failsafe mode.

Diagnostic Code No: 13
Fail Safe Operation: Engine speed at 0 RPM and the E-VRV OFF (Cut EGR)
Fail Safe Deactivation Conditions: Vehicle returned to normnal conditions.

Diagnostic Code No: 22
Fail Safe Operation: Water temperature is fixed to 20°c and the E-VRV OFF (Cut EGR)
Fail Safe Deactivation Conditions: Vehicle returned to normnal conditions.

Diagnostic Code No: 31
Fail Safe Operation: Intake air pressure is at 101.3kpa and the E-VRV OFF (Cut EGR)
Fail Safe Deactivation Conditions: Vehicle returned to normnal conditions.

Diagnostic Code No: 41
Fail Safe Operation: Throttle pedal is fixed at 0% and the E-VRV OFF (Cut EGR)
Fail Safe Deactivation Conditions: Closed throttle position switch is ON 0.1< VA < 4.85V

Diagnostic Code No: 42
Fail Safe Operation: A/C Cut
Fail Safe Deactivation Conditions: Vehicle returned to normnal conditions.

Diagnostic Code No: 43
Fail Safe Operation: Starter OFF
Fail Safe Deactivation Conditions: Vehicle returned to normnal conditions.

Diagnostic Code No: 71
Fail Safe Operation: E-VRV OFF (Cut EGR)
Fail Safe Deactivation Conditions: +B 11.5v, E-VRV OFF (Cut EGR)

Diagnostic Code Circuit/ Component Tests

Diagnostic Code 13 (Engine Speed Sensor Circuit Fault)
1. Check the resistance of the pick up sensor by checking the resistance between the terminals 1 and 2.
Specified Resistance: **650-970 ohms**
If the resistance is not as shown, replace the sensor
2. If no faults are found in step1, check for open and/or short in the harness and connector between the ECU and pick up sensor, if faults are found repair/replace as required.
3. If no faults are found in step2, check the sensor installation, if faults are found rectify as required.
4. If no faults are found in step3, check the condition and/or operation of the ECU, if faults are found repair/ replace as required.

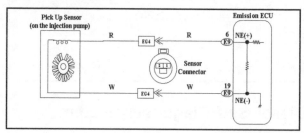

Diagnostic Code 22 (Water Temperature Sensor Circuit Test)
Please Note: If codes 22, 31 and 41 are output at the same time, the E2 (sensor ground) may be open.
1. Remove the ECU from the body panel, switch ON the ignition and check the voltage between the THW and E2 terminals (26 pin ECU connector)
Specified Voltage: **0.5-3.4v @ 20°c**
Specified Voltage: **0.2-1.0v @ 80°c**
2. If the voltage is OK in step1, check the system for intermittent faults, if faults are found reapir/replace as required.
3. If the voltage is not as shown in step1, check the operation of the temp sensor by removing the sensor from the engine, placing in a suitable container of water and checking the sensor resistance between the

terminals at varying temperatures.

Sensor Temperature (°c)	Sensor Resistance (k/ohms)
0	4.8
20	2.0
40	0.8
60	0.45
80	0.20
100	0.12

If the resistance is not as shown, repair/replace as required.

4. If the resistance in step3 is OK, check for open and/or short circuit in the harness between the ECU and water temp sensor, if faults are found repair/replace as required.

5. If no faults are found in step4, check the condition and/or operation of the ECU, if faults are found repair/replace as required.

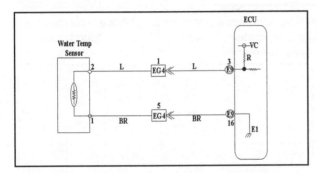

Diagnostic Code 31 (Vacuum Sensor Circuit Test)
Please Note: If codes 22, 31 and 41 are output at the same time, the E2 (sensor ground) may be open.
1. Remove the ECU from the body panel, switch ON the ignition and check the voltage between the ECU terminals VC & E2 (26 Pin ECU Connector)
Specified Voltage: 4.5-5.5v
2. If the voltage is not as shown in step1, check the condition and/or operation of the ECU, if faults are found repair/replace as required.
3. If the voltage in step1 is OK, disconnect the 26 pin ECU connector, switch ON the ignition and check the voltage between the ECU terminals PIM & E2 (26 Pin ECU Connector)
Specified Voltage: 3.3-3.9v
4. If the voltage is OK but code 31 is displayed check the condition and/or operation of the ECU, if faults are found repair/replace as required.
5. If the voltage is OK in step4, check for open and/or short circuit in the harness between the ECU and sensor, if faults are found repair/replace as required.
6. If no faults are found in step5, check the condition and/or operation of the ECU, if faults are found repair/replace as required.

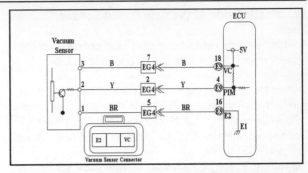

Diagnostic Code 41 (Throttle Position Circuit Test)
Please Note: If codes 22, 31 and 41 are output at the same time, the E2 (sensor ground) may be open
1. Remove the ECU from the body panel, switch ON the ignition and check the voltage between the VA and E2 terminals (26 Pin ECU Connector) when the adjusting lever is turning to the maximum speed side gradually from the idle speed.

Adjusting Lever	Voltage (V)
Idle Speed Side	0.3-1.0
Maximum Speed Side	2.7-5.2

Please Note: The voltage should increase in proportion to the adjusting valve opening angle
2. If the voltage is not as shown in step1, disconnect the throttle position sensor harness connector and record the resistance between the sensor connector terminals 1 and 2 & 2 and 3 when the adjusting lever is turning to the maximum speed side gradually from the idle speed.

Terminals	Adjusting Lever	Resistance (k/ohms)
1-2		1.8-3.42
2-3	Idle Speed Side	1.3-7.6
2-3	Maximum Speed Side	0.2-6.0

Please Note: The voltage should increase in proportion to the adjusting valve opening angle
3. If the resistance is not as shown, replace the sensor as required.
4. If the resistance is OK in step2, check for open and/or short circuit in the harness between the ECU and sensor, if faults are found repair/replace as required.
5. If no faults are found in step4, check the condition and/or operation of the ECU, if faults are found repair/replace as required.

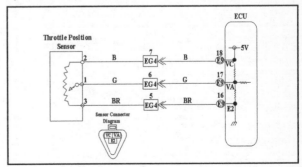

Diagnostic Code 42 (Vehicle Speed Sensor Circuit Test)

1. Road test the vehicle and check the operation of the speedometer, if faults are found repair/replace as required

2. If no faults are found in step1, remove the ECU from the body panel, put the shift lever in neutral, jack up one of the rear wheels, switch on the ignition and check the voltage between the ECU terminal SP1 and body ground (16 pin ECU connector)

Specified Voltage: Between 0v and 4.5V ±5.5v (each full turn of the wheel)

If the voltage is not as shown, check the condition of the harness and/or connector between the combination meter and the ECU, if faults are found repair/replace as required.

3. If the voltage in step2 is Ok, check the condition and/or operation of the ECU, if faults are found repair/replace as required.

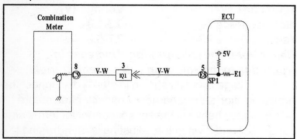

Diagnostic Code 43 (Starter Signal Circuit Test)

1. Check the voltage between the STA terminal of the ECU by removing the ECU from the body panel, starting the engine and recording the voltage between the ECU terminal STA and body ground (26 Pin ECU Connector).

Specified Voltage: 6.0v or More

2. If the voltage in step1 is not as shown, check for open circuit in the harness and/or connector between the ECU and starter relay, if faults are found repair/replace as required.

3. If no faults are found in step2 check the condition and/or operation of the ECU, if faults are found repair/replace as required.

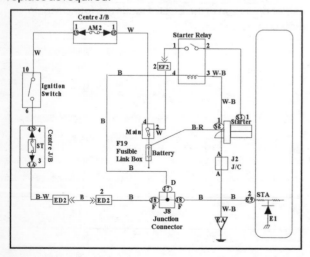

Diagnostic Code 51 (Switch Condition Signal Circuit Test)

1. Carry out self diagnosis test and check the output condition of code 51 on the glow indicator lamp.

Condition	Code
A/C Switch ON	51
A/c Switch OFF	Normal

2. If the code operation is not as shown in step1, remove the ECU from the body panel, switch ON the ignition and record the voltage between the A/C terminal and body ground on the ECU (16 Pin Connector).

Specified Voltage: 9-14v

If the voltage is OK, check the condition and/or operation of the ECU, if faults are found repair/replace as required.

3. If the voltage is not as shown in step2, check for open and/or short in the harness and/or connector between the A/C terminal body ground, if faults are found repair/replace as required.

4. If no faults are found in step3, check the condition and/or operation of the ECU, if faults are found repair/replace as required.

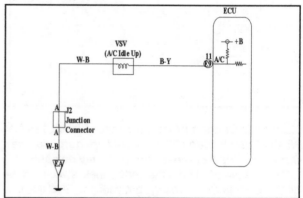

Diagnostic Code 71 (EGR System Fault)

1. Check the connection of the vacuum hose between the vacuum pump and E-VRV for the EGR, between the E-VRV for EGR and EGR valve, if faults are found repair/replace as required.

2-If no faults are found in step1, remove the ECU from the body panel, disconnect the 26 pin ECU connector from the ECU, switch ON the ignition and check the E-VRV operation by connecting a jump wire between the ECU terminal EGR and ground and ensure that air from port E is flowing through port F, disconnecting the jump wire between the ECU terminal EGR and ground and ensure that air from port E is flowing through the air filter

3. If the operation is OK in step2, check the operation of the EGR valve, if faults are found repair/replace as required.

4. If no faults are found in step3, check the operation of the EGR system, if faults are found repair/replace as required.

5. If the operation is step 2 is not OK, check the operation of the E-VRV for EGR, if faults are found repair/replace as required.

6. If no faults are found in step5, check for open and/or short in the harness and/or connector between the E-

VRV for EGR and the ECU, if faults are found repair/replace as required.

7. If no faults are found in step6, check the condition and/or operation of the ECU, if faults are found repair/replace as required.

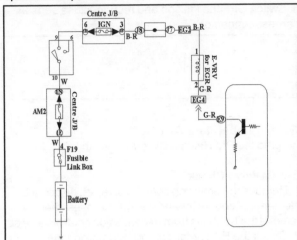

Non Diagnostic Code Related Checks

ECU Power Source Circuit Check

1-Remove the ECU from the body panel, switch ON the ignition and record the voltage between the +B & E1 terminals (26 Pin ECU Connector).

Specified Voltage: 9-14v

2-If the voltage is not as shown in step1, check for open in the harness and connector between the ECU terminal E1 and body ground, if faults are found repair/replace as required.

3-If no faults are found in step2, check the condition and/or operation if the IGN fuse, if faults are found check all relevant harneses and components connected to them, if faults are found repair/replace as required.

4-If no faults are found in step3, check the condition and/or operation of the ignition switch by disconnecting the switch harness connector and checking continuity between the terminals.

Switch Position	Terminal No	Continuity
Lock		
ACC	5-7	-
ON	4-5-7	2-3
START	1-2-4	6-7-8

If the operation is not as shown, repair/replace as required.

5-If no faults are found in step4, check for open in harness and connector between the +B terminal of the ECU connector and the ignition switch, if faults are found repair/replace as required

6-If no faults are found in step5, check the condition and/or operation of the AM2 fuse, if faults are found check all relevant harneses and components connected to them, if faults are found repair/replace as required

7-If no faults are found in step6, check for open in the

harness and connector between the ignition switch and battery, if faults are found repair/replace as required.

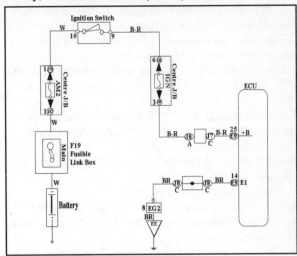

TE1 Terminal Check

1. Switch ON the ignition and record the voltage between the TE1 and E1 terminals on the check connector.

Specified Voltage: 9-14v

If the voltage is Ok. check the condition and/or operation of the ECU, if faults are found repair/replace as required.

2. If the voltage is OK in step1, check for continuity between the E1 terminal on the check connector and body ground, if faults are found repair/replace as required.

3. If no faults are found in step2, check for open and short in the harness and connector between the TE1 terminal on the ECU (16 Pin Connector) and check connector, if faults are found repair/replace as required. as required.

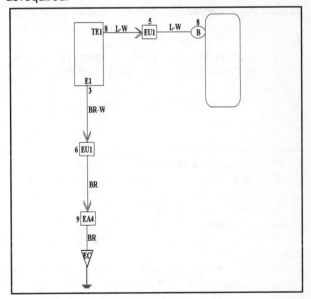

EGR System Checks and Tests
Check EGR System

1. With a 3 way conenctor connect a vacuum gauge to the vacuum hose between the EGR valve and E-VRV.

2. Check the seating of the EGR valve by starting the engine and ensuring it runs at idle.

3. Check the engine at cold operation with the coolant at 40°c, ensuring that the vacuum gauge shows zero at idle.

4. Check the engine at hot operation by ensuring that the coolant temp is more than 70°c and the vacuum gauge indicates 24kpa at idle.

5. Turn the adjusting lever on the injection pump to the full open position and ensure that the vacuum gauge needle momentarily moves to zero.

6. Keep the engine speed at more than 4200RPM or more and ensure that the needle on the vacuum gauge momentarily moves to zero.

7. If all the operations are as shown, the system is OK.

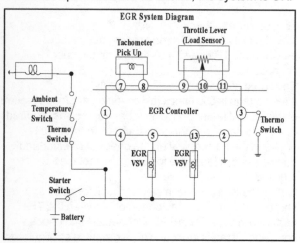

EGR System Diagram

Vacuum Pump Check

1. Disconnect the vacuum hose from the outlet pipe and install a vacuum gauge to the outlet pipe.

2. Run the engine to normal operating temperature and ensure that the vacuum gauge shows more than 86.7kpa.

3-If the operation is not as shown, repair/replace as required

Vacuum Sensor Check

1. Check the power source voltage of the sensor by disconnecting the sensor harness connector, switching on the ignition and recording the voltage between the connector termianls VC and E2.

Specified Voltage: 4.5-5.5v.

Switch off the ignition and reconnect the harness connector.

2. Check the power output of the sensor by switching on the ignition, disconnecting the vacuum hose from the sensor, connecting a voltmeter to the ECU terminals PIM and E2 (26Pin Connector) and recording the output voltage under the following conditions.

Specified Voltage: 0.2-0.8v (40kpa of vacuum applied)

Specified Voltage: 1.3-1.9v (Vacuum released)

Specified Voltage: 3.2-3.8v (69kpa of vacuum applied)

3. Switch OFF the ignition and reconnect the sensor harness connector.

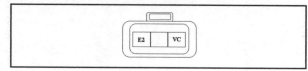

Water Temperature Sensor
Refer to the Pre Heating System Checks

E-VRV Valve Check

1. Remove the emission control valve set, disconnect the harness connector and 2 vacuum hoses, then remove the two bolts from the emission control valve set.

2. Check the E-VRV for ground by checking the resistance between the valve terminals.

Specified Resistance: 11-13ohms @ 20°c

If the resistance is not as shown, replace as required.

3. Check the E-VRV for ground by ensuring that there is no continuity between each terminal and the body, if continuity is found replace the E-VRV.

4. Check the E-VRV for air tightness by fixing a vacuum gauge to the vacuum outlet port on the valve and checking that the needle on the vacuum pump shows an increase of 46.7kpa or more, if the reading is not as shown, replace the E-VRV.

5. Check the E-VRV operation by applying 6v of DC power to the valve terminals and ensure that when vacuum is applied to the valve that the vacuum gauge needle does not move.

If the operation is not as shown, replace the valve.

EGR Valve Check

1. Remove the EGR valve from the engine, apply 26.7kpa of vacuum to the diaphram chamber and ensure that the shaft move up and that air flows from in to out.

2. With the above conditions maintained, check and ensure that there are no air leaks.

3. Ensure that the valve does not stick and/or there are no carbon deposits in the valve.

4. If the valve operation is not as shown, replace the EGR valve.

Throttle Position Sensor Check

1. Disconnect the throttle sensor harness connector and with an ohmmeter check the resistance between the harness connector terminals VC and E2

Specified Resistance: 1.84-3.45k/ohms @ 20°c

2. Check the increase and decrease in readings between the VA and E2 terminals when the adjusting lever is moved from the closed to the open position.

Refer Code No41 diagram for connector

ECU Voltage Checks
Please Note: there are two connectors on this ECU A 26 pin (Connector E09) and a 16 pin (Connector E8).

Between Terminals	Wiring Colour	Condition	Voltage
Batt & E1	B-O <> BR	Always	9-14
+B & E1	B-R <> BR	Ignition Switch ON	9-14
VC & E2	B <> BR	Ignition Switch ON	4.5-5.5
VA & E2	G <> BR	Throttle Valve Fully Closed	0.3-0.8
VA & E2	G <> BR	Throttle Valve Fully Open	3.2-4.9
PIM & E2	Y <> BR	Ignition Switch ON	3.3-3.9
PIM & E2	Y <> BR	26.7 kpa vacuum applied	2.5-3.1
THW & E2	L <> BR	At Idle Coolant Temp 80°c	0.2-1.0
STA & E1	B <> BR	Cranking	6.0 or More
NE(+) & NE(-)	R <> W	Idling	Pulse Generation
SP1 & E1	V-W <> BR	Ignition ON (Drive Wheels Turned Slow)	Pulse Generation
STA & E1	B <> BR	Ignition Switch ON	Less than 6.0
EGR & E1	G-R <> BR	26 Pin ECU Connector Disconnected (Ignition Switch ON)	9-14
SRE-L & E1	G-R <> BR	26 Pin ECU Connector Disconnected (Engine Cranking)	9-14
SRE-L & E1	G-R <> BR	At Idle	0-1.5
GIND & E1	B-W <> BR	Glow Indicator Lamp ON	0-3
GIND & E1	B-W <> BR	16 Pin ECU Connector Disconnected (Glow Indicator Lamp OFF)	9-14
TE1 & E1	L-R <> BR	Ignition ON	9-14

Table No1

Pick Up Sensor Check

1. Disconnect the sensor harness connector and check the resistance between the connector terminals 1 and 2.

Specified Resistance: **650-970ohms @ 20°c**

2. If the resistance is not as shown, replace the sensor.

Refer Code No13 diagram for connector

ECU Connector

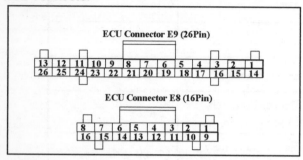

Injection System and Engine Diagnosis and Troubleshooting

Engine Does Not Crank (Hard to Start)

1. Check the operation of the starter motor, if faults are found repair/replace as required.

2. If no faults are found in step1, check the operation of the starter relay, if faults are found repair/replace as required.

No Initial Combustion (Hard to Start)

1. Check the condition and/or operation of the ECU power source circuit, if faults are found repair/replace as required.

2. If no faults are found in step1, check the operation of the pre-heat system, if faults are found repair/replace as required.

3. I no faults are found in step2, carry out an engine compression test and check the engine compression pressures.

Compression Pressure: **3138kpa**
Minimum Pressure: **1961kpa**
Difference Between Each Cylinder: **490kpa**

If the pressures are not correct, repair/replace as required.

4. If the compression pressures are OK in step3, check the condition of the ECU, if faults are found repair/replace as required.

5. If no faults are found in step4, check the condition and/or operation of the injection pump, if faults are found repair/replace as required.

Engine is Hard to Start When Cold

1. Check the condition and/or operation of the pre-heat system, if faults are found repair/replace as required.

2. If no faults are found in step1, check the condition of the "STA" signal circuit, if faults are found repair/replace as required.

3. If no faults are found in step2, check the condition and/or operation of the water temperature sensor, if

faults are found repair/replace as required.

4. If no faults are found in step3, check the condition and/or operation of the injection nozzle/s, if faults are found repair/replace as required.

5. If no faults are found in step4, check the condition and/or operation of the fuel filter, if faults are found repair/replace as required.

6. If no faults are found in step5, check the condition and/or operation of the ECU, if faults are found repair/replace as required.

7. If no faults are found in step6, check the condition and/or operation of the injection pump, if faults are found repair/replace as required.

Engine is Hard to Start When Hot

1. Check the condition of the "STA" signal circuit, if faults are found repair/replace as required.

2. If no faults are found in step1, check the condition and/or operation of the injection nozzle/s, if faults are found repair/replace as required

3. If no faults are found in step2, check the condition and/or operation of the fuel filter, if faults are found repair/replace as required.

4. If no faults are found in step3, check the condition and/or operation of the ECU, if faults are found repair/replace as required.

5. If no faults are found in step4, check the condition and/or operation of the injection pump, if faults are found repair/replace as required.

Engine Stalls Soon After Starting

1. Check the condition and/or operation of the fuel filter, if faults are found repair/replace as required.

2. If no faults are found in step1, check the condition and/or operation of the ECU, if faults are found repair/replace as required.

3. If no faults are found in step2, check the condition and/or operation of the injection pump, if faults are found repair/replace as required.

Engine Stalls Under Other Conditions

1. Check the condition and/or operation of the ECU power source circuit, if faults are found repair/replace as required.

2. If no faults are found in step1, check the condition and/or operation of the ECU, if faults are found repair/replace as required.

3. If no faults are found in step2, check the condition and/or operation of the injection pump, if faults are found repair/replace as required.

Incorrect First Idle (Poor Idling)

1. Check the condition and/or operation of the water temp sensor, if faults are found repair/replace as required.

2. If no faults are found in step1, check the condition and/or operation of the fuel filter, if faults are found repair/replace as required.

3. If no faults are found in step2, check the condition

and/or operation of the ECU, if faults are found repair/replace as required.

4. If no faults are found in step3, check the condition and/or operation of the injection pump, if faults are found repair/replace as required.

High Idle Speed (Poor Idle)

1. Check the condition and/or operation of the throttle position sensor, if faults are found repair/replace as required.

2. If no faults are found in step1, check the condition and/or operation of the water temp sensor, if faults are found repair/replace as required.

3. If no faults are found in step2, check the condition and/or operation of the vehicle speed sensor, if faults are found repair/replace as required.

4. If no faults are found in step3, check the condition and/or operation of the ECU, if faults are found repair/replace as required.

5. If no faults are found in step4, check the condition and/or operation of the injection pump, if faults are found repair/replace as required.

Low Idle Speed (Poor Idling)

1. Check the condition and/or operation of the injection nozzle/s, if faults are found repair/replace as required.

2. If no faults are found in step1, check the condition and/or operation of the EGR system, if faults are found repair/replace as required.

3. If no faults are found in step2, check the condition and/or operation of the water temp sensor, if faults are found repair/replace as required.

4. If no faults are found in step3, check the condition and/or operation of the vehicle speed sensor, if faults are found repair/replace as required.

5. I no faults are found in step4, carry out an engine compression test and check the engine compression pressures.

Compression Pressure:	**3138kpa**
Minimum Pressure:	**1961kpa**
Difference Between Each Cylinder:	**490kpa**

If the pressures are not correct, repair/replace as required.

6. If no faults are found in step5, carry out valve clearance check.

Inlet Valve Clearance:	**0.20-030mm (Cold)**
Exhaust Valve Clearance:	**0.40-0.50mm (Cold)**

If the clearances are not as shown, adjust to suit

7. If no faults are found in step6, check the condition and/or operation of the fuel line (air bleed), if faults are found repair/replace as required.

8. If no faults are found in step7, check the condition and/or operation of the ECU, if faults are found repair/replace as required.

9. If no faults are found in step8, check the condition and/or operation of the injection pump, if faults are found repair/replace as required.

Rough Idling (Poor Idling)

1. Check the condition and/or operation of the injection nozzle/s, if faults are found repair/replace as required

2. If no faults are found in step1, check the condition and/or operation of the fuel line (air bleed), if faults are found repair/replace as required.

3. If no faults are found in step2, check the condition and/or operation of the pre-heat system, if faults are found repair/replace as required.

4. If no faults are found in step3, check the condition and/or operation of the EGR system, if faults are found repair/replace as required.

5. If no faults are found in step4, check the condition and/or operation of the throttle position sensor, if faults are found repair/replace as required.

6. If no faults are found in step5, check the condition and/or operation of the pick up sensor, if faults are found repair/replace as required.

7. If no faults are found in step6, carry out an engine compression test and check the engine compression pressures.

Compression Pressure:	**3138kpa**
Minimum Pressure:	**1961kpa**
Difference Between Each Cylinder:	**490kpa**

If the pressures are not correct, repair/replace as required.

8. If no faults are found in step7, carry out valve clearance check.

Inlet Valve Clearance:	**0.20-030mm (Cold)**
Exhaust Valve Clearance:	**0.40-0.50mm (Cold)**

If the clearances are not as shown, adjust to suit

9. If no faults are found in step8, check the condition and/or operation of the ECU, if faults are found repair/replace as required.

10. If no faults are found in step9, check the condition and/or operation of the injection pump, if faults are found repair/replace as required.

Engine is Hunting When Hot (Poor Idling)

1. Check the condition and/or operation of the injection nozzle/s, if faults are found repair/replace as required.

2. If no faults are found in step1, check the condition and/or operation of the ECU power source circuit, if faults are found repair/replace as required.

3. If no faults are found in step2, check the condition and/or operation of the throttle position sensor, if faults are found repair/replace as required.

4. If no faults are found in step3, carry out an engine compression test and check the engine compression pressures.

Compression Pressure:	**3138kpa**
Minimum Pressure:	**1961kpa**
Difference Between Each Cylinder:	**490kpa**

If the pressures are not correct, repair/replace as required.

5. If no faults are found in step4, check the condition and/or operation of the fuel line (air bleed), if faults are found repair/replace as required.

6. If no faults are found in step5, carry out valve

clearance check.

Inlet Valve Clearance: 0.20-030mm (Cold)
Exhaust Valve Clearance: 0.40-0.50mm (Cold)

If the clearances are not as shown, adjust to suit

7. If no faults are found in step6, check the condition and/or operation of the ECU, if faults are found repair/replace as required.

8. If no faults are found in step7, check the condition and/or operation of the injection pump, if faults are found repair/replace as required.

Engine is Hunting When Cold (Poor Idling)

1. Check the condition and/or operation of the pre-heat system, if faults are found repair/replace as required.

2. If no faults are found in step1, check the condition and/or operation of the injection nozzle/s, if faults are found repair/replace as required.

3. If no faults are found in step2, check the condition and/or operation of the ECU power source circuit, if faults are found repair/replace as required.

4. If no faults are found in step3, check the condition and/or operation of the pick up sensor, if faults are found repair/replace as required.

5. If no faults are found in step4, check the condition and/or operation of the water temp sensor, if faults are found repair/replace as required

6. If no faults are found in step5, carry out an engine compression test and check the engine compression pressures.

Compression Pressure: 3138kpa
Minimum Pressure: 1961kpa
Difference Between Each Cylinder: 490kpa

If the pressures are not correct, repair/replace as required.

7. If no faults are found in step6, check the condition and/or operation of the fuel line (air bleed), if faults are found repair/replace as required.

8. If no faults are found in step7, carry out valve clearance check.

Inlet Valve Clearance: 0.20-030mm (Cold)
Exhaust Valve Clearance: 0.40-0.50mm (Cold)

If the clearances are not as shown, adjust to suit

9. If no faults are found in step8, check the condition and/or operation of the ECU, if faults are found repair/replace as required.

10. If no faults are found in step9, check the condition and/or operation of the injection pump, if faults are found repair/replace as required.

Engine Hesitates/Poor Acceleration (Poor Drivability)

1. Check the condition and/or operation of the injection nozzle/s, if faults are found repair/replace as required.

2. If no faults are found in step1, check the condition and/or operation of the fuel filter, if faults are found repair/replace as required.

3. If no faults are found in step2, check the condition and/or operation of the EGR system, if faults are found repair/replace as required.

4. If no faults are found in step3, check the condition and/or operation of the throttle position sensor, if faults are found repair/replace as required.

5. If no faults are found in step4, check the condition and/or operation of the pick up sensor, if faults are found repair/replace as required.

6. If no faults are found in step5, carry out an engine compression test and check the engine compression pressures.

Compression Pressure: 3138kpa
Minimum Pressure: 1961kpa
Difference Between Each Cylinder: 490kpa

If the pressures are not correct, repair/replace as required.

7. If no faults are found in step6, check the condition and/or operation of the ECU, if faults are found repair/replace as required.

8. If no faults are found in step7, check the condition and/or operation of the injection pump, if faults are found repair/replace as required.

Engine is Knocking (Poor Driveability)

1. Check the condition and/or operation of the injection nozzle/s, if faults are found repair/replace as required.

2. If no faults are found in step1, check the condition and/or operation of the EGR system, if faults are found repair/replace as required.

3. If no faults are found in step2, check the condition and/or operation of the pick up sensor, if faults are found repair/replace as required.

4. If no faults are found in step3, check the condition and/or operation of the water temperature sensor, if faults are found repair/replace as required.

5. If no faults are found in step4, check the condition and/or operation of the ECU, if faults are found repair/replace as required.

Black Smoke (Poor Driveability)

1. Check the condition and/or operation of the injection nozzle/s, if faults are found repair/replace as required.

2. If no faults are found in step1, check the condition and/or operation of the EGR system, if faults are found repair/replace as required.

3. If no faults are found in step2, check the condition and/or operation of the throttle position sensor, if faults are found repair/replace as required.

4. If no faults are found in step3, check the condition and/or operation of the ECU, if faults are found repair/replace as required.

5. If no faults are found in step4, check the condition and/or operation of the injection pump, if faults are found repair/replace as required.

White Smoke (Poor Driveability)

1. Check the condition and/or operation of the EGR system, if faults are found repair/replace as required.

2. If no faults are found in step1, check the condition and/or operation of the pre-heat system, if faults are found repair/replace as required.

3. If no faults are found in step2, check the condition and/or operation of the injection nozzle/s, if faults are found repair/replace as required.

4. If no faults are found in step3, check the condition and/or operation of the pick up sensor, if faults are found repair/replace as required.

5. If no faults are found in step4, check the condition and/or operation of the fuel filter, if faults are found repair/replace as required.

6. If no faults are found in step5, check the condition and/or operation of the water temperature sensor, if faults are found repair/replace as required.

7. If no faults are found in step6, check the condition and/or operation of the ECU, if faults are found repair/replace as required.

8. If no faults are found in step7, check the condition and/or operation of the injection pump, if faults are found repair/replace as required.

Engine is Surging/Hunting (Poor Driveability)

1. Check the condition and/or operation of the injection nozzle/s, if faults are found repair/replace as required.

2. If no faults are found in step1, check the condition and/or operation of the throttle position sensor, if faults are found repair/replace as required.

3. If no faults are found in step2, check the condition and/or operation of the ECU, if faults are found repair/replace as required.

4. If no faults are found in step3, check the condition and/or operation of the injection pump, if faults are found repair/replace as required.

VEHICLE SERVICE INFORMATION

Vehicle Filling Capacities

Engine Oil with Filter: .... 6.0 Litres
Engine Oil without Filter: .... 5.1 Litres
Cooling System: .... 8.5 Litres (Without Heater)
Cooling System: ... 11.0 Litres (With Front/Rear Heater)
Cooling System: .... 9.5 Litres (With Front Heater)
Manual Transmission: .... 2.2 Litres
Auto Transmission: ....6.5Litres (Dry Fill),
.... 2.4 Litres (Refill)
Rear Differential: .... 2.2 Litres

Vehicle Component Service Interval Changes

Timing Belt Replacement
Every 100,000kms

Check Valve Clearance:
Every 40,000kms

Engine Coolant/Anti Freeze:
Change Every 24 Months/40,000kms

Air Cleaner Element:
Change Every 24 Months/40,000kms

Fuel Filter:
Change Every 12 Months/24,000kms

Engine Oil:
Change Every 5,000kms

Engine Oil Filter:
Change Every 6 Months/10,000kms

Brake Fluid:
Change Every 24 Months/40,000kms

Manual Transmission Oil:
Change Every 24 Months/40,000kms

Auto Transmission Fluid
Change Every 24 Months/40,000kms

Rear Differential Oil:
Change Every 24 Months/40,000kms

Front Wheel Bearings
Repack Every 40,000kms

Toyota Hilux LN 85 Series 2L Engine 1988-1991

CONTENTS   PAGE

CONTENTS   PAGE

Toyota Hilux 85 Series

Toyota Hilux LN 85 Seriers
2L Engine 1988-1991

Engine Checks

Valve Clearance Check

Please Note: Before carrying out this check ensure that the engine is at normal operating temperature.

1. Remove the rocker cover, set the No1 piston to TDC on its compression stroke and ensure that the groove on the crankshaft pulley is lined up with the timing pointer on the front cover.

2. Ensure that the valve lifters on the No1 cylinder are loose and that the No4 valve lifters are tight (if they are not turn the engine on full turn (360°) and recheck).

3. Measure the valve clearances on the following valves 1&3 (Exhaust) and 1&2 (Inlet).

Inlet Valve Clearance:	**0.20-030mm (Cold)**
Exhaust Valve Clearance:	**0.40-0.50mm (Cold)**

If the clearances are not correct record the relevant readings to determine the adjusting shim required.

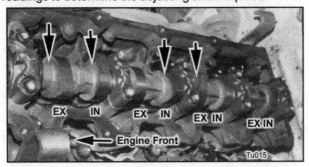

4. Turn the crankshaft one full turn (360°) and ensure that the groove on the crankshaft pulley is lined up with the timing pointer on the front cover.

5. Measure the valve clearances on the following valves 2&4 (Exhaust) and 3&4 (Inlet).

Inlet Valve Clearance: 0.20-030mm (Cold)
Exhaust Valve Clearance: 0.40-0.50mm (Cold)

If the clearances are not correct record the relevant readings to determine the adjusting shim required.

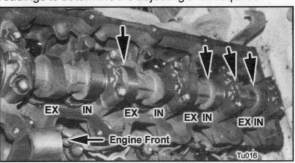

Compression Check

1. Run the engine to normal operating temperature, disconnect the fuel cut solenoid connector and remove all of the glow plugs from the engine.

2. Install an adaptor and compression gauge to the No1 cylinder, fully open the throttle, crank the engine and record the comprerssion pressure on each cylinder.

Compression Pressure:	**3138kpa**
Minimum Pressure:	**1961kpa**
Difference Between Each Cylinder:	**490kpa**

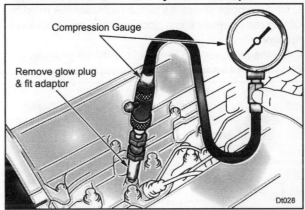

3. If the pressure on one or more cylinders is low, pour a small amount of oil into the cylinder through the glow plug hole and check the compression pressure again. If it helps the pressure there are possibly faults withy the

piston rings or cylinder bores, if the oil does not help there may be a valve sticking or not seated correctly and/or leaks past the gasket.

Cylinder Head Tightening Procedures

1. After the cylinder head has been removed and the gasket replaced, apply a thin coat of oil to all of the cylinder head bolts. Install and gradually tighten each of the bolts to its correct torque in three stages in the sequence showed in the diagram.

Specified Torque Setting: 78NM

Please Note: If any of the bolts do not reach the correct torque, check the length of the bolts.

Short Bolt:	**107mm**
Long Bolt:	**127mm**

Replace any faulty bolts as required.

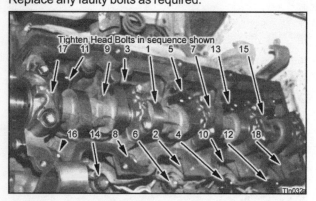

Tighten Head Bolts in sequence shown

2. Mark the front of each bolt with some paint and the tighten the bolts a further 90°. After the sequence has been completed tighten the bolts a further 90° and now ensure that the paint mark is facing to the rear.

Piston Protrusion Height Check
No1 and 4 Piston Check

1. Rotate the engine and ensure that the timing marks on the crankshaft pulley line up with the marks on the front cover.

2. Fit a dial gauge to the engine block and set the gauge at the piston measuring point.

3. Find the point where the piston protrudes the most by turning the crankshaft in a clockwise and anti clockwise direction.

4. Set the dial gauge to zero and record the protrusion measurement from the block by sliding the dial gauge.

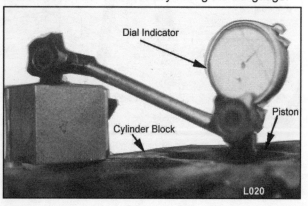

Dial Indicator

Piston

Cylinder Block

L020

Protrusion Measurement: 0.68-0.97mm

Please Note: Record the measurement at two separate measuring points.

No2 and No3 Piston Check

5. Turn the crankshaft 180°, fit a dial gauge to the engine block and set the gauge at the piston measuring point.

6. Find the point where the piston protrudes the most by turning the crankshaft in a clockwise and anti clockwise direction.

7. Set the dial gauge to zero and record the protrusion measurement from the block by sliding the dial gauge.

Protrusion Measurement: 0.68-0.97mm

Please Note: Record the measurement at two separate measuring points.

8. When the measurment has been made, to select a new head gasket follow the procedures shown.

9. There are 3 different types of head gaskets marked either "B", "D" or "F", each of them different thicknesses.

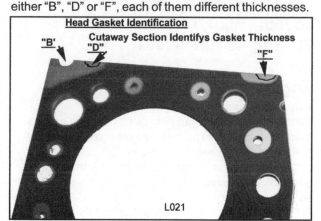

Head Gasket Identification

Cutaway Section Identifys Gasket Thickness

"B"   "D"   "F"

L021

Piston Protrusion Measurements	Gasket Thickness	Gasket Grade
0.68-0.77	1.4-1.5mm	B
0.78-0.87	1.5-1.6	D
0.88-0.97	1.6-1.7	F

Please Note: When selecting the gasket use the largest measurement of the 8 readings that are recorded.

Oil Pressure Check

1. Ensure that the engine oil level is correct, if not top up to suit.

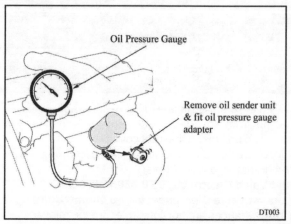

Oil Pressure Gauge

Remove oil sender unit & fit oil pressure gauge adapter

DT003

2. Remove the oil pressure switch from the engine and install a pressure gauge to the engine block.

3. Start the engine and run to normal operating temperature and then record the oil pressure shown on the gauge.

Specified Oil Pressure: **29kpa @ Idle**

Specified Oil Pressure: 294-539kpa @ 3000RPM

4. If the oil pressure is not as shown, repair/replace as required.

Cooling System Thermostat Check

1. Remove the thermostat from the engine and put into a suitable container of water.

2. Heat the water gradually and and check the valve opening temperature and valve lift.

Valve Opening Temperature: 86-90°c

Valve Lift: More than 8mm

If the operation is not as shown above replace the thermostat.

3. Check that the valve spring is tight when the thermostat is fully closed, if not replace the thermostat.

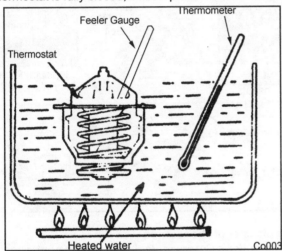

Fuel Filter Check and Replacement

1. Remove the fuel filter sensor (if fitted), drain the fuel, then remove the fuel filter.

2. Clean the fuel filter mounting bracket and then coat the fuel filter sealing ring with some diesel fuel.

3. Screw the fuel filter on until a slght resistance is felt and then turn another 2/3 of a turn or until suitably tight.

4. Install the fuel filter sensor (if fitted) to the new filter and then bleed any air present from the system.

Draining Water From The Filter

1. Loosen the drain cock 4 or 5 turns or remove the fuel filter sensor to allow the water to drain from the filter.

2. Retighten the drain cock or replace the sensor and bleed any air present from the system.

Diagram is in the next column

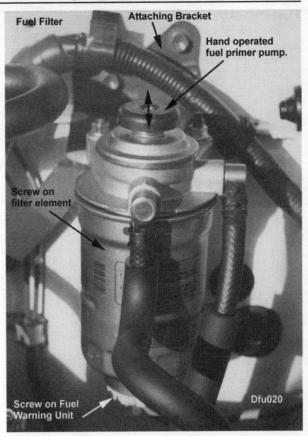

Fuel Filter Warning Lamp Check

1. Remove the switch from the filter and check that there is continuity between the terminals when the warning switch is ON (Float Up)

2. Check that there is no continuity between the terminals when the warning switch is OFF (Float Down)

3. If the operation is not as shown, repair/replace as required.

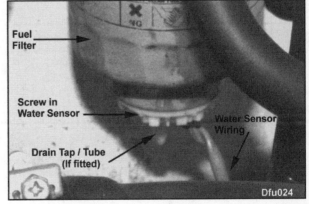

Injector Nozzle Check

1. Remove the injector from the vehicle, connect up to the pressure tester and check the initial pressure by pumping the tester handle a few times.

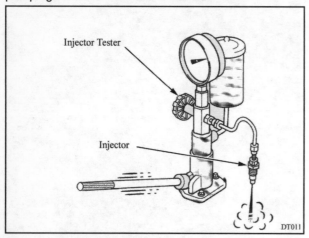

Initial Opening Pressure:
   14,808-15,593kpa (Used Nozzle)
Initial Opening Pressure:
   14,220-15,200kpa (New Nozzle).

2. If the opening pressure is not as shown above, take the injector to pieces and change the adjusting shim on the top of the injector so as the correct pressure is recorded.

Adjusted Opening Pressure: 14,220-15,200kpa
Please Note: The adjusting shims vary in 0.025mm thicknesses, each 0.05mm will adjust the pressure by 343kpa. After the shim has been changed there should be no leakage from the injector.

3. Maintain the pressure between 981-1961kpa below the opening pressure and check that there is no leakage from the injector for a period of 10seconds.

4. Check the spray pattern by pumping the pressure tester handle 4-6 times or more per second and check the injection spray pattern.

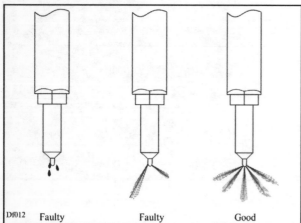

Df012 Faulty Faulty Good

5. If the operation and/or spray pattern is not as shown, repair/replace the nozzle/s as required.

Timing Belt Removal and Replacement

Removal Procedures

1. Remove the drive belts, water pump pulley, crankshaft pulley and the No1 timing cover.

2. Remove the timing belt guide, the cuurent sensor and the 4 glow plugs.

3. Set the No1 piston to TDC on its compression stroke by temporarily replacing the cranksahft pulley bolt and turning the crankshaft in a clockwise direction until the timimg mark on the camshaft gear lines up with the mark on the No2 timing belt cover.

Please Note: If the timing belt is being used again, before removing, mark a direction arrow on the timing belt and place match marks on the pulleys and the belt.

4. Loosen the No1 idler pulley mount bolts and move to the left as far as it will go. Temporarily tighten the bolt, relieve the belt tension and remove the timing belt from the engine.

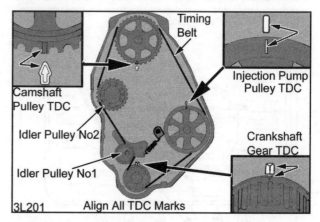

3L201 Align All TDC Marks

Replacement Procedures

Please Note: Before replacing the timimg belt check the condition and/or operation of the timing belt pulleys, tensioners and/or pulleys, if faults are found repair/replace as required.

1. Check the tensioner spring free length
Spring Free Length: **44.4-45.4mm**
Check the tension of the spring at the specified free length
Installed Tension: **59Nm at 52.1mm**

2. Install the crankshaft pulley to the engine, replace any pulleys or idlers that may have been removed for checking.

3. Set the No1 piston to TDC on its compression stroke and ensure that the timing marks on each of the pulleys line up with their relevant matchmarks.

4. Fit the timing belt onto the crankshaft pulley and No1 idler pulley, slightly turn the injection pulley in a clockwise direction, fit the timing belt onto the injection pulley and line up the marks on the injection pulley and timing belt case.

Please Note: Ensure that there is belt tension between the crankshaft timing pulley and injection pump drive pulleys.

5. Slightly turn the camshaft drive pulley in a clockwise direction, fit the timing belt onto the pulley and ensure that the marks on the pulley and timing belt case line up.

Please Note: Ensure that there is belt tension between the camshaft pulley and injection pump drive pulleys.

6. Install the timing belt to the No2 idler pulley.

7. Loosen the No1 idler pulley, stretch the timing belt and turn the crankshaft in a clockwise direction four full turns from TDC to TDC, ensuring that all of the timing marks on the drive pulleys line up with their respective match marks.

Please Note: If any of the marks do not line up, remove the belt and reinstall again.

8. Torque the No1 idler pulley bolt, refit the timing belt guide and replace any removed components in the reverse order of removal.

Timing Belt Replacement Torques

Injection Pump Drive Pulley Nut:	64Nm
No1 Idle Pulley (12mm Bolt):	19Nm
No1 Idle Pulley (14mm Bolt):	44Nm
No2 Idle Pulley:	33Nm
Crankshaft Pulley Bolt:	167Nm
Camshaft Gear Bolt:	98Nm

Timing Belt Warning Lamp Reset Procedures (Rubber Plug in the Instrument Cluster Glass)

1. Remove the grommet from the speedometer and turn off the lamp by pushing the warning lamp reset switch, then replace the grommet.

2. Start the engine and ensure that the light stays off.

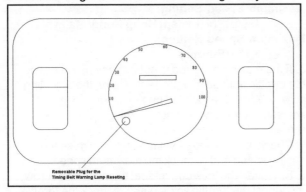

Removable Plug for the
Timing Belt Warning Lamp Reseting

Timing Belt Warning Lamp Reset Procedures (Change Screw Position on the Back of the Instrument Cluster)

1. Remove the instrument cluster from the vehicle, connect terminals A&B shown in the diagrams and then remove the CHARGE fuse from the vehicle.

2. Turn the ignition switch to ON and check that the warning lights light up, if not the check the condition and/or operation of the globe.

3. Check the condition and/or operation of the reset switches by checking that there is intermittent continuity between terminals A&B when the reset switch

is pressed, if not repair/replace the speedometer/ instrument cluster as required.

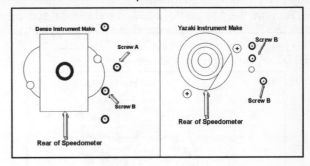

Engine Tightening Torques

Cylinder Head Tightening Torque Bolts:	78Nm (1st Stage)
Cylinder Head Tightening Torque Bolts:	. 90° (2nd Stage)
Cylinder Head Tightening Torque Bolts:	90° (3rd Stage)
Camshaft Bearing Cap:	25Nm
Exhaust Manifold Bolts and Nuts:	52Nm
Inlet Manifold Bolts and Nuts:	24Nm
Glow Plugs:	13Nm
Injection Nozzle:	64Nm
Injection Pump Drive Pulley Nut:	64Nm
No1 Idle Pulley (12mm Bolt):	19Nm
No1 Idle Pulley (14mm Bolt):	44Nm
No2 Idle Pulley:	33Nm
Flywheel Bolts:	123Nm
Drive Plate:	98Nm
Connecting Rod Caps:	54Nm (1st Stage)
Connecting Rod Caps:	90° (2nd Stage)
Main Bearings:	103Nm
Crankshaft Pulley Bolt:	167Nm
Camshaft Gear Bolt:	98Nm
Oil Pump to Timing Cover:	10Nm
Oil Pump to Block:	23Nm
Oil Pump to Injection Pump:	21Nm
Oil Sump Bolt:	18Nm

System Adjustments

Injection Timing Adjustment

1. Remove the distributive head bolt and install a special tool (SST09275-54010 plunger stroke measuring tool) to the plug hole and then set the No1 or No4 piston to 25° BTDC on its compression stroke.

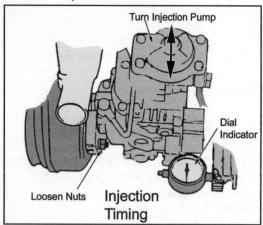

2. Please Note: (For vehicles with auto cold start device): Using a screwdriver turn the cold start lever anti clockwise about 20° and put a metal plate 8.5-10.0mm between the cold start lever and the thermo wax plunger.

3. Set the dial indicator to zero (mm) and then ensure it stays at zero (mm) while the crankshaft pulley is being moved right to left slightly.

4. Slowly turn the crankshaft pulley until crankshaft pulley groove is lined up with the timing pointer and record the plunger movement.

Injection Plunger Stroke: 0.54-0.66 (With Auto Cold Start Device)

Injection Plunger Stroke: 0.84-0.96mm (Without Auto Cold Start Device)

5. If the plunger stroke measurment is not as shown, loosen the 4 injector pipe union nuts and inlet pipe union nuts on the injection pump side.

6. Loosen the 4 injection pump mounting nuts and adjust the plunger pump stroke by slightly tilting the injection pump body. If the stroke is less than shown tilt the pump towards the engine, if the plunger strike is more than shown tilt the pump away from the engine.

7. Retighten all of the fixing bolts and union nuts, recheck the plunger stroke and then remove the plate from the cold starting lever.

8. Remove the dial indicator gauge and replace the plug bolt. Restart the engine and check for any leaks in the system.

Idle Speed Check

1. Ensure that the air cleaner is OK, the engine coolant temperature is at normal, the accessories are all switched off and that the transmission is in neutral.

2. Ensure that the adjusting screw lever touches the idle speed adjusting screw when the throttle pedal is released, if it is not adjust to suit.

3. Install a tachometer to the engine, start the engine and check the idle speed setting.

Idle Speed Setting: 700RPM (Manual 1988-1990)
Idle Speed Setting: 800RPM (Auto 1988-1990)

4. If the idle speed is not as shown in step3, disconnect the throttle linkage, loosen the lock nut of the idle adjust screw and adjust by turning the idle speed adjusting screw, re-tighten the lock nut, and reconnect the throttle linkage. Recheck the idle speed.

5. Remove the tachometer from the engine and replace any removed parts to the vehicle.

Maximum Speed Adjustment Check

1. Ensure that the adjusting lever touches the maximum speed adjusting screw when the throttle is pressed down all the way, if not adjust the throttle linkages

2. Install a tachometer to the engine, start the engine, press the throttle fully down and check the maximum speed.

Maximum Speed Setting:
    4700RPM (Hong Kong/Malaysia)
Maximum Speed Setting:
    4900RPM (Except Hong Kong/ Malaysia)
Maximum Speed Setting:
    5,150 (Europe)

3. If the maximum speed is not as shown, disconnect the throttle linkage, cut the seal wire on the adjusting screw, loosen the lock nut on the maximum speed adjusting screw and adjust by turning the adjusting screw.

4. Check the idle speed setting and then raise the engine speed and recheck the maximum speed.

5. Retighten the lock nut, re-seal the adjusting screw, reconnect the throttle linkage and recheck the throttle linkage adjustment.

6. Remove the tachometer from the engine and replace any removed parts to the vehicle.

Refer to idle speed diagram

Fuel Heater System Check

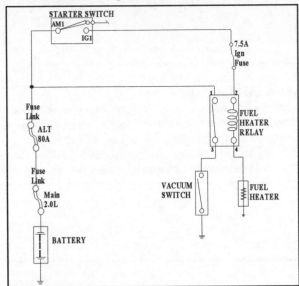

Fuel Heater Check

1. Check the fuel heater by recording the resistance between the connector terminals 1 and 2

Specified Resistance: 0.7ohms @ 20°c

If the resistance is not as shown, repair/replace as required.

Vacuum Switch Check

1. With an ohmmeter check there is no continuity between the switch terminal and switch body.

If the resistance is not as shown, repair/replace as required.

2. Apply a vacuum of 26.7±6.7kpa or more to the vacuum port and check that there is continuity between the switch terminal 1 and body.

If the operation is not as shown, repair/replace as required.

Fuel Heater Relay

1. Remove the relay (located in the engine bay relay box (LN) and check for continuity between terminals 1-3 (ensure continuity exists), and between terminals 3-4 (ensure continuity does not exist).

2. Apply battery voltage between the 1-3 terminals and ensure continuity exists between the 2-4 terminals.'

If the operation is not as shown, repair/replace as required.

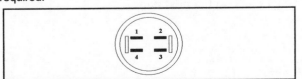

Pre-Heating System Checks

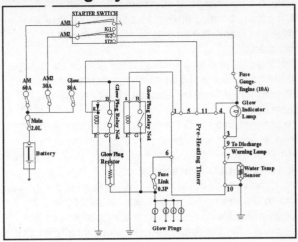

Super Glow System (Models for Europe)

Pre-Heating Timer Check

Please Note: Before starting test please ensure that the battery is fully charged, the engine cranks normally and that all the fuse links are OK.

The timer unit is located In the cowl on the LH side (LN)

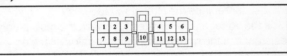

1. Check if the glow indicator lamp lights up when the starter switch is ON, (Coolant Temp is 20°c and lamp lights up for 2-3 seconds).

2. If the operation is not as shown, check to ensure that the fuse/s are OK, if they are not check for any short circuit/s and repair as required.

3. If the fuses are OK in step2, check the condition and/or operation of the indicator lamp globe, if faults are found repair/replace as required.

4. If the bulb is Ok in step3, check for battery voltage to terminal 3 on the pre-heating timer connector (on the wiring harness side), if the voltage is Ok, repair/replace the timer as required.

5. If the glow indicator lamp is OK in step1, turn off the starter switch and check for battery voltage at the pre-heater timer terminal 1 with the starter switch ON, if there is no voltage check that there is 1v or less to terminal 9, if the voltage is OK, replace the timer.

6. If the voltage in step5 is Ok, check the the voltage to the pre-heat timer terminal 1 is terminated after the engine has started, if it is not, start the engine and check for voltage present at terminal 9 of the pre heating timer, if the voltage is Ok, replace the timer, if the voltage is not Ok, repair fault/s in the vehicle charging system.

7. If the voltage is terminated in step6, turn off the starter switch and then turn on again and check for cuurent flow to terminal 5 of the timer in relation to the coolant temperature.

Current Flow: 16-26seconds @ less than 50°c

273

Current Flow: 1.7seconds @ more than 50°c
If there is no voltage at all replace the timer.

8. If the pre heating time is a lot different from what was shown in step7, the timer is faulty and should be replaced.

9. If the pre-heat time is Ok in step7, check for voltage at the timer terminal 8 when the ignition switch is in the ST position, if there is no voltage the timer needs replacing.

10. If the voltage is Ok in step9, put the starter switch in the ON position and check for voltage at the timer terminal 5 when the starter switch is at "Start", if there is no voltage at all replace the timer.

11. If the voltage in step10 is OK , switch off the ignition, switch ON the ignition and check for voltage to the glow plugs with coolant temperature a 50°c or less (a few seconds after the voltage should drop by half). If there is no voltage at all, check for battery voltage at the (+) side of the glow plug resistor, if there is no voltage present at the (+) side of the resistor replace the No1 glow plug relay.

12. If the voltage in step11 remains at battery voltage or drops to 0v, check for battery voltage at the (+) side of the glow plug resistor, if the voltage is Ok, replace the resistor, if there is no voltage present at the (+) side of the resistor replace the No2 glow plug relay.

13. If the voltage is OK in step12, check the glow plug/s resistance, if the reading is infinity, repair/replace as required, if the reading is about 0ohms, the glow plugs are OK.

Pre Heating Timer Operation Check
The timer unit is located in the cowl on the LH side (LN)
1. Disconnect the connector from the timer and check the connector harness as shown in the chart below.

Check For	Between Terminals	Condition	Specified Value
Continuity	1-ground		Continuity
Voltage	3-ground	Starter Switch OFF	No volts
Voltage	3-ground	Starter Switch ON	Battery volts
Voltage	4-ground	Starter Switch OFF	No volts
Voltage	4-ground	Starter Switch ON	Battery volts
Continuity	5-ground		Continuity
Continuity	6-ground		Continuity
Continuity	7-ground		Continuity
Continuity	10-ground		Continuity
Voltage	11-ground	Starter Switch OFF	No volts
Voltage	11-ground	Starter Switch Start	Battery volts

No1 Glow Plug Relay Check.
Please Note: The relay is located In the engine compartment on the LH side
1. With an ohmmeter check the continuity between the terminals 1-2 and ensure that it exists, check between terminals 3-4 and ensure that it does not exist.
2. Apply battery volts between terminals 1-2 and ensure that continuity exists between terminals 3-4
Diagram is in the next column

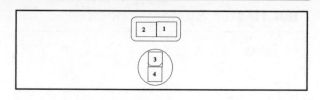

No2 Glow Plug Relay Check
1. With an ohmmeter check the continuity between the terminals 1-2 and ensure that it exists, check between terminals 3-4 and ensure that it does not exist.
2. Apply battery volts between terminals 1-2 and ensure that continuity exists between terminals 3-4

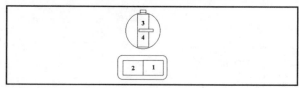

Glow Plug Check
1. With an ohmmeter check that there is continuity between the glow plug terminal and ground, if continuity does not exist, replace the faulty glow plug/s

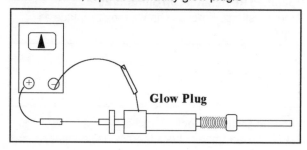

Glow Plug

Glow Plug Sensor Check
1. With an ohmmeter check that there is continuity between the sensor terminals, if no continuity exists replace the sensor.

Water Temperature Sensor Check
1. Remove the sensor harness connector and check the resistance between the sensor terminals at varying temperatures.

Sensor Temperature (°c)	Sensor Resistance (k/ohms)
0	5.0
20	2.0
40	1.0
60	0.4
80	0.14
100	0.08

2. If the resistance is not as shown, repair/replace as required.
Diagram is on the next page

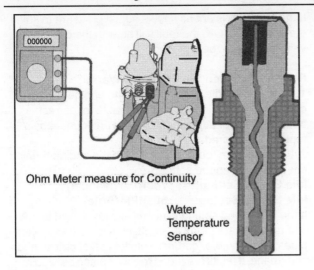

Ohm Meter measure for Continuity

Water Temperature Sensor

Pre-Heating System Checks Variable Delay System

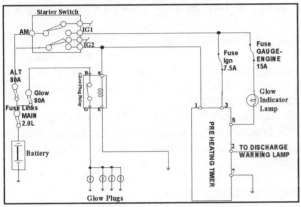

Glow Plugs

Pre-Heat Timer Check (Models Except Europe)
The timer unit is located in the cowl on the LH side (LN)
1. Disconnect the connector from the timer and check the connector harness as shown in the chart below.

Check For	Between Terminals	Condition	Specified Value
Voltage	1-ground	Starter Switch OFF	No volts
Voltage	1-ground	Starter Switch Start	Battery volts
Voltage	3-ground	Starter Switch OFF	No volts
Voltage	3-ground	Starter Switch ON	Battery volts
Continuity	7-ground		Continuity
Voltage	8-ground	Starter Switch OFF	No volts
Voltage	8-ground	Starter Switch Start	Battery volts

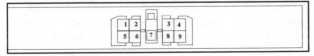

Glow Indicator Lamp Check
1. Turn the ignition switch to "Start" and check the lamp light up time.
Lamp Light Up Time: Approx 5 Seconds

Glow Plug Relay Check
1. With an ohmmeter check the continuity between the terminals 1-2 and ensure that it exists, check between terminals 3-4 and ensure that it does not exist.
2. Apply battery volts between terminals 1-2 and ensure that continuity exists between terminals 3-4
Refer previous glow plug relay diagram N o2 in the Superglow System

Glow Plug Check
1. With an ohmmeter check that there is continuity between the glow plug terminal and ground, if continuity does not exist, replace the faulty glow plug/s
Refer previous glow plug check diagrams

Injection System and Engine Diagnosis and Troubleshooting
Engine Will Not Crank
1. Check the condition and/or operation of the battery cables between the battery and starter motor, if faults are found repair/replace as required.
2. If no faults are found in step1, check the condition and/or operation of the battery, alternator output and/or drive belt, if faults are found repair/replace as required.
3. If no faults are found in step2, check the condition and/or operation of the starter motor, if faults are found repair/replace as required.

Engine Cranks Slowly or Will Not Start
1. Check the condition and/or operation of the battery cables between the battery and starter motor, if faults are found repair/replace as required.
2. If no faults are found in step1, check the condition and/or operation of the battery, alternator output and/or drive belt, if faults are found repair/replace as required.
3. If no faults are found in step2, check that the correct grade of engine oil is being used on the vehicle, if not drain and replace with the correct grade of oil.

Engine Cranks Normally But Does Not Start
1. If the engine cranks normally but does not start, check and ensure that fuel is reaching the injection nozzles by loosening any of the injection pipes, cranking the engine and ensuring that fuel is coming out of the pipe.
2. If fuel is not coming out of the pipe in step1, check the operation of the fuel cut solenoid, if faults are found repair/replace as required.
3. If no faults are found in step3, check to ensure that fuel is getting to the injection pump by disconnecting the inlet hoses from the fuel filter, feeding clean fuel from a separate container directly into the injection pump. If the engine now starts there may be blockages in the fuel filter and/or line between the fuel tank and fuel filter. If the engine does not start, check the condition and/or operation of the fuel line between the fuel filter and fuel pump. If the injection pump operation is normal it should be replaced.

4. If fuel is present in step1, check the pre-heating operation system operation by ensuring that after the ignition is turned on, the glow plug lamp lights up and that there are 6v applied to the glow plugs, if the operation is not as shown, repair/replace as required.

5. If no faults are found in step4, check the operation of the glow plug/s, if faults are found repair/replace as required.

6. If no faults are found in step5, check the fuel system pipes, hoses and/or components for leaks, cracks and/or damage, if faults are found repair/replace as required.

7. If no faults are found in step6, check the injection timing by setting either the No1 or No4 piston at TDC, releasing the cold start advance systen (where fitted) and checking the plunger stroke.

Injection Plunger Stroke: 0.84-0.96mm (Without ACSD Control)

Injection Plunger Stroke: 0.54-0.66mm (With AC SD Control)

If the timing setting is not as shown, adjust to suit.

8. If no faults are found in step7, **(With Cold Start Device Only),** check the cold start advance and fast idle system operation, if faults are found repair/replace as required.

9. If no faults are found in step7and/or 8, check the condition and/or operation of the injection nozzles, if faults are found repair/replace as required.

Idle Speed is Unstable When The Engine is Warm

1. If the idle speed is unstable when the engine is warm, check the condition and/or operation of the throttle cable and/or linkages, if faults are found repair/replace as required.

2. If no faults are found in step1, check the engine idle speed setting.

Idle Speed Setting: 700RPM (Manual)
Idle Speed Setting: 800RPM (Auto)

If the idle speed setting is not as shown, adjust to suit

3. If no faults are found in step2, check the fuel system components and/or lines for leaks and/or damage, if faults are found repair/replace as required.

4. If no faults are found in step3, check the injection timing by setting either the No1 or No4 piston at TDC, releasing the cold start advance systen (where fitted) and checking the plunger stroke.

Injection Plunger Stroke: 0.84-0.96mm (Without ACSD Control)

Injection Plunger Stroke: 0.54-0.66mm (With AC SD Control)

If the timing setting is not as shown, adjust to suit.

5. If no faults are found in step4, check the operation of the injection nozzle/s and/or the delivery valve by letting the engine run at idle speed, loosening the union nuts on each of the cylinders in order and check if there is any change of idle speed. If there is no change at any of the cylinders this will indicate that a faulty cylinder/s is present. To fix the problem check the injection nozzle pressure.

Injection Nozzle Pressure: 14,200-1520kpa

If the pressure is not as shown adjust pressure to suit. If the pressure is OK, the fault will be with the delivery valve and should be replaced.

Rough Idle When the Engine is Warm

1. If the engine idle is rough when the engine is warm, check the throttle linkages and/or cable for correct operation and/or adjustment, if faults are found repair/replace as required.

2. If no faults are found in step1, with the engine running check the idle speed setting.

Idle Speed Setting: 700RPM (Manual)
Idle Speed Setting: 800RPM (Auto)

If the idle speed setting is not as shown, adjust to suit

3. If no faults are found in step2, check the fuel system pipes, hoses and/or components for leaks, cracks and/or damage, if faults are found repair/replace as required.

4. If no faults are found in step3, check the injection timing by setting either the No1 or No4 piston at TDC, releasing the cold start advance systen (where fitted) and checking the plunger stroke.

Injection Plunger Stroke: 0.84-0.96mm (Without ACSD Control)

Injection Plunger Stroke: 0.54-0.66mm (With ACSD Control)

If the timing setting is not as shown, adjust to suit.

5. If no faults are found in step4 check the check the injection nozzle pressure.

Injection Nozzle Pressure: 14,200-1520kpa

If the pressure is not as shown adjust pressure to suit, if the pressure cannot be adjusted, replace the faulty nozzle/s

Engine Suddenly Stops

1. If the engine is running and then suddenly stops, switch off the ignition and try and start the engine, if it does not re-start, check and ensure that fuel is reaching the injection nozzles by loosening any of the injection pipes, cranking the engine and ensuring that fuel is coming out of the pipe.

2. If fuel is not coming out of the pipe in step1, check the operation of the fuel cut solenoid, if faults are found repair/replace as required.

3. If no faults are found in step3, check to ensure that fuel is getting to the injection pump by disconnecting the inlet hoses from the fuel filter, feeding clean fuel from a separate container directly into the injection pump. If the engine now starts there may be blockages in the fuel filter and/or line between the fuel tank and fuel filter. If the engine does not start, check the condition and/or operation of the fuel line between the fuel filter and fuel pump. If the injection pump operation is normal it should be replaced.

4. If fuel is present in step1, check the pre-heating operation system operation by ensuring that after the ignition is turned on, the glow plug lamp lights up and that there are 6v applied to the glow plugs, if the operation is not as shown, repair/replace as required.

5. If no faults are found in step4, check the operation of the glow plug/s, if faults are found repair/replace as required.

6. If no faults are found in step5, check the fuel system pipes, hoses and/or components for leaks, cracks and/or damage, if faults are found repair/replace as required.

7. If no faults are found in step6, check the injection timing by setting either the No1 or No4 piston at TDC, releasing the cold start advance systen (where fitted) and checking the plunger stroke.

Injection Plunger Stroke: **0.84-0.96mm (Without ACSD Control)**

Injection Plunger Stroke: **0.54-0.66mm (With ACSD Control)**

If the timing setting is not as shown, adjust to suit.

8. If no faults are found in step7, **(With ACSD Control Only),** check the cold start advance and fast idle system operation, if faults are found repair/replace as required.

9. If no faults are found in step7and/or 8, check the condition and/or operation of the injection nozzles, if faults are found repair/replace as required.

Engine Has a Lack of Power

1. If the engine has any lack of power, check the maximum speed operation by ensuring that the adjusting lever touches the maximum speed adjusting screw when the throttle is pressed down all the way, if not adjust the throttle linkages

2. Install a tachometer to the engine, start the engine, press the throttle fully down and check the maximum speed.

Maximum Speed Setting: **4700RPM Hong Kong/Malaysia**

Maximum Speed Setting: **4900RPM Except Hong Kong/ Malaysia**

Maximum Speed Setting: 5150RPM: Europe

3. If the maximum speed is not as shown, disconnect the throttle linkage, cut the seal wire on the adjusting screw, loosen the lock nut on the maximum speed adjusting screw and adjust by turning the adjusting screw.

4. Check the idle speed setting, then raise the engine speed and recheck the maximum speed.

5. Retighten the lock nut, re-seal the adjusting screw, reconnect the throttle linkage and recheck the throttle linkage adjustment.

6. Remove the tachometer from the engine and replace any removed parts to the vehicle.

7. If the maximum speed in step2 is OK, check the interchanged overflow screw (out) and inlet (no marking) are fitted into the correct positions (the screw marked out has an inner jet) and cannot be intercahnged.

8. If no faults are found in step7, check the fuel system pipes, hoses and/or components for leaks, cracks and/or damage, if faults are found repair/replace as required.

9. If no faults are found in step8, disconnect the inlet hoses from the fuel filter and pour diesel fuel directly into the injection pump, if the condition now improves replace the fuel filter. If the condition does not improve after the

fuel filter has been replaced, check the condition and/or operation of the priming pump, if faults are found repair/replace as required.

10. If no faults are found in step9, check the injection timing by setting either the No1 or No4 piston at TDC, releasing the cold start advance systen (where fitted) and checking the plunger stroke.

Injection Plunger Stroke: **0.84-0.96mm (Without ACSD Control)**

Injection Plunger Stroke: **0.54-0.66mm (With ACSD Control)**

If the timing setting is not as shown, adjust to suit.

11. If no faults are found in step10, check the check the injection nozzle pressure.

Injection Nozzle Pressure: **14,200-1520kpa**

If the pressure is not as shown adjust pressure to suit, if the pressure cannot be adjusted, replace the faulty nozzle/s

Excessive Exhaust Smoke

1. Check the condition and/or operation of the alr cleaner element, if faults are found repair/replace as required.

2. If no faults are found in step1, check the engine oil consumption, if faults are found repair/replace as required.

3. If the oil consumption is OK in step2, check the injection timing by setting either the No1 or No4 piston at TDC, releasing the cold start advance systen (where fitted) and checking the plunger stroke.

Injection Plunger Stroke: **0.84-0.96mm (Without ACSD Control)**

Injection Plunger Stroke: **0.54-0.66mm (With ACSD Control)**

If the timing setting is not as shown, adjust to suit.

(Please Note: If the exhaust smoke is black it tends to indicate that the timing is advanced and if the smoke is white that the timing is retarded).

4. If no faults are found in step3, disconnect the inlet hoses from the fuel filter and pour diesel fuel directly into the injection pump, if the condition now improves replace the fuel filter. If the condition does not improve after the fuel filter has been replaced, check the condition and/or operation of the priming pump, if faults are found repair/replace as required. *(Please Note: At between 2000-3000RPM a blocked fuel filter tends to make the exhaust smoke white).*

5. If no faults are found in step4, check the check the injection nozzle pressure.

Injection Nozzle Pressure: **14,200-1520kpa**

If the pressure is not as shown adjust pressure to suit, if the pressure cannot be adjusted, replace the faulty nozzle/s. *(Please Note: Excessive exhaust smoke is normally caused when the nozzle pressure is to low).*

Fuel Consumption is Poor

1. If the fuel consumption is poor, check the fuel system components and/or lines for leaks and/or damage, if faults are found repair/replace as required.

2. If no faults are found in step1, with the engine running check the idle speed setting.

Idle Speed Setting: **700RPM (Manual)**
Idle Speed Setting: **800RPM (Auto)**

If the idle speed setting is not as shown, adjust to suit

3. If the idle speed setting is OK in step2, check the no load maximum speed setting is OK by starting the engine, pressing down the throttle pedal to the floor and cheking the no load maximum speed setting.

Maximum Speed Setting: **4700RPM**
                                Hong Kong/Malaysia
Maximum Speed Setting: **4900RPM Except**
                                Hong Kong/ Malaysia
Maximum Speed Setting: **5150RPM Europe**

If the setting is not OK, adjust using the maximum speed adjusting screw.

4. If no faults are found in step3, check the injection timing by setting either the No1 or No4 piston at TDC, releasing the cold start advance systen (where fitted) and checking the plunger stroke.

Injection Plunger Stroke: **0.84-0.96mm (Without**
                                   ACSD Control)
Injection Plunger Stroke: **0.54-0.66mm (With**
                                   ACSD Control)

If the timing setting is not as shown, adjust to suit.

5. If no faults are found in step4, check the check the injection nozzle pressure.

Injection Nozzle Pressure: **14,200-1520kpa**

If the pressure is not as shown adjust pressure to suit, if the pressure cannot be adjusted, replace the faulty nozzle/s.

Noise When The Engine Is Warm

1. If the engine is noisey when it is warm, first check the operation of the temperature gauge if that is Ok, check the operation of the thermostat if faults are found repair/replace as required.

2. If no faults are found in step1, check the injection timing by setting either the No1 or No4 piston at TDC, releasing the cold start advance systen (where fitted) and checking the plunger stroke.

Injection Plunger Stroke: **0.84-0.96mm (Without**
                                   ACSD Control)
Injection Plunger Stroke: **0.54-0.66mm (With**
                                   ACSD Control)

If the timing setting is not as shown, adjust to suit.

3. If no faults are found in step2, check the check the injection nozzle pressure.

Injection Nozzle Pressure: **14,200-1520kpa**

If the pressure is not as shown adjust pressure to suit, if the pressure cannot be adjusted, replace the faulty nozzle/s.

Engine Will Not Return to Idle

1. Operate the adjusting lever on top of the injection pump and ensure that the engine returns to normal idle speed, if it does the throttle cable is binding or not adjusted correctly and needs fixing.

2. If the engine does not return to idle in step1, the injection pump is faulty and needs replacing.

Engine Will Not Shut Off With The Key

1. Check the fuel cut solenoid operation by disconnecting the connector on top of the fuel cut solenoid and check if the engine stops, if it does the starter switch is faulty and needs repairing and/or replacing.

2. If the engine does not stop in step1, either the fuel cut solenoid is faulty or the solenoid is blocked, if required repair/replace as required.

Diesel System Electrical Diagnosis

Engine Will Not Start When Cold

Super Glow System (LN Models for Europe)

Please Note: Before starting test please ensure that the battery is fully charged, the engine cranks normally and that all the fuse links are OK.
The timer unit is located In the cowl on the LH side (LN)

1. Check if the glow indicator lamp lights up when the starter switch is ON, (Coolant Temp is 20°c and lamp lights up for 2-3 seconds).

2. If the operation is not as shown, check to ensure that the fuse/s are OK, if they are not check for any short circuit/s and repair as required.

3. If the fuses are OK in step2, check the condition and/or operation of the indicator lamp globe, if faults are found repair/replace as required.

4. If the bulb is Ok in step3, check for battery voltage to terminal 3 on the pre-heating timer connector (on the wiring harness side), if the voltage is Ok, repair/replace the timer as required.

5. If the glow indicator lamp is OK in step1, turn off the starter switch and check for battery voltage at the pre-heater timer terminal 1 with the starter switch ON, if there is no voltage check that there is 1v or less to terminal 9, if the voltage is OK, replace the timer.

6. If the voltage in step5 is Ok, check the the voltage to the pre-heat timer terminal 1 is terminated after the engine has started, if it is not, start the engine and check for voltage present at terminal 9 of the pre heating timer, if the voltage is Ok, replace the timer, if the voltage is not Ok, repair fault/s in the vehicle charging system.

7. If the voltage is terminated in step6, turn off the starter switch, turn on again and check for current flow to terminal 5 of the timer in relation to the coolant temperature.

Current Flow: **16-26seconds @ less than 50°c**
Current Flow: **1.7seconds @ more than 50°c**

If there is no voltage at all replace the timer.

8. If the pre heating time is a lot different from what was shown in step7, the timer is faulty and should be replaced.

9. If the pre-heat time is Ok in step7, check for voltage at the timer terminal 8 when the ignition switch is in the ST position, if there is no voltage the timer needs replacing.

10. If the voltage is Ok in step9, put the starter switch in the ON position and check for voltage at the timer terminal 5 when the starter switch is at "Start", if there is no voltage at all replace the timer.

11. If the voltage in step10 is OK , switch of the ignition, switch ON the ignition and check for voltage to the glow plugs with coolant temperature a 50°c or less (a few seconds after the voltage should drop by half). If there is no voltage at all, check for battery voltage at the (+) side of the glow plug resistor, if there is no voltage present at the (+) side of the resistor replace the No1 glow plug relay.

12. If the voltage in step11 remains at battery voltage or drops to 0v, check for battery voltage at the (+) side of the glow plug resistor, if the voltage is Ok, replace the resistor, if there is no voltage present at the (+) side of the resistor replace the No2 glow plug relay.

13. If the voltage is OK in step12, check the glow plug/s resistance, if the reading is infinity, repair/replace as required, if the reading is about 0ohms, the glow plugs are OK.

Fuel Cut Solenoid Operation Check

1. Put the starter switch into the ON position and check for an operating noise from the solenoid while repeatedly connecting and disconnecting the solenoid, if a noise is heard the solenoid is OK.

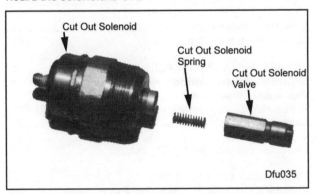

Dfu035

2. If the solenoid noise is not heard, check the condition and/or operation of the relevant fuse, if faults are found repair/replace as required.

3. If the fuse is OK in step2, apply battery volts to the solenoid and check for a noise, if a noise can be heard, check the condition of the harness between the fuse A and the fuel cut solenoid, if faults are found repair/ replace as required.

4. If no noise can be heard in step3, replace the fuel cut solenoid.

Vehicle Service Information

Vehicle Filling Capacities

Engine Oil with Filter:	5.9 Litres (Europe)
Engine Oil without Filter:	5.0 Litres (Europe)
Engine Oil dry fill :	6.4 Litres (Europe)
Engine Oil with Filter:	6.0 Litres (Except Europe)
Engine Oil without Filter:	5.0 Litres (Except Europe)
Engine Oil dry fill :	6.5 Litres (Except Europe)
Cooling System:	9.2 Litres (With Heater)
Manual Transmission:	2.2 Litres
Auto Transmission:	6.5 Litres (Dry Fill)
Auto Transmission:	2.4 Litres (Refill)
Rear Differential:	1.8 Litres

Vehicle Component Service Interval Changes

Timing Belt Replacement
> Every 100,000kms

Check Valve Clearance:
> Every 40,000kms

Engine Coolant/Anti Freeze:
> Change Every 24 Months/40,000kms

Air Cleaner Element:
> Change Every 24 Months/40,000kms

Fuel Filter:
> Change Every 12 Months/24,000kms

Engine Oil:
> Change Every 5000kms

Engine Oil Filter:
> Change Every 6 Months/10,000kms

Brake Fluid:
> Change Every 24 Months/40,000kms

Manual Transmission Oil:
> Change Every 24 Months/40,000kms

Auto Transmission Fluid
> Change Every 24 Months/40,000kms

Rear Differential Oil:
> Check Every 6 Months/10,000kms

Front Wheel Bearings
> Repack Every 40,000kms

Toyota Hilux LN 86-106-107-111
3L Engine 1988-1997

Toyota Hilux LN 86-106-107-111 3L Engine 1988-1997

CONTENTS   PAGE

CONTENTS   PAGE

Toyota HiLux LN86-111

Toyota Hilux LN 86-106-107-111 3L Engine 1988-1997

Engine Checks

Valve Clearance Check 1988 On

Please Note: Before carrying out this check ensure that the engine is at normal operating temperature.

1. Remove the rocker cover, set the No1 piston to TDC on its compression stroke and ensure that the groove on the crankshaft pulley is lined up with the timing pointer on the front cover.

2. Ensure that the valve lifters on the No1 cylinder are loose and that the No4 valve lifters are tight (if they are not turn the engine on full turn (360°) and recheck).

3. Measure the valve clearances on the following valves 1&3 (Exhaust) and 1&2 (Inlet).

Inlet Valve Clearance: 0.20-030mm (Cold)
Exhaust Valve Clearance: 0.40-0.50mm (Cold)

If the clearances are not correct record the relevant readings to determine the adjusting shim required.

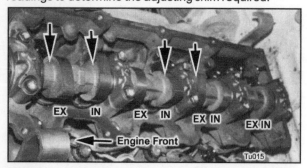

4. Turn the crankshaft one full turn (360°) and ensure that the groove on the crankshaft pulley is lined up with the timing pointer on the front cover.

5. Measure the valve clearances on the following valves 2&4 (Exhaust) and 3&4 (Inlet).

Inlet Valve Clearance: 0.20-030mm (Cold)
Exhaust Valve Clearance: 0.40-0.50mm (Cold)

If the clearances are not correct record the relevant readings to determine the adjusting shim required.

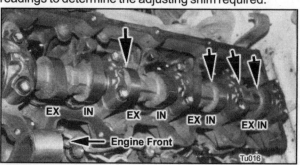

Compression Check

1. Run the engine to normal operating temperature, disconnect the fuel cut solenoid connector and remove all of the glow plugs from the engine.

2. Install an adaptor and compression gauge to the No1 cylinder, fully open the throttle, crank the engine and record the comprerssion pressure on each cylinder.

Compression Pressure: 3138kpa
Minimum Pressure: 1961kpa
Difference Between Each Cylinder: 490kpa

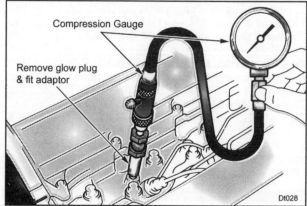

3. If the pressure on one or more cylinders is low, pour a small amount of oil into the cylinder through the glow plug hole and check the compression pressure again. If it helps the pressure there are possibly faults with the piston rings or cylinder bores, if the oil does not help there may be a valve sticking or not seated correctly and/or leaks past the gasket.

Cylinder Head Tightening Procedures

1. After the cylinder head has been removed and the gasket replaced, apply a thin coat of oil to all of the cylinder head bolts. Install and gradually tighten each of the bolts to its correct torque in three stages in the sequence showed in the diagram.

Specified Torque Setting: **78Nm**

Please Note: If any of the bolts do not reach the correct torque, check the length of the bolts.

Short Bolt: 107mm

Long Bolt: 127mm

Replace any faulty bolts as required.

2. Mark the front of each bolt with some paint and the tighten the bolts a further 90°. After the sequence has been completed tighten the bolts a further 90° and now ensure that the paint mark is facing to the rear.

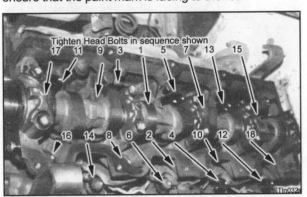

Piston Protrusion Height Check
No1 and 4 Piston Check

1. Rotate the engine and ensure that the timing marks on the crankshaft pulley line up with the marks on the front cover.

2. Fit a dial gauge to the engine block and set the gauge at the piston measuring point.

3. Find the point where the piston protrudes the most by turning the crankshaft in a clockwise and anti clockwise direction.

4. Set the dial gauge to zero and record the protrusion measurement from the block by sliding the dial gauge.

Protrusion Measurement: **0.68-0.97mm**

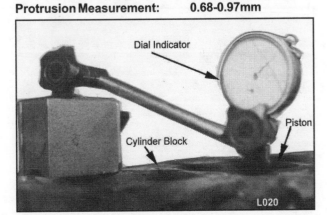

Please Note: Record the measurement at two separate measuring points.

No2 and No3 Piston Check

5. Turn the crankshaft 180°, fit a dial gauge to the engine block and set the gauge at the piston measuring point.

6. Find the point where the piston protrudes the most by turning the crankshaft in a clockwise and anti clockwise direction.

7. Set the dial gauge to zero and record the protrusion measurement from the block by sliding the dial gauge.

Protrusion Measurement: **0.68-0.97mm**

Please Note: Record the measurement at two separate measuring points.

8. When the measurment has been made, to select a new head gasket follow the procedures shown.

9. There are 3 different types of head gaskets marked either "B", "D" or "F", each of them different thicknesses.

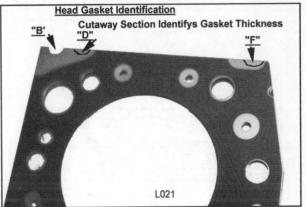

Piston Protrusion Measurements	Gasket Thickness	Gasket Grade
0.68-0.77	1.4-1.5mm	B
0.78-0.87	1.5-1.6	D
0.88-0.97	1.6-1.7	F

Please Note: When selecting the gasket use the largest measurement of the 8 readings that are recorded.

Oil Pressure Check

1. Ensure that the engine oil level is correct, if not top up to suit.

2. Remove the oil pressure switch from the engine and install a pressure gauge to the engine block.

3. Start the engine and run to normal operating temperature and then record the oil pressure shown on the gauge.

Specified Oil Pressure: **29kpa @ Idle**

Specified Oil Pressure: 294-539kpa @ 3000RPM

4. If the oil pressure is not as shown, repair/replace as required.

Diagram is on the next page

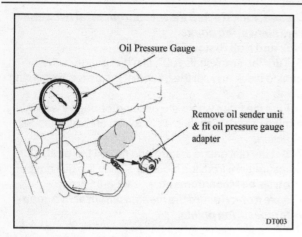

Oil Pressure Gauge

Remove oil sender unit & fit oil pressure gauge adapter

DT003

Cooling System Thermostat Check

1. Remove the thermostat from the engine and put into a suitable container of water.
2. Heat the water gradually and and check the valve

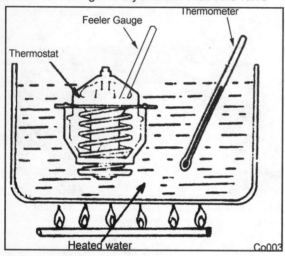

Feeler Gauge

Thermometer

Thermostat

Heated water

Co003

opening temperature and valve lift.

Valve Opening Temperature: **86-90°c**
Valve Lift: **More than 8mm**

If the operation is not as shown above replace the thermostat.

3. Check that the valve spring is tight when the thermostat is fully closed, if not replace the thermostat.

Fuel Filter Check and Replacement

1. Remove the fuel filter sensor (if fitted), drain the fuel, then remove the fuel filter.
2. Clean the fuel filter mounting bracket and then coat the fuel filter sealing ring with some diesel fuel.
3. Screw the fuel filter on until a slght resistance is felt and then turn another 2/3 of a turn or until suitably tight.
4. Install the fuel filter sensor (if fitted) to the new filter and then bleed any air present from the system.
Diagram is in the next column

Draining Water From The Filter

1. Loosen the drain cock 4 or 5 turns or remove the fuel filter sensor to allow the water to drain from the filter.
2. Retighten the drain cock or replace the sensor and bleed any air present from the system.

Fuel Filter

Attaching Bracket

Hand operated fuel primer pump.

Screw on filter element

Screw on Fuel Warning Unit

Dfu020

Fuel Filter Warning Lamp Check

1. Remove the switch from the filter and check that there is continuity between the terminals when the warning switch is ON (Float Up)
2. Check that there is no continuity between the terminals when the warning switch is OFF (Float Down)
3. If the operation is not as shown, repair/replace as required.

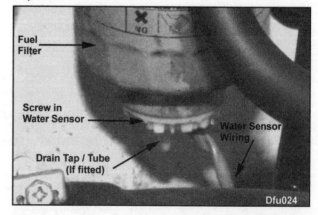

Fuel Filter

Screw in Water Sensor

Water Sensor Wiring

Drain Tap / Tube (If fitted)

Dfu024

Injector Nozzle Check

1. Remove the injector from the vehicle, connect up to the pressure tester and check the initial pressure by pumping the tester handle a few times.

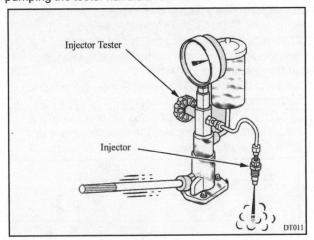

DT011

Initial Opening Pressure:
        14,220-15,200kpa (Used-1988-1996)
Initial Opening Pressure:
        14,808-15993kpa (New-1988-1996)
Initial Opening Pressure:
        13,279-15,690kpa (Used -1996On)
Initial Opening Pressure:
        14,810-15,993kpa (New-1996On)

2. If the opening pressure is not as shown above, take the injector to pieces and change the adjusting shim on the top of the injector so as the correct pressure is recorded.

Adjusted Opening Pressure:
        14,220-15,200kpa (1988-1996)
Adjusted Opening Pressure:
        13,279-15,690kpa (1996-On)

Please Note: The adjusting shims vary in 0.025mm thicknesses, each 0.025mm will adjust the pressure by 341kpa. After the shim has been changed there should be no leakage from the injector.(1988-1996)

Please Note: The adjusting shims vary in 0.05mm thicknesses, each 0.05mm will adjust the pressure by 682kpa. After the shim has been changed there should be no leakage from the injector.(1996On)

3. Maintain the pressure between 981-1961kpa below the opening pressure and check that there is no leakage from the injector for a period of 10seconds.

4. Check the spray pattern by pumping the pressure tester handle 4-6 times or more per second and check the injection spray pattern.

5. If the operation and/or spray pattern is not as shown, repair/replace the nozzle/s as required.

Diagram is in the next column

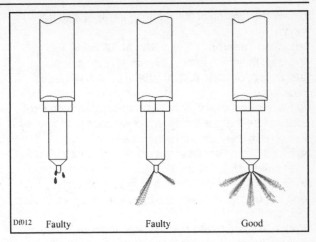

Df012   Faulty   Faulty   Good

Timing Belt Removal and Replacement

Removal Procedures

1. Remove the drive belts, water pump pulley, crankshaft pulley and the No1 timing cover.

2. Remove the timing belt guide, the cuurent sensor and the 4 glow plugs.

3. Set the No1 piston to TDC on its compression stroke by temporarily replacing the cranksahft pulley bolt and turning the crankshaft in a clockwise direction until the timimg mark on the camshaft gear lines up with the mark on the No2 timing belt cover.

Please Note: If the timing belt is being used again, before removing, mark a direction arrow on the timing belt and place match marks on the pulleys and the belt.

4. Loosen the No1 idler pulley mount bolts and move to the left as far as it will go. Temporarily tighten the bolt, relieve the belt tension and remove the timing belt from the engine.

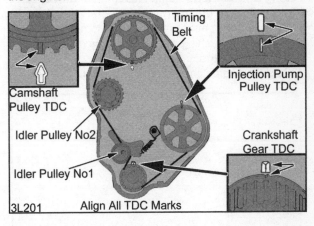

3L201   Align All TDC Marks

Replacement Procedures

Please Note: Before replacing the timimg belt check the condition and/or operation of the timing belt pulleys, tensioners and/or pulleys, if faults are found repair/replace as required.

1. Check the tensioner spring free length
Spring Free Length: **44.4-45.4mm**

Check the tension of the spring at the specified free length

Installed Tension: 59Nm at 52.1mm

2. Install the crankshaft pulley to the engine, replace any pulleys or idlers that may have been removed for checking.

3. Set the No1 piston to TDC on its compression stroke and ensure that the timing marks on each of the pulleys line up with their relevant matchmarks.

4. Fit the timing belt onto the crankshaft pulley and No1 idler pulley, slightly turn the injection pulley in a clockwise direction, fit the timing belt onto the injection pulley and line up the marks on the injection pulley and timing belt case.

Please Note: Ensure that there is belt tension between the crankshaft timing pulley and injection pump drive pulleys.

5. Slightly turn the camshaft drive pulley in a clockwise direction, fit the timing belt onto the pulley and ensure that the marks on the pulley and timing belt case line up.

Please Note: Ensure that there is belt tension between the camshaft pulley and injection pump drive pulleys.

6. Install the timing belt to the No2 idler pulley.

7. Loosen the No1 idler pulley, stretch the timing belt and turn the crankshaft in a clockwise direction four full turns from TDC to TDC, ensuring that all of the timing marks on the drive pulleys line up with their respective match marks.

Please Note: If any of the marks do not line up, remove the belt and reinstall again.

8. Torque the No1 idler pulley bolt, refit the timimg belt guide and replace any removed components in the reverse order of removal.

Timing Belt Warning Lamp Reset Procedures (Rubber Plug in the Instrument Cluster Glass)

1. Remove the grommet from the speedometer and turn off the lamp by pushing the warning lamp reset switch, then replace the grommet.

2. Start the engine and ensure that the light stays off.

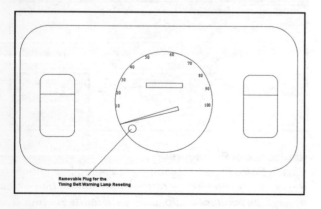

Timing Belt Warning Lamp Reset Procedures (Change Screw Position on the Back of the Instrument Cluster)

1. Remove the instrument cluster from the vehicle, connect terminals A&B shown in the diagrams and then remove the CHARGE fuse from the vehicle.

2. Turn the ignition switch to ON and check that the warning lights light up, if not the check the condition and/or operation of the globe.

3. Check the condition and/or operation of the reset switches by checking that there is intermittent continuity between terminals A&B when the reset switch is pressed, if not repair/replace the speedometer/instrument cluster as required.

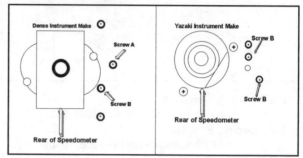

Timing Belt Replacement Torques

Injection Pump Drive Pulley Nut:	64Nm
No1 Idle Pulley (12mm Bolt):	19Nm
No1 Idle Pulley (14mm Bolt):	44Nm
No2 Idle Pulley:	33Nm
Crankshaft Pulley Bolt:	167Nm (1988-1996)
Crankshaft Pulley Bolt:	235Nm (1996ON)
Camshaft Gear Bolt:	98Nm

Engine Tightening Torques 1988-1997

Cylinder Head Tightening Torque Bolts: .... 78Nm (1st Stage)
Cylinder Head Tightening Torque Bolts: .... 90° (2nd Stage)
Cylinder Head Tightening Torque Bolts: .... 90° (3rd Stage)
Camshaft Bearing Cap: 25Nm
Exhaust Manifold Bolts and Nuts: 52Nm
Inlet Manifold Bolts and Nuts: 24Nm
Glow Plugs: 13Nm
Injection Nozzle: 64Nm
Injection Pump Drive Pulley Nut: 64Nm
No1 Idle Pulley (12mm Bolt): 19Nm
No1 Idle Pulley (14mm Bolt): 44Nm
No2 Idle Pulley: 33Nm
Flywheel Bolts: 123Nm
Drive Plate: 98Nm
Connecting Rod Caps: .... 54Nm (1st Stage)
Connecting Rod Caps: .... 90° (2nd Stage)
Main Bearings: 103Nm
Crankshaft Pulley Bolt: 167Nm (1998-1996)
Crankshaft Pulley Bolt: 235Nm (1997ON)
Camshaft Gear Bolt: 98Nm
Oil Pump to Timing Cover: 10Nm
Oil Pump to Block: 23Nm
Oil Pump to Injection Pump: 21Nm
Oil Sump Bolt: 18Nm

System Adjustments

Injection Timing Adjustment (1988-1996)

1. Remove the distributive head bolt and install a special tool (SST09275-54010 plunger stroke measuring tool) to the plug hole and then set the No1 or No4 piston to 25° BTDC on its compression stroke.

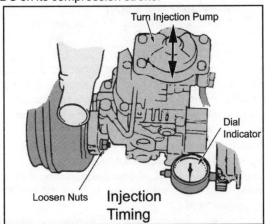

Turn Injection Pump

Dial Indicator

Loosen Nuts   Injection Timing

2. Please Note: (For vehicles with auto cold start device): Using a screwdriver turn the cold start lever anti clockwise about 20° and put a metal plate 8.5-10.0mm between the cold start lever and the thermo wax plunger.
3. Set the dial indicator to zero (mm) and then ensure it stays at zero (mm) while the crankshaft pulley is being moved right to left slightly.

4. Slowly turn the crankshaft pulley until crankshaft pulley groove is lined up with the timing pointer and record the plunger movement.
Injection Plunger Stroke:
0.54-0.66
(With Auto Cold Start Device)
Injection Plunger Stroke:
0.84-0.96mm
(Without Auto Cold Start Device)
5. If the plunger stroke measurment is not as shown, loosen the 4 injector pipe union nuts and inlet pipe union nuts on the injection pump side.
6. Loosen the 4 injection pump mounting nuts and adjust the plunger pump stroke by slightly tilting the injection pump body. If the stroke is less than shown tilt the pump towards the engine, if the plunger stroke is more than shown tilt the pump away from the engine.
7. Retighten all of the fixing bolts and union nuts, recheck the plunger stroke and then remove the plate from the cold starting lever.
8. Remove the dial indicator gauge and replace the plug bolt. Restart the engine and check for any leaks in the system.

Injection Timing Adjustment (1996 On)

1. Remove the distributive head bolt and install a special tool (SST09275-54011 plunger stroke measuring tool) to the plug hole and then set the No1 or No4 piston to 25° BTDC on its compression stroke.
2. Please Note: (For vehicles with auto cold start device): Using a screwdriver turn the cold start lever anti clockwise about 20° and put a metal plate 8.5-10.0mm between the cold start lever and the thermo wax plunger.
3. Turn the crankshaft pulley in a clockwise direction until it is between 25-30° BTDC, set the dial indicator to zero (mm).Slowly turn the crankshaft pulley until crankshaft pulley groove is lined up with the timing pointer and record the plunger movement.
Injection Plunger Stroke:
0.54-0.66: (Europe & others With Auto Cold Start Device)
Injection Plunger Stroke:
0.84-0.96mm: W/Out Auto Cold Start Device
4. If the plunger stroke measurment is not as shown, loosen the 4 injector pipe union nuts and inlet pipe union nuts on the injection pump side.
5. Loosen the 4 injection pump mounting nuts and adjust the plunger pump stroke by slightly tilting the injection pump body. If the stroke is less than shown tilt the pump towards the engine, if the plunger stroke is more than shown tilt the pump away from the engine.
6. Retighten all of the fixing bolts and union nuts, recheck the plunger stroke and then remove the plate from the cold starting lever.
7. Remove the dial indicator gauge and replace the plug bolt. Restart the engine and check for any leaks in the system.
Refer previous injection timing diagram

Idle Speed Check (1988-1996)

1. Ensure that the air cleaner is OK, the engine coolant temperature is at normal, the accessories are all switched off and that the transmission is in neutral.
2. Ensure that the adjusting screw lever touches the idle speed adjusting screw when the throttle pedal is released, if it is not adjust to suit.
3. Install a tachometer to the engine, start the engine and check the idle speed setting.

Idle Speed Setting: 700RPM (Manual 1988-1990)
Idle Speed Setting: 800RPM (Auto 1988-1990)
Idle Speed Setting: 650-750RPM (1990-1996)

4. If the idle speed is not as shown in step3, disconnect the throttle linkage, loosen the lock nut of the idle adjust screw and adjust by turning the idle speed adjusting screw, re-tighten the lock nut, and reconnect the throttle linkage. Recheck the idle speed.

Maximum Speed Adjusting Screw

Idle Speed Adjusting Screw

Dfu015

5. Remove the tachometer from the engine and replace any removed parts to the vehicle.

Idle Speed Check (1996 On)

1. Ensure that the air cleaner is OK, the engine coolant temperature is at normal, the accessories are all switched off and that the transmission is in neutral.
2. Ensure that the adjusting screw lever touches the idle speed adjusting screw when the throttle pedal is released, if it is not adjust to suit.
3. Install a tachometer to the engine, start the engine and check the idle speed setting.

Idle Speed Setting: 650-750RPM (Manual)
Idle Speed Setting: 750-850RPM (Auto)

4. If the idle speed is not as shown in step3, disconnect the throttle linkage, loosen the lock nut of the idle adjust screw and adjust by turning the idle speed adjusting screw, re-tighten the lock nut and reconnect the throttle linkage. Recheck the idle speed.
5. Remove the tachometer from the engine and replace any removed parts to the vehicle.

Refer previous idle speed diagram

Maximum Speed Adjustment Check (1988-1996)

1. Ensure that the adjusting lever touches the maximum speed adjusting screw when the throttle is pressed down all the way, if not adjust the throttle linkages
2. Install a tachometer to the engine, start the engine, press the throttle fully down and check the maximum speed.

Maximum Speed Setting:
     4400RPM: (Hong Kong/Malaysia 1988-1990)
     4600RPM: (Exc Hong Kong/ Malaysia1988-1990)

     4300-4500RPM: (Hong Kong/Malaysia 1990-1996)

     4500-4700RPM: (Exc Hong Kong/Malaysia 1990-1996)

3. If the maximum speed is not as shown, disconnect the throttle linkage, cut the seal wire on the adjusting screw, loosen the lock nut on the maximum speed adjusting screw and adjust by turning the adjusting screw.
4. Check the idle speed setting and then raise the engine speed and recheck the maximum speed.
5. Retighten the lock nut, re-seal the adjusting screw, reconnect the throttle linkage and recheck the throttle linkage adjustment.
6. Remove the tachometer from the engine and replace any removed parts to the vehicle.

Refer previous idle speed diagram

Maximum Speed Adjustment Check (1996 On)

1. Ensure that the adjusting lever touches the maximum speed adjusting screw when the throttle is pressed down all the way, if not adjust the throttle linkages
2. Install a tachometer to the engine, start the engine, press the throttle fully down and check the maximum speed.

Maximum Speed Setting:
     4670-4930RPM (Europe)
     4270-4530RPM (Hong Kong/Malaysia, Singapore)

     4470-4730RPM (Others)

3. If the maximum speed is not as shown, disconnect the throttle linkage, cut the seal wire on the adjusting screw, loosen the lock nut on the maximum speed adjusting screw and adjust by turning the adjusting screw.
4. Check the idle speed setting and then raise the engine speed and recheck the maximum speed.
5. Retighten the lock nut, re-seal the adjusting screw, reconnect the throttle linkage and recheck the throttle linkage adjustment.
6. Remove the tachometer from the engine and replace any removed parts to the vehicle.

Refer previous idle speed diagram

Fuel Heater System Check 1988-1996

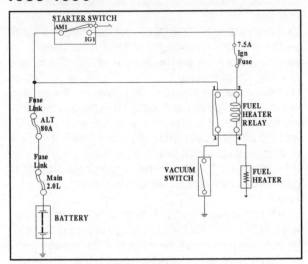

Fuel Heater Check (1988-1996)

1. Check the fuel heater by recording the resistance between the connector terminals 1 and 2

Specified Resistance: **0.7ohms @ 20°c**

2. If the resistance is not as shown, repair/replace as required.

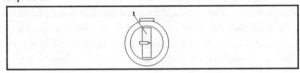

Vacuum Switch Check (1988-1996)

1. With an ohmmeter check there is no continuity between the switch terminal and switch body.
If the resistance is not as shown, repair/replace as required.
2. Apply a vacuum of 26.7±6.7kpa or more to the vacuum port and check that there is continuity between the switch terminal 1 and body.
If the operation is not as shown, repair/replace as required.

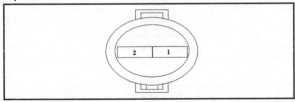

Fuel Heater Relay (1988-1996)

1. Remove the relay (located in the engine bay relay box (LN) and check for continuity between terminals 1-3 (ensure continuity exists), and between terminals 2-4 (ensure continuity does not exist).
2. Apply battery voltage between the 1-3 terminals and ensure continuity exists between the 2-4 terminals.'
If the operation is not as shown, repair/replace as

required.

Fuel Heater System Check 1996On

Fuel Heater Check (1996On)

1. Disconnect the fuel heater connector and apply a vacuum of 34.7±5.3kpa or more to the vacuum switch port.
2. With an ohmmeter record the resistance between the connector terminals 1 body.

Specified Resistance: **0.5-2.0ohms @ 20°c**

If the resistance is not as shown, repair/replace as required.

Refer 1988-1996 diagram

Vacuum Switch Check (1996On)

1. Remove the vacuum switch from the fuel filter cap.
With an ohmmeter check there is no continuity between terminal 1 and switch body.
If the resistance is not as shown, repair/replace as required.
2. Apply a vacuum of 26.7±6.7kpa or more to the vacuum switch port and check that there is continuity between the switch terminal 1 and body.
If the operation is not as shown, repair/replace as required.

Refer 1988-1996 diagram

Fuel Heater Relay (1996On)

1. Remove the relay and check for continuity between terminals 1-2 and ensure that it exists.
If continuity does not exist, replace the relay.
2. Check that there is no continuity between terminals 3 and 5
If continuity does exist, replace the relay.
3. Check the relay operation by applying battery voltage between the 1-2 terminals and ensure continuity exists between the 3-5 terminals.'
If the operation is not as shown, repair/replace as required.

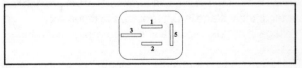

Pre-Heating System Checks
1988-1996

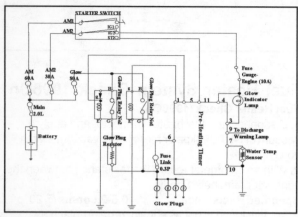

Super Glow System (Europe)
Pre-Heating Timer Check
Please Note: Before starting test please ensure that the battery is fully charged, the engine cranks normally and that all the fuse links are OK.
The timer unit is located In the cowl on the LH side (LN)

1. Check if the glow indicator lamp lights up when the starter switch is ON, (Coolant Temp is 20°c and lamp lights up for 2-3 seconds).
2. If the operation is not as shown, check to ensure that the fuse/s are OK, if they are not check for any short circuit/s and repair as required.
3. If the fuses are OK in step2, check the condition and/or operation of the indicator lamp globe, if faults are found repair/replace as required.
4. If the bulb is Ok in step3, check for battery voltage to terminal 3 on the pre-heating timer connector (on the wiring harness side), if the voltage is Ok, repair/replace the timer as required.
5. If the glow indicator lamp is OK in step1, turn off the starter switch and check for battery voltage at the pre-heater timer terminal 1 with the starter switch ON, if there is no voltage check that there is 1v or less to terminal 9, if the voltage is OK, replace the timer.
6. If the voltage in step5 is Ok, check the the voltage to the pre-heat timer terminal 1 is terminated after the engine has started, if it is not, start the engine and check for voltage present at terminal 9 of the pre heating timer, if the voltage is Ok, replace the timer, if the voltage is not Ok, repair fault/s in the vehicle charging system.
7. If the voltage is terminated in step6, turn off the starter switch, then turn on again and check for current flow to terminal 5 of the timer in relation to the coolant temperature.
Current Flow: 16-26seconds @ less than 50°c
Current Flow: 1.7seconds @ more than 50°c
If there is no voltage at all replace the timer.
8. If the pre heating time is a lot different from what was shown in step7, the timer is faulty and should be replaced.

9. If the pre-heat time is Ok in step7, check for voltage at the timer terminal 8 when the ignition switch is in the ST position, if there is no voltage the timer needs replacing.
10. If the voltage is Ok in step9, put the starter switch in the ON position and check for voltage at the timer terminal 5 when the starter switch is at "Start", if there is no voltage at all replace the timer.
11. If the voltage in step10 is OK , switch off the ignition, switch ON the ignition and check for voltage to the glow plugs with coolant temperature a 50°c or less (a few seconds after the voltage should drop by half). If there is no voltage at all, check for battery voltage at the (+) side of the glow plug resistor, if there is no voltage present at the (+) side of the resistor replace the No1 glow plug relay.
12. If the voltage in step11 remains at battery voltage or drops to 0v, check for battery voltage at the (+) side of the glow plug resistor, if the voltage is Ok, replace the resistor, if there is no voltage present at the (+) side of the resistor replace the No2 glow plug relay.
13. If the voltage is OK in step12, check the glow plug/s resistance, if the reading is infinity, repair/replace as required, if the reading is about 0ohms, the glow plugs are OK.

Pre Heating Timer Operation Check
The timer unit is located in the cowl on the LH side
1. Disconnect the connector from the timer and check the connector harness as shown in the chart below.

Check For	Between Terminals	Condition	Specified Value
Continuity	1-ground		Continuity
Voltage	3-ground	Starter Switch OFF	No volts
Voltage	3-ground	Starter Switch ON	Battery volts
Voltage	4-ground	Starter Switch OFF	No volts
Voltage	4-ground	Starter Switch ON	Battery volts
Continuity	5-ground		Continuity
Continuity	6-ground		Continuity
Continuity	7-ground		Continuity
Continuity	10-ground		Continuity
Voltage	11-ground	Starter Switch OFF	No volts
Voltage	11-ground	Starter Switch Start	Battery volts

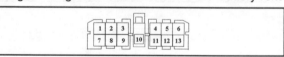

No1 Glow Plug Relay Check.
Please Note: The relay is located In the engine compartment on the LH side (LN Models).
1. With an ohmmeter check the continuity between the terminals 1-2 and ensure that it exists, check between terminals 3-4 and ensure that it does not exist.
2. Apply battery volts between terminals 1-2 and ensure that continuity exists between terminals 3-4
Diagram is on the next page

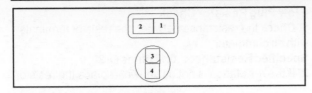

Sensor Temperature (°c)	Sensor Resistance (k/ohms)
0	5.0
20	2.0
40	1.0
60	0.4
80	0.14
100	0.08

2-If the resistance is not as shown, repair/replace as required.

No2 Glow Plug Relay Check

1. With an ohmmeter check the continuity between the terminals 1-2 and ensure that it exists, check between terminals 3-4 and ensure that it does not exist.
2. Apply battery volts between terminals 1-2 and ensure that continuity exists between terminals 3-4

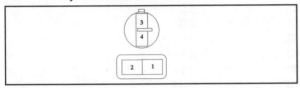

Glow Plug Check

1. With an ohmmeter check that there is continuity between the glow plug terminal and ground, if continuity does not exist, replace the faulty glow plug/s

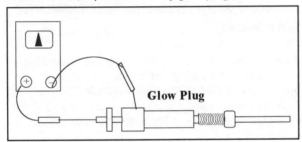

Glow Plug

Glow Plug Sensor Check

1. With an ohmmeter check that there is continuity between the sensor terminals, if no continuity exists replace the sensor.

Water Temperature Sensor Check

1. Remove the sensor harness connector and check the resistance between the sensor terminals at varying temperatures.

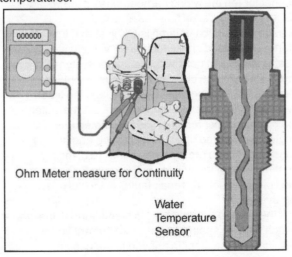

Ohm Meter measure for Continuity

Water Temperature Sensor

Pre-Heating System Checks (1996On)

Super Glow System With Resistor (LN8#/LN1## Series Models)
Pre-Heating Timer Check
Please Note: Before starting test please ensure that the battery is fully charged, the engine cranks normally and that all the fuse links are OK.
1. Disconnect the water temperature sensor and check if the glow indicator lamp lights up when the starter switch is ON
Lamp Light Up Time: 6 Seconds
2. If the operation is not as shown, check to ensure that the fuse/s are OK, if they are not check for any short circuit/s and repair as required.
3. If the fuses are OK in step2, check the condition and/or operation of the indicator lamp globe, if faults are found repair/replace as required.
4. If the bulb is Ok in step3, check for battery voltage to terminal 3 on the pre-heating timer connector (on the wiring harness side), if the voltage is Ok, repair/replace the timer as required.
5. If the glow indicator lamp is OK in step1, turn off the starter switch and check for battery voltage at the pre-heater timer terminal 5 with the starter switch ON, if there is no voltage check that there is 1v or less to terminal 10, if the voltage is OK, replace the timer.
6. If the voltage in step5 is Ok, check the the voltage to the pre-heat timer terminal 5 is terminated after the engine has started, if it is not, start the engine and check for voltage present at terminal 10 of the pre heating timer, if the voltage is Ok, replace the timer, if the voltage is not Ok, repair fault/s in the vehicle charging system.
7. If the voltage is terminated in step6, turn off the starter switch, turn on again and check for cuurent flow to terminal 1 of the timer in relation to the coolant temperature.
Current Flow: 22.5seconds
If there is no voltage at all replace the timer.
8. If the pre heating time is a lot different from what was shown in step7, the timer is faulty and should be replaced.
9. If the pre-heat time is Ok in step7, check for voltage at the timer terminal 1 when the ignition switch is in the ST position, if there is no voltage the timer needs replacing.

10. If the voltage is Ok in step9, put the starter switch in the OFF position, turn back on the ignition and check for voltage to the glow plugs (a few seconds after the voltage should drop by half), if there is no voltage at all replace the NO1 and No2 glow plug relays.

11. If the voltage in step10 stays at battery voltage or at 1/2 voltage for 32 seconds replace the No1 glow plug relay.

12. If the voltage is OK in step11, check the glow plug/s resistance, if the reading is infinity, repair/replace as required, if the reading is about 0ohms, the glow plugs are OK.

Pre Heating Timer Operation Check
Super Glow System (LN8#/LN1## Series Models)

1. Disconnect the connector from the timer and check the connector harness as shown in the chart below.

Check For	Between Terminals	Condition	Specified Value
Voltage	4-ground	Starter Switch OFF	No volts
Voltage	4-ground	Starter Switch ON	Battery volts
Voltage	2-ground	Starter Switch OFF	No volts
Voltage	2-ground	Starter Switch ON	Battery volts
Voltage	7-ground	Starter Switch OFF	No volts
Voltage	7-ground	Starter Switch ON	Battery volts
Continuity	1/5-ground		Continuity
Continuity	6-ground		Continuity
Continuity	12-ground		Continuity
Continuity	9-ground		Continuity
Continuity	11-ground		Continuity

No1 and No2 Glow Plug Relay Check

1. With an ohmmeter check there is no continuity between the terminals 1-2
If there is continuity replace the relay

2. Check that there is continuity between terminals 3-4
If there is no continuity replace the relay.

3. Apply battery volts between terminals 3-4 and ensure that continuity exists between terminals 1-2
If there is no continuity replace the relay

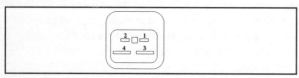

Glow Plug Check

1. With an ohmmeter check that there is continuity between the glow plug terminal and ground
Specified Resistance: 0.65ohms @ 20°c
2. If continuity does not exist, replace the faulty glow plug/plugs
Refer previous glow plug check diagrams

Glow Plug Resistor Check

1. Check the resistance between the resistor terminals with an ohmmeter
Specified Resistance: 0.17ohms @ 20°c
2. If the resistance is not as shown, replace the resistor

Water Temperature Sensor Check

1. Remove the sensor harness connector and check the resistance between the sensor terminals at varying temperatures.

Sensor Temperature (°c)	Sensor Resistance (k/ohms)
0	5.0
20	2.0
40	1.0
60	0.4
80	0.14
100	0.08

2. If the resistance is not as shown, repair/replace as required.
Refer previous water temp sensor diagrams

Super Glow System Without Resistor (LN8#/LN1## Series Models)
Pre-Heating Timer Check

Please Note: Before starting test please ensure that the battery is fully charged, the engine cranks normally and that all the fuse links are OK.

1. Disconnect the water temperature sensor and check if the glow indicator lamp lights up when the starter switch is ON
Lamp Light Up Time: 6 Seconds
2. If the operation is not as shown, check to ensure that the fuse/s are OK, if they are not check for any short circuit/s and repair as required.
3. If the fuses are OK in step2, check the condition and/or operation of the indicator lamp globe, if faults are found repair/replace as required.
4. If the bulb is Ok in step3, check for battery voltage to terminal 3(wire harness side) on the pre-heating timer connector (on the wiring harness side), if the voltage is Ok, repair/replace the timer as required.
5. If the glow indicator lamp is OK in step1, turn off the starter switch and check for battery voltage at the pre-heater timer terminal 1 with the starter switch ON, if there is no voltage check that there is 1v or less to terminal 10, if the voltage is OK, replace the timer.
6. If the voltage in step5 is Ok, check the the voltage to the pre-heat timer terminal 1 is terminated after the engine has started, if it is not, start the engine and check for voltage present at terminal 10 of the pre heating timer, if the voltage is Ok, replace the timer, if the voltage is not Ok, repair fault/s in the vehicle charging system.
7. If the voltage is terminated in step6, turn off the starter switch, turn on again and check for current flow to terminal 1 of the timer in relation to the coolant temperature.
Current Flow: 120.0seconds

If there is no voltage at all replace the timer.

8. If the pre heating time is a lot different from what was shown in step7, the timer is faulty and should be replaced.

9. If the pre-heat time is Ok in step7, check for voltage at the timer terminal 1 when the ignition switch is in the START position, if there is no voltage the timer needs replacing.

10. If the voltage is Ok in step9, put the starter switch in the OFF position, turn back on the ignition and check for voltage to the glow plugs, if there is no voltage check the operation of then glow plug relay/s and/or the glow plugs, if faults ae found repair/replace as required.

11. If the voltage in step10 is OK, reconnect the coolant temperature sensor.

Pre Heating Timer Operation Check
Super Glow System (LN8#/LN1## Series Models)
1. Disconnect the connector from the timer and check the connector harness as shown in the chart below.

Check For	Between Terminals	Condition	Specified Value
Voltage	3-ground	Starter Switch OFF	No volts
Voltage	3-ground	Starter Switch ON	Battery volts
Voltage	2-ground	Starter Switch OFF	No volts
Voltage	2-ground	Starter Switch ON	Battery volts
Voltage	7-ground	Starter Switch OFF	No volts
Voltage	7-ground	Starter Switch ON	Battery volts
Continuity	1-ground		Continuity
Continuity	12-ground		Continuity
Continuity	9-ground		Continuity
Continuity	11-ground		Continuity

Glow Plug Relay Check
1. With an ohmmeter check there is no continuity between the terminals 1-2
If there is continuity replace the relay
2. Check there is continuity between terminals 3-4 and ensure that it does exist
If there is no continuity replace the relay.
3. Apply battery volts between terminals 3-4 and ensure that continuity exists between terminals 1-2
If there is no continuity replace the relay.
Refer to previous glow plug relay diagram

Glow Plug Check
1. With an ohmmeter check that there is continuity between the glow plug terminal and ground
Specified Resistance: **0.65ohms @ 20°c**
2. If continuity does not exist, replace the faulty glow plug/plugs
Refer previous glow plug check diagram

Water Temperature Sensor Check
1. Remove the sensor harness connector and check the resistance between the sensor terminals at varying temperatures.

Sensor Temperature (°c)	Sensor Resistance (k/ohms)
0	5.0
20	2.0
40	1.0
60	0.4
80	0.14
100	0.08

2. If the resistance is not as shown, repair/replace as required.
Refer previous water temp sensor diagrams

Pre-Heating System Checks (1988-1996) Variable Delay System

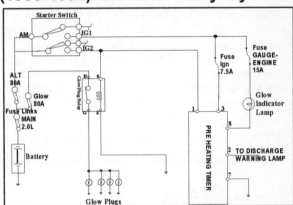

Pre-Heat Timer Check (Models Except Europe)
The timer unit is located in the cowl on the LH side
1. Disconnect the connector from the timer and check the connector harness as shown in the chart below.

Check For	Between Terminals	Condition	Specified Value
Voltage	1-ground	Starter Switch OFF	No volts
Voltage	1-ground	Starter Switch Start	Battery volts
Voltage	3-ground	Starter Switch OFF	No volts
Voltage	3-ground	Starter Switch ON	Battery volts
Continuity	7-ground		Continuity
Voltage	8-ground	Starter Switch OFF	No volts
Voltage	8-ground	Starter Switch Start	Battery volts

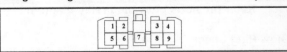

Glow Indicator Lamp Check
1. Turn the ignition switch to "Start" and check the lamp light up time.
Lamp Light Up Time: **Approx 5 Seconds**

Glow Plug Relay Check
1. With an ohmmeter check the continuity between the terminals 1-2 and ensure that it exists, check between terminals 3-4 and ensure that it does not exist.

2. Apply battery volts between terminals 1-2 and ensure that continuity exists between terminals 3-4
Refer previous glow plug relay diagram N o2 in the Superglow System

Glow Plug Check

1. With an ohmmeter check that there is continuity between the glow plug terminal and ground, if continuity does not exist, replace the faulty glow plug/s
Refer previous glow plug check diagrams

Pre Heating System Checks (1996On) Variable Delay System

Pre-Heat Timer Check (LN8#/LN1## Series Models)
1. Disconnect the connector from the timer and check the connector harness as shown in the chart below.

Check For	Between Terminals	Condition	Specified Value
Voltage	4–ground	Starter Switch OFF	No volts
Voltage	4–ground	Starter Switch ON	Battery volts
Voltage	1–ground	Starter Switch OFF	No volts
Voltage	1–ground	Starter Switch ON	Battery volts
Continuity	3–ground		Continuity
Continuity	5–ground		Continuity

After Glow Time Check

1. Turn the ignition switch to "Start" and record the time battery voltage is applied to the terminal 1 on the timer
After Glow Time: 18 Seconds

Glow Plug Relay Check

1. With an ohmmeter check that there is no continuity between the terminals 1-2
If there is continuity replace the relay
2. Check and enaure that there is continuity between terminals 3-4
If there is no continuity replace the relay.
3. Apply battery volts between terminals 3-4 and ensure that continuity exists between terminals 1-2
If there is no continuity replace the relay
Refer previous glow plug relay diagram

Glow Plug Check

1. With an ohmmeter check that there is continuity between the glow plug terminal and ground
Specified Resistance: 0.65ohms @ 20°c
2. If continuity does not exist, replace the faulty glow plug/plugs
Refer previous glow plug check diagram

Pre-Heating System Checks (1996On) Fixed Delay System

Pre-Heat Timer Check (LN80/LN100 Series Models)
1. Disconnect the connector from the timer and check the connector harness as shown in the chart below.

Check for	Between Terminals	Condition	Specified Value
Voltage	5–ground	Ignition Switch OFF	No volts
Voltage	5–ground	Ignition Switch ON	Battery volts
Voltage	6–ground	Ignition Switch OFF	No volts
Voltage	6–ground	Ignition Switch ON	Battery volts
Continuity	2–Ground		Continuity

Glow Plug Light Up Time Check

1. Switch ON the ignition and check the indicator lamp light up time.
Light Up Time: 5 Seconds

Injection System and Engine Diagnosis and Troubleshooting

Engine Will Not Crank (1988On)

1. Check the condition and/or operation of the battery cables between the battery and starter motor, if faults are found repair/replace as required.

2. If no faults are found in step1, check the condition and/or operation of the battery, alternator output and/or drive belt, if faults are found repair/replace as required.

3. If no faults are found in step2, check the condition and/or operation of the starter motor, if faults are found repair/replace as required.

Engine Cranks Slowly or Will Not Start (1988On)

1. Check the condition and/or operation of the battery cables between the battery and starter motor, if faults are found repair/replace as required.

2. If no faults are found in step1, check the condition and/or operation of the battery, alternator output and/or drive belt, if faults are found repair/replace as required.

3. If no faults are found in step2, check that the correct grade of engine oil is being used on the vehicle, if not drain and replace with the correct grade of oil.

Engine Cranks Normally But Does Not Start (1988-1996)

1. If the engine cranks normally but does not start, check and ensure that fuel is reaching the injection nozzles by loosening any of the injection pipes, cranking the engine and ensuring that fuel is coming out of the pipe.

2. If fuel is not coming out of the pipe in step1, check the operation of the fuel cut solenoid, if faults are found repair/replace as required.

3. If no faults are found in step3, check to ensure that fuel is getting to the injection pump by disconnecting the inlet hoses from the fuel filter, feeding clean fuel from a separate container directly into the injection pump. If the engine now starts there may be blockages in the fuel filter and/or line between the fuel tank and fuel filter. If the engine does not start, check the condition and/or operation of the fuel line between the fuel filter and fuel pump. If the injection pump operation is normal it should be replaced.

4. If fuel is present in step1, check the pre-heating operation system operation by ensuring that after the ignition is turned on, the glow plug lamp lights up and that there are 6v applied to the glow plugs, if operation is not as shown, repair/replace as required.

5. If no faults are found in step4, check the operation of the glow plug/s, if faults are found repair/replace as required.

6. If no faults are found in step5, check the fuel system pipes, hoses and/or components for leaks, cracks and/or damage, if faults are found repair/replace as required.

7. If no faults are found in step6, check the injection timing by setting either the No1 or No4 piston at TDC, releasing the cold start advance systen (where fitted) and checking the plunger stroke.

Injection Plunger Stroke:
  0.84-0.96mm (Without ACSD Control)
Injection Plunger Stroke:
  0.54-0.66mm (With ACSD Control)

If the timing setting is not as shown, adjust to suit.

8. If no faults are found in step7, **(With Cold Start Device Only),** check the cold start advance and fast idle system operation, if faults are found repair/replace as required.

9. If no faults are found in step7and/or 8, check the condition and/or operation of the injection nozzles, if faults are found repair/replace as required.

Engine Cranks Normally But Does Not Start (1996On)

1. If the engine cranks normally but does not start, check and ensure that fuel is reaching the injection nozzles by loosening any of the injection pipes, cranking the engine and ensuring that fuel is coming out of the pipe.

2. If fuel is not coming out of the pipe in step1, check the operation of the fuel cut solenoid, if faults are found repair/replace as required.

3. If no faults are found in step3, check to ensure that fuel is getting to the injection pump by disconnecting the inlet hoses from the fuel filter, feeding clean fuel from a separate container directly into the injection pump. If the engine now starts there may be blockages in the fuel filter and/or line between the fuel tank and fuel filter. If the engine does not start, check the condition and/or operation of the fuel line between the fuel filter and fuel pump. If the injection pump operation is normal it should be replaced.

4. If fuel is present in step1, check the pre-heating operation system operation by ensuring that after the ignition is turned on, the glow plug lamp lights up and that there are 6v applied to the glow plugs, if operation is not as shown, repair/replace as required.

5. If no faults are found in step4, check the operation of the glow plug/s, if faults are found repair/replace as required.

6. If no faults are found in step5, check the fuel system pipes, hoses and/or components for leaks, cracks and/or damage, if faults are found repair/replace as required.

7. If no faults are found in step6, check the injection timing by setting either the No1 or No4 piston at TDC, releasing the cold start advance systen (where fitted) and checking the plunger stroke.

Injection Plunger Stroke: 0.54-0.66 (Europe and others With Auto Cold Start Device)
Injection Plunger Stroke: 0.84-0.96mm (Without Auto Cold Start Device)

If the timing setting is not as shown, adjust to suit.

8. If no faults are found in step7, **(Auto Cold Start Device Only),** check the cold start advance and fast idle system operation, if faults are found repair/replace as required.

9. If no faults are found in step7and/or 8, check the

condition and/or operation of the injection nozzles, if faults are found repair/replace as required.

Idle Speed is Unstable When The Engine is Warm (1988-1996)

1. If the idle speed is unstable when the engine is warm, check the condition and/or operation of the throttle cable and/or linkages, if faults are found repair/replace as required.

2. If no faults are found in step1, check the engine idle speed setting.

Idle Speed Setting: 700RPM (Manual 1988-1990)
Idle Speed Setting: 800RPM (Auto 1988-1990)
Idle Speed Setting: 650-750RPM (1990-1996)

If the idle speed setting is not as shown, adjust to suit

3. If no faults are found in step2, check the fuel system components and/or lines for leaks and/or damage, if faults are found repair/replace as required.

4. If no faults are found in step3, check the injection timing by setting either the No1 or No4 piston at TDC, releasing the cold start advance systen (where fitted) and checking the plunger stroke.

Injection Plunger Stroke:
        0.84-0.96mm (Without ACSD Control)
Injection Plunger Stroke:
        0.54-0.66mm (With ACSD Control)

If the timing setting is not as shown, adjust to suit.

5. If no faults are found in step4, check the operation of the injection nozzle/s and/or the delivery valve by letting the engine run at idle speed, loosening the union nuts on each of the cylinders in order and check if there is any change of idle speed. If there is no change at any of the cylinders this will indicate that a faulty cylinder/s is present. To fix the problem check the injection nozzle pressure.

Injection Nozzle Pressure: 14,200-1520kpa

6. If the pressure is not as shown adjust pressure to suit. If the pressure is OK, the fault will be with the delivery valve and should be replaced.

Idle Speed is Unstable When The Engine is Warm (1996On)

1. If the idle speed is unstable when the engine is warm, check the condition and/or operation of the throttle cable and/or linkages, if faults are found repair/replace as required.

2. If no faults are found in step1, check the engine idle speed setting.

Idle Speed Setting: 650-750RPM (Manual)
Idle Speed Setting: 750-850RPM (Auto)

If the idle speed setting is not as shown, adjust to suit

3. If no faults are found in step2, check the fuel system components and/or lines for leaks and/or damage, if faults are found repair/replace as required.

4. If no faults are found in step3, check the injection timing by setting either the No1 or No4 piston at TDC, releasing the cold start advance systen (where fitted) and checking the plunger stroke.

Injection Plunger Stroke: 0.54-0.66 (Europe and

others With Auto Cold Start Device)
Injection Plunger Stroke: 0.84-0.96mm
(Without Auto Cold Start Device

If the timing setting is not as shown, adjust to suit.

5. If no faults are found in step4, check the operation of the injection nozzle/s and/or the delivery valve by letting the engine run at idle speed, loosening the union nuts on each of the cylinders in order and check if there is any change of idle speed. If there is no change at any of the cylinders this will indicate that a faulty cylinder/s is present. To fix the problem check the injection nozzle pressure.

Injection Nozzle Pressure:
        13,729-15,690kpa (New Nozzle)
Injection Nozzle Pressure:
        14,810-15,950kpa (Reused Nozzle)

6. If the pressure is not as shown adjust pressure to suit. If the pressure is OK, the fault will be with the delivery valve and should be replaced.

Rough Idle When the Engine is Warm (1988-1996)

1. If the engine idle is rough when the engine is warm, check the throttle linkages and/or cable for correct operation and/or adjustment, if faults are found repair/replace as required.

2. If no faults are found in step1, with the engine running check the idle speed setting.

Idle Speed Setting: 700RPM (Manual 1988-1990)
Idle Speed Setting: 800RPM (Auto 1988-1990)
Idle Speed Setting: 650-750RPM (1990-1996)

If the idle speed setting is not as shown, adjust to suit

3. If no faults are found in step2, check the fuel system pipes, hoses and/or components for leaks, cracks and/or damage, if faults are found repair/replace as required.

4. If no faults are found in step3, check the injection timing by setting either the No1 or No4 piston at TDC, releasing the cold start advance systen (where fitted) and checking the plunger stroke.

Injection Plunger Stroke:
        0.84-0.96mm (Without ACSD Control)
Injection Plunger Stroke:
        0.54-0.66mm (With ACSD Control)

If the timing setting is not as shown, adjust to suit.

5. If no faults are found in step4 check the check the injection nozzle pressure.

Injection Nozzle Pressure: 14,200-1520kpa

6. If the pressure is not as shown adjust pressure to suit, if the pressure cannot be adjusted, replace the faulty nozzle/s

Rough Idle When the Engine is Warm (1996On)

1. If the engine idle is rough when the engine is warm, check the throttle linkages and/or cable for correct operation and/or adjustment, if faults are found repair/replace as required.

2. If no faults are found in step1, with the engine running check the idle speed setting.

Idle Speed Setting: 650-750RPM (Manual)
Idle Speed Setting: 750-850RPM (Auto)

If the idle speed setting is not as shown, adjust to suit.
3. If no faults are found in step2, check the fuel system pipes, hoses and/or components for leaks, cracks and/or damage, if faults are found repair/replace as required.
4. If no faults are found in step3, check the injection timing by setting either the No1 or No4 piston at TDC, releasing the cold start advance systen (where fitted) and checking the plunger stroke.
Injection Plunger Stroke: 0.54-0.66 (3L Europe and others With Auto Cold Start Device)
Injection Plunger Stroke: 0.84-0.96mm (Without Auto Cold Start Device
If the timing setting is not as shown, adjust to suit.
5. If no faults are found in step4 check the check the injection nozzle pressure.
Injection Nozzle Pressure:
    13,729-15,690kpa (New Nozzle)
Injection Nozzle Pressure:
    14,810-15,950kpa (Reused Nozzle)
6. If the pressure is not as shown adjust pressure to suit, if the pressure cannot be adjusted, replace the faulty nozzle/s

Engine Suddenly Stops. (1988-1996)
1. If the engine is running and then suddenly stops, switch off the ignition and try and start the engine, if it does not re-start, check and ensure that fuel is reaching the injection nozzles by loosening any of the injection pipes, cranking the engine and ensuring that fuel is coming out of the pipe.
2. If fuel is not coming out of the pipe in step1, check the operation of the fuel cut solenoid, if faults are found repair/replace as required.
3. If no faults are found in step3, check to ensure that fuel is getting to the injection pump by disconnecting the inlet hoses from the fuel filter, feeding clean fuel from a separate container directly into the injection pump. If the engine now starts there may be blockages in the fuel filter and/or line between the fuel tank and fuel filter. If the engine does not start, check the condition and/or operation of the fuel line between the fuel filter and fuel pump. If the injection pump operation is normal it should be replaced.
4. If fuel is present in step1, check the pre-heating operation system operation by ensuring that after the ignition is turned on, the glow plug lamp lights up and that there are 6v applied to the glow plugs, if the operation is not as shown, repair/replace as required.
5. If no faults are found in step4, check the operation of the glow plug/s, if faults are found repair/replace as required.
6. If no faults are found in step5, check the fuel system pipes, hoses and/or components for leaks, cracks and/or damage, if faults are found repair/replace as required.
7. If no faults are found in step6, check the injection timing by setting either the No1 or No4 piston at TDC, releasing the cold start advance systen (where fitted) and checking the plunger stroke.

Injection Plunger Stroke:
    0.84-0.96mm (Without ACSD Control)
Injection Plunger Stroke:
    0.54-0.66mm (With ACSD Control)
If the timing setting is not as shown, adjust to suit.
8. If no faults are found in step7, **(With ACSD Control Only),** check the cold start advance and fast idle system operation, if faults are found repair/replace as required.
9. If no faults are found in step7and/or 8, check the condition and/or operation of the injection nozzles, if faults are found repair/replace as required.

Engine Suddenly Stops. (1996On)
1. If the engine is running and then suddenly stops, switch off the ignition and try and start the engine, if it does not re-start, check and ensure that fuel is reaching the injection nozzles by loosening any of the injection pipes, cranking the engine and ensuring that fuel is coming out of the pipe.
2. If fuel is not coming out of the pipe in step1, check the operation of the fuel cut solenoid, if faults are found repair/replace as required.
3. If no faults are found in step3, check to ensure that fuel is getting to the injection pump by disconnecting the inlet hoses from the fuel filter, feeding clean fuel from a separate container directly into the injection pump. If the engine now starts there may be blockages in the fuel filter and/or line between the fuel tank and fuel filter. If the engine does not start, check the condition and/or operation of the fuel line between the fuel filter and fuel pump. If the injection pump operation is normal it should be replaced.
4. If fuel is present in step1, check the pre-heating operation system operation by ensuring that after the ignition is turned on, the glow plug lamp lights up and that there are 6v applied to the glow plugs, if the operation is not as shown, repair/replace as required.
5. If no faults are found in step4, check the operation of the glow plug/s, if faults are found repair/replace as required.
6. If no faults are found in step5, check the fuel system pipes, hoses and/or components for leaks, cracks and/or damage, if faults are found repair/replace as required.
7. If no faults are found in step6, check the injection timing by setting either the No1 or No4 piston at TDC, releasing the cold start advance systen (where fitted) and checking the plunger stroke.
Injection Plunger Stroke: 0.54-0.66 (3L Europe and others With Auto Cold Start Device)
Injection Plunger Stroke: 0.84-0.96mm (Without Auto Cold Start Device
If the timing setting is not as shown, adjust to suit.
8. If no faults are found in step7, **(With Auto Cold Start Device Only),** check the cold start advance and fast idle system operation, if faults are found repair/replace as required.
9. If no faults are found in step7and/or 8, check the condition and/or operation of the injection nozzles, if faults are found repair/replace as required.

Engine Has a Lack of Power (1988-1996)

1. If the engine has any lack of power, check the maximum speed operation by ensuring that the adjusting lever touches the maximum speed adjusting screw when the throttle is pressed down all the way, if not adjust the throttle linkages

2. Install a tachometer to the engine, start the engine, press the throttle fully down and check the maximum speed.

Maximum Speed Setting:
4400RPM
(Hong Kong/Malaysia 1988-1990)
4600RPM
(Except Hong Kong/ Malaysia 1998-1990)
4300-4500RPM
(Hong Kong/Malaysia 1990-1996)
4500-4700RPM
(Except Hong Kong/Malaysia 1990-1996)

3. If the maximum speed is not as shown, disconnect the throttle linkage, cut the seal wire on the adjusting screw, loosen the lock nut on the maximum speed adjusting screw and adjust by turning the adjusting screw.

4. Check the idle speed setting, raise the engine speed and recheck the maximum speed.

5. Retighten the lock nut, re-seal the adjusting screw, reconnect the throttle linkage and recheck the throttle linkage adjustment.

6. Remove the tachometer from the engine and replace any removed parts to the vehicle.

7. If the maximum speed in step2 is OK, check the interchanged overflow screw (out) and inlet (no marking) are fitted into the correct positions (the screw marked out has an inner jet) and cannot be intercahnged.

8. If no faults are found in step7, check the fuel system pipes, hoses and/or components for leaks, cracks and/ or damage, if faults are found repair/replace as required.

9. If no faults are found in step8, disconnect the inlet hoses from the fuel filter and pour diesel fuel directly into the injection pump, if the condition now improves replace the fuel filter. If the condition does not improve after the fuel filter has been replaced, check the condition and/or operation of the priming pump, if faults are found repair/ replace as required.

10. If no faults are found in step9, check the injection timing by setting either the No1 or No4 piston at TDC, releasing the cold start advance systen (where fitted) and checking the plunger stroke.

Injection Plunger Stroke:
0.84-0.96mm (Without ACSD Control)
Injection Plunger Stroke:
0.54-0.66mm (With ACSD Control)

If the timing setting is not as shown, adjust to suit.

11. If no faults are found in step10, check the check the injection nozzle pressure.

Injection Nozzle Pressure: 14,200-1520kpa

12. If the pressure is not as shown adjust pressure to suit, if the pressure cannot be adjusted, replace the faulty nozzle/s

Engine Has a Lack of Power (1996On)

1. If the engine has any lack of power, check the maximum speed operation by ensuring that the adjusting lever touches the maximum speed adjusting screw when the throttle is pressed down all the way, if not adjust the throttle linkages

2. Install a tachometer to the engine, start the engine, press the throttle fully down and check the maximum speed.

Maximum Speed Setting:
4270-4530RPM
(Hong Kong/Malaysia,Singapore & LY General)
4470-4730RPM
(Others)

3. If the maximum speed is not as shown, disconnect the throttle linkage, cut the seal wire on the adjusting screw, loosen the lock nut on the maximum speed adjusting screw and adjust by turning the adjusting screw.

4. Check the idle speed setting and then raise the engine speed and recheck the maximum speed.

5. Retighten the lock nut, re-seal the adjusting screw, reconnect the throttle linkage and recheck the throttle linkage adjustment.

6. Remove the tachometer from the engine and replace any removed parts to the vehicle.

7. If the maximum speed in step2 is OK, check the interchanged overflow screw (out) and inlet (no marking) are fitted into the correct positions (the screw marked out has an inner jet) and cannot be intercahnged.

8. If no faults are found in step7, check the fuel system pipes, hoses and/or components for leaks, cracks and/ or damage, if faults are found repair/replace as required.

9. If no faults are found in step8, disconnect the inlet hoses from the fuel filter and pour diesel fuel directly into the injection pump, if the condition now improves replace the fuel filter. If the condition does not improve after the fuel filter has been replaced, check the condition and/or operation of the priming pump, if faults are found repair/ replace as required.

10. If no faults are found in step9, check the injection timing by setting either the No1 or No4 piston at TDC, releasing the cold start advance systen (where fitted) and checking the plunger stroke.

Injection Plunger Stroke: 0.54-0.66 (3L Europe and others With Auto Cold Start Device)
Injection Plunger Stroke: 0.84-0.96mm (Without Auto Cold Start Device

If the timing setting is not as shown, adjust to suit.

11. If no faults are found in step10, check the check the injection nozzle pressure.

Injection Nozzle Pressure:
13,729-15,690kpa (New Nozzle)
Injection Nozzle Pressure:
14,810-15,950kpa (Reused Nozzle)

12. If the pressure is not as shown adjust pressure to suit, if the pressure cannot be adjusted, replace the faulty nozzle/s

Excessive Exhaust Smoke (1988-1996)

1. Check the condition and/or operation of the alr cleaner element, if faults are found repair/replace as required.

2. If no faults are found in step1, check the engine oil consumption, if faults are found repair/replace as required.

3. If the oil consumption is OK in step2, check the injection timing by setting either the No1 or No4 piston at TDC, releasing the cold start advance systen (where fitted) and checking the plunger stroke.

Injection Plunger Stroke:
      0.84-0.96mm (Without ACSD Control)
Injection Plunger Stroke:
      0.54-0.66mm (With ACSD Control)

If the timing setting is not as shown, adjust to suit. *(Please Note: If the exhaust smoke is black it tends to indicate that the timing is advanced and if the smoke is white that the timing is retarded).*

4. If no faults are found in step3, disconnect the inlet hoses from the fuel filter and pour diesel fuel directly into the injection pump, if the condition now improves replace the fuel filter. If the condition does not improve after the fuel filter has been replaced, check the condition and/or operation of the priming pump, if faults are found repair/replace as required. *(Please Note: At between 2000-3000RPM a blocked fuel filter tends to make the exhaust smoke white).*

5. If no faults are found in step4, check the check the injection nozzle pressure.

Injection Nozzle Pressure: 14,200-1520kpa

6. If the pressure is not as shown adjust pressure to suit, if the pressure cannot be adjusted, replace the faulty nozzle/s. *(Please Note: Excessive exhaust smoke is normally caused when the nozzle pressure is to low).*

Excessive Exhaust Smoke (1996On)

1. Check the condition and/or operation of the alr cleaner element, if faults are found repair/replace as required.

2. If no faults are found in step1, check the engine oil consumption, if faults are found repair/replace as required.

3. If the oil consumption is OK in step2, check the injection timing by setting either the No1 or No4 piston at TDC, releasing the cold start advance systen (where fitted) and checking the plunger stroke.

Injection Plunger Stroke: 0.54-0.66 (3L Europe and others With Auto Cold Start Device)
Injection Plunger Stroke: 0.84-0.96mm (Without Auto Cold Start Device

If the timing setting is not as shown, adjust to suit. *(Please Note: If the exhaust smoke is black it tends to indicate that the timing is advanced and if the smoke is white that the timing is retarded).*

4. If no faults are found in step3, disconnect the inlet hoses from the fuel filter and pour diesel fuel directly into the injection pump, if the condition now improves replace

the fuel filter. If the condition does not improve after the fuel filter has been replaced, check the condition and/or operation of the priming pump, if faults are found repair/replace as required. *(Please Note: At between 2000-3000RPM a blocked fuel filter tends to make the exhaust smoke white).*

5. If no faults are found in step4, check the check the injection nozzle pressure.

Injection Nozzle Pressure:
      13,729-15,690kpa (New Nozzle)
Injection Nozzle Pressure:
      14,810-15,950kpa (Reused Nozzle)

6. If the pressure is not as shown adjust pressure to suit, if the pressure cannot be adjusted, replace the faulty nozzle/s. *(Please Note: Excessive exhaust smoke is normally caused when the nozzle pressure is to low)*

Fuel Consumption is Poor (1988-1996)

1. If the fuel consumption is poor, check the fuel system components and/or lines for leaks and/or damage, if faults are found repair/replace as required.

2. If no faults are found in step1, with the engine running check the idle speed setting.

Idle Speed Setting: 700RPM (Manual 1988-1990)
Idle Speed Setting: 800RPM (Auto 1988-1990)
Idle Speed Setting: 650-750RPM (1990-1996)

If the idle speed setting is not as shown, adjust to suit

3. If the idle speed setting is OK in step2, check the no load maximum speed setting is OK by starting the engine, pressing down the throttle pedal to the floor and cheking the no load maximum speed setting.

Maximum Speed Setting:
   4400RPM
   (Hong Kong/Malaysia 1988-1990)
   4600RPM
   (Except Hong Kong/ Malaysia 1998-1990)
   4300-4500RPM
   (Hong Kong/Malaysia 1990-1996)
   4500-4700RPM
   (Except Hong Kong/Malaysia 1990-1996)

If the setting is not OK, adjust using the maximum speed adjusting screw.

4. If no faults are found in step3, check the injection timing by setting either the No1 or No4 piston at TDC, releasing the cold start advance systen (where fitted) and checking the plunger stroke.

Injection Plunger Stroke:
      0.84-0.96mm (Without ACSD Control)
Injection Plunger Stroke:
      0.54-0.66mm (With ACSD Control)

If the timing setting is not as shown, adjust to suit.

5- If no faults are found in step4, check the check the injection nozzle pressure.

Injection Nozzle Pressure: 14,200-1520kpa

6. If the pressure is not as shown adjust pressure to suit, if the pressure cannot be adjusted, replace the faulty nozzle/s.

Fuel Consumption is Poor (1996On)

1. If the fuel consumption is poor, check the fuel system components and/or lines for leaks and/or damage, if faults are found repair/replace as required.

2. If no faults are found in step1, with the engine running check the idle speed setting.

Idle Speed Setting: **650-750RPM (Manual)**
Idle Speed Setting: **750-850RPM (Auto)**

If the idle speed setting is not as shown, adjust to suit.

3. If the idle speed setting is OK in step2, check the no load maximum speed setting is OK by starting the engine, pressing down the throttle pedal to the floor and cheking the no load maximum speed setting.

Maximum Speed Setting:
4270-4530RPM
(3L Hong Kong/Malaysia, Singapore)
4470-4730RPM
(Others)

If the setting is not OK, adjust using the maximum speed adjusting screw.

4. If no faults are found in step3, check the injection timing by setting either the No1 or No4 piston at TDC, releasing the cold start advance systen (where fitted) and checking the plunger stroke.

Injection Plunger Stroke: **0.54-0.66 (Europe and others With Auto Cold Start Device)**
Injection Plunger Stroke: **0.84-0.96mm (Without Auto Cold Start Device**

If the timing setting is not as shown, adjust to suit.

5. If no faults are found in step4, check the check the injection nozzle pressure.

Injection Nozzle Pressure:
13,729-15,690kpa (New Nozzle)
Injection Nozzle Pressure:
14,810-15,950kpa (Reused Nozzle)

6. If the pressure is not as shown adjust pressure to suit, if the pressure cannot be adjusted, replace the faulty nozzle/s.

Noise When The Engine Is Warm (1988-1996)

1. If the engine is noisey when it is warm, first check the operation of the temperature gauge if that is Ok, check the operation of the thermostat if faults are found repair/replace as required.

2. If no faults are found in step1, check the injection timing by setting either the No1 or No4 piston at TDC, releasing the cold start advance systen (where fitted) and checking the plunger stroke.

Injection Plunger Stroke:
0.84-0.96mm (Without ACSD Control)
Injection Plunger Stroke:
0.54-0.66mm (With ACSD Control)

If the timing setting is not as shown, adjust to suit.

3. If no faults are found in step2, check the check the injection nozzle pressure.

Injection Nozzle Pressure: **14,200-1520kpa**

4. If the pressure is not as shown adjust pressure to suit, if the pressure cannot be adjusted, replace the faulty nozzle/s.

Noise When The Engine Is Warm (1996On)

1. If the engine is noisey when it is warm, first check the operation of the temperature gauge if that is Ok, check the operation of the thermostat if faults are found repair/replace as required.

2. If no faults are found in step1, check the injection timing by setting either the No1 or No4 piston at TDC, releasing the cold start advance systen (where fitted) and checking the plunger stroke.

Injection Plunger Stroke: **0.54-0.66 (Europe and others With Auto Cold Start Device)**
Injection Plunger Stroke: **0.84-0.96mm (Without Auto Cold Start Device**

If the timing setting is not as shown, adjust to suit.

3. If no faults are found in step2, check the check the injection nozzle pressure.

Injection Nozzle Pressure:
13,729-15,690kpa (New Nozzle)
Injection Nozzle Pressure:
14,810-15,950kpa (Reused Nozzle)

4. If the pressure is not as shown adjust pressure to suit, if the pressure cannot be adjusted, replace the faulty nozzle/s.

Engine Will Not Return to Idle (1988 On)

1. Operate the adjusting lever on top of the injection pump and ensure that the engine returns to normal idle speed, if it does the throttle cable is binding or not adjusted correctly and needs fixing.

2. If the engine does not return to idle in step1, the injection pump is faulty and needs replacing.

Engine Will Not Shut Off With The Key (1988On)

1. Check the fuel cut solenoid operation by disconnecting the connector on top of the fuel cut solenoid and check if the engine stops, if it does the starter switch is faulty and needs repairing and/or replacing.

2. If the engine does not stop in step1, either the fuel cut solenoid is faulty or the solenoid is blocked, if required repair/replace as required.

Diesel System Electrical Diagnosis (1988-1996)

Engine Will Not Start When Cold

Super Glow System (LN Models for Europe)

Please Note: Before starting test please ensure that the battery is fully charged, the engine cranks normally and that all the fuse links are OK.
The timer unit is located In the cowl on the LH side (LN)

1. Check if the glow indicator lamp lights up when the starter switch is ON, (Coolant Temp is 20°c and lamp lights up for 2-3 seconds).

2. If the operation is not as shown, check to ensure that the fuse/s are OK, if they are not check for any short circuit/s and repair as required.

3. If the fuses are OK in step2, check the condition and/ or operation of the indicator lamp globe, if faults are found repair/replace as required.

4. If the bulb is Ok in step3, check for battery voltage to terminal 3 on the pre-heating timer connector (on the wiring harness side), if the voltage is Ok, repair/replace the timer as required.

5. If the glow indicator lamp is OK in step1, turn off the starter switch and check for battery voltage at the pre-heater timer terminal 1 with the starter switch ON, if there is no voltage check that there is 1v or less to terminal 9, if the voltage is OK, replace the timer.

6. If the voltage in step5 is Ok, check the the voltage to the pre-heat timer terminal 1 is terminated after the engine has started, if it is not, start the engine and check for voltage present at terminal 9 of the pre heating timer, if the voltage is Ok, replace the timer, if the voltage is not Ok, repair fault/s in the vehicle charging system.

7. If the voltage is terminated in step6, turn off the starter switch, turn on again and check for cuurent flow to terminal 5 of the timer in relation to the coolant temperature.

Current Flow: 16-26seconds @ less than 50°c
Current Flow: 1.7seconds @ more than 50°c

If there is no voltage at all replace the timer.

8. If the pre heating time is a lot different from what was shown in step7, the timer is faulty and should be replaced.

9. If the pre-heat time is Ok in step7, check for voltage at the timer terminal 8 when the ignition switch is in the ST position, if there is no voltage the timer needs replacing.

10. If the voltage is Ok in step9, put the starter switch in the ON position and check for voltage at the timer terminal 5 when the starter switch is at "Start", if there is no voltage at all replace the timer.

11. If the voltage in step10 is OK , switch of the ignition, switch ON the ignition and check for voltage to the glow plugs with coolant temperature a 50°c or less (a few seconds after the voltage should drop by half), if there is no voltage at all, check for battery voltage at the (+) side of the glow plug resistor, if there is no voltage present at

the (+) side of the resistor replace the No1 glow plug relay.

12. If the voltage in step11 remains at battery voltage or drops to 0v, check for battery voltage at the (+) side of the glow plug resistor, if the voltage is Ok, replace the resistor, if there is no voltage present at the (+) side of the resistor replace the No2 glow plug relay.

13. If the voltage is OK in step12, check the glow plug/s resistance, if the reading is infinity, repair/replace as required, if the reading is about 0ohms, the glow plugs are OK.

Diesel System Electrical Diagnosis (1996On)

Engine Will Not Start When Cold

Super Glow System (With Resistor)

Please Note: Before starting test please ensure that the battery is fully charged, the engine cranks normally and that all the fuse links are OK.

1. If the engine will not start when cold, disconnect the water temperature sensor and check if the glow indicator lamp lights up when the starter switch is ON

Lamp Light Up Time: 6 Seconds

2. If the operation is not as shown in step1, check to ensure that the fuse/s are OK, if they are not check for any short circuit/s and repair as required.

3. If the fuses are OK in step2, check the condition and/ or operation of the indicator lamp globe, if faults are found repair/replace as required.

4. If the bulb is Ok in step3, check for battery voltage to terminal 3 on the pre-heating timer connector (on the wiring harness side), if the voltage is Ok, repair/replace the timer as required.

5. If the glow indicator lamp is OK in step1, turn off the starter switch and check for battery voltage at the pre-heater timer terminal 5 with the starter switch ON, if there is no voltage check that there is 1v or less to terminal 10, if the voltage is OK, replace the timer.

6. If the voltage in step5 is Ok, check the the voltage to the pre-heat timer terminal 5 is terminated after the engine has started, if it is not, start the engine and check for voltage present at terminal 10 of the pre heating timer, if the voltage is Ok, replace the timer, if the voltage is not Ok, repair fault/s in the vehicle charging system.

7. If the voltage is terminated in step6, turn off the starter switch, turn on again and check for cuurent flow to terminal 1 of the timer in relation to the coolant temperature.

Current Flow: 22.5seconds

If there is no voltage at all replace the timer.

8. If the pre heating time is a lot different from what was shown in step7, the timer is faulty and should be replaced.

9. If the pre-heat time is Ok in step7, check for voltage at the timer terminal 1 when the ignition switch is in the ST position, if there is no voltage the timer needs replacing.

10. If the voltage is Ok in step9, put the starter switch in the OFF position, turn back on the ignition and check for voltage to the glow plugs, a few seconds after (the voltage should drop by half), if there is no voltage at all replace the NO1 and No2 glow plug relays.

11. If the voltage in step10 stays at battery voltage or at 1/2 voltage for 32 seconds replace the No1 glow plug relay.

12. If the voltage is OK in step11, check the glow plug/s resistance, if the reading is infinity, repair/replace as required, if the reading is about 0ohms, the glow plugs are OK.

Engine Will Not Start When Cold
Super Glow System (Without Resistor)

1. If the engine will not start when it is cold, disconnect the water temperature sensor and check if the glow indicator lamp lights up when the starter switch is ON

Lamp Light Up Time: 6 Seconds

2. If the operation is not as shown in step1, check to ensure that the fuse/s are OK, if they are not check for any short circuit/s and repair as required.

3. If the fuses are OK in step2, check the condition and/or operation of the indicator lamp globe, if faults are found repair/replace as required.

4. If the bulb is Ok in step3, check for battery voltage to terminal 3(wire harness side) on the pre-heating timer connector (on the wiring harness side), if the voltage is Ok, repair/replace the timer as required.

5. If the glow indicator lamp is OK in step1, turn off the starter switch and check for battery voltage at the pre-heater timer terminal 1 with the starter switch ON, if there is no voltage check that there is 1v or less to terminal 10, if the voltage is OK, replace the timer.

6. If the voltage in step5 is Ok, check the the voltage to the pre-heat timer terminal 1 is terminated after the engine has started, if it is not, start the engine and check for voltage present at terminal 10 of the pre heating timer, if the voltage is Ok, replace the timer, if the voltage is not Ok, repair fault/s in the vehicle charging system.

7. If the voltage is terminated in step6, turn off the starter switch, turn on again and check for cuurent flow to terminal 1 of the timer in relation to the coolant temperature.

Current Flow: 120.0seconds

If there is no voltage at all replace the timer.

8. If the pre heating time is a lot different from what was shown in step7, the timer is faulty and should be replaced.

9. If the pre-heat time is Ok in step7, check for voltage at the timer terminal 1 when the ignition switch is in the START position, if there is no voltage the timer needs replacing.

10. If the voltage is Ok in step9, put the starter switch in the OFF position, turn back on the ignition and check for voltage to the glow plugs, if there is no voltage check the operation of then glow plug relay/s and/or the glow plugs, if faults ae found repair/replace as required.

11. If the voltage in step10 is OK, reconnect the coolant temperature sensor.

Fuel Cut Solenoid Operation Check (1988On)

1. Put the starter switch into the ON position and check for an operating noise from the solenoid while repeatedly connecting and disconnecting the solenoid, if a noise is heard the solenoid is OK.

2. If the solenoid noise is not heard, check the condition and/or operation of the relevant fuse, if faults are found repair/replace as required.

3. If the fuse is OK in step2, apply battery volts to the solenoid and check for a noise, if a noise can be heard, check the condition of the harness between the fuse A and the fuel cut solenoid, if faults are found repair/replace as required.

4. If no noise can be heard in step3, replace the fuel cut solenoid.

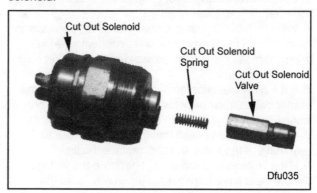

Cut Out Solenoid

Cut Out Solenoid Spring

Cut Out Solenoid Valve

Dfu035

VEHICLE SERVICE INFORMATION (1988-1996)

Vehicle Filling Capacities

Engine Oil with Filter: ....5.9 Litres (Europe)
Engine Oil without Filter: ....5.0 Litres (Europe)
Engine Oil dry fill : ....6.4 Litres (Europe)
Engine Oil with Filter: .... 6.0 Litres (Except Europe)
Engine Oil without Filter: ..... 5.0 Litres (Except Europe)
Engine Oil dry fill: .... 6.5 Litres (Except Europe)
Cooling System: .... 9.0 Litres (With Heater)
Manual Transmission: .... 2.2 Litres (LN 8#)
Manual Transmission: ....3.9 Litres (LN1##)
Front Differential: ....
.... 1.9 Litres (LN1## With Auto Engaging Diff)
Front Differential:
.... 1.6 Litres (LN1## Without Auto Engaging Diff)
Rear Differential: .... 1.8 Litres (LN8#)
Rear Differential: ....2.0 Litres (LN1##)
Transfer Case: 1.1 Litres (LN1## With Auto Engaging Diff)
Transfer Case: ....
.... 1.6 Litres (LN1## Without Auto Engaging Diff)

Vehicle Component Service Interval Changes

(LN8# Series 3L 1988-1996)

Timing Belt Replacement
  Every 100,000kms
Check Valve Clearance:
  Every 40,000kms
Engine Coolant/Anti Freeze:
  Change Every 24 Months/40,000kms
Air Cleaner Element:
  Change Every 24 Months/40,000kms
Pre-Air Cleaner Element (If Fitted):
  Change Every 24 Months/40,000kms
Fuel Filter:
  Change Every 12 Months/24,000kms
Engine Oil:
  Change Every 5000kms
Engine Oil Filter:
  Change Every 6 Months/10,000kms
Brake Fluid:
  Change Every 24 Months/40,000kms
Manual Transmission Oil:
  Change Every 24 Months/40,000kms
Auto Transmission Fluid
  Change Every 24 Months/40,000kms
Rear Differential Oil:
  Check Every 6 Months/10,000kms
Front Wheel Bearings
  Repack Every 40,000kms

Vehicle Component Service Interval Changes

(LN1## Series 3L 1988-1996)

Timing Belt Replacement
  Change Every 100,000kms
Check Valve Clearance:
  Every 40,000kms
Engine Coolant/Anti Freeze:
  Change Every 24 Months/40,000kms
Air Cleaner Element:
  Change Every 24 Months/40,000kms
Pre-Air Cleaner Element (If Fitted):
  Change Every 24 Months/40,000kms
Fuel Filter:
  Change Every 12 Months/24,000kms
Engine Oil:
  Change Every 5000kms
Engine Oil Filter:
  Change Every 6 Months/10,000kms
Brake Fluid:
  Change Every 24 Months/40,000kms
Manual Transmission Oil:
  Change Every 24 Months/40,000kms
Auto Transmission Fluid (If Fitted)
  Change Every 24 Months/40,000kms
Front Differential Oil:
  Change Every 24 Months/40,000kms
Transfer Case Oil
  Change Every 24 Months/40,000kms
Rear Differential Oil/LSD Fluid
  Check Every 24 Months/40,000kms
Front Wheel Bearings
  Repack Every 20,000kms

VEHICLE SERVICE INFORMATION (1996On)

Vehicle Filling Capacities

Engine Oil with Filter: .... 5.8 Litres (2WD)
Engine Oil without Filter: .... 4.8 Litres (2WD)
Engine Oil dry fill : .... 6.5 Litres (2WD)
Engine Oil with Filter: ....
.. 6.8 Litres (4WD with Independant Front Suspension)
Engine Oil without Filter: ....
. 5.8 Litres (4WD with Independant Front Suspension)
Engine Oil dry fill : ....
.. 7.5 Litres (4WD with Independant Front Suspension)
Engine Oil with Filter: ....
5.3 Litres (4WD without Independant Front Suspension)
Engine Oil without Filter: ....
4.3 Litres (4WD without Independant Front Suspension)
Engine Oil dry fill : ....
6.0 Litres (4WD without Independant Front Suspension)
Cooling System:9.2 Litres (2WD with Front/Rear Heater)
Cooling System: ... 8.9 Litres (2WD With Front Heater)
Cooling System: .... 8.8 Litres (2WD Without Heater)
Cooling System:9.0 Litres (4WD 3L With Front Heater)
Cooling System: ...8.1 Litres (4WD 3L Without Heater)
Manual Transmission: .... 2.2 Litres (LN8#)
Manual Transmission: .... 3.9 Litres (LN1##)
Auto Transmission: ....
.... 6.5Litres (Dry Fill), 2.4 Litres (Refill) (LN8#)
Front Differential: ....
.... 1.9 Litres (LN1## With Auto Engaging Diff)
Front Differential: ....
.... 1.6 Litres (LN1## Without Auto Engaging Diff)
Rear Differential: .... 2.2 Litres (LN8#)
Rear Differential: .... 2.2 Litres (LN1##)
Transfer Case:1.1Litres (LN1## With Auto Engaging Diff)
Transfer Case: ....
.... 1.6Litres (LN1## Without Auto Engaging Diff)

Vehicle Component Service Interval Changes
LN8# 3L 1996On

Timing Belt Replacement
   Every 100,000kms
Check Valve Clearance:
   Every 40,000kms
Engine Coolant/Anti Freeze:
   Change Every 24 Months/40,000kms
Air Cleaner Element:
   Change Every 24 Months/40,000kms
Pre-Air Cleaner Element (If Fitted):
   Change Every 24 Months/40,000kms
Fuel Filter:
   Change Every 12 Months/24,000kms
Engine Oil:
   Change Every 5000kms
Engine Oil Filter:
   Change Every 6 Months/10,000kms
Brake Fluid:
   Change Every 24 Months/40,000kms

Manual Transmission Oil:
   Change Every 24 Months/40,000kms
Auto Transmission Fluid
   Change Every 24 Months/40,000kms
Rear Differential Oil:
   Check Every 6 Months/10,000kms
Front Wheel Bearings
   Repack Every 40,000kms

Vehicle Component Service Interval Changes
(LN1## 3L 1996On)

Timing Belt Replacement
   Change Every 100,000kms
Check Valve Clearance:
   Every 40,000kms
Engine Coolant/Anti Freeze:
   Change Every 24 Months/40,000kms
Air Cleaner Element:
   Change Every 24 Months/40,000kms
Pre-Air Cleaner Element (If Fitted):
   Change Every 24 Months/40,000kms
Fuel Filter:
   Change Every 12 Months/24,000kms
Engine Oil:
   Change Every 5000kms
Engine Oil Filter:
   Change Every 6 Months/10,000kms
Brake Fluid:
   Change Every 24 Months/40,000kms
Manual Transmission Oil:
   Change Every 24 Months/40,000kms
Auto Transmission Fluid (If Fitted)
   Change Every 24 Months/40,000kms
Front Differential Oil:
   Change Every 24 Months/40,000kms
Transfer Case Oil
   Change Every 24 Months/40,000kms
Rear Differential Oil/LSD Fluid
   Check Every 24 Months/40,000kms
Front Wheel Bearings
   Repack Every 20,000kms

Toyota Landcruiser HDJ80# Series 1HD-T Engine 1990 ON

CONTENTS   PAGE

CONTENTS   PAGE

Toyota Landcruiser Early 80's Series

Toyota Landcruiser HDJ80# Series 1HD-T Engine 1990 ON

Engine Checks

Valve Clearance Check

1. Remove the intake pipe and the cylinder head cover.
2. See the No1 piston to TDC/Compression by turning the crankshaft pulley clockwise and line up is groove with the timing gear cover groove.
3. Check that the valve lifters on the No1 cylinder are loose and the exhaust valve lifters on the No6 cylinder is tight.
If this is not the case, turn the crankshaft one full turn in a clockwise direction and then line up the grooves as shown in step2.
4. Check the valve clearances on the 1,5,8 inlet valves and 2,4,7 exhaust valves with a feeler gauge and record the measurments between the valve lifter and camshaft that need adjusting. **(Measurements will be used to determine new shim thickneses that are required).**

Specified Inlet Valve Clearance: **0.15-0.25mm**
Specified Outlet Valve Clearance: **0.35-0.45mm**

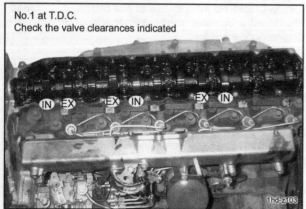

No.1 at T.D.C.
Check the valve clearances indicated

5. Turn the crankshaft in a clockwise direction one full turn (360°) and check the valve clearances on the 3, 7,

11 inlet valve and 6,10, 12 on the exhaust valve. with a feeler gauge and record the measurments between the valve lifter and camshaft that need adjusting. **(Measurements will be used to determine new shim thickneses that are required).**

Specified Inlet Valve Clearance: **0.15-0.25mm**
Specified Outlet Valve Clearance: **0.35-0.45mm**

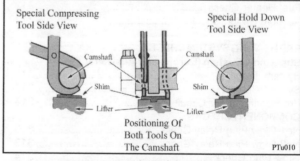

No.6 at T.D.C.
Check the valve clearances indicated

6. To complete the adjustment remove any adjusting shim that need replacement by using a valve liter (part no 09248-64011).

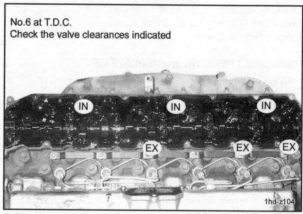

Special Compressing Tool Side View

Special Hold Down Tool Side View

Camshaft

Camshaft

Shim

Shim

Lifter

Lifter

Positioning Of Both Tools On The Camshaft

7. Turn the crankshaft to position the cam lobe of the camshaft on the adjusting valve is facing upwards. Remove the shim with a small screwdriver and magnetic tool.
8. To calculate the shim needed to adjust the valve clearance, measure the thickness of the old shim, and

306

calculate the the thickness of the new shim as shown below.

Inlet Valve Shim:
     Old shim thickness plus 0.20mm.
Exahust Valve Shim:
     Old shim thickness plus 0.40mm.

9. Once the shim thickness has been calculated, replace the shim using the valve lifter (part no 09248-64011) and then remove the lifter.

10. Recheck the valve clearance, then replace any removed parts in the reverse order of removal.

Compression Check

1. Run the engine to normal operating temperatures, disconnect the injection pump cut off solenoid connector and then remove the glow plugs.

2. Check each cylinder compression by installing a compression tester to the engine, fully opening the throttle valve, cranking the engine and recording the pressure on each cylinder.

Specified Compression Pressure: **3432kpa or more**
Minimum Pressure: **2452kpa or more**
Difference Between Each Cylinder: 490kpa or less

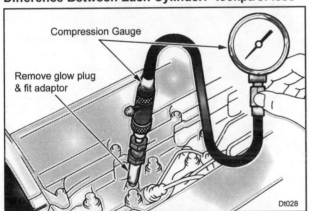

3. If the pressure is less than shown on one or more cylinders, pour a small amount of oil through the glow plug hole and recheck the pressure. If the pressure is now OK, check the condition of the piston rings and/or cylinder bore. If the pressure is still low, check for a sticking valve and/or bad valve seating.

4. Replace any removed parts in the reverse order of removal.

Piston Protrusion Check

1. Clean the cylinder block, set the No1 piston to TDC, place a dial gauge on the block and set the dial gauge to zero.

2. Find the point where the piston top protrudes the most by turning the crankshaft slightly the the left and right.

3. Measure each cylinder in two places as shown and record the average of the two measurments on each cylinder.

Specified Protrusion Measurement:
            0.405-0.655mm.

4. If the protrusion measurement is not as shown, remove the piston and con rod and replace it.

5. There are 5 types of head gaskets used on this vehicle, but only type 1,3,5 are supplied as replacement parts.

6. Select the largest of the protrusion measurements and select the gasket to suit as shown below.

Protrusion Measurement	Gasket Size
0.525mm or less	**1.15-1.25mm**
0.526-625mm	**1.25-1.35mm**
0.626mm or more	**1.35-1.45mm**
Gasket No1:	**Thickness is 1.15-1.25mm**
Gasket No3:	**Thickness is 1.25-1.35mm**
Gasket No5:	**Thickness is 1.35-1.45mm**

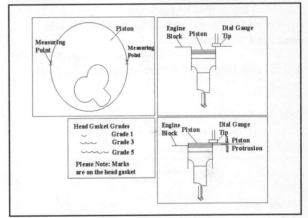

Cylinder Head Tightening Procedures

1. With the cylinder head inplace, tighten the bolts in three steps, if any of the bolts break or deform replace them as required.

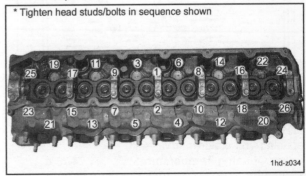

2. Apply a light coat of oil to each bolt thread, and using a torque wrench tighten the 26 bolts in three separate stages to a tor**que of 69Nm.**

3. Mark the front of the cylinder head bolts with white paint, **tighten each bolt another 90°** in the sequence shown, and **then tighten each bolt a further 90°** in the same sequence and now ensure that the paint marks on all of the bolts are facing to the rear.

Oil Pressure Check

1. Remove the oil pressure switch from the block and install a pressure gauge in its place.

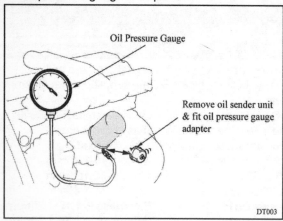

Oil Pressure Gauge

Remove oil sender unit & fit oil pressure gauge adapter

DT003

2. Run the engine to normal operating temperature and the check the engine oil pressure.
Specified Oil Pressure: 29kpa or more @ Idle
Specified Oil Pressure:
         245kpa or more @ 3000RPM.
3. If the pressure is not as shown, repair/replace as required

Cooling System Thermostat Check

1. Remove the thermostat from the engine and put into a suitable container of water.

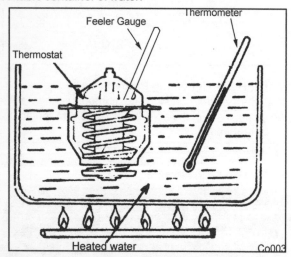

Feeler Gauge
Thermometer
Thermostat
Heated water
Co003

2. Heat the water gradually and and check the valve opening temperature and valve lift.
Valve Opening Temperature: **74-78°c**
Valve Lift: **10mm or more @ 90°c**
If the operation is not as shown above replace the thermostat.
3. Check that the valve spring is tight when the

thermostat is fully closed, if not replace the thermostat

Fuel Filter Check and Replacement

1. Remove the fuel filter sensor, drain the fuel, then remove the fuel filter.
2. Clean the fuel filter mounting bracket and then coat the fuel filter sealing ring with some diesel fuel.
3. Screw the fuel filter on until a slght resistance is felt and then turn another 2/3 of a turn or until suitably tight.
4. Install the fuel filter sensor (if fitted) to the new filter and then bleed any air present from the system.

Draining Water Fron The Filter

1. Loosen the drain cock 4 or 5 turns or remove the fuel filter sensor to allow the water to drain from the filter.

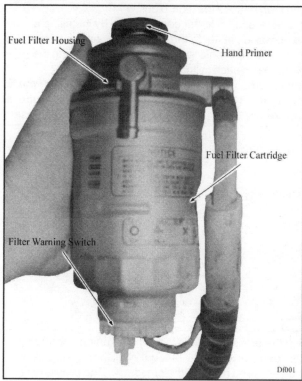

Fuel Filter Housing
Hand Primer
Fuel Filter Cartridge
Filter Warning Switch
Df001

2. Retighten the drain cock or replace the sensor and bleed any air present from the system.

Fuel Filter Warning Lamp Check

1. Remove the switch from the filter and check that there is continuity between the terminals when the warning switch is ON (Float Up)
2. Check that there is no continuity between the terminals when the warning switch is OFF (Float Down)
3. If the operation is not as shown, repair/replace as required.
Photo is on the next page

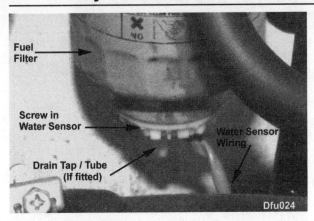

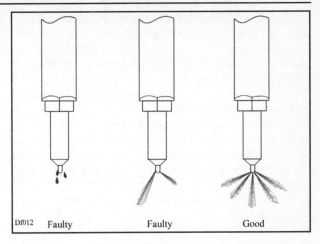

Df012   Faulty   Faulty   Good

Injector Nozzle Check

1. Remove the injector from the vehicle, connect up to the pressure tester and check the initial pressure by pumping the tester handle a few times.

Opening Pressure:

12,945-13,533kpa (No2 Opening Pressure)

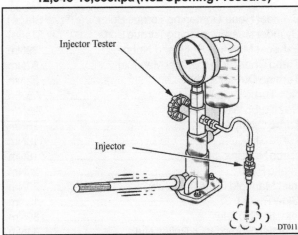

Timing Belt Removal and Replacement

Removal Procedures

1. Remove the timing belt cover and set the No1 piston to BDC by turning the crankshaft pulley in a clockwise direction until the No1 and No2 camshaft pulley groves line up at each position.

2. Remove the timing belt from the engine by removing the tension spring, the spring bolt on the timing belt idler and then the timing belt.

Please Note: If the timing belt is being re-used, draw on the belt an arrow undicating the direction of rotation, and match marks on the pulley as well as the belt.

2. If the opening pressure is not as shown above, take the injector to pieces and change the adjusting shim on the top of the No2 pressure spring so as the correct pressure is recorded.

3. After the pressure in step3 is correct disassemble the nozzle for the adjustment of the No1 opening pressure.

Opening Pressure:

17,650-18,633kpa (No1 Opening Pressure)
Please Note: The adjusting shims vary in 0.01mm thicknesses, each 0.025mm will adjust the pressure by 147kpa. After the shim has been changed there should be no leakage from the injector.

4. Maintain the pressure between 981-1961kpa below the opening pressure and check that there is no leakage from the injector for a period of 10seconds.

5. Check the spray pattern by pumping the pressure tester handle 4-6 times or more per second and check the injection spray pattern.

Diagram is in the next column

6. If the operation and/or spray pattern is not as shown, repair/replace the nozzle/s as required.

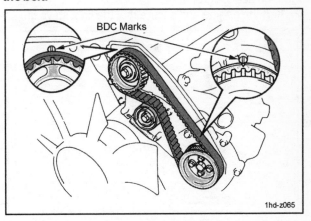

Replacement Procedures
Please Note: Before replacing the timimg belt check the condition and/or operation of the timing belt pulleys, tensioners and/or pulleys, if faults are found repair/replace as required.

1. Check the tensioner spring free length

Spring Free Length: **72.7mm**

Check the tension of the spring at the specified free length

Installed Tension: **275m at 90.1mm**

Please Note: Diagram is on the next page

2. Before fitting the belt to the engine, set the No1 piston to BDC by turning the crankshaft pulley in a clockwise direction until the No1 and No2 camshaft pulley groves line up at each position.

3. Fit the timing belt to the engine firstly on the No2 camshaft pulley, then the No1 pulley and finally the timing belt idler pulley.

4. Install the tension spring and then install and torque the idler pulley bolt to 26Nm.

5. Check the valve timing by turning the crankshaft pulley in a clockwise direction and ensure that all of the timing marks on each of the pulleys all line up. If they do not remove the belt and re-start the insatllation process again.

6. Replace any more removed parts in the reverse order of removal

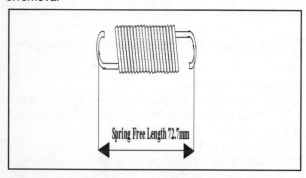

Spring Free Length 72.7mm

Timing Belt Warning Lamp Reset Procedures (Rubber Plug in the Instrument Cluster Glass)

1. Remove the grommet from the speedometer and turn off the lamp by pushing the warning lamp reset switch, then replace the grommet.

2. Start the engine and ensure that the light stays off.

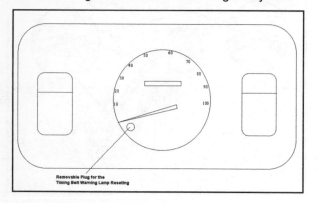

Removable Plug for the
Timing Belt Warning Lamp Reseting

Timing Belt Warning Lamp Reset Procedures (Change Screw Position on the Back of the Instrument Cluster)

1. Remove the instrument cluster from the vehicle, connect terminals A&B shown in the diagrams and then remove the CHARGE fuse from the vehicle.

2. Turn the ignition switch to ON and check that the warning lights light up, if not the check the condition and/or operation of the globe.

3. Check the condition and/or operation of the reset switches by checking that there is intermittent continuity between terminals A&B when the reset switch is pressed, if not repair/replace the speedometer/

instrument cluster as required.

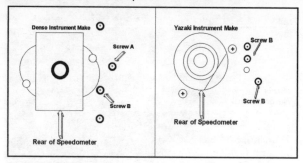

Timing Belt Replacement Torques

No1 Camshaft Pulley:	98Nm
No2 Camshaft Pulley:	31Nm
Idle Pulley:	26Nm

Engine Tightening Torques

Cylinder Head Tightening Torque Bolts:	69Nm (Tighten in 3 Stages)
Cylinder Head Tightening Torque Bolts:	90° (2nd Stage)
Cylinder Head Tightening Torque Bolts:	90° (3rd Stage)
Exhaust Manifold Bolts and Nuts:	39Nm
Turbo Charger to Exhaust Manifold:	52Nm
Turbine Outlet Elbow:	52Nm
No1 Turbo Water Pipe:	7.8Nm
No2 Turbo Water Pipe:	7.8Nm
Turbo Oil Pipe:	25Nm
Turbo Stay:	118Nm
Turbo Heat Insulator:	18Nm
Intake Pipe:	20Nm
Inlet Manifold Bolts and Nuts:	20Nm
Glow Plugs:	13Nm
Injection Nozzle:	39Nm
Injection Pump Drive Pulley Nut:	64Nm
Idle Pulley:	26Nm
Flywheel Bolts:	127Nm
Drive Plate:	127Nm
Connecting Rod Caps:	37Nm
Connecting Rod Caps:	90° (2nd Stage)
Main Bearings:	103Nm
Main Bearings:	90° (2nd Stage)
Crankshaft Pulley Bolt No1 to Crankshaft:	490Nm
Crankshaft Pulley No2 to No1 Pulley :	25Nm
Camshaft Gear No1 Bolt:	98Nm
Camshaft Gear No2 Bolt:	31Nm
Oil Pump to Block:	20Nm
Oil Pump to Injection Pump:	18Nm
Oil Pan to Cylinder Block:	10Nm

System Adjustments

Idle Speed Check

1. Before checking the idle speed, ensure that the engine is at normal operating temperature, the air cleaner OK and fitted, all of the accessories are fitted, all vacuum lines are OK, valve clearance and injection timing are set correctly and that the transmission is in "N".

2. Install a tachometer to the engine, ensure that the adjusting lever touches the idle speed adjusting screw when the throttle pedal is released, if it does not adjust to suit.

3. Start the engine, let it run and check the idle speed.

Idle Speed:	**600-700RPM (Manual)**
Idle Speed:	**750-850RPM (Auto)**

4. If the idle speed is not as shown, disconnect the throttle linkage, loosen the lock nut on the idle speed adjusting screw and adjust the idle speed by turnning the idle speed adjusting screw.

Idle Speed:	**650RPM (Manual)**
Idle Speed:	**800RPM (Auto)**

5. Tighten the lock nut, recheck the idle speed, reconnect the throttle linkage and then re-check the idle speed.

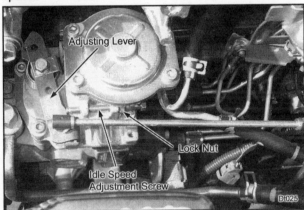

6. Remove the tachometer from the engine and replace any other removed parts in the reverse order of removal.

Injection Timing Check

1. Set the No1 or No6 piston to TDC on the compression stroke by turning the crankshaft pulley in a clockwise direction and lining up the groove on the pulley with the mark on the timing gear cover.

2. Remove the Air Control Valve, loosen the No5 injector pipe unioun nut, remove the plug bolt from the distributor head of the injection pump and install a dial gauge to the bolt hole.

3. (For Vehicles with ACSD Only), Turn the cold start lever in an anti clockwise direction about 20° and put a metel plate of between 3.5-7.5mm between the cold start lever and the thermo wax plunger.

4. Turn the crankshaft in an anti-clockwise direction, set the dial gauge to zero when it reaces its minimum value.

Specified Minimum Value: 0mm

5. Slowly turn the crankshaft in a clockwise direction until the groove on the crankshaft pulley lines up with the mark on the timing cover, then record the plunger stroke.

Specified Plunger Stroke: 1.29-1.35mm

6. If the timing needs adjustment, loosen the 5 remaining injection pipe union nuts on the injection pump side, the bolt holding the pump to the pump bracket, the two nuts holding the pump to the timing gear.

7. If the plunger stroke is less than shown, turn the pump towards the engine, if it more turn away from the engine.

8. Retighten the two nuts holding the pump to the timing gear, the bolt holding the pump to the pump bracket and then recheck the injection pump plunger stroke.

9. If fitted remove the plate from the ACSD device, the dial gauge and replace the bolt plug, tighten the union nuts on the injection pipes and replace any more removed parts in the reverse order of removal.

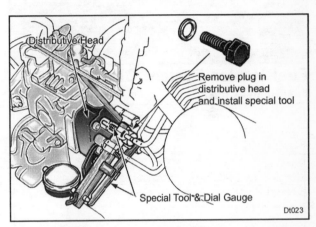

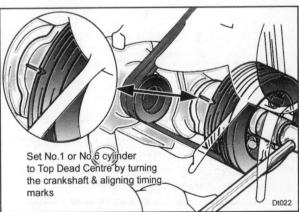

Maximum Speed Adjustment

1. With a tachometer installed to the engine, check that the adjusting lever touches the maximum speed screw when the throttle pedal is pressed down all of the way, if not adjust to suit.

2. Start the engine, press down the throttle pedal all the way and check the maximum speed.

Specified Maximum Speed: 4300-4500RPM.

3. If the maximum speed is not as shown, disconnect the throttle linkages, cut the seal on the maximum speed adjusting screw, loosen the lock nut and then adjust by turning the maximum speed adjusting screw.

Specified Maximum Speed: **4400RPM.**

4. After adjustment, check the idle speed, race the engine and then recheck the maximum speed again.

5. Reconnect the throttle linkage and adjust to suit, seal the maximum speed screw again and then replace any more removed parts in the reverse order of removal.

6. Remove the tachometer from the engine.

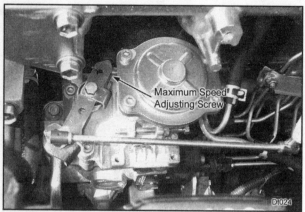

Fuel Heater System Check
Fuel Heater Check

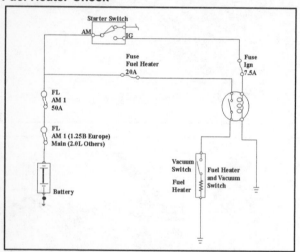

1. Apply 46.7±6.7kpa or more of vacuum to the vacuum switch and with an ohmmeter check the resistance between the No1 terminal and the switch body
Specified Resistance: **0.5-2.0ohms @ 20°c**
2. If the resistance is not as shown, replace the fuel heater and vacuum switch assembly.

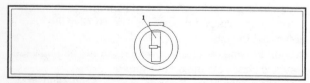

Vacuum Switch Check
1. With an ohmmeter check that there is no continuity between the No1 terminal and the switch body, if there is replace the fuel heater and vacuum switch assembly.
2. Apply 46.7± 6.7kpa or more of vacuum to the vacuum

switch and with an ohmmeter check that there is continuity between the No1 terminal and the switch body, if there is no continuity, replace the fuel heater and vacuum switch assembly.
Use fuel heater diagram

Fuel Heater Relay Check
1. With an ohmmeter check that there is continuity between terminals 1 and 3 and that there is no continuity between terminals 2 and 4.
If the continuity is not as shown above, replace the relay.
2. Apply battery volts between the continuity between terminals 1 and 3 and that there is no continuity between terminals 2 and 4.
If the operation is not as shown above, replace the relay.

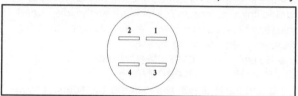

Pre-Heating System Checks
Pre Heating System Check (Superglow System Europe and Australia)

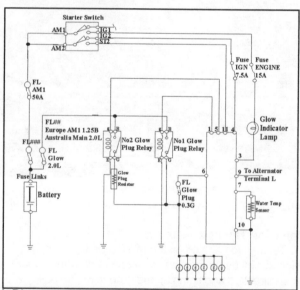

1. Disconnect the water temperature sensor and check if the indicator lamp lights up when the starter switch is in the ON position.
Specified Light Up Time: **6-7seconds**
2. If the light up time is not as shown in step1, check the condition of the relevant system fuse, if the fuse is blown, check for short circuit in the harness and repair as required.
3. If the fuse is OK in step2, check the condition and/or operation of the glow indicator lamp globe, if faults are found repair/replace as required.
4. If the bulb is OK in step3, check for battery voltage to the terminal 3 (harness side) of the pre-heating timer connector, if the voltage is OK, replace the timer

assembly.

5. If the light up time in step1 is OK, put the starter switch to OFF, and check for battery voltage to terminal 1of the pre heating timer with the ignition switch in the ON position.

6. If there is NO voltage in step5, check that there is 1v or less to terminal 9 on the timer, if there is the timer is faulty and needs replacing.

7. If the voltage in step5 is OK, check if voltage to the terminal 1of the pre heating timer is terminated after the engine has started, if it does not, start the engine and check if there is voltage at terminal 9 of the pre heating timer, if there is not, repair fault in the charging system. If there is voltage the timer is faulty and should be replaced.

8. If the voltage operation is OK in step7, put the starter switch to the OFF position, put the starter switch into the ON position and check the current flow to the terminal 5 of the timer.

Current Flow: 120 Seconds.

9. If the pre-heat time differs from above or there is NO voltage at all in step8, replace the timer.

10. If the current flow is OK in step8, after completing pre-heating check for voltage at terminal 5, check again this time when the starter switch is in the Start position.

11. If there is no voltage in step10, replace the timer.

12. If the voltage is OK in step10, put the starter switch into the off position, place the starter switch into the ON position and check for voltage to the glow plugs a few seconds later (the the voltage should drop by about 50%).

13. If there is no voltage at all in step12, check for battery voltage at the (-) side of the glow plug resistor, if there is no voltage, replace the No1 glow plug relay.

14. If the voltage in step12 stays at battery voltage or falls to 0v, check for battery voltage to the (+) side of the glow plug resistor, if there is no voltage replace the No2 glow plug relay.

15. If the voltage is OK in step12, check the glow plug resistance.

Specified Resistance: Approx. 0ohms

If the resistance is not OK, replace the glow plug/s as required.

16. If the glow plug resistance is OK in step15, the glow plug/s are OK, then replace the water temperature sensor harness connector.

Pre Heating Timer Circuit Check
Please Note: The timer is located under the instrument panel on the LH side

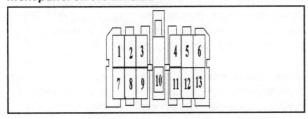

1. Disconnect the harness connector from the timer and

check the connector on the harness side as shown in the chart below.

Check For	Between Terminals	Condition	Specified Value
Continuity	1-ground		Continuity
Voltage	3-ground	Starter switch OFF	No Volts
Voltage	3-ground	Starter switch ON	Battery Volts
Voltage	4-ground	Starter switch OFF	No Volts
Voltage	4-ground	Starter switch ON	Battery Volts
Continuity	5-ground		Continuity
Continuity	6-ground		Continuity
Continuity	7-ground		Continuity
Continuity	10-ground		Continuity
Voltage	11-ground	Starter switch OFF	No Volts
Voltage	11-ground	Starter switch ON	Battery Volts

No1 Glow Plug Relay Check
Please Note: The relay is located in the engine compartment on the LH Side

1. With an ohmmeter check that there is continuity between terminals 1 and 2 and that there is no continuity between terminals 3 and 4.

If the continuity is not as shown above, replace the relay.

2. Apply battery volts between terminals 1 and 2 and that there is no continuity between terminals 3 and 4.

If the operation is not as shown above, replace the relay.

No2 Glow Plug Relay

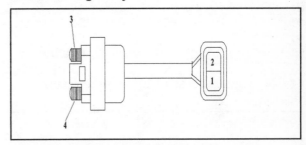

Please Note: The relay is located in the engine compartment on the LH Side

1. With an ohmmeter check that there is continuity between terminals 1 and 2 and that there is no continuity between terminals 3 and 4.

If the continuity is not as shown above, replace the relay.

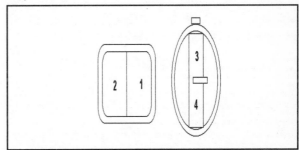

2. Apply battery volts between terminals 1 and 2 and that there is no continuity between terminals 3 and 4.

If the operation is not as shown above, replace the relay.

Glow Plug Check

1. With an ohmmeter check that there is continuity between the glow plug terminal and ground.
2. If there is no continuity replace the glow plug/s as required.

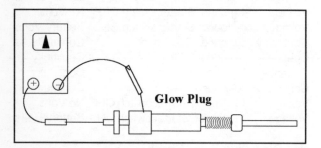

Glow Plug

Glow Plug Resistor Check

1. With an ohmmeter check that there is continuity between the resistor terminals.
2. If there is no continuity replace the resistor as required.

Water Temperature Sensor Check

1. Disconnect the sensor harness connector and check the resistance between the terminals at varying temperatures.

Coolant Temperature (°c)	Resistance(k/ohms)
-20	10-20
0	4-7
20	2-3
40	0.9-1.3
60	0.4-0.7
80	0.2-0.4

If the resistance is not as shown, repair/replace as required.

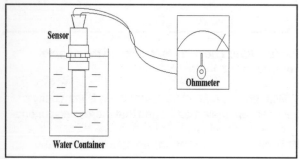

Sensor

Ohmmeter

Water Container

Pre-Heating System Checks

Pre Heating Timer Circuit Check (Fixed Delay System Execpt Europe and Australia)

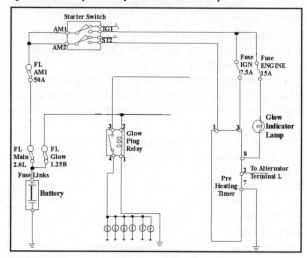

Please Note: The timer is located under the instrument panel on the LH side.

1. Disconnect the harness connector from the timer and check the connector on the harness side as shown in the chart below.

Check For	Between Terminals	Condition	Specified Value
Voltage	1-ground	Starter switch OFF	No Volts
Voltage	1-ground	Starter switch ON	Battery Volts
Voltage	3-ground	Starter switch OFF	No Volts
Voltage	3-ground	Starter switch ON	Battery Volts
Continuity	7-ground		Continuity
Voltage	8-ground	Starter switch OFF	No Volts
Voltage	8-ground	Starter switch ON	Battery Volts

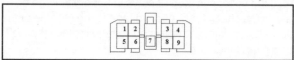

Glow Indicator Lamp Check

1. Put the starter switch into the ON position and check the light up time.
Specified Light Up Time: **Approx.5secs**
2. Put the starter switch into the ON position and measure the time that battery voltage is applied to terminal 1 of the preheat timer.
Specified Pre-Heating Time: **Approx.18secs**

Glow Plug Relay Check

Please Note: The relay is located in the engine compartment on the LH Side
1. Refer previous information for the No2 glow plug relay in the previous Superglow System.

Glow Plug Check

1. Refer previous information for the glow plug check in the previous Superglow System.

Turbocharger System Checks

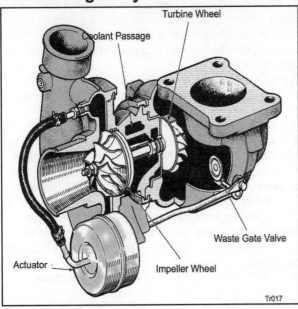

Turbine Wheel
Coolant Passage
Waste Gate Valve
Actuator
Impeller Wheel
Tr017

Intake Air System Check

1. Check for leaks and/or blockages between the air cleaner and turbo charger inlet, and between the turbo charger outlet and cylinder head

2. Check for blocked air cleaner, damaged or leaking hoses and/or connections, damage in any of the components.

3. If faults are found repair/replace as required.

Exhaust System Checks.

1. Check for leaks and/or blockages between the air cleaner and turbo charger inlet, and between the turbo charger outlet and the exhaust pipe.

2. Check for damage to any of the components, any foreign objects in the passages, leaks and/or cracks in any of the components.

3. If faults are found repair/replace as required.

Turbocharger Pressure Check

1. Install a 3 way union to the intake pipe pressure hose and install a pressure gauge to it.

2. Press down the clutch pedal, then press down the throttle pedal fully down. Run the engine at maximum speed (4400RPM) and then check the pressure.

Specified Turbo Pressure: 49-64kpa

3. If the pressure is less than shown, check the operation of the intake air system and exhaust system, if no leaks are found replace the turbocahrger.

4. If the pressure is more than shown, check the condition and/or operation of the actuator hose, if no faults are found replace the turbocharger as required.

Turbo Impeller Wheel Check

1. Disconnect the air cleaner hose and try and turn the impeller wheel.

2. If the wheel does not turn or turns with a drag, replace the turbocharger as required.

Turbocharger System Diagnosis and Troubleshooting

Poor Fuel Consumption, Lack of Power or Excessive Fuel Consumption

1. If the turbo charger system pressure is low, carry out a system pressure test.

Specified Turbo Pressure: 49-64kpa

If the pressure is not as shown, repair/replace turbocharger as required.

2. If no faults are found in step1, check the operation of the air intake system, if faults are found repair/replace as required.

3. If no faults are found in step2, check the condition and/or operation of the exhaust system, if faults are found repair/replace as required.

4. If no faults are found in step3, check the condition and/or operation of the turbocharger, if faults are found repair/replace as required.

Abnormal Noise From The Turbocharger

1. Check the condition and/or installation of the turbo insulator and/or bolts, if faults are found repair/replace as required.

2. If no faults are found in step1, check the condition and/or installation of the exhaust system, if faults are found repair/replace as required.

3. If no faults are found in step2, check the condition and/or operation of the turbocharger, if faults are found repair/replace as required.

Poor Oil Consumption or White Exhaust

1. If there are oil leaks found from the turbo seal, check for oil leaks into the exhaust system by removing the turbine elbow and checking for excessive carbon deposits on the turbine wheel, if faults are found repair/replace the turbocharger as required.

2. If no faults are found in step1, check for oil leaks into the intake air system by checking the axial play in the impeller wheel.

Specified Axial Play: 0.13mm

3. If faults are found repair/replace the turbocharger as required.

Turbo Indicator Light and Warning Light Operation Check

1. Does the green indicator lamp and orange warning lamp come on when the ignition switch is in the ON position.

2. If the lamps in step1 do not come on, check the condition and/or operation of the gauge fuse, if faults are found repair/replace as required.

3. If no faults are found in step2, check the condition and/or operation of the 7.5 CHARGE and ENGINE fuses, if faults are found repair/replace as required.

4. If no faults are found in step3, is the charging lamp out, if it is not, repair faults in the charging system.

5. If the charging lamp is out in step4, repair/replace the combination meter as required.

6. If both lamps come on in step1, do they go out when the engine is idling.

7. If both lamps stay on in step6, check if the charging lamp goes out, if it does not repair faults in the charging system.

8. If the green lamp stays on in step6, check for open circuit between the low pressure switch and the tachometer, if faults are found repair/replace as required. If no faults are found replace the low pressure switch.

9. If only the orange lamp comes on in step6, check for open circuit between the high pressure switch and the tachometer, if faults are found repair/replace as required. If no faults are found replace the high pressure switch.

10. If both lamps do go out in step6, does the green lamp come on when 13.7kpa of pressure ia applied to both pressure switches.

11. If the green lamp in step10 does not come on, check for short circuit between the low pressure switch and the tachometer, if faults are found repair/replace as required. If no faults are found replace the low pressure switch.

12. If the orange lamp comes on in step10, does the green lamp come on when 105.9kpa of pressure is applied to both switches, if it does not replace the high pressure switch, if it does replace the combination meter.

13. If the green lamp does come on in step10, does the orange lamp come on when 105.9kpa of pressure is applied to both switches, if it does not check for short circuit between the high pressure switch and the tachometer, if faults are found replace the high pressure switch.

14. If the orange indicator lamp does come on in step13, the indicator and warning lamp system is OK.

Injection System and Engine Diagnosis and Troubleshooting

Engine Will Not Crank

1. Check the condition and/or operation of the battery cables between the battery and starter motor, if faults are found repair/replace as required.

2. If no faults are found in step1, check the condition and/or operation of the battery, alternator output and/or drive belt, if faults are found repair/replace as required.

3. If no faults are found in step2, check the condition and/or operation of the starter motor, if faults are found repair/replace as required.

Engine Cranks Slowly or Will Not Start

1. Check the condition and/or operation of the battery cables between the battery and starter motor, if faults are found repair/replace as required.

2. If no faults are found in step1, check the condition and/or operation of the battery, alternator output and/or drive belt, if faults are found repair/replace as required.

3. If no faults are found in step2, check that the correct grade of engine oil is being used on the vehicle, if not drain and replace with the correct grade of oil.

Engine Cranks Normally But Does Not Start

1. If the engine cranks normally but does not start, check and ensure that fuel is reaching the injection nozzles, by loosening any of the injection pipes, cranking the engine and ensuring that fuel is coming out of the pipe.

2. If fuel is not coming out of the pipe in step1, check the operation of the fuel cut solenoid, if faults are found repair/replace as required.

3. If no faults are found in step3, check to ensure that fuel is getting to the injection pump by disconnecting the inlet hoses from the fuel filter, feeding clean fuel from a separate container directly into the injection pump. If the engine now starts there may be blockages in the fuel filter and/or line between the fuel tank and fuel filter. If the engine does not start, check the condition and/or operation of the fuel line between the fuel filter and fuel pump. If the injection pump operation is normal it should be replaced.

4. If fuel is present in step1, check the fuel system pipes, hoses and/or components for leaks, cracks and/or damage, if faults are found repair/replace as required.

5. If there are no faults in step4, check the pre-heating operation system operation by ensuring that after the ignition is turned on and the glow plug lamp lights up that there is voltage applied to the glow plugs, if the operation is not as shown, repair/replace as required.

6. If no faults are found in step5, check the operation of the glow plug/s, if faults are found repair/replace as required.

7. If no faults are found in step6, check the injection timing by (releasing the cold start advance system where fitted) and checking the plunger stroke.

Injection Plunger Stroke: **1.29-1.35mm**

If the timing setting is not as shown, adjust to suit.

8. If no faults are found in step7, check the fast idle system operation **(vehicle with ACSD only)**, if faults are found repair/replace as required.

9. If no faults are found in step8, check the condition and/or operation of the injection nozzles

Injection Nozzle Pressure:
     17,652-18,633kpa (No1 Opening Pressure)
Injection Nozzle Pressure:
     12,945-13,533kpa (No2 Opening Pressure)

10. If faults are found repair/replace as required.

Idle Speed is Unstable When The Engine is Warm

1. If the idle speed is unstable when the engine is warm, check the condition and/or operation of the throttle cable and/or linkages, if faults are found repair/replace as required.

2. If no faults are found in step1, check the engine idle speed setting.

Idle Speed: **600-700RPM (Manual)**
Idle Speed: **750-850RPM (Auto)**

If the idle speed is not as shown, adjust to suit

3. If no faults are found in step2, check the fuel system components and/or lines for leaks and/or damage, if faults are found repair/replace as required.

4. If no faults are found in step3, check the injection timing by (releasing the cold start advance system where fitted) and checking the plunger stroke.

Injection Plunger Stroke: **1.29-1.35mm**

If the timing setting is not as shown, adjust to suit.

5. If no faults are found in step4, check the operation of the injection nozzle/s and/or the delivery valve by letting the engine run at idle speed, loosening the union nuts on each of the cylinders in order and check if there is any change of idle speed. If there is no change at any of the cylinders this will indicate that a faulty cylinder/s is present. To fix the problem check the injection nozzle pressure.

Injection Nozzle Pressure:

        17,652-18,633kpa (No1 Opening Pressure)

Injection Nozzle Pressure:

        12,945-13,533kpa (No2 Opening Pressure)

6. If the pressure is not as shown adjust pressure to suit. If the pressure is OK, the fault will be with the delivery valve and should be replaced.

Engine Suddenly Stops.

1. If the engine is running and then suddenly stops check and ensure that fuel is reaching the injection nozzles by loosening any of the injection pipes, cranking the engine and ensuring that fuel is coming out of the pipe.

2. If fuel is not coming out of the pipe in step1, check the operation of the fuel cut solenoid, if faults are found repair/replace as required.

3. If no faults are found in step3, check to ensure that fuel is getting to the injection pump by disconnecting the inlet hoses from the fuel filter, feeding clean fuel from a separate container directly into the injection pump. If the engine now starts there may be blockages in the fuel filter and/or line between the fuel tank and fuel filter. If the engine does not start, check the condition and/or operation of the fuel line between the fuel filter and fuel pump. If the injection pump operation is normal it should be replaced.

4. If fuel is present in step1, check the pre-heating operation system operation by ensuring that after the ignition is turned on and the glow plug lamp lights up ensure that there are 6v applied to the glow plugs, if the operation is not as shown, repair/replace as required.

5. If no faults are found in step4, check the operation of then glow plug/s, if faults are found repair/replace as required.

6. If no faults are found in step5, check the fuel system pipes, hoses and/or components for leaks, cracks and/or damage, if faults are found repair/replace as required.

7. If no faults are found in step6, check the injection timing by setting either the No1 or No4 piston at TDC, releasing the cold start advance systen (where fitted) and checking the plunger stroke.

Injection Plunger Stroke: **1.29-1.35mm**

If the timing setting is not as shown, adjust to suit.

8. If no faults are found in step7, check the fast idle system operation, if faults are found repair/replace as

required.

9. If no faults are found in step8, check the operation of the injection nozzle/s and/or the delivery valve by letting the engine run at idle speed, loosening the union nuts on each of the cylinders in order and check if there is any change of idle speed. If there is no change at any of the cylinders this will indicate that a faulty cylinder/s is present. To fix the problem check the injection nozzle pressure.

Injection Nozzle Pressure:

        17,652-18,633kpa (No1 Opening Pressure)

Injection Nozzle Pressure:

        12,945-13,533kpa (No2 Opening Pressure)

10. If the pressure is not as shown adjust pressure to suit. If the pressure is OK, the fault will be with the delivery valve and should be replaced.

Engine Has a Lack of Power

1. If the engine has any lack of power, press down the throttle fully and ensure that the adjusting lever is in contact with the maximum speed adjusting screw, if it is not adjust to suit.

2. If no faults are found in step1, start the engine, press the throttle down to the floor and check that the no load maximum RPM is OK, if it is not, adjust using the maximum speed adjusting screw.

No Load Maximum Speed Setting:

        4300-4500RPM

3. If no faults are found in step2, ensure that the interchange overflow screw (Out) and the inlet (No Mark) are fitted in the correct positions, if not refit in correct positions.

4. If no faults are found in step3, check the fuel system components and/or lines for leaks and/or damage, if faults are found repair/replace as required.

5. If no faults are found in step4, disconnect the inlet hoses from the fuel filter and pour diesel fuel directly into the injection pump, if the condition now improves replace the fuel filter. If the condition does not improve after the fuel filter has been replaced, check the condition and/or operation of the priming pump, if faults are found repair/replace as required.

6. If no faults are found in step5, check the injection timing by releasing the cold start advance systen (where fitted) and checking the plunger stroke.

Injection Plunger Stroke: **1.29-1.35mm**

If the timing setting is not as shown, adjust to suit

7. If no faults are found in step6, check the injection nozzle pressure.

Injection Nozzle Pressure:

        17,652-18,633kpa (No1 Opening Pressure)
        12,945-13,533kpa (No2 Opening Pressure

If the pressure is not as shown adjust pressure to suit, if the pressure cannot be adjusted replace the faulty injector nozzle/s as required.

Excessive Exhaust Smoke

1. Check the condition and/or operation of the air cleaner element, if faults are found repair/replace as required.

2. If no faults are found in step1, check the engine oil consumption, if faults are found repair/replace as required.

3. If the oil consumption is OK in step2, check the injection timing by releasing the cold start advance system (where fitted) and checking the plunger stroke.

Injection Plunger Stroke: 1.29-1.35mm

If the timing setting is not as shown, adjust to suit.

(Please Note: If the exhaust smoke is black it tends to indicate that the timing is advanced and if the smoke is white that the timing is retarded).

4. If no faults are found in step3, disconnect the inlet hoses from the fuel filter and pour diesel fuel directly into the injection pump, if the condition now improves replace the fuel filter. If the condition does not improve after the fuel filter has been replaced, check the condition and/or operation of the priming pump, if faults are found repair/replace as required. *(Please Note: At between 2000-3000RPM a blocked fuel filter tends to make the exhaust smoke white).*

5. If no faults are found in step4, check the injection nozzle pressure.

Injection Nozzle Pressure:
      17,652-18,633kpa (No1 Opening Pressure)
Injection Nozzle Pressure:
      12,945-13,533kpa (No2 Opening Pressure)

6. If the pressure is not as shown adjust pressure to suit, if the pressure cannot be adjusted replace the faulty injector nozzle/s as required. *(Please Note: Excessive exhaust smoke is normally caused when the nozzle pressure is to low)*

Fuel Consumption is Poor

1. If the fuel consumption is poor, check the fuel system components and/or lines for leaks and/or damage, if faults are found repair/replace as required.

2. If no faults are found in step1, check the engine idle speed setting is correct.

Idle Speed: 600-700RPM (Manual)
Idle Speed: 750-850RPM (Auto)

If the idle speed setting is not correct adjust to suit.

3. If the idle speed setting is OK in step2, check the no load maximum speed setting is OK by starting the engine, pressing down the throttle pedal to the floor and cheking the no load maximum speed setting.

No Load Maximum Speed Setting: 4300-4500RPM

If the setting is not OK, adjust using the maximum speed adjusting screw.

4. If no faults are found in step3, check the injection timing by releasing the cold start advance systen (where fitted) and checking the plunger stroke.

Injection Plunger Stroke: 1.29-1.35mm

If the timing setting is not as shown, adjust to suit.

5. If no faults are found in step4, check the injection nozzle pressure.

Injection Nozzle Pressure:
      17,652-18,633kpa (No1 Opening Pressure)
Injection Nozzle Pressure:
      12,945-13,533kpa (No2 Opening Pressure)

6. If the pressure is not as shown adjust pressure to suit, if the pressure cannot be adjusted replace the faulty injector nozzle/s as required.

Noise When The Engine Is Warm

1. If the engine is noisy when it is warm, first check the operation of the temperature gauge if that is Ok, check the operation of the thermostat if faults are found repair/replace as required.

2. If no faults are found in step1, check the injection timing by releasing the cold start advance systen (where fitted) and checking the plunger stroke.

Injection Plunger Stroke:
            1.29-1.35mm

If the timing setting is not as shown, adjust to suit.

3. If no faults are found in step2, check the injection nozzle pressure.

Injection Nozzle Pressure:
      17,652-18,633kpa (No1 Opening Pressure)
Injection Nozzle Pressure:
      12,945-13,533kpa (No2 Opening Pressure)

4. If the pressure is not as shown adjust pressure to suit, if the pressure cannot be adjusted replace the faulty injector nozzle/s as required.

Engine Will Not Return to Idle

1. Operate the adjusting lever on top of the injection pump and ensure that the engine returns to normal idle speed, if it does the throttle cable is binding or not adjusted correctly and needs fixing.

2. If the engine does not return to idle in step1, the injection pump is faulty and needs replacing.

Engine Will Not Shut Off With The Key

1. Check the fuel cut solenoid operation by disconnecting the connector on top of the fuel cut solenoid and check if the engine stops, if it does the starter switch is faulty and needs repairing and/or replacing.

2. If the engine does not stop in step1, either the fuel cut solenoid is faulty or the solenoid is blocked, if required repair/replace as required.

Diesel System Electrical Diagnosis

Engine Will Not Start When Cold (Superglow System Europe and Australia)

Please Note: Before starting test please ensure that the battery is fully charged, the engine cranks normally and that all the fuse links are OK.

1. Disconnect the water temperature sensor and check if the indicator lamp lights up when the starter switch is in the ON position.

Specified Light Up Time: **6-7seconds**

2. If the light up time is not as shown in step1, check the condition of the relevant system fuse, if the fuse is blown, check for short circuit in the harness and repair as required.

3. If the fuse is OK in step2, check the condition and/or operation of the glow indicator lamp globe, if faults are found repair/replace as required.

4. If the bulb is OK in step3, check for battery voltage to the terminal 3 (harness side) of the pre-heating teimer connector, if the voltage is OK, replace the timer assembly.

5. If the light up time in step1 is OK, put the starter switch to OFF, and check for battery voltage to terminal 1of the pre heating timer with the ignition switch in the ON position.

6. If there is NO voltage in step5, check that there is 1v or less to terminal 9 on the timer, if there is the timer is faulty and needs replacing.

7. If the voltage in step5 is OK, check if voltage to the terminal 1of the pre heating timer is terminated after the engine has started, if it does not, start the engine and check if there is voltage at terminal 9 of the pre heating timer, if there is not, repair fault in the charging system. If there is voltage the timer is faulty and should be replaced.

8. If the voltage operation is OK in step7, put the starter switch to the OFF position, put the starter switch into the ON position and check the current flow to the terminal 5 of the timer.

Current Flow: **120 Seconds.**

9. If the pre-heat time differs from above or there is NO voltage at all in step8, replace the timer.

10. If the current flow is OK in step8, after completing pre-heating check for voltage at terminal 5, check again this time when the starter switch is in the Start position.

11. If there is no voltage in step10, replace the timer.

12. If the voltage is OK in step10, put the starter switch into the off position, place the starter switch into the ON position and check for voltage to the glow plugs a few seconds later (the the voltage should drop by about 50%).

13. If there is no voltage at all in step12, check for battery voltage at the (-) side of the glow plug resistor, if there is no voltage, replace the No1 glow plug relay.

14. If the voltage in step12 stays at battery voltage or falls to 0v, check for battery voltage to the (+) side of the glow plug resistor, if there is no voltage replace the No2 glow plug relay.

15. If the voltage is OK in step12, check the glow plug resistance.

Specified Resistance: **Approx. 0 ohms**

If the resistance is not OK, replace the glow plug/s as required.

16. If the glow plug resistance is OK in step15, the glow plug/s are OK, then replace the water temperature senson harness connector.

VEHICLE SERVICE INFORMATION

Vehicle Filling Capacities

Engine Oil with Filter: .... 9.3 Litres
Engine Oil without Filter: .... 8.0 Litres
Engine Oil with Dry Fill: 9.6Litres
Cooling System: ... 10.4 Litres (Without Heater Manual)
Cooling System: .... 10.2 Litres (Without Heater Auto)
Cooling System: .... 11.1 Litres (With Heater Manual)
Cooling System: .... 10.9 Litres (With Heater Auto)
Cooling System: .... 11.9 Litres
      (With Front/Rear Heater Manual Except Europe)
Cooling System: .... 11.7 Litres
         (With Front/Rear Heater Auto Except Europe)
Cooling System: .... 12.0 Litres
            (With Front/Rear Heater Manual Europe)
Cooling System: .... 11.8 Litres
            (With Front/Rear Heater Auto Europe)
Manual Transmission: .... 2.7 Litres (5 Speed)
Auto Transmission:15.0 Litres (Dry Fill) 6.0 Litres (Refill)
Front Differential: .... 2.6 Litres
Rear Differential: .... 2.5 Litres
Transfer Case: 1.3Litres

Vehicle Component Service Interval Changes

Timing Belt:
      Change Every 60Months/100,000kms

Check Valve Clearance:
      Every 24Months/40,000kms

Engine Coolant/Anti Freeze:
      Change at 24 Months/40,000kms

Air Cleaner Element:
      Change Every 60 Months/100,000kms

Fuel Filter:
      Change Every 24 Months/40,000kms

Engine Oil:
      Change Every 3 Months/5,000kms

Engine Oil Filter:
      Change Every 6 Months/10,000kms

Brake Fluid:
      Change Every 24 Months/40,000kms

Manual Transmission Oil:
      Change Every 18 Months/30,000kms

Auto Transmission Oil:
      Change Every 24 Months/40,000kms

Front Differential Oil:
      Change Every 18 Months/30,000kms

Transfer Case Oil
      Change Every 18 Months/30,000kms

Rear Differential Oil:
      Change Every 18 Months/30,000kms

Front/Rear Wheel Bearings
      Repack Every 12Months/20,000kms

Toyota Landrcuiser HDJ80 Series 1HD-FT Engine 1995 ON

Toyota Landcruiser Late 80's Series

Toyota Landrcuiser HDJ80 Series 1HD-FT Engine 1995 ON

Engine Checks

Valve Clearance Check

1. Remove cylinder head cover.

2. Set the No1 piston to TDC/Compression by turning the crankshaft pulley clockwise and line up the groove on the pulley with the timing gear cover groove.

3. Check that the valverockers on the No1 cylinder are loose and the valve rockers on the No6 cylinder are tight.

If this is not the case, turn the crankshaft 1 full turn in a clockwise direction and then line up the both grooves.

4. Check the valve clearances on the 1,5,9 inlet valves and 2,4,8 exhaust valves with a feeler gauge and record the measurements between the adjusting screw on the rocker arm and the valve bridge.

Specified Inlet Valve Clearance: 0.17-0.23mm
Specified Exhaust Valve Clearance: 0.47-0.53mm

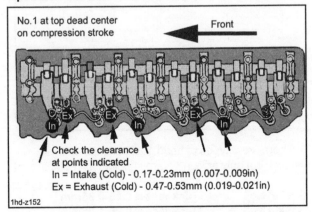

No.1 at top dead center on compression stroke

Front

Check the clearance at points indicated
In = Intake (Cold) - 0.17-0.23mm (0.007-0.009in)
Ex = Exhaust (Cold) - 0.47-0.53mm (0.019-0.021in)

1hd-z152

5. Turn the crankshaft in a clockwise direction one full turn (360°) and check the valve clearances on the 3, 7, 11 inlet valve and 6,10, 12 on the exhaust valve. with a feeler gauge and record the measurements between the adjusting screw on the rocker arm and the valve bridge.

Specified Inlet Valve Clearance: 0.17-0.23mm
Specified Exhaust Valve Clearance: 0.47-0.53mm

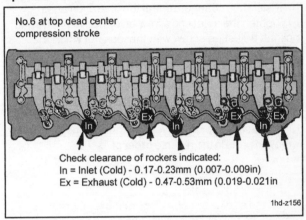

No.6 at top dead center compression stroke

Check clearance of rockers indicated:
In = Inlet (Cold) - 0.17-0.23mm (0.007-0.009in)
Ex = Exhaust (Cold) - 0.47-0.53mm (0.019-0.021in

1hd-z156

6. If the adjustments are not as shown, adjust the clearance by loosening the lock nut on the adjusting screw until the screw and the valve stem are completely separated.

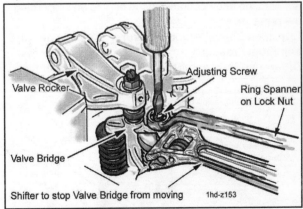

Adjusting Screw

Valve Rocker

Ring Spanner on Lock Nut

Valve Bridge

Shifter to stop Valve Bridge from moving   1hd-z153

7. Loosen the lock nut on the valve rocker arm and the loosen the adjusting screw. Insert a 0.20mm feeler gauge for the inlet valves and 0.50mm for the exhaust valves between the adjusting screw on the valve rocker and the valve bridge.

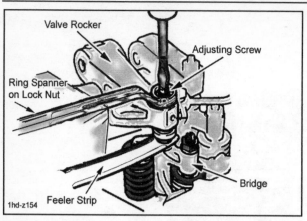

1hd-z154

Valve Rocker • Adjusting Screw • Ring Spanner on Lock Nut • Bridge • Feeler Strip

8. Turn the adjusting screw on the valve rocker arm until the feeler gauge slides in and a very slight resistance can be felt, then lock the adjusting screw with the lock nut.

9. With the feeler gauge still inserted, check that the resistance of the feeler gauge remains the same when the adjusting screw on the valve bridge is loosened. If the resistance changes repeat the operation again.

10. Tighten the adjusting screw on the valve bridge and lock the adjusting screw with the lock nut when the resistance on the feeler gauge starts to get stronger.

11. Loosen the lock nut on the valve rocker arm and turn the adjusting screw on the valve rocker arm until the feeler gauge slides with a slight resistance, then lock the adjusting screw with the lock nut.

12. Replace the rocker cover and then replace any other removed parts in the reverse order of removal.

Compression Check

1. Run the engine to normal operating temperatures, remove the rocker cover, injection pipes and the No1 nozzle leakage pipe. Disconnect the injection pump cut off solenoid connector .

2. Remove the No1 injection nozzle and then check each cylinder compression by installing a compression tester to the engine, cranking the engine and recording the pressure on each cylinder.

Specified Compression Pressure: 3432kpa or more
Minimum Pressure: 2452kpa or more
Difference Between Each Cylinder: 490kpa or less.

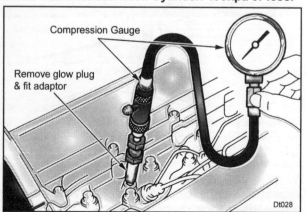

Compression Gauge • Remove glow plug & fit adaptor

Dt028

3. If the pressure is less than shown on one or more cylinders, pour a small amount of oil through the injection nozzle hole and recheck the pressure. If the pressure is now OK, check the condition of the piston rings and/or cylinder bore. If the pressure is still low, check for a sticking valve and/or bad valve seating.

4. Replace any removed parts in the reverse order of removal.

Piston Protrusion Check

1. Clean the cylinder block, set the No1 piston to TDC, place a dial gauge on the block and set the dial gauge to zero.

2. Find the point where the piston top protrudes the most by turning the crankshaft slightly the left and right.

3. Measure each cylinder in two places as shown and record the average of the two measurements on each cylinder.

Specified Protrusion Measurement: 0.175-0.425mm.

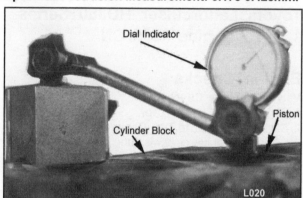

Dial Indicator • Cylinder Block • Piston

L020

4. If the protrusion measurement is not as shown, remove the piston and con rod, replace it and check again

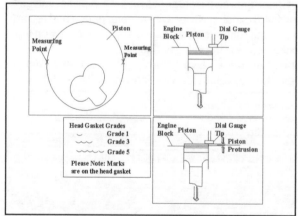

Measuring Point • Piston • Measuring Point • Engine Block • Piston • Dial Gauge Tip

Head Gasket Grades
Grade 1
Grade 3
Grade 5
Please Note: Marks are on the head gasket

Engine Block • Piston • Dial Gauge Tip • Piston • Protrusion

5. There are 5 types of head gaskets used on this vehicle, but only type 1,3,5 are supplied as replacement parts.

Gasket No1:   Thickness is 0.85-0.95mm
Gasket No3:   Thickness is 0.95-1.05mm
Gasket No5:   Thickness is 1.05-1.15mm

6. Select the largest of the protrusion measurements and select the gasket to suit as shown below.

Protrusion Measurement	Gasket Size
0.225mm or less	**0.85-0.95mm**
0.226-0.325mm	**0.95-1.05mm**
0.326mm or more	**1.05-1.15mm**

Cylinder Head Tightening Procedures

1. With the cylinder head inplace, tighten the bolts in three steps, if any of the bolts break or deform replace them as required.

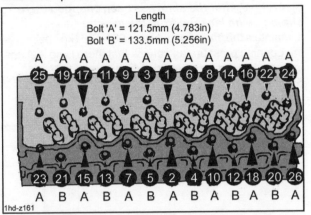

2. Apply a light coat of oil to each bolt thread, and using a torque wrench tighten the 26 bolts in three separate stages to a **torque of 68.6Nm.**

The bolts are supplied in two different lengths

Bolts (A):   121.5mm

Bolts (B):   133.5mm

If any of the bolts will not torque correctly, replace as required.

3. Mark the front of the cylinder head bolts with white paint, **tighten each bolt another 90°** in the sequence shown, and **then tighten each bolt a further 90°** in the same sequence and now ensure that the paint marks on all of the bolts are facing to the rear.

Oil Pressure Check

1. Remove the oil pressure switch from the block and install a pressure gauge in its place.

2. Run the engine to normal operating temperature and the check the engine oil pressure.

Specified Oil Pressure: 29kpa or more @ Idle

Specified Oil Pressure: 250-600kpa or more @ 3000RPM

3. If the pressure is not as shown, repair/replace as required.

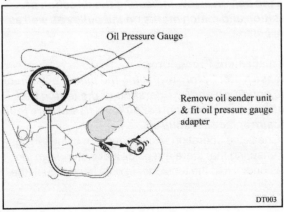

Cooling System Thermostat Check

1. Remove the thermostat from the engine and put into a suitable container of water.

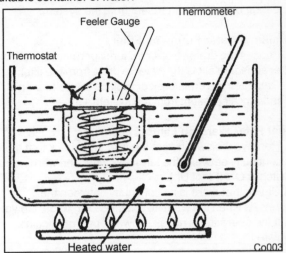

2. Heat the water gradually and check the valve opening temperature and valve lift.

Valve Opening Temperature: 74-78°c

Valve Lift: 10mm or more @ 90°c

If the operation is not as shown above replace the thermostat.

3. Check that the valve spring is tight when the thermostat is fully closed, if not replace the thermostat.

Fuel Filter Check and Replacement

1. Remove the fuel filter sensor, drain the fuel, then remove the fuel filter.

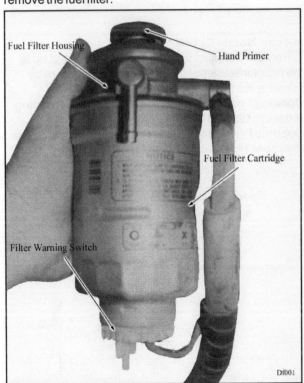

2. Clean the fuel filter mounting bracket and then coat the fuel filter sealing ring with some diesel fuel.

3. Screw the fuel filter on until a slight resistance is felt and then turn another 2/3 of a turn or until suitably tight.
4. Install the fuel filter sensor (if fitted) to the new filter and then bleed any air present from the system.

Draining Water From The Filter
1. Loosen the drain cock 4 or 5 turns or remove the fuel filter sensor to allow the water to drain from the filter.
2. Retighten the drain cock or replace the sensor and bleed any air present from the system.

Fuel Filter Warning Lamp Check
1. Remove the switch from the filter and check that there is continuity between the terminals when the warning switch is ON (Float Up)
2. Check that there is no continuity between the terminals when the warning switch is OFF (Float Down)
3. If the operation is not as shown, repair/replace as required.

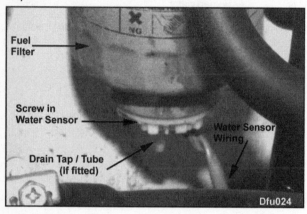

Injector Nozzle Check
1. Remove the injector from the vehicle, connect up to the pressure tester and check the initial pressure by pumping the tester handle a few times.
Opening Pressure: 23,046-24,026kpa (No2 Opening Pressure 1995-1996)
Opening Pressure: 23,144-24,124kpa (No2 Opening Pressure 1996 On)

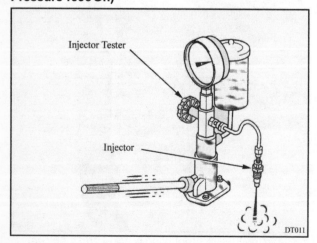

2. If the opening pressure is not as shown above, take

the injector to pieces and change the adjusting shim on the top of the No2 pressure spring so as the correct pressure is recorded.
3. After the pressure in step3 is correct disassemble the nozzle for the adjustment of the No1 opening pressure.
Opening Pressure: 17,650-18,633kpa (No1 Opening Pressure)
Please Note: The adjusting shims vary in 0.025mm thicknesses, each 0.025mm will adjust the pressure by 470kpa. After the shim has been changed there should be no leakage from the injector.
4. Maintain the pressure between 981-1961kpa below the opening pressure and check that there is no leakage from the injector for a period of 10seconds.
5. Check the spray pattern by pumping the pressure tester handle 4-6 times or more per second and check the injection spray pattern.

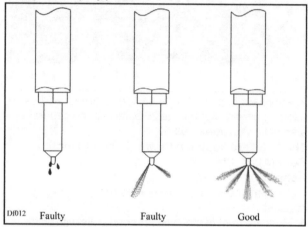

6. If the operation and/or spray pattern is not as shown, repair/replace the nozzle/s as required.

Timing Belt Removal and Replacement
Removal Procedures
1. Remove the timing belt cover and set the No1 piston to BDC/Compression by turning the crankshaft pulley in a clockwise direction until the No1 and No2 camshaft pulley groves line up with the BDC marks.
2. Remove the timing belt from the engine by alternately loosening the 2 tensioner bolts, remove them from the tensioner and then remove the timing belt.
Please Note: If the timing belt is being re-used, draw on the belt an arrow indicating the direction of rotation and match marks on the pulley as well as the belt.

Replacement Procedures
Please Note: Before replacing the timing belt check the condition and/or operation of the timing belt pulleys, tensioners and/or pulleys, if faults are found repair/replace as required.
1. Check the operation and/or condition of the tensioner by ensuring that there are no oil leaks at all from the tensioner. Hold the tensioner in both hands, push the

tensioner rod as hard as you can and ensure that the rod does not move at all. Measure the protrusion of the push rod from the end of the housing.

Specified Protrusion: **9.0-9.8mm**

If the tensioner operation is not as shown above, replace the tensioner.

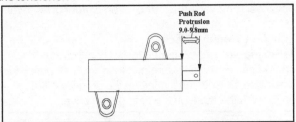

2. Before fitting the belt to the engine, set the No1 piston to BDC by turning the crankshaft pulley in a clockwise direction and ensuring that the timing mark on the No2 camshaft pulley lines up with the BDC mark, then ensure that the No1 camshaft pulley mark lines up with the BDC mark.

3. Fit the timing belt to the engine under tension between the No1 and No2 camshaft pulleys.

4. Using a press, press down the rod until the holes in the push rod line up with housing, then install a 1.5mm hex wrench into the holes to keep the rod setting into the correct position

5. Temporarily install the tensioner with the 2 bolts while pushing the idler pulley towards the timing belt. Alternately tighten the **two tensioner bolts to 13Nm** and the remove the hex wrench from the tensioner

6. Check the valve timing by turning the crankshaft pulley in a clockwise direction and ensure that all of the timing marks on each of the pulleys all line up. If they do not, remove the belt and re-start the installation process again.

7. Replace the timing cover to the engine and the replace any more removed parts in the reverse order of removal

Timing Belt Warning Lamp Reset Procedures

1. Remove the grommet from the speedometer and turn off the lamp by pushing the warning lamp reset switch, then replace the grommet.

2. Start the engine and ensure that the light stays off.

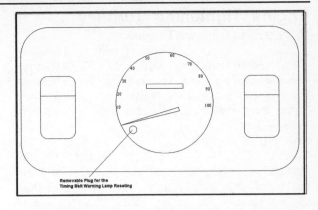

Timing Belt Warning Lamp Reset Procedures (Change Screw Position on the Back of the Instrument Cluster)

1. Remove the instrument cluster from the vehicle, connect terminals A&B shown in the diagrams and then remove the CHARGE fuse from the vehicle.

2. Turn the ignition switch to ON and check that the warning lights light up, if not the check the condition and/or operation of the globe.

3. Check the condition and/or operation of the reset switches by checking that there is intermittent continuity between terminals A&B when the reset switch is pressed, if not repair/replace the speedometer/ instrument cluster as required.

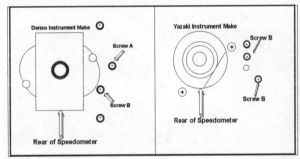

Timing Belt Replacement Torques

No1 Camshaft Pulley: 98Nm
No2 Camshaft Pulley: 31Nm
Tensioner Bolts: 13Nm

Engine Tightening Torques

Cylinder Head Tightening Torque Bolts:
.... 68.6Nm (Tighten in 3 Stages)
Cylinder Head Tightening Torque Bolts: . 90° (2ⁿᵈ Stage)
Cylinder Head Tightening Torque Bolts: . 90° (3ʳᵈ Stage)
Exhaust Manifold Bolts and Nuts: 41.7Nm
Turbo Charger to Exhaust Manifold: 52Nm
Turbine Outlet Elbow: 52Nm
No1 Turbo Water Pipe: 7.8Nm
Turbo Oil Pipe: 18.1Nm
Intake Pipe: 19.6Nm
Inlet Manifold Bolts and Nuts: 19.6Nm
Injection Nozzle: 25Nm
Tensioner Bolts: 13Nm
Idler Pulley to Timing Cover: 34.5Nm
Flywheel Bolts: 127.4Nm
Drive Plate: 127.4Nm
Connecting Rod Caps: 36.8Nm
Connecting Rod Caps: .... 90° (2ⁿᵈ Stage)
Main Bearings: .... 103Nm (12 Point Head Bolts)
Main Bearings: ...... 90° (2ⁿᵈ Stage 12 Point Head Bolts)
Main Bearings: .... 18.1Nm (6Point Head Bolts)
Crankshaft Pulley Bolt to Crankshaft: 430Nm
Camshaft Gear No1 Bolt: 98Nm
Camshaft Gear No2 Bolt: 31Nm
Oil Pump to Block: 19.6Nm

System Adjustments

Idle Speed Check

1. Before checking the idle speed, ensure that the engine is at normal operating temperature, the air cleaner OK and fitted, all of the accessories are fitted, all vacuum lines are OK, valve clearance and injection timing are set correctly and that the transmission is in "N".
2. Install a tachometer to the engine, ensure that the adjusting lever touches the idle speed adjusting screw when the throttle pedal is released, if it does not adjust to suit.
3. Start the engine, let it run and check the idle speed.
Idle Speed: 700±50RPM (Manual)
Idle Speed: 800±50RPM (Auto)
4. If the idle speed is not as shown, disconnect the throttle linkage and loosen the lock nut on the idle speed adjusting screw and adjust the idle speed by turning the idle speed adjusting screw.
5. Tighten the lock nut, recheck the idle speed, reconnect the throttle linkage and then re-check the idle speed.
6. Remove the tachometer from the engine and replace any other removed parts in the reverse order of removal.

Injection Timing Check

1. Set the No1 or No6 piston to TDC on the compression stroke by turning the crankshaft pulley in a clockwise direction and lining up the groove on the pulley with the mark on the timing gear cover.

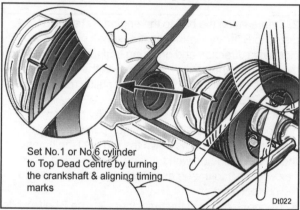

Set No.1 or No.6 cylinder to Top Dead Centre by turning the crankshaft & aligning timing marks

2. Loosen the union nuts from the No1 and No5 injector pipe, remove the plug bolt from the distributor head of the injection pump and install a dial gauge to the bolt hole.

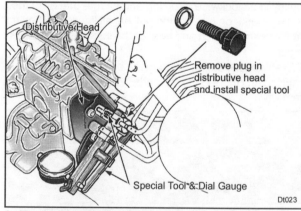

Distributive Head

Remove plug in distributive head and install special tool

Special Tool & Dial Gauge

3. (For Vehicles with ACSD Only), Turn the cold start lever in an anti clockwise direction about 20° and put a metal plate of between 9.0-10.0mm between the cold start lever and the thermo wax plunger.
4. Turn the crankshaft in an anti-clockwise direction, set the dial gauge to zero when it reaches its minimum value.
Specified Minimum Value: 0mm
5. Slowly turn the crankshaft in a clockwise direction until the groove on the crankshaft pulley lines up with the mark on the timing cover, then record the plunger stroke.
Specified Plunger Stroke: 1.37-1.43mm (Australia)
Specified Plunger Stroke: 1.52-1.58mm (Europe)

6. If the timing needs adjustment, loosen the 4 remaining injection pipe union nuts on the injection pump side, the 2bolts holding the pump to the pump bracket, the two nuts holding the pump to the timing gear.

7. If the plunger stroke is less than shown, turn the pump towards the engine, if it more turn away from the engine.

8. Retighten the two nuts holding the pump to the timing gear, the bolt holding the pump to the pump bracket and then recheck the injection pump plunger stroke.

9. If fitted remove the plate from the ACSD device, the dial gauge and replace the bolt plug, tighten the union nuts on the injection pipes and replace any more removed parts in the reverse order of removal.

Maximum Speed Adjustment
With Throttle Position Sensor

1. With a tachometer installed to the engine, press down the throttle fully and check that the adjusting lever does not move when you try and push it to the maximum speed side, if the operation is not as shown, adjust the throttle linkage as required.

Check that the adjusting lever touches the maximum speed screw when the throttle pedal is pressed down all of the way, if not adjust to suit.

Without Throttle Position Sensor

Maximum Speed Adjusting Screw

1. Check that the adjusting lever touches the maximum speed screw when the throttle pedal is pressed down all of the way, if not adjust to suit.

2. Start the engine, press down the throttle pedal all the way and check the maximum speed.

Specified Maximum Speed: 4300-4500RPM.

3. If the maximum speed is not as shown, remove the injection pump and adjust the maximum speed as required.

Fuel Heater System Check

Fuel Heater Check

1. Apply 34.7 ± 5.3kpa or more of vacuum to the vacuum switch port and with an ohmmeter check the resistance between the No1 terminal and the switch body

Specified Resistance: 0.5-2.0ohms @ 20°c

2. If the resistance is not as shown, replace the fuel heater and vacuum switch assembly.

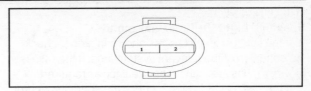

Vacuum Switch Check

1. With an ohmmeter check that there is no continuity between the No1 terminal and the switch body, if there is replace the fuel heater and vacuum switch assembly.

2. Apply 34.7± 5.3kpa or more of vacuum to the vacuum switch and with an ohmmeter check that there is continuity between the No1 terminal and the switch body, if there is no continuity, replace the fuel heater and vacuum switch assembly.

Use heater switch diagram

Fuel Heater Relay Check

1. With an ohmmeter check that there is continuity between terminals 1 and 3 and that there is no continuity between terminals 2 and 4.

If the continuity is not as shown above, replace the relay.

2. Apply battery volts between the continuity between terminals 1 and 3 and that there is no continuity between terminals 2 and 4.

If the operation is not as shown above, replace the relay.

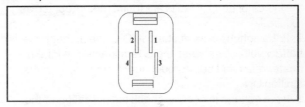

Pre-Heating System Checks
Pre Heating System Check
Power Supply Check

1. Check the operation of the intake heater system, if faults are found repair/replace as required.

2. If no faults are found in step1, disconnect the water temperature sensor, switch the ignition ON and check that the pre-heat side of the intake heater has battery voltage for 81 seconds.

3. If the pre-heat side of the intake heater does not have battery voltage for 81 seconds in step2, check the condition and/or operation of the fuse link for the intake heater, if faults are found repair/replace as required.

4. If the fuse link is OK in step3, carry out the control section check.

5. If the pre-heat side of the intake heater has battery voltage for 81 seconds, reconnect the water temperature sensor harness connector.

Control Section Check
Please Note: Carry out this check with the intake heater lead connected correctly

1. Disconnect the water temperature sensor and check if the indicator lamp lights up when the starter switch is in the ON position.

Specified Light Up Time: 6.5seconds

2. If the light up time is not as shown in step1, check the condition of the relevant system fuse, if the fuse is blown, if faults are found repair/replace as required.

3. If the fuse is OK in step2, check the condition and/or operation of the glow indicator lamp globe, if faults are found repair/replace as required.

4. If the bulb is OK in step3, check for grounding of the terminals 18, 16 and/or 25 (26Pin ECU Connector with EGR System), or the terminal 5 (pre heat timer without EGR system).

5. If there is no grounding in step4, check for open circuit or faulty ground in the harness between the terminals 18, 16 and/or 25 (26Pin ECU Connector with EGR System), or the terminal 5 (pre heat timer without EGR system) and body ground. If faults are found repair/replace as required.

6. If there is grounding in step4, check for battery voltage to the terminal 3 (harness side 16Pin ECU connector with EGR system) or the terminal 4 (harness side pre heat timer connector without EGR system) if the voltage is OK, replace the ECU or the pre-heat timer assembly. If the voltage is not OK check for open circuit between the terminal 3 (harness side 16Pin ECU connector with EGR system) or the terminal 4 (harness side pre heat timer connector without EGR system) and the indicator lamp, if faults are found repair/replace as required.

7. If the light up time in step1 is OK, check that there is battery voltage between the G terminal on the intake heater relay and body ground for 81 seconds with the ignition ON.

8. If the voltage is not OK, check the operation of the intake heater relay, if faults are found repair/replace as required.

9. If the relay is OK in step8, when the ignition is switched ON, does the terminal 2 (26Pin ECU Connector with EGR System), or the terminal 4 (pre heat timer without EGR system) have battery voltage for 81 seconds, if it does not replace the ECU or pre-heat timer.

10. If the battery voltage is OK in step9, check for open circuit in the harness between the terminal 2 (26Pin ECU Connector with EGR System), or the terminal 4 (pre heat timer without EGR system) and terminal g of the intake heater relay and/or open circuit or faults in the ground circuit between the terminal e of the intake heater relay and body ground, if faults are found repair/replace as required.

11. If the voltage is OK in step7, reconnect the water temperature sensor connector and carry out the power supply check

Fuel Cut Solenoid Operation Check

1. Put the starter switch into the ON position and check for an operating noise from the solenoid while repeatedly connecting and disconnecting the solenoid, if a noise is heard the solenoid is OK.

2. If the solenoid noise is not heard, check the condition and/or operation of the relevant fuse, if faults are found repair/replace as required.

3. If the fuse is OK in step2, apply battery volts to the solenoid and check for a noise, if a noise can be heard, check the condition of the harness between the fuse and the fuel cut solenoid, if faults are found repair/replace as required.

4. If no noise can be heard in step3, replace the fuel cut solenoid.

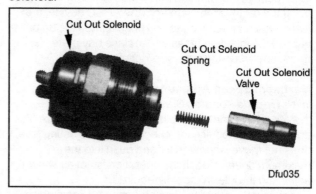

Cut Out Solenoid

Cut Out Solenoid Spring

Cut Out Solenoid Valve

Dfu035

Emission ECU Check (With EGR System)

Please Note: There are two connectors on this ECU, one with 26 pins (connector A) and one with 16 pins (connector B)

1. Disconnect the harness connector from the timer and check the connector on the harness side as shown in the chart below.

Check For	Between Terminals	Condition	Specified Value
Voltage	B7 - ground		Battery Volts
Voltage	B3 - ground	starter switch OFF	No Volts
Voltage	B3 - ground	starter switch ON	Battery Volts
Voltage	A15, A26 -gnd	starter switch OFF	No Volts
Voltage	A15, A26 -gnd	starter switch ON	Battery Volts
Continuity	A12 -ground	starter switch OFF	No Volts
Continuity	A12 -ground	starter switch ON	Battery Volts
Continuity	A6 - ground	starter switch OFF	No Volts
Continuity	A6 - ground	starter switch ON	Battery Volts
Continuity	A2 - ground		Continuity
Continuity	11 - 24		Continuity
Voltage	A18, A16, A25 - ground		Continuity

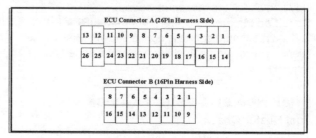

ECU Connector A (26Pin Harness Side)

13	12	11	10	9	8	7	6	5	4	3	2	1
26	25	24	23	22	21	20	19	18	17	16	15	14

ECU Connector B (16Pin Harness Side)

8	7	6	5	4	3	2	1
16	15	14	13	12	11	10	9

Pre Heating Timer Circuit Check (Without EGR System)

Please Note: There is only one connector (8Pin) on the pre-heating timer

1. Disconnect the harness connector from the timer and check the connector on the harness side as shown in the chart below.

Check For	Between	Condition Terminals	Specified Value
Voltage	4 - ground	starter switch OFF	No Volts
Voltage	4 - ground	starter switch ON	Battery Volts
Voltage	1 - ground	starter switch OFF	No Volts
Voltage	1 - ground	starter switch ON	Battery Volts
Voltage	7 - ground	starter switch OFF	No Volts
Voltage	7 - ground	starter switch ON	Battery Volts
Voltage	6 - ground	starter switch OFF	No Volts
Voltage	6 - ground	starter switch ON	Battery Volts
Continuity	3 - ground		Continuity
Continuity	8 - ground		Continuity

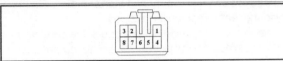

No1 Intake Heater Relay Check

1. With an ohmmeter check that there is continuity between terminals e and g, and that there is no continuity between terminals B and G.

If the continuity is not as shown above, replace the relay

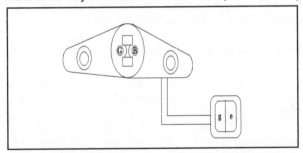

2. Apply battery volts between the continuity between terminals e and g, and that there is continuity between terminals B and G.

If the operation is not as shown above, replace the relay.

Intake Heater Check.

1. Remove the intake heater harness connector and check for continuity between the terminal of the heater and ground.
2. If there is no continuity, replace the intake heater

Water Temperature Sensor Check

1. Disconnect sensor harness connector and check the resistance between terminals at varying temperatures.

Coolant Temperature (°c)	Resistance(k/ohms)
-20	10-20
0	4-7
20	2-3
40	0.9-1.3
60	0.4-0.7
80	0.2-0.4

If the resistance is not as shown, repair/replace as required.

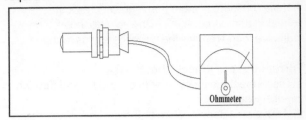

Turbocharger System Checks

Intake Air System Check

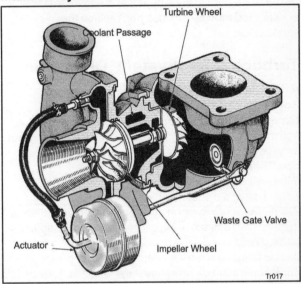

1. Check for leaks and/or blockages between the air cleaner and turbo charger inlet, and between the turbo charger outlet and cylinder head
2. Check for blocked air cleaner, damaged or leaking hoses and/or connections, damage in any of the components.
3. If faults are found repair/replace as required.

Exhaust System Checks.

1. Check for leaks and/or blockages between the air cleaner and turbo charger inlet, and between the turbo charger outlet and the exhaust pipe.
2. Check for damage to any of the components, any foreign objects in the passages, leaks and/or cracks in any of the components.
3. If faults are found repair/replace as required.

Turbocharger Pressure Check

1. Install a 3 way union to the to the hose between the vacuum pipe and the vacuum pipe and install a pressure gauge to it.
2. Press down the clutch pedal, then press down the throttle pedal fully down. Run the engine at maximum speed (4400RPM) and then check the pressure.
Specified Turbo Pressure: 38.6-50.0kpa
3. If the pressure is less than shown, check the opera-

tion of the intake air system and exhaust system, if no leaks are found replace the turbocharger.

4. If the pressure is more than shown, check the condition and/or operation of the actuator hose, if no faults are found replace the turbocharger as required.

Turbo Impeller Wheel Check

1. Disconnect the air cleaner hose and try and turn the impeller wheel.

2. If the wheel does not turn or turns with a drag, replace the turbocharger as required.

Actuator Check

1. Disconnect the actuator hose and apply between 88-96kpa of vacuum to the actuator and ensure that the actuator rod moves, if it dose not, replace the turbocharger

Turbocharger System Diagnosis and Troubleshooting

Poor Fuel Consumption, Lack of Power or Excessive Fuel Consumption

1. If the turbo charger system pressure is low, carry out a system pressure test.

Specified Turbo Pressure: 38.6-50.0kpa

If the pressure is not as shown, repair/replace turbocharger as required.

2. If no faults are found in step1, check the operation of the air intake system, if faults are found repair/replace as required.

3. If no faults are found in step2, check the condition and/or operation of the exhaust system, if faults are found repair/replace as required.

4. If no faults are found in step3, check the condition and/or operation of the turbocharger, if faults are found repair/replace as required.

Abnormal Noise From The Turbocharger

1. Check the condition and/or installation of the turbo insulator and/or bolts, if faults are found repair/replace as required.

2. If no faults are found in step1, check the condition and/or installation of the exhaust system, if faults are found repair/replace as required.

3. If no faults are found in step2, check the condition and/or operation of the turbocharger, if faults are found repair/replace as required.

Poor Oil Consumption or White Exhaust

1. If there are oil leaks found from the turbo seal, check for oil leaks into the exhaust system by removing the turbine elbow and checking for excessive carbon deposits on the turbine wheel, if faults are found repair/replace the turbocharger as required.

2. If no faults are found in step1, check for oil leaks into the intake air system by checking the axial play in the impeller wheel.

Specified Axial Play: 0.13mm

3. If faults are found repair/replace the turbocharger as required.

Injection System and Engine Diagnosis and Troubleshooting

Engine Will Not Crank

1. Check the condition and/or operation of the battery cables between the battery and starter motor, if faults are found repair/replace as required.

2. If no faults are found in step1, check the condition and/or operation of the battery, alternator output and/or drive belt, if faults are found repair/replace as required.

3. If no faults are found in step2, check the condition and/or operation of the starter motor, if faults are found repair/replace as required.

Engine Cranks Slowly or Will Not Start

1. Check the condition and/or operation of the battery cables between the battery and starter motor, if faults are found repair/replace as required.

2. If no faults are found in step1, check the condition and/or operation of the battery, alternator output and/or drive belt, if faults are found repair/replace as required.

3. If no faults are found in step2, check that the correct grade of engine oil is being used on the vehicle, if not drain and replace with the correct grade of oil.

Engine Cranks Normally But Does Not Start

1. If the engine cranks normally but does not start, check and ensure that fuel is reaching the injection nozzles, by loosening any of the injection pipes, cranking the engine and ensuring that fuel is coming out of the pipe.

2. If fuel is not coming out of the pipe in step1, check the operation of the fuel cut solenoid, if faults are found repair/replace as required.

3. If no faults are found in step3, check to ensure that fuel is getting to the injection pump by disconnecting the inlet hoses from the fuel filter, feeding clean fuel from a separate container directly into the injection pump. If the engine now starts there may be blockages in the fuel filter and/or line between the fuel tank and fuel filter. If the engine does not start, check the condition and/or operation of the fuel line between the fuel filter and fuel pump. If the injection pump operation is normal it should be replaced.

4. If fuel is present in step1, check the fuel system pipes, hoses and/or components for leaks, cracks and/or damage, if faults are found repair/replace as required.

5. If there are no faults in step4, check the pre-heating operation system operation by ensuring that after the ignition is turned on and the glow plug lamp lights up that there is voltage applied to the glow plugs, if the operation is not as shown, repair/replace as required.

6. If no faults are found in step5, check the operation of the glow plug/s, if faults are found repair/replace as required.

7. If no faults are found in step6, check the injection

timing by (releasing the cold start advance systen where fitted) and checking the plunger stroke.

Specified Plunger Stroke: 1.37-1.43mm (Australia)
Specified Plunger Stroke: 1.52-1.58mm (Europe)

If the timing setting is not as shown, adjust to suit.

8. If no faults are found in step7, check the fast idle system operation **(vehicle with ACSD only)**, if faults are found repair/replace as required.

9. If no faults are found in step8, check the condition and/or operation of the injection nozzles

Injection Nozzle Pressure:	17,652 - 18,633kpa (No1 Opening Pressure)
Opening Pressure:	23,046-24,026kpa (No2 Opening Pressure 1995-1996)
Opening Pressure:	23,144-24,124kpa (No2 Opening Pressure 1996 On)

10. If faults are found repair/replace as required.

Idle Speed is Unstable When The Engine is Warm

1. If the idle speed is unstable when the engine is warm, check the condition and/or operation of the throttle cable and/or linkages, if faults are found repair/replace as required.

2. If no faults are found in step1, check the engine idle speed setting.

Idle Speed:	**700±50RPM (Manual)**
Idle Speed:	**800±50RPM (Auto)**

If the idle speed is not as shown, adjust to suit

3. If no faults are found in step2, check the fuel system components and/or lines for leaks and/or damage, if faults are found repair/replace as required.

4. If no faults are found in step3, check the injection timing by (releasing the cold start advance system where fitted) and checking the plunger stroke.

Specified Plunger Stroke: 1.37-1.43mm (Australia)
Specified Plunger Stroke: 1.52-1.58mm (Europe)

If the timing setting is not as shown, adjust to suit.

5. If no faults are found in step4, check the operation of the injection nozzle/s and/or the delivery valve by letting the engine run at idle speed, loosening the union nuts on each of the cylinders in order and check if there is any change of idle speed. If there is no change at any of the cylinders this will indicate that a faulty cylinder/s is present. To fix the problem check the injection nozzle pressure.

Injection Nozzle Pressure:	17,652 - 18,633kpa (No1 Opening Pressure)
Opening Pressure:	23,046-24,026kpa (No2 Opening Pressure 1995-1996)
Opening Pressure:	23,144-24,124kpa (No2 Opening Pressure 1996 On)

6. If the pressure is not as shown adjust pressure to suit. If the pressure is OK, the fault will be with the delivery valve and should be replaced.

Engine Suddenly Stops.

1. If the engine is running and then suddenly stops check and ensure that fuel is reaching the injection nozzles by loosening any of the injection pipes, crank-

ing the engine and ensuring that fuel is coming out of the pipe.

2. If fuel is not coming out of the pipe in step1, check the operation of the fuel cut solenoid, if faults are found repair/replace as required.

3. If no faults are found in step3, check to ensure that fuel is getting to the injection pump by disconnecting the inlet hoses from the fuel filter, feeding clean fuel from a separate container directly into the injection pump. If the engine now starts there may be blockages in the fuel filter and/or line between the fuel tank and fuel filter. If the engine does not start, check the condition and/or operation of the fuel line between the fuel filter and fuel pump. If the injection pump operation is normal it should be replaced.

4. If fuel is present in step1, check the pre-heating operation system operation by ensuring that after the ignition is turned on and the glow plug lamp lights up that there are 6v applied to the glow plugs, if the operation is not as shown, repair/replace as required.

5. If no faults are found in step4, check the operation of the glow plug/s, if faults are found repair/replace as required.

6. If no faults are found in step5, check the fuel system pipes, hoses and/or components for leaks, cracks and/or damage, if faults are found repair/replace as required.

7. If no faults are found in step6, check the injection timing by setting either the No1 or No6 piston at TDC, releasing the cold start advance system (where fitted) and checking the plunger stroke.

Specified Plunger Stroke: 1.37-1.43mm (Australia)
Specified Plunger Stroke: 1.52-1.58mm (Europe)

If the timing setting is not as shown, adjust to suit.

8. If no faults are found in step7, check the fast idle system operation, if faults are found repair/replace as required.

9. If no faults are found in step8, check the operation of the injection nozzle/s and/or the delivery valve by letting the engine run at idle speed, loosening the union nuts on each of the cylinders in order and check if there is any change of idle speed. If there is no change at any of the cylinders this will indicate that a faulty cylinder/s is present. To fix the problem check the injection nozzle pressure.

Injection Nozzle Pressure:	17,652 - 18,633kpa (No1 Opening Pressure)
Opening Pressure:	23,046-24,026kpa (No2 Opening Pressure 1995-1996)
Opening Pressure:	23,144-24,124kpa (No2 Opening Pressure 1996 On)

10. If the pressure is not as shown adjust pressure to suit. If the pressure is OK, the fault will be with the delivery valve and should be replaced.

Engine Has a Lack of Power

1. If the engine has any lack of power, press down the throttle fully and ensure that the adjusting lever is in contact with the maximum speed adjusting screw, if it is not adjust to suit.

2. If no faults are found in step1, start the engine, press the throttle down to the floor and check that the no load maximum RPM is OK, if it is not, adjust using the maximum speed adjusting screw.

No Load Maximum Speed Setting: 4300-4500RPM

3. If no faults are found in step2, ensure that the interchange overflow screw (Out) and the inlet (No Mark) are fitted in the correct positions, if not refit in correct positions.

4. If no faults are found in step3, check the fuel system components and/or lines for leaks and/or damage, if faults are found repair/replace as required.

5. If no faults are found in step4, disconnect the inlet hoses from the fuel filter and pour diesel fuel directly into the injection pump, if the condition now improves replace the fuel filter. If the condition does not improve after the fuel filter has been replaced, check the condition and/or operation of the priming pump, if faults are found repair/replace as required.

6. If no faults are found in step5, check the injection timing by releasing the cold start advance system (where fitted) and checking the plunger stroke.

Specified Plunger Stroke: 1.37-1.43mm (Australia)
Specified Plunger Stroke: 1.52-1.58mm (Europe)
If the timing setting is not as shown, adjust to suit

7. If no faults are found in step6, check the injection nozzle pressure.

Injection Nozzle Pressure: 17,652 - 18,633kpa
                                (No1 Opening Pressure)
Opening Pressure: 23,046-24,026kpa (No2
                   Opening Pressure 1995-1996)
Opening Pressure: 23,144-24,124kpa (No2
                   Opening Pressure 1996 On)

8. If the pressure is not as shown adjust pressure to suit, if the pressure cannot be adjusted replace the faulty injector nozzle/s as required.

Excessive Exhaust Smoke

1. Check the condition and/or operation of the air cleaner element, if faults are found repair/replace as required.

2. If no faults are found in step1, check the engine oil consumption, if faults are found repair/replace as required.

3. If the oil consumption is OK in step2, check the injection timing by releasing the cold start advance system (where fitted) and checking the plunger stroke.

Specified Plunger Stroke: 1.37-1.43mm (Australia)
Specified Plunger Stroke: 1.52-1.58mm (Europe)
If the timing setting is not as shown, adjust to suit.

(Please Note: If the exhaust smoke is black it tends to indicate that the timing is advanced and if the smoke is white that the timing is retarded).

4. If no faults are found in step3, disconnect the inlet hoses from the fuel filter and pour diesel fuel directly into the injection pump, if the condition now improves replace the fuel filter. If the condition does not improve after the fuel filter has been replaced, check the condition and/or operation of the priming pump, if faults are found repair/

replace as required. *(Please Note: At between 2000-3000RPM a blocked fuel filter tends to make the exhaust smoke white).*

5. If no faults are found in step4, check the injection nozzle pressure.

Injection Nozzle Pressure: 17,652 - 18,633kpa
                                  (No1 Opening Pressure)
Opening Pressure: 23,046-24,026kpa (No2
                     Opening Pressure 1995-1996)
Opening Pressure: 23,144-24,124kpa (No2
                     Opening Pressure 1996 On)

6. If the pressure is not as shown adjust pressure to suit, if the pressure cannot be adjusted replace the faulty injector nozzle/s as required. *(Please Note: Excessive exhaust smoke is normally caused when the nozzle pressure is to low)*

Fuel Consumption is Poor

1. If the fuel consumption is poor, check the fuel system components and/or lines for leaks and/or damage, if faults are found repair/replace as required.

2. If no faults are found in step1, check the engine idle speed setting is correct.

Idle Speed: 700±50RPM (Manual)
Idle Speed: 800±50RPM (Auto)
If the idle speed setting is not correct adjust to suit.

3. If the idle speed setting is OK in step2, check the no load maximum speed setting is OK by starting the engine, pressing down the throttle pedal to the floor and checking the no load maximum speed setting.

No Load Maximum Speed Setting: 4300-4500RPM
If the setting is not OK, adjust using the maximum speed adjusting screw.

4. If no faults are found in step3, check the injection timing by releasing the cold start advance system (where fitted) and checking the plunger stroke.

Specified Plunger Stroke: 1.37-1.43mm (Australia)
Specified Plunger Stroke: 1.52-1.58mm (Europe)
If the timing setting is not as shown, adjust to suit.

5. If no faults are found in step4, check the injection nozzle pressure.

Injection Nozzle Pressure: 17,652 - 18,633kpa
                                  (No1 Opening Pressure)
Opening Pressure: 23,046-24,026kpa (No2
                     Opening Pressure 1995-1996)
Opening Pressure: 23,144-24,124kpa (No2
                     Opening Pressure 1996 On)

6. If the pressure is not as shown adjust pressure to suit, if the pressure cannot be adjusted replace the faulty injector nozzle/s as required.

Noise When The Engine Is Warm

1. If the engine is noisy when it is warm, first check the operation of the temperature gauge if that is Ok, check the operation of the thermostat if faults are found repair/replace as required.

2. If no faults are found in step1, check the injection timing by releasing the cold start advance system (where fitted) and checking the plunger stroke.

Specified Plunger Stroke: 1.37-1.43mm (Australia)
Specified Plunger Stroke: 1.52-1.58mm (Europe)
If the timing setting is not as shown, adjust to suit.
3. If no faults are found in step2, check the injection nozzle pressure.
Injection Nozzle Pressure: 17,652 - 18,633kpa
(No1 Opening Pressure)
Opening Pressure: 23,046-24,026kpa (No2 Opening Pressure 1995-1996)
Opening Pressure: 23,144-24,124kpa (No2 Opening Pressure 1996 On)
4. If the pressure is not as shown adjust pressure to suit, if the pressure cannot be adjusted replace the faulty injector nozzle/s as required.

Engine Will Not Return to Idle

1. Operate the adjusting lever on top of the injection pump and ensure that the engine returns to normal idle speed, if it does the throttle cable is binding or not adjusted correctly and needs fixing.
2. If the engine does not return to idle in step1, the injection pump is faulty and needs replacing.

Engine Will Not Shut Off With The Key

1. Check the fuel cut solenoid operation by disconnecting the connector on top of the fuel cut solenoid and check if the engine stops, if it does the starter switch is faulty and needs repairing and/or replacing.
2. If the engine does not stop in step1, either the fuel cut solenoid is faulty or the solenoid is blocked, if required repair/replace as required.

Diesel System Electrical Diagnosis

Engine Will Not Start When Cold
Power Supply Check

1. Check the operation of the intake heater system, if faults are found repair/replace as required.
2. If no faults are found in step1, disconnect the water temperature sensor, switch the ignition ON and check that the pre-heat side of the intake heater has battery voltage for 81 seconds.
3. If the pre-heat side of the intake heater does not have battery voltage for 81 seconds in step2, check the condition and/or operation of the fuse link for the intake heater, if faults are found repair/replace as required.
4. If the fuse link is OK in step3, carry out the control section check.
5. If the pre-heat side of the intake heater has battery voltage for 81 seconds, reconnect the water temperature sensor harness connector.

Control Section Check
Please Note: Carry out this check with the intake heater lead connected correctly

1. Disconnect the water temperature sensor and check if the indicator lamp lights up when the starter switch is in the ON position.
Specified Light Up Time: 6.5seconds

2. If the light up time is not as shown in step1, check the condition of the relevant system fuse, if the fuse is blown, if faults are found repair/replace as required.
3. If the fuse is OK in step2, check the condition and/or operation of the glow indicator lamp globe, if faults are found repair/replace as required.
4. If the bulb is OK in step3, check for grounding of the terminals 18, 16 and/or 25 (26Pin ECU Connector with EGR System), or the terminal 5 (pre heat timer without EGR system).
5. If there is no grounding in step4, check for open circuit or faulty ground in the harness between the terminals 18, 16 and/or 25 (26Pin ECU Connector with EGR System), or the terminal 5 (pre heat timer without EGR system) and body ground. If faults are found repair/replace as required.
6. If there is grounding in step4, check for battery voltage to the terminal 3 (harness side 16Pin ECU connector with EGR system) or the terminal 4 (harness side pre heat timer connector without EGR system) if the voltage is OK, replace the ECU or the pre-heat timer assembly. If the voltage is not OK check for open circuit between the terminal 3 (harness side 16Pin ECU connector with EGR system) or the terminal 4 (harness side pre heat timer connector without EGR system) and the indicator lamp, if faults are found repair/replace as required.
7. If the light up time in step1 is OK, check that there is battery voltage between the G terminal on the intake heater relay and body ground for 81 seconds with the ignition ON.
8. If the voltage is not OK, check the operation of the intake heater relay, if faults are found repair/replace as required.
9. If the relay is OK in step8, when the ignition is switched ON, does the terminal 2 (26Pin ECU Connector with EGR System), or the terminal 4 (pre heat timer without EGR system) have battery voltage for 81 seconds, if it does not replace the ECU or pre-heat timer.
10. If the battery voltage is OK in step9, check for open circuit in the harness between the terminal 2 (26Pin ECU Connector with EGR System), or the terminal 4 (pre heat timer without EGR system) and terminal g of the intake heater relay and/or open circuit or faults in the ground circuit between the terminal e of the intake heater relay and body ground, if faults are found repair/replace as required.
11. If the voltage is OK in step7, reconnect the water temperature sensor connector and carry out the power supply check

VEHICLE SERVICE INFORMATION

Vehicle Filling Capacities

Engine Oil with Filter: .... 9.7 Litres
Engine Oil without Filter: .... 8.4 Litres
Engine Oil with Dry Fill: 10.0Litres
Cooling System: ....
.... 10.7 Litres (Without Heater Manual 1995-1996)
Cooling System: ....
.... 10.4 Litres (Without Heater Manual 1996 ON)
Cooling System: .... 10.2 Litres (Without Heater Auto)
Cooling System: ....
.... 11.1 Litres (With Heater Manual 1995-1996)
Cooling System: ....
.... 10.9 Litres (With Heater Auto 1995-1996)
Cooling System: ....
.... 11.5 Litres (With Heater Manual 1996ON)
Cooling System: ....
.... 11.00 Litres (With Heater Auto 1996ON)
Cooling System: ....
12.0 Litres (With Front/Rear Heater Manual 1995-1996)
Cooling System: ....
... 11.8 Litres (With Front/Rear Heater Auto 1995-1996)
Cooling System: ....
... 12.5 Litres (With Front/Rear Heater Manual 1996ON)
Cooling System: ....
.... 12.0 Litres (With Front/Rear Heater Auto 1996ON)
Manual Transmission: .... 2.7 Litres (5 Speed)
Auto Transmission: .... 15.0 Litres (Dry Fill)
.... 6.0 Litres (Refill)
Front Differential: .... 2.6 Litres
Rear Differential: .... 2.5 Litres
Transfer Case: 1.3Litres

Vehicle Component Service Interval Changes

Timing Belt:
Change Every 60Months/100,000kms
Check Valve Clearance:
Every 24Months/40,000kms
Engine Coolant/Anti Freeze:
Change at 24 Months/40,000kms
Air Cleaner Element:
Change Every 60 Months/100,000kms
Fuel Filter:
Change Every 24 Months/40,000kms
Engine Oil:
Change Every 3 Months/5,000kms
Engine Oil Filter:
Change Every 6 Months/10,000kms
Brake Fluid:
Change Every 24 Months/40,000kms
Manual Transmission Oil:
Change Every 18 Months/30,000kms
Auto Transmission Oil:
Change Every 24 Months/40,000kms
Front Differential Oil:
Change Every 18 Months/30,000kms
Transfer Case Oil
Change Every 18 Months/30,000kms
Rear Differential Oil:
Change Every 18 Months/30,000kms
Front/Rear Wheel Bearings
Repack Every 12Months/20,000kms

Toyota Landcruiser HZJ 100-105 1HZ/1HD-T/1HD-FTE Engine 1998 ON

Toyota Landrcuiser HZJ 100-105 1HZ/1HD-T/1HD-FTE Engine 1998 ON

Toyota Landcruiser 100's

Toyota Landcruiser HZJ 100-105 1HZ/1HD-T/1HD-FTE Engine 1998 ON

Engine Checks

Valve Clearance Check (1HZ-1HDT)

1. Remove the intake pipe and the cylinder head cover.
2. Set the No1 piston to TDC/Compression by turning the crankshaft pulley clockwise and line up the groove on the pulley with the timing gear cover groove.
3. Check that the valve lifters on the No1 cylinder are loose and the exhaust valve lifters on the No6 cylinder is tight.

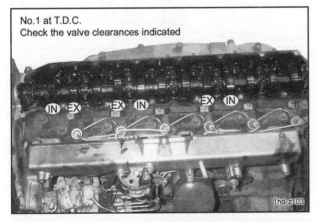
No.1 at T.D.C.
Check the valve clearances indicated
1hd-z103

If this is not the case, turn the crankshaft one full turn in a clockwise direction and then line up the groove.
4. Check the valve clearances on the 1,5,9 inlet valves and 2,4,8 exhaust valves with a feeler gauge and record the measurments between the valve lifter and camshaft that need adjusting. **(Measurements will be used to determine new shim thickneses that are required).**
Specified Inlet Valve Clearance: 0.15-0.25mm
Specified Exhaust Valve Clearance: 0.35-0.45mm
5. Turn the crankshaft in a clockwise direction one full

turn (360°) and check the valve clearances on the 3, 7, 11 inlet valve and 6,10, 12 on the exhaust valve. With a feeler gauge and record the measurments between the valve lifter and camshaft that need adjusting. **(Measurements will be used to determine new shim thickneses that are required).**
Specified Inlet Valve Clearance: 0.15-0.25mm
Specified Exhaust Valve Clearance: 0.35-0.45mm

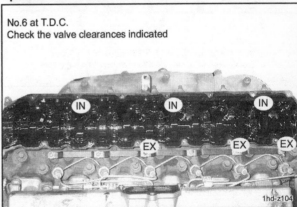
No.6 at T.D.C.
Check the valve clearances indicated
1hd-z104

6. To complete the adjustment remove any adjusting shim that need replacement by using a valve liter (part no 09248-64011).
7. Turn the crankshaft to position the cam lobe of the camshaft on the adjusting valve upwards, remove the shim with a small screwdriver and magnetic tool.
8. To calculate the shim needed to adjust the valve clearance, measure the thickness of the old shim, and calculate the the thickness of the new shim as shown below.
Inlet Valve Shim: Old shim thickness plus 0.20mm.
Exhaust Valve Shim:
Old shim thickness plus 0.40mm.
9. Once the shim thickness has been calculated, replace the shim using the valve lifter (part no 09248-64011) and then remove the valve lifter.
10. Recheck the valve clearance, then replace any removed parts in the reverse order of removal.

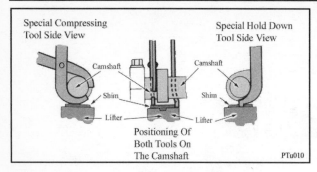

Special Compressing Tool Side View — Camshaft, Shim, Lifter

Special Hold Down Tool Side View — Camshaft, Shim, Lifter

Positioning Of Both Tools On The Camshaft

PTu010

Valve Clearance Check (1HD-FTE)

1. Remove the engine rocker cover, set the No1 piston to TDC/Compression by turning the crankshaft pulley in a clockwise direction until the groove on the pulley lines up with the groove on the timing cover.

2. Check that the No1 valve rocker arm is loose and the No6 valve rocker arm is tight. If it is not, turn the crankshaft one full turn (360°) and check again.

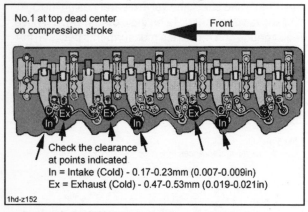

No.1 at top dead center on compression stroke

Front

Check the clearance at points indicated
In = Intake (Cold) - 0.17-0.23mm (0.007-0.009in)
Ex = Exhaust (Cold) - 0.47-0.53mm (0.019-0.021in)

1hd-z152

3. Check the valve clearance by using a feeler gauge between the adjusting screw on the valve rocker arm and the valve bridge and recording the valve clearances on the (1,5,9 inlet valves and 2,4,8 exhaust valves).

Specified Inlet Valve Clearance: 0.17-0.23mm
Specified Exhaust Valve Clearance: 0.47-0.53mm

Turn the crankshaft in a clockwise direction one full turn (360°) and check the valve clearances on the 3, 7, 11 inlet valve and 6,10, 12 on the exhaust valve.

Specified Inlet Valve Clearance: 0.17-0.23mm
Specified Exhaust Valve Clearance: 0.47-0.53mm

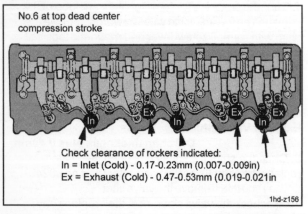

No.6 at top dead center compression stroke

Check clearance of rockers indicated:
In = Inlet (Cold) - 0.17-0.23mm (0.007-0.009in)
Ex = Exhaust (Cold) - 0.47-0.53mm (0.019-0.021in)

1hd-z156

4. If the valve clearnces are not as shown, loosen the

lock nut on the valve bridge and loosen the adjusting screw until the adjusting screw and the valve stem are completely separated.

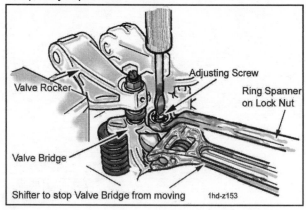

Valve Rocker

Adjusting Screw

Ring Spanner on Lock Nut

Valve Bridge

Shifter to stop Valve Bridge from moving   1hd-z153

5. Loosen the lock nut on the valave rocker arm and loosen the adjusting screw.
Insert a 0.20mm feeler gauge (inlet) or 0.50mm feeler gauge (exhaust) between the adjusting screw and the valve bridge, turn the adjusting screw on the rocker arm until the feeler gauge slides with a very slight drag and then lock the adjusting screw with the lock nut.

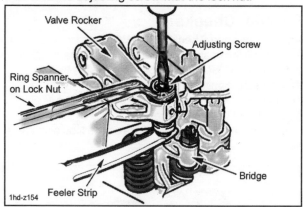

Valve Rocker

Adjusting Screw

Ring Spanner on Lock Nut

Bridge

1hd-z154   Feeler Strip

6. With the feeler gauge installed. Check the resistance of the feeler gauge remains the same when the adjusting screw on the valve bridge is loosened. If the resistance changes repeat the adjusting process again.

7. Tighten the adjusting screw on the valve bridge and lock the adjusting screw with the lock nut when the resistance of the feeler gauge begins to get stronger.

8. Loosen the lock nut on the valve rocker arm, turn the adjusting screw on the valve rocker arm until the feeler gauge slides with a slight drag, then lock the adjustung screw with the lock nut.

Please Note: Diagram is on the next page

9. Replace the engine rocker cover and any other removed parts.

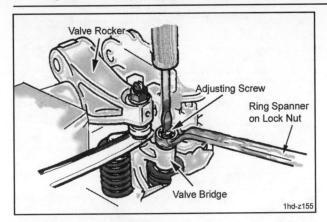

1hd-z155

Compression Check (All)

1. Run the engine to normal operating temperatures, remove the intake pipe, remove the rocker cover, remove the injection pipes and nozzle leakage pipes and then disconnect the injection pump cut off solenoid connector

2. Check each cylinder compression by removing the No1 fuel injector (leaving all the others inatalled to the engine), installing a compression tester to the engine, crank the engine and recording the pressure on each cylinder. After checking the pressure, replace the injector and repeat the operation on each cylinder.

Specified Compression Pressure:
        3628kpa or more (1HZ)
Specified Compression Pressure:
        3432kpa or more (1HD-T/1HD-FTE)
Minimum Pressure:
        2648kpa or more (1HZ)
Minimum Pressure:
        2452kpa or more (1HD-T/1HD-FTE)
Difference Between Each Cylinder:
        490kpa or less.

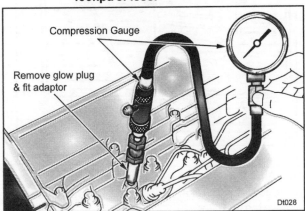

Dt028

3. If the pressure is less than shown on one or more cylinders, pour a small amount of oil through the injector nozzle hole and recheck the pressure. If the pressure is now OK, check the condition of the piston rings and/or cylinder bore. If the pressure is still low, check for a sticking valve and/or bad valve seating.

4. Replace any removed parts in the reverse order of removal.

Piston Protrusion Check (All)

1. Clean the cylinder block, set the No1 piston to TDC, place a dial gauge on the block and set the dial gauge to zero.

2. Find the point where the piston top protrudes the most by turning the crankshaft slightly the the left and right.

3. Measure each cylinder in two places as shown and record the average of the two measurments on each cylinder.

Specified Protrusion Measurement: 0.175-0.425mm

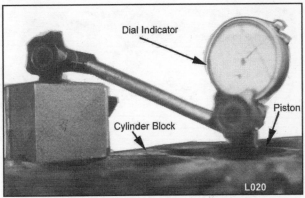

L020

4. If the protrusion measurement is not as shown, remove the piston and con rod and replace it.

5. There are 5 types of head gaskets used on this vehicle, but only type 1,3,5 are supplied as replacement parts.

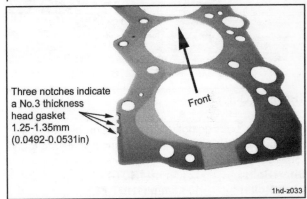

1hd-z033

Gasket No1: Thickness is 1.15-1.25mm (1HZ/1HD-T)
Gasket No3: Thickness is 1.25-1.35mm (1HZ/1HD-T)
Gasket No5: Thickness is 1.35-1.45mm (1HZ/1HD-T)
Gasket No1: Thickness is 0.85-0.95mm (1HD-FTE)
Gasket No3: Thickness is 0.95-1.05mm ((1HD-FTE)
Gasket No5: Thickness is 1.05-1.15mm (1HD-FTE)

6. Select the largest of the protrusion measurements and select the gasket to suit as shown below.

Protrusion Measurement	Gasket Size
0.455mm or less	1.15-1.25mm (1HZ)
0.456-0.555mm	1.25-1.35mm (1HZ)
0.566mm or more	1.35-1.45mm (1HZ)
0.525mm or less	1.15-1.25mm (1HD-T)
0.526-0.625mm	1.25-1.35mm (1HD-T)
0.626mm or more	1.35-1.45mm (1HD-T)
0.225mm or less	0.85-0.95mm (1HD-FTE)
0.226-0.325mm	0.95-1.05mm (1HD-FTE)

0.326mm or more   **1.05-1.15mm (1HD-FTE)**

Cylinder Head Tightening Procedures (All)

1. With the cylinder head inplace, tighten the bolts in three steps, if any of the bolts break or deform replace them as required.

2. Apply a light coat of oil to each bolt thread, and using a torque wrench tighten the 26 bolts in three separate stages to a tor**que of 68.6Nm.**

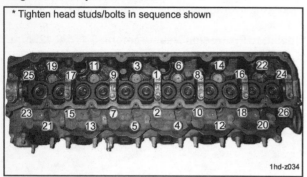

* Tighten head studs/bolts in sequence shown

1hd-z034

1HZ-1HDT (Only)

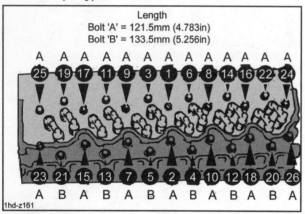

Length
Bolt 'A' = 121.5mm (4.783in)
Bolt 'B' = 133.5mm (5.256in)

1hd-z161

1HD-FTE (Only)

If any of the bolts do not reach torque figures, check the condition and/or length of the bolts and if faults are found repair/replace as required.

Short Bolts: **121.5mm (1HDT-FE)**
Long Bolts: **133.5mm (1HDT-FE)**

3. Mark the front of the cylinder head bolts with white paint, **tighten each bolt another 90°** in the sequence shown, and **then tighten each bolt a further 90°** in the same sequence and now ensure that the paint marks on all of the bolts are facing to the rear.

Oil Pressure Check (All)

1. Remove the oil pressure switch from the block and install a pressure gauge in its place.

2. Run the engine to normal operating temperature and the check the engine oil pressure.

Specified Oil Pressure:

            250-600kpa or more @ 3000RPM

3. If the pressure is not as shown, repair/replace as required

Oil Filter

Oil Pressure Gauge Sender Unit

1hd-z005

Cooling System Thermostat Check (All)

1. Remove the thermostat from the engine and put into a suitable container of water.

2. Heat the water gradually and and check the valve opening temperature and **valve lift.**

Valve Opening Temperature: **74-78°c**
Valve Lift: **10mm or more @ 90°c**

If the operation is not as shown above replace the thermostat.

3. Check that the valve spring is tight when the thermostat is fully closed, if not replace the thermostat.

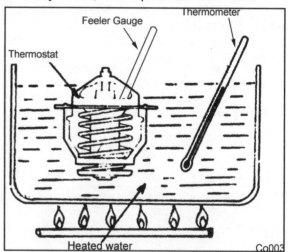

Thermometer

Feeler Gauge

Thermostat

Heated water

Co003

Fuel Filter Check and Replacement (All)

1. Remove the fuel filter sensor, drain the fuel, then remove the fuel filter.

2. Clean the fuel filter mounting bracket and then coat the fuel filter sealing ring with some diesel fuel.

3. Screw the fuel filter on until a slght resistance is felt and then turn another 2/3 of a turn or until suitably tight.

4. Install the fuel filter sensor (if fitted) to the new filter and then bleed any air present from the system.

Diagrams are on the next page

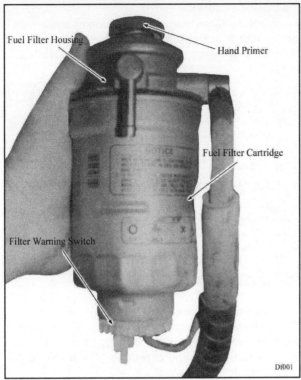

Fuel Filter Housing
Hand Primer
Fuel Filter Cartridge
Filter Warning Switch

Df001

Draining Water Fron The Filter (All)

1. Loosen the drain cock 4 or 5 turns or remove the fuel filter sensor to allow the water to drain from the filter.
2. Retighten the drain cock or replace the sensor and bleed any air present from the system.

Fuel Filter Warning Lamp Check

1. Remove the switch from the filter and check that there is continuity between the terminals when the warning switch is ON (Float Up)
2. Check that there is no continuity between the terminals when the warning switch is OFF (Float Down)
3. If the operation is not as shown, repair/replace as required.

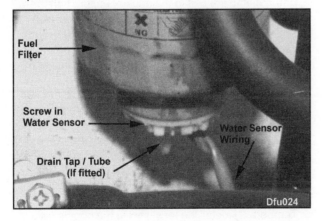

Fuel Filter
Screw in Water Sensor
Water Sensor Wiring
Drain Tap / Tube (If fitted)

Dfu024

Injector Nozzle Check (1HZ)

1. Remove the injector from the vehicle, connect up to the pressure tester and check the initial pressure by pumping the tester handle a few times.

Initial Opening Pressure: 14,710-15690kpa (New Nozzle) 1HZ White Ring (Man/Auto)
Initial Opening Pressure: 15,690-16,671kpa (New Nozzle) 1HZ Brown Ring (Auto)
Initial Opening Pressure: 14,220-15,200kpa (Used Nozzle) 1HZ White Ring (Man/Auto)
Initial Opening Pressure: 15,200-16,181kpa (Used Nozzle) 1HZ Brown Ring (Auto)

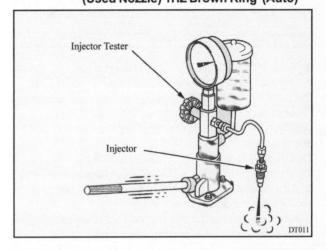

Injector Tester
Injector

DT011

2. If the opening pressure is not as shown above, take the injector to pieces and change the adjusting shim on the top of the injector so as the correct pressure is recorded.

Adjusted Opening Pressure: 14,220-15,200kpa 1HZ White Ring (Man/Auto)
Adjusted Opening Pressure: 15,200 - 16,181kpa 1HZ Brown Ring (Auto)

Please Note: The adjusting shims vary in 0.025mm thicknesses, each 0.05mm will adjust the pressure by 470kpa. After the shim has been changed there should be no leakage from the injector.

3. Maintain the pressure between 981-1961kpa below the opening pressure and check that there is no leakage from the injector for a period of 10seconds.
4. Check the spray pattern by pumping the pressure tester handle 4-6 times or more per second and check the injection spray pattern.

Diagram is on the next page

5. If the operation and/or spray pattern is not as shown, repair/replace the nozzle/s.

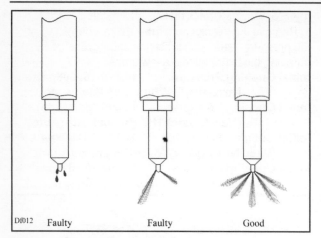

Df012   Faulty   Faulty   Good

Injector Nozzle Check (1HD-T/1HDT-FE)

1. Remove the injector from the vehicle, connect up to the pressure tester and bleed air feom the uniioon nut. Check the opening pressure by pumping the tester handle a few times and reading the pressure just as it starts to drop

Opening Pressure:	**17,652-18,663kpa (1HD-T)**
Opening Pressure:	**17,162-18,142kpa (1HDT-FE)**

2. If the opening pressure is not as shown above, replace the capsule sub assembly

3. After the pressure in step3 is correct disassemble the capsule sub assembly and tighten the plug screw.

4.

nozzle for the adjustment of the No1 opening pressure.

Opening Pressure:	**17,650-18,633kpa (No1 Opening Pressure)**

Please Note: The adjusting shims vary in 0.01mm (1HD-T) or 0.025mm (1HDT-FE) thicknesses, each 0.01mm will adjust the pressure by 147kpa (1HD-T), or 373kpa (1HDT-FE). After the shim has been changed there should be no leakage from the injector.

4. Maintain the pressure between 981-1961kpa below the opening pressure and check that there is no leakage from the injector for a period of 10seconds.

5. Check the spray pattern by pumping the pressure tester handle 4-6 times or more per second and check the injection spray pattern.

6. If the operation and/or spray pattern is not as shown, repair/replace the nozzle/s as required.

Use Previous Injector Test Diagrams

Timing Belt Removal and Replacement (All)

Removal Procedures

1. Remove the intake pipe, remove the timing belt cover and set the No1 piston to BDC by turning the crankshaft pulley in a clockwise direction until the No1 and No2 camshaft pulley marks line up with the BDC marks.

2. Remove the timing belt from the engine by loosening alternately the 2 tensioner bolts and then remove them with the tensioner.

3. After removing the tensioner from the engine, remove

the timing belt from the engine.

Please Note: If the timing belt is being re-used draw on the belt an arrow undicating the direction of rotation and match marks on the pulley as well as the belt.

Timing Marks

1hd-z076

Replacement Procedures

Please Note: Before replacing the timimg belt check the condition and/or operation of the timing belt pulleys, tensioners and/or pulleys, if faults are found repair/replace as required.

1. Check the tensioner operation by first ensuring that there are no sign of any oil leaks from the tensioner assembly. Hold the tensioner with both hands and push the rod with both hands, ensuring that the rod does not move. Check the protrusion of the tensioner push rod.

Push Rod Protrusion:	**9.0-9.8mm**

If the protrusion is not as shown, replace the tensioner

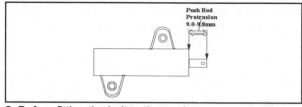

Push Rod Protrusion 9.0-9.8mm

2. Before fitting the belt to the engine, ensure that the timing mark on the No2 camshaft pulley lines up with the BDC mark, and that the No1 camshaft pulley mark lines up with the BDC mark.

Do not turn the crankshaft at this point as the valve heads will hit the tops of the pistons

3. Line up any match marks that you may have marked on the belt. Fit the timing belt under tension between the No1 and No2 camshaft pulleys.

4. Using a press, slowly press in the tensioner rod with between 220-2205ft lb of force, line up the holes on the push rod and the hosuing and then put a 1.5mm hex wrench through the holes to keep the setting position of the push rod, then release the press.

5. Temporarily install the tensioner to the engine with the two bolts while pushing the pulley towards the timimg belt, alternatley tighten the two tensioner bolts to 13Nm.After the bolts have been tightened remove the hex wrench from the tensioner.

6. Check the valve timing by turning the crankshaft pulley in a clockwise direction and ensuring that each of the timing marks line up with their respective match marks.

7. If the marks do not line up, remove the timing belt from the engine and start the installation process again.

8. Refit the timing cover and replace any more removed parts in the reverse order of removal

Timing Belt Warning Lamp Reset Procedures

1. Remove the grommet from the speedometer and turn off the lamp by pushing the warning lamp reset switch, then replace the grommet.

2. Start the engine and ensure that the light stays off.

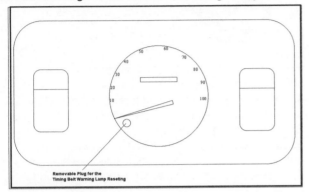

Removable Plug for the
Timing Belt Warning Lamp Reseting

Timing Belt Warning Lamp Reset Procedures (Change Screw Position on the Back of the Instrument Cluster)

1. Remove the instrument cluster from the vehicle, connect terminals A&B shown in the diagrams and then remove the CHARGE fuse from the vehicle.

2. Turn the ignition switch to ON and check that the warning lights light up, if not the check the condition and/or operation of the globe.

3. Check the condition and/or operation of the reset switches by checking that there is intermittent continuity between terminals A&B when the reset switch is pressed, if not repair/replace the speedometer/instrument cluster as required.

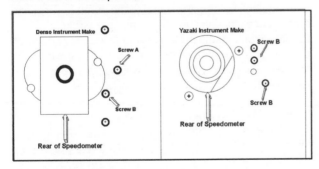

Timing Belt Replacement Torques

No1 Camshaft Pulley:	98Nm
No2 Camshaft Pulley:	31Nm
Tensioner Bolts:	13Nm
Tensioner Pulley Bolt:	34.5Nm

Engine Tightening Torques

Cylinder Head Tightening Torque Bolts:	68.6Nm (Tighten in 3 Stages)
Cylinder Head Tightening Torque Bolts:	90° (2nd Stage)
Cylinder Head Tightening Torque Bolts:	90° (3rd Stage)
Exhaust Manifold Bolts and Nuts:	41.7Nm
Inlet Manifold Bolts and Nuts:	19.6Nm
Glow Plugs:	12.7Nm
Injection Nozzle:	63.7Nm
Injection Pump Drive Gear to Pump:	103Nm (1HZ-1HD-T)
Injection Pump Drive Gear to Pump:	137Nm (1HD-FTE)
EGR Pipe to Intake Pipe:	19.6Nm (1HD-FTE)
EGR Pipe to Exhaust Manifold:	39.2Nm (1HD-FTE)
Idle Pulley:	34.5Nm
Flywheel Bolts:	127.4Nm
Drive Plate:	127.4Nm
Connecting Rod Caps:	36.8Nm
Connecting Rod Caps:	90° (2nd Stage)
Main Bearings:	103Nm (12 Point Bolt 1st Stage)
Main Bearings:	90° (12 Point Bolt 2nd Stage)
Main Bearings:	18Nm (6 Point Bolt)
Crankshaft Pulley Bolt:	430Nm
Camshaft Gear No1 Bolt:	98Nm
Camshaft Gear No2 Bolt:	31Nm
Oil Pump to Block:	19.6Nm
Oil Pan to Cylinder Block:	15.7Nm

System Adjustments

Idle Speed Check (1HZ-1HD-T)

1. Before checking the idle speed, ensure that the

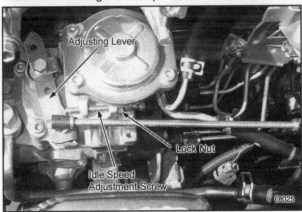

engine is at normal operating temperature, the air cleaner OK and fitted, all of the accessories are fitted, all vacuum lines are OK, valve clearance and injection timing are set correctly and that the transmission is in "N".

2. Install a tachometer to the engine, ensure that the adjusting lever touches the idle speed adjusting screw when the throttle pedal is released, if it does not adjust to suit.

3. Start the engine, let it run and check the idle speed.

Idle Speed:	**650±50RPM (1HZ Manual)**
Idle Speed:	**710±50RPM (1HZ Auto)**
Idle Speed:	**650±50RPM (1HD-T Manual)**
Idle Speed:	**700±50RPM (1HD-T Auto)**

4. If the idle speed is not as shown, disconnect the throttle linkage and loosen the lock nut on the idle speed adjusting screw and adjust the idle speed by turnning the idle speed adjusting screw.

5. Tighten the lock nut, recheck the idle speed, reconnect the throttle linkage and then re-check the idle speed.

6. Remove the tachometer from the engine and replace any other removed parts in the reverse order of removal.

Idle Speed Check (1HD-FTE)

1. Ensure that the engine is at normal operating temperature, the air cleaner is fitted, all pipes and hoses on the air induction system are connected, all accessories are turned off, all vaccum hoses are connected, the ECD warning system conenctors are connected and the valve clearances and ignitioon timing is set.

2. Install a tachometer tester probe to the TAC terminal on the self diagnosis connetor (located under the steering column on the lower dash panel).

3. Start the engine and check the idle speed
Specified Idle Speed: 550-650RPM.

4. If the idle speed is not as shown, adjust to suit

Injection Timing Check (1HZ-1HDT)

1. Set the No1 or No6 piston to TDC on the compression stroke by turning the crankshaft pulley in a clockwise direction and lining up the groove on the pulley with the mark on the timing gear cover

2. Remove the plug bolt from the distributor head of the injection pump and install a dial gauge to the bolt hole.

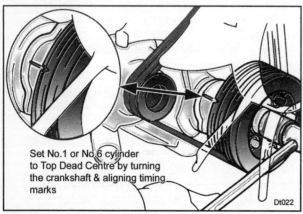

Set No.1 or No.6 cylinder to Top Dead Centre by turning the crankshaft & aligning timing marks

Dt022

3. (For Vehicles with ACSD Only), Turn the cold start lever in an anti clockwise direction about 20° and put a

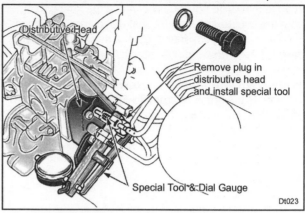

metel plate of between 9.0-10.0mm between the cold start lever and the thermo wax plunger.

4. Turn the crankshaft in an anti-clockwise direction, set the dial gauge to zero when it reaces its minimum value.
Specified Minimum Value: 0mm

5. Slowly turn the crankshaft in a clockwise direction until the groove on the crankshaft pulley lines up with the mark on the timing cover, then record the plunger stroke.

Specified Plunger Stroke:
**   0.65-0.71mm (1HZ with ACSD)**
Specified Plunger Stroke:
**   0.85-0.91mm (1HZ without ACSD)**
Specified Plunger Stroke:
**   1.18-1.24mm (1HD-T)**

6. If the timing needs adjustment, loosen the 6 union nuts on the injection pump side, the bolt holding the pump to the pump bracket, the two nuts holding the pump to the timing gear.

7. If the plunger stroke is less than shown, turn the pump towards the engine, if it more turn away from the engine.

8. Retighten the two nuts holding the pump to the timing gear, the bolt holding the pump to the pump bracket and then recheck the injection pump plunger stroke.

9. If fitted remove the plate from the ACSD device, the dial gauge and replace the bolt plug, tighten the union nuts on the injection pipes and replace any more removed parts in the reverse order of removal.

Injection Timing Check (1HD-FTE)

1. Using a mirror, check that the punching line on the injection pump flange lines up with the punching line on the water pump.

2. If the marks do not line up, loosen the 2 bolts holding the injection pump to the pump to the pump stay, the 4 nuts atht hold the injection pump to the timing belt case.

3. Line up the punching lien marks by slightly turning the injection pump, then retighten the loosened nuts and bolts.

Diagram is on the next page

Diesel Injection Pump

Alignment marks on injection pump and water pump shown at point of pen

Dt029

Maximum Speed Adjustment (1HZ-1HD-T)
With Throttle Position Sensor
1. With a tachometer installed to the engine, press down the throttle fully and check that the adjusting lever does not move when you try to push it to the maximum speed side, it it does, adjust to suit.
Without Throttle Position Sensor
1. Check that the adjusting lever touches the maximum speed screw when the throttle pedal is pressed down all of the way, if not adjust to suit.
2. Start the engine, press down the throttle pedal all the way and check the maximum speed.
Specified Maximum Speed: 4600±100RPM (1HZ)
Specified Maximum Speed: 4400±100RPM (1HD-T)
3. If the maximum speed is not as shown, remove the injection pump and adjust the maximum speed to suit.

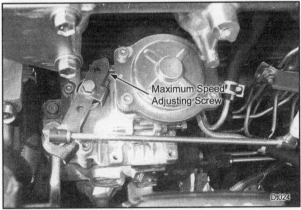

Maximum Speed Adjusting Screw

D1024

4. Remove the tachometer from the engine, and then replace any more removed parts in the reverse order of removal.

Maximum Speed Check (1HD-FTE)
1. Ensure that the engine is at normal operating temperature, the air cleaner is fitted, all pipes and hoses on the air induction system are connected, all accessories are turned off, all vaccum hoses are connected, the ECD warning system conenctors are connected and the valve clearances and ignitioon timing is set.
2. Install a tachometer tester probe to the TAC terminal on the self diagnosis connetor (located under the steering column on the lower dash panel).
3. Start the engine and check the idle speed

Specified Idle Speed: 550-650RPM.
4. Check the engine maximum speed by pressing down the throttle fully and record the speed.
Specified Maximum Speed: 4300-4500RPM
5. If the maximum speed is not as shown, adjust to suit
Use idle speed diagram

Fuel Heater System Check
Please Note: See system diagram on the next page
Fuel Heater Check
1. Apply 34.7±5.3kpa or more of vacuum to the vacuum switch and with an ohmmeter check the resistance between the No1 terminal and the switch body
Specified Resistance: 0.5-2.0ohms @ 20°c
2. If the resistance is not as shown, replace the fuel heater and vacuum switch assembly.

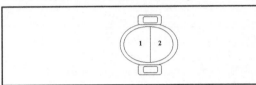

Vacuum Switch Check
1. With an ohmmeter check that there is no continuity between the No1 terminal and the switch body, if there is replace the fuel heater and vacuum switch assembly.
2. Apply 34.7±5.3kpa or more of vacuum to the vacuum switch port and with an ohmmeter check that there is continuity between the No1 terminal and the switch body, if there is no continuity, replace the fuel heater and vacuum switch assembly.
Use fuel heater diagram

Pre-Heating System Checks

Please Note: See system diagram on the next page
Pre Heating System Check (Superglow System)
1. Disconnect the water temperature sensor and check if the indicator lamp lights up when the starter switch is in the ON position.
Specified Light Up Time: Appx: 1.0secs @ 20°c
2-Switch on the ignition and record the time battery voltage is applied to the No1 terminal on the pre heat timer.
Voltage Time: Appx 6.0 secs
3. Check the pre-heating timer circuit by disconnecting the harness connector (12 Pin) from the timer and check the connector on the harness side as shown in the chart below.

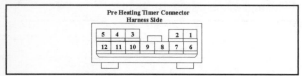

Check For	Between Terminals	Condition	Value
Voltage	3-ground	starter switch	OFF No Volts
Voltage	3-ground	starter switch	ON Battery Volts
Voltage	2-ground	starter switch	OFF No Volts
Voltage	2-ground	starter switch	ON Battery Volts
Voltage	7-ground	starter switch	OFF No Volts
Voltage	7-ground	starter switch	ON Battery Volts
Continuity	1-ground		Continuity
Continuity	12-ground		Continuity
Continuity	9-ground		Continuity

Glow Plug Relay Check

1. With an ohmmeter check that there is no continuity between terminals 1 and 2 and that there is continuity between terminals 3 and 4.
If the continuity is not as shown above, replace the relay.
2. Apply battery volts between the continuity between terminals 3 and 4 and that there is no continuity between terminals 1 and 2.
If the operation is not as shown above, replace the relay.

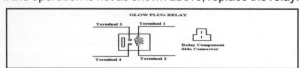

Glow Plug Check

1. With an ohmmeter check that there is continuity between the glow plug terminal and ground.
Specified Resistance: 0.75ohms @ 20°c
2. If there is no continuity replace the glow plug/s as required.
Diagram is on the next page

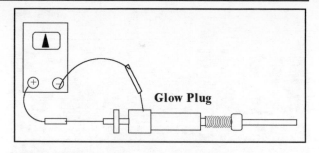

Water Temperature Sensor Check

1. Disconnect the sensor harness connector and check the resistance between the terminals at varying temperatures.

Coolant Temperature (°c)	Resistance(k/ohms)
-20	10-20
0	4-7
20	2-3
40	0.9-1.3
60	0.4-0.7
80	0.2-0.4

2. If the resistance is not as shown, repair/replace as required.

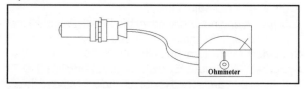

Intake Air System Checks

Intake Heater Inspection
1-With an ohmmeter, check that there is continuity between the intake heater terminal and ground.
2-If there is no continuity, replace the heater

Intake Heater Relay Check

1. With an ohmmeter check that there is continuity between terminals e and g, and that there is no continuity between terminals B and G.
If the continuity is not as shown above, replace the relay.
2. Apply battery volts between the continuity between terminals e and g and that there is continuity between terminals B and G.
If the operation is not as shown above, replace the relay.

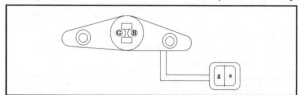

Continued on page 348

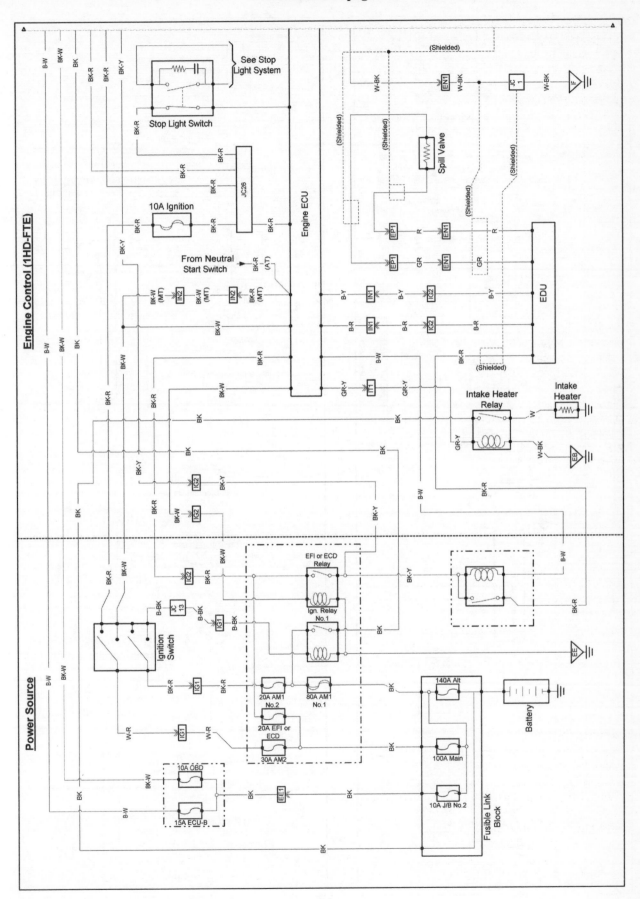

347

Continued on page 349

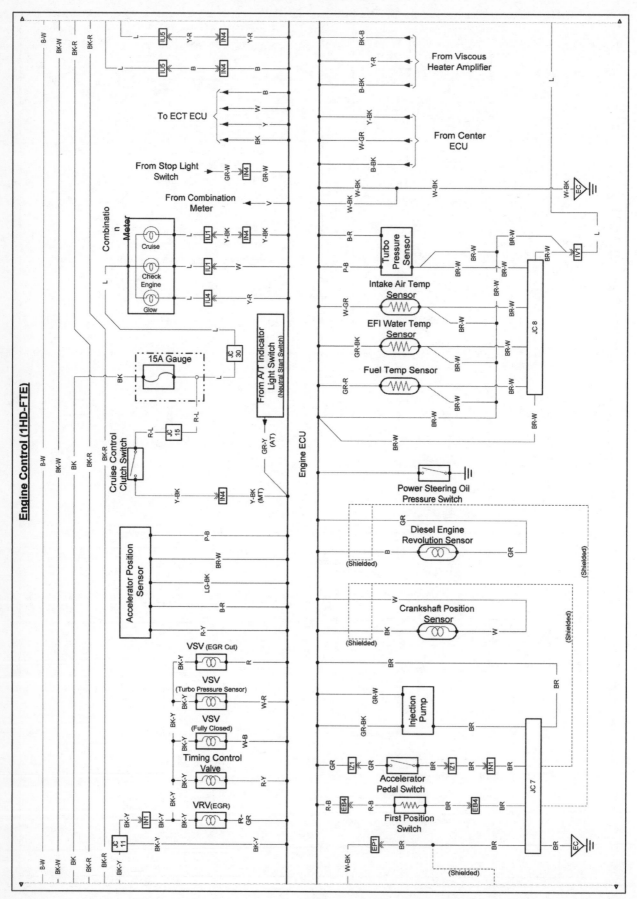

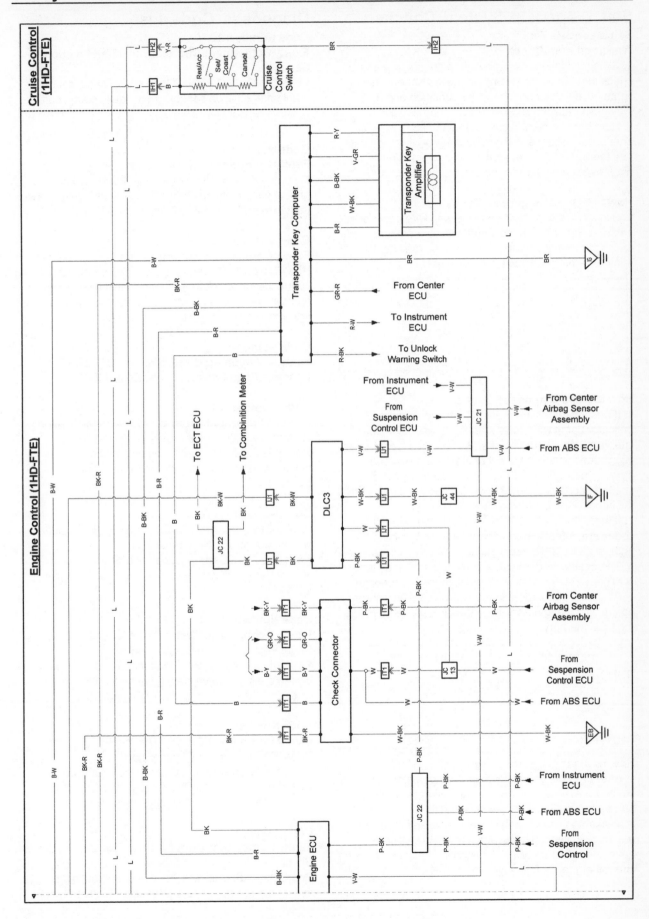

Self Diagnosis System Checks

Self Diagnosis Test
Warning Lamp Check

1. Switch on the ingition (don't start the engine) and check that the warning lamp on the instrument cluster lights up, if it does not check the condition of the indicator lamp globe and/or relevant harness/s.
2. Start the engine and ensure that the light goes out after a few seconds. If the lamp stays on it will indicate that there are faults present in the system and the diagnostic codes need to be extracted.

How to Extract Diagnostic Codes

1. Switch on the ignition, install a jump wire between the 13 and 4 terminals on the diagnostic connector and read the codes that are being output through the check engine warning lamp on the dash panel.

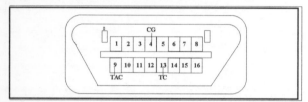

How to Read Diagnostic Codes.

1. If no fault codes are present in the system the Glow Indicator Lamp will flash continuously at 0.25 second intervals. If faults codes are present (For Example Code 13), in the system there will at first be a 4.5 second pause, there will then be a 0.5 second flash, a 1.5 second pause and then 3 more 0.5 second flashes on the check engine warning lamp.
2. If more than one code is present in the system the codes are output in numerical sequence lowest to highest with a 2.5 second pause between each code.
3. The codes will continue to be output until the jump wire has been removed from the diagnostic connector.
4. All codes that appear in the code list below will light up the check engine warning lamp and will be stored in the ECU memory.

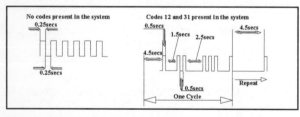

How to Clear Diagnostic Codes

1. After all of the codes have been output, clear all codes from the system by disconnecting the battery terminals for at least 30 seconds and then replacing. It is advisable to now roadtest the vehicle and then carry out the self diagnosis test again to ensure all codes have been cleared from the system and that there are no intermittent faults in the system

Diagnostic Code List

Code Number: 12
Faulty Component/Circuit: Crankshaft Position Sensor
Possible Fault Causes: Open and/or short in the crankshaft position sensor circuit, faulty crankshaft position sensor or faulty ECU.

Code Number: 13
Faulty Component/Circuit: Engine Speed Sensor
Possible Fault Causes: Open and/or short in the engine speed sensor circuit, faulty engine speed sensor, fault in the STA circuit or faulty Engine ECU.

Code Number: 14
Faulty Component/Circuit: Timing Control System
Possible Fault Causes: Open and/or short in the timing control circuit, blocked fuel filter, fuel freezing or air in, faults in the injection pump (internal pressure and/or timing control valve), or faulty Engine ECU.

Code Number: 17
Faulty Component/Circuit: Interior IC Failure
Possible Fault Causes: Faulty Engine ECU.

Code Number: 19 (1)
Faulty Component/Circuit: Throttle Pedal Position Sensor Circuit (Open or Short)
Possible Fault Causes: Open and/or short in the sensor sensor circuit, faulty sensor or faulty Engine ECU.

Code Number: 19 (2)
Faulty Component/Circuit: Throttle Pedal Position Sensor Circuit (IDL Switch/Range)
Possible Fault Causes: Open and/or short in the sensor sensor circuit, faulty sensor or faulty Engine ECU.

Code Number: 19 (3)
Faulty Component/Circuit: Throttle Pedal Closed Pedal Position Switch Circuit (Short)
Possible Fault Causes: Short in the throttle pedal closed position switch circuit, faulty throttle pedal closed position switch, or faulty Engine ECU.

Code Number: 19 (4)
Faulty Component/Circuit: Throttle Pedal Closed Pedal Position Switch Circuit (Short)
Possible Fault Causes: Open in the throttle pedal closed position switch circuit, faulty throttle pedal closed position switch, or faulty Engine ECU.

Code Number: 22
Faulty Component/Circuit: Water Temperature Sensor Circuit
Possible Fault Causes: Open and/or short in the sensor sensor circuit, faulty sensor or faulty Engine

Code Number: 24
Faulty Component/Circuit: Intake Air Temperature Sensor Circuit
Possible Fault Causes: Open and/or short in the sensor sensor circuit, faulty sensor or faulty Engine ECU.

Code Number: 32
Faulty Component/Circuit: Injection Pump System
Possible Fault Causes: Open and/or short in the injection pump correction control circuit, faulty injection pump correction unit or faulty Engine ECU.

Code Number: 33
Faulty Component/Circuit: Intake Shutter Control Circuit
Possible Fault Causes: Open and/or short in the VSV for the shutter control circuit, faulty VSV for the shutter control circuit or faulty Engine ECU.

Code Number: 35 (1HD-T)
Faulty Component/Circuit: Turbo Pressure Sensor Circuit
Possible Fault Causes: Open and/or short in the sensor circuit, faulty sensor, or faulty Engine ECU..

Code Number: 39
Faulty Component/Circuit: Fuel Temperature Sensor Circuit
Possible Fault Causes: Open and/or short in the sensor circuit, faulty sensor, or faulty Engine ECU..

Code Number: 42
Faulty Component/Circuit: Vehicle Speed Sensor Signal
Possible Fault Causes: Open and/or short in the vehicle speed sensor circuit, faulty vehicle speed sensor, faulty instrument cluster or Engine ECU.

Code Number: 89
Faulty Component/Circuit: Interior IC Fault
Possible Fault Causes: Faulty Engine ECU.

Code Number: 97
Faulty Component/Circuit: EDU Circuit Fault
Possible Fault Causes: Open and/or short in the EDU circuit, faulty spill control valve or faulty Engine ECU

Code Number: 99
Faulty Component/Circuit: Engine Immobiliser System Fault
Possible Fault Causes: Open or short in the imobiliser system circuit, faults in the transponder key amplifier, computer, key coil and/or Engine ECU.

Fail Safe Mode

1-If any of the following codes DTC12, 13, 19, 22, 24, 35, 39, and/or 42 are recorded the ECU will automatically be placed into failsafe mode.
Diagnostic Code No: 12
Fail Safe Operation: TCV duty is fixed at 30%
Fail Safe Deactivation Conditions: 2 or more TDC signals are detected for 4 engine revolutions.

Diagnostic Code No: 13
Fail Safe Operation: Fuelcut, TCV duty is fixed at 1.0%, Closed diesel throttle valve
Fail Safe Deactivation Conditions: 2 or more NE signals are detected for 0.5secs.

Diagnostic Code No: 19(1)
Fail Safe Operation: Throttle pedal is in the closed position (SW ON) and throttle pedal is fixed at 0%
Fail Safe Operation: Throttle pedal is in the closed position (SW ON) and throttle pedal is fixed at 8%
Fail Safe Deactivation Conditions: (+)B OFF

Diagnostic Code No: 19(2)
Fail Safe Operation: Throttle pedal is in the closed position (SW ON) and throttle pedal is fixed at 0%
Fail Safe Operation: Throttle pedal is in the closed position (SW ON) and throttle pedal is fixed at 8%
Fail Safe Operation: Throttle pedal position is less than 10%
Fail Safe Deactivation Conditions: (+)B OFF.

Diagnostic Code No: 19(3)
When the Idle Switch is Faulty
Fail Safe Operation: Throttle pedal is in the closed position (SW ON) and throttle pedal is fixed at 0%
Fail Safe Operation: Throttle pedal is in the closed position (SW OFF) and throttle pedal is fixed at 8%
When the Idle Switch is OK
Fail Safe Operation: (Idle Switch ON)
Throttle pedal is in the closed position (SW ON) and throttle pedal is fixed at 0%
Fail Safe Operation: (Idle Switch OFF)
Throttle pedal is in the closed position (SW OFF) and throttle pedal is less than 10%
Fail Safe Deactivation Conditions: (+)B OFF.

Diagnostic Code No: 19(4)
Fail Safe Operation: Throttle pedal position less than 10%
Fail Safe Deactivation Conditions: (+) B OFF

Diagnostic Code No: 22
Fail Safe Operation: Water temperature is fixed at 100°c
Fail Safe Deactivation Conditions: Vehicle returned to normal conditions.

Diagnostic Code No: 24
Fail Safe Operation: Intake air temperature is fixed at 20°c
Fail Safe Deactivation Conditions: Vehicle returned to normal conditions.

Diagnostic Code No: 35
Fail Safe Operation: Intake air pressure is at 101.3kpa
Fail Safe Deactivation Conditions: Vehicle returned to normal conditions.

Diagnostic Code No: 39
Fail Safe Operation: Fuel temperature is fixed to 60°c
Fail Safe Deactivation Conditions: Vehicle returned to normal conditions.

Diagnostic Code No: 42
Fail Safe Operation: Vehicle speed is set at 0kmh
Fail Safe Deactivation Conditions: Vehicle speed >0kmh.

ECU Voltage Checks
Please Note: there are four connectors on this ECU.
Connector (A) is 22 pin, Connector (B) is 12 pin,
Connector (C) is 16 pin, Connector (D) is 26 pin

See next 4 pages for voltage readings

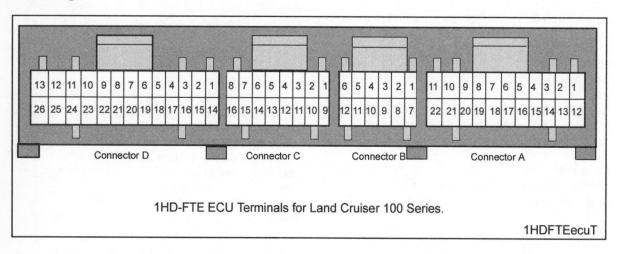

1HD-FTE ECU Terminals for Land Cruiser 100 Series.

1HDFTEecuT

Between Terminals	Wiring Colour	Condition	Specified Value (v)
A01 - D14	B-R-BR	Always	9-14
A02 - D14	G-Y-BR	Ignition Switch ON	0-3
A02 - D14	G-Y-BR	Air Intake Heater ON	9-14
A03 - D13	B-W-W-B	Ignition Switch ON	9-14
A04 - D14	P-B-BR	Ignition Switch ON	9-14
A05 - D14	W-BR	Check engine lamp ON	0-3
A05 - D14	W-BR	Check engine lamp not ON	9-14
A06 - D14	L-B-BR	Engine started for a few seconds	Pulse Generation
A07 - D14			
A08 - D14	Y-B-BR	Ignition ON	Pulse Generation
A09 - D14	V-BR	Ignition ON, Drive wheels turning slowly	Pulse Generation
A10 - D14			
A11 - D14	B-W-BR	Engine Cranking	6.0 or More
A12 - D14	B-Y-BR	Ignition Switch ON	9-14
A13 - D14	L-W-BR	Ignition Switch ON	0-1.5
A14 - D14	B-R-BR	Ignition Switch ON	9-14
A15 - D14	V-W-BR	Hand held tester connected	Pulse Generation
A16 - D14			
A17 - D14	L-B-BR	Idling	Pulse Generation
A18 - D14			
A19 - D14			
A20 - D14	B-L-BR	Power heater switch ON	0-3
A20 - D14	B-L-BR	Power heater switch OFF	9-14
A21 - D14			
A22 - D14			

Between Terminals	Wiring Colour	Condition	Specified Value
B01 - D14	Y-R-BR	Glow indicator lamp ON	0-3
B01 - D14	Y-R-BR	Glow indicator lamp Not ON	9-14
B02 - D14	W-G-BR	A/C Switch ON (Idling)	0-1.5
B02 - D14	W-G-BR	A/C Switch OFF	9-14
B03 -D14	GR-BR	Throttle pedal fully closed	9-14
B03 - D14	GR-BR	Throttle pedal fully opened	0-3
B04 - D14			
B05 - B04	R-Y-BR-W	Throttle pedal fully closed	0.6-1.3
B05 - B04	R-Y-BR-W	Throttle pedal fully opened	2.8-4.5
B06 - B04	L-R-BR-W	Ignition ON	4.5-5.5
B07 - D14	B-BR	Idling	Pulse Generation
B08 - D14	L-B-BR	Ignition ON	9-14
B08 - D14	L-B-BR	A/C Cut Controlled (Driving at less than 30kmh and throttle opened fully for 5 secs)	0-3
B09 - B04	LG-B-BR-W	Throttle pedal fully closed	9-14
B09 - B04	R-Y-BR-W	Throttle pedal fully opened	0-3
B10 - D14			
B11 - D14			
B12 - B04	LG-B-BR-W	Throttle pedal fully closed	0.6-1.3
B12 - B04	P-L-BR-W	Throttle pedal fully opened	2.8-4.5

Between Terminals	Wiring Colour	Condition	Specified Value
C01 - C09	L-R-BR-W	Ignition Switch ON	4.5-5.5
C02 - C09	P-L-BR-W	40kpa of vacuum applied	1.0-1.8
C02 - C09	P-L-BR-W	135kpa of vacuum applied	2.3-4.2
C03 - C09	W-G-BR-W	Engine idling (intake air temp @ 0°c)	0.2-3.8
C04 - C09	W-G-BR-W	Engine idling (coolant temp @ 60°c)	0-1.5
C05 - C09	B-R-BR-W (LHD)	Ignition switch ON (Engine Cold)	0.5-3.8
C05 - C09	G-R-BR-W (RHD)	Ignition switch ON (Engine Cold)	0.5-3.8
C06 - D14	G-B-BR	For 0.5secs after the Ignition switch is ON	Pulse Generation
C07 - D14	L-B-BR	Heater Blower Switch ON	0-3
C07 - D14	L-B-BR	Heater Blower Switch OFF	9-14
C08 - D14	L-B-BR	Engine idling, steering wheel turning	0-3
C08 - D14	L-B-BR	Ignition ON	9-14
C09 - D14			
C10 - D14			
C11 - D14			
C12 - D14			
C13 - D14			
C14 - D14	G-W-BR	For 0.5secs after the Ignition switch is ON	Pulse Generation
C15 - D14			
C16 - D14			

Between Terminals	Wiring Colour	Condition	Specified Value
D01 – D14			
D02 – D14			
D03 – D14	R-BR	Ignition Switch ON	0-3
D03 – D14	R-BR	Maintain engine speed at 1500RPM after warm up	9-14
D04 – D13			
D05 – D14			
D06 – D14			
D07 – D14	R-L-BR	Auto shift in the 1st gear position	9-14
D07 – D14	R-L-BR	Auto shift in any other position	0-3
D08 – D14			
D09 – D13	W-R-W-B	VSV for atmospheric pressure leaning OFF	9-14
D09 – D13	W-R-W-B	VSV for atmospheric pressure leaning ON	0-3
D10 – D13	W-L-W-B	VSV (OFF) Idling	9-14
D10 – D13	W-L-W-B	VSV ON (after Ign Sw is OFF for 2 secs)	0-3
D11 – D13	R-Y-W-B	Ignition Switch ON	9-14
D11 – D13	R-Y-W-B	Idling	Pulse Generation
D12 – D14	L-Y-BR	Ignition Switch ON	9-14
D12 – D14	L-Y-BR	Idling	Pulse Generation
D13 – D14			
D14 – D14			
D15 – D14			
D16 – D14			
D17 – D16	B-W	Idling	Pulse Generation
D18 – D14			
D19 – D18	L-G	Idling	Pulse Generation
D20 – D14			
D21 – D14			
D22 – D14			
D23 – D14	Y-R-BR	Heater Blower Switch ON	0-3
D23 – D14	Y-R-BR	Heater Blower Switch OFF	9-14
D24 – D14	R-G-W-B	Ignition Switch ON	9-14
D24 – D13	EGR ON	Idling	Pulse Generation
D25 – D14	L-B-BR	Ignition Switch ON	Pulse Generation
D26 – D14			

Diagnostic Code Circuit/Component Tests

Diagnostic Code 12 (Crankshaft Position Sensor Circuit Fault)

1. Check the resistance of the sensor by removing the harness connector and checking the resistance between the sensor terminals.

Specified Resistance: 19-32ohms (cold)
Specified Resistance: 24-37ohms (hot)

If the resistance is not as shown, replace the sensor.

2. If the sensor is OK in step1, check for open and/or short in the harness and connector between the engine ECU and crankshaft position sensor, if faults are found repair/replace as required.

3. If no faults are found in step2, check for correct installation of the sensor, if faults are found repair/replace as required.

4. If no faults are found in step3, check the condition and/or operation of the engine ECU, if faults are found repair/replace as required.

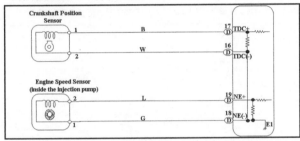

Diagnostic Code 13 (Engine Speed Sensor Circuit Fault)

1. Check the resistance of the pick up sensor by checking the resistance between the sensor terminals.

Specified Resistamce: 205-255ohms

If the resistance is not as shown, check the condition and/or replace the injection pump

2. If no faults are found in step1, check for open and/or short in the harness and connector between the ECU and speed sensor, if faults are found repair/replace as required.

3. If no faults are found in step2, check the sensor installation, if faults are found rectify as required.

4. If no faults are found in step3, check the condition and/or operation of the engine ECU, if faults are found repair/replace as required.

Use above diagram

Diagnostic Code 14 (Timing Control System Fault)

1. Check the operation of the timing control valve by disconnecting the timing control valve harness connector and checking the resistance between the terminals.

Specified Resistance: 10-14ohms @ 20°c

If the resistance is not as shown, check and/or replace the injection pump.

2. If no faults are found in step1, remove the 26pin engine ECU connector (D) and record the voltage between the connector terminal D11 and body ground.

Specified Voltage: 9-14v

3. If the voltage is not as shown in step2, check for open and/or short in the harness and connector between the timing control valve and the engine ECU and between the timing control valve and the ECD main relay, if faults are found repair/replace as required.

4. If the voltage is OK in step2, switch on the ignition and check the voltage between the 26 pin ECU conenctor (D) terminal 11 and body ground (harness connected)

Specified Voltage: 9-14v

If the voltage is not as shown, check the condition and/or operation of the engine ECU, if faults are found repair/replace as required.

5. If the voltage is OK in step4, check the condition and/or operation of the fuel filter, fuel freezing and/or air in the fuel, if faults are found repair/replace as required.

6. If no faults are found in step5, check the condition and/or operation of the fuel injection pump, if faults are found repair/replace as required.

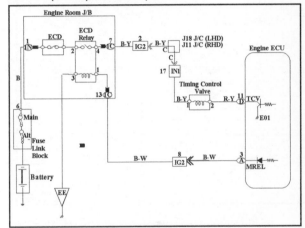

Diagnostic Code 19(1) (Throttle Pedal Position Sensor Circuit Fault) (Open and/or Short)
Diagnostic Code 19(3) (Throttle Pedal Closed Position Switch Circuit Fault) (Open and/or Short)
Diagnostic Code 19(4) (Throttle Pedal Closed Position Switch Circuit Fault) (Open and/or Short)

1. Disconnect the throttle pedal position sensor harness connector and check the voltage between the terminals 4 and body ground (harness side).

Specified Voltage: 4.5-5.5v

2. If the voltage is step1 is Ok, switch ON the ignition and check the voltage between the 12 pin ECU connector (B) terminals 5, 12 and 4.

Specified Voltage:
0.6-1.3v (Throttle Pedal Fully Closed)
Specified Voltage:
2.8-4.5v (Throttle Pedal Fully Open)

If the voltage is OK, check the condition and/or operation of the engine ECU, if faults are found repair/replace as required.

3. If the voltage in step2 is not as shown, check for open and/or short in the harness and connector between the engine ECU and throttle pedal position sensor (VA,VAS line), if faults are found repair/replace as required.

4. If no faults are found in step3, replace the throttle pedal position sensor.

5. If the voltage in step1 is not as shown, check for voltage between the the 12 pin ECU connector (B) terminals 6 and 4 (harness connected).

Specified Voltage: 4.5-5.5v

If the voltage is not as shown, check the condition and/or operation of the engine ECU, if faults are found repair/replace as required.

6. If the voltage is Ok in step5, check for open and/or short in the harness between the engine ECU and throttle pedal position sensor (VCC line), if faults are found repair/replace as required.

Diagnostic Code 19(2) (Throttle Pedal Position Sensor Circuit Fault) (IDL Switch/Range Fault)

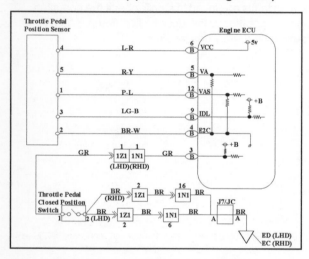

1. Check the voltage between the 12 pin ECU connector (B) terminals 9 and 4 (harness connected).

Specified Voltage: 9-14v (Throttle Pedal Fully Closed)

Specified Voltage: 0-3v (Throttle Pedal Fully Open)

2. If the voltage is not as shown in step1, check for open and/or short in the harness between the engine ECU and throttle pedal position sensor (IDL line), if faults are found repair/replace as required.

3. If no faults are found in step2, replace the throttle pedal position sensor

4. If the voltage is OK in step1, check the voltage between the terminals 4 and body ground (harness side).

Specified Voltage: 4.5-5.5v

5. If the voltage is OK in step4, check the voltage between the 12 pin ECU connector (B) terminals 5, 12 and 4.

Specified Voltage: 0.6-1.3v (Throttle Pedal Fully Closed)

Specified Voltage: 2.8-4.5v (Throttle Pedal Fully Open)

If the voltage is OK, check the condition and/or operation of the engine ECU, if faults are found repair/replace as required.

6. If the voltage in step5 is not as shown, check for open

and/or short in the harness and connector between the engine ECU and throttle pedal position sensor (VA,VAS line), if faults are found repair/replace as required.

7. If no faults are found in step6, replace the throttle pedal position sensor.

8. If the voltage is not as shown in step4, check for voltage between the the 12 pin ECU connector (B) terminals 6 and 4 (harness connected).

Specified Voltage: 4.5-5.5v

If the voltage is not as shown, check the condition and/or operation of the engine ECU, if faults are found repair/replace as required.

9. If the voltage is Ok in step8, check for open and/or short in the harness between the engine ECU and throttle pedal position sensor (VCC line), if faults are found repair/replace as required.

Use First Code 19 Diagram

Diagnostic Code 22 (Water Temperature Sensor Circuit Test)

Please Note: If codes 22, 24 and 39 are output at the same time, the E2 (sensor ground) may be open.

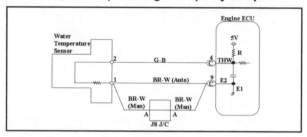

1. Remove the ECU from the body panel, switch ON the ignition and check the voltage between 16 pin ECU connector (C) terminals 4 and 9 terminals (harness connected)

Specified Voltage: 0.2-3.8v @ 20°c

Specified Voltage: 0.1-1.5v @ 80°c

2. If the voltage is OK in step1, check the system for intermittent faults, if faults are found reapir/replace as required.

3. If the voltage is not as shown in step1, check the operation of the temp sensor by removing the sensor from the engine, placing in a suitable container of water and checking the sensor resistance between the terminals at varying temperatures.

Sensor Temperature (°c)	Sensor Resistance (k/ohms)
-20	10-20
0	4-7
20	2-3
40	0.9-1.3
60	0.4-0.7
80	0.2-0.4

If the resistance is not as shown, repair/replace as required.

4. If the resistance in step3 is OK, check for open and/or short circuit in the harness between the ECU and water temp sensor, if faults are found repair/replace as required.

5. If no faults are found in step4, check the condition and/or operation of the ECU, if faults are found repair/ replace as required.

Diagnostic Code 24 (Intake Air Temperature Sensor Circuit Test)

Please Note: If codes 22, 24 and 39 are output at the same time, the E2 (sensor ground) may be open.

1. Remove the ECU from the body panel, switch ON the ignition and check the voltage between 16 pin ECU connector (C) terminals 3 and 9 terminals (harness connected)

Specified Voltage: **0.2-3.8v @ 20°c**
Specified Voltage: **0.1-1.5v @ 80°c**

2. If the voltage is OK in step1, check the system for intermittent faults, if faults are found reapir/replace as required.

3. If the voltage is not as shown in step1, check the operation of the sensor by removing the sensor from the engine, placing in a suitable container of water and checking the sensor resistance between the terminals at varying temperatures.

Sensor Temperature (°c)	Sensor Resistance (k/ohms)
-20	10-20
0	4-7
20	2-3
40	0.9-1.3
60	0.4-0.7
80	0.2-0.4

If the resistance is not as shown, repair/replace as required.

4. If the resistance in step3 is OK, check for open and/ or short circuit in the harness between the ECU and sensor, if faults are found repair/replace as required.

5. If no faults are found in step4, check the condition and/or operation of the ECU, if faults are found repair/ replace as required.

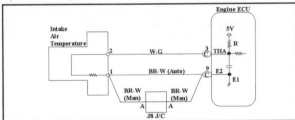

Diagnostic Code 32 (Injection Pump Correction System Fault)

1. Remove the injection pump correction unit from the injection pump and install another control unit to the pump. Clear diagnostic codes from the system, switch on the ignition and check for diagnostic codes again.

2. If code 32 is not output, in step1, check the condition and/or operation of the injection pump, if faults are found repair/replace as required.

3. If code 32 is output in step1, check the condition and/ or operation of the ECU, if faults are found repair/replace as required.

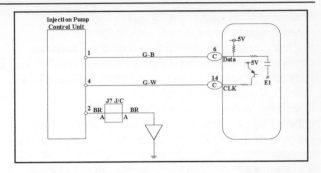

Diagnostic Code 33 (Intake Shuuter Control Circuit Fault)

Please Note: If codes 22, 31 and 41 are output at the same time, the E2 (sensor ground) may be open

1. Remove the glovebox compartment door and disconnect the 26 pin ECU connector (D). Switch ON the ignition and check the VSV function by connecting a jump wire between the 26 pin ECU connector (D) terminal 10 and body ground (VSV ON), then disconnect the wire between the 26 pin ECU connector (D) terminal 10 and body ground (VSV ON). Ensure that when the VSV is ON that air flows from through the rear port to the front port and that when the VSV is OFF that air flows through the rear port to the air filter at the rear of the VSV.

2. If the operation is of the VSV is OK in step1, check the condition and/or operation of the ECU, if faults are found repair/replace as required.

3. If the operation of the VSV is not OK in step1, check for open and/or short in the harness and connector between the engine ECU and VSV for intake shutter and between the VSV and the ECD main relay, if faults are found repair/replace as required.

4. If no faults are found in step3, replace the VSV.

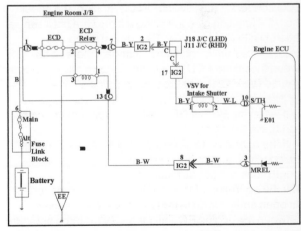

Diagnostic Code 35 (Turbo Pressure Sensor Circuit Fault)

Please Note: If codes 22, 24, 35 and 39 are output at the same time, the E2 (sensor ground) may be open

1. Disconnect the sensor harness connector, switch ON the ignition ansd with a voltmeter check the voltage between the connector terminals VC and E2 (harness side).

Specified Voltage: 4.75-5.25v.

If the voltage is not as shown, replace the sensor.

2. If the voltage is OK in step1, remove the glovebox compartment door, switch ON the ignition and check the voltage between the 16 pin ECU connector (C) terminal 1 and 9 (harness connected).

Specified Voltage: 4.5-5.5v.

If the voltage is not as shown, check the condition and/ or operation of the ECU, if faults are found repair/replace as required.

3. If the voltage is OK in step2, switch ON the ignition and check the voltage between the 16 pin ECU connector (C) terminal 2 and 9 (harness connected).

Specified Voltage: 1.7-2.9v.

If the voltage is not as shown, check the condition and/ or operation of the ECU, if faults are found repair/replace as required.

4. If the voltage is Ok in step3, check for open and/or short in the harness and connector between the the engine ECU and the turbo pressure sensor, if faults are found repair/replace as required.

5. If no faults are found in step4, check the connection of the vacuum hose between the turbo pressure sensor and the VSV for the turbo pressure sensor, VSV for the pressure sensor and the intake manifold, if faults are found repair/replace as required.

6. If no faults are found in step5, check the resistance of the VSV for the turbo pressure sensor by disconnecting the harness connector and checking that there is continuity between the terminals.

Specified Resistance: 37-44ohms @ 20°c

If the resistance is not as shown, replace the sensor.

7. If the resistance in step6 is Ok, check the operation of the VSV for Turbo Pressure Sensor by removing the glovebox compartment door and disconnect the 26 pin ECU connector (D). Switch ON the ignition and check the VSV function by connecting a jump wire between the 26 pin ECU connector (D) terminal 9 and body ground (VSV ON), and then disconnect the wire between the 26 pin ECU connector (D) terminal 9 and body ground (VSV ON). Ensure that when the VSV is ON that air flows from through the rear port to the airfilter, and that when the VSV is OFF that air flows through the rear port to the front port of the VSV.

8. If the operation is of the VSV is OK in step7, check the condition and/or operation of the ECU, if faults are found repair/replace as required.

9. If the operation of the VSV is not OK in step1, check for open and/or short in the harness and connector between the engine ECU and the VSV for turbo pressure sensor and the ECD main relay, if faults are found repair/replace as required.

10. If no faults are found in step9, replace the VSV.

Diagram is in the next column

Diagnostic Code 39 (Fuel Temperature Sensor Circuit Fault)

Please Note: If codes 22, 24, 35 and 39 are output at the same time, the E2 (sensor ground) may be open

1. Remove the glovebox compartment door, switch ON the ignition and check the voltage between the 16 pin ECU connector (C) terminal 5 and 9 (harness connected) at varying temperatures.

Fuel Temperature (°c)	Voltage (v)
20 (engine is cool)	0.2-3.8
80 (engine is hot)	0.1-1.5

If the voltage is OK, check the system for intermittent faults, if faults are found repair/replace as required.

2. If the voltage is Ok in step1, check the operation of the fuel temperature sensor by by removing the sensor from the engine, placing in a suitable container of water and checking the sensor resistance between the terminals at varying temperatures.

Sensor Temperature (°c)	Sensor Resistance (k/ohms)
-20	10-20
0	4-7
20	2-3
40	0.9-1.3
60	0.4-0.7
80	0.2-0.4

If the resistance is not as shown, repair/replace as required.

3. If the resistance in step2 is OK, check for open and/ or short circuit in the harness between the ECU and sensor, if faults are found repair/replace as required.

4. If no faults are found in step3, check the condition and/or operation of the ECU, if faults are found repair/ replace as required.

Diagram is on the next page

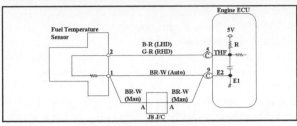

Diagnostic Code 42 (Vehicle Speed Sensor Circuit Test)

1. Road test the vehicle and check the operation of the speedometer, if faults are found repair/replace as required

2. If no faults are found in step1, remove the glovebox compartment door, put the shift lever in neutral, jack up one of the front wheels, switch on the ignition and check the voltage between the 22 Pin ECU connector (A) terminal 9 and body ground (harness connected) with the wheel being turned slowly.

Specified Voltage: Between 0v and 4.5V ±5.5v (each full turn of the wheel)

If the voltage is not as shown, check the condition of the harness and/or connector between the combination meter and the engine ECU, if faults are found repair/replace as required.

3. If the voltage in step2 is Ok, check the condition and/or operation of the engine ECU, if faults are found repair/replace as required.

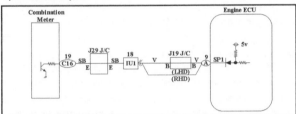

Diagnostic Code 97 (EDU Circuit Fault)

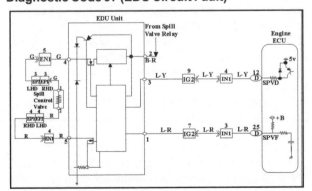

1. Disconnect the EDU harness connector, switch ON the ignition and check the voltage between the connector No2 terminal and body ground (harness side)

Specified Voltage: 10-14v

If the voltage is not as shown, carry out "**Power Source Circuit Check**" shown in the "**Non Diagnostic Code Related Checks**".

2. If the voltage is Ok in step1, check the continuity

between the EDU ground bolt and body ground, if faults are found tighten bolt as required.

3. If no faults are found in step2, record the resistance between the EDU connector terminals 4 and 5 (harness side)

Specified Resistance: 1.7ohms

4. If the resistance is not as shown in step3, check the operation of the spill control valve by disconnect the valve harness connector and checking the resistance between the terminals.

Specified Resistance: 10-14ohms @ 20°c

If the resistance is not as shown, replace the injection pump

5. If no faults are found in step4, check for open and/or short in the harness and connector between the spill control valve and the EDU, if faults are found repair/replace as required.

6. If no faults are found in step5, check for open and/or short in the harness and connector between the engine ECU and the EDU, if faults are found repair/replace as required.

7. If no faults are found in step6, remove the glovebox compartment door, switch on the ignition and check the voltage between the 26 Pin ECU connector (D) terminal 12 and body ground (harness connected).

Specified Voltage: 9-14v

If the voltage is not as shown, check the condition and/or operation of the engine ECU, if faults are found repair/replace as required.

8. If the voltage is Ok in step7, switch ON the ignition and check the voltage between the 26 Pin ECU connector (D) terminal 25 and body ground (harness connected).

Specified Voltage: 9-14v

If the voltage is not as shown, check the condition and/or operation of the engine ECU, if faults are found repair/replace as required.

9. If the voltage is OK in step8, check the condition and/or operation of the EDU, if faults are found repair/replace as required.

10. If the resistance is Ok in step3, check for open and/or short in the harness and connector between the engine ECU and the EDU, if faults are found repair/replace as required.

11. If no faults are found in step10, remove the glovebox compartment door, switch on the ignition and check the voltage between the 26 Pin ECU connector (D) terminal 12 and body ground (harness connected).

Specified Voltage: 9-14v

If the voltage is not as shown, check the condition and/or operation of the engine ECU, if faults are found repair/replace as required.

12. If the voltage is Ok in step11, switch ON the ignition and check the voltage between the 26 Pin ECU connector (D) terminal 25 and body ground (harness connected).

Specified Voltage: 9-14v

If the voltage is not as shown, check the condition and/or operation of the engine ECU, if faults are found repair/

replace as required.

13. If the voltage is OK in step12, check the condition and/or operation of the EDU, if faults are found repair/replace as required.

Non Diagnostic Code Related Checks

ECU Power Source Circuit Check

1. Remove the glove compartment door, switch ON the ignition and record the voltage between the 22 pin ECU connector (A) terminals 12 and the 26 pin connector (D) terminal 14 (harness connected)

Specified Voltage: **9-14v**

2. If the voltage is not as shown in step1, check for open in the harness and connector between the ECU connector (D) terminal 17 and body ground (harness connected), if faults are found repair/replace as required.

3. If no faults are found in step2, check the operation of the ECD main relay, if faults are found repair/replace as required.

4. If no faults are found in step3, check the condition and/or operation of the ECD fuse, if faults are found check for shorts in all of the harness/s connected to the fuse, if faults are found repair/replace as required.

5. If no faults are found in step4, check for open in harness and connector between the engine ECU and the ECD main relay, between the ECD main relay and battery, if faults are found repair/replace as required.

6. If no faults are found in step5, switch ON the ignition and check the voltage between the 22 pin ECU connector (A) terminal 14 and the the 26 pin ECU connector (D) terminal 14 (harness connected), if faults are found repair/replace as required.

Specified Voltage: **9-14v**

If the voltage is not as shown, check the condition and/or operation of the ignition switch, if faults are found repair/replace as required.

7. If no faults are found in step6, check for open in the harness and connector between the emmision ECU, ignition switch and battery, if faults are found repair/replace as required.

8. If no faults are found in step7, check for open and/or short in the harness and connector between the ignition switch and the engine ECU, if faults are found repair/replace as required.

9. If no faults are found in step8, switch ON the ignition and check the voltage between the 22 pin ECU connector (A) terminal 3 and body ground (harness connected).

Specified Voltage: **9-14v**

If the voltage is Ok, check the condition and/or operation of the engine ECU, if faults are found repair/replace as required.

10. If the voltage is not as shown in step9, check for open in the harness and connector between the engine ECU and the ECD main relay, between the ECD main relay and body ground, if faults are found repair/replace as required./

11. If the voltage is Ok in step10, switch ON the ignition

and check the voltage between the 22 pin ECU connector (A) terminal 3 and body ground (harness connected).

Specified Voltage: **9-14v**

If the voltage is Ok, check the condition and/or operation of the engine ECU, if faults are found repair/replace as required.

12. If the voltage is not as shown in step9, check for open in the harness and connector between the engine ECU and the ECD main relay, between the ECD main relay and body ground, if faults are found repair/replace as required.

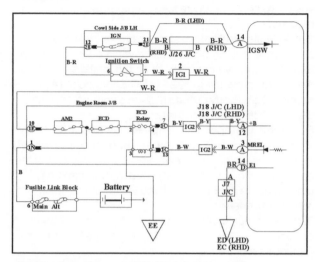

Intake Heater Control Circuit Fault

1. Switch ON the ignition and check if the glow indicator lamp lights up for 0.5seconds or more

2. If the glow indicator lamp in step1, does light up for 0.5 seconds or more check the glow indicator lamp lighting up time

Specified Light Up Time: **1.0 seconds or more @ 20°c**

If the light up time is not as shown, check the condition and/or operation of the engine ECU, if faults are found repair/replace as required.

3. If the light up time in step2 is OK, run the self diagnosis check and see if there are any codes present in the system, if there are repair the faults before carrying on with this test.

4. If no codes are present in step3, check the condition and/or operation of the intake heater relay, if faults are found repair/replace as required.

5. If no faults are found in step4, remove the glove compartment door, disconnect the 26 pin engine ECU connector (D) and record the voltage between the 26 pin ECU connector (A) terminals 2 and body ground while the engine is cranking.

Specified Voltage: **9-14v**

If the voltage is not as shown, check the condition and/or operation of the engine ECU, if faults are found repair/replace as required.

6. If the voltage is OK in step5, check for open and/or short in the harness and connector between the intake heater relay and the engine ECU, between the intake heater relay and body ground, if faults are found repair/replace as required.

7. If no faults are found in step6, disconnect the intake heater connector and check there is continuity between the intake heater termimnal and ground, if there is no continuity repair/replace as required.

8. If no faults are found in step7, check the installation of the intake heater, if faults are found repair/replace as required.

9. If no faults are found in step8, check for open and/or short in the harness between the intake heater relay and the intake heater, if faults are found repair/replace as required.

10. If the glow indicator lamp light up OK in step1, remove the glovebox door disconnect the 12 pin engine ECU harness connector (B), switch ON the ignition and check the voltage between the the 12 pin engine ECU harness connector (B) terminal 1 and body ground.

Specified Voltage: 9-14v

If the voltage is OK check the condition and/or operation of the engine ECU, if faults are found repair/replace as required.

11. If the voltage is not as shown in step10, check the condition and/or operation of the GAUGE fuse, if faults are found check for shorts in all of the relevant harness/s that connect to the fuse, if faults are found repair/replace as required.

12. If the fuse is OK in step11, check the condition and/or operation of the glow indicator lamp globe, if faults are found repair/replace as required.

13. If the globe is OK in step12, check for open in the harness and connector between the combination meter and the engine ECU and between the combination meter and the GAUGE fuse, if faults are found repair/replace as required.

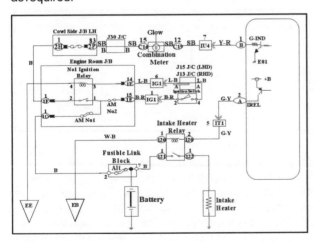

EGR Control Circuit Check

1. Check the condition and/or operation of the system vacuum hoses, if faults are found repair/replace as required.

2. If no faults are found on step1, check for vacuum between the EGR valve and the VSV for the EGR at 1500RPM by installing a 3way connector to the hose between the VSV and the EGR valve, install a vacuum gauge to the 3 way connector check the vacuum reading at 1500RPM under varying conditions. (Type (I) at 0kpa, Type (II) at between 0 and 28kpa, Type(III) at more than 28kpa).

3. If the vacuum reading in step2 is Type(I) check the operation of the E-VRV by removing the glovebox door, disconnecting the 26pin ECU connector(D), turning ON the ignition installing a jumpwire between the 26pin ECU connector(D) terminal 24 and body ground, then disconnecting the jumpwire between the 26pin ECU connector(D) terminal 24 and body ground. Air should flow through the rear port and out of the front port with the wire connected and the ignition ON, Air should flow through the rear port with the wire disconnected and the ignition ON.

4. If no faults are found in step3, check the operation of the EGR valve, if faults are found repair/replace as required.

5. If no faults are found in step4, check the condition and/or operation of the engine ECU, if faults are found repair/replace as required.

6. If the operation of the E-VRV is not as shown in step3, check the condition of the E-VRV, if faults are found repair/replace as required.

7. If no faults are found in step6, check for open and/or short in the harness and/or connector between the E-VRV and the engine ECU, and between the E-VRV and the ECD main relay, if faults are found repair/replace as required.

8. If no faults are found in step7, check the operation of the EGR valve, if faults are found repair/replace as required.

9. If no faults are found in step8, check the condition and/or operation of the engine ECU, if faults are found repair/replace as required.

10. If the reading in step2 is Type (III), check the operation of the EGR valve, if faults are found repair/replace as required.

11. If no faults are found in step10, check the condition and/or operation of the engine ECU, if faults are found repair/replace as required.

12. If the reading in step2 is Type (II), check the operation of the VSV for the EGR, if faults are found repair/replace as required.

13. If no faults are found in step12, check the voltage between the 26pin ECU connector(D) terminal 24 and body ground.

Specified Voltage: 9-14v (Ignition ON)
Specified Voltage: Pulse Generation (EGR ON)

If the voltage is not as shown, check the condition and/or operation of the engine ECU, if faults are found repair/replace as required.

14. If the voltage is OK in step 13, check for open and/or short in the harness and connector between the VSV for EGR and engine ECU, if faults are found repair/replace as required.

15. If no faults are found in step14, check the operation of the E-VRV by removing the glovebox door, disconnecting the 26pin ECU connector(D), turning ON the ignition installing a jumpwire between the 26pin ECU connector(D) terminal 24 and body ground, then disconnecting the jumpwire between the 26pin ECU connector(D) terminal 24 and body ground. Air should flow through the rear port and out of the front port with the wire connected and the ignition ON, Air should flow through the rear port with the wire disconnected and the ignition ON.

16. If no faults are found in step15, check the operation of the EGR valve, if faults are found repair/replace as required.

17. If no faults are found in step16, check the condition and/or operation of the engine ECU, if faults are found repair/replace as required.

18. If no faults are found in step17, check the condition of the E-VRV, if faults are found repair/replace as required.

19. If no faults are found in step18, check for open and/or short in the harness and/or connector between the E-VRV and the engine ECU, and between the E-VRV and the ECD main relay, if faults are found repair/replace as required.

20. If no faults are found in step19, check the operation of the EGR valve, if faults are found repair/replace as required.

21. If no faults are found in step20, check the condition and/or operation of the engine ECU, if faults are found repair/replace as required.

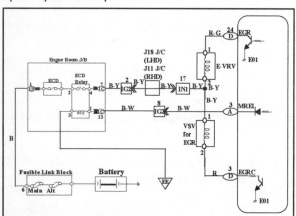

A/C Signal Circuit Fault

1. Remove the glove compartment door, start the engine and record the voltage between the 12 pin ECU connector (B) terminal 2 and body ground when the A/C switch is being turned to ON and OFF.

A/C Switch Condition	Voltage (v)
ON	Less than 1.5
OFF	9-14

2. If the voltage is not as shown in step1, check for open and/or short in the harness and connector between the engine ECU and the A/C amplifier, if faults are found repair/replace as required.

3. If no faults are found in step2, check the condition and/or operation of the A/C amplifier, if faults are found

repair/replace as required.

4. If the voltage in step1 is OK, carry out the "**Lower Engine Idle Speed Check**" shown in the **Injection System and Engine Diagnosis and Troubleshooting section.**

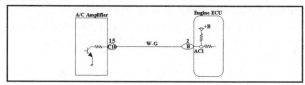

A/C Cut Control Circuit Check

1. Check the voltage between the 12 pin ECU connector (B) terminal 8 and body ground.

Specified Voltage: **9-14v (Ignition ON)**

Specified Voltage: **0-3v (at A/C cut controlled)**
   driving at less than 30khm and the throttle pedal fully down for 5 seconds

2. If the voltage in step1 is OK, check the condition and/or operation of the engine ECU, if faults are found repair/replace as required.

3. If the voltage in step1 is not as shown, check the voltage between the 22 pin ECU connector (A) terminal 8 and body ground.

Specified Voltage: Pulse Generation (Ignition ON)

4. If the voltage in step3 is OK, check the condition and/or operation of the engine ECU, if faults are found repair/replace as required.

5. If the voltage is OK in step4, check for open and short in the harness and connector between the engine ECU and the A/C amplifier, if faults are found repair/replace as required.

6. If no faults are found in step5, check the condition and/or operation of A/C amplifier, if faults are found repair/replace as required.

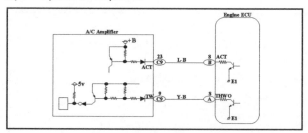

Diagnostic Connector (DLC3) Circuit Check

1. Switch On the ignition, install a jump wire between the TC and CG terminals on the diagnostic connector and ensure that the check engine warning lamp is blinking, if it is the system is OK, if any diagnostic codes are present in the system, carry out those repairs before carrying on with this test.

2. If the check engine warning lamp is not blinking in step1, switch ON the ignition and check the voltage between the TC and CG terminals on the diagnostic connector.

Specified Voltage: **9-14v**

3. If the voltage is OK in not OK in step2, check the continuity between the diagnostic connector connector teminal CG and body ground, if the continuity is not OK, repair/replace harness and/or connector as required.

4. If the continuity is OK in step3, check for open and short in the harness between diagnostic connector terminal TC and the 22 pin diagnostic connector (A) terminal 4, if faults are found repair/replace as required.

5. If no faults are found in step4, check the condition and/or operation of the engine ECU, if faults are found repair/replace as required.

6. If the voltage in step2 is OK, remove the glove box door, disconnect the 22 pin ECU connector (A), switch ON the ignition and check the voltage between the 22 pin ECU connector (A) terminal 5 and body ground.

Specified Voltage: **9-14v**

If the voltage is OK, check the condition and/or operation of the engine ECU, if faults are found repair/replace as required.

7. If the voltage is not as shown in step6, check the condition and/or operation of the check engine warning lamp globe, if faults are found repair/replace as required.

8. f no faults are found in step7, check for open and/or short in the harness and connector between the 22 pin ECU connector (A) terminal 5 and the combination meter, if faults are found repair/replace as required.

RHD Diagram

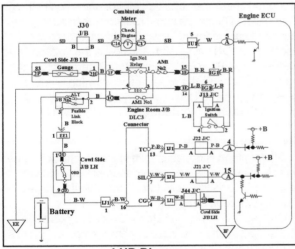

LHD Diagram

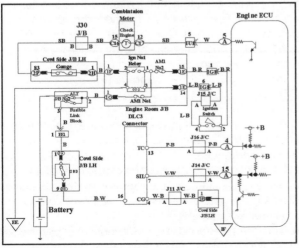

Starter Signal Test

1. Check the starter signal by removing the glove box door, disconnecting the 22 pin ECU connector (A), switch ON the ignition and checking the voltage between the 22 pin ECU connector (A) terminal 11 and body ground (harness connected) while the engine is being cranked.

Specified Voltage: **6.0v or more.**

2. If the voltage is OK in step1, carry out the "Engine Does Not Crank" check that is shown in the **Injection System and Engine Diagnosis and Troubleshooting section.**

3. If the voltage is not as shown in step2, check for open in the harness and connector between the ECU and the starter relay, if faults are found repair/replace as required.

4. If no faults are found in step3, check the condition and/or operation of the engine ECU, if faults are found repair/replace as required.

Neutral Start Switch Test

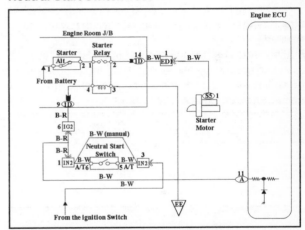

1. Disconnect the neutral start switch harness connector and check the continuity between each terminal as shown below.

Shift Lever Position	Terminal No to Continuity
P	5-6 / 2-7
R	2-8
N	5-6 / 2-9
D	2-10
2	2-3
L	2-4

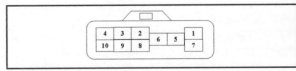

If the continuity is not as shown, replace the neutral start switch.

2. If the switch operation is OK in step1, check the voltage between the 22 pin ECU connector (A) terminal 22 and body ground (harness connected)

Shift Lever Position	Voltage (v)
P or N	0-3
L,2,D or R	9-14

3. If the voltage is not as shown in step2, check the condition and/or operation of the engine ECU, if faults are found repair/replace as required.

4. If the voltage is OK in step2, check for short and open in the harness and connector between the neutral start switch and the engine ECU, if faults are found repair/replace as required.

1st Gear Position Switch Circuit Check (Manual Only)

1. Check the operation of the shift position switch by disconnecting the harness connector and with an ohmmeter check the switch continuity as shown below.

Trasmisssion Position	Continuity
1st gear	Continuity
Other Positions	No Continuity

If the operation is not as shown, replace the switch as required.

2. If the switch operation ion step1 is Ok, check for short and open in the harness and connector between the shift position switch and the engine ECU, if faults are found repair/replace as required.

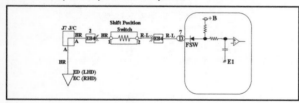

Spill Valve Relay Circuit Check

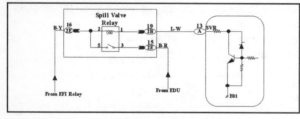

1. Check the operation of the spill valve relay by removing the relay from the vehicle and checking that there is continuity between terminals 1 and 2 and not between terminals 3 and 5.

If the operation is not as shown, replace the relay.

Apply battery volts between between terminals 1 and 2 and ensure that there is continuity between terminals 3 and 5.

If the operation is not as shown, replace the relay.

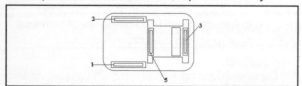

2. If the relay operation in step1 is OK, check the voltage between the ECU 26 Pin Connector (A) terminal A13 and body ground

Specified Voltage: 0-1.5v

3. If the Voltage is step2 is not OK, check for open in the harness and connector between the ECU and Spill Valve Relay, if faults are found repair/replace as required.

4. If the voltage in step2 is OK, check the condition and operation of the ECU, if faults are found, repair/replace as required.

Heater Idle Up Switch Circuit Check

1. Check the operation of the power switch by removing the switch and checking the continuity between the terminals as shown below.

Switch Position	Between Terminals	Condition
OFF	3-4	No Continuity
ON	3-4	Continuity
Illuminated Circuit	1-2	Continuity

If the operation is not as shown, replace the switch.

2. If the switch operation is OK in step1, carry out the A/C Cut Control Circuit test listed in this section, if faults are found check the condition and/or operation of the A/C amplifier, if faults are found repair/replace as required.

3. If no faults are found in step2, remove the glove box door, switch ON the ignition and check the voltage between the 26 pin ECU connector (D) terminal 23 and body ground when the heater blower switch is being turned to OFF and ON.

Heater Switch	Voltage (v)
OFF	9-14
ON	0-3

4. If the voltage is not as shown in step3, check for open and short in the harness and connector between the engine ECU and viscous heater amplifier, if faults are found repair/replace as required.

5. If no faults are found in step4, check the condition and/or operation of the viscous heater amplifier, if faults are found repair/replace as required.

6. If the voltage is OK in step3, remove the glove box door, switch ON the ignition and check the voltage between the 16 pin ECU connector (C) terminal 7 and body ground when the heater blower switch is being turned to OFF and ON.

Heater Switch	Voltage (v)
OFF	9-14
ON	0-3

7. If the voltage is OK in step6, check the condition and/or operation of the engine ECU, if faults are found repair/replace as required.

8. If the voltage is not a shown in step7, check for short and open in the harness and connector between engine ECU and the viscous heater amplifier, if faults are found repair/replace as required.

9. If no faults are found in step8, remove the glove box door, switch ON the ignition and check the voltage between the 22 pin ECU connector (A) terminal 20 and body ground when the heater blower switch is being turned to OFF and ON.

Heater Switch	Voltage (v)
OFF	9-14
ON	0-3

10. If the voltage is OK in step9, check the condition and/or operation of the engine ECU, if faults are found repair/replace as required.

11. If the voltage is not a shown in step10, check for short and open in the harness and connector between injection pump and the viscous heater amplifier, if faults are found repair/replace as required.

12. If no faults are found in step11, check the condition and/or operation of the injection pump, if faults are found repair/replace as required.

RHD Diagram

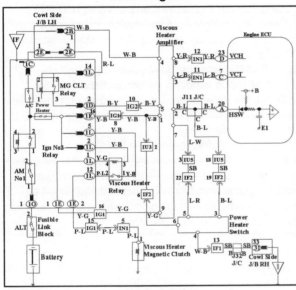

LHD Diagram

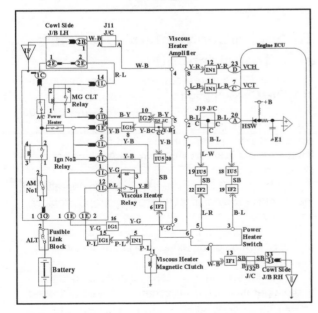

Turbocharger System Checks

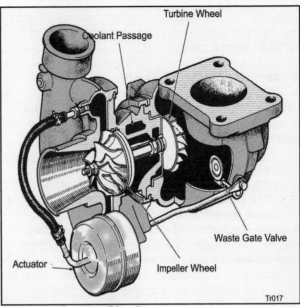

Tr017

Intake Air System Check

1. Check for leaks and/or blockages between the air cleaner and turbo charger inlet, and between the turbo charger outlet and cylinder head

2. Check for blocked air cleaner, damaged or leaking hoses and/or connections, damage in any of the components.

3. If faults are found repair/replace as required.

Exhaust System Checks.

1. Check for leaks and/or blockages between the cylinder head and turbo charger inlet, and between the turbo charger outlet and the exhaust pipe.

2. Check for damage to any of the components, any foreign objects in the passages, leaks and/or cracks in any of the components.

3. If faults are found repair/replace as required.

Turbocharger Pressure Check

1. Install a 3 way union to the hose leading to the VSV for the turbo pressure sensor, and install a pressure gauge to it.

2. Press down the clutch pedal, then press down the throttle pedal fully down. Run the engine at maximum speed (4400RPM) and then check the pressure.

Specified Turbo Pressure: 38.6-50.0kpa (1HD-T)
Specified Turbo Pressure: 50-70kpa (1HD-FTE)

3. If the pressure is less than shown, check the operation of the intake air system and exhaust system, if no leaks are found replace the turbocahrger.

4. If the pressure is more than shown, check the condition and/or operation of the actuator hose, if no faults are found replace the turbocharger as required.

Turbo Impeller Wheel Check

1. Disconnect the air cleaner hose and try and turn the impeller wheel.

2. If the wheel does not turn or turns with a drag, replace the turbocharger as required.

Turbo Actuator Check (1HD-T)
1. Disconnect the actuator hose and using a hand vacuum pump apply 92.7kpa to the actuator valve and ensure that the rod moves, if the rod does not move, replace the turbo charger.

Turbo Actuator Check (1HD-FTE)
1. Disconnect the actuator hose and using a hand vacuum pump apply 114kpa to the actuator valve and ensure that the rod moves, if the rod does not move, replace the turbo charger.

Intake Shutter Check (1HD-FTE)
1. Check that the intake shutter linkage moves smoothly, check that the diaphram rod is pulled when a vacuum of about 60kpa is applied to the actuator.
2. Apply about 60kpa of vacuum directly to the the actuator when the engine is idling and check that the engine either runs rough or stalls.
3. Remove the VSV for the intakle shutter and check the VSV for an open circuit by checking the resistance between the VSV terminals.
Specified Resistance: 33-39ohms @ 20°c
If the resistance is not as shown, replace the VSV.
4. Check the VSV for ground by using an ohmmeter and checking that there is no continuity between the VSV terminals and the body.
If there is continuity, replace the VSV.
5. Check the VSV operation by checking that air flows from the rear port of the valve to the filter, apply battery volts across the terminals and check that air flows from the rear to the front port on the valve, if the operation is not as shown, replace the VSV.

Turbo Pressure Sensor Test (1HD-FTE)
1. Check the power source voltage of the pressure sensor by disconnecting the sensor harness connector, switching on the ignition and with a voltmeter record the voltage between the VC and E2 terminal (harness side).
Specified Voltage: 4.75-5.25v
2. If the voltage is not as shown, replace the sensor
3. Check the power source of the turbo pressure sensor by switching ON the ignition and disconnecting the vacuum hose from the turbo pressure sensor.
4. Install a voltmeter between the 16 pin ECU connector (C) terminals 2 and 9 and record the output voltage under ambient atmospheric pressure.
Specified Voltage: 1.0-1.8v (40kpa or more applied)
Specified Voltage: 2.3-4.2v (135kpa of vacuum applied)
5. Apply vacuum to the sensor in 13.3kpa segments up to 66.7kpa and measure the voltage drop from step4 for each segment

Vacuum Applied	Voltage Drop
13.3	0.1-0.3
26.7	0.3-0.5
40	0.5-0.7

6. Using a turbo charger pressure gauge, apply pressure to the turbo pressure sensor in 9.8kpa units to 49.0kpa and measure the voltage drop from step4.

Vacuum Applied	Voltage Drop
19.6	0.15-0.45
39.2	0.4-0.7
56.8	0.7-1.0
78.5	1.0-1.3
98.0	13.-1.6

7. Reconnect the vacuum hoses to the pressure sensor and replace any more removed parts.

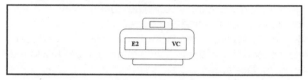

Turbo Charger Pressure Control VSV (1HD-FTE)
1. Remove the VSV from the engine and check the VSV for an open circuit by checking the resistance between the VSV terminals.
Specified Resistance: 37-44ohms @ 20°c
If the resistance is not as shown, replace the VSV.
2. Check the VSV for ground by using an ohmmeter and checking that there is no continuity between the VSV terminals and the body.
If there is continuity, replace the VSV.
3. Check the VSV operation by checking that air flows from the rear port of the valve to the front port, apply battery volts across the terminals and check that air flows from the rear port through the filter, if the operation is not as shown, replace the VSV.

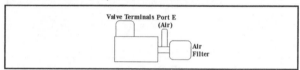

Turbocharger System Diagnosis and Troubleshooting
Poor Fuel Consumption, Lack of Power or Excessive Fuel Consumption
1. If the turbo charger system pressure is low, carry out a system pressure test.
Specified Turbo Pressure: 38.6-50kpa
If the pressure is not as shown, repair/replace turbocharger as required.
2. If no faults are found in step1, check the operation of the air intake system, if faults are found repair/replace as required.
3. If no faults are found in step2, check the condition and/or operation of the exhaust system, if faults are found repair/replace as required.
4. If no faults are found in step3, check the condition and/or operation of the turbocharger, if faults are found repair/replace as required.

Abnormal Noise From The Turbocharger

1. Check the condition and/or installation of the turbo insulator and/or bolts, if faults are found repair/replace as required.

2. If no faults are found in step1, check the condition and/or installation of the exhaust system, if faults are found repair/replace as required.

3. If no faults are found in step2, check the condition and/or operation of the turbocharger, if faults are found repair/replace as required.

Poor Oil Consumption or White Exhaust

1. If there are oil leaks found from the turbo seal, check for oil leaks into the exhaust system by removing the with the exhaust manifold converter or the turbine elbow and checking for excessive carbon deposits on the turbine wheel, if faults are found repair/replace the turbocharger as required.

2. If no faults are found in step1, check for oil leaks into the intake air system by checking the axial play in the impeller wheel.

Specified Axial Play: 0.13mm

3. If faults are found repair/replace the turbocharger as required.

BACS Control System Checks(1HD-T)

BACS Control System Check

1. Check the operation of the EGR system, if faults are found repair/replace as required.

2. If no faults are found in step1, install a 3 way connector and vacuum gauge between the BACS union and the high altitude compensator

3. Run the engine to normal operating temperature and when the adjusting lever on the injection pump is quickly pushed to fully open, check that the vacuum gauge slowly increases from 0 to 40kpa.

4. If the vacuum reading is OK, the system operation is OK, if the reading is not as shown, check each port.

EGR System Checks and Tests (Europe)

Check EGR System

1. With a 3 way conenctor connect a vacuum gauge to the vacuum hose between the EGR valve and E-VRV.

2. Check the seating of the EGR valve by starting the engine and ensuring it runs at idle.

3. Check the engine at cold operation with the coolant at less than 20°c, ensuring that the vacuum gauge shows zero at idle.

4. Check the engine at hot operation by ensuring that the coolant temp is more than 70°c and less than 96°c, the vacuum gauge indicates more than 28kpa at idle and then increases another 28kpa at 1500RPM.

5. Press down the throttle fully and check that the vacuum gauge drops momentarily.

6. Keeping the engine speed at more than 4000RPM,

check that the vacuum gauge drops to Zero.

7. When the throttle pedal is released, ensure that the vacuum gauge drops momentarily while the engine speed decreases from 4000RPM to idle.

Vacuum Pump Check

1. Disconnect the vacuum hose from the outlet pipe and install a vacuum gauge to the outlet pipe.

2. Run the engine to normal operating temperature and ensure that the vacuum gauge shows more than 86.7kpa.

3. If the operation is not as shown, repair/replace as required.

E-VRV Valve Check

1. Remove the emission control valve set, disconnect the harness connector and 2 vacuum hoses, then remove the two bolts from the emission control valve set.

2. Check the E-VRV for open circuit by checking the resistance between the valve terminals.

Specified Resistance: 11-13ohms @ 20°c

If the resistance is not as shown, replace as required.

3. Check the E-VRV for ground by ensuring that there is no continuity between the terminals and the body, if continuity is found replace the E-VRV.

4. Check the E-VRV for air tightness by fixing a vacuum gauge to the vacuum outlet port on the front of the valve and checking that the needle on the vacuum pump shows an increase of 66.7kpa or more, if the reading is not as shown, replace the E-VRV.

5. Check the E-VRV operation by applying 6v of DC power to the valve terminals and ensure that when vacuum is applied to port at the front of the valve that the vacuum gauge needle does not move.

If the operation is not as shown, replace the valve.

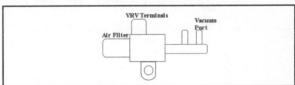

EGR Cut VSV Check

1. Remove the VSV from the engine and check the VSV for a open circuit by checking the resistance between the VSV terminals.

Specified Resistance: 37-44ohms @ 20°c

If the resistance is not as shown repair/replace as required.

2. If no faults are found in step1, check the VSV for ground by ensuring that there is no continuity between each terminal and body. If there is continuity, replace the VSV.

3. If no faults are found in step2, check the VSV operation by checking that air flows from port E to the filter. Apply battery volts across the terminals and ensure that air flows from port E to the filter.

4. If the operation is not as shown, repair/replace as required. *Diagram is on the next page*

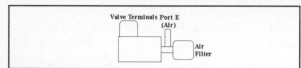

EGR Valve Check

1. Remove the EGR valve from the engine and check the EGR valve operation by applying vacuum to the valve and checking for ventilation between the in and out outlets

No Ventilation: Less than 13kpa of vacuum applied
With Ventilation: More than 27kpa of vacuum applied.

2. Apply more than 67kpa of vacuum to the valve and ensure that there is no leakage of vacuum.
3. Check for the valve sticking and/or heavy carbon deposits in the valve.

Throttle Position Sensor Check
Refer to Diagnostic Code 19 Check

Engine Speed Sensor Check
Refer to Diagnostic Code 13 Check

Water Temperature Sensor
Refer to the Diagnostic Code 22 Check

ECD System Test

ECD Main Relay Check

1. Remove the ECD main relay from the vehicle and with an ohmmeter check that there is continuity between terminals 1 and 3, and that there is no continuity between terminals 2 and 4.
If continuity exists, replace the relay
2. Apply battery volts across terminals 1 and 3 and ensure that there is continuity between terminals 2 and 4.

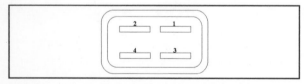

3. If there is no continuity replace the relay.

Spill Relay Check

1. Remove the relay from the vehicle and with an ohmmeter check that there is continuity between terminals 1 and 2, and that there is no continuity between terminals 3 and 5.
If continuity exists, replace the relay

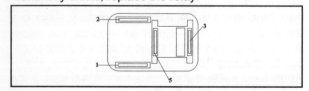

2. Apply battery volts across terminals 1 and 2 and ensure that there is continuity between terminals 3 and 5.
If there is no continuity replace the relay.

Water Temperature Sensor Check
Refer to Diagnostic Code 22 in the "self diagnosis system checks"

Fuel Temperature Sensor Check
Refer to Diagnostic Code 39 in the "self diagnosis system checks"

Intake Air Temperature Sensor Check
Refer to Diagnostic Code 24 in the "self diagnosis system checks"

Crankshaft Position Sensor Check
Refer to Diagnostic Code 12 in the "self diagnosis system checks"

Shift Position Switch Check
Refer to Shift Position Switch Check in the "non self diagnosis system checks

ECD Engune ECU Unit Resistance Check
Please Note: there are four connectors on this ECU.
Connector (A) is 22 pin, Connector (B) is 12 pin,
Connector (C) is 16 pin, Connector (D) is 26 pin

Terminal No	Condition	Resistance(ohms)
A02-D14		4-8
A03-D13		60-80
A13-D14		60-80
C03-C09	Intake air temp 20°c	2.0-3.0 k/ohms
C04-C09	Coolant temp 80°c	200-400
C05-C09	Fuel temp 20°c	2.0-3.0 k/ohms
D03-D14	25°c	30-40
D09-D13	25°c	30-40
D10-D13	25°c	30-40
D11-D13		10-16
D17-D16	-10 to 50°c (Cold)	19-32
D17-D16	50 to 100°c	24-37
D19-D18		205-255
D24-D13		11-18

See ECU Connector Diagarm in the Terminal Voltage Section

Injection System and Engine Diagnosis and Troubleshooting

Engine Will Not Crank (Hard to Start)

1. Check the condition and/or operation of the battery cables between the battery and starter motor, if faults are found repair/replace as required.
2. If no faults are found in step1, check the condition and/or operation of the battery, alternator output and/or drive belt, if faults are found repair/replace as required.
3. If no faults are found in step2, check the condition and/or operation of the starter motor, if faults are found repair/replace as required.
4. If no faults are found in step3, check the condition and/or operation of the starter relay, if faults are found repair/replace as required.
5. If no faults are found in step4, check the condition

and/or operation of the neutral start switch (auto only), if faults are found repair/replace as required.

Hard to Start (Cold Engine)
1. Check the condition and/or operation of the intake heater control unit, if faults are found repair/replace as required.
2. If no faults are found in step1, check the condition and/or operation of the STA signal circuit, if faults are found repair/replace as required.
3. If no faults are found in step2, check the condition and/or operation of the heater idle up switch circuit, if faults are found repair/replace as required.
4. If no faults are found in step3, check the condition and/or operation of the injection nozzle, if faults are found repair/replace as required.
5. If no faults are found imn step4, check the condition and/or operation of the fuel filter, if faults are found, repair/replace as required.
6. If no faults are found in step5, check the condition and/or operation of the engine ECU, if faults are found repair/replace as required.
7. If no faults are found in step6, check the condition and/or operation of the injection pump, if faults are found repair/replace as required.

Hard to Start (Hot Engine)
1. Check the condition and/or operation of the STA signal circuit, if faults are found repair/replace as required.
2. If no faults are found in step1, check the condition and/or operation of the injection nozzle, if faults are found repair/replace as required.
3. If no faults are found in step2, check the condition and/or operation of the fuel filter, if faults are found, repair/replace as required.
4. If no faults are found in step3, carry out an engine compression test, if faults are found repair/replace as required.
5. If no faults are found in step4, check the condition and/or operation of the engine ECU, if faults are found repair/replace as required.
6. If no faults are found in step5, check the condition and/or operation of the injection pump, if faults are found repair/replace as required.

Engine Stalls Soon After Starting
1. Check the condition and/or operation of the fuel filter, if faults are found, repair/replace as required.
2. If no faults are found in step1, check the condition and/or operation of the ECU power source circuit, if faults are found repair/replace as required.
3. If no faults are found in step2, check the condition and/or operation of the engine ECU, if faults are found repair/replace as required.
4. If no faults are found in step3, check the condition and/or operation of the injection pump, if faults are found repair/replace as required.

Engine Stalls (Other Conditions)
1. Check the condition and/or operation of the ECU power source circuit, if faults are found repair/replace as required.
2. If no faults are found in step1, check the condition and/or operation of the spill valve relay circuit, if faults are found repair/replace as required.
3. If no faults are found in step2, check the condition and/or operation of the engine ECU, if faults are found repair/replace as required.
4. If no faults are found in step3, check the condition and/or operation of the injection pump, if faults are found repair/replace as required.

Poor Idling (Incorrect First Idle)
1. Check the condition and/or operation of the fuel filter, if faults are found, repair/replace as required.
2. If no faults are found in step1, check the condition and/or operation of the engine ECU, if faults are found repair/replace as required.
3. If no faults are found in step2, check the condition and/or operation of the injection pump, if faults are found repair/replace as required.

Poor Idling (High Engine Idle Speed)
1. Check the condition and/or operation of the A/C signal circuit, if faults are found repair/replace as required.
2. If no faults are found in step1, check the condition and/or operation of the STA signal circuit, if faults are found repair/replace as required.
3. If no faults are found in step2, check the condition and/or operation of the engine ECU, if faults are found repair/replace as required.
4. If no faults are found in step3, check the condition and/or operation of the injection pump, if faults are found repair/replace as required.

Poor Idling (Low Engine Idle Speed)
1. Check the condition and/or operation of the A/C signal circuit, if faults are found repair/replace as required.
2. If no faults are found in step1, check the condition and/or operation of the injection nozzle, if faults are found repair/replace as required.
3. If no faults are found in step2, check the condition and/or operation of the EGR control circuit, if faults are found repair/replace as required.
4. If no faults are found in step3, carry out an engine compression test, if faults are found repair/replace as required.
5. If no faults are found in step4, check the engine valve clearances, if faults are found, adjust to suit.
6. If no faults are found in step5, check the condition and/or operation of the fuel line (air bleed), if faults are found repair/replace as required.
7. If no faults are found in step6, check the condition and/or operation of the engine ECU, if faults are found repair/replace as required.

8. If no faults are found in step7, check the condition and/or operation of the injection pump, if faults are found repair/replace as required.

Poor Idling (Rough Idle)

1. Check the condition and/or operation of the injection nozzle, if faults are found repair/replace as required.
2. If no faults are found in step1, check the condition and/or operation of the fuel line (air bleed), if faults are found repair/replace as required.
3. If no faults are found in step2, check the condition and/or operation of the intake heater control unit, if faults are found repair/replace as required.
4. If no faults are found in step3, check the condition and/or operation of the EGR control circuit, if faults are found repair/replace as required.
5. If no faults are found in step4, carry out an engine compression test, if faults are found repair/replace as required.
6. If no faults are found in step5, check the engine valve clearances, if faults are found, adjust to suit.
7. If no faults are found in step6, check the condition and/or operation of the engine ECU, if faults are found repair/replace as required.
8. If no faults are found in step7, check the condition and/or operation of the injection pump, if faults are found repair/replace as required.

Poor Idling (Engine is Hunting When the Engine is Hot)

1. Check the condition and/or operation of the injection nozzle, if faults are found repair/replace as required.
2. If no faults are found in step1, check the condition and/or operation of the ECU power source circuit, if faults are found repair/replace as required.
3. If no faults are found in step2, carry out an engine compression test, if faults are found repair/replace as required.
4. If no faults are found in step3, check the condition and/or operation of the fuel line (air bleed), if faults are found repair/replace as required.
5. If no faults are found in step4, check the engine valve clearances, if faults are found, adjust to suit.
6. If no faults are found in step5, check the condition and/or operation of the engine ECU, if faults are found repair/replace as required.
7. If no faults are found in step6, check the condition and/or operation of the injection pump, if faults are found repair/replace as required

Poor Idling (Engine is Hunting When the Engine is Cold)

1. Check the condition and/or operation of the injection nozzle, if faults are found repair/replace as required.
2. If no faults are found in step1, check the condition and/or operation of the ECU power source circuit, if faults are found repair/replace as required.
3. If no faults are found in step2, check the condition and/or operation of the intake heater control unit, if faults are found repair/replace as required.

4. If no faults are found in step3, carry out an engine compression test, if faults are found repair/replace as required.
5. If no faults are found in step4, check the condition and/or operation of the fuel line (air bleed), if faults are found repair/replace as required.
6. If no faults are found in step5, check the engine valve clearances, if faults are found, adjust to suit.
7. If no faults are found in step6, check the condition and/or operation of the engine ECU, if faults are found repair/replace as required.
8. If no faults are found in step7, check the condition and/or operation of the injection pump, if faults are found repair/replace as required.

Poor Drivability (Engine Hesitates/Poor Acceleration)

1. Check the condition and/or operation of the injection nozzle, if faults are found repair/replace as required.
2. If no faults are found in step1, check the condition and/or operation of the fuel filter, if faults are found repair/replace as required.
3. If no faults are found in step2, check the condition and/or operation of the EGR control circuit, if faults are found repair/replace as required.
4. If no faults are found in step3, carry out an engine compression test, if faults are found repair/replace as required.
5. If no faults are found in step4, check the condition and/or operation of the engine ECU, if faults are found repair/replace as required.
6. If no faults are found in step5, check the condition and/or operation of the injection pump, if faults are found repair/replace as required.

Poor Drivability (Engine Knocking)

1. Check the condition and/or operation of the injection nozzle, if faults are found repair/replace as required.
2. If no faults are found in step1, check the condition and/or operation of the EGR control circuit, if faults are found repair/replace as required.
3. If no faults are found in step2, check the condition and/or operation of the engine ECU, if faults are found repair/replace as required.

Poor Drivability (Black Smoke)

1-Check the condition and/or operation of the injection nozzle, if faults are found repair/replace as required.
2-If no faults are found in step1, check the condition and/or operation of the EGR control circuit, if faults are found repair/replace as required.
3-If no faults are found in step2, check the condition and/or operation of the engine ECU, if faults are found repair/replace as required.
4-If no faults are found in step3, check the condition and/or operation of the injection pump, if faults are found repair/replace as required.

Poor Drivability (White Smoke)

1-Check the condition and/or operation of the EGR

control circuit, if faults are found repair/replace as required.

2-If no faults are found in step1, check the condition and/or operation of the intake heater control unit, if faults are found repair/replace as required.

3- If no faults are found in step2, check the condition and/or operation of the injection nozzle, if faults are found repair/replace as required.

4-If no faults are found in step3, check the condition and/or operation of the fuel filter, if faults are found repair/replace as required.

5-If no faults are found in step4, check the condition and/or operation of the engine ECU, if faults are found repair/replace as required.

6-If no faults are found in step5, check the condition and/or operation of the injection pump, if faults are found repair/replace as required.

Poor Drivability (Engine is Hunting/Surging)

1-Check the condition and/or operation of the injection nozzle, if faults are found repair/replace as required.

2-If no faults are found in step1, check the condition and/or operation of the engine ECU, if faults are found repair/replace as required.

3-If no faults are found in step2, check the condition and/or operation of the injection pump, if faults are found repair/replace as required.

Vehicle Component Service Interval Changes

Timing Belt:
Change Every 150,000kms

Check Valve Clearance:
Every 24Months/40,000kms

Engine Coolant/Anti Freeze:
Change every 24 Months

Air Cleaner Element:
Change Every 60 Months/100,000kms

Fuel Filter:
Change Every 12 Months/20,000kms

Engine Oil:
Change Every 6 Months/10,000kms

Engine Oil Filter:
Change Every 6 Months/10,000kms

Brake Fluid:
Change every 24 Months

Manual Transmission Oil:
Drain and Refil as Required

Front Differential Oil:
Change Every 24 Months/40,000kms

Transfer Case Oil
Drain and Refil as Required

Rear Differential Oil:
Change Every 24 Months/40,000kms

Front/Rear Wheel Bearings
Repack Every 12Months/20,000kms

Drive Belts
Change Every 24 Months/40,000kms

VEHICLE SERVICE INFORMATION

Vehicle Filling Capacities

Engine Oil with Filter: ....9.3 Litres (1HZ Engine)
Engine Oil without Filter: ....8.0 Litres (1HZ Engine)
Engine Oil with Dry Fill: ....10.4Litres (1HZ Engine)
Engine Oil with Filter: .... 11.4 Litres (1HD-T Engine)
Engine Oil without Filter: ..... 10.1 Litres (1HD-T Engine)
Engine Oil with Dry Fill: .... 11.7 Litres (1HD-T Engine)
Engine Oil with Filter: ...... 11.4 Litres (1HD-FTE Engine)
Engine Oil without Filter: . 10.1 Litres (1HD-FTE Engine)
Engine Oil with Dry Fill: ... 12.1 Litres (1HD-FTE Engine)
Cooling System: ....
12.4 Litres (1HZ Engine) (GCC Countries with Heater)
Cooling System: ....
...... 12.9 Litres (1HZ Engine) (GCC Countries with Rear Heater)
Cooling System: ....
12.4 Litres (1HZ Engine) (Australia/Other Countries with Heater, Manual)
Cooling System: ....
12.0 Litres (1HZ Engine) (Australia/Other Countries with Heater, Auto)
Cooling System: ....
12.9 Litres (1HZ Engine) (Australia/Other Countries with Rear Heater, Manual)
Cooling System: ....
12.5 Litres (1HZ Engine) (Australia/Other Countries with Rear Heater, Auto)
Cooling System: ....
12.5 Litres (1HD-T Engine) (With Heater, Manual)
Cooling System: ....
12.1 Litres (1HD-T Engine) (With Heater, Auto)
Cooling System: ....
13.0 Litres (1HD-T Engine) (With Rear Heater, Manual)
Cooling System: ....
12.6 Litres (1HD-T Engine) (With Rear Heater, Auto)
Cooling System: ....
13.2 Litres (1HD-T Engine) (With Heater, Manual)
Cooling System: ....
12.8 Litres (1HD-T Engine) (With Heater, Auto)
Cooling System: ....
13.7 Litres (1HD-T Engine) (With Viscous Heater, Manual)
Cooling System: ....
13.3 Litres (1HD-T Engine) (With Viscous Heater, Auto)
Manual Transmission: ....2.2 Litres
Auto Transmission: ....15.0 Litres (Dry Fill)
Auto Transmission: ....6.0 Litres (Re-Fill)
Front Differential: ....2.7 Litres (With FRS)
Front Differential: .... 1.7 Litres (With IFS)
Rear Differential: ....3.2 Litres
Transfer Case: 1.5Litres

Toyota Landcruiser PJ70-75 Series 1PZ Engine 1990 ON

CONTENTS   PAGE

CONTENTS   PAGE

PZJ70-75

Toyota Landcruiser PJ70-75 Series 1PZ Engine 1990 ON

Engine Checks

Valve Clearance Check

1. Remove the intake pipe and the cylinder head cover.
2. Se the No1 piston to TDC/Compression by turning the crankshaft pulley clockwise and lining up the groove on the pulley with the timing gear cover groove.
3. Check that the valve lifters on the No1 cylinder are loose and the exhaust valve lifyers on the No5 cylinder is tight.
If this is not the case, turn the crankshaft 1 full turn in a clockwise direction and then line up the grooves again..
4. Check the valve clearances on the 1,5,9 inlet valves and 2,4,8 exhaust valves with a feeler gauge and record the measurments between the valve lifter and camshaft that need adjusting. **(Measurements will be used to determine new shim thicknesses that are required).**
Specified Inlet Valve Clearance: 0.15-0.25mm
Specified Inlet Valve Clearance: 0.35-0.45mm
5. Turn the crankshaft in a clockwise direction one full turn (360°) and check the valve clearances on the 3, 7 inlet valve and 6,10 on the exhaust valve. with a feeler gauge and record the measurments between the valve lifter and camshaft that need adjusting. **(Measurements will be used to determine new shim thickneses that are required).**
Specified Inlet Valve Clearance: 0.15-0.25mm
Specified Inlet Valve Clearance: 0.35-0.45mm

No1 Piston at TDC
Front of Engine — Inlet / Exhaust
No5 Piston at TDC
Front of Engine — Inlet / Exhaust

6. To complete the adjustment remove any adjusting

shim that need replacement by using a valve liter (part no 09248-64011).
7. Turn the crankshaft to position the cam lobe of the camshaft on the adjusting valve upwards, remove the shim with a small screwdriver and magnetic tool.
8. To calculate the shim needed to adjust the valve clearance, measure the thickness of the old shim, and calculate the the thickness of the new shim as shown below.
Inlet Valve Shim:
     Old shim thickness plus 0.20mm.
Exahust Valve Shim:
     Old shim thickness plus 0.40mm.
9. Once the shim thickness has been calculated, replace the shim using the valve lifter (part no 09248-64011) and then remove the lifter.
10. Recheck the valve clearance, then replace any removed parts in the reverse order of removal

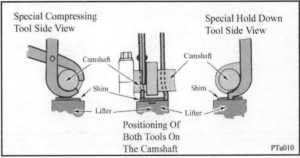

Special Compressing Tool Side View — Camshaft — Shim — Lifter
Special Hold Down Tool Side View — Camshaft — Shim — Lifter
Positioning Of Both Tools On The Camshaft — PTu010

Compression Check

1. Run the engine to normal operating temperatures, disconnect the injection pump cut off solenoid connector and then remove the glow plugs.
2. Check each cylinder compression by installing a compression tester to the engine, fully opening the throttle valve, cranking the engine and recording the pressure on each cylinder.
Specified Compression Pressure: 3628kpa or more
Minimum Pressure: 2648kpa or more
Difference Between Each Cylinder: 490kpa or less.
3. If the pressure is less than shown on one or more

cylinders, pour a small amount of oil through the glow plug hole and recheck the pressure. If the pressure is now OK, check the condition of the piston rings and/or cylinder bore. If the pressure is still low, check for a sticking valve and/or bad valve seating.

4. Replace any removed parts in the reverse order of removal.

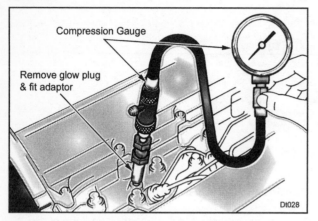

Compression Gauge

Remove glow plug & fit adaptor

Dt028

Piston Protrusion Check

1. Clean the cylinder block, set the No1 piston to TDC, place a dial gauge on the block and set the dial gauge to zero.

2. Find the point where the piston top protrudes the most by turning the crankshaft slightly the the left and right.

3. Measure each cylinder in two places as shown and record the average of the two measurments on each cylinder.

Specified Protrusion Measurement: 0.405-0.655mm.

Dial Indicator

Cylinder Block

Piston

L020

4. If the protrusion measurement is not as shown, remove the piston and con rod and replace it.

5. There are 5 types of head gaskets used on this vehicle, but only type 1,3,5 are supplied as replacement parts.

Gasket No1:	**Thickness is 1.16-1.24mm**
Gasket No3:	**Thickness is 1.26-1.34mm**
Gasket No5:	**Thickness is 1.36-1.44mm**

6. Select the largest of the protrusion measurements and select the gasket to suit as shown below.

Protrusion Measurement	Gasket Size
0.405mm or less	1.16-1.24mm
0.456-0.555mm	1.26-1.34mm
0.556mm or more	1.36-1.44mm

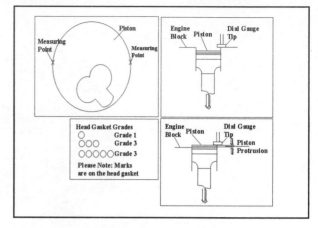

Cylinder Head Tightening Procedures

1. With the cylinder head inplace, tighten the bolts in three steps, if any of the bolts break or deform replace them as required.

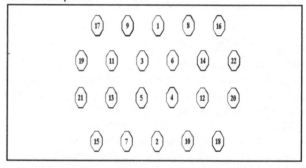

2. Apply a light coat of oil to each bolt thread, and using a torque wrench tighten the 22 bolts in three separate stages to a tor**que of 69Nm.**

3. Mark the front of the cylinder head bolts with white paint, **tighten each bolt another 90°** in the sequence shown, and **then tighten each bolt a further 90°** in the same sequence and now ensure that the paint marks on all of the bolts are facing to the rear.

Oil Pressure Check

1. Remove the oil pressure switch from the block and install a pressure gauge in its place.

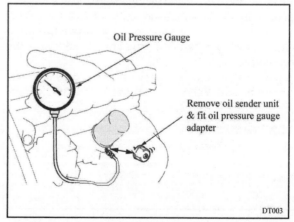

Oil Pressure Gauge

Remove oil sender unit & fit oil pressure gauge adapter

DT003

2. Run the engine to normal operating temperature and the check the engine oil pressure.

Specified Oil Pressure: 29kpa or more @ Idle
Specified Oil Pressure:245kpa or more @ 3000RPM.

3. If the pressure is not as shown, repair/replace.

Cooling System Thermostat Check

1. Remove the thermostat from the engine and put into a suitable container of water.

2. Heat the water gradually and and check the valve opening temperature and **valve lift.**

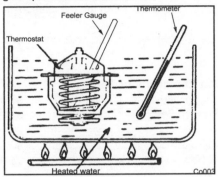

Valve Opening Temperature: 74-78°c
Valve Lift: 10mm or more @ 90°c

If the operation is not as shown above replace the thermostat.

3. Check that the valve spring is tight when the thermostat is fully closed, if not replace the thermostat.

Fuel Filter Check and Replacement

1. Remove the fuel filter sensor, drain the fuel, then remove the fuel filter.

2. Clean the fuel filter mounting bracket and then coat the fuel filter sealing ring with some diesel fuel.

3. Screw the fuel filter on until a slght resistance is felt and then turn another 2/3 of a turn or until suitably tight.

4. Install the fuel filter sensor (if fitted) to the new filter and then bleed any air present from the system.

Draining Water From The Filter

1. Loosen the drain cock 4 or 5 turns or remove the fuel filter sensor to allow the water to drain from the filter.

2. Retighten the drain cock or replace the sensor and bleed any air present from the system.

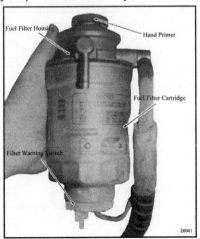

Fuel Filter Warning Lamp Check

1. Remove the switch from the filter and check that there is continuity between the terminals when the warning switch is ON (Float Up)

2. Check that there is no continuity between the terminals when the warning switch is OFF (Float Down)

3. If the operation is not as shown, repair/replace as required.

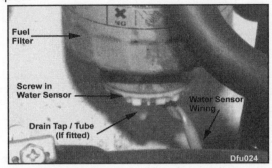

Injector Nozzle Check

1. Remove the injector from the vehicle, connect up to the pressure tester and check the initial pressure by pumping the tester handle a few times.

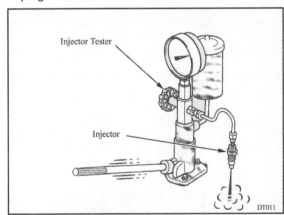

Initial Opening Pressure:
          13,239-15,200kpa (Used Nozzle)
Initial Opening Pressure:
          14,220-15,200kpa (New Nozzle).

2. If the opening pressure is not as shown above, take the injector to pieces and change the adjusting shim on the top of the injector so as the correct pressure is recorded.

Adjusted Opening Pressure: 13,239-15,200kpa
Please Note: The adjusting shims vary in 0.025mm thicknesses, each 0.025mm will adjust the pressure by 441kpa. After the shim has been changed there should be no leakage from the injector.

3. Maintain the pressure between 981-1961kpa below the opening pressure and check that there is no leakage from the injector for a period of 10seconds.

4. Check the spray pattern by pumping the pressure tester handle 4-6 times or more per second and check the injection spray pattern.

5. If the operation and/or spray pattern is not as shown, repair/replace the nozzle/s as required.

Illustration on next page.

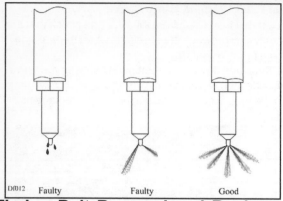

Df012 Faulty   Faulty   Good

Timing Belt Removal and Replacement

Removal Procedures

1. Remove the timing belt cover and set the No1 piston to BDC by turning the crankshaft pulley in a clockwise direction until the No1 and No2 camshaft pulley groves line up at each position.

2. Remove the timing belt from the engine by removing the tension spring, the spring bolt on the timing belt idler and then the timing belt.

Please Note: If the timing belt is being re-used, draw on the belt an arrow undicating the direction of rotation and match marks on the pulley as well as the belt.

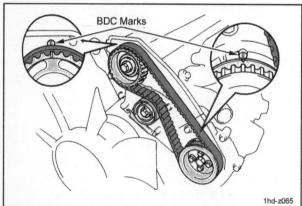

1hd-z065

Replacement Procedures

Please Note: Before replacing the timimg belt check the condition and/or operation of the timing belt pulleys, tensioners and/or pulleys, if faults are found repair/replace as required.

1. Check the tensioner spring free length
Spring Free Length: **72.7mm**
Check the tension of the spring at the specified free length

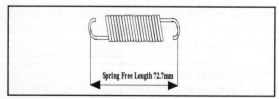

Installed Tension: **275Nm at 90.1mm**
2. Before fitting the belt to the engine, set the No1

piston to BDC by turning the crankshaft pulley in a clockwise direction until the No1 and No2 camshaft pulley groves line up at each position.

3. Fit the timing belt to the engine firstly on the No2 camshaft pulley, then the No1 pulley and finally the timing belt idler pulley.

4. Install the tension spring and then install and torque the idler pulley bolt to 26Nm.

5. Check the valve timing by turning the crankshaft pulley in a clockwise direction and ensure that all of the timing marks on each of the pulleys all line up. If they do not remove the belt and re-start the insatllation process again.

6. Replace any more removed parts in the reverse order of removal

Timing Belt Replacement Torques

No1 Camshaft Pulley:	98Nm
No2 Camshaft Pulley	31Nm
Idle Pulley:	26Nm
Crankshaft Pulley Bolt No1 to Crankshaft:	90Nm
Crankshaft Pulley No2 to No1 Pulley :	25Nm

Timing Belt Warning Lamp Reset Procedures (Rubber Plug in the Instrument Cluster Glass)

1. Remove the grommet from the speedometer and turn off the lamp by pushing the warning lamp reset switch, then replace the grommet.

2. Start the engine and ensure that the light stays off.

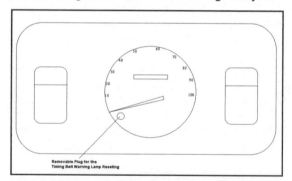

Timing Belt Warning Lamp Reset Procedures (Change Screw Position on the Back of the Instrument Cluster)

1. Remove the instrument cluster from the vehicle, connect terminals A&B shown in the diagrams and then remove the CHARGE fuse from the vehicle.

2. Turn the ignition switch to ON and check that the warning lights light up, if not the check the condition and/or operation of the globe.

3. Check the condition and/or operation of the reset

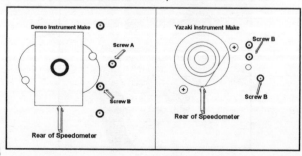

switches by checking that there is intermittent continuity between terminals A&B when the reset switch is pressed, if not repair/replace the speedometer/instrument cluster as required.

Engine Tightening Torques

Cylinder Head Tightening Torque Bolts: .... 69Nm (Tighten in 3 Stages)
Cylinder Head Tightening Torque Bolts: .... 90° (2nd Stage)
Cylinder Head Tightening Torque Bolts: .... 90° (3rd Stage)
Exhaust Manifold Bolts and Nuts: 39Nm
Inlet Manifold Bolts and Nuts: 20Nm
Glow Plugs: 13Nm
Injection Nozzle: 64Nm
Injection Pump Drive Pulley Nut: 64Nm
Idle Pulley: 26Nm
Flywheel Bolts: 127Nm
Drive Plate: 127Nm
Connecting Rod Caps: 37Nm
Connecting Rod Caps: .... 90° (2nd Stage)
Main Bearings: 103Nm
Main Bearings: .... 90° (2nd Stage)
Crankshaft Pulley Bolt No1 to Crankshaft: 490Nm
Crankshaft Pulley No2 to No1 Pulley : 25Nm
Camshaft Gear No1 Bolt: 98Nm
Camshaft Gear No2 Bolt: 31Nm
Oil Pump to Block: 20Nm
Oil Pump to Injection Pump: 18Nm
Oil Pan to Cylinder Block: 10Nm

System Adjustments

Idle Speed Check

1. Before checking the idle speed, ensure that the engine is at normal operating temperature, the air cleaner OK and fitted, all of the accessories are fitted, all vacuum lines are OK, valve clearance and injection timing are set correctly and that the transmission is in "N".
2. Install a tachometer to the engine, ensure that the adjusting lever touches the idle speed adjusting screw when the throttle pedal is released, if it does not adjust to suit.

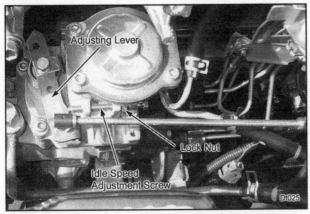

3. Start the engine, let it run and check the idle speed.
Idle Speed: **600-700RPM**

4. If the idle speed is not as shown, disconnect the throttle linkage, loosen the lock nut on the idle speed adjusting screw and adjust the idle speed by turning the idle speed adjusting screw.
Idle Speed: **650RPM**
5. Tighten the lock nut, recheck the idle speed, reconnect the throttle linkage and then re-check the idle speed.
6. Remove the tachometer from the engine and replace any other removed parts in the reverse order of removal.

Injection Timing Check

1. Remove the timing belt cover and set the No1 piston to TDC on the compression stroke by turning the crankshaft pulley in a clockwise direction and lining up each of the pulley groves with each of the timing marks on the engine.

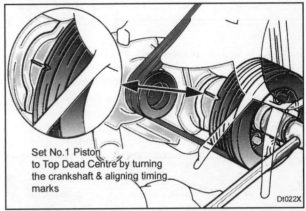

Set No.1 Piston to Top Dead Centre by turning the crankshaft & aligning timing marks

2. Remove the plug bolt from the distributor head of the injection pump and install a dial gauge to the bolt hole.

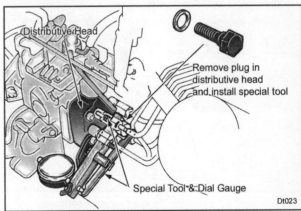

Distributive Head

Remove plug in distributive head and install special tool

Special Tool & Dial Gauge

3. **(For Vehicles with ACSD Only),** Turn the cold start lever in an anti clockwise direction about 20° and put a metel plate of between 3.5-7.5mm between the cold start lever and the thermo wax plunger.
4. Turn the crankshaft in an anti-clockwise direction, set the dial gauge to zero when it reaces its minimum value.
Specified Minimum Value: **0mm**
5. Slowly turn the crankshaft in a clockwise direction until the groove on the crankshaft pulley lines up with the mark on the timing cover, then record the plunger stroke.
Specified Plunger Stroke: **0.82-0.88mm**

6. If the timing needs adjustment, loosen the 5 union nuts on the injection pump side, the bolt holding the pump to the pump bracket, the two nuts holding the pump to the timing gear.

7. If the plunger stroke is less than shown, turn the pump towards the engine, if it more turn away from the engine.

8. Retighten the two nuts holding the pump to the timing gear, the bolt holding the pump to the pump bracket and then recheck the injection pump plunger stroke.

9. If fitted remove the plate from the ACSD device, the dial gauge and replace the bolt plug, tighten the union nuts on the injection pipes and replace any more removed parts in the reverse order of removal.

Maximum Speed Adjustment

1. With a tachometer installed to the engine, check that the adjusting lever touches the maximum speed screw when the throttle pedal is pressed down all of the way, if not adjust to suit.

2. Start the engine, press down the throttle pedal all the way and check the maximum speed.

Specified Maximum Speed: 4500-4700RPM.

3. If the maximum speed is not as shown, disconnect the throttle linkages, cut the seal on the maximum speed adjusting screw, loosen the lock nut and then adjust by turning the maximum speed adjusting screw.

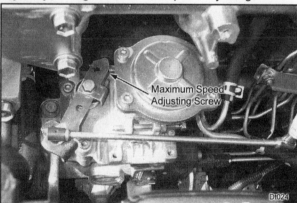

Specified Maximum Speed: 4600RPM.

4. After adjustment, check the idle speed, race the engine and then recheck the maximum speed again.

5. Reconnect the throttle linkage and adjust to suit, seal the maximum speed screw again and then replace any more removed parts in the reverse order of removal

6-Remove the tachometer from the engine

Fuel Heater System Check

Fuel Heater Check

1. Apply 46.7±6.7kpa or more of vacuum to the vacuum switch and with an ohmmeter check the resistance between the No1 terminal and the switch body

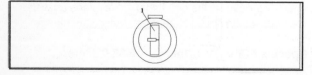

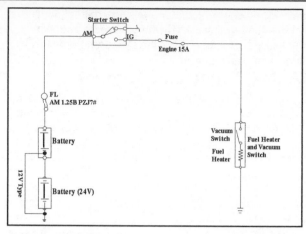

Specified Resistance: 0.5-2.0ohms @ 20°c

2. If the resistance is not as shown, replace the fuel heater and vacuum switch assembly.

Vacuum Switch Check

1. With an ohmmeter check that there is no continuity between the No1 terminal and the switch body, if there is replace the fuel heater and vacuum switch assembly.

2. Apply 46.7± 6.7kpa or more of vacuum to the vacuum switch and with an ohmmeter check that there is continuity between the No1 terminal and the switch body, if there is no continuity, replace the fuel heater and vacuum switch assembly.

Use Fuel Heater Switch Diagram

Pre-Heating System Checks

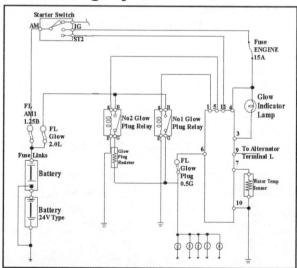

Pre Heating System Check (Superglow System Europe and Australia)

1. Disconnect the water temperature sensor and check if the indicator lamp lights up when the starter switch is in the ON position.

Specified Light Up Time: 6-7seconds

2. If the light up time is not as shown in step1, check the condition of the relevant system fuse, if the fuse is blown, check for short circuit in the harness and repair as required.

3. If the fuse is OK in step2, check the condition and/or operation of the glow indicator lamp globe, if faults are found repair/replace as required.

4. If the bulb is OK in step3, check for battery voltage to the terminal 3 (harness side) of the pre-heating timer connector, if the voltage is OK, replace the timer assembly.

5. If the light up time in step1 is OK, put the starter switch to OFF, and check for battery voltage to terminal 1 of the pre heating timer with the ignition switch in the ON position.

6. If there is NO voltage in step5, check that there is 1v or less to terminal 9 on the timer, if there is the timer is faulty and needs replacing.

7. If the voltage in step5 is OK, check if voltage to the terminal 1of the pre heating timer is terminated after the engine has started, if it does not, start the engine and check if there is voltage at terminal 9 of the pre heating timer, if there is not, repair fault in the charging system. If there is voltage the timer is faulty and should be replaced.

8. If the voltage operation is OK in step7, put the starter switch to the OFF position, put the starter switch into the ON position and check the current flow to the terminal 5 of the timer.

Current Flow: **120 Seconds.**

9. If the pre-heat time differs from above or there is NO voltage at all in step8, replace the timer.

10. If the current flow is OK in step8, after completing pre-heating check for voltage at terminal 5, check again this time when the starter switch is in the Start position.

11. If there is no voltage in step10, replace the timer.

12. If the voltage is OK in step10, put the starter switch into the off position, place the starter switch into the ON position and check for voltage to the glow plugs a few seconds later (the the voltage should drop by about 50%).

13. If there is no voltage at all in step12, check for battery voltage at the (-) side of the glow plug resistor, if there is no voltage, replace the No1 glow plug relay.

14. If the voltage in step12 stays at battery voltage or falls to 0v, check for battery voltage to the (+) side of the glow plug resistor, if there is no voltage replace the No2 glow plug relay.

15. If the voltage is OK in step12, check the glow plug resistance.

Specified Resistance: Approx. 0ohms

If the resistance is not OK, replace the glow plug/s as required.

16. If the glow plug resistance is OK in step15, the glow plug/s are OK, then reconnect the water temperature senson harness connector.

Pre Heating Timer Circuit Check
Please Note: The timer is located under the instrument panel on the LH side.

1. Disconnect the harness connector from the timer and check the connector on the harness side as shown in the chart below.

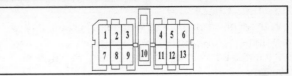

Check For	Between Terminals	Condition	Specified Value
Continuity	1-ground		Continuity
Voltage	3-ground	starter switch OFF	No Volts
Voltage	3-ground	starter switch ON	Battery Volts
Voltage	4-ground	starter switch OFF	No Volts
Voltage	4-ground	starter switch ON	Battery Volts
Continuity	5-ground		Continuity
Continuity	6-ground		Continuity
Continuity	7-ground		Continuity
Continuity	10-ground		Continuity
Voltage	11-ground	starter switch OFF	No Volts
Voltage	11-ground	starter switch ON	Battery Volts

Component Checks
No1 Glow Plug Relay Check
Please Note: The relay is located in the engine compartment on the LH Side

1. With an ohmmeter check that there is continuity between terminals 1 and 2 and that there is no continuity between terminals 3 and 4.
If the continuity is not as shown above, replace the relay.

2. Apply battery volts between the continuity between terminals 1 and 2 and that there is no continuity between terminals 3 and 4.

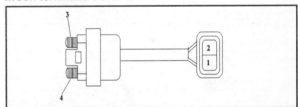

If the operation is not as shown above, replace the relay.

No2 Glow Plug Relay
Please Note: The relay is located in the engine compartment on the LH Side

1. With an ohmmeter check that there is continuity between terminals 1 and 2 and that there is no continuity between terminals 3 and 4.
If the continuity is not as shown above, replace the relay.

2. Apply battery volts between the continuity between terminals 1 and 2 and that there is no continuity between terminals 3 and 4.

If the operation is not as shown above, replace the relay.

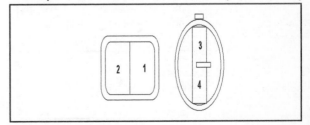

Glow Plug Check

1. With an ohmmeter check that there is continuity between the glow plug terminal and ground.
2. If there is no continuity replace the glow plug/s as required.

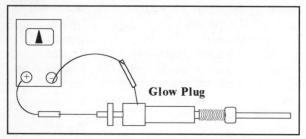

Glow Plug

Glow Plug Resistor Check

1. With an ohmmeter check that there is continuity between the resistor terminals.
2. If there is no continuity replace the resistor as required.

Water Temperature Sensor Check

1. Disconnect the sensor harness connector and check the resistance between the terminals at varying temperatures.

Coolant Temperature (°c)	Resistance(k/ohms)
-20	10-20
0	4-7
20	2-3
40	0.9-1.3
60	0.4-0.7
80	0.2-0.4

2. If the resistance is not as shown, repair/replace as required.

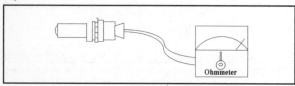

Ohmmeter

Pre-Heating System Checks

Pre Heating Timer Circuit Check (Fixed Delay System Execpt Europe and Australia)
Please Note: The timer is located under the instrument panel on the LH side.

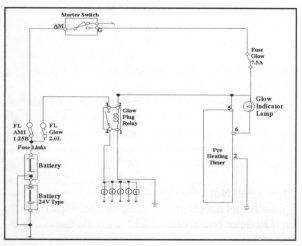

1. Disconnect the harness connector from the timer and check the connector on the harness side as shown in the chart below.

Check For	Between Terminals	Condition	Specified Value
Continuity	2-ground		Continuity
Voltage	5-ground	starter switch OFF	No Volts
Voltage	5-ground	starter switch ON	Battery Volts
Voltage	6-ground	starter switch OFF	No Volts
Voltage	6-ground	starter switch ON	Battery Volts

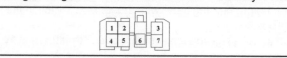

Glow Indicator Lamp Check

1. Put the starter switch into the G position and check the light up time.

Specified Light Up Time:	**Approx.6secs (12v)**
Specified Light Up Time:	**Approx.5secs (24v)**

Glow Plug Relay Check

Refer previous information for the No2 glow plug relay in the previous Superglow System.

Glow Plug Check

Refer previous information for the glow plug check in the previous Superglow System.

Injection System and Engine Diagnosis and Troubleshooting

Engine Will Not Crank

1. Check the condition and/or operation of the battery cables between the battery and starter motor, if faults are found repair/replace as required.
2. If no faults are found in step1, check the condition and/or operation of the battery, alternator output and/or drive belt, if faults are found repair/replace as required.
3. If no faults are found in step2, check the condition and/or operation of the starter motor, if faults are found repair/replace as required.

Engine Cranks Slowly or Will Not Start

1. Check the condition and/or operation of the battery cables between the battery and starter motor, if faults are found repair/replace as required.
2. If no faults are found in step1, check the condition and/or operation of the battery, alternator output and/or drive belt, if faults are found repair/replace as required.
3. If no faults are found in step2, check that the correct grade of engine oil is being used on the vehicle, if not draon and replace with the correct grade of oil.

Engine Cranks Normally But Does Not Start

1. If the engine cranks normally but does not start, check and ensure that fuel is reaching the injection nozzles, by loosening any of the injection pipes, cranking the engine and ensuring that fuel is coming out of the pipe.
2. If fuel is not coming out of the pipe in step1, check

the operation of the fuel cut solenoid, if faults are found repair/replace as required.

3. If no faults are found in step2, check to ensure that fuel is getting to the injection pump by disconnecting the inlet hoses from the fuel filter, feeding clean fuel from a separate container directly into the injection pump. If the engine now starts there may be blockages in the fuel filter and/or line between the fuel tank and fuel filter.

4. If fuel is present in step1, check the fuel system pipes, hoses and/or components for leaks, cracks and/or damage, if faults are found repair/replace as required.

5. If there are no faults in step4, check the pre-heating operation system operation by ensuring that after the ignition is turned on and the glow plug lamp lights up ensure that there is voltage applied to the glow plugs, if the operation is not as shown, repair/replace as required.

6. If no faults are found in step5, check the operation of then glow plug/s, if faults are found repair/replace as required.

7. If no faults are found in step6, check the injection timing by (releasing the cold start advance systenwhere fitted) and checking the plunger stroke.

Injection Plunger Stroke: **0.82-0.88mm**
If the timing setting is not as shown, adjust to suit.

8. If no faults are found in step7, check the fast idle system operation **(vehicle with ACSD only)**, if faults are found repair/replace as required.

9. If no faults are found in step8, check the condition and/or operation of the injection nozzles

Injection Nozzle Pressure: **13,239 to 15200kpa**
10. If faults are found repair/replace as required.

Rough Idle When The Engine is Warm

1. If the idle speed is unstable when the engine is warm, check the condition and/or operation of the throttle cable and/or linkages, if faults are found repair/replace as required.

2. If no faults are found in step1, check the engine idle speed setting.

Idle Speed: **600-700RPM**
If the idle speed is not as shown, adjust to suit

3. If no faults are found in step2, check the fuel system components and/or lines for leaks and/or damage, if faults are found repair/replace as required.

4. If no faults are found in step3, check the injection timing by (releasing the cold start advance system where fitted) and checking the plunger stroke.

Injection Plunger Stroke: **0.82-0.88mm**
If the timing setting is not as shown, adjust to suit.

5. If no faults are found in step4, check the operation of the injection nozzle/s and/or the delivery valve by letting the engine run at idle speed, loosening the union nuts on each of the cylinders in order and check if there is any change of idle speed. If there is no change at any of the cylinders this will indicate that a faulty cylinder/s is present. To fix the problem check the injection nozzle pressure.

Injection Nozzle Pressure: **13,239 to 15200kpa**
6. If the pressure is not as shown in step5, the injector

pressure needs adjusting, if the pressure cannot be adjusted, replace nozzle/s as required.

7. If the pressure is OK in step6, replace the delivery valve

Fuel Consumption is Poor

1. If the fuel consumption is poor, check the fuel system components and/or lines for leaks and/or damage, if faults are found repair/replace as required.

2. If no faults are found in step1, check the engine idle speed setting is correct.

Idle Speed: **600-700RPM**
If the idle speed setting is not correct adjust to suit.

3. If the idle speed setting is OK in step2, check the no load maximum speed setting is OK by starting the engine, pressing down the throttle pedal to the floor and cheking the no load maximum speed setting.

No Load Maximum Speed Setting: **4500-700RPM**
If the setting is not OK, adjust using the maximum speed adjusting screw.

4. If no faults are found in step3, check the injection timing by releasing the cold start advance systen (where fitted) and checking the plunger stroke.

Injection Plunger Stroke: **0.82-0.88mm**
If the timing setting is not as shown, adjust to suit.

5. If no faults are found in step4, check the injection nozzle pressure.

Injection Nozzle Pressure: **13,239 to 15200kpa**
6. If the pressure is not as shown adjust pressure to suit, if the pressure cannot be adjusted replace the faulty injector nozzle/s as required.

Noise When The Engine Is Warm

1. If the engine is noisy when it is warm, first check the operation of the temperature gauge if that is Ok, check the operation of the thermostat if faults are found repair/replace as required.

2. If no faults are found in step1, check the injection timing by releasing the cold start advance systen (where fitted) and checking the plunger stroke.

Injection Plunger Stroke: **0.82-0.88mm)**
If the timing setting is not as shown, adjust to suit.

3. If no faults are found in step2, check the injection nozzle pressure.

Injection Nozzle Pressure: **13,239 to 15200kpa**
4. If the pressure is not as shown adjust pressure to suit, if the pressure cannot be adjusted replace the faulty injector nozzle/s as required.

Engine Will Not Return to Idle

1. Operate the adjusting lever on top of the injection pump and ensure that the engine returns to normal idle speed, if it does the throttle cable is binding or not adjusted correctly and needs fixing.

2. If the engine does not return to idle in step1, the injection pump is faulty and needs replacing.

Engine Will Not Shut Off With The Key

1. Check fuel cut solenoid operation by disconnecting the connector on top of the fuel cut solenoid and check if the engine stops, if it does the starter switch is faulty and needs repairing and/or replacing.

2. If the engine does not stop in step1, either the fuel cut solenoid is faulty or the solenoid is blocked, if required repair/replace as required.

Diesel System Electrical Diagnosis
Engine Will Not Start When Cold (Superglow System Europe and Australia)
Please Note: Before starting test please ensure that the battery is fully charged, the engine cranks normally and that all the fuse links are OK.

1. Disconnect the water temperature sensor and check if the indicator lamp lights up when the starter switch is in the ON position.
Specified Light Up Time: 6-7seconds
2. If the light up time is not as shown in step1, check the condition of the relevant system fuse, if the fuse is blown, check for short circuit in the harness and repair as required.

3. If the fuse is OK in step2, check the condition and/or operation of the glow indicator lamp globe, if faults are found repair/replace as required.

4. If the bulb is OK in step3, check for battery voltage to the terminal 3 (harness side) of the pre-heating timer connector, if the voltage is OK, replace the timer assembly.

5. If the light up time in step1 is OK, put the starter switch to OFF, and check for battery voltage to terminal 1of the pre heating timer with the ignition switch in the ON position.

6. If there is NO voltage in step5, check that there is 1v or less to terminal 9 on the timer, if there is the timer is faulty and needs replacing.

7. If the voltage in step5 is OK, check if voltage to the terminal 1of the pre heating timer is terminated after the engine has started, if it does not, start the engine and check if there is voltage at terminal 9 of the pre heating timer, if there is not, repair fault in the charging system. If there is voltage the timer is faulty and should be replaced.

8. If the voltage operation is OK in step7, put the starter switch to the OFF position, put the starter switch into the ON position and check the current flow to the terminal 5 of the timer.
Current Flow: 120 Seconds.
9. If the pre-heat time differs from above or there is NO voltage at all in step8, replace the timer.

10. If the current flow is OK in step8, after completing pre-heating check for voltage at terminal 5, check again this time when the starter switch is in the Start position.

11. If there is no voltage in step10, replace the timer.

12. If the voltage is OK in step10, put the starter switch into the off position, place the starter switch into the ON position and check for voltage to the glow plugs a few seconds later (the voltage should drop by about 50%).

13. If there is no voltage at all in step12, check for battery voltage at the (-) side of the glow plug resistor, if there is no voltage, replace the No1 glow plug relay.

14. If the voltage in step12 stays at battery voltage or falls to 0v, check for battery voltage to the (+) side of the glow plug resistor, if there is no voltage replace the No2 glow plug relay.

15. If the voltage is OK in step12, check the glow plug resistance.
Specified Resistance: Approx. 0ohms
If the resistance is not OK, replace the glow plug/s as required.

16. If the glow plug resistance is OK in step15, the glow plug/s are OK, then reconnect the water temperature senson harness connector.

VEHICLE SERVICE INFORMATION
Vehicle Filling Capacities
Engine Oil with Filter: .... 9.0 Litres
Engine Oil without Filter: .... 7.7 Litres
Engine Oil with Dry Fill: 9.3Litres
Cooling System: .... 9.6 Litres (Without Heater)
Cooling System: .... 10.3 Litres (With Heater)
Cooling System: 11.3 Litres (With Front/Rear Heater)
Cooling System: .... 9.8 Litres (With Heater)
Manual Transmission: .... 3.0 Litres
Front Differential: .... 2.6 Litres
Rear Differential: .... 2.5 Litres
Transfer Case: 2.2Litres

Vehicle Component Service Interval Changes
Timing Belt:
    Change Every 60Months/100,000kms
Check Valve Clearance:
    Every 24Months/40,000kms
Engine Coolant/Anti Freeze:
  Change at 36Months/60,000kms thenevery 40,000kms
Air Cleaner Element:
    Change Every 18 Months/30,000kms
Fuel Filter:
    Change Every 12 Months/20,000kms
Engine Oil:
    Change Every 3 Months/5,000kms
Engine Oil Filter:
    Change Every 6 Months/10,000kms
Brake Fluid:
    Change Every 24 Months/40,000kms
Manual Transmission Oil:
    Change Every 18 Months/30,000kms
Front Differential Oil:
    Change Every 18 Months/30,000kms
Transfer Case Oil:
    Change Every 18 Months/30,000kms
Rear Differential Oil:
    Change Every 18 Months/30,000kms
Front/Rear Wheel Bearings
    Repack Every 12Months/20,000kms